# NORTH AMERICAN BORDERLANDS

Since the early colonial period, historians have been fascinated with North America's borderlands—places where people interacted across multiple, independent political and legal systems. Today the scholarship on these regions is more robust and innovative than ever before.

*North American Borderlands* introduces students to exemplary recent scholarship on this vital topic, showcasing work that delves into the complexities of borderland relationships. Essays range from the seventeenth through the late twentieth century, touch on nearly every region of the continent, and represent a variety of historical approaches and preoccupations. Anchored by a substantial introduction that walks students through the terminology and historiography, the collection presents the major debates and questions most prominent in the field today.

**Brian DeLay** is Associate Professor of History at the University of California, Berkeley, and the author of *War of a Thousand Deserts: Indian Raids and the U.S.-Mexican War*

Rewriting Histories focuses on historical themes where standard conclusions are facing a major challenge. Each book presents papers (edited and annotated when necessary) at the forefront of current research and interpretation, offering students an accessible way to engage with contemporary debates.

Series editor Jack R. Censer is Professor of History at George Mason University.

# REWRITING HISTORIES
Edited by Jack R. Censer

ATLANTIC AMERICAN SOCIETIES: FROM COLUMBUS THROUGH ABOLITION
*Edited by J R McNeill and Alan Karras*

COMPARATIVE FASCIST STUDIES: NEW PERSPECTIVES
*Edited by Constantin Iordachi*

DECOLONIZATION: PERSPECTIVES FROM NOW AND THEN
*Edited by Prasenjit Duara*

DIVERSITY AND UNITY IN EARLY NORTH AMERICA
*Edited by Philip Morgan*

THE FRENCH REVOLUTION: RECENT DEBATES AND NEW CONTROVERSIES
*Edited by Gary Kates*

FROM ROMAN PROVINCES TO MEDIEVAL KINGDOMS
*Edited by Thomas F.X. Noble*

GENDER AND AMERICAN HISTORY SINCE 1890
*Edited by Barbara Melosh*

GLOBAL ENVIRONMENTAL HISTORY
*Edited by John R. McNeill and Alan Roe*

GLOBAL FEMINISMS SINCE 1945
*Edited by Bonnie G. Smith*

GLOBALIZING FEMINISMS, 1789–1945
*Edited by Karen Offen*

THE HOLOCAUST: ORIGINS, IMPLEMENTATION, AFTERMATH
*Edited by Omer Bartov*

HAITIAN HISTORY: NEW PERSPECTIVES
*Edited by Alyssa Sepinwall*

THE INDUSTRIAL REVOLUTION AND WORK IN NINETEENTH-CENTURY EUROPE
*Edited by Lenard R. Berlanstein*

THE ISRAEL/PALESTINE QUESTION
*Edited by Ilan Pappé*

MEDIEVAL RELIGION: NEW APPROACHES
*Edited by Constance Hoffman Berman*

NAZISM AND GERMAN SOCIETY, 1933–1945
*Edited by David Crew*

THE NEW SOUTH: NEW HISTORIES
*Edited by J. William Harris*

THE OLD SOUTH: NEW STUDIES OF SOCIETY AND CULTURE
*Edited by J. William Harris*

THE ORIGINS OF THE BLACK ATLANTIC
*Edited by Larent DuBois and Julius S. Scott*

THE ORIGINS OF THE COLD WAR: AN INTERNATIONAL HISTORY
*Edited by David Painter and Melvyn Leffler*

PRACTICING HISTORY: NEW DIRECTIONS IN HISTORICAL WRITING
*Edited by Gabrielle M. Spiegel*

REFORMATION TO REVOLUTION
*Edited by Margo Todd*

THE RENAISSANCE: ITALY AND ABROAD
*Edited by John Jeffries Martin*

REVOLUTIONARY RUSSIA: NEW APPROACHES TO THE RUSSIAN REVOLUTION
*Edited by Rex A. Wade*

THE REVOLUTIONS OF 1989
*Edited by Vladimir Tismaneanu*

SEGREGATION AND APARTHEID IN TWENTIETH CENTURY SOUTH AFRICA
*Edited by William Beinart and Saul Dubow*

SOCIETY AND CULTURE IN THE SLAVE SOUTH
*Edited by J. William Harris*

STALINISM: NEW DIRECTIONS
*Edited by Sheila Fitzpatrick*

TWENTIETH CENTURY CHINA: NEW APPROACHES
*Edited by Jeffrey N. Wasserstrom*

# NORTH AMERICAN BORDERLANDS

*Edited by Brian DeLay*

NEW YORK AND LONDON

First published 2013
by Routledge
711 Third Avenue, New York, NY 10017

Simultaneously published in the UK
by Routledge
2 Park Square, Milton Park, Abingdon, Oxon OX14 4RN

*Routledge is an imprint of the Taylor & Francis Group, an informa business*



*Library of Congress Cataloging in Publication Data*

North American borderlands / edited by Brian DeLay.
p. cm. — (Rewriting histories)
Includes bibliographical references and index.
1. Borderlands—North America—History. 2. Borderlands—United States—History. 3. North America—Historical geography. 4. United States—Historical geography. 5. North America—Boundaries. 6. United States—Boundaries. I. DeLay, Brian, 1971–
E46.N67 2012
973—dc23
2012023196

ISBN: 978-0-415-80865-1 (hbk)
ISBN: 978-0-415-80866-8 (pbk)

Typeset in Sabon
by Apex CoVantage, LLC

For
Laurel Thatcher Ulrich
&
Fred Anderson

& in Memory of David J. Weber

# CONTENTS

# SERIES EDITOR'S PREFACE

Rewriting history, or revisionism, has always followed closely in the wake of history writing. In their efforts to re-evaluate the past, professional as well as amateur scholars have followed many approaches, most commonly as empiricists, uncovering new information to challenge earlier accounts. Historians have also revised previous versions by adopting new perspectives, usually fortified by new research, which overturn received views.

Even though rewriting is constantly taking place, historians' attitudes towards using new interpretations have been anything but settled. For most, the validity of revisionism lies in providing a stronger, more convincing account that better captures the objective truth of the matter. Although such historians might agree that we never finally arrive at the "truth," they believe it exists and over time may be better approximated. At the other extreme stand scholars who believe that each generation or even each cultural group or subgroup necessarily regards the past differently, each creating for itself a more usable history. Although these latter scholars do not reject the possibility of demonstrating empirically that some contentions are better than others, they focus upon generating new views based upon different life experiences. Different truths exist for different groups. Surely such an understanding, by emphasizing subjectivity, further encourages rewriting history. Between these two groups are those historians who wish to borrow from both sides. This third group, while accepting that every congeries of individuals sees matters differently, still wishes somewhat contradictorily to fashion a broader history that incorporates both of these particular visions. Revisionists who stress empiricism fall into the first of the three camps, while others spread out across the board.

Today the rewriting of history seems to have accelerated to a blinding speed as a consequence of the evolution of revisionism. A variety of approaches has emerged. A major factor in this process has been the enormous increase in the number of researchers. This explosion has reinforced and enabled the retesting of many assertions. Significant ideological shifts have also played a major part in the growth of revisionism. First, the crisis of Marxism, culminating in the events in Eastern Europe in 1989, has given rise to doubts about explicitly Marxist accounts. Such doubts have spilled over into the entire field of social history which has been a dominant subfield of the discipline for several decades. Focusing on society and its class divisions implied that these are the most important elements in historical analysis. Because Marxism was built on the same claim, the whole basis of social history has been questioned, despite the very many studies that directly had little to do with Marxism. Disillusionment with social history, simultaneously opened the door to cultural and linguistic approaches largely developed in anthropology and literature. Multiculturalism and feminism further generated revisionism. By claiming that scholars had, wittingly or not, operated from a white European/American male point of view, newer researchers argued that other approaches had been neglected or misunderstood. Not surprisingly, these last historians are the most likely to envision each subgroup rewriting its own usable history, while other scholars incline towards revisionism as part of the search for some stable truth.

Rewriting Histories will make these new approaches available to the student population. Often new scholarly debates take place in the scattered issues of journals which are sometimes difficult to find. Furthermore, in these first interactions, historians tend to address one another, leaving out the evidence that would make their arguments more accessible to the uninitiated. This series of books will collect in one place a strong group of the major articles in selected fields, adding notes and introductions conducive to improved understanding. Editors will select articles containing substantial historical data, so that students—at least those who approach the subject as an objective phenomenon—can advance not only their comprehension of debated points but also their grasp of substantive aspects of the subject.

Borderlands have been defining subjects of historical inquiry in North America since the early colonial period. In the 1890s Frederick Jackson Turner transformed the study of borderlands with his influential frontier thesis, which focused on the outlook of European settlers as they forged ahead with little recognition of those in their way. Although scholarly inquiry continued for many years in the direction taken by Turner, over time research on borderlands throughout the world emerged and inflected the study of North America.

In this extraordinary collection of essays, Brian DeLay provides a snapshot of the current state of the examination of borderlands in North America. First and foremost, he defines borderlands as "zones of plural sovereignty," where people interacted with one another across more than one legal and political system. DeLay has selected essays that focus on relationships in borderlands regions, and he organizes the book around various themes: the development of authority; the impact of alien flora and fauna; and the construction of boundaries, as inflected by different understandings of gender. The second half of the book considers three further topics, including those contestations over sovereignty that resulted in violence and war. Concomitant with such struggles was the development of ideas of conquest, extermination, and resistance. Likewise, in such circumstances, individuals and groups continued to attempt to turn borders to their own purposes even as such limits more clearly emerged in the nineteenth and twentieth centuries.

While bringing together essays exploring disparate themes, the volume charts a lucid picture of borderland research as it has emerged in the past generation.

# INTRODUCTION

Borderlands history has been a venerable, even defining pursuit of American historical writing since the early contact era. Judging from the upswing in recent publications, prizes, and job openings, borderlands history is also reasonably fashionable right now. Focused by definition on the territorial margins of empires, states, and nonstate polities, borderlands history should also be seen as a central worksite for that great preoccupation of postwar American historiography, pluralism. Venerable and trendy, marginal and central: what exactly *is* borderlands history?

Self-described borderlands historians often don't agree on what the label signifies. Judging from historiography and much of our contemporary cultural production, one could easily conclude that "the borderlands" means the present-day American Southwest. Whether the border itself or intergroup relations figure meaningfully into the analysis or not, according to current usage most any kind of historical inquiry classifies as 'borderlands history' so long as it takes place in what's now New Mexico, Arizona, Texas, or California. This convention has the momentum of history behind it. Herbert Eugene Bolton first popularized the phrase "Spanish Borderlands" in 1921. Thereafter he and his many students (over 100 PhDs) produced scholarship that deepened the equation of term and region.[1] The U.S. media's on-again off-again preoccupation with the Mexican border during the twentieth and twenty-first centuries helped to define the Southwest as *the* borderlands rather than *a* borderland for most of Americans. Even today, despite a marked increase in scholarship on the U.S.-Canadian borderlands, historians probably use the term more often in reference to the Southwest than to all other regions combined.[2]

And yet scholars regularly apply the term to other places around the continent and indeed around the world. A quick sampling of article and book titles from the past few years yields, for example, *War, Judgment, and Memory in the Basque Borderlands;* "Conquering the Past: Postwar Archaeology and Nationalism in the Borderlands of Chile and Peru;" *The Lands Between: Conflict in the East European Borderlands*; *Changing Places: Society, Culture, and Territory in the Saxon-Bohemian Borderlands*; "The

'Minority Problem' and National Classification in the French and Czechoslovak Borderlands;" *Borderlines in Borderlands: James Madison and the Spanish-American Frontier*; *The Soviet Counterinsurgency in the Western Borderlands*; *Encounter, Transformation, and Identity: The Peoples of the Western Cameroon Borderlands*; and many, many more besides.[3] Works like these employ *borderlands* to mean regions surrounding the borders of modern nation states, anywhere in the world. It is an intuitive use of the term, and one implied by the bulk of self-defined borderlands scholarship outside the Southwest. Indeed, the interdisciplinary Association of Borderland Studies, initially focused on the U.S.-Mexican borderland but now global in scope, dedicates itself to the "systematic interchange of ideas and information relating to international border areas."[4]

But like the stubborn equation of borderlands with the American Southwest, this usage comes with a severe if often unexamined limitation. By seeing borderlands only where one finds the territorial limits of modern states; by taking a fairly recent governing technology (fixed, surveyed, internationally-recognized borders) as the starting point, this approach necessarily excludes the vast majority of history and historic societies. For millennia prior to the rise of nation states, distinct neighboring polities interacted with each other in landscapes where boundaries were usually less precise than modern borders but nonetheless critical to collective identity, access to resources, and patterns of interchange and conflict. In other words, linking "borderlands" to modernity walls off the study of state border regions from an immensity of comparative possibilities. It also forces a question about terms. If borderlands require nation states, what then do we call zones of interaction between distinct polities prior to the modern era?

The reliable answer—*frontier*—has been losing appeal among academic historians of North America for a variety of reasons. For one, the term's association with Frederick Jackson Turner became a decided liability after the "New Western Historians" leveled their assault upon his famous Frontier Thesis in the 1980s and 1990s. Insofar as *frontier* still conjures up a historiographic tradition with a nearly exclusive focus on the westward expansion of Euro-American pioneers, it seems too narrow, subjective, and problematic a term to signify the continent's contested places.[5] Moreover, *frontier* is spatially insufficient for the task at hand. Administrators in Washington D.C. or historians crafting grand narratives might have found utility in identifying *the* frontier dividing colonial British North American or U.S. society from others. But the past generation of scholarship has recast North America as a continent of dizzying and hyper-dynamic geo-political complexity prior to the twentieth century. All its independent polities had territorial limits and had alien neighbors occupying or using territory beyond those horizons. Most peoples in North American history had to be mindful of *multiple* frontiers. So we still need the word, but it has rather precise work to do. What's been missing is another term that can signify both broader regions of interaction between polities and the scholarship dedicated to the history of these regions. *Borderland* has become that term for an increasing number of historians.

Borderlands history as it's emerging is therefore broader than the study of the American Southwest, and deeper than the study of modern state border regions. It is most fundamentally the history of a spatial context: of places where people interacted across multiple, independent political and legal systems. Put more succinctly, borderlands are zones of plural sovereignty.[6] While such liminal places have existed throughout human history and around the world, nowhere is the literature about them more established, diverse, and vibrant than in North America. Today there are a great number of historians doing this work, whether or not they embrace the borderlands label. Among others, they include many scholars of Native American and Latina/o history; students of diplomatic, international, and transnational history; historians of empire and colonialism; Early Americanists and scholars of the early republic specializing in the colonial 'backcountry;' historians of science, law, and culture in contact zones; and military historians exploring cross-cultural conflict in North America. The scale and diversity of contemporary work centered on borderland regions defies tidy categorization, or distillation into a single, representative volume.[7]

This book has a humbler aim. Its purpose is to showcase a development in borderlands history that has come into its own in the past ten or fifteen years. That development is the pursuit of *shared stories*—histories of relationships, aimed at recovering the contexts and perspectives of multiple peoples interacting in a borderland.

A degree of multi-vocality has inevitably characterized what I've defined here as borderlands history from its earliest beginnings in the colonial era, through the increasingly professionalized work of the nineteenth century (epitomized by Francis Parkman's multi-volume borderland masterpiece *France and England in America*), to the traditions established by Turner and Bolton and elaborated upon by their respective legions of students during the first half of the twentieth century. Some of this work achieved subtle evocations of more than one colonial perspective—Parkman's great contest between the French and English, or some of the Bolton school's work on inter-imperial competition in Florida, Texas, and the Gulf Coast, for example. The same cannot be said, however, for histories of Native Peoples. With a few notable exceptions, academic historical scholarship from these eras approached indigenous actors with only a fraction of the seriousness, depth, and curiosity with which it treated Europeans and European-Americans. This was partly a consequence of enduring prejudice and indifference, of course, but disciplinary turfs played a role, too. Anthropologists were the ones who were supposed to study Indians and, as it happened, few anthropologists studying Indians prior to the 1950s had much interest in history.[8]

This rigid state of affairs began to crack at the edges with the advent of Ethnohistory. Called together to research and testify in a variety of Indian land claims cases, a cohort of anthropologists and historians found their conversations fruitful and in 1954 established the American Society for Ethnohistory "for the interdisciplinary investigation of the histories of the Native Peoples of the Americas." Ethnohistory sought the marriage of sensibilities and techniques characteristic of anthropology with questions, methods, and source materials more familiar to history. This meeting of the minds coincided with the early stages of the Civil Rights Movement, which would have profound consequences for American historiography, including the historical study of native peoples. By the 1970s the publication of a handful of challenging and iconoclastic Indian-centric histories attested to the shifting intellectual, institutional, and professional landscape. Momentum built, and by the 1980s the growing cohort of historians overthrowing old assumptions about native peoples wrote with increasing subtlety and ambition, and, critically, began moving from the fringes to the center of historiographic debate. Gary Clayton Anderson, James Axtel, Colin Calloway, Albert Hurtado, Theda Perdue, Daniel Richter, Neal Salisbury, Nancy Shoemaker, and other practitioners of the "New Indian History" demolished two old conceits. First, that native peoples were bit players in early American history; and second, that whatever their significance, existing sources made native histories more or less unrecoverable.[9]

By the 1990s, with these historiographic battles seemingly won and the literature on native peoples increasingly rich and sophisticated, a new kind of North American borderlands history became possible: shared stories that emphasize *relationships* instead of privileging either colonial or native experiences and perspectives. The shift here wasn't so much revolutionary as evolutionary. Earlier work had sometimes aimed to make meaningful intervention into both indigenous and colonial histories, and much of today's Native American historiography—broader and more robust than ever—continues to do so. But the maturation of the field and the sense that it had succeeded in registering its case for relevance encouraged some of its practitioners to re-center their work around relationships rather than Indian history per se. They came to see colonial actors as comparably alien and as ripe for new analysis as the native peoples who had been the focus of so much of the energy in previous decades. Some scholars of the colonial backcountry or western pioneers accepted the invitation from the opposite direction. Hence James Merrell went from *The Indians' New World* (1989), as emblematic of the New Indian history as any work, to *Into the American Woods* (1999), a dark and marvelous meditation on the limits of cross-cultural toleration in the Pennsylvania borderlands. Elliott West pivoted from *Growing Up With the Country* (1989), on white children in the pioneer west, to *Contested Plains* (1998), a brilliant fusion of environmental, Native American, and western expansion history. No work did more to herald the potential of a borderlands history centered on relationships than Richard White's 1992 landmark monograph *The Middle Ground: Indians, Empires, and Republics in the Great Lakes Region, 1650–1815*. Though rightly celebrated as exemplary of the New Indian History (an identifier White himself accepted for the work), *The Middle Ground*'s broad influence followed more from its suggestive insights into borderland relationships than from its contribution to Indian history as such.[10]

A few years after White's book appeared, a parallel advance became apparent or at least potential in emerging scholarship on North America's great 19th and 20th-century borderlands, those surrounding the U.S.-Canadian and, especially, the U.S.-Mexican borders. Building on work by Oscar J. Martínez, David J. Weber, and others, a new cohort of Chicana/o and western historians began embracing problems that transcended national borders.[11] In so doing they responded to the call for a transnational turn in U.S. history, read widely in Mexican and (to a lesser extent) Canadian historiography, and took inspiration from sophisticated work in other world regions, such as Peter Sahlin's oft-cited book *Boundaries: The Making of France and Spain in the Pyrenees* (1989). By the early 2000s the fruits of this transnational borderlands work had begun to transform the historiographies of both regions. By focusing on relationships and processes transcending borders, and by taking seriously actors on both sides of the divide, it began to offer critical interventions into larger questions about race, nation, citizenship, and nation-making in borderlands more generally.[12]

The pages that follow bring together fourteen essays exemplary of this new, multi-vocal borderlands scholarship. They are organized into six themes: authority, Columbian Exchange, gender, war, ideas, and crossings. Some compelling themes are absent, perhaps most obviously exchange, labor and slavery, and identity. In the process of assembling this volume I concluded that these themes in particular were so fundamental to the literature and so ubiquitous throughout it that setting them apart made little sense—all three are addressed in multiple essays in this volume. The chapters represent a wide variety of historical approaches. They were chosen for their excellence and for the light they shed on the six themes, but also with an eye to broad geographic and temporal coverage. Together the chapters in this volume explore relationships in borderland regions throughout North America, from the early contact period through the late twentieth century. Concentrating only on the past generation of scholarship and on that subsection of the literature that pivots on shared stories; balancing the six themes as well as different methodological approaches, geographic coverage, and chronological breadth; and working with inevitable constraints on length—all of this has meant excluding authors and essays that I admire and that have been influential and even celebrated in the historiography. Some of this work is mentioned in the notes to the section introductions, but these are in no sense comprehensive. My consoling hope is that this collection will whet readers' appetites for further exploration into North American borderlands history.[13]

***

A note on editing. Most of the following essays, particularly those derived from monographs, have been edited down for length. In all essays, original illustrations, maps, charts, acknowledgements, and sub-headings have been omitted, as have most discursive endnotes. Cuts to the main text are indicated by ellipses, and my own occasional explanatory comments are enclosed in brackets.

## NOTES

1 For Bolton and Borderlands, see David J. Weber, "John Francis Bannon and the Historiography of the Spanish Borderlands: Retrospect and Prospect," *Journal of the Southwest* 29:4 (1987): 331–363; Albert L. Hurtado, "Parkmanizing the Spanish Borderlands: Bolton, Turner, and the Historians' World," *Western Historical Quarterly* 26:2 (1995): 149–67.

2 For the northern borderland, see the essays in Sterling Evans, ed., *The Borderlands of the American and Canadian Wests: Essays on Regional History of the Forty-Ninth Parallel* (Lincoln: University of Nebraska Press, 2006); and Benjamin H. Johnson and Andrew Graybill, eds., *Bridging National Borders in North America: Transnational and Comparative Histories* (Durham: Duke University Press, 2010).

3 Sandra Ott, *War, Judgment, and Memory in the Basque Borderlands, 1914–1945* (Reno: University of Nevada Press, 2008); Stefanie Gänger, "Conquering the Past: Post-War Archaeology and Nationalism in the Borderlands of Chile and Peru, C. 1880–1920," *Comparative Studies in Society and History* 51:4 (2009): 691–714; Alexander Victor Prusin, *The Lands Between: Conflict in the East European Borderlands, 1870–1992* ( Oxford: Oxford University Press, 2010); Caitlin E. Murdock, *Changing Places: Society, Culture, and Territory in the Saxon-Bohemian Borderlands, 1870–1946* ((Ann Arbor: University of Michigan Press, 2010); Tara Zahra, "The 'Minority Problem' and National Classification in the French and Czechoslovak Borderlands," *Contemporary European History* 17:2 (2008): 137–165; J. C. A. Stagg, *Borderlines in Borderlands: James Madison and the Spanish-American Frontier, 1776–1821* (New Haven: Yale University Press, 2009); Alexander Statiev, *The Soviet Counterinsurgency in the Western Borderlands* (Cambridge: Cambridge University Press, 2010); Ian Fowler and Verkijika G. Fanso, *Encounter, Transformation and Identity: Peoples of the Western Cameroon Borderlands, 1891–2000* (Oxford: Berghahn Books, 2009).

4 See the ABS website: http://www.absborderlands.org/2about.html (accessed April 6, 2012).

5 See especially Patricia Nelson Limerick, *The Legacy of Conquest: The Unbroken Past of the American West* (New York: W.W. Norton & Company, 1987). Not all western historians found Turner (and "frontier") so unredeemable. See for example William Cronon, George A. Miles, and Jay Gitlin, eds., *Under an Open Sky: Rethinking America's Western Past* (New York: W.W. Norton, 1992); and the introduction in John Mack Faragher, ed., *Rereading Frederick Jackson Turner: The Significance of the Frontier in American History, and Other Essays* (New

York: H. Holt, 1994). These should be read alongside the trenchant critique of how some New Western historians historicized 'frontier' in Kerwin Lee Klein, "Reclaiming the 'F' Word, Or Being and Becoming Postwestern," *Pacific Historical Review* 65:2 (1996): 179–215; and the influential essay by Jeremy Adelman and Stephen Aron, "From Borderlands to Borders: Empires, Nation-States, and the Peoples in Between in North American History," *American Historical Review* 104 (1999): 814–841.

6 Legal scholars have historicized and complicated the contested and enormously consequential notion of sovereignty, recovering in particular the ways in which colonial actors mobilized it against non-European peoples. See for example Lauren A. Benton, *A Search for Sovereignty: Law and Geography in European Empires, 1400–1900* (Cambridge: Cambridge University Press, 2010); Lisa Ford, *Settler Sovereignty: Jurisdiction and Indigenous People in America and Australia, 1788–1836* (Cambridge, Mass: Harvard University Press, 2010). Douglas Howland and Luise White go so far as to abjure an "overarching and totalizing definition of sovereignty—one that is ahistorical and transnational." [Howland and White, eds., *The State of Sovereignty: Territories, Laws, Populations.* Bloomington: (Indiana University Press, 2009), 1.] But we ought to be able to engage the term on multiple registers; attending to its historicity and to the great variability in how human communities have organized themselves throughout history, but also availing ourselves of a shared vocabulary generic enough to be applicable to very different kinds of societies. Too often historians normalize European-derived practice, defining basic terms like "politics," "war," "diplomacy," etc., so that only Europeans and their offshoots can really have them. Sovereignty, then, I define simply as ultimate political authority over people and/or space.

7 The very range of 'borderlands' work invites some understandable skepticism about its coherence as a field. Recently Stephen Aron, observing profligate use of the term *borderland* in scholarship ("sexual borderlands," "surfing borderlands," etc.), predicted that "a backlash against the 'b-word' may be brewing." Aron, "Frontiers, Borderlands, Wests," in Eric Foner and Lisa McGirr, eds., *American History Now* (Philadelphia: Temple University Press, 2011), 261–81.

8 For the intellectual history behind this progression, see Kerwin Lee Klein, *Frontiers of Historical Imagination: Narrating the European Conquest of Native America, 1890–1990* (Berkeley: University of California Press, 1997).

9 For iconoclasm, see Francis Jennings' influential battle cry *The Invasion of America: Indians, Colonialism, and the Cant of Conquest* (Chapel Hill: University of North Carolina Press, 1975). In the decades after its inception, ethnohistory occasioned many historiographic and methodological essays. See for example Calvin Martin, "Ethnohistory: A Better Way to Write Indian History," *The Western Historical Quarterly* 9:1 (January, 1978): 41–56. For the New Indian history in context, see R. David Edmunds, "Native Americans, New Voices: American Indian History, 1895–1995," *The American Historical Review* 100:3 (June, 1995): 717–740.

10 James Hart Merrell, *The Indians' New World: Catawbas and Their Neighbors from European Contact Through the Era of Removal* (Chapel Hill: University of North Carolina Press, 1989); Merrell, *Into the American Woods: Negotiators on the Pennsylvania Frontier* (New York: Norton, 1999); Elliott West, *Growing up with the Country: Childhood on the Far-Western Frontier* (Albuquerque: University of New Mexico Press, 1989); West, *The Contested Plains: Indians, Goldseekers, & the Rush to Colorado* (Lawrence: University Press of Kansas, 1998); Richard White, *The Middle Ground: Indians, Empires, and Republics in the Great Lakes Region, 1650–1815* (Cambridge: Cambridge University Press,

1991). Another early and influential example of this multi-vocal approach to borderlands history is Daniel H. Usner, *Indians, Settlers, and Slaves in a Frontier Exchange Economy: The Lower Mississippi Valley Before 1783* (Chapel Hill: University of North Carolina Press, 1992).

11 Oscar J. Martínez, *Troublesome Border* (Tucson: University of Arizona Press, 1988); David J. Weber, *The Mexican Frontier, 1821–1846: The American Southwest Under Mexico* (Albuquerque: University of New Mexico Press, 1982); Weber, *The Spanish Frontier in North America* (New Haven: Yale University, 1992); Weber, *Bárbaros: Spaniards and their Savages in the Age of Enlightenment* (New Haven: Yale University Press, 2005).

12 Peter Sahlins, *Boundaries: The Making of France and Spain in the Pyrenees* (Berkeley: University of California Press, 1989). Samuel Truett and Elliott Young's edited volume *Continental Crossroads: Remapping U.S.-Mexico Borderlands History* (Durham: Duke University Press, 2004) highlighted much of this emerging work, and framed it in an insightful introduction. Other books in this important wave of U.S.-Mexican borderlands history include Benjamin Herber Johnson, *Revolution in Texas: How a Forgotten Rebellion and its Bloody Suppression Turned Mexicans into Americans* (New Haven: Yale University Press, 2003); Elliott Young, *Catarino Garza's Revolution on the Texas-Mexico Border* (Durham: Duke University Press, 2004); Andrés Reséndez, *Changing National Identities at the Frontier: Texas and New Mexico, 1800–1850* (Cambridge: Cambridge University Press, 2005); Samuel Truett, *Fugitive Landscapes: The Forgotten History of the U.S.-Mexico Borderlands* (New Haven: Yale University Press, 2006).

13 To that end, over the past few years several historiographic pieces have been published and serve as able guides to relevant literature. These include Sterling Evans's introduction to *Borderlands of the American and Canadian Wests*; Claudio Saunt, "Go West: Mapping Early American Historiography," *The William and Mary Quarterly* 65:4 (October 2008): 745–78; Benjamin H. Johnson and Andrew Graybill, "Borders and their Historians in North America," in Johnson and Graybill, eds., *Bridging National Borders in North America*, 1–29; Ramon A. Gutiérrez and Elliott Young, "Transnationalizing Borderlands History," *The Western Historical Quarterly* 41:1 (Spring, 2010): 26–53; Eric Hinderaker and Rebecca Horn, "Territorial Crossings: Histories and Historiographies of the Early Americas," *The William and Mary Quarterly* 67:3 (July, 2010): 395–432; "Latino History: An Interchange on Present Realities and Future Prospects, *Journal of American History,* 97 (2010): 424–63; Aron, "Frontiers, Borderlands, Wests;" Ned Blackhawk, "American Indians and the Study of U.S. History," in Foner and McGirr, eds., *American History Now*, 376–99; Pekka Hämäläinen and Samuel Truett, "On Borderlands," *Journal of American History* 98:2 ( September, 2011): 338–361.

# Part I

# AUTHORITY

Borderlands are places with multiple claims to final authority. Oftentimes these are also places of striking contrasts in language and culture, in legal and economic systems, in religion, gender relations, and lifeways. But the defining quality of borderlands regions is plural sovereignty—the presence of multiple polities claiming and exercising ultimate *de facto* authority over place and people. In the borderlands of many modern nation states, the spatial geography of sovereignty has been delimited on maps and demarcated by border monuments, signs, barbed wire, walls, and armed guards. If you're paying attention, you usually know where you are. Before the modern era, however, the connection between space and authority was seldom as transparent or as fixed. Indigenous and European authorities alike conceived of sovereignty as jurisdiction over people and resources more than jurisdiction over fixed space.[1] The distinction ought not be taken too far; people and resources always occupy space, after all, and that space is always finite and hence bounded in one way or another. But in a world where ecological change, migration, war, diplomacy, shifting allegiances, and barriers to communication frequently muddied or remade the shape of spatial authority, obsessing over territorial delimitation served little purpose. Geopolitical dynamism and territorial ambiguity could facilitate and encourage contact and exchange. But it also meant that representatives of different sovereign peoples encountered profound challenges in negotiating social and economic relations with one another. These challenges and varied responses to them have been a central preoccupation in the last generation of borderlands scholarship.

Richard White presented an enormously influential model for understanding the navigation of these challenges in *The Middle Ground*. White's book begins in trauma and warfare, as tens of thousands of native peoples from the Ohio Country, the Great Lakes region (what the French called the *pays d'en haut*), and beyond were killed, captured, or made refugees in wars with the expansive Iroquois confederacy. Survivors tried to rebuild lives for themselves in new, multi-ethnic villages established in the *pays d'en haut*.

Colonial authorities in New France, meanwhile, worked to create and maintain alliances with these fractious groups as part of their broader economic and geopolitical strategy in North America. Even when all involved valued the relationship, however, the erstwhile partners often found cooperation, or even comprehension, extraordinarily difficult. White's essay introduces his concept of the middle ground, and examines how it worked to protect relationships in the face of two complex stresses: marriage and homicide.

The French had only very modest territorial designs upon the *pays d'en haut*, and generally recognized that it was neither in their interest nor in their power to formally colonize the indigenous people living there. In chapter two Cynthia Radding explores the evolution of a more intrusive and transformational Spanish authority among the native peoples of northwestern New Spain. Mines and missions, expropriation of land and water, demands for labor and military service, and various efforts at social engineering remade key aspects of life for the region's peoples. Yet, crucially, Radding demonstrates that indigenous compromises in this borderland were always partial and always conditional. When Spaniards or Mexicans violated what she calls the "colonial pact," nonviolent resistance and even full-blown rebellion illuminated the very real limits of colonial authority.[2]

Colonial Pennsylvania presents still another context for the consideration of borderlands authority. Unlike the endeavors of the French in the *pays d'en haut* or the Spanish in Sonora, the colonial project in Pennsylvania came to rely less and less on partnership with or colonization of Indians. More and more what it required was land. Authorities in Philadelphia desired good relations with the region's native peoples for ideological and tactical reasons. But by the mid-eighteenth century native population movements on the one hand and European immigration and westward expansion on the other had made indigenous and colonial interests appear incompatible. James Merrell's chapter "Conversations in the Woods" recovers the practical challenges of navigating divided authority on this increasingly tense borderland. He does so by introducing us to the go-betweens responsible for handling communication and defusing crisis. His chapter opens with two of the region's most storied and experienced intermediaries, the trader Conrad Weiser and the prominent Iroquois (Oneida) Shickellamy.

## NOTES

1 For jurisdictional sovereignty, see Peter Sahlins, *Boundaries: The Making of France and Spain in the Pyrenees* (Berkeley: University of California Press, 1989).

2 For elaboration of the argument Radding outlines in her essay, see her book *Wandering Peoples: Colonialism, Ethnic Spaces, and Ecological Frontiers in Northwestern Mexico, 1700–1850* (Durham: Duke University Press, 1997).

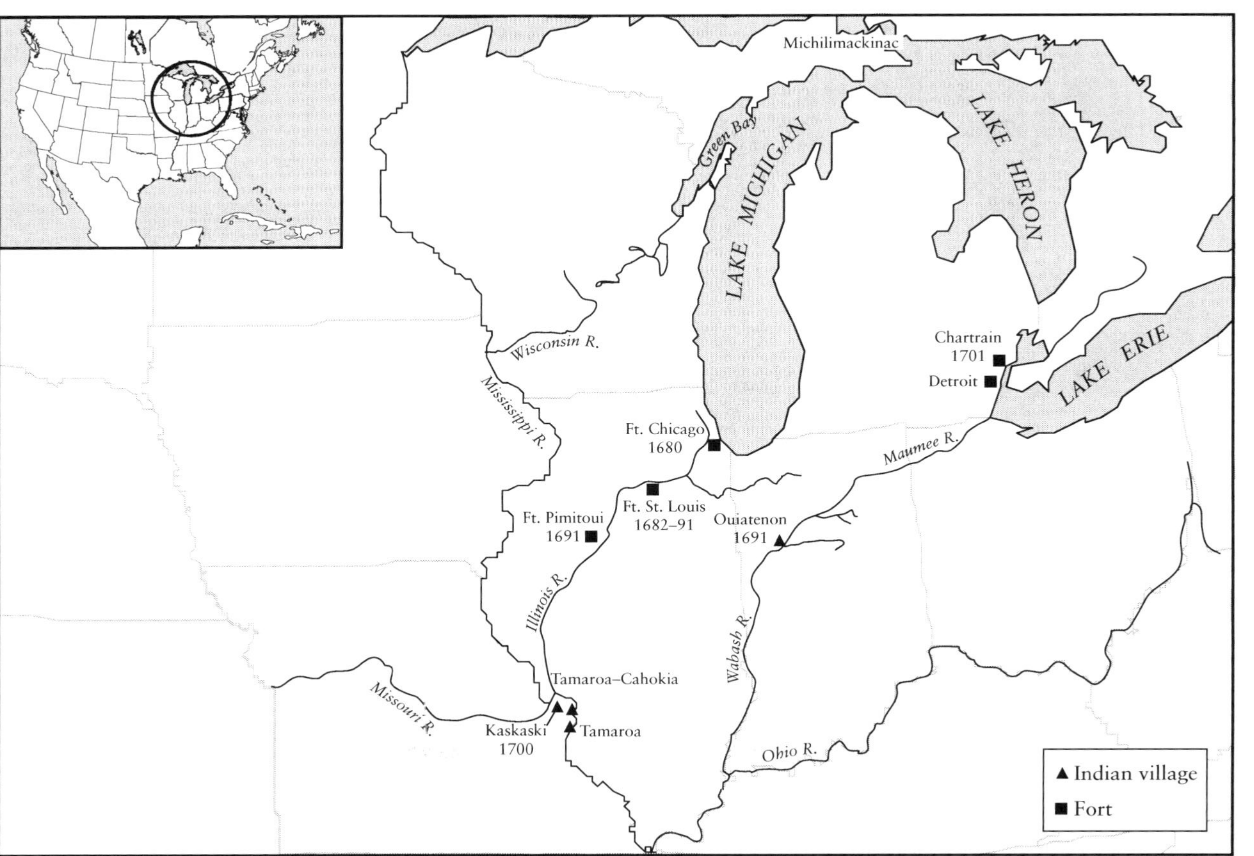


*Map 1.1* The Great Lakes Region

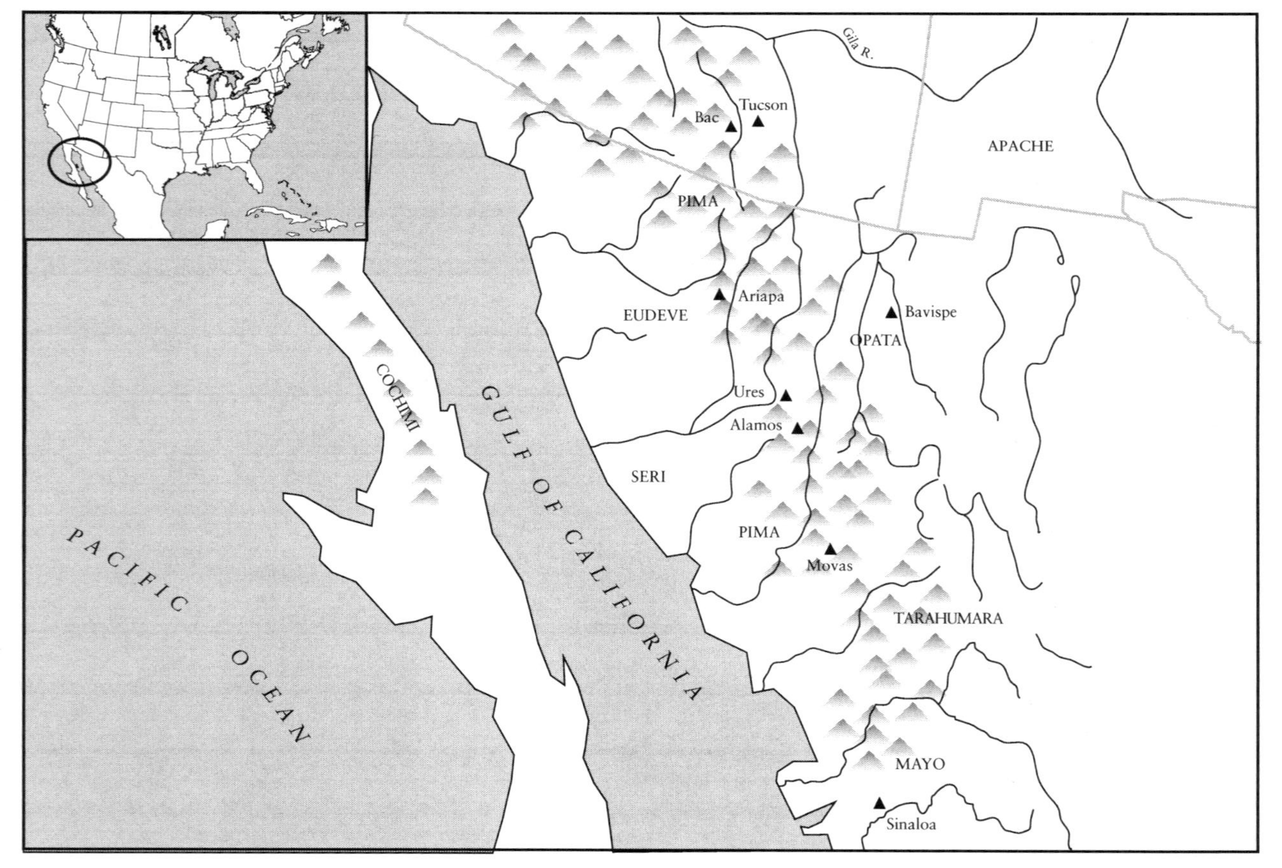


*Map 1.2* Sonora

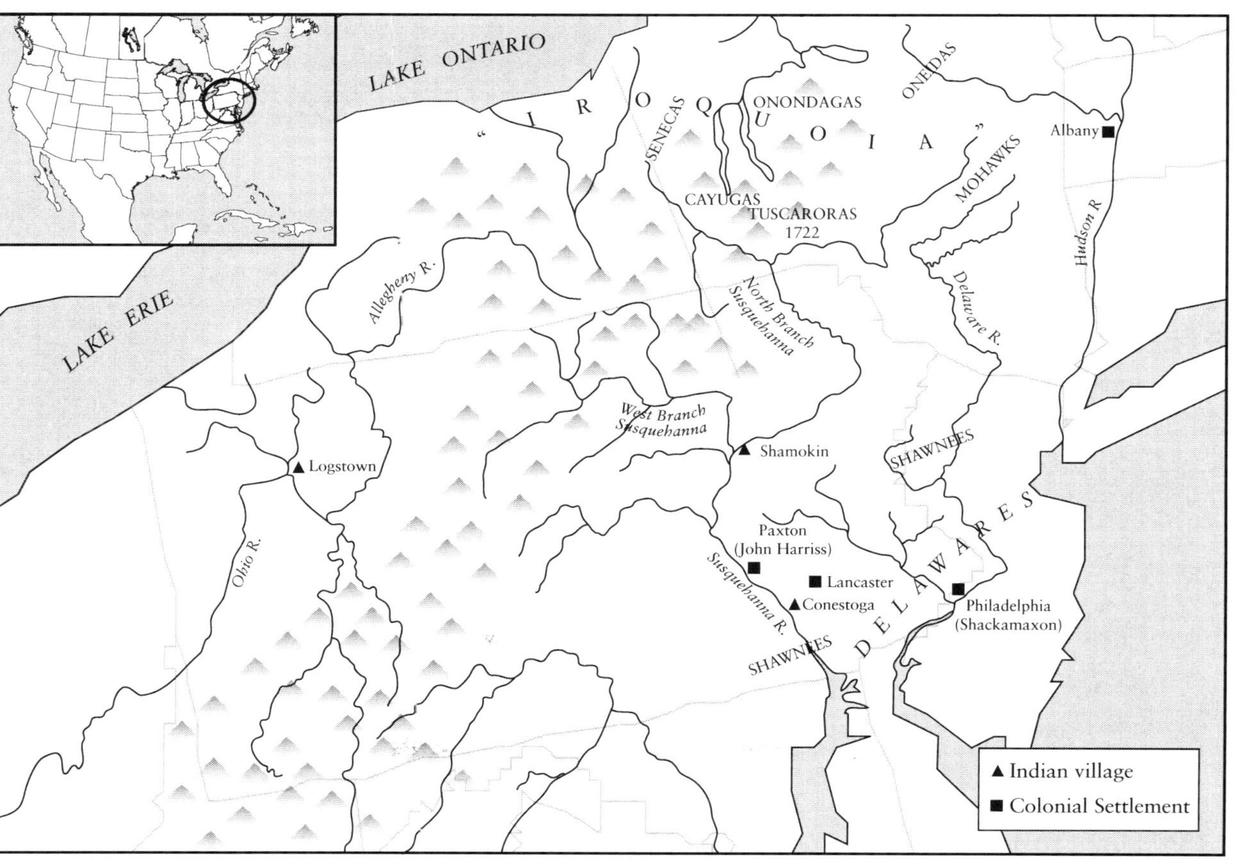


*Map 1.3* Western Pennsylvania

# 1

# MARRIAGE AND HOMICIDE ON THE MIDDLE GROUND

*Richard White*

Because the French and Algonquians were trading partners and allies, the boundaries of the Algonquian and French worlds melted at the edges and merged. Although identifiable Frenchmen and identifiable Indians obviously continued to exist, whether a particular practice or way of doing things was French or Indian was, after a time, not so clear. This was not because individual Indians became "Frenchified" or because individual Frenchmen went native, although both might occur. Rather, it was because Algonquians who were perfectly comfortable with their status and practices as Indians and Frenchmen, confident in the rightness of French ways, nonetheless had to deal with people who shared neither their values nor their assumptions about the appropriate way of accomplishing tasks. They had to arrive at some common conception of suitable ways of acting; they had to create what I [refer] to as a middle ground.[1]

The creation of the middle ground involved a process of mutual invention by both the French and the Algonquians. This process passed through various stages, of which the earliest is at once the most noticed and the least interesting. It was in this initial stage that the French, for example, simply assimilated Indians into their own conceptual order. Indians became *sauvages,* and the French reduced Indian religion to devil worship and witchcraft. Algonquians, for their part, thought of the first Europeans as manitous. On both sides, new people were crammed into existing categories in a mechanical way.

Literacy gave this initial stage a potency and a durability for Europeans it might otherwise have lacked. Because the French were literate, knowledge of Indians was diffused far from the site of actual contact. Such knowledge, unchallenged by actual experience with Indians, survived as a potent cultural relict. Long after it ceased to govern the actions of those who actually lived among Indians, the idea of Indians as literally *sauvages,* or wild men embodying either natural virtue or ferocity, persisted among intellectuals and statesmen in France. Assimilated into European controversies, these imaginary Indians became the Indians of Chateaubriand and Rousseau. They took on importance, but it was one detached from the continuing processes of contact between real Algonquians and real Europeans. In the *pays d'en haut,* actual Indians and whites of widely different social class and status had, for a variety of reasons, to rely on each other in order to achieve quite specific ends. It was these Frenchmen (for Frenchwomen would not appear until much later) and Algonquian men and women who created a common ground—the middle ground—on which to proceed.[2]

This process of creation resulted quite naturally from attempts to follow normal conventions of behavior in a new situation. Each side sought different goals in a different manner. French officials and merchants sought to rationalize and order what they saw as the unpredictable world of the *sauvage;* Algonquians sought, in a sense, the opposite. They wanted to change or readjust the given order by appeals for personal favor or exemption. In much the same way that they sought special power to readjust the order of the world of plants, animals, and spirits by appealing to the manitous, so they sought beneficial changes in the social world by appeals to the French. Often, in the examples that follow, when the French sought the imposition of hard-and-fast rules, the Algonquians sought the "power" that comes from knocking the order off balance, from asserting the personal, the human exception. The result of each side's attempts to apply its own cultural expectations in a new context was often change in culture itself. In trying to maintain the conventional order of its world, each group applied rules that gradually shifted to meet the exigencies of particular situations. The result of these efforts was a new set of common conventions, but these conventions served as a basis for further struggles to order or influence the world of action.[3]

The middle ground depended on the inability of both sides to gain their ends through force. The middle ground grew according to the need of people to find a means, other than force, to gain the cooperation or consent of foreigners. To succeed, those who operated on the middle ground had, of necessity, to attempt to understand the world and the reasoning of others and to assimilate enough of that reasoning to put it to their own purposes. Particularly in diplomatic councils, the middle ground was a realm of constant invention, which was just as constantly presented as convention. Under the new conventions, new purposes arose, and so the cycle continued.[4]

Perhaps the central and defining aspect of the middle ground was the willingness of those who created it to justify their own actions in terms of what they perceived to be their partner's cultural premises. Those operating in the middle ground acted for interests derived from their own culture, but they had to convince people of another culture that some mutual action was fair and legitimate. In attempting such persuasion people quite naturally sought out congruences, either perceived or actual, between the two cultures. The congruences arrived at often seemed—and, indeed, were—results of misunderstandings or accidents. Indeed, to later observers the interpretations offered by members of one society for the practices of another can appear ludicrous. This, however, does not matter. Any congruence, no matter how tenuous, can be put to work and can take on a life of its own if it is accepted by both sides. Cultural conventions do not have to be true to be effective any more than legal precedents do. They have only to be accepted. . . .

The middle ground itself . . . did not originate in councils and official encounters; instead, it resulted from the daily encounters of individual Indians and Frenchmen with problems and controversies that needed immediate solution. Many of these problems revolved around basic issues of sex, violence, and material exchange. The need to resolve these problems, perhaps even more than the problems of alliance, forced the middle ground into existence. But even this misstates the issue, for the distinction between official dealings and personal dealings was a hazy and confusing one in Algonquian society, where coercive mechanisms and hierarchical structures were notoriously weak.

Although French officials spoke of their relationship with the Algonquians in economic, political, and, less often, religious terms, paradoxically economic and political institutions could not control the context of contact. In the day-to-day relations of the western country, the relationships of Algonquians and Frenchmen as trading partners and allies were abstractions, pertinent, perhaps, to Indians and French as aggregates, but having little to do with actual people in face-to-face relationships. In another society, with more coercive mechanisms at an elite's disposal, personal relations between intruders such as the French and the members of the host society might be kept to a minimum and mattered little. Traders might be isolated in special quarters and granted special privileges; they might be governed by separate rules and taxed at stated rates. Isolation, however, was impossible among the Algonquians, who lacked a state with coercive institutions and in whose society obedience to authority was usually neither a social fact nor a social virtue. . . .[5]

The operation of the middle ground must be understood within a dual context. First, there was the weakness of hierarchical controls within Algonquian villages and the frailty of any authority French officials exerted over Frenchmen in the West. Second, there was the cultural threat each society seemed to pose to the elite of the other. What this meant in practice was that both the extent and meaning of social relations between Frenchmen and Algonquians were often negotiated largely on a face-to-face level within the villages themselves, and that these relations were not what either French authorities or Algonquian elders might have preferred them to be. This does not mean that there was no official element involved, but rather that official decisions could not determine the course of actual relations.

The array of relations negotiated in the middle ground was quite large, but leaving aside for now the liquor trade, problems in two arenas of contact—sex and violence—seem to have been particularly acute. Sexual relations between

Frenchmen and Indian women and violence between French and Indians, both men and women, accompanied trade throughout the West. One facilitated trade, and the other threatened to destroy it; both presented problems of cultural interaction that had to be negotiated. Sex and violence are thus important not only in their own right but also as avenues for understanding how cultural accommodation on the middle ground, in fact, worked.

What made sexual relations between Frenchmen and Indian women so central to contact in the West was that until the 1730s relatively few Frenchwomen ever came west. Frenchwomen were a curiosity in the upper country. The appearance of Madame Le Sueur at Fort Saint Louis in the 1690s created such an uproar that she, like Indians visiting Europe, had to consent to a public display so that the curious could see her. The absence of Frenchwomen meant that French males actively sought out Indian women as sexual partners. Not all French males did so, of course. The Jesuits and often their donnés were celibate. This was a condition which, if not unknown among the Algonquians, was regarded by them with the same combination of curiosity and revulsion with which the French regarded the berdaches of the Illinois and the acceptance of homosexual relations among many Algonquian peoples.[6]

Algonquians eventually accepted Jesuit celibacy, but the Jesuits never accepted Algonquian sexual mores, particularly when other Frenchmen proved so enthusiastic about them. Sex was hardly a personal affair; it was governed and regulated by the appropriate authorities. The supreme arbiters of sex among the French were precisely those who, theoretically, had the least practical experience, the priests. The Jesuits took a vocal and active interest in the sexual activities of both the French and the Indians. . . .[7]

Despite their differing purposes, nearly all French accounts were united, first, by their inability to understand the status of women vis-à-vis men except in terms of conjugal relations and, second, by their tendency to group actual sexual relations in terms of two opposite poles of conduct, with marriage at one extreme and prostitution and adultery at the other. In attempting to impose their own cultural categories on the actions of Algonquian women, the French tended to select material that made the women seem merely a disorderly and lewd set of Europeans, not people following an entirely different social logic. The immediate result was to define a woman in terms of a person—her actual or potential husband—who may not have been anywhere near being the most significant figure in the woman's life. Depending on her tribal identity, an Algonquian woman often had a more durable and significant relationship with her mother, father, brothers, sisters, or grandparents, or with other, unrelated women than with her husband or husbands. Nor was an Algonquian woman's status dependent solely on her husband. Her own membership in ritual organizations or, among some tribes such as the Shawnees, Huron-Petuns, and Miamis, her own political status in offices confined to women had more influence on her social position than the status of her husband did. . . .[8]

Younger women and hunting women . . . enjoyed substantial freedom in engaging in sexual relations with Frenchmen and played a major part in establishing the customary terms of sexual relationships between the Algonquians and the French. Initially, many Frenchmen, like the Jesuits, may have viewed this sort of relationship as simple prostitution or as a loose, easily dissolved marriage, but by the 1690s they recognized it as a separate, customary form for sexual relationships in the fur trade. Basically, women adapted the relationship of hunting women to hunters to the new conditions of the fur trade. Such women not only had sexual intercourse with their French companions, they also cooked and washed for them, made their clothes, and cut their wood. . . .

These women did not solicit customers, and they did not sell discrete sexual acts. Sex accompanied a general agreement to do the work commonly expected of women in Algonquian society. Nor was the relationship a temporary marriage. In marriage a wife received no payment from her husband, nor was she as free as a hunting woman to dissolve one relationship and begin another. Finally, these relationships were not contracts between families. They were, instead, a bridge to the middle ground, an adjustment to interracial sex in the fur trade where the initial conceptions of sexual conduct held by each side were reconciled in a new customary relation. The appeal of unions that offered both temporary labor and sexual companionship to the coureurs de bois [unauthorized French traders] is obvious, but these relationships also may have flourished because of the badly skewed sex ratios within Algonquian societies, apparently the result of warfare. . . .

Hunting women, as a group, carried and modified one Algonquian pattern of sexual relations into the fur trade in their liaisons with the coureurs de bois, but a smaller group of Christian Indian women were also influential in creating other patterns of sexual conduct through their own relationships with both Algonquian men and Frenchmen. The influence of these women was not felt everywhere; necessarily, it was confined to groups in which the Jesuits had succeeded in making a significant number of converts: the Huron-Petuns, the" Kiskakon Ottawas, and above all the Kaskaskias of the Illinois confederation.[9]

The influence of Christian women emerged most clearly among the Illinois. In the late seventeenth and early eighteenth centuries, there were signs of sexual crisis among the Illinois. They had a badly skewed sex ratio, which Deliette, probably exaggerating, estimated at four women to each man. The Illinois themselves thought that their traditional marriage pattern was in decay, and in French accounts, they combined draconian punishments for adultery with widespread sexual liaisons between Frenchman and Indian women. By 1692 the Illinois had largely abandoned Starved Rock and had built villages at the southern end of Lake Peoria, thus creating a new collection of villages at Pimitoui. The French who accompanied the Illinois had built the second Fort Saint Louis near these villages. Pimitoui also served as the headquarters for Jesuit mission activity among the Illinois and surrounding nations. Father Gravier, missionary to the Illinois since 1688 or 1689, established a permanent mission there in 1693. By 1696 the priest estimated that over the preceding six years he had baptized some two thousand persons. Even allowing for large numbers of deathbed baptisms and baptisms of infants who did not grow up to be practicing Catholics, this is a substantial figure. Much of Gravier's lasting success took place among the Illinois, particularly among the young women, who, according to Deliette, "often profit by their teaching and mock at the superstitions of their nation. This often greatly incenses the old men."[10]

By the 1690s the differential sexual appeal of Catholic teaching began to have significant repercussions among the Illinois. This, in turn, influenced the way the French and Illinois societies were linked. Jesuit teaching among the Illinois in the 1690s stressed the cult of the Virgin Mary, and with it came a heavy emphasis on chastity and virginity. This stress on a powerful female religious figure, whose power, like that of the Jesuits, was connected with sexual abstinence, attracted a congregation composed largely of women, particularly young women and older girls. How these young women understood Christianity and the cult of the Virgin is not entirely clear. They may have identified it in terms of women's ritual organizations, but given their tendency to mock Illinois traditions, they also clearly saw it in opposition to existing religious practices. During a period of warfare, direct cultural challenge by the Jesuits, population decline, and, if French accounts are correct, widespread violence of men against women, the actions of these women had direct social and cultural implications. Women took the common Algonquian dictum that unmarried women were "masters of their own body" and justified not sexual experimentation but sexual abstinence. They then assayed the religious powers they derived from prayer and Catholic doctrine against the powers the elders derived from visions and tradition. Their actions outraged both the young men, who found their own sexual opportunities diminished, and the elders and shamans who were directly challenged.[11]

In this dispute, Christianity and the Algonquians' social and cultural world were becoming part of a single field of action, and the outcome influenced not just Algonquian but also French society. Frenchmen in the West were no more enthusiastic about the new Christian influence among Illinois women than were Illinois men. Frenchmen, too, resented the new ability of Jesuits, through their influence over women, to control the sexual lives of the coureurs de bois and the voyageurs. Their resentment went beyond this.

Jesuit influence threatened not only sexual activity but also the ability of traders and coureurs de bois to create the ties to Algonquian society on which their trade, and perhaps their lives, depended. The critical issue here was not casual liaisons, but marriage. Formal marriages between Indian women and Frenchmen were quite rare during the seventeenth century. Marriage *à la façon du pays,* that is, according to local Algonquian custom, may have occurred, but there are few references to interracial marriage of any kind until the 1690s. In 1698 Father St. Cosme mentioned voyageurs with Illinois wives, and about the same time Father Carheil mentioned other voyageurs at Michilimackinac who had married among the Indians. In theory, the Jesuits and the colonial elite in general might have been expected to approve marriage between Frenchmen and Indian women as an alternative to the unregulated sexual relationships of the *pays d'en haut.* Along the same line, the French voyageurs, operating in a world of abundant sexual opportunities, might have been expected to be indifferent to formal conjugal ties. In fact, however, their positions were nearly the opposite during the 1690s. The seemingly sudden rise of interracial marriages in the 1690s may be connected with the increasingly serious attempts of the French to force the coureurs de bois out of the *pays d'en haut.* These culminated in the French abandonment of most western posts in the late 1690s. Through marriage, the coureurs de bois may have been attempting to establish the necessary kin connections with Indians that would be vital to the ability of any Frenchman to remain safely in the West.[12]

Such attempts met with considerable sympathy from French commanders, usually with trading interests of their own, who were responsible not for larger policies but for day-to-day relations with the Indians. Both Henry de Tonti and the Sieur de la Forest at Fort Saint Louis supported attempts to fortify ties with the Illinois through intermarriage. Cadillac's plan for Detroit in the early eighteenth century included the promotion of marriages between soldiers and Indian women. He explained: "Marriages of this kind will strengthen the friendship of these tribes, as the alliances of the Romans perpetuated peace with the Sabines through the intervention of the women whom the former had taken from the others."[13]

Indians, like the commanders, saw marriage as an integral part of their alliance with the French. Male heads of families, at least, greeted marriages enthusiastically. Marriage, far more than the prevailing French liaisons with hunting women, put sex firmly in the political arena. As both sides recognized, marriage was an alliance between families that concerned many more people than the marital partners. Not only did property move into the hands of the bride's family, but kinship relations were established that enabled both families to call on their relatives for aid and protection. Because of the wider social implications of marriage, as compared to relations with hunting women, a woman found her family much more interested in her choice of a permanent French partner than in her casual liaisons.[14]

Jesuits and higher French officials, however, were unenthusiastic about marriage both because it gave voyageurs and coureurs de bois an independent hold in the *pays d'en haut* and also for racist reasons. The Jesuits did not favor interracial marriage in the seventeenth century. Their preferred solution to the problems of sexual morality was to banish most Frenchmen from the upper country and to place those who remained under strict Jesuit supervision. Gradually, however, the Jesuits and other priests in upper Louisiana came to condone interracial marriage if the wife was Catholic. Of twenty-one baptisms recorded at the French village of Kaskaskia between 1704 and 1713, the mother was Indian and the father was French in eighteen cases. In 1714, the Sieur de la Vente, the curé for Louisiana, praised intermarriage as a way to people the colony. He contended that, the women of the Illinois and neighboring tribes were "whiter, more laborious, more adroit, better housekeepers, and more docile" than Indian women found elsewhere in the West and the South.[15]

Leading colonial officials were much more consistent in their opposition to intermarriage than the priests were. In Canada they preferred that Frenchmen marry and settle around Quebec or Montreal. As long as official policy involved the suppression of the coureurs de bois and their removal from the West, officials could not be openly enthusiastic about marriages there. They coupled such policy considerations with racist disgust at the results of French-Indian intermarriage. As Governor [Philippe de Rigaud] de Vaudreuil explained in opposing interracial marriage at Detroit in 1709: "Bad should never be mixed with good. Our experience of them in this country ought to prevent us from permitting marriages of this kind, for all the Frenchmen who have married savages have been licentious, lazy and intolerably independent; and their children have been characterized by as great a slothful-ness as the savages themselves." By the time he was governor of Louisiana, [Antoine Laumet de La Mothe, Sieur de] Cadillac, who had once advocated intermarriage, and his intendant, Duclos, opposed intermarriage in the same terms. Indian women were, they said, licentious and would leave men who did not please them, and even if the marriage lasted, the result would be a population of "mulattos [*mulâtres*], idlers, libertines, and even more knaves than [there] are in the Spanish colonies."[16]

Given this range of social and cultural concerns, the divisions within each society, and the inevitability of members of both societies being integral figures in deciding outcomes, it is not surprising that the prospect of a marriage between a Christian Illinois woman and a Frenchman precipitated a crisis that was ultimately decided on the middle ground. In 1694 Michel Accault's attempt to wed Aramepinchieue brought to light both the full complexity of the relations between the two societies and the processes by which the middle ground was emerging.

The controversy over the marriage of Accault and Aramepinchieue did not pit the Illinois against the French. Rather, it divided each group in a way that can only be grasped by looking at the social positions of the bride and the groom. Aramepinchieue was the daughter of Rouensa, a leading Kaskaskia chief. She was a fervent Christian and the pride of the Illinois mission. Michel Accault was a Frenchman who had first come west with [René Robert Cavelier, Sieur de] La Salle. He had later accompanied [a] voyage to the Sioux. Afterward, he had traded widely in the West and had established a reputation among the Jesuits as a libertine and an enemy of the faith. Aramepinchieue thus had links both with the Kaskaskia elite and Father Gravier. Accault was leagued with Henry de Tonti and the Frenchmen around him at Fort Saint Louis and was an enemy of Gravier's. His marriage with Aramepinchieue would strengthen the connections of a prominent Kaskaskia family with the French to the benefit of both. Rouensa announced the marriage in precisely those terms. He was strengthening his alliance with the French.[17]

The problem was that this proposed union, while it might link French and Algonquians, also emphasized the internal divisions within each group. Aramepinchieue refused to marry Accault. Father Gravier supported her decision. His immediate target was Accault. He would not sanction the influence within Indian society of a Frenchman he regarded as dissolute. He might grudgingly permit the marriage of Catholic Frenchmen with Christian Indian women, but he would do so only in circumstances that would advance the cause of the true faith. He told Aramepinchieue's parents and her suitor that "God did not command her not to marry, but also that she could not be forced to do so; that she alone was mistress to do the one or the other." Gravier's statement demonstrates that no matter how repressive Catholic morality may appear in retrospect, it could be used to buttress women's influence over their lives and their families. Women like Aramepinchieue had always had some control over their choice of marriage partners, but Christianity presented them with a new mechanism of control. What made this unique was not the woman's ability to reject unwanted suitors but, rather, the allies who could be mustered to maintain her decision against family pressures.[18]

In one sense, Aramepinchieue's decision represents a clear rejection of Algonquian norms and an appeal to an alien set of standards, but in another sense Aramepinchieue was appealing to such standards only to strengthen a very Algonquian sense of a woman's autonomy. Gravier's assertion that she was "mistress to do either the one or the other" did, after all, echo the Algonquian tenet that unmarried women were "masters" of their own bodies. Gravier, who sought to subvert traditional Illinois sexual practices because they contradicted Catholicism, and Aramepinchieue, who used Catholicism to maintain the values that supported those same practices, thus found themselves allies. By definition, then—the involvement of both French and Indians, the need for members of each group to get assistance from members of the other to fulfill desires arising within their own society, and the inability of either French or Indian norms to govern the situation—this was a conflict of the middle ground.

The initial result of the bride's refusal was a standoff, which both Rouensa and the French commander tried to break with the limited coercive means available to them. Rouensa drove Aramepinchieue from his house, but she was protected by Father Gravier, who secured her shelter with a neophyte family. Her rejection of her parents' wishes pained her deeply, but she justified her actions by appeals to Catholic doctrine. The chiefs in council retaliated by attempting to halt Catholic services at the chapel. At least fifty persons, virtually all of them women and girls, persisted in going to church. The council then (although they denied it) appears to have dispatched a warrior armed with a club to disrupt the services. The women defied him. Among the Illinois, me opposing sides had clearly formed along gender lines. Not all of the women abandoned the chiefs, but Christianity was, for the moment, a women's religious society acting in defiance of a male council. Among the French, the division was necessarily among males. The French commander, far from stopping this interference with the mission, gloated over it and denounced Gravier publicly before both me French and the Indians. When these tactics failed to sway the priest, neither the commander nor Rouensa felt confident enough to escalate the level of violence, although the Kaskaskias left the option of further coercion open.[19]

Such a face-off did not serve the interests of either side. Aramepinchieue was in turmoil over her alienation from her parents, to whom she was closely attached. Gravier found further missionary activities virtually impossible in the face of council opposition, which threatened to confine his promising mission to a besieged group of young women and girls. On the other hand, Gravier and the bride together blocked a marriage that both the Kaskaskias and the French deeply wanted.

The situation, in the end, was solved by a series of trade-offs. Aramepinchieue, in effect, negotiated a compromise with her father. She told Gravier, "I think that if I consent to the marriage, he will listen to you in earnest, and will induce all to do so," and she consented to the marriage on the terms that her parents, in turn, "grant me what I ask." They agreed. Rouensa disavowed his opposition to Christianity in full council and urged those present to "obey now the black gown." His agreement was sincere, and he and his wife began instruction for baptism. Accault, too, became a practicing Catholic once more and an ally of the Jesuits'. In return, the Kaskaskia chief, as he informed the other headmen of the confederation with considerable presents, was "about to be allied to a Frenchman."[20]

The marriage, therefore, was a great coup for Gravier. It brought into the church the most prominent Kaskaskia civil leader and his brother, an equally prominent war leader, and opened the way for making the Kaskaskias the most Catholic of the western Algonquians. The main agent in these events was a seventeen-year-old woman who appealed to alien standards both to control her condition and, eventually, to alter the condition of her nation. By 1711 the Kaskaskias were supposedly virtually all Catholic, and missionaries had made significant inroads among other Illinois groups. Aramepinchieue had maintained and strengthened the relationships that mattered most to her—those with her parents and the Christian congregation of women. The price was marriage to Accault, but this may very well have remained for her a subsidiary social arrangement. Christianity did not immediately transform marriage. French officials would later claim that Christian Illinois women less devout than Aramepinchieue still felt free to leave their French husbands whenever they chose.[21]

Women like Aramepinchieue are rarely visible in the documents, but their traces appear everywhere. Diplomatic negotiations and warfare, the large trading expeditions, these were the work of men, but the Frenchmen who appeared in Algonquian villages either traveled with Algonquian women or had liaisons with them there. Much of their petty trading was probably with women. The labor they purchased was usually that of women. On a day-today basis, women did more than men to weave the French into the fabric of a common Algonquian-French life. Both in and out of marriage, these women bore children with the French, some of whom in time would come to form a separate people, the *métis,* who themselves mediated between French and Algonquians and became of critical importance to the area.

Gravier himself would continue to make his greatest gains among the women of the Illinois, but in other tribes of the confederation he would not acquire allies of the status of Aramepinchieue. In 1706 Gravier returned to Pimitoui. The Kaskaskias had by now left to resettle on the Mississippi, the French had abandoned Fort Saint Louis, and the Peorias who remained at the site resented Gravier's aggressive tactics enough to attack him physically. They wounded him and, revealingly, left him in the care of "some praying women" until Kaskaskias sent by Rouensa rescued the priest. Father Gravier never fully recovered from his wounds, and eventually he died of complications. His death, a reminder of how tentative and tenuous the middle ground could be, also serves as a transition to the second issue demanding French-Algonquian cooperation—violence and interracial murder.[22]

Although not all murders, as the killing of Father Gravier demonstrates, grew out of the trade, violence and interracial murder as a whole were inextricably bound up with commerce. In 1684 alone, the only year for which a summary is given, thirty-nine Frenchmen trading in the West died at the hands of their Algonquian allies. Indians murdered Frenchmen during robberies, killed them in disputes over debt or gift exchanges, attacked them in attempts to stop weapons from going to their enemies, killed them to avenge killings by the French, and, as the liquor trade expanded, killed them in drunken quarrels. The French, in turn, used force against thieves, which did not prevent theft from becoming as established a part of the exchange as gifts or bargaining. . . .[23]

Perhaps the most perplexing intercultural concern of the French and the Algonquians was how to settle and limit the number of murders arising from the trade, when there was no authority in the West capable of creating a monopoly on violence and establishing order. Violence became one of the central concerns of the middle ground. When murders occurred between Algonquians and Frenchmen, each side brought quite different cultural formulas to bear on the situation. For northeastern Indians, both Algonquians and Iroquoians, those people killed by allies could be compensated for with gifts or by slaves or, failing these, by the killing of another member of the offending group. The decision about how to proceed was made by the dead person's kin, but extensive social pressure was usually exerted to accept compensation short of blood revenge, since killing a person of the offending group often only invited future retaliation. Among the French the matter was simpler. Society at large took the responsibility for punishing murder. Punishment was not left to the kin of the victim but rather to the state. The expected compensation for murder was the death of the murderer.[24]

Of the obvious differences here, two were particularly important. In the French scheme of things, exactly who committed the murder was of supreme importance, since the individual killer was held responsible for the crime. Only when a group refused to surrender a known murderer did collective responsibility arise. For the Indians, identifying the murderer was not as important as establishing the identity of the group to which the murderer belonged, for it was the group—family, kin, village, or nation—that was held responsible for the act. Both sides established cultural measures of equivalence in compensating for the dead, but the French equivalence was invariably another death. As the French emphasized again and again . . . death could only be compensated for by more death. Indians would, if necessary, also invoke a similar doctrine of revenge, but their preference was always either, in their words, "to raise up the dead," that is, to restore the dead person to life by providing a slave in the victim's place, or "to cover the dead," that is, present the relatives with goods that served as an equivalent.[25]

Most murders in the West left no trace in the documents, but an examination of those that are recorded can be rewarding. Three incidents in particular offer enough documentation for cultural analysis. The first occurred in 1682 or 1683, when two Frenchmen were waylaid on the Keweenaw Peninsula in Lake Superior and murdered by a Menominee and several Chippewas. These murders took place when the *pays d'en haut* was in a state of near chaos. Iroquois attacks, which had devastated the Illinois, had so far gone unavenged. Iroquois parties had recently struck the Illinois and the Mascoutens and were edging closer to Green Bay itself. Not only did the French seem unable to protect their allies, but an epidemic that the Potawatomis blamed on Jesuit witchcraft had recently ravaged the villages around the bay. The Potawatomis had murdered two French donnés in retaliation and had begun efforts to create a larger anti-French alliance. A recent alliance between the Saulteurs and the Sioux, which Daniel Greysolon Dulhut had helped orchestrate, had further inflamed the peoples of Green Bay against the French. They attempted to block French trade with the Sioux.

The Fox had already fought and defeated a large Sioux-Chippewa force at a considerable loss to themselves, and a full-scale Chippewa-Fox war seemed imminent. But apparently not all the Chippewas relished the new alignment. Achiganaga, an important headman at Keweenaw, had attacked the Sioux and planned further attacks. His war parties, as well as those of the peoples at Green Bay, threatened the lives of French voyageurs.[26]

In the midst of this turmoil a party led by Achiganaga's sons and including at least one Menominee, a member of a Green Bay tribe, murdered, two Frenchmen. Their motive may have been robbery. Or Achiganaga may have sought to disrupt the Sioux trade, break the new alliance of other proto-Ojibwa bands with the Sioux, and join with the peoples of the bay in a larger anti-French movement. In any case, his sons murdered two Frenchmen and stole their goods. Dulhut, despite the powerful kin connections of the accused murderers, seized the Menominee at Sault Sainte Marie and sent out a party that successfully captured Achiganaga and all his children at Keweenaw. The local Algonquian peoples reacted to Dulhut's acts by resorting to customary procedures. The Saulteurs offered the French the calumet—the standard ceremony for establishing peace and amity—and then they offered slaves to resurrect the dead Frenchmen and end the matter. Dulhut's emissary refused all such offers and denied the legitimacy of such cultural equivalence, telling them "that a hundred slaves and a hundred packages of beaver could not make him traffic in the blood of his brothers."[27]

Up to this point, all seems to be merely another example of something that appears in the literature many times: an ethnocentric European imposing by force proper cultural forms on a people he regards as savages. Savagism as a way of looking at Indians was, however, of limited utility in the woods. Dulhut was hardly in a position to act as if Indians were without culture. The French state did not command a monopoly of violence in the West and its authority was feeble. Dulhut did not have an established judicial system to appeal to, unless he wished to try to convey his prisoners to Quebec or Montreal. When the murderers had been disposed of, he and his men would remain to travel among the surrounding Indians who were not likely to forget whatever action he took. Their thoughts on the matter could not be safely ignored, and Dulhut having rejected Indian norms, relaxed his own considerably.

What followed at Michilimackinac was a series of rather extraordinary improvisations as Dulhut and various Ottawa, Huron-Petun, and Chippewa headmen and elders struggled to create a middle ground where the matter could be resolved. Dulhut's primary appeal throughout was to French law and custom, but he tried repeatedly, if necessarily somewhat ignorantly, to justify his recourse to law and custom by equating them with Indian practices. Having rejected the preferred means of settling killings among allies—the covering or raising up of the dead—he insisted on the penalty exacted from enemies: blood revenge. The Indians, for their part, paid little attention to what mattered most to the French, the proper way of establishing guilt and punishing the perpetrator. They only sought to offer suitable compensation to the living and reestablish social peace.[28]

The result was a series of bizarre cultural hybrids. The various Ottawa, Chippewa, and Huron-Petun bands convened in council with Dulhut only to find themselves transformed into a jury by the French for the trial of the Menominee, Achiganaga, and two of his sons. Kinsmen of the accused were drafted as lawyers, testimony was given and written down, and the murderers, with the exception of Achiganaga, freely admitted the crime. The elders cooperated with this French ritual, apparently believing that after it was performed the French would accept appropriate compensation. Instead, Dulhut demanded that the Indians themselves execute the murderers. To the Indians, Achiganaga's failure to confess constituted acquittal, and he was no longer part of the proceedings, but execution of the remaining three men, after compensation had been refused, would have been the equivalent of a declaration of war on the Saulteurs and Menominees by the executioners. The elders were so shocked and confused by this demand that they did not even make an answer.[29]

Dulhut, at this point, decided unilaterally to execute the Menominee and the two sons of Achiganaga as the admittedly guilty parties. This decision not only upset the Indians at Michilimackinac, it also appalled the French wintering at Keweenaw, who sent Dulhut a message warning that if he executed the murderers, the Indians' relatives would take revenge on the French. They begged him to act with restraint. French standards simply could not be imposed with impunity. Dulhut, after consulting with the Sieur de La Tour, the man longest among the lake tribes and most familiar with their customs, sought once more to appeal to Indian custom and return the matter to the middle ground. He again tried to find some connection between French law and what he regarded as Indian custom. Since two Frenchmen had died, Dulhut would execute only two Indians—the Menominee and the eldest of the two sons of Achiganaga—for "by killing man for man, the savages would have nothing to say, since that is their own practice." He announced this decision in the cabin of an Ottawa headman the French called Le Brochet, adding that although French law and custom demanded the execution of all the men involved in the robbery, he would be content with a life for a life.[30]

By his decision, Dulhut established a tenuous connection between Algonquian and French customs—a life for a life—but he also revealed the very different meanings such a dictum had in each culture. Only now, according to Dulhut, did the Ottawas believe that the French would actually execute two of the men. The headmen of the Sable Ottawas and the Sinago Ottawas, themselves uninvolved in the murder, begged Dulhut to spare the murderers. They, too, sought a middle ground and appealed to French precedent. At the request of Onontio, the Ottawas had spared an Iroquois prisoner. The French should now do the same for them. Dulhut denied the situations were equivalent. The

Iroquois was a prisoner of war; these men were murderers. Here the glaring differences between Ottawa and French cultural categories emerged in action.[31]

Blood revenge was appropriate in each society but for different categories of killing. For the Algonquians there were two kinds of killings—deaths at the hands of enemies and deaths at the hands of allies. The appropriate response depended on the identity of the group to whom the killer belonged. If the killer belonged to an allied group, then the dead were raised or covered. If the murderers refused to do this, then the group became enemies and the price appropriate to enemies, blood revenge, was exacted. For the French also there were two kinds of killings—killings in war and murders. Killing enemies in war theoretically brought no retribution once the battle ended. For them, the battlefield was a cultural arena separate from the rest of life. Releasing the Iroquois was thus only appropriate; he was a soldier, not a murderer. Algonquians in practice recognized no such cultural arena as a battlefield; they killed their enemies when and where they found them unless they were ritually protected. For the French it was murder that demanded blood revenge; for the Algonquians, it was killings by enemies, killings which the French saw as warfare. The French insistence on blood revenge in an inappropriate category, therefore, created great confusion. To the Ottawas the logic of such a response—that enemies should be spared but that allies should be killed—was incomprehensible.[32]

The way out of this deadlock was created by a man named Oumamens, a headman of the Amikwas (a proto-Ojibwa group). He spoke for the Saulteurs in council and resorted to the kind of cultural fiction that often disguises the beginnings of cultural change. He got up and praised, of all things, Dulhut's mercy, because he had released Achiganaga and all but one of his children. In effect, Oumamens chose to emphasize those of Dulhut's actions which conformed to Algonquian custom. He announced that the Saulteurs were satisfied. Dulhut, for his part, stressed not mercy but deterrence. If the elders "had from the beginning made known to the young men that in case they committed any evil deed the tribe would abandon them, they would have been better advised, and the Frenchmen would still be alive." Both sides thus tended to stress the aspect of the affair that made cultural sense to them. An hour later, at the head of forty-eight Frenchmen with four hundred warriors watching, Dulhut had the two Indians executed.[33]

The executions did not establish the legitimacy of French justice. Indeed, in the days that followed the executions, the Indians treated them as two more murders to be resolved, and Dulhut consented to their proceedings. Because Achiganaga's son and the Menominee had been executed in the territory of the Huron-Petuns and the Ottawas, these groups were implicated, and they took steps to settle the whole affair.[34]

Three Ottawa tribes—the Sables, Sinagos, and Kiskakons—gave two wampum belts to the French to cover their dead and two other belts to Achiganaga and to the Menominee's relatives. The next day the Huron-Petuns did the same. Dulhut, for his part, held a feast for Le Brochet, the Sable headman, to "take away the pain that I had caused him by pronouncing the death sentence of the two savages in his cabin, without speaking to him of it." Dulhut then loaded Achiganaga with presents, and the Saulteurs gave the French at Keweenaw additional belts "to take good care that no trouble be made over the death of their brother; and in order, should any have evil designs, to restrain them by these collars, of which they are bearers."[35]

The incident is revealing precisely because it was so indecisive, so improvised, precisely because neither French nor Algonquian cultural rules fully governed the situation. Both French and Algonquian customs were challenged, consciously explained, and modified in practice. Dulhut did not establish the primacy of French law, and he did not prevent further killings. What he did do was to shake, but not eliminate, the ability of Algonquian norms to govern murders of Frenchmen by Indians. Both sides now had to justify their own rules in terms of what they perceived to be the practices of the other. What happened in 1683 was, in the end, fully in accordance with neither French nor Indian conceptions of crime and punishment. Instead, it involved considerable improvisation and the creation of a middle ground at a point where the cultures seemed to intersect, so that the expectations of each side could find at least some satisfaction. At Green Bay the next spring, Father Nouvel thought that Dulhut's executions had produced a good effect, but at the same time he attributed the Potawatomi and Sauk desire for reconciliation with the French to their growing fear of the Iroquois, not their fear of French reprisals. Nouvel, for his part, demanded no further executions; he was willing to accept the Potawatomi and Sauk offer to cover the deaths of the two French donnés they had murdered.[36]

At Michilimackinac in 1683, Dulhut had operated without specific authority from the French government for his actions. He had improvised his solutions. The killings at Detroit, some twenty years later, in 1706, led to negotiations with the highest colonial officials, at a time when the French-Algonquian alliance had created a considerably more elaborate middle ground on which Indians and Frenchmen might work. Indeed, it was the alliance itself that both created the conditions that caused the murders and provided the ceremonial forms that compensated for them.

In 1706, as Ottawa warriors departed to attack the Sioux, a Potawatomi warned them that in their absence the Huron-Petuns and the Miamis would fall on the Ottawa village and kill those who remained. The Ottawa war leaders consulted with the civil leaders and, although some wavered, the old and powerful Sable chief whom the French called Le Pesant convinced them to strike first. The Ottawas ambushed a party of Miami chiefs, killing five of them, and then attacked the Miami village, driving the inhabitants into the French fort. The French fired on the attacking Ottawas and killed a young Ottawa who had just been recognized as a war leader. Although the

Ottawa leaders tried to prevent any attacks on the French, angry warriors killed a French Recollect priest outside the fort and a soldier who came out to rescue him.[37]

The Ottawas tried all the ceremonial means at their disposal to effect a reconciliation with the French, but they were rebuffed by the man commanding in Cadillac's absence. In subsequent fighting, the French sided with the Miamis, as did the Huron-Petuns (the nation the Ottawas claimed had actually organized the plot against them). Before the Ottawas withdrew to Michilimackinac, three Frenchmen, about thirty Ottawas, fifty Miamis, and an unknown number of Huron-Petuns were dead. The critical issue between the French and Ottawas, however, was the men killed during the first exchange: the young Ottawa leader, another Ottawa man with powerful kin connections at Michilimackinac, the Recollect, and the first French soldier killed. . . .[38]

The prominence of the dead on both sides intensified the difficulties of settling the killings. The dead Ottawas had powerful kinspeople; the French stressed the particular horror of killing a priest; and Cadillac promised the Miamis and Huron-Petuns the destruction of the Ottawas as revenge for their own dead. The negotiations to resolve these killings would be, according to Governor de Vaudreuil, one of the most important affairs in the history of the upper country.[39]

The ceremonial forms of the Ottawa-French alliance shaped the negotiations from the beginning. The alliance was centered on Quebec, the home of Onontio, and it was formulated in the language of kinship to which both the French and the Algonquians attached great significance. Leaders of both the French and the Algonquians negotiated according to ritual forms which placed the French governor, Onotio, in the position of father to the Indians, of whom the Ottawas were his eldest sons. The French were quite at home with such patriarchal formulations and attached quite specific meanings to them. For them all authority was patriarchal, from God the Father, to the king (the father of his people), to the father in his home. Fathers commanded; sons obeyed. The Ottawas understood the relationship somewhat differently. A father was kind, generous, and protecting. A child owed a father respect, but a father could not compel obedience. In establishing a middle ground, one took such congruences as one could find and sorted out their meanings later.[40]

Within the alliance, these ritual forms for father and son thus had a built-in ambiguity that would influence the course of the negotiations that followed the fighting at Detroit. Negotiations in the West (at Sault Sainte Marie and Michilimackinac) covered the Ottawa dead to that nation's satisfaction, but covering the French dead proved more difficult. Many of the matters at issue here revolved around questions of the proper way for a father to act toward his errant sons. At Quebec, Vaudreuil, in his negotiations with the Ottawas in the fall of 1706 and the spring of 1707, insisted on phrasing the alliance arid Ottawa obligations in terms of Christian patriarchy. The governor demanded that the Ottawas appear before him as penitent sinners appear before the Christian God. The customary Ottawa compensation for the dead was inadequate and inappropriate.

> I am a good father and as long as my children listen to my voice, no evil ever befalls them. . . . It is not belts that I require, Miscouaky, nor presents when my children have disobeyed me and committed such a fault as yours; the blood of Frenchmen is not to be paid for by beaverskins. It is a great trust in my kindness that I demand; a real repentance for the fault that has been committed, and complete resignation to my will. When your people entertain those feelings, I will arrange everything.[41]

The Ottawa response to these demands, in the usual manner of the middle ground, was to seek cultural congruence. They, too, focused on patriarchy, but of a different kind. Otontagan (or Jean le Blanc), the Sable chief second in influence to Le Pesant, spoke for the Ottawas when they came to Quebec the next summer. He admitted his guilt (even though he had, in fact, tried to save the Recollect) but attempted to place the primary responsibility for the affair with Le Pesant. Otontagan's major concern, however, was to get Vaudreuil to act like an Ottawa, not a French, father. He stressed Vaudreuil's beneficence. Vaudreuil certainly had the power to kill him, but "I have nothing to fear because I have a good father." Since Vaudreuil had specifically rejected covering the dead, Otontagan concluded that he must want the dead raised up. The delegation accordingly brought two adopted captives to give to Vaudreuil "to bring the gray coat again to life." Vaudreuil held out for a stricter patriarchy. He demanded vengeance; he demanded the head of Le Pesant because "the blood of French is usually repaid among us only by blood." But such a demand, Otontagan told Vaudreuil, was impossible. Le Pesant was allied to all the nations of the Great Lakes. They would prevent his delivery and execution.[42]

On the surface, the negotiations at Quebec appear to be another example of a stubborn French refusal to compromise. The situation was, in fact, much more complex. Vaudreuil knew that no Ottawa leader possessed sufficient authority to hand over anyone, let alone someone of Le Pesant's stature. His intention was not to secure Le Pesant's death, rather it was to cut him off from the French alliance, destroy his influence, and demonstrate that any chief held responsible for the death of a Frenchman would suffer the same fate. Since Vaudreuil did not expect Le Pesant to be surrendered, the actual restoration of the Ottawas to the alliance would involve a compromise of some sort. Since patriarchs do not compromise, he sent the Ottawas back to Detroit, telling them to negotiate a peace with Cadillac. He would approve such a peace as long as Le Pesant was not included in any pardon Cadillac granted. By this maneuver Vaudreuil could make an impossible demand, while leaving the responsibility of negotiating what might be an embarrassing compromise to his rival and subordinate, Cadillac.[43]

At Detroit the larger issue remained—how the alliance could be restored within the cultural parameters of the parties involved. Le Pesant was called "that great bear, that malicious bear," and Vaudreuil's demand for his execution loomed over the proceedings. The people struggling with this problem were themselves political actors who were not necessarily wedded to the welfare of either Le Pesant or Vaudreuil. The chief Ottawa negotiators, Otontagan and Onaske from Michilimackinac, were Le Pesant's political rivals. They protected him not out of love but because they had no means at their disposal to deliver him, and they feared the repercussions if they tried. Cadillac, for his part, was a long-standing opponent of Vaudreuil and only too glad to use the affair to benefit himself and embarrass the governor. Both Cadillac and the Ottawa chiefs could conceivably use the cultural demands of outsiders to advance their interests within their own society while simultaneously renewing the alliance.[44]

The willingness of both Cadillac and the Ottawa negotiators to move from their initial positions reflects this sense of their own political advantage. They could also violate the usual norms of their own cultures because the alliance, itself the middle ground, created cultural demands of its own. Cadillac shifted his position first. He indicated that the surrender of Le Pesant was more important than his death. "I wish him to be in my power, either to grant him his life or put him to death," he told Otontagan. Cadillac was, in effect, putting Le Pesant in the place of the slaves or captives usually given to raise the dead. Such cultural logic was more comprehensible to the Ottawas than a demand for execution, even if the surrender of a chief was without precedent. These were unusual conditions; the alliance itself was at stake. Otontagan agreed to deliver Le Pesant: "He is my brother, my own brother, but what can we do?" Since Otontagan and Kinouge, another headman, were, like Le Pesant, Sable Ottawas, they agreed to take responsibility for his surrender, thus making the matter an internal Sable matter and limiting the repercussions. In effect, a cultural fiction was agreed on. Cadillac and the Ottawas agreed to act as if Le Pesant were a slave being offered to the French in compensation for their dead. Cadillac would then determine if he lived or died. This made cultural sense in a way that Le Pesant's execution did not; it preserved the alliance, and it served the personal interests of both French and Ottawa negotiators.[45]

There were two formidable obstacles to this solution. The first was the Miamis and the Huron-Petuns, whom Cadillac had made simple observers of the whole affair. For their benefit, Cadillac treated the Ottawa delegation imperiously. He gave the Huron-Petuns—and tried to give the Miamis—the Ottawa captives intended for Vaudreuil in order "to revive your dead a little—I do not say altogether." He even, in council, made the Huron-Petuns the elder brothers of the French alliance in place of the Ottawas. But he denied them revenge. He warned both nations that with the delivery of Le Pesant, he would consider the matter closed. "There shall be no blood left to be seen."[46]

The second obstacle was a practical one: Who exactly would persuade or force Le Pesant to consent to serve as a slave to the French? Who provided the solution to this problem is not known, but how it was solved is clear enough. A proceeding that had been half theater and half negotiation now became fully theater. After considerable negotiations at Michilimackinac, Le Pesant agreed to come to Detroit and surrender himself as a slave to the French. According to Vaudreuil, all that followed was prearranged between Le Pesant and an emissary of Cadillac. How much the other Ottawas or other Frenchmen knew of these arrangements is not clear.[47]

Cadillac compared the astonishment provoked by the appearance of Le Pesant at Detroit to that produced by the arrival of the Doge of Genoa in France. To evoke such a response, to make the Indians marvel at the culturally unimaginable things Cadillac and the French could achieve, was, in fact, the sole point of the drama now enacted at Detroit. Cadillac's production of "The Surrender of Le Pesant," however, had to play to a suspicious and critical audience of Miamis, Huron-Petuns, and those French officials who watched from afar. All of them were concerned not so much with the plot as with the culturally symbolic details that gave the drama its meaning. Vaudreuil delivered the most extended review of the performance, although, as shall be seen, the Miamis were the most critical.[48]

Le Pesant, until now the Godot of this drama, put in his appearance at Detroit on September 24, 1707. He delivered his only recorded lines while looking to shore from the canoe that brought him. He trembled, either from malaria or fear, and said, "I see I am a dead man." Yet what Vaudreuil noted was his escort. He came with ten warriors who were not Kiskakon or Sinago Ottawas, but Sable Ottawas from his own village. They were sent, Vaudreuil said, not to deliver him but to protect him from angry Huron-Petuns and Miamis. Cadillac verbally abused Le Pesant, referring to him as his slave, but Cadillac spoke to Le Pesant on a wampum belt. One did not speak to slaves on wampum. One spoke to representatives of nations in that manner. The Ottawas then asked for Le Pesant's life and, offering a young slave, asked that they be allowed to return to Detroit.[49]

With Le Pesant's ritual submission, the first act ended. Le Pesant, Vaudreuil pointed out, had served his purpose. His continued presence now became a problem for Cadillac. Vaudreuil had ordered his death and Cadillac had earlier promised the Miamis and Huron-Petuns that he would kill him. But if Cadillac actually killed Le Pesant, he risked conflict with the Sable Ottawas and their allies on the Great Lakes. Le Pesant's surrender was useful; his continued presence was not.[50]

Cadillac and the Ottawas solved the problem by writing Le Pesant out of the script. That night, leaving behind his shoes, his knife, and his shabby hat, Le Pesant escaped from the fort at Detroit. Cadillac, in retaliation, locked up his escorts for a day and then released them, contending that Le Pesant would perish in the woods, and, in any case, his influence was now gone. Vaudreuil was skeptical. Le Pesant—whose name translates from the French as the heavy one, or the fat one—was notoriously obese and nearly seventy years old. That a seventy-year-old fat man whose surrender had been the object of French policy in the upper country for more than a year could escape past sentinels from a French fort on the first night of his captivity strained credibility. Cadillac's only explanation was that Le Pesant had lost a lot of weight lately. With Le Pesant gone, Cadillac assured the Ottawas that he had intended to pardon him anyway, thus freeing himself from complicity in his death if the Huron-Petuns or Miamis should catch him.[51]

Vaudreuil, skeptical and critical as he was, appreciated good acting and clever staging, even as he deciphered the drama and explained away the illusions it sought to create. With both the Ottawas and the French acting according to script, the cultural demands of each had been met by creating an artificial and controlled stage, a special kind of middle ground. Vaudreuil appreciated this.[52]

The Miamis and Huron-Petuns were less enthusiastic. Their response to the drama was so harsh that Cadillac did not choose to fully report it. Instead, he reported only the closing part of the council that followed Le Pesant's escape and was attended by the Miamis, the Huron-Petuns, the French, and the Ottawas. In council, following the usual ritual forms, he calmed the waters, removed the fallen trees, smoothed the land, and opened the way for peace and the return of the Ottawas to Detroit.[53]

Unfortunately for Cadillac, the audience in historical dramas of this sort must consent to the script, for they always have the option of adding a final act. Le Pesant returned to Michilimackinac in the same canoe and with the same warriors who had escorted him down to Detroit, but this did not close the play. Cadillac had gained the Ottawas but lost the Miamis, who soon killed not only Ottawas but also Frenchmen, and so began yet another round of negotiations. The resolution of the killings at Detroit was thus only partially successful, but the negotiations are, nevertheless, illuminating. They reveal the substantial and expanding middle ground the French-Algonquian alliance had created. Here common problems could be worked out and mutually comprehensible solutions arrived at. The negotiations also reveal the extent to which solutions could be elaborately scripted cultural fictions, political theater. Such fictions deeply influenced events in both societies. . . .[54]

Separately, the stories of Dulhut and Achiganaga's sons [and] of Le Pesant and Cadillac . . . are incidents widely scattered over time and space, but together they form an evolving ritual of surrender and redemption that would be central to the French-Algonquian alliance. This ritual of the middle ground clearly drew elements from both cultures but fully corresponded to neither. The ritual operated by analogy. The murderer was to the governor as a sinner was to God. The governor was to the murderer as a stern but forgiving father was to an erring son. Such analogies were hooks, both attaching the new ritual to the purely Algonquian or French way of settling murders and pulling elements of the older process into the middle ground. As under the French system, Indian murderers would be imprisoned while their crimes were investigated; as under the Algonquian system, Indian and French dead would be covered or raised up.

Once formulated, this ritual of surrender and redemption became a centerpiece of the middle ground. Orders from Governor Duquesne to the Sieur de Pean in 1754 expressed its basic elements well: "He must manage to see that he obtains the murderers, to whom he will grant pardon in the customary manner." The ritual, however, was under constant pressure from Frenchmen who, having seen to it that murderers were surrendered, wished to see these murderers executed, and from Algonquians who hesitated to surrender kinspeople for even temporary imprisonment before their pardon "in the customary manner." Each murder, each surrender, and each pardon thus became a test of the health of the alliance. Onontio's failure to pardon and his children's failure to surrender signaled crises that only a renewal of the ritual could resolve. Like all structural elements of culture, the ritual remained meaningful only insofar as it was constantly replicated in action.[55]

What was being created in social action was a world very different from the one historians would expect to find if they relied on the older ethnographies. Nor does the evolution of this world conform to much acculturation literature with the gradual adoption by Indians of certain European values. Instead, members of two cultures established an alliance that they both thought furthered interests generated within their own societies. They maintained this alliance through rituals and ceremonials based on cultural parallels and congruences, inexact and artificial as they originally may have been. These rituals and ceremonials were not the decorative covering of the alliance; they were its sinews. They helped bind together a common world to solve problems, even killings, that threatened the alliance itself. These solutions might have been, as at Detroit, elaborate cultural fictions, but through them change occurred. Such changes, worked out on the middle ground, could be remarkably influential, bringing important modifications in each society and blurring the boundaries between them.

## NOTES

1 The impossibility of considering any society in isolation is one of the major themes of Eric Wolf in *Europe and the People Without History* (Berkeley: University of California Press, 1982), 3–23, 385. It is also a position taken by Anthony Giddens, *A Contemporary Critique of Historical Materialism* (Berkeley: University of California Press, 1981), 23–24.

2 Cornelius J. Jaenen, "Les Sauvages Ameriquians: Persistence into the Eighteenth Century of Traditional French Concepts and Constructs for Comprehending Amerindians," *Ethnohistory* 29 (1982): 43–56.

3 A useful discussion of these processes is found in Roy Wagner, *The Invention of Culture* (Chicago: University of Chicago Press, 1981), 1–70, particularly 46–52, 87–88. Many Frenchmen of peasant backgrounds were probably closer to what Wagner calls the differentiating mode of tribal peoples than to the systematizing mode of French officials. Attempts to get around the confining model of a basically static structure which is combined with an ephemeral history has been most thoroughly developed by Anthony Giddens, *Central Problems in Social Theory: Action, Structure and Contradiction in Social Analysis* (Berkeley: University of California Press, 1979); *Critique of Historical Materialism;* and *The Constitution of Society* (Berkeley: University of California Press, 1984). It has simultaneously emerged in anthropology, see Marshall Sahlins, *Islands of History* (Chicago: University of Chicago Press, 1985).

4 For this, see Wagner, *Invention of Culture*, 52–55.

5 "Narrative of . . . Occurrences . . . 1694, 1695," in E. B. O'Callaghan, ed., *Documents Relative to the Colonial History of the State of New York; Procured in Holland, England, and France, by John R. Brodhead* (Albany, NY: Parsons, Weed, 1853–1857), 9:608 [Hereafter NYCD]. For the development of trading enclaves, see Philip D. Curtin, *Cross-Cultural Trade in World History* (Cambridge: Cambridge University Press, 1984), 11–12, 38, 46–49, 111–15.

6 For Madame Le Sueur, see De Garnnes (Deliette) Memoir, *Collections of the Illinois Historical Library* (Springfield, IL: Trustees of the Illinois State Historical Library, 1915–1940), 23:338 [hereafter *IHC*]. For berdaches and homosexuality, see De Garnies (Deliette) Memoir, *IHC* 23:329–30; Chrestien Le Clercq, *First Establishment of the Faith in New France* (New York: J. G. Shea, 1881), 35; Relations des découvertes, in Pierre Margry, *Découvertes et établissements des Français . . . de l'Amérique Septentrionale, 1614–1698*, 6 vols. (Paris: Maisonneuve et Cie, 1879, repr. New York, AMS, 1974). 1:488.

7 Reuben Gold Thwaites, ed., The Jesuit Relations and Allied Documents (Cleveland, OH: Burrows Brothers, 1898), 54:179–83 [hereafter *JR*]; *JR* 65:235–45; Cadillac, Account of Detroit, Sept. 25, 1702, in *Michigan Pioneer Historical Society: Collections and Research* (Lansing, MI: The Society, 1877–1920), 33:143 [hereafter *MPHC*]. Ordonnance du M. le Comte de Frontenac pour la traite et commerce du outaouacs . . . 8 avril 1690 (avec remarques faites par l'intendant), AN, F3, v. 6, f. 366.

8 For general difficulties with European observations on Indian women, see Katherine Weist, "Beasts of Burden and Menial Slaves: Nineteenth-Century Observations of Northern Plains Indian Women," and Alice Kehoe, "The Shackles of Tradition," both in Patricia Albers and Beatrice Medicine, *The Hidden Half: Studies of Plains Indian Women* (Washington, D.C.: University Press of America, 1983), 29–52, 53–73. Women among the Illinois gained power from visions and could become shamans. The culturally very similar Miami had female chiefs whose duties paralleled the male chiefs'. They inherited their status from their fathers and did not obtain it through their husbands. See William C. Sturtevant, ed., *Handbook of North American Indians* (Washington, D.C.: Smithsonian Institution, 1978–), 15:675, 677, 684–85 [hereafter *HBNI*].

9 *JR* 65:67, 79; De Gannes (Deliette) Memoir, *IHC* 23:361. For emphasis Jesuits placed on sexual conduct among Kiskakon Ottawas and Kaskaskias, see *JR* 54:179–83, and *JR* 65:67–69.

10 De Garnies (Deliette) Memoir, *IHC* 23:329–30, 335–37; Joutel Memoir, in Isaac Joslin Cox, ed., *The Journeys of Réné Robert Cavelier, Sieur De La Salle . . .* (New York: A. S. Barnes & company, 1905), 2:222. Emily Blasingham estimates the ratio of adult warriors to the rest of the population at 1:3.17 which obviously would not allow for Deliette's estimate, but her estimate is perhaps even more of a guess than his. Emily J. Blasingham, "The Depopulation of the Illinois Indians. Part 2, Concluded," *Ethnohistory* 3:4 (October 1, 1956): 361–412, p. 364. For village sites, see J. Joe Bauxar, "The Historic Period," in Elaine Bluhm (ed.), *Illinois Archaeology Bulletin No. 1*, Illinois Archaeological Survey, Urbana (Carbondale, III.: Southern Illinois University Press, 1959), 49. For Gravier's mission, see Mary Borgian Palm, "The Jesuit Missions of the Illinois Country (1673–1763)," Ph.D. diss., St. Louis University, 1931 (Cleveland, privately printed, Sisters of Notre Dame, 1931), 22, 24–25. For Father Gravier's claim of baptism, see *JR* 65:33. For conflict, see *JR* 65:67, and Fr. Rale quoted in Mary Elizabeth Good, "The Guebert Site: An Eighteenth-Century Historic Kaskaskia Indian Village in Randolph County, Illinois," *Central States Archaeological Societies Memoir*, 2 (n.p., 1972), 14.

11 For Virgin Mary, see *JR* 59:187; 193, 201, 207, *JR* 63:217–19. For opposition of young men, see *JR* 65:67.

12 For marriages, see *JR* 65:241; *JR* 65:69; St. Cosme, in Louise P. Kellogg, ed., *Early Narratives of the Northwest, 1634–1699* (New York: Charles Scribner's Sons, 1917), 251. The best work on intermarriage on the Great Lakes is by Jacqueline Peterson, "Prelude to Red River: A Social Portrait of the Great Lakes Metis," *Ethnohistory* 25 (1978): 41–68. For intermarriage in the Northwest, see Olive Dickason, "From One Nation in the Northeast to New Nation in the Northwest: A Look at the Emergence of the Metis" in Jacqueline Peterson and Jennifer S. H. Brown, *The New Peoples; Being and Becoming Metis in North America* (Lincoln: University of Nebraska Press, 1985). Interracial marriage within the later fur trade has been the subject of two recent books, but both studies look at situations significantly different from those of the late seventeenth-century West, where many of the earliest Catholic marriages were solemnized by priests. See Sylvia Van Kirk, *Many Tender Ties: Women in Fur-Trade Society, 1670–1870* (Norman: University of Oklahoma Press, 1980), and Jennifer S. Brown, *Strangers in the Blood: Fur Trade Company Families in Indian Country* (Vancouver: University of British Columbia Press, 1980).

13 *JR* 64:201–03; Cadillac to Minister, 18 Oct. 1700, *MPHC* 33:189. For Cadillac's later opposition, see Mariage des francais avec les sauvagesses, 1 sept. 1716, AN, C13A, v.4, f. 255. Who was commanding at Fort. St. Louis in the Illinois at the time is unclear. Tonti was there in April 1694, Declaration de Henri de Tonti, 11 avril 1694, AN, C13A, Louisiana, v. 1 (fol, 27), but in the fall of 1693 he was in Montreal. Engagement of Viau to La Forest and Tonti, Sept. 11, 1693, *IHC* 23:273–75. Given the absence of Tonti and La Forest, Deliette may have been in command.

14 *JR* 64:195, 197, 207, 211. Milo Milton Quaife, ed., *The Western Country in the 17th Century; the Memoirs of Lamothe Cadillac and Pierre Liette* (Chicago: Lakeside Press, 1947), 39, 45; Nicolas Perrot, Memoir on the Manners, Customs, and Religion of the Savages of North America, in Emma Helen Blair, ed., *The Indian Tribes of the Upper Mississippi Valley and Region of the Great Lakes . . .* (Cleveland, Ohio: The Arthur H. Clark Company, 1911), 64–69; Joseph-François Lafitau, *Customs of the American Indians Compared with the Customs of Primitive Times* (Toronto: Champlain Society, 1974–1977), 1:336–37.

15 For official attitudes toward marriage, see Cornelius J. Jaenen, *Friend and Foe: Aspects of French-Amerindian Cultural Contact in the Sixteenth and Seventeenth Centuries* (New York: Columbia University Press, 1976), 164. For Father de la

Vente, see Manage des francais avec les sauvagesses, 1 sept. 1716, AN, C13A, v. 4. For banishment and supervision, see *JR* 65:233–45. For baptism, see Mary Borgian Palm, "The Jesuit Missions of the Illinois Country, 1673–1763," Ph.D. diss, St. Louis University, 1931 (Cleveland, privately printed, Sisters of Notre Dame, 1931), 43–45.

16 For governor's opposition, see Vaudreuil and Raudot to Minister, Nov. 14, 1709, *MPHC* 33:454. For Duclos and Cadillac, see Mariage des francais avec les sauvagesses, 1 sept. 1716, AN, C13A, v. 4, f. 255. For renewed concern in 1730, see Bienville et Salmon au Ministre, 16 mai 1735, AN, C13A, v. 20, f. 85. Memoire concernant les Illinois, 1732 AN, F3, v. 24.

17 For Accault, see *JR* 64:213, 180. For Aramepinchieue and Rouensa, see *JR* 64: 179–81, 193–237. Aramepinchieue took the Christian name Mary or Marie; see Palm, "Jesuit Missions," 38.

18 *JR* 64:205–07, 213, 280. *JR* 64:211, 95. For Aramepinchieue, see *JR* 64:193–95, 205–07, 213–29.

19 *JR* 64:195–205.

20 For Aramepinchieue quotations, see *JR* 64:207–9; otherwise, *JR* 64:179, 213, 211.

21 *JR* 64:79–81, 231–35; Palm, "Jesuit Missions," 38; André Penicault, *Fleur de Lys and Calumet: Being the Penicault Narrative of French Adventure in Louisiana*, ed. Richebourg Gaillard McWilliams (Baton Rouge: Louisiana State University Press, 1953), 139–40. For claims of success among other Illinois nations, see Callières et de Champigny au Ministre, 18 oct. 1700, AN, C11A, v. 18.

22 *JR* 65:101–03; Palm, "Jesuit Missions," 36, 47; Blàsingham, "Depopulation of the Illinois," 201; Bauxar, "Historic Period," 49. For Gravier, see *JR* 66:51–63.

23 Some historians continue to divide Indian-white relations between peaceful commerce and violent conflict. For such a position, see Francis Jennings, *The Ambiguous Iroquois Empire* (New York: W. W. Norton, 1984), 83. In fact, violence cannot be separated from the trade. The larger question of the role of violence in commerce has recently been raised by Curtin, *Cross-Cultural Trade*, 41–45. It is a question still illuminated by the work of Frederic Lane, *Venice and History* (Baltimore: Johns Hopkins University Press, 1966), 412–28; see, particularly, the "Economic Consequences of Organized Violence." For the number of murders, see Raisons qu'on a proposee a la Cour, 1687?, AN, C11A, v. 15, f. 271.

24 In the cases that follow both sides try to make these positions clear. See, e.g., extract from a letter by Dulhut, April 12, 1684, in Lyman C. Draper and Reuben G. Thwaites, eds., *Collections of the State Historical Society of Wisconsin* (Madison, WI: The Society, 1855–1911) [Hereafter *WHC*], 16:120, hereafter cited as Dulhut's letter. For Algonquian custom, see Jaenen, *Friend and Foe*, 123. For a discussion of murder, revenge, and compensation that stresses revenge rather than compensation among the Cherokee, see John Phillip *Reid, A Law of Blood: The Primitive Law of the Cherokee Nation* (NewYork: New York University Press, 1970), 73–112. Reid says that a retaliatory killing does not bring revenge (78). This does not appear to have been true among the Algonquians. Note how in the Dulhut case below Achiganaga is given presents to compensate for his son's death.

25 Report of Boisbriant Diron Desursins Legardeur De L'isle Ste. Therese Langloisere, June 17, 1723, in J. H. Schlarman, *From Quebec to New Orleans: Fort De Chartres* (Belleville, Ill.: Beuchler, 1929), 226–31. See also Jaenen, *Friend and Foe*, 97. Jaenen makes the distinction between the French emphasis on punishment and the Indian emphasis on compensation.

26 For conditions at Green Bay, see Enjalran à Lefevre de La Barre, 16 aoust 1683, Margry, *Découvertes*, 5:4–5. For Saulteur-Fox conflict, see ibid., 5; Claude Charles

Le Roy, Sieur de Bacqueville de la Potherie, *History of the Savage Peoples Who Are the Allies of New France*, in Emma Helen Blair, ed., *The Indian Tribes of the Upper Mississippi Valley and Region of the Great Lakes*, 2 vols. (Cleveland: Arthur H. Clark, 1912), 1:358–63; Dulhut letter, *WHC* 16:114. Durantaye à A. de la Barre, 11 avril 1684, AN, C11A, v. 6, 1.521–22. For activities of French traders and danger they were in, see Denonville au Ministre, aoust 1688, AN, C11A, v. 10, (f. 66); Nouvel à M. de la Barre, 23 avril 1684, AN, C11A, v. 6.

27 The only detailed account of this murder is Dulhut's own, but since he was in a position to justify his actions, he provided considerable detail. See Dulhut letter, April 12, 1684, *WHC*, 16:114–15, 123.

28 Dulhut letter, April 12, 1684, *WHC* 16:119.

29 Ibid., 118–20.

30 Ibid., 119–21.

31 Ibid., 120–21.

32 Ibid., See also Jaenen, *Friend and Foe*, 132–34. It should be noted that by 1690 the French had begun imitating the Iroquois and were torturing and killing prisoners of war, Narrative of . . . Occurrences 1690, 1691, *NYCD* 9:518.

33 Ibid., 120–21.

34 Ibid., 124.

35 Ibid., 124–25.

36 Fr. Nouvel à M. de la Barre, 23 avril 1684, AN, C11A, v. 6, f. 523. Reconciliation was also forwarded by Governor de la Barre who approved of Dulhut's actions, but the French court, which often had only a shaky grasp of what was going on in the upper country, confused Dulhut's executions with the killing of an Iroquois at Michilimackinac and denounced Dulhut and his presence in the backcountry, De la Barre au Ministre, 5 juin 1684, AN, C11A, v.6. Louis XIV to De La Barre, July 21, 1684, *DHNY*, 1:108–9.

37 For the Ottawa version of these events, see Speech of Miscouaky, Sept. 26, 1706, *MPHC* 33:288–92. For the French investigation, see Report of D'Aigremont, *MPHC* 33:435. For Cadillac's account, see Cadillac to de Vaudreuil, Aug. 27, 1706; E. M. Sheldon, *The Early History of Michigan from the First Settlement to 1815* (New York: A. S. Barnes, 1956), 219. For mention of a second French soldier killed later, see Instructions to D'Aigremont, June 30, 1707, *WHC* 16:243.

38 For Ottawa attempts to negotiate, see Speech of Miscouaky, 26 Sept. 1706, *MPHC* 133:290–92; Report of D'Aigremont, *MPHC 33*:435–36. For various casualty figures in the fight, see "Council with Ottawas, June 18, 1707," in Sheldon, *Early History of Michigan*, 228, where Jean le Blanc puts the Ottawa dead at 30; Speech of Miscouaky, Sept. 26, 1706, *MPHC* 33:294, where the figure is 26 for the Ottawas and 50 dead and wounded for the Miamis. For the significant Ottawa dead, see Speech of Miscouaky, Sept. 26, 1706, *MPHC* 33:290, and Fr. Marest to Vaudreuil, Aug. 14, 1706, *MPHC* 33:262–69. For the French emphasis on the priest and the first soldier killed, see Council with the Ottawas, June 20, 1707, Speech of Vaudreuil, Sheldon, *Early History of Michigan*, 242; Speech of Vaudreuil, June 21, 1707, ibid., 245.

39 For difficulties, see Father Marest to Vaudreuil, Aug. 14, 1706, *MPHC* 33:262–69; Council with the Ottawas, Speech of Vaudreuil, June 20, 1707, Sheldon, *Early History of Michigan*, 242. Cadillac to Vaudreuil, Aug. 27, 1706, ibid., 228–29. For importance of negotiations, see Vaudreuil to Father Marest, n.d. (1707), Sheldon, *Early History of Michigan*, 273.

40 Many examples of the French councils survive. For examples for the period under consideration here, see Parolles des sauvages . . ., Archives Nationales, Archives Coloniales, F3, v. 8, f. 136–41; Talk between Marquis de Vaudreuil

and Onaskin . . ., Aug. 1, 1707, *MPHC* 33:258–62; Speech of Miscouaky . . . to Marquis de Vaudreuil, Sept. 26, 1706, *MPHC* 33:288–96; Conference with Ottawas, June 18, 1707, in Sheldon, *Early History of Michigan*, 232–50. For the differences in how the Great Lakes Indians and the French perceived the relationship between parents and children, see Father Gabriel Sagard, *The Long Journey to the Country of the Hurons* (Toronto: Champlain Society 1939, facsimile ed., Greenwood Press), 130–31; Pierre de Charlevoix, *Journal of a Voyage to North America* (London: R. & J. Dodsley, 1761, Readex microprint facsimile ed., 1966), 2:55, 89–90, 109, 114–15; Lafitau, *Customs of the American Indian* 1:362; Perrot, *Memoir* 1:67; Louis Armand de Lom d'Arce Lahontan, *New Voyages to North-America*, ed. Reuben Gold Thwaites (Chicago: A.C. McClurg, 1905), 2:458. See also Jaenen, *Friend and Foe*, 94–97.

41 Kischkouch, the young Sinago chief killed at Detroit, had a brother, Merasilla, who had actually gone among the Saulteurs and Amikwas to raise a party to avenge his brother "and restore the name of Kischkouch." In the end, Merasilla excused himself from the war party, despite reproaches that he showed "no love for his brother," and helped negotiate a peace. The war party went to Detroit, accompanied by other Ottawas, but did not attack. Another Ottawa killed at Detroit had as relatives two of the principal women at Michilimackinac, and they went from cabin to cabin, weeping and demanding the deaths of Frenchmen there until negotiations covered their loss. Marest to Vaudreuil, Aug. 14, 1706, *WHC* 16:232–34; Marest to Vaudreuil, Aug. 16, 1706, and Aug. 27, 1706, *MPHC* 33:262–71; Cadillac to Vaudreuil, Aug. 27, 1706, Sheldon, *Early History of Michigan*, 226–27. For quote, see Reply of Vaudreuil to Miscouaky, Nov. 4, 1706, *MPHC* 33:295.

42 For Otontagan, see Vaudreuil to Minster, July 24, 1707; *MPHC* 33:328–29, Council with Ottawas, June 18, 1707, Speech of Jean le Blanc, Sheldon, *Early History of Michigan*, 233–39. For Vaudreuil's position, see Council with Ottawas, June 20, 1707, Reply of Vaudreuil, Sheldon, *Early History of Michigan*, 242; Reply of Jean le Blanc, June 21, 1707, ibid., 243–44.

43 See the speech of Vaudreuil to Jean le Blanc, June 22, 1707, Sheldon, *Early History of Michigan*, 245–47; Vaudreuil to Minster, July 24, 1707, *MPHC* 33:328–30. For the rivalry of Vaudreuil and Cadillac, see Vaudreuil to Minister, Nov. 12, 1707, *MPHC* 33:371–72.

44 Otontagan (Jean le Blanc), Kinouge, Meatinan, and Menukoueak were joined partway through the proceedings by Kataolauibois (Koutaouileone) and Onaske, who was headman of the Kiskakon Ottawas at Michilimackinac. Council held at Detroit, Aug. 6, 1707, Aug. 8, 1707, *MPHC* 33:331, 334; Speeches of Three Indians from Michilmackina [*sic*] Oct. 7, 1707, *MPHC* 33:362–64.

45 Council Held at Detroit, Aug. 6, 1707, Speech of Cadillac *MPHC* 33:332. Council Held at Detroit, Replies of Otontagan, Aug. 6, 1707, Seventh Council, Speech of Onaske, *MPHC* 33:332–33. 335–36. Speeches of Three Indians from Michilimakina [*sic*], Oct. 7, 1707, *MPHC* 33:363-64.

46 The Huron-Petuns and Miamis wondered out loud why Cadillac should bother to demand Le Pesant when there were so many Ottawa chiefs in Detroit upon whom they could take revenge. Council Held at Detroit, Aug. 7, 1707, Aug. 9, 1707, *MPHC* 33:333–35; Speeches of Three Indians from Michilimakina [*sic*], Oct. 7, 1707, *MPHC* 33:363–64.

47 How Le Pesant was persuaded, or forced, to come was not clear. Kataolauibois told Vaudreuil that it was Onaske, Sakima, Meyavila, and himself, all of them Kiskakons and Sinago Ottawas from Michilimackinac, who compelled Le Pesant to embark. He minimized the role of Otontagan, even though Onaske

had stressed at Detroit that the surrender of Le Pesant was Otontagan's responsibility. Kataolauibois's account of negotiations is, however, sketchy and he told Vaudreuil that he would leave it to the Sieur de St. Pierre, who had been present, to give a full account. It appears clear, however, that Le Pesant in reaching his decision to come had to deal with strong pressure from leading men that he go. The pressure was strong enough so that Kataloauibois feared Le Pesant's revenge if Cadillac did not execute him. Speeches of Three Indians from Michilimakina [*sic*], Oct. 7, 1707, *MPHC* 33:365. Vaudreuil, deriving his account from the Sieur de St. Pierre, says that Le Pesant made private arrangements with the Sieur d'Argenteuil, Cadillac's emissary, to come to Detroit. Vaudreuil to Minister, Oct. 1, 1707, *MPHC* 33:354.

48 Cadillac to Vaudreuil (copy made), Oct. 1, 1707, *MPHC* 33:352–52. Words of the Ottawas to Cadillac, Sept. 24, 1707, *MPHC* 33:346–50. Vaudreuil to Minister, Oct. 1, 1707, *MPHC* 33:350–53.

49 Cadillac to Vaudreuil (copy made), Oct. 1, 1707, *MPHC* 33:351–52; Words of the Ottawas to Cadillac, Sept. 24, 1707, *MPHC* 33:346–48; Vaudreuil to Minister, Oct. 1, 1707, *MPHC* 33: 354–57.

50 Vaudreuil to Minister, Oct. 1, 1707, *MPHC* 33:355–58.

51 Cadillac to Vaudreuil (copy made), Oct. 1, 1707, *MPHC* 33:351; Vaudreuil to Minister, Oct. 1, 1707, *MPHC* 33:355; Words of Ottawas to Cadillac Sept. 25, 1707, *MPHC* 33:348–50.

52 Vaudreuil to Minister, Oct. 1, 1707, *MPHC* 33:355.

53 Words of Ottawas to Cadillac, Sept. 25, 1707, *MPHC* 33:348–50.

54 For the retaliation of the Miamis and the events which followed, see Vaudreuil and Raudot—to Minister, Nov. 14, 1708, *MPHC* 33:403–5, 408; Father Marest to De Vaudreuil, June 4, 1708, *MPHC* 33:383–87; De Vaudreuil to Minister, Nov. 5, 1708, *MPHC* 33:395–99; Report of D'Agremont, Nov. 14, 1708, *MPHC* 33:937—40. For the reaction of the Ottawas to Le Pesant's surrender, see Speeches of Three Indians from Michilimakina (*sic*), Oct. 7, 1707, *MPHC* 33:365.

55 Instruction de Duquesne à Pean, 9 may 1754, in Fernand Grenier (ed.), *Papiers Contrecoeur, el autres documents concernant le conflit anglo-français sur l'Ohio de 1745 à 1756* (Quebec: Les presses universitaires, Laval, 1952), 122.

# 2
# THE COLONIAL PACT

*Cynthia Radding*

This essay focuses on social and cultural change in eastern and central Sonora during the late colonial and early national periods. Its discussion of frontier ecology, rooted in historical struggles over scarce productive resources in the semiarid environment of the Sonoran Desert, addresses the following questions: What was the colonial pact between the Spanish state and Indians in northwestern Mexico, and how did its rupture influence ethnic and class relations in the region? How significant were legal, economic, and cultural distinctions between *indio* and *vecino* in highland Sonora during this century? What was the impact of military service and the Apache wars on the indigenous and Hispanic peasant population? By substantiating the material basis for social conflict, the present study documents a secular process of class formation that cut across racial lines and created new constellations of power.

The *colonial pact* signifies the political ties between the Spanish Crown and Indian communities through which the communities asserted certain basic claims to their means of livelihood and to a degree of local autonomy for their internal governance. Indigenous community leaders understood this relationship as being regulated by a reciprocal arrangement through which Indians provided labor for Spanish enterprises and auxiliary warriors for military defense in return for protection from enslavement and the loss of village lands.[1] Such a pact could not be assumed nor was it consistently observed; rather, it had to be negotiated and tenaciously defended over two centuries of colonial rule.

The dissolution of the colonial pact during the Bourbon colonial administration and the formative years of the Mexican Republic affected particularly the Opata and Eudeve peoples of Sonora. These highland villagers competed with seminomadic bands of hunter-gatherers and with Spanish and mestizo landowners and small farmers for both desert and riverine resources; they relied on irrigable cropland, forests and scrubland for hunting and gathering, and pasture for grazing.[2] The unequal struggle for survival during the transitional period of the eighteenth and nineteenth centuries transformed the social structures through which ethnic communities recreated their cultures and the political implications of resource allocation in the region.

The Sonoran Desert and its surrounding uplands comprised an area of geographic, demographic, cultural, and political frontiers. The ecological bonds between the physical environment and the peoples who inhabited it changed the landscape over time through both destructive and regenerative processes, processes which underlay the alliances and conflicts that punctuated their history. Migrations, conquest, and the imperial economy created distinct zones of production which, in turn, established changing and often conflictual frontiers through the countervailing forces of population dispersal and concentration. The serrano (upland) village peoples of the western foothills of the Sierra Madre Occidental had settled the area several millennia before the arrival of European conquerors. Organized in rival chieftaincies, serrano peoples had fought among themselves for territory, scarce agricultural resources, and control of trade routes.[3] The relative aridity of the environment meant that both foraging and horticulture were essential to survival and, for this reason, cyclical migratory patterns within the region marked the peoples' way of life. Nevertheless, highland Sonoran villagers on the northern frontier of Mesoamerica were settled peoples whose cultures distinguished them from the nomadic bands of the North American Great Plains and the central *cordilleras* of the northern Mexican plateau.[4]

The colonial province of Sonora extended from the Río Yaqui in the south to the river basins of the Gila and Colorado in the north. It was shared (and disputed) by village agriculturalists, who settled in the river valleys, and by gatherers, hunters, and fishermen, who camped along the California gulf coast and in the rugged terrain of the Sierra Madre. These indigenous peoples gleaned their sustenance from the abundant flora of the desert and from the coastal estuaries; likewise, the low scrub forest of the hills and canyons of the sierras provided shelter, medicine, food, fiber, game, and small, irregular plots for planting. Nomadic bands moved in seasonal patterns, creating defined territories in proximity to the established villages where they traded. All groups depended on a variety of resources in order to assure subsistence, especially since climatic variations from year to year affected planting cycles and crop yields. For this reason, as well as the ritual visitations associated with ancient migratory patterns, the movements of different peoples blurred and altered the ethnic boundaries that crossed and re-crossed the Sonoran map.

The *Opatería,* identified as an ethnic territory, comprised various clusters of agrarian communities which, under colonial rule, converged into a "nation" with common linguistic roots and cultural traditions. At the time of European contact, the Opatas controlled the major river valleys of central Sonora, and maintained contested boundaries with the Sobaipuri Pima, Lower Pima, and Cahita peoples to the north, west, and south, and with nomadic groups of the eastern Sierra Madre.[5] They engaged in territorial wars among groups of villages for control over individual valleys or mountain ranges. Serrano political structures and alliances were fluid, largely because their ethnic organization was rooted in the community. The Opatas' relatively high population densities, their ties to long-distance trade networks, and their territorial expansion implied both a well-developed peasant base and a degree of social stratification which, in altered form, endured through colonial institutions.[6]

*Eudeves,* highland villagers similar to the Opatas in their culture and economy, but distinct in their language, formed discernible clusters of communities in two separate zones located to the southeast and northwest of the Opatería proper.[7] *Nebomes,* highland Pima speakers who held territory between the Opata and Cahita nations, adapted their farming methods to the ecological conditions of the Sonoran piedmont in much the same way as the Opatas. Linguistically related to the O'odham (Papago) farmers and gatherers of the desert plains, their villages and rancherías covered the upland terrain of the middle portion of the Yaqui drainage. Together, the Opata, Eudeve, and Nebome peoples constituted the settled peasantry of central and southern Sonora.

The Apaches, diverse bands of hunter-gatherers related linguistically to the Athapaskan speakers of Alaska and western Canada, appeared in the Mexican northwest after European conquest. In the seventeenth and eighteenth centuries, they displaced or assimilated other groups of hunter-gatherers known as the Sumas, Mansos, Chinarras, Jumanos, Jocomes, and Janos, who did not speak Athapaskan languages.[8] The Apaches and their allies hunted and raided along the ill-defined mountainous frontier between Sonora, Chihuahua, and New Mexico. The pressure of constant warfare waged against these nomads coalesced in an imperial policy to maintain presidios, armed garrisons of paid soldiers, in Janos (Chihuahua) and in Fronteras, Terrenate, Pitic, Horcasitas, Altar, and Tubac (Sonora). The Apaches, in turn, responded to increased hostilities with important adaptations in their mode of subsistence, warfare, and social organization. As they became skilled horsemen, men and women formed highly mobile bands that eluded presidial troops.[9]

Spaniards first invaded Sonora in the early sixteenth century, lured by the promise of mineral wealth. In contrast to central and southern Mesoamerica—where Spanish dominion rested on native tribute and a colonial aristocracy sought the privileges of encomienda—the colonial economy of the northern provinces relied on mining and ranching. On the mining frontier of Nueva Vizcaya, centered on Zacatecas, Durango, and Chihuahua, Spaniards imported Indian, mulatto, and mestizo laborers and created settlements in the course of waging war against the Chichimecas. Mining reached Sonora from Chihuahua during the second quarter of the seventeenth century and spread gradually throughout the western Cordilleras of the Sierra Madre. Silver strikes in Bacanuchi, Nacozari, San Juan Bautista, San Miguel, Trinidad, and San Ildefonso de Ostimuri attracted Spanish prospectors and free workers from Nueva Vizcaya; however, the main source of labor for mining and ranching in Sonora was local serrano communities.[10]

With the northward advance of the mining frontier, colonial governors turned to the mission enterprise of the Society of Jesus to bring the northwestern provinces under Spanish dominion. Jesuit missionaries pursued a program of religious evangelization and sociopolitical stabilization based on the serrano villages. They concentrated the population of numerous small hamlets in nuclear towns that controlled sufficient cropland to support a compact community, a policy known as *reductión.* In the interests of conquest the Crown supported the missions financially and provided the legal framework to protect the Indians' land-use rights and shield them from the worst abuses of forced labor.

For nearly 250 years, first the Jesuit (1591–1767) and then the Franciscan (1768–1842) missions served as effective political linkages between the Spanish monarch and his Native American subjects in the frontier provinces. Notwithstanding the cultural conflicts that surfaced repeatedly over differences between the missionaries' objectives and native practices, the institution of the mission came to symbolize a colonial pact of reciprocal obligations, as revealed by the Indians' protests against the nineteenth-century liberal reforms regarding land tenure and village governance.

Highland peasants contested the asymmetrical distribution of power under colonial rule and negotiated their ethnic territory on a number of fronts. Sonoran indigenous peoples demanded autonomy and respect for their territory in return for their labor and provision of militias to fight the unconquered tribes on the margins of Spanish dominion.[11] Furthermore, Sonoran peoples defended their ethnic space and claimed new territory through their physical mobility.[12] They faced repeated threats from Spanish officials and miners, who tried to overrun the missions to gain access to land and cheap labor. When their lands were overrun or rendered unproductive by the expanding frontier of colonial mining and ranching, however, serrano peasants created new rancherías (hamlets) related to the parent villages through kinship and visitation, and thereby maintained the essential contours of their communities in new settings. Migratory patterns and shifting ethnic frontiers comprised both a way of life and a means of resistance for Sonoran peasants, who could survive through hunting and gathering in the monte away from their fields. Indeed, temporary flight from the pueblos afforded them relief from hunger, crop failure, and epidemic disease.

The ethnic boundaries of this northern peasantry were fluid, comprising a number of Indian groups as well as a mixed population of vecinos, *castas,* and *gente de razón.*[13] Culturally, the demarcation between "Indians" and "non-Indians" was ambiguous, but the terms were not meaningless. Their significance derived from a combination of race, kinship, and effective participation in the life of the community. Ethnic identity vied with market relations of production as defining principles for securing access to the land in the closing decades of colonial rule. The struggle over land in Sonora, as elsewhere in Mexico, had strong political and economic significance. Arable cropland represented a tangible village patrimony that supported the ethnic autonomy of serrano peoples. Village leaders' defense of communal lands before Spanish and Mexican authorities concerned not only the material wealth of this productive resource, but also their status as the recognized governors of their people. At stake were the opposing concepts of land-use rights predicated on recognized membership in the ethnic community versus property rights held by virtue of purchase or juridical title.

After Mexican independence, these highland Indian communities faced a new political alignment in their confrontations with the Sonoran notables who took control of the state government. The struggle for territory and power entered a new phase, one that was both decisive and paradoxical. During the first half of the nineteenth century, when the Mexican state was weak at both the national and provincial levels, Sonoran ethnic polities confronted powerful networks of criollo families.[14] These regional oligarchs used both legislative and military means to dissolve the colonial pact and forge new political alignments that favored their rise to power and their accumulation of private wealth.

The missions provided an institutional framework for the survival of peasant agrarian economy and ethnic polity under Spanish dominion. Mission pueblos replicated Iberian town government in a colonial setting through the election of Indian officers, who received a cane of office and the titles of *gobernador, alcalde, fiscal, topil* and, for purposes of religious instruction, of *mador* and *temastián*. Native governors wielded authority within their villages: they meted out local justice and assigned the specific tasks required to complete the work of planting and harvesting in mission fields.

Colonial law also reserved for each mission town a nucleus of arable land for the support of the mission as well as the sustenance of Indian families.[15] While individual milpas were separate from the *labores* allotted to the missions, the irrigation canals built and maintained through Indian labor benefited both the common fields and the milpas. To be sure, the *hijos del pueblo* were required to labor in the mission fields on certain days of the week, and women were assigned tasks relating to the preparation of food and the maintenance of the church and religious ornaments. Nonetheless, mission Indians also farmed their own plots and frequently sought work outside the pueblos in mining camps and haciendas, which suggests a significant degree of freedom of movement, despite their complaints over the level of work demanded of them.

Religious conversion in the missions was hardly complete nor free of conflict, as attested by the missionaries' repeated denunciations of witchcraft among their neophytes. Nevertheless, Christian ritual, visibly enacted in ceremonies, processions, and the cult of the saints, created an additional arena for Indian officers and ceremonial leaders to display their prestige before their kinsmen and *paisanos*.[16]

The Apache frontier was one of the defining principles of Spanish-Opata relations during the eighteenth century. Spaniards, Pirnas, and Opatas formed an uneasy, but necessary, alliance against the Apaches and bands of

Sibubapas and Piatos (Lower and Upper Pirnas) who abandoned the missions. Spanish settlers and authorities depended on Indian warriors to secure their dominion over what was as yet unconquered territory, while serrano peasants sought to defend their villages, livestock, and fields threatened by ever-encroaching bands of hunter-raiders. Moreover, the serrano villagers used their status as presidial auxiliaries and their military prowess on the nomadic frontier to defend their status as corporate communities.

Military service in the frontier presidios opened a new avenue for ethnic persistence in the Sonoran highlands as well. From the mid-eighteenth century onwards, Pima and Opata auxiliaries were recruited to fight in punitive expeditions mounted against the Seris and the Apaches. In addition, the Spanish bestowed the title of "Capitán General de la Nación [Opata or Pima]" on certain leaders, who exerted authority over the warriors recruited from numerous villages.

Following the establishment of the Comandancia General de Provincias Internas (1776), a high military command for the northern provinces, the creation of presidial companies manned entirely by Indian militias marked a further innovation. Colonial authorities stationed Opata troops at San Miguel de Bavispe (1781) and at San Miguel de Bacoachi (1784), turning these mission *visitas* in the upper Bavispe and Sonora river drainages into presidios. The salaries and military ranks assigned to the Indians in presidial service created a hierarchy parallel to that of the missions. Serrano men took seriously the honor that public office and military rank conferred on them, and there is some evidence that certain families monopolized these offices over several generations.[17]

Military service on the Apache frontier undeniably put Opata warriors at risk and drained manpower from the pueblos. Presidial auxiliaries found a new source of income, however, and—at Bavispe and Bacoachi—access to land as soldier-vecinos. Opata and Pima militias that fought against the nomads used the Spaniards' dependence on them to negotiate certain privileges for their leaders and protection for their communities. These privileges included honorific titles, uniforms, and a monetary salary. Finally, Indian auxiliaries preserved warfare as a unifying ligament of their societies and a means of re-creating social rankings within their communities.[18]

Despite a common enemy, however, Spanish-serrano alliances were unstable and fraught with tension. Military service itself became a point of conflict, as Indian warriors called away for extended periods of time on punitive expeditions deep in the Sierra Madre found it necessary to pay other kinsmen to tend their crops. In addition, Spanish governors, native captains, and missionaries disagreed on the amount of rations that the pueblos should supply to military expeditions, giving rise to disputes over the cost of frontier defense and over the limits of these different spheres of authority.[19] More generally, cumulative demographic and economic changes in Sonora, hastened by Bourbon policies, gave rise to deepening lines of conflict both within serrano communities and between Indians and Spaniards.

Eighteenth-century Sonora saw a significant increase in its population through both natural growth and immigration from Nueva Galicia and Nueva Vizcaya. Mining strikes at San Antonio de la Huerta, Baroyeca, and San Ildefonso de la Cieneguilla created sizable population centers; in addition, many *placeres de oro* (placer gold strikes) scattered throughout the Sonoran highlands attracted new settler-prospectors, who recruited *cuadrillas* (gangs) of Indian laborers to work in these mining camps. Furthermore, ranching operations that clustered around old and new mining centers such as Tepache, Motepore, Saracachi, Trinidad, Ráo Chico, and Alamos (in northern Sinaloa) increased the number of people and livestock that lived off the land. Military presidios brought new groups of soldier-settlers who either came with their families or married in the province and claimed farming plots in the environs of their garrisons. The presidios of San Carlos de Buenavista, San Pedro de la Conquista de Pitic, San Miguel de Horcasitas, Santa Gertrudis del Altar and, farther north, Fronteras, Tubac, and Tucson all gave rise to *villas* with a mixed Spanish, casta, and Indian population.

Just as significant was the differential growth between vecinos and Indians in Sonora during the late colonial period. Serrano population declined seriously in the sixteenth and early seventeenth centuries due to epidemics and, in later periods, recurring episodes of disease and crop failure.[20] Although serrano population was rising again by the last third of the eighteenth century, Spanish and casta populations were growing even faster.[21]

The growing number of vecinos resulted from the blurring of ethnic categories due to migration and to changes in the *calidad* or civic status of Indians who chose to leave the mission regime. *Naborías,* the pool of Indian laborers seeking wages in the mines or living as tenants on the Spaniards' haciendas, became confused with the vecinos or gente de razón, persons nominally of white or mixed racial origin who were not subject to the communal obligations imposed on Indians. Furthermore, an indeterminate number of Indians petitioned to change their status to that of vecino, motivated by the attraction of wages and commodities in Spanish settlements and by a desire to escape the burdens of communal labor obligations that seemed to outweigh the protection of traditional mission communities. In 1784, Bishop Antonio de los Reyes noted both that all the mission villages contained substantial numbers of vecinos and that many fields nominally belonging to the pueblos and assigned to the upkeep of the churches were unplanted. In Arivechi and Saguaripa, where the "vecinos and Indians who live in the class of vecinos" outnumbered the hijos del pueblo, Opatas and Eudeves had petitioned the alcalde mayor to be considered vecinos, while Indian *comuneros* of Movas, Cucurpe, and Mátape had sold or rented much of their land to private settlers.[22]

Those Indians who left their pueblos or, without abandoning their villages, changed their status to that of vecino altered the ecological and social relationships that had sustained traditional systems of land use and distribution in the serrano communities. Market arrangements of purchase and rental of fixed plots of land vied with the allotment of usufruct rights to floodplain milpas among Indian families by village leaders. Changes in land tenure eroded the efficacy of farming techniques that had followed the seasonal rhythms of flooding and drought in the Sonoran piedmont. Indian commoners lacked sufficient land to support themselves and the missions, while vecinos expanded their holdings of both farmland and pastures. The gradual privatization of communal land and unbounded rangeland, considered *realenga* or public domain, through the legal instruments of *composición* (verification of land title) and *denuncia* (filing a claim on public land) seriously threatened the economic patrimony and political integrity of highland communities. At issue were two opposing concepts of property and two distinct polities: that of vecinos, or subjects of the realm, and that of the *común,* or membership in an Indian corporate community.

During the first quarter of the eighteenth century, when privatization of land in Sonora gathered momentum through registered composiciones, Indian communities took steps to protect their holdings.[23] The missions of Nuestra Señora de la Concepción de Movas and Santa Ana de Nuri, at the confluence of the Chico and Yaqui Rivers, and the mission of San Pedro de Aconchi, in the Sonora Valley, paid for land titles authorized by the governor of Nueva Vizcaya.[24] In 1716, Pima commoners of Obiachi, Xecatacari, and Buena Vista in the mission district of San Pedro de Cumuripa, petitioned the local magistrate to restore their lands and authorize the formation of a new pueblo in Buena Vista "in order to serve both Majesties."[25]

After the mid-eighteenth century, the population of Spaniards and vecinos (of diverse ethnic origins) reached a critical mass sufficient to expand private landholdings at the expense of native communities.[26] Analysis of land titles recorded between 1790 and 1850 shows that during this period the pace of land enclosures accelerated.[27] Purchases through public auction increased after 1788, and peaked during the decades from 1810 to 1820 and 1830 to 1840. The size of realengos, measured in the number of *sitios* included in each property, tended to rise over time, and prices paid for rangeland increased noticeably throughout the period. This may be due, in part, to officially set minimum prices for land sold in public auction beginning in 1805. Nevertheless, the upward pressure on land values, especially after the turn of the nineteenth century, suggests that population growth (of people and cattle) spurred competition for land among the vecinos and created the conditions for a land market to develop on the Sonoran frontier.

Military presidios established under Bourbon rule in the central and northern portions of Sonora constituted the nuclei from which private landholding expanded. Presidial captains took advantage of their privileged position to develop family enterprises centered on ranching and local commerce. Numerous clans vigorously expanded their properties during the early decades of the nineteenth century, constituting a provincial landholding class.[28] Among the more outstanding examples are the Noriega (Pitic);

Arvizu, Aguilar, and Inigo (Horcasitas); and García, Escalante, and Elías-Gonzalez (Fronteras, Bacoachi) families. These notable families prospered under official Bourbon policies that accelerated the privatization of landholding during the final decades of colonial rule.

The legal framework for an evolving land market in Sonora was established by Visitor-General José de Gálvez, the personal representative of the king in New Spain, who decreed the formal division of mission lands in 1769. Gálvez's orders were reiterated by Intendent-Governor Pedro Corbalán in 1772; by Pedro Galindo Navarro, advisor to the Commandant-General, in 1785; and by Commandant-General Pedro de Nava in 1794.[29]

Bourbon directives for land redistribution reserved a nucleus of land for community support and, in theory, benefited each resident Indian family with a subsistence plot. In practice, however, these initiatives accelerated the transferal of land from communities to private estates and hastened population decline in the pueblos. The parallel and mutually reinforcing processes of a diminishing land base, intrusion of non-Indian squatters in the pueblos, and increased demand for wage labor in Spanish enterprises impoverished native horticulture and eroded the political foundations of Indian communities. Internal migratory patterns intensified as serrano villagers turned increasingly to paid labor as presidial auxiliaries, mineworkers, and transient day laborers or became tenants and *peones* on the haciendas that consolidated their holdings in the major river valleys during this period. Ethnic communities in Sonora experienced internal stratification and a deepening schism between vecinos and hijos del pueblo, which would lead to the breakdown of many of their corporate structures after Mexican independence.

These different lines of conflict converged in three ethnic rebellions that shook the province in the mid-eighteenth century: the Yaqui uprising of 1739–1741; the Seri revolts beginning in 1748; and the Upper Pima rebellion of 1751.[30] The Yaqui and Upper Pima rebellions were suppressed, but bands of Pima rebels, known to the Spaniards as Piatos and Sibubapas, often joined with Seris to attack Spanish communities. Sibubapa resistance intensified after the expulsion of the Jesuits in 1767, when many Lower Pirnas fled their pueblos and roamed through the highland ranges, robbing cattle and engaging in passing skirmishes with presidial troops. Their movements paralleled similar migrations across the porous ethnic boundaries of Pima, Eudeve, and Opata territories during the confused period when ordered mission life was interrupted by the removal of Jesuit missionaries from the province.[31]

Each of these revolts was sparked by different sets of grievances and circumstances. Foremost among the causes were resentment against particular missionaries' disciplinary actions, territorial claims to lands usurped or occupied by miners and ranchers, and food shortages occasioned by drought and crop failure. Taken together, however, they make evident the combined pressures on Sonoran highland communities, which mounted in intensity during the last half-century of colonial rule. While Yaquis and Upper Pirnas were not able to sustain a long-term rebellion, their revolts, combined with the prolonged resistance of the Seris and the ongoing wars on the Apache frontier, limited colonial dominion in Sonora. Spaniards never saw their ambitions for mining wealth fully developed nor brought to fruition their imperial project to hold a unified northern frontier.

The wars of independence affected the province of Sonora only indirectly, drawing presidial troops away from frontier defense to support the royalist cause against the *insurgentes* of the central plateau.[32] Nevertheless, once Mexican independence was consummated in the Republic of 1824, Sonoran landed notables exerted their influence to take control of the governorship and legislature of the state of Occidente and, later, of Sonora and Sinaloa.[33] Like other peripheral elites in early republican Mexico, the Sonoran oligarchs changed the terms of negotiation with the ethnic communities in their province and, in so doing, altered irretrievably the operative legal definition of property and the relations between the state and these serrano *naciones*. The new regime pushed aggressively to privatize the land and to change both the civic status of Indians and the internal governance of their pueblos.[34]

The deputies of Occidente and Sonora passed legislation during the decade from 1825 to 1835 that, in theory, established equality between Indians and vecinos, and defined citizenship in terms of landed property. This new legal framework sought to impose the sovereignty of the state over the pueblos through the institutions of municipal government and the division of communal lands. During the same period, the expulsion of the Spaniards from Mexico, ordered by federal law on December 20, 1827, and applied in Occidente on February 15, 1828, deprived those Sonoran pueblos that had remained under mission tutelage—primarily in the Pimería Alta—of their missionaries and left their communal property in the hands of civilian commissioners.

The most important of these laws was Decree 89 of 1828, which focused on the corporate holdings—*fundo legal—and* all arable lands in the communities. Despite the appearance of equitable treatment—as suggested by the first two articles of the decree, which called for the restitution of "those lands which have been unfairly taken" from Indian communities, and by the citation of the appropriate sections of the colonial *Recopilación* of 1681 and a similar decree issued by the Cortes de Cádiz of 1813—the root purpose of Decree 89 concerned the demarcation and division of communal lands. It stated, "The lands known as the fundo legal, as well as mission property restored to the pueblos and vacant lands in their environs, shall be reduced to private property to the exclusive benefit of the Indians."[35] The legislators recognized as legitimate property only those holdings authorized by legal title, thus favoring large landowners and undermining the ancient tradition of the común. Concerning ethnic polity, the authors of this law took note of the racially mixed population that characterized many communities and opened their councils and militias to both vecinos and Indians, altering the system of internal governance that the pueblos had received from the missions. In point of fact, contemporary observers criticized the deleterious effects of Spaniards and castas who had gained control of political offices in the communities.[36]

The state of Sonora passed a series of laws between 1831 and 1835, based on the tenets of Decree 89, which made it easier for private citizens to register "vacant lands" as their own and subordinated Indian pueblos to municipal governments.[37] That Sonoran governors enforced the new laws to the benefit of local elites is evident in the reports and correspondence that reached the president of Mexico from different sources during these years. State officials had measured and divided village lands in the Opata villages of the Sonora River valley and in the Eudeve area of eastern Sonora. These legal innovations placed valuable communal resources in private hands and set in motion two parallel processes: the consolidation of a regional landed oligarchy and the social stratification of peasant communities. The division of alluvial cropland in the pueblos separated peasant cultivators into classes of vecinos and Indians, smallholders and "proletarians." By the 1830s, villages like Mátape, Batuc, Nacameri, Cumpas, Aconchi, and Baviácora comprised dual communities of Indians and vecinos, distinguished by their opposing claims to the land. Conflicts over land arose in the former missions of Mátape, Batuc, and Tepupa over measurements begun during the colonial period and extended through purchase and inheritance over half a century, Nacameri was the scene of litigation between vecinos and a nucleus of Pima and Eudeve families who remained from the mission and, later, between non-Indian smallholders and *hacendados* from the powerful Robles, Aguilar, and Gómez del Campillo families.[38]

Taken together the legal distinction between Indian citizens and hijos del pueblo, the division of communal lands, and the dissolution of the pueblos' internal governance constituted an unprecedented invasion of Sonoran ethnic communities. Responding to events, Opata governors protested the loss of village land, the disintegration of the común, and the corrosion of their authority as concomitant parts of the same process. Indigenous leaders resisted the new political order through negotiation, political appeal, and armed revolt. Between 1825 and 1833, Opata and Yaqui warriors confronted presidial troops in numerous skirmishes in the mountain ranges between the Bavispe and Yaqui Valleys. Opata leaders Dolores Gutiérrez, Juan Güiriso, Antonio Baiza, and Miguel and Bautista Sol joined with the famed Yaqui leader Juan Banderas. They launched an ambitious rebellion to create an autonomous state in eastern Sonora. They opposed the division of communal lands and taxes imposed by the state government; furthermore, the Opatas called for restoration of the colonial mission regime and, with it, the restitution of the común. These uprisings, occurring simultaneously with new Apache incursions through the sierra, seriously shook the fledgling regime, but state troops suppressed the Indians' movement with the capture and execution of their leaders.[39]

Even while engaged in armed revolt, Opata leaders turned again to negotiation, appealing their case to the highest authorities of the Mexican nation.

In 1831, Opata representatives obtained an executive order from President Anastacio Bustamante directing the governor of Sonora to recognize their communities' fundo legal and to restore alienated land to their villages. Busta-mante's ruling had little effect, however, because state authorities ignored the federal directive. After their military defeat and several violent confrontations with landowners in different localities, the Opatas again sent representatives to Mexico City in 1836. José Anrríquez, the governor of Cumpas, and Juan Ysidro Bohórquez, "a native of Oposura representing himself and thirty-six pueblos who comprise the Opata nation," gave a formal petition to the Secretary of State and of the Interior. In the petition they reasoned that the core problem of land was linked with their status as leaders and legitimate representatives of their people. What they defended was the land itself, valued as an ethnic territory, and a political order that was receding from their grasp in a time of transition marked by changing agrarian structures and a new configuration of power.[40]

The Secretary of State reiterated Bustamante's directive of 1831, but in ambiguous terms referring merely to compliance with the law. By midcentury, the Opatas had lost their communal lands, and within several decades their ethnic territory was considerably eroded. The Opata nation suffered disintegration not because its leaders lacked political acumen or a sense of their own history, but rather because the power structure they confronted had economically and militarily surpassed the resources they could marshal in defense of their ethnic community.

Diverse ecological, cultural, and political frontiers collided in Sonora during the century between 1740 and 1840. After Mexican independence Sonoran provincial elites overturned the colonial pact between Indian communities and the state. Leading frontier families buttressed their rise to power with the ideological tenets of liberalism and federalism, which supported their regional autonomy vis-à-vis the central government and defined citizenship as a status conferred on individuals independent of corporate entities such as ethnic communities, guilds, or the Church. Equally significant, the juridical bases of land tenure were irrevocably changed, elevating private property over communal holdings.

But early republican liberalism did not go uncontested. Peasant cultivators of the Sonoran highlands articulated a different discourse rooted in the común. Their ethnic polity evolved from pre-Hispanic origins, and was remolded and preserved through colonial institutions. Serrano villagers persisted in their defense of ethnic autonomy, linked to communal agrarian structures and the physical mobility that permitted them to live in the semiarid environment of the Sonoran piedmont. Ethnic traditionalists confronted emerging social classes which, in turn, developed from an expanding market economy and the privatization of the land.

Agrarian conflict would continue in the Sonoran highlands throughout the nineteenth century, contributing to the explosive events of the Revolution of 1910. The social landscape and ethnic frontiers of this frontier province were never fixed or immutable; indeed, the piedmont and desert lowlands of Sonora have remained contested ground. It was during the transition from colony to republic, however, that serrano peoples ceased to be a peasantry based on ethnic ties to the común and became rural workers and producers—*rancheros*, tenants, and sharecroppers—whose claim to the land depended on contractual relations of purchase, rental, and service.

## NOTES

1 Nils Jacobsen, "Campensinos y tenencia de la tierra en el altiplano peruano en la transición de la Colonia a la República," *Allpanchis* 23 (1991), 25–93.

2 Thomas E. Sheridan, *Where the Dove Calls: The Political Ecology of a Peasant Corporate Community in Northwestern Mexico* (Tucson: University of Arizona Press, 1988).

3 Daniel T. Reff, *Disease, Depopulation, and Culture in Northwestern New Spain, 1518-1764* (Salt Lake City: University of Utah Press, 1991); Carroll Riley, *The Frontier People: The Greater Southwest in the Protohistoric Period* (Albuquerque: University of New Mexico Press, 1987).

4 William B. Griffen, *Culture Change and Shifting Populations in Central Northern Mexico*. Anthropological Papers of the University of Arizona, #13 (Tucson: University of Arizona Press, 1969); Thomas D. Hall, *Social Change in the Southwest, 1350-1880* (Lawrence: University Press of Kansas, 1989); Elizabeth A. H. John, *Storms Brewed in Other Men's Worlds: The Confrontation of Indians, Spanish, and French in the Southwest, 1540–1795* (College Station: Texas A&M University Press, 1975).

5 Thomas Barnes, Thomas Naylor, and Charles Polzer, *Northern New Spain: A Research Guide* (Tucson: University of Arizona Press, 1981) 81, 87; Riley, *Frontier People*, 50, 295-98; Edward H. Spicer, *Cycles of Conquest: The Impact of Spain, Mexico, and the United States on the Indians of the Southwest, 1533–1960* (Tucson: University of Arizona Press, 1962), 23.

6 William E. Doolittle, *Oasis in the Gran Chichimeca: Pre-Hispanic Occupance in the Valley of Sonora*. Anthropological Papers of the University of Arizona, No. 48 (Tucson: University of Arizona Press, 1988); Peter Gerhard, *The North Frontier of New Spain*. Rev. Ed. (Norman: University of Oklahoma Press, 1993); Riley, *Frontier People*; Carl Ortwin Sauer, *Aboriginal Population of Northwestern Mexico* (Berkeley, CA: University of California Press, 1935).

7 Campbell W. Pennington, ed., *Arte y cocabulario de la lengua dohema, heve o eudeva. Anónimo (siglo xvii)*. (México, D. F.: UNAM, 1981); Pennington, *La cultura de los eudeve del noroeste de México* (Hermosillo: INAH, 1982).

8 Patrick H. Beckett and Terry L. Corbett, *The Manso Indians* (Las Cruces, NM: COAS Publishing and Research, 1992); Diana Hadley and Thomas E. Sheridan, "Land Use History of the San Ráfael Valley, Arizona (1540–1960)," General Technical Report RM-GTR-269 (Fort Collins, CO: U.S. Dept. of Agriculture, 1995); Thomas Naylor, "Athapaskans They Weren't: The Suma Rebels Executed at Casas Grandes in 1685," in David R. Wilcox and W. Bruce Masse, eds., *The Protohistoric Period in the North American Southwest, A.D. 1540–1700* (Tempe, AZ: Arizona State University Press, 1981); Spicer, *Cycles of Conquest*.

9 William B Griffen, *Apaches at War and Peace: The Janos Presidio, 1750–1858* (Albuquerque: University of New Mexico, 1988); Charles H. Lange, Carroll L.

Riley, and Elizabeth M. Lange, eds., *The Southwestern Journals of Adolph F. Bandelier, 1883–1884* (Albuquerque, NM. University of New Mexico Press, 1970); Louis Lejeune, *La guerra Apache en Sonora*, ed., Michael Antochiew (Hermosillo: Gobierno de Estado de Sonora, 1984); Carl Lumholtz, *Unknown Mexico: Explorations in the Sierra Madre and Other Regions, 1890–1898* (New York: Scribners, 1902); Spicer, *Cycles of Conquest*; Ignacio Zúñiga, *Rápida ojeada al estado de Sonora* (Mexico: Juan Ojeda, 1835). Memoria del XI Simposio de Historia y Antropología de Sonora 22 (1987).

10 Ignacio del Río, "Sobre la aparición y desarrollo del trabajo libre asalariado en el norte de Nueba España (siglos XVI–XVII)," in Elsa Cecilia Frost, Michael Meyer, and Josefina Vázquez, eds., *El trabajo y los trabajadores en la historia de México* (Tucson: University of Arizona Press, 1979), 92–111.

11 Juan Mateo Manje, *Diario de las exploraciones en Sonora. Luz de tierra incógnita* (Hermosillo: Gobierno del Estado de Sonora); Sergio Ortega Noriega, "El sistema de misiones jesuíticas, 1591–1699," in *Historia general de Sonora, II: De la conquista al estado libre y soberano de Sonora* (Mexico: Gobierno del Estado de Sonora, 1985), 37–75; Andres Pérez de Ribas, *Historia de los triunfos de nuestra santa fé entre gentes las más bárbaras y fieras del Nuevo orbe* [1645] (Hermosillo: Gobierno del Estado de Sonora, 1985).

12 The concept of ethnic space is developed by Marcello Carmagnani, El regreso de los dioses: El proceso de reconstitución de la identidad étnica en Oaxaca, Siglos xvii y xviii (Mexcio: Fondo de Cultura Económica, 1988), 15, 52–108. John Tutino, *From Insurrection to Revolution: Social Bases of Agrarian Violence, 1750–1940* (Princeton: Princeton University Press, 1986), 25–29, identifies mobility as a value defended by peasants in different cultural milieux.

13 These three terms refer to non-Indians of different racial categories in colonial society. Vecinos were landholding residents of a given locality; whether or not they were actually of Spanish origin, they were Hispanic in their cultural and political orientation. Gente de razón ("people of reason") were distinguished from Indians in their civil status and legal obligations; racially they could be Spanish, criollo (whites born in the New World), or mestizo (a mixture of white and Indian). *Castas,* a term that appeared frequently in colonial documents generated in Sonora, included persons of mixed racial composition with Amerindian, European, and African antecedents.

14 Ruggiero Romano, "Algunas consideraciones alrededor de nación, estado, y libertad en europa y America centro-meridional," in Antonio Annino et al., America Latino: del estado colonial al estado nación, 1750–1940, Vol. 1 (Milano: Franco Angeli, 1987); Stuart Voss, "Northwest Mexico," in Diane Balmori, Stuart Voss, and Miles Wortman, eds., *Notable Family Networks in Latin America* (Chicago: University of Chicago Press, 1984), 79–128.

15 *Recopilación de las leyes de Indias,* 1680, Título doce. De la venta, composición, y repartimiento de tierras, solares y aguas, ley V; Título tercero, De las reducciones y pueblos de indios, ley VIII, Madrid, Marcialo Pons, 1973.

16 Pérez de Ribas, *Historia de los triunfos*; Ignaz Pfefferkorn, *Descripción de la Provincia de Sonora [1794–1795]*, ed., Armando Hopkins Durazo (Hermosillo: Gobierno del Estado de Sonora, 1983–84); Charles W. Polzer, *Rules and Precepts of the Jesuit Missions of Northwestern New Spain, 1600–1767* (Tucson: University of Arizona Press, 1976); Cynthia Radding, *Wandering Peoples*; Spicer, *Cycles of Conquest.*

17 Fray Antonio Angel Núñez, "Carta edificante histórico-curiosa," Biblioteca Nacional Fondo Franciscano (hereafter BNFF) *Noticias de Varias Misiones,* vol. 76.

18 José Luis Mirafuentes Galván, "Seris, apaches y españoles en Sonora: Consideraciones sobre su confrontación military en el siglo XVIII," *Historias* 22 (1987),

18–29; Mirafuentes Galván, "Elite y defensa en la provincia de Sonora, siglo XVIII," in *Memoria del XI Simposio de Historia y Antropología de Sonora* 22 (1987), 411–23.

19 Juan Bautista de Anza to Brigadier Teodoro de Croix, Comandante General de Provincias Internas, 30 June 1777, BNFF 34/734, f. 1–5; Pedro Garrido y Durán, Intendente de Sonora to Don Ygnacio de Noperi, Capitán General de la Nación Opata, BNFF 35/767; "Representación del Padre Comisario de las misiones fray Juan Prestamero sobre quejas de los ópatas contra el padre ministro de Opodepe," 17 July 1777, BNFF 34/735.

20 Robert H. Jackson, *Indian Population Decline: The Missions of Northwestern New Spain, 1687–1840* (Albuquerque: University of New Mexico Press, 1994); Reff, *Disease, Depopulation, and Culture Change.*

21 Figures for Sonora are sketchy at best, because of the general mobility of this frontier population and the absence of systematic tribute collection. Although a few well-documented Jesuit and diocesan visitations produced estimates of the number of families and "souls" in each mission pueblo, these are not exact and, more to the point, do not account for an indeterminate number of Indian *naborías* and mestizos living outside the missions.

22 Bishop Reyes, 1784, BNFF 34/759, f. 31.

23 Evidence of composiciones comes from the archives of the Audiencia de Guadalajara, conserved in the Archivo de Instrumentas Públicos (hereafter AIPJ) and in the Biblioteca Pública del Estado de Jalisco (BPEJ), and the Archivo de Hidalgo de Parral (AHP), the latter consulted in microfilm at the University of Arizona.

24 AIPJ Libros de Gobierno de la Audiencia de Guadalajara, Libro 47, f. 218–20; Archivo de la Mitra, Hermosillo (AMH), Archivo del Sagrario 1, 1666–1828.

25 BPEJ Real Audiencia de Guadalajara RC 27–9–259, 15ff, 1716.

26 Peter Gerhard, *The North Frontier of New Spain* (Princeton: Princeton University Press, 1982); Radding, *Wandering Peoples.*

27 My analysis is based on the following sources: AGN, Tierras [AHGES TP], and Archivo Histórico del Gobierno del Estado de Sonora, Títulos Primordiales. Romero (1991) analyzes a similar body of material.

28 Stuart Voss, *On the Periphery of Nineteenth-Century Mexico* (Tucson: University of Arizona Press, 1982); Voss, "Northwest Mexico."

29 Patricia Escandón, "Economía y sociedad en Sonora, 1767–1821," in *Historia General de Sonora, Vol. 2: De la conquista al estado libre y soberano de Sonora* (Mexico: Gobierno del Estado de Sonora, 1985), 258-64; John L. Kessell, *Friars, Soldiers, and Reformers* (Tucson: University of Arizona Press, 1976); Ignacio del Río, "El noroeste novohispano y la nueva política imperial española," in *Historia General de Sonora, Vol. 2: De la conquista al estado libre y soberano de Sonora*, 209–219. BNFF 34/738, 740, 741.

30 Alejandro Figueroa Valenzuela, *Los que hablan fuerte: El desarrollo de la sociedad yaqui* (Hermosillo: Instituto Nacional de Antropología e Historia, 1986); Evelyn Hu-DeHart, *Missionaries, Miners, and Indians: Spanish Contact with the Yaqui Nation of Northwestern New Spain, 1533–1820* (Tucson: University of Arizona Press, 1981); John L. Kessell, *Mission of Sorrows: Jesuit Guevavi and the Pimas, 1691–1767* (Tucson: University of Arizona Press, 1970); José Luis Marafuentes Galván, "Elite y defensa en la provincia de Sonora, Siglo XVIII," *Memoria del XI Simposio de Historia y Antropología de Sonora* 22 (1987), 411–23; Marafuentes Galván, "El 'enemigo de las casas de adobe': Luis de Sáric y la rebellion de los pimas altos en 1751," *Memoria del XIII Simposio de Historia y Antropología de Sonora* 1 (1989), 103–24; Spicer, *Cycles of Conquest*; Spicer, *The Yaquis: A Cultural History* (Tucson: University of Arizona Press, 1980).

31 Pennington, *Arte y vocabulario*. Military reports on the movements of Sibubapas and presidial captains' negotiations with them are in AGN, Provincias Internas, vols. 48 and 86.

32 James E. Officer, *Hispanic Arizona, 1536–1856* (Tucson: University of Arizona Press, 1987), 84–86; Juan Domingo Vidargas del Moral, "Sonora y Sinaloa como provincias independientes y como estado interno de occidente," in *Historia general de Sonora*, 11, 321–27; Eduardo W. Villa, *Historia del Estado de Sonora* (Hermosillo: Gobierno del Estado de Sonora, 1984), 153–60.

33 During the wars of independence, Sonora remained nominally under the administration of the Intendencia de Arispe and the Comandancia de Provincias Internas de Occidente. After 1821, the northwestern provinces sent delegates to the Deputatión Provincial convened under the auspices of Iturbide. In 1824, Sonora and Sinaloa became part of the constitutional Republic of Mexico as the unified Estado de Occidente, but they divided into two separate states in 1831.

34 Tutino, *From Insurrection*, 216–28; Voss, *On the Periphery*.

35 "Decreto No. 89 del Estado de Occidente, Alamos, 30 de septiembre de 1828: Ley para el repartimiento de los pueblos indígenas, reduciéndolos a propiedad particular," in F. Pesqueira, *Documentes para la historia de Sonora,* Serie II, Tomo I, 1821–1845.

36 Cynthia Radding, *Las estructuras socioeconómicas de las misiones de la Pimería Alta, 1768–1850* (Mexico: Instituto Nacional de Antropología e Historia, 1979), 28–29, 88–90; Juan de Gándara, Protector de indios de Opodepe, to Fiscal Protector General de Indios, 24 July 1818, BPEJ ARAG RC 264–5–3600; Fernando Ma. Grande, Visitador de las misiones de la Pimería Alta, to gobernador del Estado de Occidente, 1828. I consulted a copy of this document through the courtesy of Kieran R. McCarty.

37 Sonoran state decrees were consulted in AHGES caja 36–1, exp. 1052. Laws directly concerning land tenure are 3 (1833), 10 (1834), 41, 47, 62, and 75 (1835).

38 Radding, *Las Estructuras*, 234–38; BNFF 32/659, 1803; Governor Manuel Escalante y Arvizu used the term *proletario* in a letter to the president of Mexico, 4 June 1836, in AGN, Gobernación, caja 3, exp. s/n.; AHGES TP Tomo IV, exp. 40, f. 899–947; leg. 1, exp. I, 1831; leg. 7, exp. 87, f. 1304–1350; exp. 83, f. 1188–1218; exp. 84, 85, f. 1219–1289; AGN, Tierras, leg. 1416, exp. 11, 18; leg. 1422, exp. 3; leg. 1424, exp. 7, 10.

39 Spicer, *Cycles of Conquest*, 61–64, 100–03; AGN, Gobernación caja 3, exp. s/c, s/n, 1837. Governor Escalante to the Secretary of State and of the Interior.

40 The language of Anrríquez's and Bohórquez's petitions illustrates well the tenets of the moral economy literature. See especially Eric Hobsbawm, "Peasants and Politics," *Journal of Peasant Studies* 1:1 (1973), 3–22; James C. Scott, *Weapons of the Weak: Everyday Forms of Peasant Resistance* (New Haven: Yale University Press, 1985); Scott, *Domination and the Arts of Resistance: Hidden Transcripts* (New Haven: Yale University Press, 1990); Gavin Smith, *Livelihood and Resistance: Peasants and the Politics of Land in Peru* (Berkeley: University of California Press, 1989); and Ward Stavig, "Ethnic Conflict, Moral Economy, and Population in Rural Cuzco on the Eve of The Tupac Araru II Rebellion," *Hispanic American Historical Review* 68:4 (1988), 737–70.

# 3

# CONVERSATIONS IN THE WOODS

*James H. Merrell*

At [Conrad] Weiser's Tulpehocken home, at Shickellamy's Shamokin lodge and at farmhouses, hunting cabins, and mills in between, the Oneida and the German met to smoke a pipe and "talke a great deal." Matters large and small came up, from a mysterious black wampum belt making the rounds to a Delaware's stolen peltry, from battles over the mountains to the clash of armies and empires beyond the seas. One winter night in 1746, when the two "sat down to discourse" by the headman's fire, was typical: over dinner the Iroquois asked "what news accured among the white people"; the Pennsylvanian, answering, went on and "asked what news accured among the Indians."[1]

Such quiet chats, through many seasons and many years, were the essence of what everyone from Weiser to Shawnee headmen to William Penn himself called "a Kind Correspondents" or "a Good Correspondance" between peoples.[2] To be sure, not every encounter between colonist and Indian was really "Correspondance." Pennysylvania traders who headed out in search of customers or Indians who trooped into a colonial settlement to peddle their wares; Moravians setting up a model farm in Indian country or coaxing natives to live in a model town on Bethlehem's outskirts; a colonial farmer who fed a passing war party or let an Indian family camp in his field—these people needed no go between to write the script and direct the actors.

But those contacts did require the congenial climate that a negotiator helped sustain. As the calamities in the late 1720s and early 1740s attest, that climate was prone to sudden squalls. Rumors of war put colonists or Indians to flight. Missionaries, too, carefully scouted Shamokin, Onondaga, and Philadelphia for signs of trouble before sending the Lord's servants to live among natives. And colonial settlers only appreciated how much their lives had depended on what Iroquois called "frequent Opportunities of conferring and discoursing with their Brethren" when after 1754, conversation having stopped, peace disappeared beneath a torrent of blood and fire. . . .[3]

Keeping paths open was easier said than done. That evening at Shickellamy's house in 1746 was in fact made possible by a remarkable series of negotiations that got people past their linguistic and cultural differences. Like travel, talk was difficult, dangerous, thankless—and largely forgotten. But eavesdropping on the murmur of conversation, like following go-betweens into the woods, can offer a new angle of vision on the frontier experience, can reinforce the combination of concord and discord that recruitment and travel uncovered. On the one hand, negotiators, prodded by a general consensus on the need for regular contact, developed an eclectic yet powerful set of tools—pieces of paper and strings of wampum, along with linguistic dexterity and a knack for improvising—that got messages across. On the other hand, however, those beads and those pages also pick up, in the lower registers, a deepening unease and distrust. By midcentury, wampum and writing, made marvelously complementary in go-betweens' hands, became increasingly contentious as it appeared that people did not always speak (or write) "truly and freely." While negotiators became more conversant with channels of communication, the woods' static became more pronounced until, after 1750, frontier war ended Penn's "Kind Correspondence. . . ."

Pack up and head out, listen in and report back—the art of inter-cultural converse sounds simple, but it was in fact a dauntingly complex transaction. The first and most basic obstacle was language; a simple hello, not to mention a chat, required people to remove the language barrier. With Indians insisting that formal talks be in their tongue, that chore usually fell to colonists.[4] Natives believed that having an interpreter gave them "more dignity," one Pennsylvanian explained, just as use of "proper grammatical language" lent "their words . . . greater weight and effect . . . , while some are afraid of committing mistakes when speaking in an idiom not their own." Capturing and conveying an Indian talk's finer points demanded great skill. "Particularly when they have a joke to pass, a hint to give, or a shrewd remark to make, they wish it to have all the advantages of a good translation, and that their wit may not be spoiled by a foreign accent, improper expression, or awkward delivery."[5]

The trick was finding a good translator, for Indian languages were notoriously hard to learn.[6] A student of Iroquois discovered "that they have various modes of speech and phrases peculiar to each age and sex"—a hungry man announced his hunger with one word, a hungry child with another—"which they strictly observe." Similarly, Delaware had ten terms for *bear,* depending on the animal's age and sex, and *to eat* varied according to whether the food required chewing. Those trying to figure out such nuances had to cope with the fact that some native speakers habitually dropped syllables, much depended on the right accent, and Indians sometimes were reluctant teachers. To acquire what one native called "an Indian *ear*" was a long and difficult apprenticeship. . . .[7]

The sense of being lost got worse if the language gap required more than one translator. Even toward the end of the colonial era, makeshift arrangements could be found. An August 1761 meeting in Philadelphia heard Seneca

George speak Seneca to Kanak't (Last Night), a Conoy, who converted the words to Delaware so that Isaac Stille could, finally, bear them across to waiting colonists. "When we met at Easton [earlier this month]," Seneca George said at that talk in the provincial capital, "we did not fully understand one another, we are therefore come here now, that we may understand each other more clearly." With Kanak't and Stille at his side, poised to haul his words over two linguistic spans, the Seneca's confidence seems misplaced.[8]

It did not help that Indians were known for obfuscation. Raised in a culture that discouraged open confrontation—"[a] person might be among them 30 years and even longer," wrote Conrad Weiser, "and not once see two sober Indians dispute or quarrel; when one of them has a deadly hatred to another, they endeavor to smother their anger"—natives often resorted to indirection to avoid unpleasantness.[9] They can "express themselves with great clearness and precision" when they want to, one observer noted, but they were also masters of the "art of dissembling." "If they intend to speak in an obscure manner, they can speak so cleverly and with so much circumstance that even Indians must puzzle out the true sense of their allusions."[10]

Communication problems were compounded by the rumors that flourished in the frontier's volatile atmosphere. Colonists picked up "various and Contradictory" stories from Indian country; natives might get good news from Penn's people, then bad news, then good once again.[11] The French, Pennsylvanians heard, are massing on the frontier. No, Indians had been told, they are sailing up the Delaware. The Iroquois are about to sweep down on the province and its native friends. Virginia is poised to invade the Susquehanna Valley.[12] Unnamed war parties are about to strike. Pennsylvania is plotting "to cutt off the Indians" by sending them poison blankets or luring them to Philadelphia in order to enslave them.[13] Rumors ran rampant, keeping everyone on edge. . . .

The only way to cope with rumor and gossip was to send someone out (or call someone in) to "sift" stories, "to enquire and find out the Truth of the matter, and of every other thing that passes." Enter the go-between, "our true Corespondent."[14]

Those trying to converse amid rumor mongers and frontier frictions had powerful assistance, for an accepted code governed correct communication between peoples. Indians and colonists alike expected to be spoken to "in form," in a "regular manner." If protocol were ignored, Indians would say that "heretofore they had only heard from the English as a Noise in the Woods unintelligible"—and might even insist that they had heard nothing at all. Colonists, too, dismissed messages improperly sent as "only a transient discourse."[15]

"[R]ight understanding of one Another" meant not only finding "some suitable Person in whom we can place a Confidence" but also conforming to Indian custom. This, in turn, meant, striking a passive pose that left the locals to invite you here and there, telling you where to wait and when to leave. On approaching his destination the wise messenger went along with the custom of firing guns in salute, and he learned to wait as a delegation of important men came out to greet him, to smoke a friendly pipe with him, and to escort him into town amid more gunfire. Similarly, a Delaware or Iroquois emissary approaching a colonial city was often "received . . . according to the Forms in use with Indians."[16]

Once a traveler was in the village, the Condolence began. Even if one side had already condoled the other immediately on hearing about the death of an important person—each time Shickellamy lost a son, Pennsylvania sent a gift to dry his tears, and in the spring of 1749 Weiser headed to Shamokin yet again, this time to console the Oneida's children at the death of their father—no message got through until hearts were healed "according to old Custom."[17] Indians insisted that "they cou'd not see the Road [to Philadelphia] nor hear what the Governor . . . had to say to them till that Ceremony had been done."[18] With tears dried and broken hearts mended, conversation could commence.

To pursue those talks, go-betweens surmounted the language barrier. It helped that, whatever the native tongue used in formal discourse, more and more Indians picked up some English—enough, at least, that they might serve as a check on a translator's accuracy. Watch what you say around the Iroquois here, a negotiator would warn a colonist visiting an Indian camp during a treaty; "most of them understand English."[19] English speakers were common in the Ohio country, and even Shickellamy knew some English. "[L]ye still *John*," the Oneida "called out" to John Bartram when that False Face paid them a call in Onondaga. "I never heard him speak so much plain *English* before," the astonished naturalist remarked.[20] Neither did anyone else, apparently; no other colonist so much as mentioned the Oneida's knowing English. But Bartram was not the only colonist surprised when familiar words came from foreign mouths. "[T]hey mostly all Spake English," a Pennsylvanian said of Delaware warriors who captured him in 1758, and "one spoke as good English as I can."[21]

Colonial mediators, meanwhile, were not only more fluent in the Indian languages, they also had a surer grasp of native metaphor. So comfortable was one woodsman that, filling Pennsylvania officials in on Shawnee politics, he lapsed into Indian phrasing: "they have had a Tast of the Friench,"he wrote, "and finde them Sweet in the Mouth and bitter in the Heart." Having heard this sort of talk for so long, those officials had come to know "the meaning of these Indian Expressions" well enough that translators bothered less with the usual parenthetical explanation of, say, "a clear & open road . . . (by this meaning a friendly communication)."[22] Thus Indians and colonists, driven by a powerful urge to communicate, enrolled in a vast, diffuse, and unnoticed educational experiment. But learning to let Indians lead and picking up the jargon was only the first course in the curriculum of the woods.

Tradition has it that Hiawatha, when he helped found the Great League by convincing the Iroquois nations to unite, was the first to place shell beads on a string.[23] Ever since that distant day, these seashells—harvested on the beaches of Long Island Sound, then drilled to make beads before being placed on strings or woven into belts—had great spiritual power in Indian America. Offered to propitiate the dead and other beings, wampum linked the visible and invisible worlds; passed to the living to patch up differences or ease the minds of the bereaved, it mended the torn social fabric of a town or clan; arranged in patterns and kept to recall formal conversations, it connected past to present.

Use of wampum reached beyond clan or town to embrace strangers; it became a filament connecting disparate peoples across Indian country. Though Hiawatha's Iroquois heirs might claim pride of invention, many native groups considered shells "potent medicine. . . ."[24]

In diplomacy, wampum worked its magic in various ways. Indian messengers would say that it served to "confirm" or "enforce" their words, it guaranteed that "we speak truth" and ensured that a speech would "have Credit with you," would "have its full Effect on" the listener's "Mind."[25] Natives might even have thought strings and belts more powerful still, so powerful that the shells themselves held the message. Thus an Iroquois or Delaware council spoke words directly into a string or belt as we would into a tape recorder; then a messenger, reaching his destination, merely turned the beads on and became their mouthpiece. So animated, a belt took on a mind and life of its own. The wampum, Indian envoys might say, "has been leading us by the arm." One Iroquois go-between even talked of how "this day a Belt of Wampum (black) came to Shamokin from Oneida from the Six Nations," as if it had floated down the Susquehanna on its own.[26]

The delicate beads, then, carried heavy freight in formal conversation. "Without Wampum," one colonist observed, "Nothing is to be done Amongst the Indians."[27] The number of beads needed to conduct diplomacy was staggering. Some messengers had just a string or two in a pocket or pouch, but others crammed a bag or "casket" with ten, twenty, even thirty or more belts, each bearing part of a talk, each containing anywhere from several hundred to ten thousand beads that, woven into a belt, might be a foot wide and six feet long.[28] "It is amazing to think what a Quantity of Wampum this Journey will take in Strings & Belts," Richard Peters grumbled as he prepared to dispatch messengers into the Indian countries. Demand at midcentury was so great that Philadelphia merchants asked contacts in New York City for 100,000 beads, and a "wampum maker"—a Delaware or Philadelphia woman, James Sympson in New York, or one of the Montour women on the Pennsylvania frontier—was kept busy.[29]

Wampum's value as a communications medium stemmed in part from its versatility. Just as it had many uses within a town, so between peoples one string might mark a messenger's status while another sanctioned part of a speech and—carefully stored in a "Counsel Bagg," then regularly pulled out for rehearsal of its message—kept words alive far into the future.[30] Better still, wampum could take many forms. A large belt or long string meant something important. White shells denoted peace, "black" (actually purple) ones war, though words of war also came in as scalps tied to a white belt, red paint splashed across it, or a hatchet woven into its face. . . .[31]

However clear the message, making belts talk was an art. Pulling them out, a messenger would set them "in order on the Table," then pick up each one in turn and hold it while speaking its words. Wampum virtuosos had a certain flair. During the war an Onondaga messenger named Ogaghradarisha, to mark how far up the Susquehanna his people wanted Pennsylvania to build a fort, left a wampum belt folded in half to designate the road to Shamokin; then, at the right moment, he opened it full length to stretch, metaphorically, all the way upriver past Wyoming. Sometimes an Indian made a point of "*turning* . . . the belt" when halfway through his talk, by which, one impressed colonist remarked, "it may be as well known . . . how far the speaker has advanced in his speech, as with us on taking a glance at the pages of a book or pamphlet while reading." Having finished, a messenger would then return the belt or string to the table, tie it to a stick, drape it over a pole laid across the rafters of a longhouse, or pass it to his listeners.[32]

If an envoy bearing an unpopular message tried to hand over the belt, his hostile audience kept it "talking" in equally dramatic fashion. Indians might refuse to touch a belt if they opposed its words. When one party of "war messengers" trying to recruit more men draped a belt over the shoulder or thigh of a headman, the recipient, "after shaking it off without touching it with his hands, . . . with a stick, threw it after them, as if he threw a snake or a toad out of his way." Peace belts might get the same cold treatment, as natives using tobacco pipes or sticks "throwed them on one side."[33]

Figures of speech so rich in expressive possibility and so thoroughly embedded in native life were bound to sweep colonists into their embrace. Pennsylvania was born too late for the frenzied days when wampum was money in New England and New Netherland, but Indian use of belts and strings in early conversations with the English along the Delaware quickly taught the newcomers its importance. The colony soon started dispatching messengers with the beads as a "Credential," and in 1700 William Penn himself was handing wampum to visiting Iroquois "in token of amitie & friendship wt ym. . . ."[34]

Colonists on the frontier, too, knew the spell wampum cast. Pennsylvania troops raiding an Indian village in 1756 systematically destroyed houses and burned crops, but they knew enough to bring the town's "Council Belts" back to Philadelphia. Whether the looters took the wampum because of its spiritual and historical significance to Indians—knowing its loss would be a blow to native morale—or because it would fetch a high price in a capital always needing more shells, they appreciated beads' importance.[35]

By the close of the colonial era, Pennsylvanians had grown so attached to the new medium that they sent wampum belts to Iroquoia explaining the Stamp Act crisis. From this confidence came a desire to experiment with form; some Pennsylvania belts bore decidedly non-native designs as colonists added touches of their own. Instead of hands or diamonds, belts might display the Penn family crest or a provincial fort. Instead of paths or hearts, they sported dates or initials immortalizing everyone from King George (*G.R.*) and Teedyuscung (*D.K.*, for Delaware King) to a provincial army officer (*W.C.*, for William Clapham).[36]

Whatever their design and their message, shells were a go-between's stock in trade. He advised wampum makers on the size, color, and pattern of belts, kept beads on hand just in case, and, before setting out with a message, packed hundreds, even thousands of the shells among the "nessecarys . . . to Facilitate the Success of his Journey." To run short or run out was to court disaster. Weiser fretted that one emissary bound for the Indian countries "was without wampum for accidents," and in February 1760 Teedyuscung, preparing for another trip, complained "that he has not got Wampum enough" to carry Pennsylvania's words of peace.[37]

Making their way through the Susquehanna Valley with Teedyuscung and those words of peace that June, Christian Frederick Post, John Hays, Isaac Stille, and Moses Tatamy met just the misfortune Weiser had dreaded and the Delaware leader had predicted: they ran low on beads. To Post's relief, local Indians, testifying to their desire for an end to war, "Laid Down A Blanket and Preaclemed A Publick colection[,] and for Joy the Wemen and Girels and children throd in wampom till There Wase 14 fathem for to helpe For strings on our Jorney." That women and children tossed beads onto the blanket suggests how each finished string or belt represented large segments of a community, including not just the messenger delivering it or the council sending it but also those who obtained and strung the shells. For Post and the rest that day, it meant the chance to resume "our old Buisiness of Belt makeing," which had already occupied much of their time during three days of bad weather on the road from Philadelphia.[38]

While the others in that 1760 embassy continued "to Make Ready Belts and Strings and Speeches," Post sat down to write out those speeches "in a Large Hand that Isaac Still might Read them" at Indian councils farther west. A few days later, as the emissaries went on with their preparations for a push deeper into Indian country, the Nanticoke headman of a nearby village sent them "a Letter and Belt and string and Very Agreeable Speeches." At the time, no one thought either Post's scribbling or that Nanticoke message remarkable, for by then envoys routinely had paper in one pocket and wampum—tagged and numbered to correspond to particular written speeches—in the other.[39] While Pennsylvanians learned beadwork, they taught natives how writing, too, encouraged conversation.

Some Indians refused to go along, sending messages on wampum and insisting that "This is my Letter, Being I don't understand writing." But many embraced the new way of talking.[40] Like colonists learning about wampum, natives proved quick studies, and in Lasse Cocke's day Indian messengers joined their colonial counterparts to negotiate the borderlands with both letters and strings.[41] In 1715, Sassoonan, trying to dam the river of rum drowning his people, asked the governor for written permission to "stave all the rum that came amongst them." When that campaign failed and Shickellamy launched another Susquehanna temperance crusade, he made sure, before confronting provincial liquor dealers, to bring along a copy of the Pennsylvania law against selling alcohol to Indians. . . .[42]

Jonnhaty and the rest demanded a document not just because it carried weight among colonists; in Indian country, too, the black scratches on paper took on an aura of authority. "A letter," wrote David Zeisberger, "especially if it is sealed, is considered a very important thing" among Indians; one that arrived in Onondaga generated such excitement, that "[t]he whole town was full of it," and on hearing it read aloud natives "Suck'd in every paragraph." With writing acquiring talismanic power, Indian raiders who during the war lugged off French, German, and English Bibles from frontier settlements might have acted on impulses akin to their Pennsylvania counterparts who stole a town's council wampum: keenly aware of the objects' potency, they sought to capture it for themselves.[43]

Warriors hauling Bibles out of a burning farmhouse, townsfolk enraptured by a letter—these suggest the respect Indians had for the written word. Some scholars, reading that respect as awe, have posited an unbridgeable gulf between colonial and Indian media. Turning page upon page of merchants' account books, hefting the stacks of correspondence and council minutes European colonists bequeathed us, one can glimpse a vast chasm between a European world built on writing and a native American universe confined to word of mouth. But the frontier was not so simple. Its means of expression had no obvious divide between literate and oral, but rather a spectrum—anchored at one end by thoroughgoing mastery of a curriculum of books and paper, at the other by immersion in oral culture—with negotiators, like almost everyone else, arrayed at various points between. . . .[44]

Woodsmen who had learned to speak in pictures would have scoffed at the notion that natives could neither read nor write. Indian country was littered with evidence to the contrary. Beside the path stood those "archives," those "Indian histories" where natives chronicled their adventures taking deer and scalps, while at home in the village a "Jurnal" recounting a man's exploits sat on his bed. All of these depictions are "as intelligible to them," one colonist admitted, "as a written account is to us."[45]

For an Indian handy with picture-writing, pen and ink in some ways was no radical departure. Men who once had issued threats by "Marcking on a Board Certain Indian figures" began to put, in "a little Book," "the Picture and Marks of an Indian Warriour with his Gun and Spear."[46] Other natives cushioned the shock of the new by directing it into customary channels, drawing parallels between marks made on paper and figures made from shells. Like wampum, paper brought an author into direct contact with his audience, however many miles actually separated them. "[W]e look on" the belts you sent "as if we had seen your Kings in Person," Cherokees assured the Six Nations in 1758, just as in a letter Indians would say that "We now Speak to you, and we speak as in your presence, even face to face."[47]

Like belts and strings, too, papers went into a council bag for safekeeping. At first natives thought the object itself more important than the scratches on its surface, for some Indians kept a document even after "it was so defaced that" a colonist "could not read any more of it than a word here and there." Puzzled looks from Pennsylvanians unable to make out the faded ink taught natives to shield the pages from wear and tear. At Shamokin in 1748, Shickellamy brought out an old letter of recommendation from the governor of Pennsylvania and listened, "much pleas.d," as a colonist read it aloud.[48]

Paper so carefully preserved took its place beside wampum in the conversation between cultures. Headmen who got a letter inviting them to meet with Pennsylvania would keep it, sometimes for years, so that when they finally did come in they could return it to their host as they would an "invitation string" of wampum. That done, the visitor might pull out an old letter or treaty and pass it around as proof "that we have always been your fast Friends" or, clutching it in his hand, "speak on it" as he would a belt of beads.[49] Shawnees once went farther still, hauling out an old "Certificate of the renewal of our Friendship" and trying to get colonial officials to sign the document "afresh" as an endorsement of continued good relations. The startled governor and councilors declined the honor, but the request itself, with an Indian pushing a quill pen into a reluctant colonial hand, suggests how far native peoples had gone in making this medium their own. . . .[50]

Intercultural communication was plagued by ignorance and folly, fraud and mistrust, cupidity and arrogance; indeed, as time wore on, the interference got worse rather than better. A closer look reveals that not even Shickellamy and Weiser were as devoted to truth as they appeared; if these two putative paragons fell short of the ideal, imagine how far short others fell. All were human: they made mistakes, both honest and dishonest, and their agendas clashed as often as coincided. . . .

Many obstacles stood in the way of conversation. Sickness or bad weather might stop an envoy, as did a hunting or trading expedition and—among Indian messengers—a bad dream.[51] So did drink. The Pennsylvania fur traders in August 1728 who paused to slake their thirst (and spill their news) at a Philadelphia tavern had kindred spirits a generation later in Teedyuscung, who bartered his wampum for liquor, and Andrew Montour, who, having lost his dispatches, was (co-incidentally?) held in Carlisle on a tavern debt.[52]

Sometimes Pennsylvania traders, perfectly sober, found good reason to fail as messengers. Charles Poke and Thomas Hill neglected to carry a belt from Allegheny Indians to Philadelphia, since that wampum told provincial officials how these two traders had "abused" the very people who now sent them east to turn themselves in! A request for more English goods sent by Ohio leaders in the 1740s met a similar oblivion, perhaps because the men toting (and burying) that plea wanted to keep the trade to themselves. . . .[53]

Even a sober and skilled emissary found wampum hard to handle. However long a belt was, however elaborate its design, it was not a letter that could simply be picked up and deciphered by anyone familiar with the medium. A negotiator using wampum had to tie in his mind a particular speech with a particular belt's size, color, and pattern; if not, the beads were struck dumb. Surely, then, written documents were an improvement—an open book, as it were, to any educated eye? A belt wore obscure symbols; a page—any page—bore letters, words, sentences, all awaiting a trained glance to unveil its secrets.

But a document only looked more reliable. As Indians learned through painful experience, much depended on who did the writing; some scribes penned "loose Letters." In 1739 Shawnees visiting the capital found this out when provincial officials accused them, "from your own Letters," of favoring the French. There must be some mistake, the Indians replied; that letter "was not wrote agreeable to their Minds, nor as they designed." What happened is that "being merry over a Cup of good Liquor at Alleghenny, they then said they would write to you, their Brothers [in Philadelphia], which two white Men who were in Company undertook to do." Only now do we discover that those two, for reasons of their own, "so wrote what they themselves thought proper."[54]

In 1753 other Pennsylvania traders, living up to their worst reputation, strayed even farther from native intentions by slipping into an innocuous letter, marked by headmen, a paragraph in which Indians supposedly agreed to sell their lands on the Ohio River's east side to pay off trade debts. The governor and council, though always happy to buy more territory, were so amazed by this extraordinary proposal and so distrustful of the traders who penned it that they wondered if the Indians had been "in a sober, thoughtful mood" when their scruffy amanuenses took it down. Sure enough, inquiries confirmed that natives had said no such thing.[55]

By midcentury the Ohio country, where Pennsylvania's ambitions clashed with those of Virginia, France, and assorted Indian nations, was particularly fertile soil for such chicanery. First came the debate over Britain building a fort there. Thomas Penn (long since returned to England to stay) and his loyalists in Philadelphia considered a stronghold "a mark of Possession" that would counter both French and Virginians; for their part, George Croghan and his fellow fur traders longed for the protection a garrison could provide. Thus in January 1751 Croghan arrived in the provincial capital to announce that Ohio Indians at Logstown "are of opinion that their Brothers the English ought *to have a fort on this River* to secure the Trade." Sent back that spring only to "sound the Indians in a private manner that he might know their Sentiments" about this venture, the trader surprised everyone by returning with the natives' formal request for "a Strong House." Governor James Hamilton was pleased; the Quaker-dominated assembly, opposed both to war and to spending money, was not. Imagine, then, its delight when Andrew Montour, who had been at Croghan's side throughout the Ohio visit, came in to deny that Indians had said any such thing.[56]

Who was lying? It is as hard to tell now as it was then. Croghan, publicly humiliated, fought hard to clear his name (he even persuaded Montour to change his story), but matters never got sorted out. Wherever truth lay, this chapter in the cross-cultural concourse reveals how tangled the lines of communication were becoming as the number of players on the frontier stage grew and the stakes mounted.

Conrad Weiser, who had visited the assembly with Montour to hear the *métis* embarrass Croghan, soon found out how unpredictable a fellow Montour was, and how unfathomable the politics of the Ohio country. At Logstown in 1752, Montour pressed Indian leaders to accept the expansive interpretation of an Iroquois land sale that Virginia and Weiser had obtained at Lancaster in 1744, a reading that would have given Ohio to the Old Dominion. But at another council Montour, reversing himself, insisted that "the Indians never Sold nor released it [the territory beyond the mountains;] If they did they were imposed upon by the Interpreter"—none other than the now "very angry" Weiser himself. Once again truth is elusive, and once again it is less important than what the dispute reveals about confusion in formal conversations.[57]

A return visit to the banks of the Ohio in December 1758 finds truth more evident and some go-betweens' efforts to evade it more obvious. Croghan and Montour, having long since patched up their differences, stood with General John Forbes's army on the ruins of Fort Duquesne at the Forks of the Ohio, just captured from the French. It was a pivotal moment in American history. British success in taking the stronghold owed much to their messengers' ability to convince Ohio Indians that, upon ousting the French, the British army would obey the natives' demand to leave Ohio. Believing that promise, natives sat out the contest and the French fell.[58] Now, meeting the triumphant Forbes, Ohio leaders repeated, several times, their insistence "that he should go back over the mountains." Forbes did turn around: desperately ill, he headed east to die. But he left behind Colonel Henry Bouquet and two hundred troops to build a stronghold, to be christened Fort Pitt. Now Bouquet, unhappy with the Indians' insistence on his retreat, wanted them to "alter their mind."

When native leaders refused, Croghan and Montour stepped in. As traders and, more recently, Crown Indian agents, both were keen to see the soldiers stay. First they simply refused to "tell Colonel *Bouquet* the *Indians'* answer." Then Croghan insisted that, in private talks with Bouquet, the headmen had indeed changed their minds about the troops. When Christian Frederick Post, who was also there, expressed doubts about that story, "Mr. Croghn grew very angry" and said any other account of Indian wishes "was a d—d lie." The Ohio natives, informed of Croghan's version, "said, Mr. *Croghn* and *Henry Montour* had not spoke and acted honestly and uprightly." Honest or not, Montour and Croghan—and Bouquet—got their wish: the army stayed. Ohio leaders learned the hard way that among a go-between's tricks was making *no* mean *yes* and *yes, no.*[59]

Croghan and Montour, caught by Post that winter day, offer the best example of how a negotiator could put words in someone's mouth. With Post's help, it is easy to see where, and why, something got lost in translation. But without a Post standing by at every conversation to point out where an interpreter strayed, it is harder to tell how much of what Croghan called "Indian Form" and Weiser termed "Indian Phrases" fell by the way.[60] It is clear, however, that even an interpreter committed to accurate translation had a difficult time getting messages through the cultural and linguistic interference, through the profound difference in agendas and customs.

Just a month after the Ohio Indians' meeting with Bouquet, one of the native leaders at that council, a Delaware named Custaloga, gave a French officer his version of the conversation.[61] It bore little resemblance to Bouquet's. While both accounts of the talks mentioned trade, peace, and return of colonial captives, they painted Bouquet and Britain in very different colors. Bouquet had himself boasting that "the English are . . . the most powerfull People on this Continent," insisting that the two hundred soldiers had to stay to protect traders, agreeing that the Indians must soon return their prisoners, and instructing natives to drive out all of the remaining French.

Custaloga's Bouquet was a more contrite fellow. "I . . . [am] going to be quite different from what you have seen and experienced of me up to the present," he allegedly promised. "It is," this Bouquet admitted, "unreasonable that we have come to stain your lands with blood . . . , we should have respected your lands." But fear not: we will leave soon, for "The King himself . . . forbids us to cross to the other side of the [Ohio] river, and orders us even to come away from it." Two hundred soldiers in a fort? No, only "a trading house here without a stockade." Drive away your French friend? "I shall be delighted to be door to door with him." Prisoners? Keep those "you have adopted as your relatives." But perhaps you might surrender the older ones, "who would be in the way, or of very little use to you." It is almost as if Custaloga and Bouquet were remembering different conversations.

This was hardly the first time transmission was garbled. In 1743 Oneidas told New York officials that, though the treaty minutes said nothing about it, during the council at Onondaga Virginia had actually admitted that colonists were to blame for the skirmish with Jonnhaty's men. And in 1756 the Onondaga envoy Ogaghradarisha, recalling his visit to Pennsylvania to request a colonial fort at Shamokin and propose another above Wyoming, had the governor say "*That as he found by woeful experience, that making purchases of Lands was the cause of much blood having been shed,* he was determined to buy no more."[62]

The line between true and false is harder to draw in these cases than it was with Post at the Ohio Forks. Did Custaloga consciously change Bouquet's words? Or was the Delaware offering an accurate (if not verbatim) account of the treaty, based on his own design or on a slanted interpretation by Andrew Montour? Ogaghradarisha's message begs the same questions. Was he putting words in the governor's mouth? Perhaps the fault lay in Weiser's interpretation that day, or in the gap between Weiser's Mohawk and Ogaghradarisha's Onondaga. Or maybe Ogaghradarisha mistook Pennsylvania's reluctance to accept at once his invitation to build a fort above Wyoming, so deep in Iroquois territory, as a policy statement against ever again buying native land. At this remove, one can only pose the questions; the rest is a guessing game. But it is no idle pastime. Pondering it, we approach the heart of translation's mystery, where words become malleable and imprecise, prey to the skills, schemes, and memories of those doing the talking.

Even in the best of times, interpretation is not an exact science. The equation that manufactures sentences from sounds has a host of variables, from the setting and audience to the translator's ability and sobriety or his agenda and attention span, not to mention the means of recording his work for future reference. The colonial era was not the best of times, even if an interpreter intended only the most faithful rendering of a speaker's words. Go-betweens were often tired, afraid, drunk, or bored—and sometimes all four at once. Their linguistic gifts ranged from fluency to ignorance, such as that exhibited by the Delaware Joseph Peepy, a regular translator in the last two decades of the colonial period who, near the end of his career, was said to speak only broken English. Moreover, fluency, so difficult to attain, was also easy to lose. In 1754 Weiser asked to be relieved of his duties "as a principal Interpreter" because "he is no longer Master of that Fluency he formerly had, and finding himself at a Loss for proper Terms to express himself is frequently obliged to make Use of Circumlocution." With rusty or inept translators, one colonist lamented how much of a native's eloquence was reduced to dross by an interpreter able to distill only "the sense" of it.[63]

It seems likely, then, that many an Indian speaker would have been disappointed to learn how much of his wisdom and wit were "spoiled" by a lousy accent, poor choice of words, and clumsy delivery. While we cannot measure the full extent of this impediment to understanding, we can identify elements of native speechmaking that, if not altogether abandoned by interpreters and scribes, at least received less emphasis, and therefore made less impact, than native American orators intended.

The first is repetition. Rehearsal of key words and phrases is vitally important to oral cultures intent on retaining their knowledge.[64] To natives like Tongocone and the other Delawares condoling Tenohwangogue in 1761, intoning phrases over and over again was, like regular renewal of friendship at councils, the very lifeblood of conversation. Colonists saw words differently. Like a treaty that stood for all time once it was written down and marked or signed by the right people, so a phrase, once spoken and inscribed, had no need to reappear. Only colonial inconsistency in translating and recording Indian speeches—with some interpreters and scribes more prone to include everything—exposes the gap, providing occasional glimpses of what must have been a consistent Indian reiteration:[65]

- The Delaware leader Sassoonan, 1715 (interpreter and scribe unknown): *added to the same effect, . . . further added, . . . added, . . . Continued in the same strain, . . . repeated the same.*
- Sassoonan again, 1740 (scribe unknown, interpreter "Thomas Freeman, an Indian"): *now we are come down; we are come into your House . . . . [W]e are glad now we are come; and my Uncles the Mingoes, came along with Us from Alleghany . . . . I tell you again that our Friends, the Mingoes, came along with Us, and are come into your House.*
- Ohio Delawares, 1758 (Christian Frederick Post, translator and scribe): *You have talked of that Peace and Friendship which we had formerly with you . . . . [A]lways remember that Friendship which we had formerly . . . . [O]ur good Friendship and Peace we had formerly. . . . [T]hat Friendship we formerly had . . . . [T]hat Friendship with you we formerly had . . . . [T]he Peace and Friendship we had Formerly . . . . [T]he Friendship which we had formerly amongst our Fathers and Grandfathers . . . . That Friendship . . . which was formerly between us . . . . [T]hat Peace and Friendship which we formerly had with you.*
- An Oneida named Saghughsuniunt (Thomas King), 1762 (interpreter uncertain, scribe Richard Peters?): *call your Soldiers away from Shamokin. . . . [T]ake away your Soldiers. . . . I must tell you again these Soldiers must go away from Shamokin Fort. . . . [T]here is no occasion for Soldiers to live there any longer. . . . [W]e must press you to take away your Soldiers from Shamokin.*

Having skimmed these lines, the reader may now, perhaps, be readier to forgive colonial translators and scribes who usually saved their breath and their ink, even if that meant altering the rhythms and accents of native discourse.

A second strand of speech only occasionally found its way into the record due to colonial delicacy, not colonial boredom. A native speaker's use of the body as metaphor usually enraptured colonial auditors, accustomed as they were to thinking in terms of a *body politic.* Thus interpreters conveyed—and scribes recorded—metaphors from head to foot. But amid all the body parts, private parts are conspicuously absent from surviving accounts of speeches; they come up just enough to suggest that colonists routinely bowdlerized Indian talks.

Much of this discourse centered on insults about turning men into women. Why fight Catawbas? Because, a Cayuga said (through Weiser), those southern Indians "sent us word that . . . they were men and double men for they had two P——s; that they could make Women of Us." During the war with colonists another Iroquois explained that Delawares attacking Pennsylvania had boasted that "We are Men" and shall keep fighting; do not try to stop us, "lest we cut off your private Parts and make Women of you."[66]

Two other references to private parts confirm the suspicion that colonists, not Indians, were responsible for keeping such talk to a minimum. The Pennsylvanian John Hays, with Christian Post at a council on the Susquehanna in 1760, noted in his diary that one native stood to complain about British exchange rates for furs. Prices are so high, the Indian argued, that *he got but 6 fills of a Measure for a ribboned Stroud, and it was so little that his Cock could Not Go in it, and he had But A little one.* Significantly, polishing his grammar and spelling for the final report on their mission, Hays omitted this speech altogether.[67]

Conrad Weiser, translating for the Seneca go-between Newcastle, went in the opposite direction in his report, not away from the explicit but toward it. Newcastle says, the Pennsylvanian explained, that the Iroquois sent a message to Delawares that included talk of how those Delawares

> have Suffered the string that tied your petticoat to be cut loose by the French, and you lay with them, & so became a common Bawd, . . . and as you have thrown off the Cover of your modesty and become stark naked, . . . We now give you a little Prick and put it into your private Parts, and so let it grow there till you shall be a compleat man.

The speech has attracted scholarly attention for the light it sheds on Iroquois talk of Delawares as women. But its significance also lies in how Weiser handled it. Before repeating Newcastle's message, the negotiator was at pains to say that the image was not his, but the Seneca's: I only "took down in words . . . the literal Interpretation of what Newcastle said." Weiser's skittish way with those words makes one wonder how often he and others censored an Indian speech before it ever reached colonists' tender ears.[68]

Perhaps, given all the obstacles in the way—differences in language and emphasis, a metaphorical wilderness, the temptation to censor or edit speeches—we should be surprised that native voices from colonial times come through as clearly as they do. But at the time, Indians and colonists alike were frustrated by the enduring language barrier between them.

In 1748 one Indian woman befriending Moravians at Shamokin broke down and wept because she "could not understand & Speake with" them better. Leaders on both sides knew the feeling. . . . But tedium or merely getting the gist of it was, in some sense, not the worst thing happening to the good correspondence. More ominous still, Indian and colonist were coming to understand one another only too well.[69]

The farther one goes in exploring frontier conversation, the darker the prospect appears. People lied; they made up letters and mishandled wampum; their incompetence or chicanery meant that countless words were "lost by the way & never told." Even writing and wampum, complementary as they could be in capable hands, ended up in contention as Indians came to fear the power of the pen and colonists insisted more shrilly on paper's primacy.

Contention between the two media was always there, in the weight each side accorded them. Where Indians considered written documents supplementary, colonists thought the opposite. "They were glad," Iroquois told Pennsylvania in 1722, "the Govr. sent them a Letter for that was like two tongues, and *confirmed* what the Messenger said to them." Two decades later Governor Thomas let slip the prevailing colonial view when he informed Shawnees that "I send you this not only under the Seal of our Government, but for *a further Confirmation* have added four Strings of Wampum."[70]

Like any literate people, colonists thought reliance on the spoken word a mistake. Speech, they insisted, is transitory and intangible; it lingers in the air for a heartbeat, then dies there, to be followed either by silence or by other evanescent sounds in the flow of thoughts expressed.[71] But putting those thoughts down on paper is, it seemed to Europeans, a different matter. Here, they believed, words make an indelible mark, become tangible objects that, years hence, can resurrect the talk of men long dead. Here, on the page, lies truth, a record of deeds, of wisdom, just waiting to be revived in order to enlighten generations to come. And here, in the ink, the message comes through clearly to sustain "Kind Correspondents."

Or so European colonists wished to believe. However close colonial and Indian modes of communication might look, however adept Pennsylvanians became with shell beads or Indians with writing, colonists nonetheless thought that literacy, civilization's hallmark, set them off from their native neighbors.[72] A spectrum of communicative forms there indeed was, but at its center lay, to the European (and, in the end, to the Indian) way of thinking, a divide separating peoples that could read and write from those that could not. While literacy is indeed a tool of communication, it is also "a mode of excommunication," a weapon that literally wrote off groups. . . .[73]

Some Indians sounded awed, even cowed, by a document's power to carry thoughts across space or time. When I die I am going to hell, one aged Delaware solemnly told a missionary. "Ask'd . . . how he came to belive so, Said he I have liv'd with white People, (who can reed & Know many things from

God), & they all Say so." In formal discourse, too, Indians might genuflect before the paper altar Penn and Logan erected for them. If we "make any Blunders, or have forgot any part of the Speech," Saghughsuniunt told Pennsylvania's governor in 1757, please "excuse" it, "as they cou'd not write, therefore, were obliged to keep every thing in their Memory."[74]

These two may have been putting colonists on, for alongside such obeisance were louder, more common Indian expressions of confidence in their own ways of recording and recalling things. In Philadelphia an Iroquois named Kanickhungo insisted that writing was not the only way to make the past live. "We who are now here are old Men," he said to Thomas Penn, James Logan, and a crowd of colonists in October 1736, "who have the Direction of Affairs in our own Nations, & as we are old, it may be thought that the Memory of these things may be lost with us, who have not like you the Art of preserving it, by committing all Transactions to writing"; not so, Kanickhungo continued, for "we nevertheless have Methods of transmitting from Father to Son an account of all these things, whereby you will find the Remembrance of them is faithfully preserved."[75]

Natives defending their own method of seeing that "succeeding Generations are made acquainted with what has passed" also came to doubt writing's capacity for capturing and conveying truth. Growing familiarity with the literate cosmos bred distrust. One reason Susquehanna Shawnees took such a dislike to Count Zinzendorf in 1742 was the Moravian's habit of holing up in a tent with his books and papers; it looked to Indians like sorcery, with the writings a tool of that malevolent craft. Around this time Canasatego, too, sounded the alarm. Waxing nostalgic for the days when Indians had the continent to themselves, the Onondaga told colonial leaders that "We are now . . . lyable to many . . . Inconveniences since the English came among Us, and particularly from the Pen and Ink work that is going on at the Table [pointing to the Secretarys]" scratching away there.[76]

In the years to come, suspicions of that work grew, pushed by traders' "loose Letters," by how documents, so fixed in appearance, could be so easily misread, by deeds whose boundaries on the page diverged from native memory of an agreement. Paper's power to pluck territory from Indian hands seemed particularly sinister.[77] "They say," remarked Post, "that they have been robbed of the lands by the writing of the whites." Indians leveled the charge time and again. "[W]hen You have gott a writing [confirming a land sale] from us," Delawares complained, "you lock it up in ye. Chest & no body Knows what you have bought or what you paid for it." We have "an Uneasiness on our Minds . . . concerning our Land," an Iroquois speaker told colonists in 1754. Our elders deny ever having sold it, yet now "We understand that there are Writings for all our Lands."[78]

During the war, fear of a literate world became so acute in the Indian countries that someone pulling out a book might have it knocked from his grasp or stolen. "I Durst Not Reead But sum times When they were in A

Good Umer," wrote one colonial envoy, "and Not Long at A tim." Do not even let Indians know that you have books with you, another advised.[79]

Though reading was provocative, writing was worse. In the early 1760s Post warned colonists venturing into the Ohio country that "Indians are very suspicious of those white people whom they see engaged in reading and writing, especially the latter; believing that it concerns them or their territory." The go-between spoke from hard experience. During delicate wartime negotiations, he and his companions had drawn suspicious looks every time they picked up a pen. "[W]hat had they to write there?" the "very jealous" natives demanded.[80]

Jealousy was compounded by natives' growing dependence on books and papers. Like a headman holding an old piece of paper or an Iroquois warrior with a passport tucked away in his pack, Indians knew and used literacy's power. At the same time, however, they could not unlock all of its secrets, could neither abandon it nor fully embrace and exploit it. The result, among illiterate messengers, was occasional embarrassment and perpetual uneasiness. In the late 1750s the Ohio Delaware Tamaqua went from village to village, papers in hand, speaking words of peace, only to be told by some fur traders that what he carried was not a peace treaty but a land agreement.[81] Tamaqua's brother Pisquetomen knew the feeling. He once strode grandly into the provincial council chamber to lay belts and strings on the table, then faltered when it turned out that the accompanying paper he handed the governor did not, in fact, contain "the Substance" of that wampum; someone had given him the wrong document. Pressed to go ahead and "deliver what they had to say from their Memory," he and his companions declined; "he depended upon that Paper to Assist his Memory in what he had to say," Pisquetomen replied, "he could not do without it."[82]

*He could not do without it*—yet he could not even read it. The dilemma preoccupied and infuriated natives. No colonist saw this more clearly than Post, when Ohio leaders summoned him so that they could dictate a letter. "The jealousy natural to the *Indians* is not to be described," the messenger remarked; "for though they wanted me to write for them, they were afraid I would, at the same time, give other information, and this perplexed them."[83]

Indians thus perplexed came up with a variety of ways to master or counter writing's power. Some learned to read and write. "[T]hey had Writers among themselves," Teedyuscung, thinking of Isaac Stille and Joseph Peepy, reminded provincial officials. But literate natives were rare, even at the end of the colonial era, so other groups adopted an educated colonist. In 1761 an Onondaga named Jenochiaada sent a messenger to Pennsylvania to say (on a wampum string) that "When I receive a Letter from you I cannot understand it, which I think very hard." Was the solution to insist on wampum, then? Not for Jenochiaada. "[W]e ought to have somebody living among us," he went on, "who can understand and interpret your Messages & the Letters you send to us." His candidate was "my [adopted] Child, James Sherlock"; please give him "your leave . . . [to] live amongst us."[84]

Ironically, even Indians who accepted the triumph of writing were often rebuffed when they wanted to learn its mysteries for themselves. Colonial officials, far from welcoming such overtures, sought to shore up the barrier between bookish people and everyone else.[85] When Oneidas in 1753 asked David Zeisberger to write a letter to Conrad Weiser, the Moravian refused, "adding, that if they had any message to send to Weiser, they should do it by means of a belt, which was a much better and surer way than by letter." Similarly, when Teedyuscung nine years later wished aloud that the peace just made among the Indians at Lancaster had been written down and "signed by all of us [headmen] . . . , that we might have it always to shew to our Children and Grand Children," Pennsylvania's governor "reminded him that it was not the Custom for Indians to sign writings to one another." The natives' ambivalence about writing was matched by colonial ambivalence about their having it.[86]

By then Teedyuscung was accustomed to British officials deflecting his tentative forays into the written universe. Since 1757, pressed by Moses Tatamy and Isaac Stille, he had struggled to get a clerk of his own in order to ensure an accurate account of his conversations with colonists. The contest began innocently enough at a treaty in July 1757 when the Delaware, pleading a faulty memory and a desire to "have things done regularly," asked for "a Copy of all the Proceedings." To this, provincial leaders agreed readily enough.[87]

But Teedyuscung's other request created a stir. I also want, he said, speaking (of course) on a wampum string, "a Clerk to take Minutes along; with the Governor's Clerk." This was a rather different matter: handing over a copy of the minutes the governor's man takes is one thing, two clerks—and therefore two versions of the same speech—quite another. Governor William Denny, counseled by Croghan and Weiser, refused. "No Indian Chief, before you, ever demanded to have a Clerk," Denny replied, "and none has ever been appointed for Indians in former Treaties."[88]

Resistance only confirmed Delaware suspicions about writing. "[H]e looked on it both unjust and unkind," Teedyuscung said, "to attempt . . . by this refusal to lead him on Blindfold and in the Dark." In the end the Indians got their wish, and Charles Thomson, headmaster of a Quaker school in Philadelphia, took a seat at the scribe's table. Croghan, in charge of keeping the minutes, was furious. "As to his having a Clerk or not having one I think it is a matter of little consequence," the old trader fumed, "but the having a Clerk was not the thing." That second scribe thrust an illegitimate voice (and pen) into official business; to Croghan, that was the crux of the matter.[89]

And yet in a larger sense the secretary was indeed "the thing," because he was a teacher that could guide illiterate Indians through the forbidden recesses of the written world, a world colonial leaders wanted to keep to themselves. Looking ahead, Croghan feared worse to come. Will Thomson now sit with Indians to help draft a speech, then read it in council as colonists did? Teedyuscung, no fool, proceeded along precisely those lines, asking Thomson, a distraught Croghan reported, "to read it off as a lawyer would put in a plea at the bar." This is "very extraordinary and the most unprecedented procedure ever known at an Indian treaty," the Pennsylvanian spluttered. He managed to talk the Delaware out of it this time, but what next? Sitting over in England, Thomas Penn knew. They will not stop at getting copies of treaties or their own clerk, Penn warned. Soon any disgruntled Indian—knowing that, as that Delaware had put it, documents are "in ye. Chest" under lock and key—will demand to see our land records. Forbid it, the proprietor ordered: "if they make a charge, they should make that charge good from the evidence they have, and not be allowed to search into the Cabinets of any Persons for Causes of Complaint."[90]

Some Indians, listening to squabbles over clerks, came to believe that there was another way, a better way, to embrace the strange new world of books while rejecting its colonial authors and authorities. In an effort to steal writing's spell for themselves, natives began to compose books of their own. "[H]e would Read Like Mad ofe it in the Morning," remarked one colonist after watching an Indian with a "Book of Pickters." Spiritual leaders began using texts to inspire others. One Delaware "had drawn, as he pretended, by the direction of the great Spirit, a kind of map on a piece of deer skin, somewhat dressed like parchment, which he called 'the great Book or Writing.' . . . This map he held before him while preaching, frequently pointing to particular marks and spots upon it, and giving explanations as he went along." Increasingly, Indians making and reading such books counseled "total Seperation from" European colonists.[91]

It had come to this, then, William Penn's "Kind Correspondence." Indians rejected a colonial symbol system that they had come to read as a tool of oppression, turning to competing books, and competing visions, as an antidote to poison pens. Other natives sought to play the game by the newcomers' rules, only to be forbidden by colonists who, insisting that Truth lay on the face of their papers, also insisted on remaining Truth's sole custodian. The conversational aids—wampum and freedom, paper and words—had spawned mistrust and contempt, had driven a wedge between Indians and colonists that went deeper than a message lost or gone astray, deeper than rumor, ignorance, or incompetence, to touch the frontier's very heart.

After 1750, peoples in and around Penn's Woods were doing more than talking, more, even, than wrangling about clerks and copies, about whose books spoke truth, about where wisdom resided and deceit lurked: they were killing each other with terrible fury. Frontier war—known ever since as the Seven Years' War or the French and Indian War—erupted because a combination of new conditions and old unhappiness proved more than even the most gifted conversationalist could handle. With so many voices clamoring to be heard, conversation lapsed into cacophony, and finally into war cries and terrified shrieks.

Gone, by 1750, were the days when Conrad Weiser and Shickellamy could manage most of the business between Pennsylvania and its Indian neighbors; the frontier was becoming too vast, the number of peoples involved too large, the lines of communication too long, for that. The Delaware, Shawnee, and Iroquois emigration into the Ohio country had altered the diplomatic landscape. While these groups kept up their trade and their talk of friendship with Pennsylvania, many of them—especially Shawnees and Delawares—also remembered all too well how Penn's people had driven them away. Mingled with fond memories of amity that, one Pennsylvania governor hoped, "remain stamp'd on your Minds, never to be forgott," were unhappy recollections of land fraud and trade abuse along the Delaware and the Lehigh, the Tulpehocken and the Susquehanna. It did not help that Indians, according to Croghan and many others who knew them, were "Jealous and Revengefull[,] Never forgett & seldom forgive where they think they are Ingered."[92]

And now colonists—not just Pennsylvanians but Virginians, with their newly-formed cadre of land speculators called the Ohio Company—were casting a hungry eye beyond the mountains, too, sending out surveyors to prepare, in secret, the way for further European settlement. "I took an Opportunity to set my Compass privately . . . ," wrote their agent, Christopher Gist, in November 1750, "for I understood it was dangerous to let a Compass be seen among these Indians." Memories of past misdeeds were so keen that shortly before war broke out, Indians at a town beside the Allegheny River "found a Rat & Kill'd it, at which ye antiants of them seem'd Concearned," saying "that ye French or English should get that Land from them, ye same prediction being made by their Grandfathers' on finding a Rat on Delaware before ye White People Came there." No wonder France, sending troops and traders into the Ohio at midcentury in order to check the English advance that threatened to cut French Canada off from French Louisiana, convinced natives that the British were up to no good.[93]

Complicating the frontier further, to the north sat William Johnson, his influence among the Iroquois growing steadily, while the Iroquois themselves kept trying to make good their claims to suzerainty over the increasingly populous and independent Ohio peoples. Even Pennsylvania was becoming a more complicated place to do Indian business. Proprietary officials sought money for arms and other gifts to counter the French and keep natives loyal; Quaker-dominated assemblies, which controlled the purse, refused. "As these [Indian] Affairs take up more time, and give more trouble to a Government, than almost all other Business put to gether," sighed Governor James Hamilton during one "dangerous Season" in November 1753, "it is a pity they afford so little Satisfaction in transacting them." A few months later a weary Conrad Weiser, listening to the hubbub, longed for the day when "I Shall not trouble my head any longer" about "Indian affairs. . . . [T]here is now So many Cookes in that Kitchen that the brothe is allready Spoiled."[94]

As late as 1750, Richard Peters had boasted to his superior, proprietor Thomas Penn, of Weiser's being so thoroughly in command that "I verily believe it is in his power to turn the Indian Councils which way he pleases." Hyperbole, of course; no one ever had that much say. Yet Peters captured the look of the Pennsylvania frontier in the recent past. Beginning in the late 1740s, however, as things started to fall apart for Weiser and for the world he knew, Pennsylvania's Indian agent began talking retirement. Indians pestered him with land and trade complaints, yet Philadelphia did nothing. "I shall be sick of Indian Affairs," the German colonist had warned Peters in June 1747, "If no medium is found to do them Justice."[95]

To make things worse, the colony's diplomatic opening to the Ohio country left Weiser overburdened and out of his depth. He was a Six Nations man, a veteran of the trail running from Philadelphia through Tulpehocken and Shamokin to Onondaga; the western paths and peoples lay beyond his ken. "I should think meselve happy if I had nothing to do in public affairs, and could turn farmer entirely," a frustrated Weiser wrote after meeting some Ohio folk in Lancaster during the summer of 1748. Then, that fall, Shickellamy died, robbing the colony of its closest Indian ally and Weiser of his best guide. The Pennsylvania agent who had handled the Shenandoah Valley and Armstrong messes was a different man from the one who, early in 1754, admitted that "I Can not force things to go as I will, but must Submit to accidents. . . . I am perplects with Indians affairs, and Can not say Such or Such is best."[96]

Nor was Weiser alone in his perplexity. Onondaga and Ohio, Quakers and proprietary men, Pennsylvania and Virginia, not to mention France and Britain—with so many contending forces, events were spinning out of any go-between's control. The surest proof of negotiators' impotence was that though they saw war coming, none could prevent it. Beginning in the late 1740s, Scarouyady, Croghan, Weiser, and Montour all warned Pennsylvania authorities that if no one answered the French offensive in the Ohio with guns and other gifts, even with troops and forts, those French would secure a foothold west of the mountains and turn Indians there against Pennsylvania in particular and Britain in general.[97] Quaker reluctance to finance war and British reluctance to provoke an incident worked against taking a hard line. So did squabbles among the go-betweens themselves about how to proceed. Weiser and Croghan have a "difference of Opinion" about which nations out there should get presents, a disgusted Hamilton wrote in 1750; this, the governor observed, arose "between Two persons who are suppos'd to understand Indian Affairs the best."[98] And that was before Croghan fought Montour about building forts, and Montour quarreled with Weiser about which land Indians had relinquished. All these squabbles left negotiators less able to sustain the conversation.

Disputes between negotiators, between governor and assembly, between Pennsylvania and New York, between Pennsylvania and Virginia, between

Ohio nations and the Iroquois, between France and Britain—in the end all of these spelled a breakdown in correspondence, a breakdown more sinister than loose letters and mislaid wampum, misapprehension and mistranslation. Some thought the communications media specifically to blame. One native messenger said that Susquehanna Indians had joined the war in 1755 because Teedyuscung lacked wampum to send Pennsylvania word of their continuing allegiance. Teedyuscung himself, meanwhile, blamed writing for the bloodshed: "Somebody must have wrote wrong," he explained, "and that makes the Land all Bloody." But Scarouyady argued that the wave of fury and fear broke over Pennsylvania's frontier because of a longer, more pronounced failure of the conversation common for more than two generations. Pennsylvanians "had been too negligent of Cultivating . . . Friendship with the Indians . . . ," the Oneida scolded an audience in Philadelphia in the spring of 1756 ; conflict might have been avoided "If we had been more Conversant with each other."[99]

## NOTES

1 *Pennsylvania Archives*, 9 Series, 138 vols., (Harrisburg and Philadelphia: 1853–1949) [hereafter *PA*, cited by series and vol. number] 1st, I, 671 ("talke"); Weiser to Peters[?], 24 Jan. 1745/6, Eugene Du Simitiere Papers [hereafter DSP], 966. F.24 ("discourse"; see also *Minutes of the Provincial Council of Pennsylvania, From the Organization to the Termination of the Proprietary Government*, 10 vols., (Harrisburg, PA: 1851–1852) [Hereafter *MPCP*], V, 136–39, 162, 167, 212, 222–23; *PA*, 1st, 1, 750–51, 756–69; Weiser to [?], 15 Apr. 1746, Correspondence of Conrad Weiser, in the Papers of Conrad Weiser [hereafter CCW], Historical Society of Pennsylvania [hereafter HSP], I, 14).

2 Weiser to Peters, 27 Oct. 1754, quoted in Paul A. W. Wallace, *Conrad Weiser, 1696–1760: Friend of Colonist and Mohawk* (Philadelphia: University of Pennsylvania Press, 1945), 372. See also "Sentements of Ohio," n.d., CCW, II, 27; *PA,* 1st, I, 551; Albert Cook Myers, ed., *William Penn: His Own Account of the Lenni Lenape or Delaware Indians, 1683* (Moylan, Pa., 1937), 87.

3 *MPCP*, III, 440.

4 "Witham Marshe's Journal of the Treaty held With the Six Nations . . ." Collections of the Massachusetts Historical Society, For the Year MDCCC, 1st ser., VII, 171–201 [hereafter Marshe], p. 180; John Gottlieb Ernestus Heckewelder, *History, Manners, and Customs of the Indian Nations: Who Once Inhabited Pennsylvania and the Neighboring States*, rev. ed., (Philadelphia, 1881) [hereafter Heckewelder, *History*], 311–12; *PA*, 2d, VI, 650.

5 Heckewelder, *History*, 311–12.

6 Some was probably pidgin, but it is doubtful that pidgin sufficed for formal talks. Ives Goddard, "The Delaware Jargon," in Carol E. Hoffecker et al., eds., *New Sweden in America* (Newark, Del., 1995), 137–49.

7 E. B. O'Callaghan, ed., *The Documentary History of the State of New York. . . .*, 4 vols., (Albany, NY: 1849–1851) [hereafter *DHNY*], IV, 435 (Iroquois); Archer Butler Hulbert and William Nathaniel Schwarze, eds., "David Zeisberger's History of North American Indians," *Ohio Archaeological and Historical Publications*, XIX (1910) [hereafter Zeisberger, *History*], 144; Heckewelder, *History*, xliii, 320.

8 *MPCP*, VIII, 655–56. See also III, 199; John W. Jordan, trans., "Bishop J.C.F. Cammerhoff's Narrative of the Journey to Shamokin, Penna., in the Winter of 1748," *Pennsylvania Magazine of History and Biography*, XXIX (1905) [hereafter Cammerhoff], 174; "Journal of James Pemberton at the Lancaster Treaty, 1762," in Julian P. Boyd, ed., *Indian Treaties Printed by Benjamin Franklin, 1732–1762* (Philadelphia, 1938) [hereafter Pemberton 1762], 319; Journal of Joseph Shippen, Building of Fort Augusta, 1756, 11 Oct., Small Books, no. 4, Papers of the Shippen Family, HSP [hereafter PSF].

9 Abraham H. Cassell, comp., Helen Bell, trans., "Notes on the Iroquois and Delaware Indians: Communictions from Conrad Weiser . . . ." *Pennsylvania Magazine of History and Biography* [hereafter *PMHB*] I (1877), 163–67, 319–23, II (1878), 407–10 [hereafter Weiser, "Notes,"], 322. William Penn himself noted that "they are great Concealers of their own resentments" (Richard S. Dunn et al., eds., *The Papers of William Penn*, 5 vols. (Philadelphia, 1981–1986) [hereafter *PWP*], II, 449). And see Anthony F. C. Wallace, *The Death and Rebirth of the Seneca* (New York, 1970), Part I.

10 Zeisberger, *History*, 143 (also Heckewelder, *History*, 150).

11 *MPCP*, VIII, 305 (also 310), 709.

12 *MPCP*, I, 299–301, 396–97, 435–36, II, 471 (French attacks), 474–75 (by sea); 145, 204, 509–10; Logan to Col. Burnet, 18 Apr. 1728, James Logan Letterbooks [hereafter JLLB], James Logan Papers, HSP, III [1721–1732], 202; *PWP*, III, 451–55 (other attacks). *MPCP*, III, 504, 509–10; William M. Beauchamp, ed., *Moravian Journals Relating to Central New York, 1745–1766* (Syracuse, NY: 1916) [hereafter *MJNY*], 204 (Virginia).

13 *MPCP*, III, 501. Meeting between Gov. Hamilton and Brothers Joseph, Herman, and Rogers, 17 June 1752, Moravian Church Archives: Records of the Moravian Mission Among the Indians of North America (microfilm, 40 reels) [hereafter MCA], 34/317/1/3. For other fears of attack, see *MPCP*, I, 157–58, 396, 448–49, II, 71, 245; Narrative of John Budd, 4 July 1694, in Penn Letters and Ancient Documents, 274, American Philosophical Society [hereafter APS]; Nash, ed., "First Decade," *PMHB*, XC (1966), 333.

14 *PA*, 1st, II, 23.

15 *MPCP*, VI, 613; VII, 48 ("in form"; also IV, 657); Peters to "Hond Sir," 5 July 1753, Penn Manuscripts, Official Correspondence, HSP (and microfilm) [hereafter PMOC], VI, 73 ("regular"). "Journal of Daniels Journey to the Allegheny," Pemberton Papers, Frank M. Etting Collection, HSP [hereafter PPEC], II, 29 ("Noise"). Heckewelder, *History*, 109. James Hamilton to Weiser, 27 Apr. 1751, Richard Peters Papers, HSP [hereafter RPP], III, 38 ("transient").

16 *MPCP*, VIII, 639 ("understanding"), IV, 568 ("suitable"). *PA*, 1st, III, 505–507; Hays, *passim* (passive). *MPCP*, II, 386, V, 349–50, 530, VI, 151 (firing). VII, 137, VIII, 150 (colonial city).

17 *MPCP*, VI, 152 ("Custom"). For Shickellamy, *PA*, 1st, I, 241–42, 665–66, 673, II, 23; Indian Charges, 1744, CCW, I, II. And see Croghan to Peters, 16 Oct. 1764, George Croghan Papers, Cadwalader Collection, HSP [hereafter GCP], 5/19; Croghan to Maj. Gen. Monckton, 3 Oct. 1761, Ibid., 5/23.

18 *MPCP*, V, 474, VI, 152, 180 (quotation), VII, 47, 68.

19 Marshe, 180. See also *PA*, 1st, II, 724, III, 107.

20 John Bartram, *Observations on the Inhabitants, Climate, Soil, Rivers, Productions, Animals, and other Matters Worthy of Notice. Made by John Bartram, In his Travels from Pennsilvania to Onondago, Oswego and the Lake Ontario, in Canada . . .* (London, 1751) [hereafter Bartram, *Observations*], 43. John W. Jordan, ed., "The Journal of James Kenny, 1761–1763," PMHB, XXXVII (1913),

1–47, 152–201 [hereafter Kenny 1761–63], 12, 18, 21, 154; James Smith, *An Account of the Remarkable Occurrenc es in the Life and Travels of Col. James Smith During his Captivity with the Indians . . .* (Cincinnati, OH: 1907) [hereafter Smith, *Account*], 6, 8, 10, 15, 20, 2 22–23, 25 (Ohio country).

21 *PA*, 1st, III, 397.

22 George Miranda Report, n.d., Provincial Council Papers, N.D. file, HSP ("Sweet"). *MPCP*, II, 600 ("friendly"), III, 319 ("Expressions"). When in doubt, colonists would ask Indians to elaborate, also furthering the educational process (VII, 209, VIII, 88).

23 Lynn Ceci, "The Value of Wampum among the New York Iroquois: A Case Study in Artifact Analysis," *Journal of Anthropological Research*, XXXVIII (1982), 102–3.

24 Frank G, Speck, *A Study of the Delaware Indian Big House Ceremony*, 2 vols. (Harrisburg, Pa., 1931), II, 64.

25 *MPCP*, V, 537 ("Mind"), 615, VII, 156 ("confirm"); VIII, 470 ("enforce"); *PA*, 1st, I, 737 ("truth"); Seneca George to Gov. Denny, 25 June 1758, Records of the Provincial Council in the Pennsylvania State Archives, Executive Correspondence (microfilm, Harrisburg, Pa.) [hereafter RPCEC], B9, 1947 ("Credit").

26 Foster, "Another Look at Wampum," in Jennings et al., eds., *History and Culture of Iroquois Diplomacy*, esp. 104–106; *MPCP*, VI, 615 ("this day").

27 Information regarding Teedyuscung delivered to Spangenberg from a Delaware Indian (Augustus), 30 July 1756, Penn Manuscripts, Indian Affairs, HSP [hereafter PMIA], II, 98 (and see *DHNY*, II, 625).

28 *MPCP*, II, 387 (20 belts), 546–49 (32), VI, 194–98 (10); Proceedings of the Council at Conestoga, 31 July 1710, PMIA, I, 34, in Francis Jennings et al., eds., *Iroquois Indians: A Documentary History of the Six Nations and their League*, microfilm edition, 50 reels (Woodbridge, CT: 1985) [hereafter *Iroq. Ind.*], Reel 7 (26 belts, 2 strings, 31 sticks). For the number of beads, see Helga Dobler and William A. Starna, trans. and eds., *The Journals of Christian Daniel Claus and Conrad Weiser: A Journey to Onondaga, 1750*, in *Transactions of the American Philosophical Society*, LXXXIV, Part 2 (Philadelphia, 1994) [hereafter *Journals of Claus and Weiser*], 12–13; *PA*, 1st, II, 17, III, 555; *Collections of the Illinois Historical Society Library*, XI, 21; Peters, Diary, 2–4, 6, 7, 9, 15, 22, 25 Oct. 1758, RPR. *MPCP*, VIII, 508 (pocket). Account of the Easton Treaty, June 1762, Friendly Association Mss., Swarthmore College Library (pouch). James Sullivan et al., eds., *The Papers of Sir William Johnson*, 14 vols. (Albany, NY: 1921–1965) [hereafter *PWJ*], II, 860–861 (casket or chest).

29 Peters to the Proprietaries, 15 Nov. 1755, Richard Peters Letters to the Proprietaries of Pennsylvania, 1755–1757, 17, Simon Gratz Collection, Case 2, Box 33-a, HSP ("amazing"). Israel Pemberton to Geo. Browne, 22 May 1758, Philadelphia Yearly Meeting, Indian Committee Records, Friendly Association for Regaining and Preserving Peace with the Indians by Pacific Measures, vols. AA1-AA5, Quaker Collection, Haverford College [hereafter FA], I, 494; Peters to Weiser, 13 7ber 1758, CCW, II, 135 (100,000). Edward Shippen to Joseph Shippen, 19 June 1751, PSF, I (Sympson, "a wampum maker"; it is unclear whether Sympson drilled the wampum or was among those who wove it into belts). Peters to Croghan, 23 Apr. 1755, RPCEC, B5, 801 (Philadelphia woman). Peters, Diary, 6–7 Oct. 1758, RPP (Montour). For women, see Israel Pemberton to Christian Frederick Post, 65 mo. 1760, Pemberton Papers, Folder 2, Haverford College Library; *MPCP*, VII, 216–218; Beauchamp, "Wampum in Council," *American Antiquarian and Oriental Jnl.*, XX (1898), 9.

30 *PA*, 1st, I, 762 ("Bagg"); Heckewelder, *History*, 186. Sassoonan allegedly selling wampum from the council bag was a sort of sacrilege, especially since his other

name, Alumapees, meant "preserver of the records" (Francis Jennings, "The Delaware Interregnum,"*PMHB*, LXXXIX [1965], 174).

31 *PA*, 1st, I, 741–742; *MPCP*, VI, 195, 686 (hatchets), VII, 66 (scalps). Those agreeing with a message could also "add Strength to" a belt by tying a string to it. Conference at Israel Pemberton's, 23 Apr. 1756, LP, II/41; Minutes of a Conference at Easton, 12 Oct. 1758, RPCEC, B9, 2024; *MPCP*, VI, 685–686, IX, 47; Nathaniel Holland to Israel Pemberton, 16 Oct. 1760, FA, IV, 43.

32 Conference at Armstrong's, 10 June 1756, Between Col. William Clapham and Ogaghradarisha, PMIA, II, 92. Heckewelder, *History*, 108 (*"turning"*). *MPCP*, II, 387 (hang belts or strings on a line), 471 (board), VIII, 174, 179 (in order); Wallace, *Weiser*, 91 (stick); Bartram, *Observations*, 60 (pole).

33 Heckewelder, *History*, 109–110 ("snake"). *MPCP*, VII, 49, 65–66 ("throwed"). See also VI, 197–198; "Two Journals of Western Tours, by Charles [sic] Frederick Post . . ." in Rueben Gold Thwaites, ed., *Early Western Travels, 1748–1846*, vol. 1 (Cleveland, OH: 1904), 175–291 [hereafter Post 1758], 256; Kenny 1761–63, 24; Peters to the Proprietors, 26 Oct. 1749, PMOC, IV, 245.

34 *MPCP*, I, 586 ("amitie"), II, 141, 145, 204 ("Credential"), 387, 461; Logan Account Book, 1712–1720, 99, 112, 115, 169, LP.

35 Peters to Thomas Penn, 30 Oct. 1756, PMOC, VIII, 185.

36 *PWJ*, V, 201; XII, 75 (Stamp Act). Julian P. Boyd, "Indian Affairs in Pennsylvania, 1 736 1762," in idem, ed., *Indian Treaties Printed by Benjamin Franklin*, 1736–1762 (Philadelphia, 1938), xxvi (Penn Family); Journal of Shippen, Building of Fort Augusta, 1756, 28 July, PSF (Clapham, forts); *MPCP*, VII, 701 (G.R., D.K.). For (G.K. on Indian belts, *MPCP.* VII, 522; "Substance of a Conversation with Gray Eyes, a Delaware Indian Messenger," 24 May 1761, FA, IV, 123.

37 Croghan to Gage, 22 Mar. 1765, GCP, 5/27 ("nessecarys"), For advising, Peters to Croghan, 23 Apr. 1755, RPCEC, B5, 801. For string on hand, *MPCP*, VI, 150–51, VIII, 468. Weiser to Peters, 28 Jan. 1754, CCW, I, 43 ("accidents"); *PA*, 1st, III, 701 ("Wampum enough").

38 Hays, 79, 66 67. See also 69–70, 76, 78; Post 1760, 6, 13 14, 16 May, 11–12 June. For wampum having the sanction of many people, see Daniel K. Richter, *The Ordeal of the Longhouse: The Peoples of the Iroquois League in the Era of European Colonization* (Chapel Hill, NC: 1992), 47–48.

39 *PA*, 1st, III, 737; Hays, 68–69; Post 1760, 30–31 May (1760). For combining, see *MPCP*, III, 459, VI, 150,VII, 147, VIII, 212; Post 1758, 243; *PA*, 1st, 1, 229–30, II, 193 194, III, 556; *CVSP*, I, 231; Kenneth P. Bailey, ed., *The Ohio Company Papers, 1753–1817* . . . (Arcata, Calif., 1947), 21; Instructions to Post and Thomson, 7 June 1758, MCA, 28/219/8/2; Joseph Shippen, Jr., to John Jacob Schmick, 28 Jan. 1768, Joseph Shippen, Jr., Letterbook, 1763–1773, 28, APS.

40 William P. Palmer, ed., *Calendar of Virginia State Papers and Other Manuscripts, 1652–1781* . . . Vol. 1 (Richmond, VA: 1875) [hereafter *CVSP*], I, 232 ("don't understand"; see also Weiser to Logan, 16 Sept. 1736, LP, 10/62; *MJNY*, 95; *MPCP*, III, 362). Examples of Indians sending letters and strings are in *MPCP*, III, 103 504–5, IV, 656–58, V, 568–70, 691–92; *PA*, 1st, IV, 60–61.

41 Peter Wraxall, *An Abridgement of the Indian Affairs Contained in Four Folio Volumes, Transacted In the Colony of New York, From the Year 1678 to the Year 1751*, ed. Charles Howard Mcllwain (Cambridge, Mass., 1915), 33; Albert Cook Myers, ed., *Narratives of Early Pennsylvania, West New Jersey, and Delaware, 1630–1707* (New York, 1912), 173; Logan Account Book, 1712–1720, 217, LP; *MPCP*, III, 154, 609; Council at Philadelphia, 25 and 28 Jan. 1722/3, Eugene du Simitiere Papers, [hereafter DSP], Library Company of Philadelphia [hereafter LCP] 966.F.6.

42 *MPCP*, II, 604 (also III, 276, 581); *PA*, 1st, I, 455 (and see 425).

43 Zeisberger, *History*, 145 ("very important"); *MJNY*, 212 ("whole town"); *PWJ*, IX, 407 ("Suck'd in"). *PA*, 2d, VII, 430; Smith, *Account*, 24; Kenny 1761–63, 178.
44 Harvey J. Graff, *The Legacies of Literacy: Continuities and Contradictions in Western Culture and Society* (Bloomington, Ind., 1987), 5.
45 John Woolman, *The Journal of John Woolman* (Boston, 1909 [orig. pub. 1871]), 190–91 ("histories"); William A. Hunter, ed., "John Hays' Diary and Journal of 1760," Pennsylvania Archaeologist, XXIV (1954), 63–83 [hereafter Hays], 77 ("Jurnal"); George Henry Loskiel, *History of the Mission of the United Brethren Among the Indians in North America* (London: 1794) [hereafter Loskiel, *History*], Part I, 25 ("intelligible"). And see Baron de Lahontan [Louis-Armand de Lom d'Arce], *New Voyages to North-America*, ed. Reuben Gold Thwaites, 2 vols. (Chicago, 1903 [orig. pub. 1703]), II, 510–514; Lafitau, *Customs,* II, 36–37; "Christopher Gist's First and Second Journals . . .," in Lois Mulkearn, ed., *George Mercer Papers Relating to the Ohio Company of Virginia* (Pittsburgh, PA: 1954) [hereafter Gist], 28; Heckewelder, *History*, 130–31; Nicholas Cresswell, *The Journal of Nicholas Cresswell, 1774–1777* (London, 1925), 110–11.
46 Timothy Horsfield to Gov. Hamilton, 5 Sept. 1761, HP, II, 445; Edward Shippen to Hamilton, 29 Oct. 1763, Correspondence of Edward and Joseph Shippen, 1750–1778, Shippen Papers, APS.
47 *PWJ*, II, 861, VII, 348. On wampum having this quality, see Foster, "Another Look at Wampum," in Jennings et al., eds., *History and Culture of Iroquois Diplomacy*, 107.
48 Zeisberger, *History*, 93–94; Edmund De Schweinitz, *The Life and Times of David Zeisberger, The Western Pioneer and Apostle of the Indians* (Philadelphia, 1870), 217; *MPCP*, IX, 102 (council bag). Depositions, 1725, LP, 11/12 ("defaced"). Shamokin Diary, 28 Feb. 1748, MCA, 6/121/4/1 (Shickellamy; see *also Journals of Claus and Weiser*, 43). For other examples of documents being saved, see *MPCP*, III, 94, IV, 433, V, 316, VIII, 668–669; *PWJ*, XI, 463; S. K. Stevens et al., eds., *The Papers of Henry Bouquet*, 6 vols. (Harrisburg, PA: 1972–1994) OR S. K. Stevens et al., eds., *The Papers of Col. Henry Bouquet*, 19 vols (Harrisburg, 1940–1943) [hereafter *PHB*], VI, 96.
49 *MPCP*, III, 334, IV, 433 (invitation; for invitation strings of wampum being handled in this way, see III, 437); III, 599, VII, 7–9 (Conestogas pulling out documents; for the documents, see eh. VII). For speaking on paper, see Council with the Indians at Contestoga, 6 Apr. 1722, DSP, 966.F.4.
50 *MPCP*, V, 316. Shawnees at a different council again pulled out "an old Treaty" and "several Letters from Mr. Logan—and one or two from you" (Peters to Thomas Penn [copy], 18 Feb. 1756, PMOC, VIII, 41).
51 *PA*, 2d, II, 653; *MPCP*, VIII, 98. For snow, see *MPC*, VIII, 87, 92; /M, 2d, II, 650-654. Post 1758, 186; *MPCP* V, 486, 599–600; R. A. Brock, ed., *The Official Records of Robert Dinwiddie, Lieutenant-Governor of the Colony of Virginia, 1750–1758* . . . , 2 vols., Virginia Historical Society, *Collections*, new ser., III–IV (Richmond, Va., 1883), I, 22, 398 (illness). Weiser to Col. Gale, [Spring 1743], RPP, II, 5 (hunting).
52 *MPCP*, III, 329 (1728); Minutes of an Indian Treaty at Pittsburgh, 18 Aug. 1760, Rees. Mor. Miss., Box 323, Folder 7, Item 1, in *Iroq. Ind.*, Reel 23 (Teedyuscung); *PWJ*, X, 148 (Montour). See also Post 1758, 185, 236; *PA*, 1st, III, 420; Israel Pemberton to Christian Frederick Post, 65 mo. 1760, Pemberton Pprs., Haverford College Library; Nathaniel Holland to (Israel Pemberton], 16 Oct. 1760, FA, IV, 431.
53 *PA*, 1st, I, 425 (Poke and Hill); Weiser 1748, 43, n.42; *MPCP*, V, 438 (Ohio).
54 Ibid., 293 ("loose Letters"), IV, 343 (Shawnees).

55 Ibid., V, 691–95, 703 ("mood"), 734; Peters to Proprietaries, 26 Nov. 1753, PMOC, VI, 133; George Croghan to "Your Honour," 3 Feb. 1754, ibid., 155; *PA*, 1st, II, 119.
56 *MPCP*, V, 514 ("sound"), 538 ("Strong House"). See Nicholas B. Wainwright, *George Croghan, Wilderness Diplomat* (Chapel Hill, N.C., 1959), 35, 41–44; Michael N. McConnell, *A Country Between: The Upper Ohio and its Peoples, 1724–1774* (Lincoln, NE: 1992), 93–95.
57 "The Treaty of Logg's Town, 1752," Commission, Instructions, &c., Journal of Virginia Commissioners, and Text of Treaty," *Virginia Magazine of History and Biography*, XIII (1905–1906), 143–74 (hereafter Logstown Treaty], 171–72; Peters to Weiser, 6 Feb. 1753, CCW, I, 38; Weiser to [?], [1753–1754], CCW, II, 25; Peters to the Proprietor, 6 Nov. 1753, PMOC, VI, 115; Wallace, *Weiser*, 348.
58 See Merrell, *Into the American Woods*, ch. VI.
59 Post 1758, 282–85. Sec David L. Ghere, "Mistranslations and Misinformation: Diplomacy on the Maine Frontier, 1725 to 1775, *American Indian Culture and Research Journal*, VIII (1984), 3–26.
60 *MPCP*, VII, 683; Weiser, "Observations;" See David Murray, *Forked Tongues: Speech, Writing, and Representation in North American Indian Texts* (Bloomington, Ind.: 1991), ch. 3.
61 *PHB*, II, 621–626. For Custaloga, see McConnell, *A Country Between*, 102, 105, 108. Another account of the Bouquet conference is in *PA*, 1st, III, 571–74.
62 Minutes of the New York Commissioners of Indian Affairs, 14 Aug. 1743, in *Iroq. Ind.*, Reel 11 (Oneidas). *DRCNY*, VII, 197 (1756). For additional remarks on this meeting, see *MPCP*, VII, 156–60, 170–72, 182, 184; *PA*, 2d. VI, 521–22; *PWJ*, II, 488, 491,521–22. Another example is 439–40, IX, 347 383; *MPCP*, VII, 41 42, 46–47, 67, 69, 71, 106.
63 David McClure, *Diary of David McClure, Doctor of Divinity, 1748–1820*, ed. Franklin B. Dexter (New York, 1899), 59 (Peepy); *MPCP*, VI, 49 (Weiser); Cadwallader Colden, *The History of the Five Indian Nations Depending on the Province of New-York in America* (Ithaca, N.Y., 1958 [orig. pub. 1727 and 1747]), xi ("sense").
64 My thinking here owes much to Walter J. Ong, *Orality and Literacy: The Technologizing of the World* (London: 1982), ch. 3.
65 *MPCP*, II, 600, IV, 433–34, VIII, 188, 753. Compare Sassoonan's speeches at IV, 307–8, 643, 680.
66 Ibid., IV, 721, VII, 522.
67 Hays, 81.
68 *MPCP*, VII, 217–218.
69 Shmokin Diary, 16 Jan. 1748, MCA, 6/121/4/1 (Indian woman).
70 Ibid., III, 189 (emphasis added); Gov. George Thomas to the Shawnees, 16 Aug. 1742, RPP, I, 93 (emphasis added).
71 This and the following paragraph owe a great debt to Ong, *Literacy and Orality*, especially ch. 3.
72 Stephen J. Greenblatt, *Marvelous Possessions: The Wonder of the New World* (Chicago, 1991), 9–10; Harbsmeier, "Writing and the Other," in Schousboe and Larsen, eds., *Literacy and Society*, 199–203; Jack Goody, *The Interface Between the Written and the Oral* (New York: 1987).
73 Harbsmeier, "Writing and the Other," in Schousboe and Larsen, eds., *Literacy and Society*, 203 (emphasis added).
74 Shamokin Diary, 21 Feb. 1748, MCA, 6/121/4/1 (aged Delaware); *MPCP*, VII, 521 (King). On Indian awe, on writing as sacred, see Loskiel, *History*, Part I, 23–24.
75 *MPCP*, IV, 84 (see also II, 574).
76 Wallace, *Weiser*, 141 (Zinzendorf); *MPCP*, IV, 708 (Canasatego).

77 See Goody, *Interface*, xv; Nicholas Hudson, *Writing and European Thought, 1600–1830* (Cambridge: 1994), 162–63; Claude Lévi-Strauss, *Tristes Tropiques*, trans. John Weightman and Doreen Weightman (New York, 1974), 296–300.
78 Wallace, ed., *Travels of Heckewelder*, 64 (Post); Moses Tatamy, Declaration, [1757], FA, I, 405–8 (Delawares); MPCP, VI, 74 (Iroquois).
79 Hays, 80 (knocked; "Durst Not Reead"); Smith, *Account*, 28 (stolen, though he also noted—3, 24, 39—that Indians sometimes let him read); Wallace, ed., *Travels of Heckewelder*, 64 (hide books).
80 Wallace, ed., *Travels of Heckewelder*, 64 ("suspicious"; see also Post to Israel Pemberton, 8 Aug. 1761, FA, IV, 167). Post 1758, 252 (see also 226–27, 247; "Journal of Captain Thomas Morris, Detroit, September 25, 1764," in Reuben Gold Thwaites, ed., *Early Western Travels, 1748–1846* [Cleveland, Ohio, 1904], I, 322).
81 *PA*, 1st, IV, 96.
82 *MPCP*, VIII, 174.
83 Post 1758, 201.
84 *PA*, 1st, III, 343 (Teedyuscung). *MPCP*, VIII, 630, 632, 638–639 (1761). And see Meeting with Killbuck, 105 mo. 1771, FA, IV, 419; his official visit is *in MPCP*, IX, 735–42.
85 Jane Merritt and I have, independently, come to this conclusion, and come to it using the same examples. Merritt, "The Power of Language," 26–27.
86 *MJNY*, 179 (Zeisberger); *MPCP*, IX, 8 (Teedyuscung).
87 *MPCP*, VII, 652–655. For the clerk fight, see Jennings, *Empire of Fortune*, 342–345; Theodore Thayer, *Israel Pemberton, King of the Quakers* (Philadelphia, 1943), 140. The debate can be found in *MPCP*, VII, 648–65, 689 690, VIII, 30–31, 47, 50; Charles Thomson to the Governor, 23 Aug. 1736, Charles Thomson, Correspondence, Gratz Collection, IISP; *PA*, 2d, VI, 570–571; *DRCNY*, VII, 322–23; Charles Thomson to William Franklin, 13 Mar. 1758, Papers of Benjamin Franklin, B: F85, v. 488, f. 122, APS; Peters to Penn, 19 Mar. 1758, Lardner Family Papers, IISP; *PHJ*. III, 766, 771–73.
88 *MPCP*, VII, 664.
89 *MPCP*, VII, 656 (Teedyuscung); *PA*, 2d, VI, 570–571 (Croghan).
90 *PA*, 2d, VI, 570–571; Penn to Peters, 14 Nov. 1757, RPP, IV, 122.
91 Hays, 76–77 ("Read Like Mad"); Heckewelder, *History*, 291–293 ("great Book"). Kenny 1761–63, 171, 173, 175 ("Seperation"); Zeisberger, *Diaries*, 25.
92 *MPCP*, III, 311 ("stamp'd). Croghan to Franklin (copy), 2 Oct. 1767, GCP, 5/29 ("Jealous"; see also Croghan to Gen. Monekton, 26 July 1761, GCP, *5/23*; *PWJ*, III, 964 965; PHB, VI, 137–38).
93 Gist, 9–10; Kenny 1761, 63, 45.
94 Hamilton to the Proprietary, 26 Nov. 1753, PMOC, VI, 139 ("a pity"); *MPCP*, V, 696 ("dangerous Season"); Weiser to Peters, 28 Jan. 1764, CCW, I, 43 ("Cookes").
95 Peters to Penn, 28 Sept. 1750, PMOC, V, 57 ("pleases"). *PA*, 1st, I, 751 ("sick"; see also 758–59, 761–62, II, 15, 23–24; *MPCP*, V, 87–88).
96 *PA*, 1st, II, 12 ("happy"); Weiser to Peters, 7 Feb. 1754, Berks and Montgomery Counties, Miscellaneous Manuscripts, 1693–1869, 55, HSP ("perplects").
97 For examples of the warnings, see *PA*, 1st, II, 144, 173 174, 2d, VI, 548–54 (Croghan); *MPCP*, VI, 46 (Montour); Wallace, *Weiser*, 372–73; Weiser to [?], [1753–1754], CCW, II, 25; *MPCP*, V, 147, VI, 589–90.
98 Hamilton to Thomas Penn, 18 Nov. 1750, PMOC, V, 89.
99 Information regarding Teedyuscung delivered to Spangenberg . . . from a Delaware Indian (Augustus), 30 July 1756, PMIA, II, 98 (wampum); *PWJ*, III, 767 ("wrote wrong"); Conference at Pemberton's, 19 23 Apr. 1756, LP, 11/41 (Scarouyady).

# Part II

# COLUMBIAN EXCHANGE

Alfred W. Crosby's 1972 book *The Columbian Exchange* introduced a simple but enduring idea into the historiography: that the most important consequences of European expansion were biological. To make any sense of the immense global transformations of the past five hundred years, historians had to attend not just to the movement of people but to the broader collision of biological systems inaugurated in 1492. The new and quickening circulation of animals, plants, and microbes that attended human journeys between Eurasia, Africa, and the Americas proved to be far too momentous and interdependent for anyone to control, predict, or even understand. But they transformed human life in profound ways. 1983 William Cronon's landmark work *Changes in the Land* demonstrated the potential for environmental history to illuminate relationships in contested zones. Over the past generation, attention to changes in the nonhuman world has reoriented the study of borderland regions across North America.[1] The chapters in this section highlight both the variety of this work and the insights revealed by it.

Virginia DeJohn Anderson's focus on "creatures of empire" transforms our understanding of Metacom's (or "King Philip's") War, colonial New England's watershed conflict. Unused to thinking of domestic animals as important variables in political or diplomatic history, historians had long ignored the many references to them in colonial correspondence. But Anderson demonstrates that imported pigs, horses, cattle, and sheep had become a chronic source of friction between colonists and Indians by the late seventeenth century. Recovering the rise and development of these tensions does much to explain the origins of the war.[2]

Though Spaniards first visited the coast of California more than a century before Metacom's War, not until the 1780s had they embarked on a formal colonization project there. Built around a steadily expanding chain of missions along California's coast, Spain's colonial endeavor there never involved large armies or mass colonization. But as Steven Hackel explains, it nonetheless ushered in a "dual revolution" that transformed indigenous polities throughout coastal California. Eurasian animals and the invasive plant species that they unwittingly brought with them displaced native flora and fauna, remaking landscapes and precipitating subsistence crises that drove Indian families into missions. At the same time, old-world diseases led to devastating epidemics, high infant mortality, and a collapsing birth rate among indigenous women. On the borderlands of coastal California, then, the same forces driving Indians into missions ultimately undid the mission project along with its native subjects.

## NOTES

1 Nowhere has environmental history been more critical to rethinking borderland relationships than the Great Plains. See Dan Flores, "Bison Ecology and Bison Diplomacy: The Southern Plains from 1800 to 1850," *Journal of American History* 78:3 (September, 1991): 465–85; Elliott West, *The Way West: Essays on the Central Plains* (Albuquerque: University of New Mexico Press, 1995); West, *The Contested Plains: Indians, Goldseekers, & the Rush to Colorado* (Lawrence: University Press of Kansas, 1998); Andrew C. Isenberg, *The Destruction of the Bison: An Environmental History,* 1750–1920 (Cambridge: Cambridge University Press, 2000); Theodore Binnema, *Common and Contested Ground: A Human and Environmental History of the Northwestern Plains* (Norman: University of Oklahoma Press, 2001); Pekka Hämäläinen, "The Rise and Fall of Plains Indian Horse Cultures," *Journal of American History* 90:3 (Dec., 2003): 833–62; Sterling Evans, *Bound in Twine: The History and Ecology of the Henequen-Wheat Complex for Mexico and the American and Canadian Plains, 1880-1950* (College Station: Texas A&M University Press, 2007); Dan Flores, "Bringing Home All the Pretty Horses: The Horse Trade and the Early American West, 1775–1825," *Montana: The Magazine of History* 58:1 (2008): 3–21.

2 For an elaboration of Anderson's argument, see her innovative book *Creatures of Empire: How Domestic Animals Transformed Early America* (New York: Oxford University Press, 2004).

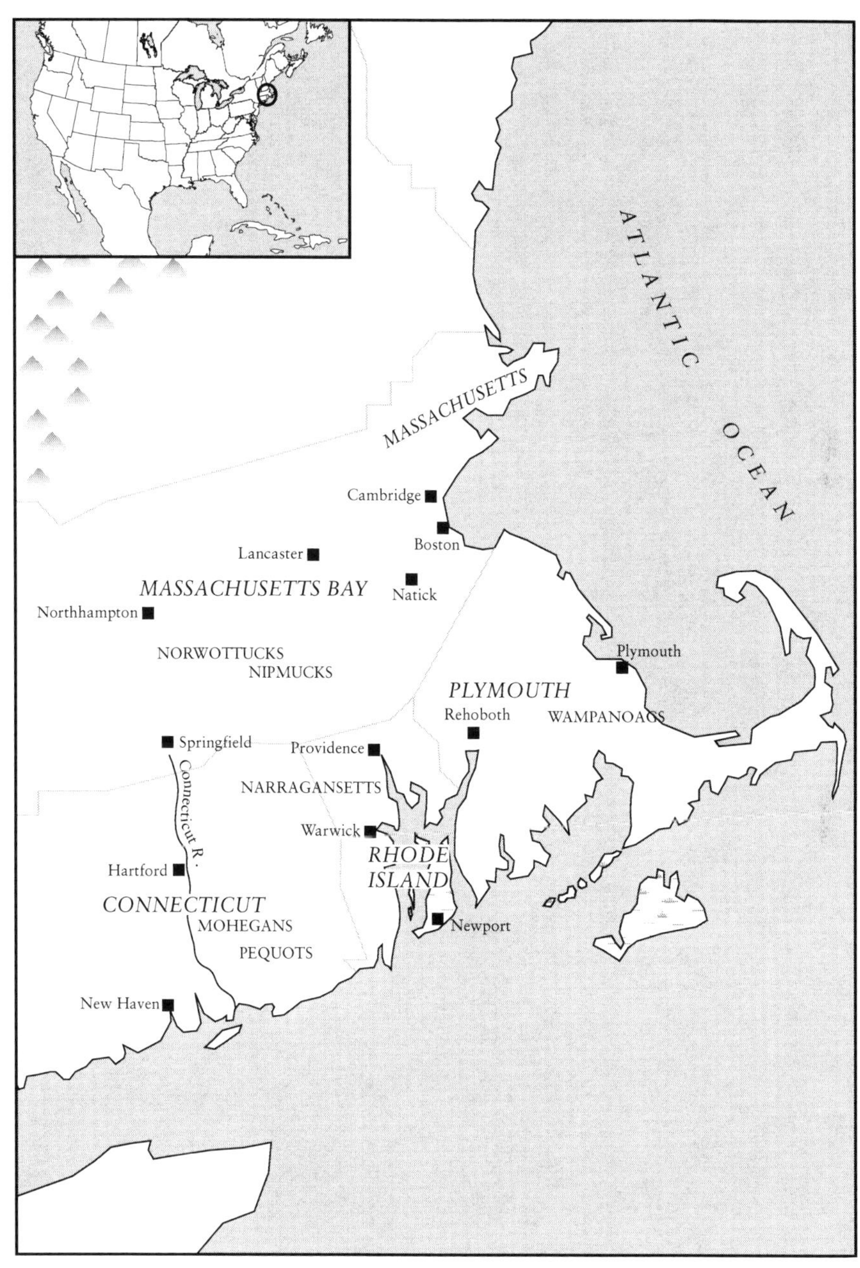


*Map 2.1* New England

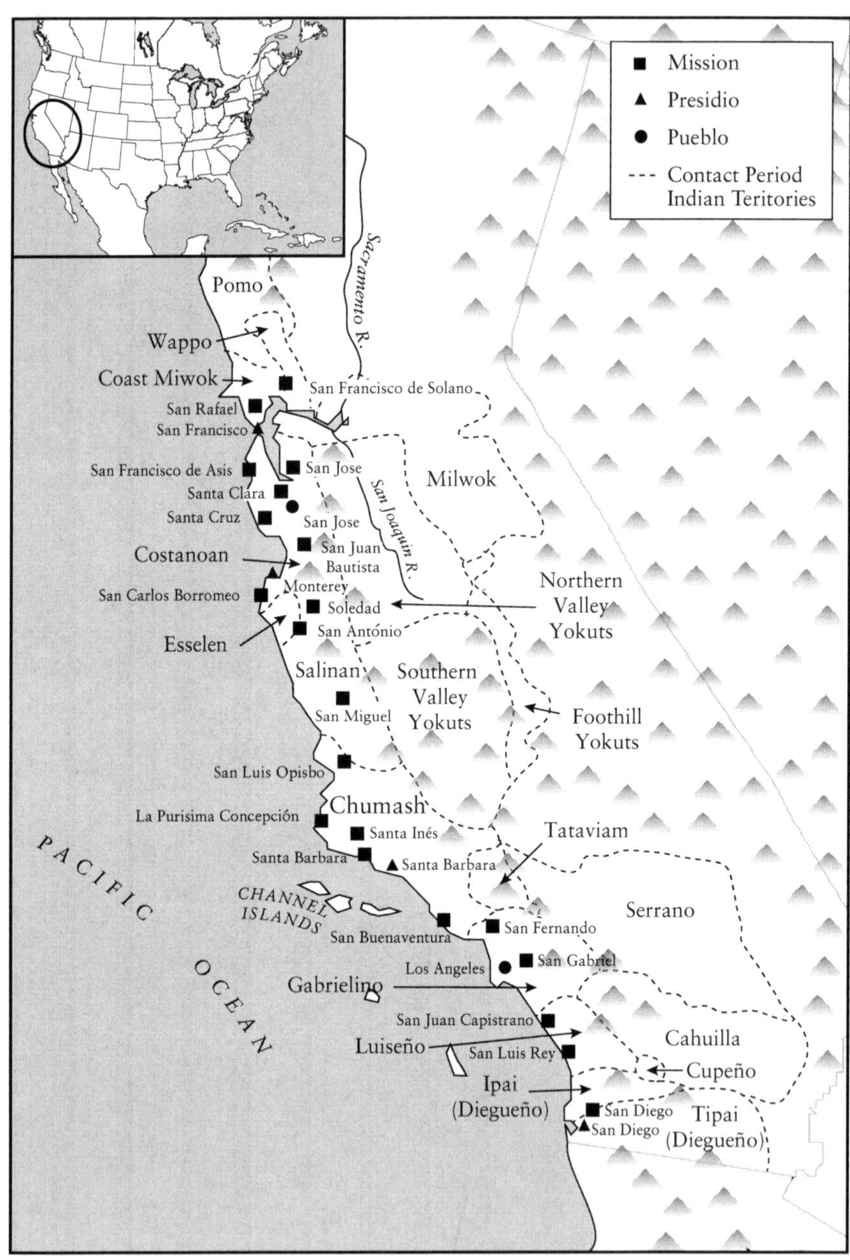


*Map 2.2* California

# 4

# KING PHILIP'S HERDS

*Virginia DeJohn Anderson*

On a late spring day in 1669, the ambitious younger son of a prominent Rhode Island family received a letter from the town clerk of Portsmouth. Like many of his neighbors, the young man raised livestock and followed the common practice of placing his pigs on a nearby island where they could forage safe from predators. But that was what brought him to the attention of Portsmouth's inhabitants, who ordered the clerk to reprimand him for "intrudeinge on" the town's rights when he ferried his beasts to "hog-Island." The townsmen insisted that he remove "Such Swine or other Catle" as he had put there, on pain of legal action. They took the unusual step of instructing the clerk to make two copies of the letter and retain the duplicate—in effect preparing their legal case even before the recipient contested their action.[1]

It was by no means unusual for seventeenth-century New Englanders to find themselves in trouble with local officials, particularly when their search for gain conflicted with the rights of the community. But this case was different. We can only wonder what Metacom, whom the English called King Philip, made of the peremptory directive from the Portsmouth town clerk—for indeed it was to him, son of Massasoit and now sachem of the Wampanoags himself, that the letter was addressed. Because the records (which directed no comparable order to any English swine owner) do not mention the outcome of the dispute, we may suppose that Philip complied with the town's demand. The episode was thus brief, but it was no less important for that, because it involved the man whose name would soon be associated with what was, in proportion to the populations involved, the most destructive war in American history.[2]

For three centuries, historians have depicted Philip in many ways—as a savage chieftain, an implacable foe of innocent Christian settlers, and a doomed victim of European aggressors—but never as a keeper of swine. Although the Hog Island episode may seem unrelated to the subsequent horrors of King Philip's War, the two events were in fact linked. Philip resorted to violence in 1675 because of mounting frustrations with colonists, and no problem vexed relations between settlers and Indians more frequently in the years before the



What caused Kings Phillip's war? What did livestock have to do with this?

war than the control of livestock.[3] English colonists imported thousands of cattle, swine, sheep, and horses (none of which is native to North America) because they considered livestock essential to their survival, never supposing that the beasts would become objectionable to the Indians. But the animals exacerbated a host of problems related to subsistence practices, land use, property rights and, ultimately, political authority. Throughout the 1660s, Philip found himself caught in the middle, trying to defend Indian rights even as he adapted to the English presence. The snub delivered by Portsmouth's inhabitants showed him the limits of English flexibility, indicating that the colonists ultimately valued their livestock more than good relations with his people. When Philip recognized that fact, he took a critical step on the path that led him from livestock keeper to war leader.

Successful colonization of New England depended heavily on domestic animals. Nowhere is this better seen than in the early history of Plymouth Colony. Not until 1624—four years after the *Mayflower*'s arrival—did Edward Winslow bring from England "three heifers and a bull, the first beginning of any cattle of that kind in the land." This date, not coincidentally, marked the end of the Pilgrims' "starving times" as dairy products and meat began to supplement their diet. By 1627, natural increase and further importations brought the Plymouth herd to at least fifteen animals, whose muscle power increased agricultural productivity.[4] The leaders of Massachusetts Bay Colony, perhaps learning from Plymouth's experience, brought animals from the start. John Winthrop regularly noted the arrival of settlers and livestock during the 1630s, often recording levels of shipboard mortality among animals as well as people. Edward Johnson estimated that participants in the Great Migration spent £12,000 to transport livestock across the ocean, not counting the original cost of the animals. . . .[5]

The size of a town's herds soon became an important measure of its prosperity. As early as 1634, William Wood noted that Dorchester, Roxbury, and Cambridge were particularly "well stored" with cattle. Other commentators added to the list of towns with burgeoning herds. In 1651, Edward Johnson tallied the human and livestock populations for several communities as a measure of divine favor. His enumeration revealed that towns with three or four dozen families also contained several hundred head of livestock.[6] Like Old Testament patriarchs, New England farmers counted their blessings as they surveyed their herds.

Their interest in livestock grew in part from their English experience. Many settlers came from England's wood-pasture region, where they had engaged in a mixed husbandry of cattle and grain. In New England, the balance in that agrarian equation tipped toward livestock because the region's chronic labor shortage made raising cattle a particularly efficient use of resources. Selectmen usually hired one or two town herdsmen, freeing other livestock owners to clear fields, till crops, and construct buildings and fences. Until settlers managed to plant English hay, livestock foraged on the abundant, though less nutritious, native grasses, converting otherwise worthless herbage into milk and meat for consumption and sale. Livestock were so important to survival that New Englanders reversed the usual English fencing practices. English law required farmers to protect their crops by confining livestock within fenced or hedged pastures, but New England farmers were enjoined to construct and maintain sufficiently sturdy fences around cornfields to keep their peripatetic beasts out.[7]

Raising livestock had cultural as well as economic ramifications. For colonists, the absence of indigenous domestic animals underscored the region's essential wildness. "The country is yet raw," wrote Robert Cushman in 1621, "the land untilled; the cities not builded; the cattle not settled." The English saw a disturbing symmetry between the savagery of the land and its human and animal inhabitants. America, noted Cushman, "is spacious and void," and the Indians "do but run over the grass, as do also the foxes and wild beasts."[8] Such evaluations ultimately fueled colonists' own claims to the land. The "savage people," argued John Winthrop, held no legitimate title "for they inclose no ground, neither have they cattell to maintayne it, but remove their dwellings as they have occasion." Winthrop's objection to the Indians' seminomadic habits stemmed from a cultural assumption that equated civilization with sedentarism, a way of life that he linked to the keeping of domesticated animals. Drawing on biblical history, Winthrop argued that a "civil" right to the earth resulted when, "as men and cattell increased, they appropriated some parcells of ground by enclosing and peculiar manurance." Subduing—indeed, domesticating—the wilderness with English people and English beasts thus became a cultural imperative. New England could become a new Canaan, a land of milk and honey, only if, Thomas Morton wryly observed, "the Milke came by the industry" of its civilizing immigrants and their imported livestock.[9]

Accordingly, only those Indians who submitted to "domestication" could live in the New England Canaan. They had to accept Christianity, of course; in addition, colonists insisted that they adopt English ways entirely, including the keeping of domestic animals. Roger Williams urged natives to move "from Barbarism to Civilitie, in forsaking their filthy nakednes, in keeping some kind of Cattell."[10] John Eliot offered livestock, among other material incentives, to entice Indians to become civilized. He admonished one native audience: "if you were more wise to know God, and obey his Commands, you would work more then [sic] you do." Labor six days a week, as God commanded and the English did, and, Eliot promised, "you should have cloths, houses, cattle, riches as they have, God would give you them."[11]

To assist Indians in making this transformation, Puritan officials established fourteen "praying towns" where they could proceed toward conversion as they earned the material rewards Providence would bestow. The inhabitants of these communities not only would learn to worship God as the English did but also would wear English clothes, live in English framed houses, and farm with English animals. Among the goods sent from England to support this civilizing program were seven bells for oxen, to be distributed to Indian farmers who exchanged their traditional hoe agriculture for the plow.[12] Soon the increase in livestock became as much a hallmark of the success of the praying towns as it was of English communities. Daniel Gookin reported in 1674 that the praying town of Hassanamesitt (Grafton) was "an apt place for keeping of cattle and swine; in which respect this people are the best stored of any Indian town of their size." He went on to observe, however, that though these natives "do as well, or rather better, than any other Indians" in raising crops and animals, they "are very far short of the English both in diligence and providence."[13]

Praying Indians raised livestock as participants in what may be called an experiment in acculturation. By moving to places such as Natick or Hassanamesitt, they announced their intention to follow English ways—including animal husbandry—in hopes of finding favor with the Christian God.[14] But the praying towns never contained more than a tiny minority of the native population; most Indians rejected the invitation to exchange their ways for English ones. For the vast majority, the cattle and swine that served as emblems of the praying Indians' transformation had a very different meaning. They became instead a source of friction, revealing profound differences between Indians and colonists.

As Indians encountered these unfamiliar animals, they had to decide what to call them. Williams reported that the Narragansetts first looked for similarities in appearance and behavior between an indigenous animal and one of the new beasts and simply used the name of the known beast for both animals. Thus *ockqutchaun-nug,* the name of a "wild beast of a reddish haire about the bignesse of a Pig, and rooting like a Pig," was used for English swine. Finding no suitable parallels for most domestic animals, however, the Narragansetts resorted to neologisms such as "cowsnuck," "goatesuck," and eventually "hogsuck" or "pigsuck." The "termination *suck,* is common in their language," Williams explained, "and therefore they adde it to our English Cattell, not else knowing what names to give them."[15]

Giving these animals Indian names in no way implied that most Indians wanted to own livestock. In fact, contact with domestic animals initially produced the opposite reaction, because livestock husbandry did not fit easily with native practices. Indians could hardly undertake winter hunting expeditions accompanied by herds of cattle that required shelter and fodder to survive the cold weather. Swine would compete with their owners for nuts, berries, and roots, and the presence of livestock of any kind tended to drive away deer.[16] Moreover, the Indians, for whom most beasts were literally fair game, struggled with the very notion of property in animals. They assumed that one could own only dead animals, which hunters shared with their families.[17]

Further, the adoption of livestock would alter women's lives in crucial ways by affecting the traditional gender-based division of labor. Would women, who were mainly responsible for agricultural production, assume new duties of animal husbandry? If not, how would men's involvement with livestock rearing alter women's powerful role as the primary suppliers of food? Who would protect women's crops from the animals? How would the very different temporal cycle of livestock reproduction and care be reconciled with an Indian calendar that identified the months according to stages in the planting cycle?[18]

Animal husbandry also challenged native spiritual beliefs and practices. Because their mental universe assumed no rigid distinction between human and animal beings, the Indians' hunting rituals aimed to appease the spirits of creatures that were not so much inferior to, as different from, their human killers. Such beliefs helped to make sense of a world in which animals were deemed equally rightful occupants of the forest and whose killing required an intimate knowledge of their habits. Would Indians be able to apply these ideas about animals as *manitous*, or other-than-human persons, to domestic beasts as well? Or would those beasts' English provenance and dependence on human owners prohibit their incorporation into the spiritual world with bears, deer, and beaver?[19]

Finally, a decision to keep livestock ran counter to a powerful hostility toward domestic animals that dated from the earliest years of English settlement. Because colonists often established towns on the sites of former Indian villages depopulated by the epidemics that preceded their arrival, no line of demarcation separated English from Indian habitation. Native villages and colonial towns could be quite close together, and the accident of propinquity made for tense relations. At least at first, friction between these unlikely neighbors grew less from the very different ideas that informed Indian and English concepts of property than from the behavior of livestock. Let loose to forage in the woods, the animals wandered away from English towns into Indian cornfields, ate their fill, and moved on.

Indians, who had never had to build fences to protect their fields, were unprepared for the onslaught. Even their underground storage pits proved vulnerable, as swine "found a way to unhinge their barn doors and rob their garners," prompting native women to "implore their husbands' help to roll the bodies of trees" over the pits to prevent further damage.[20] Hogs attacked another important food source when they "watch [ed] the low water (as the Indian women do)" along the shoreline and rooted for clams, making themselves "most hatefull to all Natives," who called them "filthy cut throats, &c."[21] In Plymouth Colony, settlers in Rehoboth and their Indian neighbors engaged in a long-running dispute over damages from trespassing animals. At first, in 1653, the colonists claimed to "know nothing of" the Indian complaints. By 1656, settlers had erected a fence along the town boundary, but because a stream—across which livestock were "apte to swime"—also separated English and native lands, the animals still made their way into Indian cornfields. Four years later, Philip's older brother Wamsutta, known to the English as Alexander, was still bringing the Indians' complaints to the attention of Plymouth authorities.[22]

English livestock also proved to be a nuisance as they roamed through the woods. Cattle and swine walked into deer traps, and the English held the Indians liable for any injuries they sustained.[23] Similarly, in 1638, when William Hathorne of Salem found one of his cows stuck with an arrow, he insisted on restitution. Salem officials demanded the exorbitant sum of £100 from local Indians at a time when a cow was generally valued at about £20. Roger Williams pleaded the natives' case with John Winthrop, explaining that the colonists had charged the wrong Indians and that the sachems were outraged because the English held them personally responsible for the fine levied for their subjects' purported offense. "Nor doe they believe that the English Magistrates doe so practice," Williams reported, "and therefore they hope that what is Righteous amongst our Selves we will accept of from them."[24]

Williams went on to observe that "the Busines is ravelld and needes a patient and gentle hand to rectifie Misunderstanding of Each other and misprisions." He foresaw that endless recriminations would flow from colonists' attempts to raise livestock in the same space where Indians hunted. Native leaders, finding Williams a sympathetic listener, informed him of the "feares of their Men in hunting or travelling," for they had reason to believe they would be held responsible for every domestic animal found hurt or dead in the woods. Williams urged Winthrop to work with the Indians to contrive an equitable procedure to be followed in similar cases so that Indian hunters would not feel so much at risk from the rigors of a judicial system that appeared biased against them.[25]

Instead of recognizing the fundamental incompatibility of English and Indian subsistence regimes, colonial authorities repeatedly permitted joint use of land.[26] In so doing, they assumed that Indians would agree that the colonists' livestock had, in effect, use rights to the woods and fields too. Indians could hunt on lands claimed by the English only if they accepted certain restrictions on their activities. Indians who set traps within the town of Barnstable, for instance, had "fully and dilligenttly" to visit their traps daily to check for ensnared livestock and, if any were found, "thaye shall speedyli lett them out."[27] The Connecticut government imposed stricter limits on Indian hunters when the town of Pequot was founded in 1649. Uncas, the Mohegan sachem, was instructed "that no trapps [should] bee sett by him or any of his men" within the town, although colonial officials saw no reason completely "to prohibitt and restraine Uncus and his men from hunting and fishing" unless they did so on the Sabbath. Connecticut authorities acquired meadow land from the Tunxis Indians in 1650 and similarly recognized native rights of hunting, fishing, and fowling on the property so long as such activities "be not dun to the breach of any orders in the country to hurt cattle."[28] As late as 1676, in the aftermath of King Philip's War, Connecticut officials allowed "friendly" Indians "to hunt in the conquered lands in the Narrogancett Country, provided they sett not traps to prejudice English cattell."[29]

Joint use was doomed to failure, not by Indian unwillingness to comply with English conditions, but by the insurmountable problems that arose from grazing livestock on hunting lands. Accidental injuries were bound to occur and to disturb colonists, while Indians resented the damage done by domestic animals wandering out of the woods and into their cornfields. The behavior of livestock—creatures as indispensable to the English as they were obnoxious to the Indians—undermined the efforts of each group to get along with the other. Attempts to resolve disputes stemming from trespassing livestock led only to mutual frustration.

The Indians were doubtless the first to recognize the difficulties inherent in the joint use of land and the unrestricted foraging of colonists' animals. One Connecticut sachem actually attempted to restrict the *settlers'* use of land that he was willing to grant them outright. When Pyamikee, who lived near Stamford, negotiated with town officials, he tried to make the English agree not to put their livestock on the tract, for he knew that "the English hoggs would be ready to spoyle their [the Indians'] corne" in an adjacent field, "and that the cattell, in case they came over the said five mile river," would do likewise. But the colonists would only assure Pyamikee that livestock would always travel under the supervision of a keeper. . . .[30]

Many Indians used colonial courts to seek redress for damage caused by trespassing livestock. English authorities, in turn, often recognized the legitimacy of such complaints and granted restitution, as in 1632 when the Massachusetts General Court ordered Sir Richard Saltonstall to "give Saggamore John a hogshead of corne for the hurt his cattell did him in his corne."[31] Trespass complaints were so frequent, however, that colonial governments instructed individual towns to establish procedures for local arbitration lest the courts be overwhelmed. In Plymouth Colony, the task of reviewing such cases fell either to town selectmen or to ad hoc committees. If the livestock owner ignored their orders to pay damages, the aggrieved Indian could "repaire to some Majestrate for a warrant to recover such award by distraint."[32] Massachusetts and Connecticut adopted similar measures.[33]

But the colonists were less accommodating than they seemed. They insisted that Indians resort to an English court system that was foreign to them, the proceedings of which were conducted in an incomprehensible language necessitating the use of not-always reliable translators. (In the case described above, one of Pumham's objections to using the Plymouth court was his mistrust of the court interpreters.) Moreover, the English soon required Indians to fence their cornfields before they could seek reparations. As early as 1632,

Sagamore John, who received the award of damages from Saltonstall, had to promise "against the next yeare, & soe ever after" to fence his fields.[34] In 1640 Massachusetts law required settlers to help their Indian neighbors "in felling of Trees, Ryving & sharpning railes, and holing of posts" for fences, but this friendly gesture was coupled with stern provisos. Any Indian who refused to fence his fields after such help was offered forfeited his right to sue for damages. In addition, Indian complainants had to identify which beasts had trampled their corn—an impossible task if the animals had come and gone before the damage was discovered.[35] Beginning in the 1650s, Plymouth magistrates allowed Indians to impound offending beasts, but this meant either that they had to drive the animals to the nearest English pound or construct one on their own land and walk to the nearest town to give "speedy notice" of any animals so confined.[36]

Even if they complied with English conditions, Indians could not depend on the equitable enforcement of animal trespass laws. The coercive power of colonial governments was limited—magistrates could hardly march off to view every downed fence and ruined field—and reliance on local adjudication meant that townsmen had to police themselves. New England colonists were notoriously litigious, but it was one thing to defend against the charges of an English neighbor and quite another to judge impartially an Indian's accusations of trespass. When problems arose near the centers of colonial government, Indians could generally get a fair hearing, as did Sagamore John near Boston. But the enforcement of animal trespass laws became more haphazard toward the edges of settlement. Indians in the praying town of Okommakamesit (Marlborough)—thirty miles from Boston—abandoned a 150-acre tract with an apple orchard for "it brings little or no profit to them, nor is ever like to do; because the Englishmen's cattle, &c. devour all in it, because it lies open and unfenced," and they clearly expected no redress.[37] Along the disputed border between Rhode Island and Plymouth, settlers could scarcely agree among themselves who was in charge. Under such circumstances, as Pumham and his fellow Shawomets discovered, cudgel-wielding Englishmen all too easily took the law into their own hands. Farther away—in Maine, for example—even the pretense of due process could vanish. In 1636, Saco commissioners empowered one of their number to "excecut any Indians that ar proved to have killed any swyne of the Inglishe" and ordered all settlers summarily to "apprehend, execut or kill any Indian that hath binne known to murder any English, kill ther Cattell or any waie spoyle ther goods or doe them violence."[38]

Given the deficiencies of the colonial legal system, it is not surprising that many Indians dealt with intrusive livestock according to their own notions of justice. Indians who stole or killed livestock probably committed such deeds less as acts of wanton mischief, as the English assumed, than in retribution for damages suffered. In their loosely knit village bands, Indians placed a premium on loyalty to kin rather than to the larger social group. The strength of these kinship bonds at once limited the authority of sachems (a point lost on the magistrates who had ordered sachems to pay for Hathorne's cow) and sanctioned acts of violence undertaken in revenge for wrongs done to family members.[39] English authorities did not bother to inquire into Indian motives for theft and violence toward animals. But when, for instance, Pumham and other Shawomets—who had previously encountered irascible colonists and ineffective courts—were later charged with "killing cattle, and forceable entry" on settlers' lands, it takes little imagination to suspect that they were exacting their own retributive justice.[40]

Once they took matters into their own hands, Indians could be charged with theft and destruction of property with the full force of English law turned against them. The penalties for such offenses further corroded relations between the groups. Unable to pay the requisite fines—often levied in English money—Indians found themselves imprisoned or sentenced to corporal punishment.[41] Thus their options shrank even as livestock populations grew. Retaliation against the animals brought severe sanctions from the English, while efforts to accommodate the beasts on English terms required unacceptable alterations in Indian agriculture and the virtual abandonment of hunting. By the middle of the seventeenth century it was clear to the Indians that the English and their troublesome animals would not go away. The English, for their part, assumed that the solution was for Indians to abandon their ways and become livestock keepers themselves.

Some Indians—most notably King Philip—adopted livestock husbandry, though not in capitulation to English example and exhortation. Their adaptation was not a step, either intentional or inadvertent, toward acculturation, for they refused to make the complete transformation advocated by Englishmen who linked animal husbandry to the acquisition of civilized ways. The natives' decision instead fit into a broader pattern of intercultural borrowing that formed an important theme in Anglo-Indian relations during the first decades of contact. Much as settlers incorporated native crops and farming techniques into their agricultural system, Indians selected from an array of English manufactures such items as guns, cloth, and iron pots that were more efficient substitutes for bows and arrows, animal skins, and earthenware. Neither group forfeited its cultural identity in so doing, and when some Indians began to raise livestock—again largely for practical considerations—they deliberately selected the English beast that would least disrupt their accustomed routines.

Indians who raised livestock overwhelmingly preferred hogs.[42] More than any other imported creatures, swine resembled dogs, the one domesticated animal that Indians already had. Both species scavenged for food and ate scraps from their owners' meals. Although hogs also competed with humans for wild plants and shellfish and could damage native cornfields, these disadvantages were offset by the meat they supplied and the fact that Indians could deal with their own swine however they wished. Like dogs, swine aggressively fended off predators, such as wolves. Roger Williams recorded an instance of "two English Swine, big with Pig," driving a wolf from a freshly killed deer and devouring the prey themselves. Hogs could also be trained like dogs to come when called, a useful trait in an animal that foraged for itself in the woods.[43]

Swine keeping required relatively few adjustments to native subsistence routines—far fewer than cattle rearing would have involved. It made minimal demands on labor, rendering moot the issue of who—men or women—would bear primary responsibility for their care. Keeping cattle would have either dramatically increased women's work loads or involved men in new types of labor tying them more closely to the village site. Cattle needed nightly feeding, and cows had to be milked daily. Most male calves would have had to be castrated, and the few bulls required careful handling. Since cattle needed fodder and shelter during the winter, Indians would have had to gather and dry hay and build and clean barns—activities that infringed on their mobility during the hunting season. Some members of each village would have had to become herdsmen. Losing a cow in the woods was a more serious matter than losing a pig, for pigs had a far higher rate of reproduction.[44]

In return for a limited investment in labor, native hog keepers acquired a year-round supply of protein that replaced the meat they could no longer get from a dwindling deer population. These Indians may in fact have enjoyed an improved diet, avoiding the seasonal malnutrition resulting from their former dependence on corn and game.[45] Swine also provided products that replaced items formerly obtained from wild animals. Gookin noted in 1674 that Indians "used to oil their skins and hair with bear's grease heretofore, but now with swine's fat." And in at least one instance, Indians fashioned moccasins from "green hogs skinns" in place of deerskin. Settlers, in contrast, valued cattle for reasons that had little appeal for Indians. They plowed with oxen, but Indians who farmed with hoes did not need them. Colonists also prized the meat and dairy products supplied by their herds; although Indians would eat beef, most native adults were physiologically unable to digest lactose except in tiny amounts and would have learned to avoid milk products.[46]

Settlers raised hogs and ate pork, but they did not share the Indians' preference for swine over cattle. Cattle were docile and, to the English mind, superior beasts. Swine, on the contrary, were slovenly creatures that wallowed in mud, gobbled up garbage, and were rumored to kill unwary children. Colonists named their cows Brindle and Sparke and Velvet; no one named pigs. The English kept swine as if on sufferance, tolerating their obnoxious behavior in order to eat salt pork, ham, and bacon. Most of all, swine keeping did not promote hard work and regular habits so well as cattle rearing did. Writers who extolled the civilizing benefits of livestock husbandry doubtless envisioned sedentary Indian farmers peacefully gathering hay and tending herds of cattle alongside their English neighbors, but the reality was hardly so bucolic.[47]

Settlers instead encountered Indians who lived much as they always had, but who now had swine wandering across their lands—and occasionally into English cornfields.[48] The colonists recognized only grudgingly the Indians' property in animals and usually assumed that the natives' hogs were stolen. In 1672, Bay Colony officials insisted that Indians pilfered swine although they acknowledged that "it be very difficult to proove" that they had done so. Other explanations—that the Indians had captured feral animals or had purchased hogs from settlers—were seldom advanced. The fact that "the English, especially in the inland plantations, . . . loose many swine" and that Indians had hogs invited suspicion.[49]

To discourage the theft of animals among themselves and to identify strays, settlers used earmarks. Each owner had a distinctive mark that was entered in the town records, to be checked when an animal was reported stolen or a stray was found. The proliferation of town and colony orders requiring earmarks, as well as the increasing intricacy of the marks themselves—a mixture of crops, slits, "forks," "half-pennies," and so on—provides as good a measure as any of the growing livestock population. The earmark itself became a form of property handed down from one generation to the next.[50] Instead of assigning earmarks to native owners, however, magistrates ordered that "no Indians shall give any ear mark to their Swine, upon the penalty of the forfeiture" of the animal. An Indian who wished to sell a hog had to bring it with its ears intact; if he sold pork, he had to produce the unmarked ears from the carcass. This practice made native purchases of English hogs problematic, for the animals would already have marked ears. Should the Indian subsequently desire to sell such an animal, he could be required to "bring good Testimonies that he honestly obtained such Swine so marked, of some English." Moreover, Indian owners were at the mercy of unscrupulous settlers who might steal their animals and mark them as their own. Colonists did not prohibit Indian ownership of swine, but they denied Indians the acknowledged symbol of legitimate possession.[51]

The Indians' selective involvement with animal husbandry scarcely improved relations between natives and colonists. To the previous list of problems new and equally vexing issues were added, including trespasses by Indian animals, theft, and difficulties with proving ownership of animal property. For settlers, probably the least welcome change appeared when enterprising Indians started selling swine and pork in competition with English producers of the same commodities. Many orders pertaining to earmarks begin with a preamble that assumes that native competition went hand in hand with native dishonesty. In the Bay Colony, there was "ground to suspect that some of the Indians doe steale & sell the English mens swine;" in Plymouth, settlers complained "of Indians stealing of live Hogs from the

English, and selling them." Thus magistrates urged colonists to mark their animals to protect their property from native thieves. In fact, the charges of theft were not substantiated; the real problem was commercial, not criminal. Earmark regulations aimed at least as much to make Indian sales difficult as to make Indians honest.[52]

Competition with Indians was more than colonists had bargained for. In 1669—just six years before the start of King Philip's War—the Plymouth General Court proposed to license certain colonists "to trade powder, shott, guns, and mony (now under prohibition) with the Indians" as a means of discouraging the local Indians' pork trade. The magistrates complained that "a greate parte of the porke that is now carryed by the Indians to Boston" was "sold there at an under rate," hurting Plymouth pork sellers. The court felt no need to make explicit connections between its proposal to sell arms and its complaint about competition, but the likeliest explanation is that Plymouth Indians were using the proceeds of their Boston pork sales to purchase guns from licensed Bay Colony sellers, tapping into an arms trade that the Massachusetts General Court had established in the previous year. If the Indians could obtain arms from Plymouth suppliers, they presumably would cede the Boston pork trade to Old Colony producers. The court expressed no particular interest in helping out Boston consumers who spurned the wares of their fellow Englishmen in order to buy cheaper meat; its explicit aim was to ensure that the pork trade would "fall into the hands of some of our people, and soe the prise may be kept up."[53]

The Plymouth government's concern in this instance testifies to a remarkable set of native adaptations. If the Indians indeed brought pork and not live animals to the Bay Colony, they had learned to preserve meat in a way that appealed to English consumers. Some colonists, noting native ignorance of salting techniques, had assumed that Indians did not know how to preserve food.[54] We do not know whether Plymouth Indians had learned to salt as well as to sell pork, but there is no doubt that they had identified Boston as New England's most lucrative food market. Almost from the start, Boston merchants and shopkeepers vied with farmers over the relatively scarce amount of land on the small peninsula occupied by the town. As early as 1636, officials prohibited families from grazing more than two cows on the peninsula itself, and in 1647, the town herd was fixed at seventy beasts.[55] By 1658, swine had become such a public nuisance that Boston officials required owners to keep them "in their owne ground," effectively limiting the number of hogs each family could maintain.[56] Given these restrictions, many Bostonians apparently gave up raising animals and bought meat from livestock producers in nearby towns, who were also raising stock for the West Indies market.[57] Did the Plymouth Indians know this when they went to Boston? Their business acumen should not be underestimated. Although he did not refer specifically to the meat trade, Williams noticed that Indian traders "will beate all markets and try all places, and runne twenty thirty, yea forty mile, and more, and lodge in the Woods, to save six pence." Ironically, native enterprise met with suspicion rather than approbation from colonists who liked the Indians less the more like the English they became.[58]

The extent of native livestock husbandry is difficult to measure because colonial records mainly preserve instances in which animals became a source of conflict. The evidence does suggest that Indians residing near English settlements had a greater tendency to raise domestic animals than did those farther away. The Wampanoags, living in the Mount Hope area between Plymouth Colony and Rhode Island, apparently began to raise hogs by the middle of the seventeenth century, after some thirty years of contact with English settlers.[59] The location and timing of their adaptation were scarcely accidental.

The Wampanoags had close contact with settlers and, accordingly, a greater need for livestock than did native peoples living elsewhere. The ecological changes caused by English settlers steadily converting woodland into fenced fields and open meadows around Mount Hope reduced the deer population on which the Wampanoags depended; their swine keeping substituted one form of protein for another. Their trade in hogs and pork may also have been intended to offer a new commodity to settlers as other trade items disappeared or diminished in value. By the 1660s, the New England fur trade had ended with the virtual extinction of beaver. At the same time, English demand for wampum sharply declined as an improving overseas trade brought in more hard currency and colonies ceased accepting wampum as legal tender.[60] But hogs and pork failed as substitutes for furs and wampum. Most colonists owned swine themselves and—as the response of the Plymouth magistrates in 1669 suggests—evidently preferred to limit the market in animals to English producers.

Wampanoag swine keeping also contributed to growing tensions with colonists over land, creating disputes that were even harder to resolve than those concerning trade. Land that diminished in usefulness to Indians as it ceased to support familiar subsistence activities regained value for raising hogs; indeed, such places as offshore islands held a special attraction to keepers of swine. The Wampanoags' desire to retain their land awakened precisely when settlers evinced an interest in acquiring it. By the 1660s, a younger generation of settlers had reached maturity and needed farms. In Plymouth Colony, bounded on the north by the more powerful Bay Colony and on the west by an obstreperous Rhode Island, aggressive settlers eyed the lands of their Wampanoag neighbors. During the 1660s, new villages were formed at Dartmouth, Swansea, and Middleborough, while established towns such as Rehoboth and Taunton enlarged their holdings—and in effect blockaded the Wampanoags on Mount Hope peninsula.[61]

No man was harder pressed by these developments than King Philip. As sachem of the Wampanoags since 1662, he had tried to protect his people and preserve their independence in the face of English intrusion. Over time, his tasks became far more difficult. The number of occasions when the interests of Indians and settlers came into conflict grew as his ability to mediate diminished. Since Wampanoag land bordered on Massachusetts, Rhode Island, and Plymouth, Philip had to contend at various times with three, often competing, colonial governments. Even more problematic were his relations with neighboring towns, whose inhabitants pursued their economic advantage with little fear of intervention from any colony government and no regard for how their actions would affect Indian welfare.

Philip confronted the implications of New England localism most directly in cases of trespass. Colonial governments ordered towns to address Indian grievances but could not or would not enforce compliance. For six years, beginning in the mid-1650s, Rehoboth's inhabitants virtually ignored complaints from nearby Indians about damage from livestock, despite orders from the Plymouth court to solve the problem. In 1664, more than a decade after the issue first arose, Philip himself appeared at court—this time to complain about Rehoboth men trespassing on Wampanoag land to cut timber—and even then he may have hoped for a favorable outcome.[62] But if he did, the court soon compounded his problems by deciding to refer trespass cases to the selectmen of the towns involved. From then on, Philip and his people would have to seek justice at the hands of the very people who might well own the offending beasts.[63]

The Wampanoag leader's problems in dealing with townsmen whose attitudes ranged from unsympathetic to hostile worsened after the colony government declared its hands-off policy on trespass and reached a low point in 1671, when Plymouth officials charged Philip with stockpiling arms and conspiring with other Indian groups to attack the colonists. He denied the charges and appealed to Bay Colony magistrates to confirm his innocence. But Plymouth threatened coercion if he did not submit to its authority, and Philip signed a compact that further eroded his ability to safeguard Wampanoag interests. This agreement compelled him to seek Plymouth's approval before he disposed of any native territory, but colony officials were not similarly constrained by the need for Philip's permission before they approached Indians to purchase land. He also agreed that differences between natives and settlers would be referred to the colony government for resolution, although the magistrates' record in dealing even with straightforward cases of trespass gave little cause for optimism.[64]

The Plymouth court intended to subvert Philip's authority over his people in order to facilitate the acquisition of Wampanoag land by a new generation of colonists who would, in turn, raise new generations of livestock. As early as 1632, William Bradford recognized that settlers who owned animals required a lot of land to support their beasts. He complained when families abandoned Plymouth to form new towns where meadow was available, but he could not stop them. Instead, he could only lament that "no man now thought he could live except he had cattle and a great deal of ground to keep them."[65] Expansion accelerated during the 1660s and early 1670s, once again fueled by a burgeoning livestock population. During the two decades before King Philip's War, Plymouth officials approached local Indians at least twenty-three times to purchase land, often mentioning a specific need for pasture. Sometimes they only wanted "some small parcells"; on other occasions they desired "all such lands as the Indians can well spare."[66]

The need to sustain their herds drove the English to seek Indian land, and their expansionary moves collided with an urgent Wampanoag need to preserve what remained of their territory. Joint use of land, although fraught with problems, at least recognized mutual subsistence needs; by the 1660s, however, the practice had greatly diminished. Now the English not only wanted more land but demanded exclusive use of it. They asserted their property rights even in situations when accommodating Indian interests would have presented little threat. Allowing Philip to put his swine on Hog Island probably would not have harmed Portsmouth's inhabitants and might have improved relations between Indians and settlers. But what was Philip to think of the townsmen's summary refusal to share land, even when he proposed to use it for precisely the same purpose as they did? In that spring of 1669, Philip personally experienced the same English intransigence that he encountered as the representative of his people. After the Hog Island episode, and even more after his forced submission to Plymouth in 1671, he could not fail to see that while the colonists insisted that he yield to them, they would not yield in any way to him.

In an atmosphere of increasing tension, trespass assumed new significance. As colonists moved closer to native villages, the chances that livestock would stray onto Indian lands multiplied. With both groups competing for a limited supply of land, colonists did not restrain their animals from grazing wherever they could, while Indians grew ever more sensitive to such intrusions. Whenever livestock were concerned, the English ignored the Indians' property rights, while demanding that the natives recognize English rights. Indians resented encroachment by beasts that usually presaged the approach of Englishmen requesting formal ownership of land that their animals had already informally appropriated. Faced with the manifest inability—or unwillingness—of New England towns to solve the problem of trespass, and discouraged from seeking help from colony governments, Indians often resorted to their own means of animal control; they killed the offending beasts. This response would once have landed Indians in court, but by 1671 they faced far more serious consequences.

In that year, a group of angry colonists living near Natick very nearly attacked the Wampanoags of Mount Hope for killing livestock that had trespassed on Indian land. Interceding on behalf of the Indians, the Bay Colony's Indian commissioner, Daniel Gookin, begged for forbearance from the settlers, arguing that it was not worth "*fighting with Indians about horses and hogs,* as matters too low to shed blood." He urged the settlers to keep their animals on their own land; if any strayed into native territory and were killed, the owners should make a record of the fact, presumably to facilitate legal recovery.[67] War was averted, but this incident nonetheless showed that tension over livestock had reached dangerously high levels.

Both sides now understood that disputes over trespassing animals epitomized differences so profound as to defy peaceful solution. Whenever Indians killed livestock that had damaged their cornfields, colonists denounced such acts as willful violations of English property rights—rights that some settlers wanted to defend by force of arms. For Indians, trespassing animals constituted an intolerable violation of *their* sovereign rights over their land. The problem intensified by the early 1670s, for the English were determined to deprive Philip of all means of ensuring the integrity of the shrinking tracts of Wampanoag land, even as they refused effectively to control their beasts. The issue of trespassing livestock generated such tension precisely because it could not be separated from fundamental questions of property rights and authority.

When war broke out in 1675, the Indians attacked first, but the underlying causes resembled those that had provoked English belligerence four years earlier. John Easton, a Rhode Island Quaker, sought out Philip early in the conflict to ask why he fought the colonists; Philip's response indicated that intermingled concerns about sovereignty, land, and animals had made war inevitable. He supplied Easton with a litany of grievances that recalled past confrontations with the English and particularly stressed intractable problems over land and animals. He complained that when Indian leaders agreed to sell land, "the English wold say it was more than thay agred to and a writing must be prove [proof] against all them." If any sachem opposed such sales, the English would "make a nother king that wold give or seell them there land, that now thay had no hopes left to kepe ani land." Even after they sold land, Indians suffered from English encroachments, for "the English Catell and horses still incresed that when thay removed 30 mill from wher English had anithing to do"—impossible for the native inhabitants of Mount Hope—"thay Could not kepe ther coren from being spoyled." The Indians had expected that "when the English boft [bought] land of them that thay wold have kept ther Catell upone ther owne land."[68]

Because livestock had come to symbolize the relentless advance of English settlement, the animals were special targets of native enmity during the war. Colonel Benjamin Church, who led colonial forces in several campaigns, reported that Indians "began their hostilities with plundering and destroying cattle."[69] In an attack near Brookfield, Indians burned dwellings and "made great spoyle of the cattel belonging to the inhabitants." At Rehoboth "they drove away many cattell & h[ors]es"; at Providence they "killd neer an hundered cattell"; in the Narragansett country they took away "at the least a thousand horses & it is like two thousan Cattell And many Sheep."[70] As the human toll also mounted in the summer of 1675, English forces failed to stop Philip from slipping away from Mount Hope and only managed to capture "six, eight, or ten young Pigs of King Philip's Herds."[71]

The livestock on which colonists depended exposed them to ambush. Early in the war, Indians attacked "five Men coming from Road-Island, to look up their Cattel upon Pocasset Neck." Settlers sought refuge in garrison houses and secured their cattle in palisaded yards but could not provide enough hay to sustain them for long. Sooner or later they had to drive the creatures out to pasture or bring in more hay. Philip and his forces—who had a keen understanding of the voraciousness of English livestock—would be waiting. Near Groton in March 1676 "a Parcel of Indians . . . laid an Ambush for two Carts, which went from the Garison to fetch in some Hay." At about the same time at Concord, "two men going for Hay, one of them was killed." Settlers counted themselves lucky when they escaped, even if their animals fell victim. When Hatfield inhabitants let their livestock out to graze in May 1676, they lost the entire herd of seventy cattle and horses to Indians who had anticipated the move.[72]

The Indians seized and killed cattle mainly to deprive the colonists of food, but some of their depredations also suggest an intense animosity toward the animals themselves. One contemporary reported that "what cattle they took they seldom killed outright: or if they did, would eat but little of the flesh, but rather cut their bellies, and letting them go several days, trailing their guts after them, putting out their eyes, or cutting off one leg, &c."[73] Increase Mather described an incident near Chelmsford when Indians "took a Cow, knocked off one of her horns, cut out her tongue, and so left the poor creature in great misery."[74] Such mutilations recalled the tortures more often inflicted on human victims and perhaps similarly served a ritual purpose.[75] Certainly when Indians—who found a use for nearly every scrap of dead game animals—killed cattle "& let them ly & did neither eat them nor carry them away," they did so deliberately to send a message of terror to their enemies.[76]

Symbolic expressions of enmity, however, were a luxury that the Indians generally could not afford. As the war progressed, with cornfields ruined and hunting interrupted, Indians often needed captured livestock for food. When Church and his troops came upon an abandoned Indian encampment in an orchard, they found the apples gone and evidence of "the flesh of swine, which they had killed that day." At another site, colonial forces "found some of the English Beef boiling" in Indian kettles. In Maine, where fighting dragged on for months after Philip's death in August 1676, the "English took much Plunder from the Indians, about a thousand Weight of dried Beef, with other Things."[77] Edward Randolph, sent by the crown to investigate New England affairs in the summer of 1676, reported to the Council of Trade on the devastation caused by the war. He estimated that the settlers had lost "eight thousand head of Cattle great and small"—a tremendous reduction in the livestock population but not enough to starve the colonists into defeat or sustain the Indians to victory.[78]

The presence of livestock in New England was not the sole cause of the deterioration in relations between Indians and settlers. But because of their ubiquity and steady increase, domestic animals played a critical role in the larger, tragic human drama. The settlers had never been able to live without livestock, but as the animal population grew, Indians found it increasingly difficult to live with them. Both sides threatened violence over the issue of livestock—the English in 1671 and the Indians, who made good on the threat, in 1675. The cultural divide separating Indians and colonists would have existed without the importation to America of domestic animals. But the presence of livestock brought differences into focus, created innumerable occasions for friction, tested the limits of cooperation—and led, in the end, to war.

## NOTES

1 Clarence S. Brigham, ed., *The Early Records of the Town of Portsmouth* (Providence, R. I., 1901), 149–150. On the use of islands for grazing see Carl Bridenbaugh, *Fat Mutton and Liberty of Conscience: Society in Rhode Island, 1636–1690* (Providence, R. I., 1974), 16–17.

2 Douglas Edward Leach, *Flintlock and Tomahawk: New England in King Philip's War* (New York, 1958), 243–244; for a detailed account of the impact of the war on one town see Richard I. Melvoin, *New England Outpost: War and Society in Colonial Deerfield* (New York, 1989), 92–128.

3 Historians, when they have investigated livestock at all, have generally done so from an ecological perspective; see, for instance, William Cronon, *Changes in the Land: Indians, Colonists, and the Ecology of New England* (New York, 1983), and Alfred W. Crosby, *Ecological Imperialism: The Biological Expansion of Europe, 900–1900* (New York, 1986).

4 William Bradford, *Of Plymouth Plantation, 1620–1647,* ed. Samuel Eliot Morison (New York, 1952), 141; Nathaniel Shurtleff and David Pulsifer, eds., *Records of the Colony of New Plymouth in New England,* 12 vols. (Boston, 1855–1861), XII, 9–13. See also Darrett B. Rutman, *Husbandmen of Plymouth: Farms and Villages in the Old Colony, 1620–1692* (Boston, 1967), 6, 14–15.

5 John Winthrop, *The History of New England from 1630 to 1649,* ed. James Savage, 2 vols. (Boston, 1825–1826), I, passim; Edward Johnson, *Johnson's Wonder-Working Providence, 1628–1651,* ed. J. Franklin Jameson, Original Narratives of Early American History (New York, 1910), 54.

6 Wood, *New England's Prospect,* ed. Vaughan, 58–60; Samuel Maverick, *A Briefe Discription of New England and the Severall Townes Therein Together with the Present Government Thereof* (1660), (Boston, 1885), 8–15; Paul J. Lindholdt, ed., *John Josselyn, Colonial Traveler: A Critical Edition of "Two Voyages to New-England"* (Hanover, N. H., 1988), 110–119, 138–141; *Johnson's Wonder-Working Providence,* ed. Jameson, 68–69, 72, 110, 188–189, 195–197. In Cape Cod towns during the 17th century, a majority of householders owned cattle and swine; see Anne E. Yentsch, "Farming, Fishing, Whaling, Trading: Land and Sea as Resource on Eighteenth-Century Cape Cod," in Mary C. Beaudry, ed., *Documentary Archaeology in the New World* (New York, 1988), Table 13.8, 149.

7 Virginia DeJohn Anderson, *New England's Generation: The Great Migration and the Formation of Society and Culture in the Seventeenth Century* (New York, 1991), 30–31, 151–152, 154–156; Russell, *Long, Deep Furrow,* chap. 4; Cronon, *Changes in the Land,* 141–142; Rutman, *Husbandmen of Plymouth,* 17–19; David Thomas Konig, *Law and Society in Puritan Massachusetts: Essex County, 1629–1692* (Chapel Hill, N. C, 1979), 118–119.

8 Cushman, "Reasons and Considerations Touching the Lawfulness of Removing Out of England into the Parts of America" and "Of the State of the Colony, and the Need of Public Spirit in the Colonists," in Alexander Young, ed., *Chronicles of the Pilgrim Fathers of the Colony of Plymouth, From 1602 to 1625,* 2d ed. (Boston, 1844), 265, 243.

9 Allyn B. Forbes et al., eds., *Winthrop Papers, 1498–1654,* 6 vols. (Boston, 1929–1992), II, 120; Thomas Morton, *New English Canaan or New Canaan . . .* (1637), ed. Charles Francis Adams, Jr., *Publications of the Prince Society,* XIV (Boston, 1883), 230. The honey for the New England Canaan would also be an import, since honeybees are not native to America; see Crosby, *Ecological Imperialism,* 188–189. English concern about sedentarism and the connection to property rights is addressed in Cronon, *Changes in the Land,* 130, and Neal Salisbury, *Manitou and Providence: Indians, Europeans, and the Making of New England, 1500–1643* (New York, 1982), 176–177.

10 Glenn W. LaFantasie, ed., *The Correspondence of Roger Williams,* 2 vols. (Hanover, N. H., and London, 1988), II, 413.

11 Letter from Eliot in Thomas Shepard, "The Clear Sun-shine of the Gospel Breaking Forth upon the Indians in New-England . . ." (1648), MHS, *Colls.,* 3d Ser., IV (1834), 57–58.

12 William Kellaway, *The New England Company, 1649–1776: Missionary Society to the American Indians* (New York, 1961), 69.

13 Gookin, "Historical Collections of the Indians in New England" (1674), MHS, *Colls.,* Ist Ser., I (1792), 185; see also 184, 189, and Lindholdt, ed., *John Josselyn, Colonial Traveler,* 105. On the establishment of the praying towns see James Axtell, *The Invasion Within: The Contest of Cultures in Colonial North America* (New York, 1985), chap. 7; Francis Jennings, *The Invasion of America: Indians, Colonialism, and the Cant of Conquest* (Chapel Hill, N. C, 1975), chap. 14; Salisbury, "Red Puritans: The 'Praying Indians' of Massachusetts Bay and John Eliot," *William and Mary Quarterly,* 3d Ser., XXXI (1974), 27–54; and James P. Ronda, "Generations of Faith: The Christian Indians of Martha's Vineyard," ibid., XXXVIII (1981), 369–394.

14 The praying Indians never fully adopted the English program for their cultural transformation; see Harold W. Van Lonkhuyzen, "A Reappraisal of the Praying Indians; Acculturation, Conversion, and Identity at Natick, Massachusetts, 1646–1730," *New England Quarterly,* LXIII (1990), 396–428, and Kathleen J. Bragdon, "The Material Culture of the Christian Indians of New England, 1650–1775," in Beaudry, ed., *Documentary Archaeology,* 126–131. Their attempts to balance English prescriptions with native preferences suffered heavily after King Philip's War; see Daniel Mandell, "'To Live More Like My Christian English Neighbors': Natick Indians in the Eighteenth Century," *WMQ,* 3d Ser., XLVIII (1991), 551–579.

15 Williams, *A Key into the Language of America,* ed. John J. Teunissen and Evelyn J. Hinz (Detroit, Mich., 1973), 173–175. An "*ockqutchaun*" was a woodchuck; I am grateful to James Baker of Plimoth Plantation for this information.

16 Cronon, *Changes in the Land,* 101, 108; M. K. Bennett, "The Food Economy of the New England Indians, 1605–75," *Journal of Political Economy,* LXIII (1955), 369–397.

17 Cronon, *Changes in the Land,* 129–130.
18 Van Lonkhuyzen, "Reappraisal of the Praying Indians," 412–413; Joan M. Jensen, "Native American Women and Agriculture: A Seneca Case Study," *Sex Roles: A Journal of Research,* III (1977), 423–441; Salisbury, *Manitou and Providence,* 36. For an example of the way in which the adoption of domesticated animals—in this case, the horse—disturbed the gender-based division of labor in an Indian society see Richard White, "The Cultural Landscape of the Pawnees," *Great Plains Quarterly,* II (1982), 31–40. I thank George Phillips for this reference.
19 Kenneth M. Morrison, *The Embattled Northeast: The Elusive Ideal of Alliance in Abenaki-Euramerican Relations* (Berkeley, Calif., 1984), chap. 2; Gregory Evans Dowd, *A Spirited Resistance: The North American Indian Struggle For Unity, 1745–1815* (Baltimore, 1992), chap. 1; Salisbury, *Manitou and Providence,* 35–36; Elisabeth Tooker, ed., *Native North American Spirituality of the Eastern Woodlands: Sacred Myths, Dreams, Visions, Speeches, Healing Formulas, Rituals, and Ceremonials* (New York, 1979), 11–29.
20 Nathaniel B. Shurtleff, ed., *Records of the Governor and Company of the Massachusetts Bay in New England,* 5 vols. (Boston, 1853–1854), I, 102, 121, 133; John Noble, ed., *Records of the Court of Assistants of the Colony of the Massachusetts Bay, 1630–1692,* 3 vols. (Boston, 1901–1928), II, 46, 49; quotation from Wood, *New England's Prospect,* ed. Vaughan, 113.
21 Williams, *Key into the Language of America,* ed. Teunissen and Hinz, 182.
22 Shurtleff and Pulsifer, eds., *Plym. Col. Recs.,* III, 21, 106, 119–120, 167, 192.
23 See, for instance, Shurtleff, ed., *Mass. Bay Recs.,* I, 143; Charles J. Hoadly, ed., *Records of the Colony and Plantation of New Haven,* 2 vols. (Hartford, Conn., 1857–1858), I, 150. For a description of Indian hunting techniques see Williams, *Key into the Language of America,* ed. Teunissen and Hinz, 224–225.
24 LaFantasie, ed., *Correspondence of Williams,* I, 192.
25 Ibid., I, 193, quotations on 192.
26 On the problems of joint use see Peter A. Thomas, "Contrastive Subsistence Strategies and Land Use as Factors for Understanding Indian-White Relations in New England," *Ethnohistory,* XXIII (1976), 1–18.
27 Shurtleff and Pulsifer, eds., *Plym. Col. Rea.,* II, 130–131.
28 Quotation in Kenneth L. Feder, "'The Avaricious Humour of Designing Englishmen': The Ethnohistory of Land Transactions in the Farmington Valley," *Bulletin of the Archaeological Society of Connecticut,* No. 45 (1982), 36.
29 J. Hammond Trumbull et al., eds., *The Public Records of the Colony of Connecticut . . . . ,* 15 vols. (Hartford, Conn., 1850–1890), II, 289. Colonial officials eventually prohibited Indians from firing the woods in the autumn—a procedure that killed undergrowth and thus facilitated hunting—because of danger to the colonists' haystacks; Shurtleff, ed., *Mass. Bay Recs.,* V, 230–231.
30 Hoadly, ed. *New Haven Recs.,* II, 104–107.
31 Shurtleff, ed., *Mass. Bay Recs.,* I, 102. For similar instances of town and colony authorities granting restitution to Indians see ibid., I, 121, 133; Trumbull et al., eds., *Public Recs. of Conn.,* II, 165; III, 81; Shurtleff and Pulsifer, eds., *Plym. Col. Recs.,* III, 132; IV, 68; Howard M. Chapin, ed., *The Early Records of the Town of Warwick* (Providence, R. I., 1926), 89; and Leonard Bliss, Jr., *The History of Rehoboth, Bristol County, Massachusetts . . .* (Boston, 1836), 44. See also Yasuhide Kawashima, *Puritan Justice and the Indian: White Man's Law in Massachusetts, 1630–1763* (Middletown, Conn., 1986), chap. 7.
32 Shurtleff and Pulsifer, eds., *Plym. Col. Recs.,* V, 62; IX, 143 (quotation), 219.
33 Shurtleff, ed., *Mass. Bay Recs.,* I, 293–294; Trumbull et al., eds., *Public Recs. of Conn.,* III, 42–43.

34 Shurtleff, ed., *Mass. Bay Recs.*, I, 99.

35 William H. Whitmore, ed., *The Colonial Laws of Massachusetts, Reprinted from the Edition of 1660, with the supplements to 1672, Containing Also, the Body of Liberties of 1641* (Boston, 1889), 162. In 1662 Plymouth Colony law required settlers to help Indians build fences; see Shurtleff and Pulsifer, eds., *Plym. Col. Recs.*, XI, 137–138.

36 Trumbull et al., eds., *Public Recs. of Conn.*, III, 42–43; Shurtleff and Pulsifer, eds., *Plym. Col. Recs.*, III, 106, 192, XI, 123,137–138.

37 Gookin, "Historical Collections of the Indians in New England," 220.

38 Charles Thornton Libby et al., eds., *Province and Court Records of Maine*, 5 vols. (Portland, Me., 1928–1960), I, 2–4.

39 Salisbury, *Manitou and Providence*, 41–42; Kawashima, *Puritan Justice and the Indian*, chap. 1.

40 John Russell Bartlett, ed., *Records of the Colony of Rhode Island and Providence Plantations, in New England*, 10 vols. (New York, 1968; orig. pub. 1856–1865), I, 391.

41 For instances of Indian depredations against livestock see Trumbull et al., eds., *Public Recs. of Conn.*, I, 226; Hoadly, ed., *New Haven Recs.*, II, 361; Shurtleff, ed., *Mass. Bay Recs.*, I, 87, 88; IV, pt. 2, 54, 361; Shurtleff and Pulsifer, eds., *Plym. Col. Recs.*, IV, 92–93, 190–191, V, 80, IX, III, 209; and Samuel Eliot Morison, ed., *Records of the Suffolk County Court, 1671–1680*, Colonial Society of Massachusetts, *Publications* (Boston, 1933), XXIX, 404.

42 Virtually all references to Indian ownership of livestock specify hogs; see Chapin, ed., *Early Recs. of Warwick*, 102; Shurtleff and Pulsifer, eds., *Plym. Col. Recs.*, IV, 66; V, 6, II–12, 22, 85; Bartlett, ed., *R. I. Col. Rea.*, II, 172–173; Brigham, ed., *Early Recs. of Portsmouth*, 149–150; and Trumbull et al., ed., *Public Recs. of Conn.*, III, 55. See also Robert R. Gradie, "New England Indians and Colonizing Pigs," in William Cowan, ed., *Papers of the Fifteenth Algonquian Conference* (Ottawa, 1984), 147–169; I thank Barbara DeWolfe for this reference.

43 Juliet Clutton-Brock, *Domesticated Animals from Early Times* (Austin, Tex., 1981), 73, 74; Williams, *Key into the Language of America*, ed. Teunissen and Hinz, 226.

44 Clutton-Brock, *Domesticated Animals*, 68, 73; Russell, *Long, Deep Furrow*, 35, 88; Percy Wells Bidwell and John I. Falconer, *History of Agriculture in the Northern United States, 1620–1860* (Washington, D. C, 1925; repr. New York, 1941), 25, 31–32.

45 The evidence is sketchy but suggestive. One archaeological study of a Narragansett cemetery dating from the mid-17th century (roughly the time and location corresponding to historical evidence of Indian swine keeping) finds that the Indian skeletons show a surprising lack of iron deficiency anemia as well as little evidence of seasonal malnutrition. Such characteristics resulted from an improved diet, and although the specific content of that diet cannot be recovered, it is possible that the consumption of pork was an important factor. See Marc A. Kelley, Paul S. Sledzik, and Sean P. Murphy, "Health, Demographics, and Physical Constitution in Seventeenth-Century Rhode Island Indians," *Man in the Northeast*, No. 34 (1987), 1–25.

46 Gookin, "Historical Collections of the Indians in New England," 153; Shurtleff, ed., *Mass. Bay Recs.*, IV, pt. 2, 360. On Indians' lactose intolerance see Crosby, *Ecological Imperialism*, 27.

47 For contemporary English attitudes toward domestic animals see Keith Thomas, *Man and the Natural World: A History of the Modern Sensibility* (New York, 1983), 54, 64, 95, 96. These attitudes persisted into the 19th century; see Harriet Ritvo, *The Animal Estate: The English and Other Creatures in the Victorian Age*

(Cambridge, Mass., 1987), 21. Colonists concurred with the assessment of the danger of swine to children; see City of Boston, *Second Report of the Record Commissioners* (Boston Town Records, 1634–1660), (Boston, 1877), 145. For naming of cattle see, for instance, George Francis Dow, ed., *Records and Files of the Quarterly Courts of Essex County,* 9 vols. (Salem, Mass., 1911–1975), III, 361, 428.

48 Trumbull et al., eds., *Public Recs. of Conn.,* Ill, 55n.

49 Shurtleff, ed., *Mass. Bay Recs.,* IV, pt. 2, 512.

50 For ordinances requiring earmarks see, for example, Trumbull et al., eds., *Public Recs. of Conn.,* I, 118, 517; Shurtleff, ed., *Mass. Bay Recs.,* IV, pt. 2, 512–513; and Brigham, ed., *Early Recs. of Portsmouth,* 72–73, and for descriptions of earmarks see, for instance, ibid., 261–286, 288–295, 320–322. Cattle and horses were usually branded, and owners often entered complete descriptions of the animals in town books; see Whitmore, ed., *Col. Laws of Mass.,* 158, 258, and City of Boston, *Fourth Report of the Record Commissioners* (Dorchester Town Records), 2d ed. (Boston, 1883), 35–36.

51 John D. Cushing, ed., *The Laws of the Pilgrims: A Facsimile Edition of "The Book of the General Laws of the Inhabitants of the Jurisdiction of New-Plimouth, 1672 & 1685"* (Wilmington, Del., 1977), 44; see also Shurtleff, ed., *Mass. Bay Recs.,* IV, pt. 2, 512–513.

52 Shurtleff, ed., *Mass. Bay Recs.,* IV, pt. 2, 512; Cushing, ed., *Laws of the Pilgrims,* 44.

53 Shurtleff and Pulsifer, eds., *Plym. Col. Recs.,* V, 11–12. On the colonial arms trade see Patrick M. Malone, *The Skulking Way of War: Technology and Tactics Among the New England Indians* (Lanham, Md., 1991), 49.

54 Morton, *New English Canaan,* ed. Adams, 161.

55 Darrett B. Rutman, *Winthrop's Boston: A Portrait of a Puritan Town, 1630–1649* (Chapel Hill, N. C., 1965), 206.

56 City of Boston, *Second Report of the Record Commissioners,* 145.

57 A partial Boston tax valuation for 1676 indicates that fewer than half of household heads owned cattle or swine; see City of Boston, *First Report of the Record Commissioners of the City of Boston* (Boston, 1876), 60–67. On the development of a domestic and foreign market in live stock and meat see Karen J. Friedmann, "Victualling Colonial Boston," *Agricultural History,* XLVII (1973), 189–205, and Darrett B. Rutman, "Governor Winthrop's Garden Crop: The Significance of Agriculture in the Early Commerce of Massachusetts Bay," *WMQ,* 3d Ser., XX (1963), 396–415.

58 Williams, *Key into the Language of America,* ed. Teunissen and Hinz, 218.

59 Montauk Indians living on the eastern end of Long Island also raised hogs in the 17th century. Like the Wampanoags on the mainland, the Montauks lived in an area surrounded by English settlement and had been in contact with settlers for decades. See Jasper Dankers and Peter Sluyter, "Journal of a Voyage to New York in 1679–80," *Memoirs of the Long Island Historical Society,* I (1867), 126.

60 Cronon, *Changes in the Land,* 101; Salisbury, "Indians and Colonists in Southern New England after the Pequot War: An Uneasy Balance," in Laurence M. Hauptman and James D. Wherry, eds., *The Pequots in Southern New England: The Fall and Rise of an American Indian Nation* (Norman, Okla., 1990), 90–91.

61 On the expansion of Plymouth settlement see Rutman, *Husbandmen of Plymouth,* 21.

62 Shurtleff and Pulsifer, eds., *Plym. Col. Recs.,* III, 21, 167, IV, 54.

63 The law requiring town selectmen to decide trespass cases was passed in the mid-1660s; the record contains no specific date. See Shurtleff and Pulsifer, eds., *Plym. Col. Recs.,* XI, 143.

64 Ibid., V, 79.

65 Bradford, *Of Plymouth Plantation,* ed. Morison, 253.
66 Shurtleff and Pulsifer, eds., *Plym. Col. Recs.,* III, 84, 104, 123, 142, 216–217, IV, 18, 20, 45, 70, 82, 97, 109, 167, V, 20, 24, 24–25, 95, 96,. 97–98, 98–99, 109, 126, 151.
67 Gookin's comments were paraphrased in a letter to him from Gov. Thomas Prince of Plymouth. Gookin had heard a rumor that he was accused of inciting Philip to fight against the English; Prince's letter aimed to reassure him that that was not the case; see MHS, *Colls.,* 1st Ser., VI (1799; repr. 1846), 200–201.
68 "A Relacion of the Indyan Warre, by John Easton, 1675," in Charles H. Lincoln, ed., *Narratives of the Indian Wars, 1675–1699,* Original Narratives of Early American History (New York, 1913), 11.
69 Church, *Diary of King Philip's War, 1675–1676,* ed. Alan and Mary Simpson (Chester, Conn., 1975), 75; see also William Hubbard, *The History of the Indian Wars in New England from the First Settlement to the Termination of the War with King Philip, in 1677,* ed. Samuel G. Drake (New York, 1969; orig. pub. 1865), 64.
70 "Capt. Thomas Wheeler's Narrative of an Expedition with Capt. Edward Hutchinson into the Nipmuck Country, and to Quaboag, now Brookfield, Mass., first published 1675," *Collections of the New-Hampshire Historical Society,* II (1827), 21; Douglas Edward Leach, ed., *A Rhode Islander Reports on King Philip's War: The Second William Harris Letter of August, 1676* (Providence, R. I., 1963), 44, 46, 58. For other descriptions of attacks on livestock see Church, *Diary of King Philip's War,* ed. Simpson and Simpson, 172; Samuel G. Drake, *The Old Indian Chronicle; Being a Collection of Exceeding Rare Tracts, Written and Published in the Time of King Philip's War . . .* (Boston, 1836), 13, 35, 58; and Hubbard, *History of the Indian Wars,* 164, 192, 234, 242.
71 Drake, *Old Indian Chronicle,* 10; the anonymous author of this account subsequently refers to the capture of Philip's "Cattel and Hogs," although there is no corroborating evidence that Philip owned cattle; see p. 11. He did own a horse, given to him by the Plymouth General Court in 1665; see Shurtleff and Pulsifer, eds., *Plym. Col. Recs.,* IV, 93.
72 Quotations from Hubbard, *History of the Indian Wars,* 83, 195–196, 222; for the Hatfield raid, see George W. Ellis and John E. Morris, *King Philip's War, Based on the Archives and Records of Massachusetts, Plymouth, Rhode Island and Connecticut, and Contemporary Letters and Accounts* (New York, 1906), 227–228, and Melvoin, *New England Outpost,* 101, 107.
73 Quotation from an anonymous narrative of the war reprinted in Drake, *Old Indian Chronicle,* 102.
74 Increase Mather, *A Brief History of the War with the Indians in New-England . . .* (1676), ed. Samuel G. Drake (Boston, 1862), 132.
75 On Indian use of torture see Jennings, *Invasion of America,* 160–164.
76 Leach, ed., *A Rhode Islander Reports on King Philip's War*, 46.
77 Church, *Diary of King Philip's War,* ed. Simpson and Simpson, 133; Hubbard, *History of the Indian Wars,* 276, pt. 2, 223.
78 Randolph's report is in Nathaniel Bouton et al., eds., *Provincial Papers: Documents and Records Relating to the Province of New-Hampshire,* vol. 1 (Concord, N. H., 1867), 344. Christian Indians also suffered losses to their livestock during the war; see Gookin, "An Historical Account of . . . the Christian Indians in New England . . . ," American Antiquarian Society, *Archaeologia Americana,* II (1836), 451, 504, 512.

# 5

# DUAL REVOLUTIONS AND THE MISSIONS

*Steven W. Hackel*

In Alta California, there would be no classic military invasion that culminated in the conquest of Indians. Spanish soldiers and Indian warriors did not meet in a climactic battle that decided the fate of the region. Yet the contest for California did involve innumerable battles in villages and throughout the countryside between elements of the Old World and the New. To Alta California, just as elsewhere in New Spain, Spaniards came equipped with unwitting silent armies of pathogens, plants, and animals that rendered them and their institutions nearly invincible. These Old World agents of "ecological imperialism" proved innately suited to the new region and so conquered it with a brutal efficiency, under-cutting its peoples and the foods they relied upon through demographic and ecological revolutions that dramatically transformed California's human and natural landscape. At first, these dual revolutions and the Indian response to them precipitated and promoted the efflorescence of Franciscan missions, which initially filled with people and produced surplus foods. But, ultimately, these missions and their Indians would be undone, destroyed by the population collapse that had in part prompted their growth. The story of the rise and fall of the California missions, therefore, suggests the primacy of the biological and ecological forces that to a large degree structured the world in which Indians and Europeans shaped their encounters and communities.[1]

European diseases most likely arrived in the Monterey region in the summer of 1769. They might have been first introduced long before, perhaps in 1542 by Juan Rodríguez Cabrillo, in 1602 by Sebastián Vizcaíno, or in the seventeenth or eighteenth centuries by one of the Manila galleons during an unrecorded stop.[2] But, after the mission and presidio were founded at Monterey in 1770, bringing with them a permanent presence of soldiers and missionaries, pathogens long endemic to Europe easily multiplied and spread through the countryside as they encountered a bountiful population that had no experience with them. These diseases had enormous effects on

California Indian communities; they certainly reduced the number of laborers, thinned the leadership ranks, and ultimately forced a change in settlement patterns by helping to push Indians into the missions.[3]

Whether Indians of the Monterey region suffered from epidemic diseases in the first years of Spanish settlement is not clear. However, they came to San Carlos and other missions from villages and communities that were fragmented and frayed, most likely from disease and perhaps from warfare. A significant portion of the young recruits to San Carlos were either orphaned or fatherless; 7.4 percent of those baptized before age fifteen were orphans, and nearly 21 percent were fatherless. Every death constituted a tear in the community's social fabric; it was one less parent, one less son or daughter, one less member of a ritual society or clan. Far fewer of the children baptized at Mission San Carlos were motherless than fatherless, a fact that suggests not only that disease and warfare claimed more adult men than adult women but that widows with children especially might have found some aspects of life in the missions preferable to life outside of them. These figures, however, only hint at the social disruption within Indian communities during the early years of Spanish settlement. Many of the Indians' deaths went unrecorded by the Franciscans and are therefore lost to us: children, unmarried adults, and childless widows and widowers—any of these who died without baptism would not have been noted by the Franciscans.

Although the Franciscans' records only begin to show the losses suffered by Indian communities during colonization, they do allow for a study of the age, sex, and marital status of those who came to the missions. This analysis suggests that a majority of the migrants to Mission San Carlos were perhaps those least confident in their ability to weather the dual revolutions and the sustained upheavals they entailed: the very young, the old, and unmarried women, all of whom comprised more than 70 percent of the gentile baptisms at Mission San Carlos during its decades of recruitment. By and large, the Indians who came to the mission were young: almost half were under age fifteen, and nearly a quarter were under age five. Families with many children to feed might have come to rely on mission foodstuffs more rapidly than others. Females constituted about 53 percent of all gentile baptisms and were the majority in nearly every age cohort; males predominated only among Indians between the ages of five and nine, an occurrence perhaps tied to the absence of fathers from many Indian families but also likely related to the Franciscans' intensive recruitment of young boys because of their special importance to the missionary program. Among adults who came to the mission, marriage was a common state, but more so for men than women. Some women might have been widowed and therefore not married at baptism. As in nearly all societies, younger women were more likely to be married than younger men, and older men were more likely to be married than older women.

Although the exact date Old World pathogens began to attack the Children of Coyote went unrecorded, the arrival of European animals, namely cattle, mules, horses, and pigs, did not. Spaniards took these from missions in Baja California and brought them on the initial overland expeditions. The presidio at Monterey had horses and mules from its inception in June 1770, and in August 1771 Pedro Fages—the gobernante of Alta California—delivered to the mission a large sow, a large hog, and four piglets.[4] Four months later, the mission accepted eighteen head of cattle, and by then the presidio almost certainly had its own herd. In February 1773, the mission gained twelve mules; six months later it obtained another three mules and eleven horses. Sheep had not been brought to the mission as of 1775, but in all likelihood they were introduced soon thereafter, and, by the end of 1778, there was a small herd of forty-eight sheep at San Carlos. When presented with grasslands containing more food than they had ever needed to maintain their numbers, horses, cattle, and sheep increased in much the same way as would pathogens: they multiplied rapidly and dispersed widely throughout the region. The result was an animal population explosion—an "ungulate irruption"—that emerged from the earliest years of Spanish settlement in Alta California.[5]

By 1783, Mission San Carlos counted some 874 animals: 500 cattle, no sheep, no goats, 25 pigs, 18 mules, and 111 horses. Indians had built an adobe corral for the sheep and goats and a pen for the pigs, but the larger, more aggressive, and more numerous horses and cattle proved increasingly difficult to contain, and their corrals and stalls were constantly in need of repair and reinforcement. In January 1785, one missionary at San Carlos warned that the cattle herd of 500 now posed a threat to the mission's cultivated fields and needed to be reduced.[6] The warning went unheeded and the herd's growth continued unarrested, as did the increase of the mission's holdings of sheep, goats, and horses. As their numbers grew, the animals proved too numerous to keep corralled; most were turned loose to graze the countryside and captured only when needed. The increase went largely unchecked, and for Indians the consequences were dire. Spanish cattle, sheep, and horses not only overran Indian lands, trampling fields and encroaching on villages, but Indians who killed Spanish livestock were themselves punished severely by the padres and soldiers. Soldiers exacerbated the Indians' problems by seeking to eliminate natural predators, such as bears, which occasionally threatened the growing herds. . . .

Just as European diseases radiated from Spanish centers of settlement into remote Indian villages in the years after 1770, so too did environmental degradation, as Spanish livestock invaded and then exhausted ecological niches farther and farther from the mission and presidio. Into this disturbed environment came a host of weeds and plants that Europeans had inadvertently brought with them. These Old World plants had shown themselves adept at coexisting alongside European grazing animals elsewhere. They were hardier than native grasses and bushes and more suited to dry, compacted soil, and, as a result, they succeeded many indigenous food sources.

The near-complete displacement of native plants by European weeds has been made abundantly clear through analysis of adobe bricks manufactured in the Monterey region during the 1820s, 1830s, and 1840s: they contain much higher pollen counts of European weeds than of native plants.[7] By the turn of the nineteenth century, the hills and valleys of the Monterey region were covered with alien plants that supported Spanish livestock, but few, if any, Indian villages remained. In 1800, the mission grazed 4,000 sheep and 1,200 head of cattle, and the presidio soon counted some 1,275 cattle and more than 7,000 horses. By then, nearly all of the Indians in the area labored for their primary subsistence in mission fields, not the surrounding countryside.

The awful, if accidental, genius of Spanish colonization in California, then, was not just in creating a subsistence crisis among Indian communities through introduced diseases, plants, and animals; it was in offering what appeared to be a solution in the form of food Indians raised at the mission. Rumsen Indians had been working for food ever since June 1770, when small groups earned *panocha,* chocolate, flour, and ham for manual labor they performed at the presidio.[8] Spaniards had brought these goods north from Mexico, and in the early 1770s Indians used them to supplement a diet still largely gathered from beyond the mission; it would be another decade until Indians at the mission had cleared enough land and planted enough crops to sustain large numbers of villagers.

The Franciscans had come to California with the seeds and tools—hoes, plows, shovels, and picks—they needed to transform the land. At first, they had little success. In the year after Mission San Carlos was established, Rumsen field hands, under the directions of the missionaries, planted "all kinds of seeds" in a little enclosed garden. But nothing came of these efforts, for, as Father Junípero Serra wrote, the land was occasionally "washed over by the salt water of the estuary" and so was "fit for nothing but nettles and reeds." Later that year, in the summer of 1771, because of the bad soil—and his deteriorating relationship with Fages—Serra moved the mission several miles southwest to its present location, farther from the presidio and closer to Rumsen laborers and fresh water. Even at the new location, Serra continued to despair about the mission's progress: "With regard to crops nothing worthy of the name has as yet been achieved . . . as regards spiritual matters, much could have been accomplished if only there were something to eat."[9]

Not until the winter of 1772 did Indians plant crops at the new location on land that was, in one padre's words, "half dug and half cleared." The wheat and barley, however, yielded only small harvests, and the corn and beans were damaged by a late frost. Serra lamented: "Finding ourselves unable to give [the neophytes] food and keep them with us, we baptized very few, except when necessity demanded." Missionaries were forced to subsist on what little remained from the supplies brought north, and the few Indians at the mission relied on gathered food. Two years after its establishment, the mission owed its continued existence to the neighboring gentile Indians, who, Serra wrote, "are the main supporters of our people." But, over time, just as the dual revolutions were eroding native communities and remaking the countryside, mission fields worked by Rumsen hands began to support an increasing number of natives. Thus, Indians not only responded to changes in their world; they accelerated them.[10]

In 1774, the mission's garden, which by then had been itself blessed in honor of Saint Joseph and was referred to as a *milpa,* yielded a large and diverse crop: 225 bushels of corn, 187 bushels of wheat, 30 bushels of barley, 7.5 bushels of kidney beans, and another 1.5 bushels of broad beans. And this was only the beginning. New baptisms continued to add laborers to the mission while taking them away from native villages, and the padres found agricultural varieties suited to Monterey's soil and climate that furthered the displacement of indigenous plants. In 1775, Indians and missionaries added peas, garbanzos, and lentils to the garden, in addition to planting three different varieties of wheat. Altogether that year, Indians harvested 885 bushels of produce at the mission. In 1781, Indians spent seven months working on an irrigation system, which was largely completed by December, and they kept clearing new fields for more crops, a task that proved arduous, given that the land had been "covered with long tough grasses and thickets but also with great trees, willows, alders, and so forth."[11]

By 1783, Indians working the mission's irrigated fields, which might have comprised some 155 acres of what once was native terrain, were producing a significant surplus of food.[12] The padres boasted of a "sizeable walled garden [which produces] abundant vegetables and some fruit." In that year, Indians harvested some 4,500 bushels, a huge figure that no doubt explains why 166 gentiles came to the mission for baptism—more than in any other year. So abundant was the crop that Serra sent nearly 200 bushels of wheat to the soldiers at the presidio. More tellingly, though, the padres "gave," in their words, some 375 bushels of grain to villagers of Sargentaruc and Excelen who had worked in the mission's fields during the harvest; these more remote villages by the early 1780s were beginning to see their own numbers and economies undercut by the dual revolutions, and they were increasingly looking to the mission for subsistence. The more than 600 Indians already at the mission, according to Serra, were maintained "without any scarcity."[13]

The Indians' decision to migrate to the missions generated a momentum all its; own. In electing to move, Indians made choices for themselves and their families, but their decisions worked against others who might have wanted to stay away. The migrations could only have accelerated the collapse of villages and subsistence economies that had become unable, it seems, to support even the declining number of people living in them. Simultaneously, the Indians provided more labor for the missions' fields, which in turn then produced more crops and in so doing bolstered the missions' appearances as places of refuge, as sources of food and shelter and community.[14]

Earlier and elsewhere in colonial America, as in northeastern North America, many Indian groups had responded to the shocks of colonization by launching wars on their Indian neighbors to secure access to European trade and captives, replacing those lost to disease or war. In Alta California, as in some other parts of northern New Spain, however, Indians instead generally came to missions; they were compelled by the upheaval of the dual revolutions and lured still by the; material (in this case, food, not muskets or alcohol) and the hope of community regeneration through association with other remnant, refugee groups. Thus, what the Franciscans set out to establish as Catholic missions, California Indians originally must have viewed as resources oriented around agricultural production. In this regard, in becoming places of congregation for Indians, the California missions were unusually successful. In Baja California, by comparison, only the demographic revolution took hold: missions proved hotbeds for contagion but were unable to support the plants and animals upon which the growth of most borderlands missions so depended. This was also largely the case in Texas and Sonora, where missions rarely counted large numbers of Indian residents.[15]

This movement to the missions began almost as soon as Spaniards and their silent weapons arrived in Monterey. All told, the Children of Coyote came to Mission San Carlos from many outlying villages over nearly four decades, and, when each village is viewed separately, the distribution over time of its members' baptisms conforms to several patterns. Every *ranchería*, or village, had one or two years in which many more individuals joined the mission than in other years; in no instance did all the residents of a single village attain baptism in fewer than five years. Even in years when large numbers of Indians from one village came, their baptisms were usually spread out over several months. The gradual rate of baptisms from each village reveals that, throughout the period 1770 to 1808, individuals and family units came steadily to Mission San Carlos. Whole villages were not forced into the mission during a short period of time as some scholars have asserted; they were driven by a different sort of occupying force than one of soldiers bearing guns and lances.[16]

Indians came to the mission in what now appear as four distinct waves spread out over the thirty-nine-year period from 1770 to 1808. Each successive wave involved villages located a greater distance from Mission San Carlos. The period from 1773 to 1778 represented the first major wave of gentiles: 454 were baptized; during these years, roughly 30 percent of all the 1,525 gentiles baptized at the mission through 1808. Through 1778, 417 Rumsen Indians from Achasta and Tucutnut, the closest villages to the newly established mission, and Ichxenta, Socorronda, and Echilat, located up the river valleys, were christened at San Carlos.[17] During the 1770s, only a few dozen Indians from the more distant; Excelen, Ensen, and Sargentaruc attained baptism. The majority of the last of the local Rumsen Indians were baptized in 1778; after that, only fifteen gentiles joined; the mission in 1779, 1780, and 1781.

The period 1782–1785 constituted the second major migration of gentiles to the mission. In these years, the Franciscans expanded their reach to groups; beyond the immediate vicinity: the Excelen, Eslenajan, Ecjeajan, Sargentaruc, Kalendaruc, and Ensen. From these groups, about 400 gentiles attained baptism, approximately 26 percent of all the gentile baptisms that would occur at the mission. The third movement of gentiles to San Carlos occurred in 1790–1792, when 213 were baptized, 78 from the Costanoan group Ensen. The drop-off in baptisms between 1796 and 1803, when only 63 gentiles were baptized, can probably be explained by the Franciscans' changing leadership at the mission and the terrible epidemic that struck Mission Carmel in 1802. The last major wave took place in 1805–1807, when the final outlying villagers came into the mission.

Although certainly not exact—and only one part of a very complicated story—there is a rough correlation between when individuals from specific villages attained baptism and when cattle and other livestock spread into their territory. This relationship appears weakest in the early years of colonization, when livestock totals were lowest, and more pronounced in the years when Spanish herds multiplied. The first movements to San Carlos involved Indians from five associated Rumsen villages situated within ten miles of Mission San Carlos in the hills and valleys of the Carmel River and San Jose Creek, all early grazing areas of mission and presidio livestock. In the second half of the 1770s, Indians came to Mission San Carlos from the upper Carmel River valley and the Salinas River valley, just as these areas were becoming important sources of pasturage for European cattle. In the early 1780s, Spanish livestock extended their grazing farther up the Salinas Valley, into the upper Carmel River valley, and farther south to the Big Sur region, forcing Indians into San Carlos from the Esselen territories of Sargentaruc, Excelen, and Eslenajan. These villages were all some twenty to thirty-five miles from San Carlos. In the late 1780s and the 1790s, large numbers of Indians ventured to San Carlos and Mission Soledad from throughout the greater Monterey region as the intruding livestock expanded dramatically in number and range and remade the landscape a considerable distance from the missions. In these years, Indians moved in large numbers from the Ensen villages of the Salinas Valley—then a prime area for mission and presidio cattle—and the Esselen villages of Imunahan and Aspasniajan, both of which were situated to the south of recently established Mission Soledad and located in the valleys and canyons where its own herds grazed. By the early 1800s, after a fourth and final wave composed largely of elderly holdouts, seemingly all the Indians of the region had relocated to one of the Franciscan missions.

The missionaries and soldiers misunderstood the relationship between the spread of their diseases, animals, and plants and the mounting number of baptisms at the missions: they saw the growth of agriculture and a pastoral economy as drawing Indians to the missions rather than pushing them there. But they were fully aware by the mid-1790s that the Monterey region's natural environment was in a period of transformation and crisis. In the early 1790s, the number of cattle: and sheep kept by San Carlos nearly doubled, increasing from 1,082 cattle and 900 sheep in 1790 to 2,300 and 1,577, respectively, in 1794. And, by that same year, Missions Santa Cruz and Soledad (both founded in 1791) together held nearly 700 cattle and 900 sheep. Furthermore, the presidio's horses and cattle numbered in the thousands. When drought gripped the overgrazed region in 1793, 1794, and 1795, suddenly there was inadequate pasture to support the steadily increasing herds. Soon, the royal herd of cattle grazed in the lower Salinas Valley was declining in numbers and producing far fewer calves, a sure sign of its mal-nourishment. The resulting diminution in the presidio's herd prompted an investigation by the governor. Soldiers, who doubled as cowherds and shepherds, all described a region that had not seen rain in years, where the pasturage had become "infinitely" reduced. By the mid-1790s, the native vegetation of the region had been severely damaged, if not totally destroyed, by the introduced animals and the lack of rain. Sheep and their ability to eat grasses down to the ground proved especially damaging to the pasturage in and around Monterey. "What the livestock had not eaten, they had trampled.[18]

Ironically, the environmental crisis of the mid-1790s served only to complete the ungulates' dominance of the land. Thousands of horses, cattle, and sheep ranged farther and farther in search of pasture, scouring the valleys and hills, rooting out any remaining pockets of native grasses. Indians who had not yet moved to San Carlos, Santa Cruz, or Soledad, and therefore still relied upon the countryside for their subsistence, were hit especially hard. Suffering from what the soldiers described as their great "hunger" as a result of the disappearance of the acorns and other seeds, Indians increasingly turned to cattle as a source of food. Soldiers asserted that their own horses were simply too weak and too scrawny to allow them to look after so many animals and prevent Indians from attacking them.[19]

Spanish livestock recovered quickly after the drought; native vegetation and the Indians who depended upon it could not. Once rains returned, as in 1798, nonnative grasses and introduced livestock solidified their hold, and by then nearly all the Indians of the region had relocated to one of its missions. Now it became a pastoral paradise, with its mild climate, its wet but cool winters, and its rich covering of grasses well adapted to both drought and aggressive grazing. In 1800, Missions Santa Cruz, San Carlos, Soledad, and San Juan Bautista grazed some 3,811 cattle, 11,082 sheep, and 2,678 horses; two decades later, they counted nearly three times as many animals—some 22,000 cattle, 23,200 sheep, and 2,533 horses. This process played itself out throughout the rest of Spanish California in the decades after 1770, as more missions and their animals came to dominate and then transform the countryside. Herds of horses increased so rapidly that, by 1805, Father President Estevan Tapis was asking the governor to slaughter them. One visitor to Monterey in 1806 reported that the governor had recently sent out a party of soldiers to kill 20,000 head of cattle "wherever they found them, because he feared that they would multiply to the point that there would not be enough pasture to feed them." Such practices reduced for a moment the number of cattle in the region, but, by the end of the Spanish period, missions in California collectively held some 193,234 sheep, 149,730 cattle, and 19,830 horses. The presidios, a small number of private ranchos, and numerous wild herds held countless more.[20]

Faced with declining numbers and an inability to maintain their annual subsistence, California Indians elected to move to missions such as San Carlos Borromeo because doing so at first allowed them to survive and to hold on to crucial elements of their culture. When Indians left their villages, they brought to missions many things, including their music, dances, architecture, and what remained of their subsistence economies. Although the Franciscans objected to dances that brought men and women together after dark, they rarely prevented those that occurred in broad daylight, and thus they signalled to Indians the important native practices were compatible with life at the missions. Dancers at San Carlos with some regularity painted their bodies, donned regalia, and came together as they created spectacles for themselves and foreign visitors to the region.[21]

When Georg Heinrich von Langsdorff came to Mission San Jose in 1806 Father Pedro de la Cueva gave the Indians the day off from mission work to prepare a dance in honor of the visitor. To secure the participation of the mission's best dancers, De la Cueva gave them "finery." The morning of the dance the men gathered beyond the mission, by a creek, where some decorated themselves "with cinders, red clay, and chalk." Others painted figures on their chests, stomachs, thighs, and backs. Several covered their naked bodies with down. Women adorned themselves with "mussels, feathers, and coral." For the better part of the day, the Costanoan of Mission San Jose danced for Langsdorff and themselves, "jumping rhythmically and making all kinds of body movements and grimaces" as they portrayed "scenes from war and domestic life with the help of bows and arrows and with feathers held in their hands and on their heads. The women had their own songs and way of dancing, hopping near the men and "sliding their thumb and index finger rhythmically from one side to the other of their abdomens." As rich as this description is of the Indians' music, costumes, and preparations, elements of these dances must have spoken uniquely to the Indians' beliefs and concerns. Clearly, though, Indian dances at the missions were elaborate affairs through which participants told stories of their history and affirmed native beliefs and hierarchies.[22]

Although modern reconstructions of Spanish missions give the impression that all baptized Indians resided within a closed quadrangle under the padres' surveillance, from 1770 until 1807 Indians at San Carlos inhabited a village of their own construction on a bluff just beyond the main buildings. Pedro Fages observed in 1773 that the village was "built after the manner of the country": it was composed of huts clustered together and made of thatch and straw. . . .[23]

The entrance to these huts was low and narrow; a small hearth stood in the middle of the structure, and smoke escaped through a small hole in the roof. For decades, the desires of the Indians to remain in their own lodgings overrode the missionaries' plans to place Indian families in separate adobe cabins. In 1792, one of the diarists of a Spanish naval expedition reported that the Franciscans had offered to help the Indians build Spanish-style houses, but "they just continued not wanting to live in them, preferring to live in the open."[24]

The Indians' decision to remain in their own huts testifies to their affinity for their own architecture, a style that reflected their way of life: families overlapped, slept as one on pelts on the ground; villagers came and went; and villages relocated as seasons changed. . . .[25] The Indians' preference for their own huts also suggests a desire to maintain distance between themselves and the Franciscans, who were not welcome inside. Virtually all the Franciscan and military officials who traveled throughout Alta California stated that the Indians did not allow them to enter their homes.

What convinced the Indians to abandon their straw huts is unclear, but in 1806 and 1807 they built ninety-three small adobe houses as part of the quadrangle adjacent to the mission church.[26] Perhaps the grasses and brush were not so readily available in the transformed landscape. And, similarly, the expertise necessary to build these huts might also have been scarce in an Indian community increasingly composed of those raised in and around the mission. The completion of the last of the adobes in 1807 was followed a year later by the baptism of the Monterey region's last gentile Indians. By 1806, Indians must have realized that the mission was to be their home year-round for the foreseeable future; permanent lodgings therefore would have had an appeal and logic not present, decades earlier. Significantly, by then the Indians' numbers and families were smaller, and perhaps the family unit had taken on a more nuclear structure. The mission's population in 1807 was approximately 562. Each of the newly constructed houses, therefore, could have held a family of six, a family unit far smaller than the extended households living together in the brush huts. The movement into the adobes, therefore, came only after decades of gradual changes and adaptation.

Just as it was many years before Indians at Mission San Carlos abandoned' straw huts for adobe lodgings, Indians in general only gradually gave up their lives outside the missions. In particular, they continued subsistence gathering, hunting, and related activities even though they depended upon such practices for sustenance less and less each year. At some times, the Indians' continuation of these habits was rooted in a need to overcome temporary shortages of food, especially in the missions' first years. Franciscans encouraged Indians to fend for themselves during times of need: "It may be necessary" Serra stated during one very lean time, "to send the greater part, or all, of our new Christians who can do so to look for food in the mountains, or on the beach, as they did not so many years ago."[27] What the Franciscans viewed as a necessity in times of shortfall was ; in all likelihood seen by the Indians as an affirmation that the missions represented a blending of old and new practices. Moreover, Indians might have even seen their settlement in the missions as the padres saw the Indians' continued subsistence gathering: as a temporary strategy to weather a crisis. . . .

The amount of time the Indians spent away from the missions varied: at Mission San Diego, perhaps the least agriculturally productive of the California missions, the vast majority spent only a week or two a year at the mission; at San Carlos Borromeo, by contrast, most Indians left for only two weeks a year. At Santa Barbara, at least in 1800, one-fifth of the mission population was usually away on *paseo*. Every Sunday after Mass in front of the church, the padres would read the names of the fifth of the community that would be allowed to leave. Indians from distant villages would take two weeks; those from nearby would go for a week. Only during the wheat harvests did missionaries deny Indians leaves, and, once the harvest was completed in the summer, everyone was given two weeks off. Clearly, by the early 1800s, in the face of the Indians' continued insistence on leaving, the Franciscans realized that more than hunger lay behind the Indians' desires. In one revealing exchange, Father [Fermín Francisco de] Lasuén responded with annoyance when Indians who he believed were well fed said they were hungry and therefore needed to leave the mission for a week to gather foods. "Why, you make me think that if one were to give you a young bull, a sheep, and a *fanega* of grain every day you would still be yearning for your mountains and beaches," Lasuén responded. Then, "the brightest of the Indians who were listening to me said, smiling and half ashamed of himself, 'What you say is true, Father. It's the truth.'"[28]

Significantly, it was not just in leaving the missions for days or weeks that Indians stuck to activities that had long been meaningful to them. Late summer months were a time when the Rumsen customarily gathered at the seashore, collected sardines, hunted birds, and socialized, and Indians continued these get-togethers after they had moved to Mission San Carlos. In the summers of the mid-1770s, baptized Indians divided their time between harvesting wheat from the mission fields and gathering sardines from the shore. . . .

Even after they moved to the missions, Indians still gave a higher priority to many of their accustomed activities and beliefs than those introduced by the missionaries. In particular, Indians harvested sardines and gathered birds over many Sundays, thereby withdrawing from and in essence subverting Catholic observances. Missionaries did not see a religious component in the Indians' gatherings by the beach; if they had, they in turn would have subverted the Indians' observances. To the missionaries, the issue seemed to be how to manage the disruption of the harvest all this entailed. . . . The missionaries were spectators, separated from the Indians not just by physical space but by a cultural gulf. In supporting activities, the full import of which they did not wholly grasp and which they were often powerless to prevent, missionaries left alone the social and economic web under-girding indigenous culture. Camping on the beach, divided into groups, each around a fire, roasting and eating what they had caught, Indians . . . celebrated the land and its bounty and reaffirmed elements of harmony, continuity, and community in what to them must have been an increasingly disharmonious and chaotic world. . . .

A unique view of the persistence of customary Indian activities long into the mission period was recorded in the testimony of several baptized Chumash who testified in the murder of an Indian from Mission San Luis Obispo in the summer of 1796. For days before the murder, Indians had traveled through the mountains, hills, and coastal areas miles from the mission. Some gathered *quiotes* (yucca stalks); others, clams. They killed and processed deer, gathered wood, and visited relatives left behind in native villages. All of this, the wide-ranging travel, the eating of familiar foods, the sleeping outdoors, the renewal of family relationships, sustained the Indians' social and cultural networks and the value system that lay beneath them.[29]

Just as neophytes headed to the countryside to pursue supplemental gathering and familiar activities, gentiles opportunistically came to the missions to augment their diet with mission-produced foods. Perhaps more Indians did not move to Mission San Carlos in the mid-1770s because of the ease with which gentiles could take advantage of the mission's economic production and maintain social contacts with baptized Indians without assuming the yoke of Catholicism. In an intersection of multiple economic and social systems, gentile Indians purchased part of the mission harvest directly from the baptized Indians. With the rise of the missions, a frontier exchange economy—one no doubt embedded in both evolving and collapsing social ties and communication networks—developed in which mission Indians peddled wheat, corn, or barley for beads. According to Father Lasuén: "Our neophytes sell one measure of wheat, or corn, etc., (it is true; they sell them, and they even keep them in order to sell them) for four strings of beads. They can buy a like quantity of seeds from the countryside for just two. The Indians themselves have established this rate of exchange; and they are in the habit of saying that among the wild seeds there are none equal to our barley." At Mission San Buenaventura, large groups of Indians from the surrounding villages came and purchased various seeds and grains from mission Indians.

Apparently, in one year, Indians from the Channel Islands off the coast of Santa Barbara came to the mission and left with some eleven canoes full of food purchased from mission Indians. The trade went both ways; mission Indians not only purchased goods from the gentiles with mission-produced foods, but they also acquired food from gentiles by using as exchange the glass beads they obtained from the padres and the soldiers.[30]

Trade between mission Indians and gentiles certainly undermined the Franciscans' goal of using food as a means of attracting Indians to Catholicism and simultaneously detaching them from indigenous society and customs. But, without this trade, the missions themselves and the supply of Indian labor upon which they depended would have been weakened. Moreover, the neophyte-gentile exchange networks were as crucial to the survival of the neophytes as they were beneficial to the gentiles. Among the native groups of Alta California, as with virtually all peoples, trade was a sign of the absence of hostility. Mission Indians' refusal to trade with gentiles might have precipitated an attack on the mission. In fact, a rupture in relations between mission and gentile Indians had led Indians to attack Mission San Gabriel in its first years. Thus, what at first appears to have been a simple economic exchange of barley for beads between different Indian groups might have been an indication of lasting social bonds and the establishment of an economic and political equilibrium between Indians at and beyond the missions.[31]

Eventually, though, over a period of decades, this blending of multiple economies—this increasingly tenuous social, economic, and political symbiosis—dissolved as the environment changed, Indians' numbers declined, and Indian customs altered. In some areas more rapidly than others, Indians at the missions came to depend almost completely on mission-produced foods just as they finally abandoned their brush huts for adobe cabins. Indications of the degree to which Old World plants and animals had actually come to replace the Indians' traditional diets exist in plant and animal remains unearthed at the missions by archaeologists. For example, at Mission Santa Cruz, less than 10 percent of the vegetal remains recovered from Indian housing came from plants native to the region. Hazelnuts were the most common nonintroduced plant recovered in the mission but constituted only 8 percent of all vegetal remains. By comparison, corn and wheat—the staple of mission agriculture—constituted nearly two-thirds of the recovered remains.[32]

Animal remains show a similar reliance by mission Indians upon nonnative livestock. Archaeological work suggests that beef and mutton made up at least 80 percent of the meat consumed by Indians in some missions. The grazing habits of domesticated livestock, together with the Spaniards' policy of punishing Indians who set fire to fields—a practice that formerly had increased the browse for deer—combined to reduce the deer population. Not surprisingly, therefore, the bones of the deer, which had been the primary source of meat for Indians before colonization, were comparatively rare among excavated remains. The only native animals that remained undiminished by European colonization and a steady part of mission Indians' diets were shellfish—most importantly clams and mussels—and fish, but these had never been the Indians' main sources of food, merely supplement to the seeds, grasses, nuts, and deer upon which subsistence in the Monterey region had formerly rested.[33]

Scores of thousands of California Indians left their native villages for Franciscan missions during the colonial period. For all Indians, the movement to the missions and the acceptance of baptism were to place one foot in a completely different world. After baptism, some found they could not straddle both worlds, and they tried to retrace their steps back to their previous villages and lives. Others came to envision their lives as a more fluid continuum between missions and rancherías, and they intended to leave the missions only briefly. Franciscans had trouble distinguishing between Indians who had completely rejected the missions and those who saw their absences as temporary In what constituted an important but exaggerated polarization, the Franciscans mistakenly interpreted all unpermitted Indian absences from the missions as a rejection of Catholicism and a challenge to their authority Branding all absentee Indians as *huidos,* or fugitives, Franciscans called upon soldiers and trusted Indians to bring them back, and they flogged Indians who repeatedly left without permission.[34]

Disease, hunger, punishments—usually inflicted after Indians fled in search of food and other comforts—and a general unhappiness with the constraints of life cumulatively drove many Indians from the missions. Only on rare occasions were the Indians' motivations investigated by Spanish officials. After at least 280 Indians abandoned Mission San Francisco in the spring of 1795 (approximately a third of the mission's Indian population), the governor launched an inquiry into the causes of this mass desertion. Twenty-three male adult Indians from the East Bay were brought back to the mission and asked why they had fled.[35] The record of testimony is spare, usually not more than a sentence or two, but, when read in the context of events, it offers insight into how Indians did and did not adjust to the missions and how and when they sought to assert autonomy and independence within a controlling system.

Put simply, for many the specter of death and illness hung over the missions. Half of the Indians cited their own sickness, the death of a family member, or a fear of death as a reason for flight. Marciano Muiayaia, a forty-three-year-old Huchiun, "offered no other reason for having fled than that he had become sick." A close look at the mission's burial register suggests that no other reason would have been necessary. In the spring of 1795, an epidemic of unknown cause struck Mission San Francisco, and Indian deaths rose dramatically. Two hundred twenty-four neophytes died in 1795,

74 in March and April alone, compared to 123 in all of 1794 and 101 in all of 1796. Thus, people like Marciano Muiayaia had good reason to flee Mission San Francisco in 1795: it was an exceptionally unhealthy place that year.[36]

Eleven of the others explained that they left because of hunger. Per capita agricultural production at Mission San Francisco did decline in 1794 and 1795 as a result of drought, but not one of the Indians testified that there was not enough food. To the contrary, two acknowledged that mission-produced food might not have been bountiful in 1795 but was certainly available. Many Indians, however, especially those most recently baptized, did not consider the mission as their only source of food. For those new to the missions, the repetitive diet of corn and grain soups offered by the Franciscans was a poor and unpalatable substitute for the traditional variety to which their bodies were accustomed. Recent migrants to the missions would indeed be hungry. In fact, hunger as a stated motive for leaving correlates inversely with time spent in the mission. Of the twenty-three fugitive men who testified, thirteen had been baptized only a few months before their flight, and, of these thirteen, eleven stated hunger as a reason for their abandonment.[37]

When Indians were denied the opportunity to leave, or when they were punished for leaving against the padres' wishes, they often fled. Indian testimony clearly reveals that many found it difficult to balance the work the padres required of them with their desire to continue elements of their lives outside the missions. At San Francisco, for example, Milan Alas stated that he had been whipped by Father Antonio Dantí one afternoon after "he left work [in the tannery] to look for clams to feed his family." And Prospero Chichis claimed that he was punished by the same padre after "he had gone one night to the lagoon to hunt ducks for food."[38] Significantly, this food gathering seems to have focused on waterfowl and marine life, two sources of food that would have been minimally affected by the spread of European plants and animals. The efforts of these men to supplement their diets are useful reminder of the risky yet pragmatic flexibility of Indian food gathering at the missions; it stood in stark contrast to the Franciscans' rigid agrarian and pastoral practices.

The Indians' testimony further suggests that these men relied on their families and in particular on their wives, not on the missionaries or their functionaries, to procure and prepare some of their food. Much of the gathering and the carrying of customary foods back to the mission seems to have been the responsibility of women. In 1801, thirty years after Mission San Carlos was founded, it was still common for Indian women to return from the beach or the hills weighted down with fish, shellfish, or seeds. At Mission San Francisco, Roman Ssumis, a fifty-year-old man, stated that, after his wife and son left the mission, "he did not have anyone to give him food." Otolon Eunucse, aged twenty-four, left Mission San Francisco in part "because his wife did not care for him or give him food." And Patabo Guecuéc, aged forty-three, claimed that, after his wife and two children died, "he had no one to care for him."[39] Indian hunger and the fugitivism it generated, therefore, were related to the disintegration in the missions of the family networks and relationships Indians depended upon for gathering and food preparation.

Although it is difficult to determine how many and how often baptized Indians fled from the missions, the absolute number of permanent fugitives has been historically overestimated, if Mission San Carlos is typical. The difference between the number of Indian baptisms minus Indian deaths and the resident mission population should approximate the maximum number of Indians who fled and never returned. This calculation suggests that, at Mission San Carlos, the maximum number of permanent fugitives through 1817 was 218, or 8.4 percent of the Indians baptized through that year. Through the end of 1831, the number was 298, or roughly 10.5 percent of the 2,844 Indians baptized at the mission. At least 80 San Carlos neophytes moved to other missions, where they died and were buried, bringing the number of permanent fugitives down to around 218, or about 7.7 percent of the Indians baptized at the mission through 1831, a figure far below the 15.6 percent suggested by previous historians.[40]

The letters of the padres and notations they left in the sacramental registers also can be used to estimate the total number of Indians who abandoned Mission San Carlos at one time or another. Some of those listed might have been coerced: into returning; others likely were not so much fugitives as individuals trying to live a transient, coexistent life between missions and native villages. Thirty-nine Indians appear in the Franciscans' correspondence as huidos from San Carlos. Many of these, however, did return after an extended period away. Others lived out their days in their native rancherías. The baptismal and burial registers also reveal other Indians who left the missions, both temporarily and permanently. Sixteen neophytes were born while their parents were classified by the missionaries as fugitives, but most of these thirty-two parents came back. Sixty-eight Indians died away from the mission, most in a distant village. Some of these may safely be considered permanent fugitives, but others might have died suddenly while on paseo, on what they intended as a temporary absence, or on flights prompted by a sense of imminent death. These different sources suggest that 139 (4.9 percent of total mission baptisms) would be a conservative estimate of the number of permanent fugitives during the period 1770 through 1831.

Missionaries occasionally provided the military with lists indicating the names of absent Indians. These suggest rates of fugitivism from specific missions in a given year. One such list from San Carlos indicates a minimum rate of 1.3 percent in 1799.[41] Surviving lists from 1818 and 1819 show that rates varied from mission to mission but were normally very low, except in highly unusual circumstances, such as at San Francisco in 1795. In 1818,

4.5 percent of the Indians at San Fernando and 9.1 percent of those at Soledad were absent; yet, at Santa Barbara, the rate of fugitivism was 1.1 percent. Similarly, in 1819, less than 1 percent of the neophytes at Mission San Jose had fled. That same year, only 1.3 percent of the Indian population at Mission San Gabriel were missing; at Santa Clara, the rate was 1.8 percent. Hence the historical estimate of a fugitivism rate of 10 percent of all Indians baptized in the missions throughout the colonial period is too high; a figure of 5 percent may be more accurate, although rates fluctuated from year to year and mission to mission.[42]

Because most mission-born Indians did not live to adulthood, and life outside required skills that many mission-born Indians did not have, fugitives were far more likely to have been baptized as adults. This, of course, is not to imply that adult mission-born Indians were more content than those who came to the missions as adults; it does, however, suggest their limited options, because life in the countryside was simply not a viable option for the mission born, especially since, by the time they came of age, the natural landscape had been transformed into one more hospitable to livestock than Indians. Of the twenty-three men who fled Mission San Francisco in 1795 and later gave testimony about their motivations, at least twenty-one were baptized as adults. Similarly, most of the forty-seven fugitives from Mission San Fernando whom the padres identified by age in 1818 had been baptized as adults. Their average age when they fled was thirty-nine, and the group included thirteen men and women over age fifty, who, like the rest, must have had extensive experience living outside the mission.

At San Carlos, Indian fugitivism seems to have peaked in the early 1790s, when the mission's population was at its historic high and imperiled by an epidemic.[43] In subsequent years, flight—especially that which was intended as permanent—just does not seem to have been a feasible solution for even the most discontented. By then, few Indians lived removed from missions in the Monterey region. Trade networks through which Indians had acquired many of their staple foods had been thoroughly disrupted or even eliminated by the establishment of missions to the north, south, and east of San Carlos. And, by the early 1800s, most adults at the mission had been born there. These mission born were almost certainly less skilled than earlier generations in constructing brush huts, cultivating wild plants, and wringing an existence out of the countryside, especially one that now had grown stingy Gradually, therefore, as the world changed around them and Indians transformed their world by relocating to the missions, they lost the ability and perhaps even the desire to balance older customary activities outside the mission with life inside it. Certainly, many Indians wanted a life away from the missions, but, increasingly during the 1810s and 1820s, Indians left, not for the countryside, but to work on a Spanish ranch or in one of California's growing pueblos, where they could ply skills or trades taught by the Franciscans or Spanish artisans. These late-colonial "fugitives" then, were not so much the displaced orphans of Spanish colonization and the dual revolutions as had been their parents and grandparents—but rather their most assimilated offspring.

Flight was in general an option taken by only a minority of Indians, and it only slightly reduced the size of mission communities. The majority of Indians who went to the missions stayed at the missions and tried to continue as before where possible; thus most looked back but did not go back, and they remained at places like San Carlos, where they died of disease or suffered drastically reduced fertility long before they could replenish their numbers and reestablish their communities. Mission populations were to prove incapable of surviving in California, as they struggled everywhere in northern New Spain, perhaps even less viable than the deteriorating village communities Indians had left behind. At Mission San Carlos, for example, the population rose for a quarter of a century after 1770—swelled as it was by a stream of adults and children from neighboring villages—but then dropped, steadily and seemingly irreversibly, once high mortality and low fertility undermined natural increases and the mission had drained its pool of local gentile Indians. There, in a nutshell, is a short history of all the California missions. They offered the promise of individual and community salvation, but they destroyed nearly all those they intended to save.

Then as now, the Indians' population collapse commanded attention—not just because it affected all aspects of colonial California, both Indian and Spanish, but because this catastrophe raised profound issues about the efficacy and morality of the Franciscan enterprise, leading contemporaries to fight over the causes and significance of the Indians' decline. Soldiers blamed missionaries. Missionaries at first blamed soldiers and Indians. And Indians, it seems, blamed missionaries and other Indians for the calamitous diseases that overtook them. In some areas of colonial America, disease and Indian depopulation had played into the hands of colonists and missionaries, who pointed to the ineffectiveness of native shamans and collective wisdom as proof of the justness of their colonial enterprise. But this does not seem to have been the case in Alta California, where padres acknowledged the utility of some Indian cures and admitted the failure of their own, and consistently high rates of Indian mortality led Indians to distrust missionaries and Franciscans to question openly the legacy of their endeavor.

Scholars have long observed that native Americans experienced a drastic population decline following European contact and colonization.[44] In the mission communities of Alta California, the decline of the Indians was documented inf greater detail and with greater accuracy than nearly anywhere else in North America during the colonial period. Annual aggregate totals of births and deaths recorded by the Franciscans at Mission San Carlos and elsewhere reveal the inability of the Indian population to sustain itself through natural increase in the face of extremely high mortality. The annual crude death rate at Mission San Carlos averaged 79 deaths per thousand between 1784 and 1831. By our standards today, these are very high, but even for the eighteenth century this was extraordinary. For example, in England between 1730 and 1820, the crude death rate dropped from 31 to 24 per thousand. During epidemics, the crude death rate at Mission San Carlos surpassed 100, and, in 1828, when nearly a quarter of the Indians at the mission died, it reached a staggering 216 per thousand. The least healthy season was winter, when rain, wind, and fog rendered the mission cold, damp, and especially lethal. Since morbidity—the incidence of disease in a population—is normally greater than mortality (unless everybody dies), in a year in which between 5 and 10 percent of the mission population succumbed to disease, a far greater percentage would have been sick and possibly incapacitated by illness. Significantly, the average annual crude death rate at the mission was nearly double the average annual crude birth rate of 45 births per thousand. Thus, in nearly every year of the mission's existence, the Indian population was failing to reproduce itself. During the mission's first decades, this population collapse was masked by new arrivals, but, once the influx began to taper off in the early 1790s, the population peaked at 876 and then went into steady decline. By 1821, the last year of Spanish rule in California, the mission population stood at 374; a decade later, it was fewer than 210.[45]

Although aggregate annual statistics and crude birth and death rates allow for an observation of gross population trends, the use of nominal records and the technique of family reconstitution provide the means for an analysis of population change. Once families have been reconstituted and the life course of individuals has been charted, this method can yield evidence as to how the high mortality at Mission San Carlos was distributed among age groups and whether it was concentrated among the very young or very old. In particular, family reconstitution is useful in measuring mortality during infancy and childhood, the periods of early life when death is most likely. Similarly, estimates of the rates of fertility—or the number of births per woman—across different age cohorts can determine the degree to which the low number of births at the mission was related to individual women's having few children or to a low number of women of reproductive age.

An analysis based on family reconstitution shows that infant mortality was extremely high at Mission San Carlos. Eleven percent of all infants died in the first month of life, and nearly all these deaths occurred in the first two weeks after delivery. These rates suggest that many infants arrived prematurely, suffered from congenital birth defects, had a very low birth weight, or contracted a lethal infection at birth or during a difficult delivery. Infants whose births followed that of an older sibling by nine to fifteen months—and therefore might have been premature—were twice as likely to die in the first month of life as those whose mothers had a longer interval between births. At the mission, infant mortality declined over the first five months of life, but it increased around the twelfth month, perhaps due to weaning, teething, and the introduction of solid foods. Many Indian women nursed their children for eighteen or twenty months, but the onset of weaning would have deprived infants of some of the immunities they received from nursing; teething and open gums would have made them more susceptible to infection; and infection might have been introduced when they began to eat solid foods and drink water.[46]

All told, 37 percent of babies born at Mission San Carlos died before their first birthday. Infant mortality was a burden shared equally by both sexes: 39 percent of males and 35 percent of females died in the first year of life. The rate varied a bit with the seasons; infants born in the winter and spring had a slightly higher mortality than those born in the summer or fall.[47] Infant mortality, however, did vary by decade, and therefore it seems to have been related to both the size of the mission population—which would have had an impact on sanitary conditions—and the type of structures the Indians lived in. Infant mortality at the mission was at its highest in the 1780s, when the population surpassed seven hundred Indians, most of whom lived in the straw-hut village. The rate was at its lowest in the 1820s, when the population dipped below three hundred and all of the Indians lived in adobe structures that provided some warmth and protection from the elements. (The infant mortality rate for the 1770s is deceptive, given the small number of births at the mission in that decade.) Indian housing was not inherently unhealthful, but, under normal circumstances, Indians of the Monterey region had seasonal encampments, moving from place to place and constantly rebuilding their villages. Most villages were not inhabited year-round. This, however, was not the case with Indian brush huts at the mission, and, over time, the Indian village at Mission San Carlos appears to have become unhealthful.

San Carlos's infant mortality rate of 366 per thousand is consistent with estimated infant mortality at other California missions. Moreover, it is consistent with the highest rates in many preindustrial communities of the past. In the late 1800s, infant mortality in Europe varied from around 100 in Norway and Sweden to 250 in Germany, Austria, and Russia. And, in the seventeenth and eighteenth centuries, many European communities experienced rates on a level with those at Mission San Carlos. In England between 1580 and 1750, roughly 10 percent of all babies died in the first month; the same was true at San Carlos. In London in the 1730s and 1740s, infant mortality was above 300 per thousand. In the French countryside during the first half of the eighteenth century, the infant mortality rate fluctuated between 120 and 360 per thousand; and, in a sample of Italian towns of the early eighteenth century, infant mortality was consistently above 320 per thousand. In some regions of eighteenth-century Spain, infant mortality was well above 200 and even topped 300 per thousand in some communities. Thus, infant mortality at Mission San Carlos is best understood as being roughly equivalent to that which characterized the most unhealthful communities in Europe through the seventeenth and eighteenth centuries. And, in all likelihood, the high infant mortality at Mission San Carlos was not a dramatic increase from rates commonly experienced by California Indians before Spanish colonization.[48]

Childhood mortality—deaths between the ages of one and five—was a different story. In most societies studied by historical demographers, the rate of childhood mortality is considerably lower than that of infant mortality. But, at Mission San Carlos, the infant mortality rate of 366 per thousand was surpassed by a childhood mortality rate of 427 per thousand. In other words, 37 percent of all newborns died in the first year, and 43 percent of those who survived the first year died before their fifth birthday. The rate of childhood mortality at Mission San Carlos was nearly four times that of England in the Seventeenth and eighteenth centuries, and nearly double that of Spain in the eighteenth century.[49]

As with infant mortality, both of the sexes suffered very high childhood mortality rates: 46 percent of boys and 39 percent of girls died between ages one and five. This meant a very low expectation of life at birth: 11.2 years. At Mission San Carlos, the healthiest years of life were those between early childhood and adulthood, yet the risk of dying between ages five and fifteen was still three to four times greater than in England during the seventeenth and eighteenth centuries. Less than 25 percent of Indians born at Mission San Carlos lived to age fifteen.[50]

The comparatively healthy years that Indians enjoyed at Mission San Carlos between ages five and fifteen did not herald the onset of a long adult life. Mortality rose dramatically for men and women during the early adult years, when they became sexually active and were exposed to a host of diseases. Mortality remained high throughout adult life and increased steadily with age. Although both sexes suffered similarly high rates of mortality as infants, children, and adolescents, the dangers of childbearing led the mortality of adult women to far outstrip that of adult men. These risks were extreme during and after the first pregnancy; nearly one in three married women who survived to age fifteen died before age nineteen. For most age cohorts, adult mortality at Mission San Carlos was two to three times that found in seventeenth- and eighteenth-century England. These exceptionally high rates, in particular among women, must have contributed to the rates of infant and childhood mortality, for the death of one or both parents could have had serious consequences for the nutrition and health of children born at the mission. Furthermore, the high mortality rates among women of reproductive age lowered the crude birth rate by reducing the number of women of childbearing age.

Decades of elevated mortality among adult women created an abnormal population structure at San Carlos. In 1780, when the mission was largely composed of recently arrived villagers, the population, when distributed by age and sex, resembled a pyramid, with women between ages twenty to forty outnumbering their male counterparts. Forty years later, however, the natural pyramidal shape of the population had been destroyed, and men outnumbered women in every age group between fifteen and sixty-four.

The high mortality rates at Mission San Carlos among all age groups, and in particular among adult married women, provide only a partial explanation of the rapid collapse of the Indian population at San Carlos and throughout Alta California. Ultimately, the constant inability of Indians to offset their deaths by births doomed them. To better understand the reasons behind population growth or decline, historical demographers frequently measure the number of children produced in a community by calculating age-specific marital fertility rates.[51] At Mission San Carlos, the age-specific marital fertility rate for women aged twenty to twenty-four was 287 per thousand, suggesting that most women between those ages would have given birth to only one child during those five years. By this measure, the fertility of women at Mission San Carlos was low, lower than; that in contemporary Spain, France, England, and Germany, where women would have most likely given birth to two children between the ages twenty and twenty-four. In fact, the fertility of women at the mission was low enough that it could only have reproduced a population that experienced very low rates of mortality. Low marital fertility rates at Mission San Carlos do not seem to have been the result of the Indians' own attempts at contraception, for the Indians' fertility patterns conform to that of a population that did not practice it.[52]

To estimate the number of children a woman would have had if her childbearing experience replicated that of all women in each specific age group, one can sum the age-specific fertility rates and arrive at what demographers call the average total marital fertility rate. By this measure, married women at Mission San Carlos who lived to age fifty and stayed married would have given birth to 6 children during their reproductive lives. By modern standards, this figure may seem high, but it is low compared to societies of the past. English women gave birth on average to 7.5 children during the seventeenth and eighteenth centuries, and French women gave birth to more than 8. And, in the nineteenth century, the average total fertility of the Euromestizo elite of Mexico City was 8.5.[53]

At Mission San Carlos, however, most Indian women gave birth to far fewer than the 6 children suggested by the rate of total fertility. The average age of first marriage for mission-born women was fifteen, the average interval between marriage and the birth of the first child was a long forty-six months, and the average interval between births was thirty-three months.[54] Women who were still married at age fifty gave birth to their last child on average at age forty-one. But less than 10 percent of women who married at the mission were alive and married at fifty. When high adult female mortality is factored into the low fertility of women at the mission, the "true" total fertility of women at Mission San Carlos, plummets to a meager 1.9 children, obviously below the necessary figure of 2.6 or 2.7 sufficient to reproduce the population. Thus, although very high mortality at the mission among infants, children, and women of reproductive age was the principal cause of the population collapse at Mission San Carlos, low fertility accelerated the decline of the Indians' numbers; it meant that surviving women were producing unusually few children at a time when the community was suffering a mortality crisis. Padres and Indians, no doubt, struggled to grasp the enormity of this problem. At San Buenaventura, from 1811 to 1815, missionaries recorded the names of pregnant women and whether the women delivered a living child. Tragically, they found that nearly one in four pregnancies ended in miscarriage or stillbirth. At La Purísima, the crisis was even more severe: in 1810, the majority of pregnant women, especially the youngest, had stillborns, according to the missionaries.[55]

Excessively high mortality and low fertility throughout Alta California were largely the result of a host of chronic infectious diseases introduced to the region by the Spaniards. Close quarters, little shelter from wind, rain, or fog, and bad water, in all likelihood fouled by Spanish livestock or the Indian village itself, proved especially lethal at San Carlos. Clearly, epidemics also exacted a terrible toll: in at least nine years between 1770 and 1831, the crude death rate approached or surpassed 100 per thousand at the mission. Through 1808, when the last gentiles attained baptism, most of these epidemics—revealed through a surge and decline in the crude death rate—coincided with the arrival of large numbers of gentiles from the surrounding area. But it is not clear whether soaring death rates were the result of previously healthy Indians' living in overcrowded conditions at the mission or whether sick Indians from the countryside came to the mission after epidemics tore through their villages. In all likelihood, both scenarios reinforced one another, and the health of Indians in and out of the missions probably deteriorated in tandem.[56]

The most detailed description of the illnesses that plagued Mission San Carlos was recorded by Claude-Nicolas Rollin, who served as surgeon to the La Pérouse expedition. Rollin was to be granted a pension if he could keep the mortality rate of the *Boussoule* under 3 percent, and, in keeping with the spirit of the expedition, he was to examine the bodies of the Indians he encountered and investigate their maladies and cures. When Rollin visited the mission in 1786, he interviewed a surgeon from the presidio, a resident Franciscan, and several neophytes. Moreover, hundreds of Indians separated by sex assembled in the mission plaza and stood for inspection. Rollin learned that, in the winter, these Indians suffered from throat and lung infections; in the spring, they endured fever and digestive ailments. Summer brought dysentery. Poor care compounded ailments such that they became grievous and lethal. Failed pregnancies were common, and infants often suffered from convulsions, whooping cough, strabismus, and diarrhea.[57]

Missionaries and government officials in California had none of Rollin's training and did little more than guess at the identity of the diseases that erupted in their midst. Their accounts, however, suggest that diphtheria, dysentery, measles, influenza, and tuberculosis were the most prevalent and dangerous illnesses in the missions. In 1802, diphtheria and pneumonia were the likely culprits in an epidemic that killed 11 percent of the Indians at San Carlos. In 1806, measles carried off another 13 percent. Both of these epidemics exacted a similarly high toll at other California missions. In July 1806, Father Mariano Payeras lamented that, at Mission La Purísima, where the disease killed 150 Indians, "the measles with the consequences has cleaned out the mission and filled the cemeteries." Smallpox, the most lethal of the diseases that scourged the Indians of the New World during the colonial period, most likely did not take hold in Alta California until the late 1820s and seems not to have hit Mission San Carlos until the 1840s, Measles might have been the cause of an epidemic that killed more than 20 percent of the Indians at San Carlos in 1828.[58]

Although deadly epidemics periodically erupted in the mission, endemic disease exacted a higher cumulative toll. So many Indians died from disease every year that even in nonepidemic years the crude death rate was disastrously high. Dysentery and other waterborne illnesses were ever present. Overcrowding and the housing of single and widowed women in a cramped separate dormitory must have aided the spread of infection. Furthermore, venereal diseases, notably gonorrhea and syphilis, both highly infectious, not only contributed to the high mortality but almost certainly contributed to the low fertility that prevented the mission population from stabilizing between epidemics.[59]

Until the middle of the nineteenth century, gonorrhea was confused with syphilis or assumed to be a different manifestation of the same illness. And syphilis itself was very difficult to diagnose until modern times, as its symptoms closely resemble those of dozens of other diseases. The Franciscans, military officers, and visitors to the region, however, were convinced that syphilis was endemic to Indians in the missions; and, although their conviction that Indians lived as sexual libertines predisposed them to see syphilis in many of the Indians' ailments, their correspondence makes a powerful case that syphilis—and in all likelihood gonorrhea—were indeed prevalent among Indians in colonial California. These Indians might have first contracted a virulent form of the diseases from Portolá's expeditionary force; one account suggests that Anza brought syphilis to the province in 1776. Although the exact date will never be known, soldiers stationed at the missions and those who traveled between the presidios had ample opportunities to infect the native population and also to become infected themselves.[60]

In health reports, the Franciscans consistently suggested that syphilis was the most serious disease afflicting the Indians. Some described conditions consistent with the symptoms of the malady: visible ulcers, coughing up blood, trouble voiding. Rollin, in 1786, found syphilis to have spread widely at San Carlos. He examined Indians who suffered from lesions, ulcers, and inflammations of the lymph glands. Some missionaries went so far as to suggest that the disease was destroying the Indian population. Typical were the comments of the Franciscans at Mission San Miguel: "The dominant malady among them is venereal disease which is carrying them to the grave rapidly . . . . now for every three births there are four deaths. I do not believe there is an effective remedy for the said malady." From the early 1790s through the 1830s, the governors of the region also noted the terrible toll that venereal diseases were taking on the mission Indians. One of the most detailed descriptions of the symptoms was provided by Langsdorff:

> The most terrible of all diseases, known world wide as syphilis, is found here in all of its variations. It is common among the Spanish and the Indians and causes even greater devastation, because absolutely no medical measures are taken to prevent it. The usual results are spots on the skin, horrible rashes, persistently running sores, painful aches in the bones, throat infections, loss of the nose, deformities and death.

Langsdorff also observed among Indians "ophthalmia, rheumatism, virulent abscesses at the corners of the mouth and chronic diseases of various types," all of which he attributed to syphilis. Ophthalmia—or irritation of the eyes—can have many origins, but syphilis is not typically one of them. It is, however, one of the primary maladies suffered by children born to mothers with gonorrhea.[61]

Gonorrhea, like syphilis, is easily transmitted through sexual contact, and it most likely played a significant role in Indian suffering and population decline at Mission San Carlos. After one or two acts of coitus with an infected partner, 20–30 percent of men and 50–70 percent of women will contract the disease. Previous infection offers little or no resistance to reinfection. Gonorrhea does not kill adults, but the disease drastically reduces the health of fetuses and newborn infants: up to a third of all infected pregnant women will spontaneously abort the fetus; and up to two-thirds of infants born to infected mothers will be premature and therefore less likely to survive the first month of life. Most important, pelvic inflammatory disease (acute salpingitis), which results when gonorrhea spreads into the uterus and fallopian tubes, can often lead to sterility. Of women with untreated gonorrhea, 15–20 percent develop pelvic inflammatory disease, and 60–70 percent of those women will be completely unable to conceive a child. Gonorrhea can also destroy the fertility of men. In the era before antibiotics, the disease probably rendered sterile up to half of its male victims. Gonorrhea, therefore, almost certainly played a large role in depressing fertility and thereby hastening the decline of Indians at Mission San Carlos.[62]

During syphilis's primary and secondary phases, which can last four years after the initial exposure, the disease is highly contagious; 10–50 percent of persons exposed to it will become infected, and pregnant women can transmit it to the fetus. Over time, usually five to twenty years after exposure to the disease, the infected individual will develop what is known as late syphilis, which is not infectious but kills or incapacitates half of its victims. Syphilis does not impair conception, but it can lead to pregnancy loss. A woman who has primary or secondary syphilis is unlikely to deliver a normal-term infant: at least 30 percent of pregnancies of women with syphilis will abort spontaneously; 20 percent of infants born to women with infectious syphilis are likely to die shortly after birth. The remainder can be born with or develop lesions in the first six months of life and subsequently suffer the effects of congenital syphilis. According to the Franciscans at Mission San Gabriel, many Indians were in fact born with indications of congenital syphilis: "Many of the children at birth give evidence immediately of the only heritage their parents give them. As a result of every four children born, three die in their first or second year, while of those who survive the majority do not reach the age of twenty-five." Furthermore, syphilitic women who have spontaneous abortions may be vulnerable to sterilizing infections. Perhaps this is one reason why about half of all Indian couples at San Carlos had no children. Transmission of syphilis to the fetus is very rare after the fourth year of maternal infection, so, in an otherwise healthy population, endemic syphilis would not have a dramatic impact on fertility and population levels, for it would most likely cost women the first, and maybe even the second, of seven or eight eventual pregnancies. But, in colonial California, where adult women rarely lived long enough to have more than one or two pregnancies, syphilis would have had a devastating effect on the population's ability to reproduce itself. When one considers that gonorrhea and syphilis often accompanied one another, the low fertility rates at the mission become understandable.[63]

When Indians left the mission and returned to their native villages, they often carried infections with them, and as a result low fertility also seems to have characterized many Indian women well before they moved to the mission. One Franciscan near the end of the Spanish period claimed that it was generally agreed upon that gentile Indian women had few children. "Young [gentile] women," observed Father Ramón Abella after two decades at Mission San Francisco, "never bring children [to the mission]," women in their late twenties rarely brought two or three, and it was quite rare for women to have five or six children, "as is common with the gente de razón."[64]

There is little in the historical record suggesting how Indians in colonial California understood the diseases that were overwhelming them. Some Indians, according to one missionary, attributed the deaths of so many to herbal poisons that the Indians gave one another. Short of abstaining from sexual contact with one another or with soldiers, the Indians at the missions could do little to prevent the spread of venereal diseases among themselves. . . . At best, Indians could treat only some of the skin disorders that accompanied syphilis. At Mission San Carlos, men daily repaired to a sweat lodge, where they perspired so profusely that upon leaving they gave the "appearance of having bathed." For men, this was as much a social as a medicinal activity. And, at first, the missionaries tried to stop this practice, but they relented when they realized its medicinal value. When the men at the mission "betook themselves to the *temescal* again scarcely a man was found afflicted with the itch." Women and children, however, did not make use of this therapy, even though, once infected, they suffered from similar skin disorders. Other curatives regularly practiced by the Indians at San Carlos and throughout Alta California—such as bloodletting and the sucking of blood out of an infected body part—were perceived by the Indians as beneficial, but they might have been detrimental to the health of the sick and even hastened the transmission of contagious diseases to the healthy. Indians at San Carlos also drank herbal infusions intended to induce vomiting or sweating. . . .[65]

Topical medicines offered by the missionaries—salves, poultices, and ointments—were of no use in either preventing or limiting the effects of venereal diseases, and nothing the padres did could avert pregnancy loss or stillbirths among infected women. Indian women, in addition to suffering the losses of their stillborn children, had blame heaped upon them by missionaries: "In the beginning it was attributed to incontinence. In order to prevent it, precautions were taken; they were taught, preached to, and perhaps even punished (tactfully); but up to now it has all been in vain, and we have not yet been able to discern the origin and cause "of such deplorable events." One missionary went so far as to publicly humiliate. and punish a childless couple, demanding to know from the Indian woman: "Why don't you bear children?" After she responded "Who knows!" and desperately resisted the Franciscan's attempts to examine her reproductive organs, he had her flogged and publicly humiliated for being childless.[66]

As early as the 1810s, Franciscans in California began to suggest that venereal diseases were not just symptomatic of the Indians' unchastity but, in fact, if left unchecked, would depopulate the missions. At San Luis Obispo, the Franciscans observed that venereal disease "puts an end to men as well as women" and warned, "If no steps are taken to check these effects this conquest will soon come to an end." Those at San Gabriel were even more direct: "If the government does not supply doctors and medicine Upper California will be without any Indians at all." However, before the discovery of penicillin in the early twentieth century, there was no effective cure for either syphilis or gonorrhea, so any medicine sent to the missions would have probably done more harm than good. In any event, during Mexico's struggle for independence between 1810 and 1821, virtually no supplies of any kind were sent from central Mexico to the missions of Alta California. This neglect would not prove salutary.[67]

In 1820, on sending to his superiors in Mexico the annual population totals from all the missions, which continued to show that deaths outnumbered births for the most part, Father President Mariano Payeras wrote a most thoughtful reflection on the legacy of a half century of Spanish and Franciscan rule in Alta California. Having served in Alta California since 1793, Payeras wrote from experience, which gave his letter a mournful quality that is in marked contrast to the optimism that characterized nearly all the Franciscans' reports to their superiors in Mexico. Payeras reported that, after fifty-one years of work, the Franciscans had baptized all the Indians between San Diego and an area just north of San Francisco. The missionaries had expected their efforts to lead to a "beautiful and flourishing church and some beautiful towns which could be the joy of the sovereign majesties of heaven and earth." But instead they found themselves "with missions or rather with a people miserable and sick, with rapid depopulation of rancherías which with profound horror fills the cemeteries." Previously healthy Indians, once baptized and resident at the missions, became feeble, lost weight, and sickened and died. This was particularly true, Payeras noted, of women, "especially those who have recently become pregnant. . . ."[68]

To arrest the spread of disease and to care for the sick, the missions had built infirmaries and acquired medicines, but, Payeras lamented, all had been in vain. Like most Franciscans before and after, he concluded that the Indians' ill health was owing to their unrestrainable sexual promiscuity and that there was "no human recourse" left other than to alert his superior in Mexico that Alta California was a dying province, which would soon be "deserted and depopulated of Indians within a century of its discovery and conquest by the Spaniards." In closing his letter, Payeras expressed his plea that perhaps his superior or even the viceroy might take some unspecified measures to free the Franciscans from the "undeserved reproach" that future generations were likely to visit upon the missionaries for their role in the decimation of the Indians. Mexican independence and the end of Spanish rule in 1821 rendered any viceregal intervention impossible, and, by 1820, when Payeras wrote his letter, it was too late anyway to reverse the population decline initiated by Spanish colonization.[69]

The transformation of places like Mission San Carlos from growing centers of Indian congregation to "skeleton" communities is especially important because of the sheer magnitude of the American Indians' decline during European expansion. The picture of population collapse I have just sketched shows in detail only one of twenty-one missions in California. But what happened at Mission. San Carlos was representative of what occurred at twenty other Alta California missions and in countless villages throughout the countryside. And it is suggestive of the demographic processes set in motion whenever and wherever Europeans attempted to colonize the native peoples of the Americas. All European colonists, however, did not react alike to the Indians' destruction. For the Franciscans, without Indians alive, working, and undergoing a process of civilization, the conquest had lost its object and could even be deemed a failure. In this regard, the views of California missionaries and those elsewhere in the Spanish Borderlands differed sharply from those of contemporary Anglo-Americans during and after the colonial period. On the frontiers in British North America, where few Europeans could ever really imagine or work toward a world with Indians meaningfully included, the demise of Indians was welcomed as progress hastened.[70]

California missions by the end of the Spanish period had become places of grief for Indians and missionaries. Payeras was haunted not only by the sheer number of Indians who had died in the missions but by the memory of those he had known personally. It was "horrible to go through the missions now," Payeras confessed, "especially those of the north and ask after the many robust and young neophytes who lived there twenty years ago" when in most there was not "one or two" living whom he could remember. Although Payeras's own horror at what the missions had wrought was no doubt profound, his sadness might have been unusual among California missionaries, and in any event it can only hint at the emotions Indians themselves experienced as they buried their own, tended to the sick, and continued to live in and around the missions—places that had appeared initially as centers of refuge but had in reality proved to be graveyards for their kin.[71]

A glimpse of the emotional despair that overcame many Indians in the wake of the illnesses and deaths of so many—and one Franciscan's intolerance of such grief—was recorded by Spanish military officials who asked some of the Indians who had abandoned Mission San Francisco in 1795 and later returned why they had fled. The Indians' words are clear and direct. Their answers, in their likely acceptability to Spanish interrogators, suggest just how notorious the missions had become as maelstroms of destruction. Bridging the colonial gulf, Indians presented a litany of grief arising out of the dislocation and disorientation that accompanied the high mortality, plunging fertility, and fraying of family and Kinship networks in the missions.

TIBURCIO OBMUSA: "He explained that after his wife and daughter died, because he was crying, on five separate occasions Father Dantí ordered him whipped. For these reasons he fled."

HOMOBONO SUMIPOCSÉ: "His motive for having fled was that his brother had died on the other shore and when he cried for him they whipped him in the mission."

LIBORATO YREE: "He fled because of the deaths of his mother, two brothers, and three nephews."

NICOLÁS ENNÓT: "He explained that he ran away only because his father had died. He had no other motive."

AND MACARIO UNCATT: "He testified that, because of the deaths of his wife and one child, he fled, no other motive than that."[72]

## NOTES

1 Elinor G. K. Melville, *A Plague of Sheep: Environmental Consequences of the Conquest of Mexico* (Cambridge, 1994), 2; Alfred W. Crosby, *Ecological Imperialism: The Biological Expansion of Europe, 900–1900* (Cambridge, 1986); Jared Diamond, *Guns, Germs, and Steel: The Fates of Human Societies* (New York, 1997). On environmental change in Monterey and Alta California, see Burton L. Gordon, *Monterey Bay Area: Natural History and Cultural Imprints*, 3d ed. (Pacific Grove, Calif., 1996), 56–62; William Preston, "Serpent in the Garden: Environmental Change in Colonial California," in Ramón A. Gutiérrez and Richard J. Orsi, eds., *Contested Eden: California before the Gold Rush* (Berkeley, Calif., 1998), 260–98.

2 Despite a lack of evidence supporting the theory that epidemics preceded Spanish colonization in California, William L. Preston has advanced this hypothesis with vigor and creativity. See his "Portents of Plague from California's Protohistoric Period," *Ethnohistory*, XLIX (2002), 69–121; see also Lisa Kealhofer, "The Evidence for Demographic Collapse in California," in Brenda J. Baker and Kealhofer, eds., *Bioarchaeology of Native American Adaptation in the Spanish Borderlands* (Gainesville, Fla., 1996), 56–92, esp. 56–64.

3 Melville, *A Plague of Sheep*, 5; Alfred W. Crosby, Jr., *The Columbian Exchange: Biological and Cultural Consequences of 1492* (Westport, Conn., 1972); Crosby, "Virgin Soil Epidemics as a Factor in the Aboriginal Depopulation in America," *WMQ*, 3d Ser., XXXIII (1976), 289–299.

4 Francisco Palóu, *Historical Memoirs of New California . . .*, ed. and trans. Herbert Eugene Bolton, 4 vols. (1926; Berkeley, Calif., 1966), I, 50–52; "Libro de cuentas, inventario de la misión," 14a, LDS film 0913303, Mission San Carlos (hereafter cited as San Carlos account book). This document has irregular and at times illegible page numbers. Horses and mules were used for transportation; cattle, for food; and labor; and sheep, for wool and food. Pigs were never raised in large numbers at the mission, since, the padres considered them dirty and their meat foul.

5 On the mission's cattle acquisitions, see "Ganado y vacuno," San Carlos account book (no clear page number), and also page 9. On the sheep, see Junípero Serra, Aug. 17, 1775, Monterey, in Antoine Tibesar, ed. and trans., *Writings of Junipero Serra*, 4 vols. (Washington, D.C., 195501966), II, 307; Serra, annual report on the missions, Aug. 15, 1779, Mission San Carlos, ibid., III, 355; and see Melville, *A Plague of Sheep*, 6–7, esp. 47–59, for the four stages of the ungulate irruption." Ungulates are "herbivores with hard horny hooves" (6).

6 Serra, report on the missions, July 1, 1784, Monterey, in Tibesar, ed. and trans., *Writings of Serra*, IV, 275; Matías de Santa Catalina Noriega, January 1785, San Carlos account book (no clear page number).

7 Rebecca Allen, *Native Americans at Mission Santa Cruz, 1791–1834: Interpreting the Archaeological Record*, Perspectives in California Archaeology, V (Los Angeles, Calif., 1998), 42–43.

8 Account of rations distributed at Monterey, June–August 1770, Archivo General de la Nación, Mexico City [hereafter AGN], Indiferente de Guerra, legajo 161b, 160b–161a.

9 San Carlos account book, 8. The mission received additional agricultural implements and seeds when the *San Antonio* arrived again in May 1771. See Serra, memorandum, June 20, 1771, Junípero Serra to Francisco Palóu, June 21, 1771, Serra to Rafael Verger, Aug. 8, 1772, all in Tibesar, ed. and trans., *Writings of Serra*, I, 227–35, 240–41 257 (my trans.).

10 San Carlos account book, 16; Serra to Palóu, Aug. 18, 1772, Serra to Antonio María de Bucareli y Ursúa, May 21, 1773, both in Tibesar, ed. and trans., *Writings of Serra*, I, 265, 353.

11 San Carlos account book, 15a, 15b; Serra, report on the missions, July 1, 1784, in Tibesar, ed. and trans., *Writings of Serra*, IV, 269, 273.

12 In consultation with faculty at Oregon State University's College of Agriculture, I determined this figure by multiplying the harvest of the principal crops by estimated harvest per acre. Wheat harvest of 835 fanegas (1.5 bushels per fanega) at 20 bushels an acre equals 62.6 acres. Corn harvest of 971 fanegas at 40 bushels an acre equals 36.4 acres. Barley harvest of 740 fanegas at 20 bushels an acre equals 55.5 acres for a total of 154.5 acres cultivated. This does not include any of the vegetables or fruit grown at the mission (San Carlos account book, 17a).

13 Serra, report on the missions, July 1, 1784, in Tibesar, ed. and trans., *Writings of Serra*, IV, 271, 273; San Carlos account book, 17a. Nearly all of the harvest was in corn, wheat, and barley. The majority of gentiles that year attained baptism in late summer, fall, and early winter, during and after the harvest.

14 For the primacy of disease in the movement of Indians to Spanish missions, see Daniel T. Reff, *Disease, Depopulation, and Culture Change in Northwestern New Spain, 1518–1764* (Salt Lake City, Utah, 1991); Reff, "The Jesuit Mission Frontier in Comparative Perspective: The Reductions of the Río de la Plata and the Missions of Northwestern Mexico, 1588–1700" in Donna J. Guy and Thomas E. Sheridan, eds., *Contested Ground: Comparative Frontiers on the Northern and Southern Edges of the Spanish Empire* (Tucson, Ariz., 1998), 16–31. Reff pays far more attention to disruptions originating in disease than to changes in the environment caused by the introduction of new plants and animals.

15 Daniel K. Richter, *Facing East from Indian Country: A Native History of Early America* (Cambridge, Mass., 2001); Harry W. Crosby, *Antigua California: Mission and Colony on the Peninsular Frontier, 1697–1768* (Albuquerque, N.Mex., 1994), 209–221; Robert H. Jackson, *Indian Population Decline: The Missions of Northwestern New Spain, 1687–1840* (Albuquerque, N.Mex., 1994), 69–83; Mardith Keithly Schuetz, "The Indians of the San Antonio Missions, 1718–1821" (Ph.D. diss., University of Texas, Austin, 1980); Schuetz, "Demography of the Mission Indians," in Clark Spencer Larsen, ed., *Native American Demography in the Spanish Borderlands*, Spanish Borderlands Sourcebooks, II (New York, 1991), 206–231. On population decline in the missions of Sonora, see Jackson, *Indian Population Decline*, 61–69; on the economy of the missions, see Cynthia Radding, *Wandering Peoples: Colonialism, Ethnic Spaces, and Ecological Frontiers in Northwestern Mexico, 1700–1850* (Durham, N.C., 1997).

16 For two extreme and divergent positions on the role of Spanish coercion in Indian baptisms in Alta California, see Sherburne F. Cook, *The Conflict between the California Indian and White Civilization* (Berkeley, Calif., 1976); Francis F. Guest, "An Examination of the Thesis of S. F. Cook on the Forced Conversion of the Indians in the California Missions," *Southern California Quarterly* [hereafter SCQ], LXI (1979), 1–77.

17 For these Indians' villages and political affiliations, see Randall Milliken, *Ethnohistory of the Rumsen*, Papers in Northern California Anthropology, no. 2 (Berkeley, Calif., 1987), 43–58. The villages of Achasta, Tucutnut, Ichxenta, Socorronda, and Echilat were located in the valleys of the Carmel River and San Jose Creek both of which flow into the sea adjacent to Mission San Carlos.

18 Letter of Joseph María Bertrán, May 2, 1798, testimony of soldiers, Dec. 1–2, 1798, Monterey Presidio, both in AGN, California [hereafter CA], XXI, expediente 12,

400a–401b, 414a–419a. By the mid-1790s, when the drought struck, the animals' needs exceeded the land's carrying capacity. The crash that ensued conforms to Stage 3 of the cycles of ungulate irruptions described by Melville, *A Plague of Sheep*, 53–55. On variability of climate in California and its potentially drastic impact upon native subsistence, see Lester B. Rowntree, "Drought during California's Mission Period, 1769–1834," *Journal of California and Great Basin Anthropology*, VII (1985), 7–20; H. C. Fritts and G. A. Gordon, "Reconstructed Annual Precipitation for California," in M. K. Hughes et al., *Climate from Tree Rings* (New York, 1982), 185–191; Daniel O. Larson, "California Climatic Reconstructions," *Journal of Interdisciplinary History*, XXV (1994), 225–253.

19 Testimony of soldiers, Dec. 1–2, 1798, Monterey Presidio, AGN, CA, XXI, expediente 12, 414a–419a.

20 Estevan Tapis to José Joaquín de Arrillaga, cited in Robert Archibald, *The Economic Aspects of the California Missions* (Washington, D.C., 1978), 180. During the drought and the following decade, nearly eight hundred Indians came to the Franciscan missions of the region, and more than a third of those went to Mission San Carlos. For animal counts, see Archibald, *Economic Aspects*, 179–181. For quote, see Georg Heinrich von Langsdorff, *Remarks and Observations on a Voyage around the World from 1803 to 1807*, ed. Richard A. Pierce, trans. Victoria Joan Moessner, 2 vols. (Kingston, Ont., 1993), II, 99.

21 Raymundo Carrillo, Oct. 13, 1802, Santa Barbara, AGN, Provincias Internas [hereafter PI], CCXVI, expediente 1, 104b–111a, est. 109a–109b.

22 Langsdorff, *Remarks and Observations*, ed. Pierce, trans. Moessner, II, 114–16.

23 For Fages's quote, see Herbert Ingram Priestley, ed. and trans., *A Historical, Political, and Natural Description of California, by Pedro Fages, Soldier of Spain . . .* (Berkeley, Calif., 1937), 64–65. Fages stated that there were 151 Indians at the mission, and the sacramental registers suggest that this must have been in the fall of 1773.

24 Claude-Nicolas Rollin, "Memoire physiologique et pathologique surles Américains," Marine, Ser. 3JJ, 387, reel 1, file 7, 13, Archives nationales, Paris (hereafter cited as Rollin, "Memoire physiologique"); Donald C. Cutter, *California in 1792: A Spanish Naval Visit* (Norman, Okla., 1990), 134. On Rollin, see Dunmore, ed. and trans., *Journal of La Pérouse*, I, lxxxi–lxxxiii.

25 Rollin, "Memoire physiologique," 13–14.

26 James Culleton, *Indians and Pioneers of Old Monterey* (Fresno, Calif., 1950), 171. Culleton puts the number of new houses at eighty-nine. For a report of ninety-three houses constructed over two years, see Robert H. Jackson and Edward D. Castillo, *Indians, Franciscans, and Spanish Colonization: The Impact of the Mission System on California Indians* (Albuquerque, N.Mex., 1995), app. 3, 146–47.

27 Serra to Fernando de Rivera y Moncada, Oct. 24, 1775, Monterey, in Tibesar, ed. and trans., *Writings of Serra*, II, 367 (my trans.). See also Serra to Bucareli, May 21, 1773, ibid., 1, 347. Later that year, Palóu noted that the food shortage was so severe that the Indians could not stay at the mission (Palóu, *Historical Memoirs*, ed. and trans. Bolton, III, 230–31).

28 Tapis and Juan Cortés to Lasuén, Oct. 30, 1800, Mission Santa Barbara, AGN, PI, CCXVT, expediente 1, 82b; Lasuén, "Refutation of Charges," June 19, 1801, Monterey, AGN, PI, CCXVI, expediente 1, 69b, and in Finbar Kenneally, ed. and trans., *Writings of Fermín Francisco de Lasuén*, 2 vols. (Washington, D.C.: 1965), II, 203–4.

29 See "Causa criminal contra Silverio y Rosa . . .," AGN, CA, LXV, expediente 6, 241a–301b.

30 Lasuén, "Refutation of Charges," June 19, 1801, Monterey, AGN, PI, CCXVI, expediente 1, 67b–68a, and in Kenneally, ed. and trans., *Writings of Lasuén*, II, 200–202; Señán and Vicente de Santa María, response to question no. 6, AGN, PI, CCXVI, expediente 1, 92b–93b. Lasuén does not specifically refer to the Indians of Mission San Carlos in his statement; he speaks of "our" Indians, which could mean all the Indians under the control of the Franciscans or those at Mission San Carlos. When he was at San Diego years earlier, he had noted a similar exchange between neophytes and gentiles. For a full investigation of a "frontier exchange economy," see Daniel H. Usner, Jr., *Indians, Settlers, and Slaves in a Frontier Exchange Economy: The Lower Mississippi Valley before 1783* (Chapel Hill, N.C., 1992).

31 Serra to Bucareli, May 21, 1773, Mexico City, in Tibesar, ed. and trans., *Writings of Serra*, I, 359–61.

32 Allen, *Native Americans at Mission Santa Cruz*, 43–47. No similar archaeological studies were undertaken for Mission San Carlos.

33 Ibid., 55–61.

34 On the missionaries' justifications of these punishments, see Hackel, *Children of Coyote*, Chapter 8.

35 For a discussion of the events surrounding this mass flight from the mission, see Milliken, *A Time of Little Choice*, 137–146. Soldiers stated that too much work, too much punishment, and too much hunger had caused the Indians to flee the mission. On the twenty-three adult Indians, see testimony of runaway Indians, Aug. 12, 1797, San Francisco Presidio, AGN, CA, LXV, expediente 2, 108a–109a. Milliken, in *A Time of Little Choice*, has provided a translation of the Indians' testimony (299–303). I have consulted the original for my quotations and used Milliken for the Indians' native names and biographical information.

36 Testimony of Marciano Muiayaia, Aug. 12, 1797, San Francisco Presidio, AGN, CA, LXV, expediente 2, 108a; Mission San Francisco de Asís libro de difuntos, 1776–1809, Bancroft Library, University of California, Berkeley [herafter BL]. In 1795, the crude death rate at Mission San Francisco was 250 (Milliken, *A Time of Little Choice*, app. 2, 266).

37 On the Costanoans' diet, see Richard Levy, "Costanoan," in William C. Sturtevant, ed., Handbook of North American Indians, VIII: California (Washington, D.C.: 1978) [hereafter *HNAI*], VIII, 491. See also Milliken, A *Time of Little Choice*; Robert F. Heizer and Albert B. Elsasser, *The Natural World of the California Indians* (Berkeley, Calif., 1980). Paleopathological studies do suggest that some Indians in the missions: might have suffered from nutritional deficiencies (Phillip L. Walker, Patricia Lambert, and Michael J. DeNiro, "The Effects of European Contact on the Health of Alta California Indians," in David Hurst Thomas, ed., *Columbian Consequences*, 3 vols. (Washington, D.C., 1989–1991) [hereafter CC], 1, 352–55). The link between population change and nutrition and the degree to which malnutrition increases the human body's susceptibility to disease is not as clear as it once appeared. See Massimo Livi-Bacci, *Population and Nutrition: An Essay on European Demographic History* (Cambridge, 1990). Indians who had been at the mission for several years suggested that it was the padres' corporal punishment that led them to flee.

38 Testimony of Milan Alas and Prospero Chichis, Aug. 12, 1797, San Francisco Presidio, AGN, CA, LXV, expedierte 2, 108b–109a; Indian names from Milliken, *A Time of Little Choice*, 302–3.

39 Lasuén, "Refutation of Charges," June 19, 1801, Mission San Carlos, in Kenneally, ed. and trans., *Writings of Lasuén*, II, 209; testimony of runaway Indians (Roman Ssumis, Otolon Eunucse, and Patabo Guecuéc), Aug. 12, 1797, San

Francisco Presidio, AGN, CA, LXV, expediente 2, 108a–108b; Indian names from Milliken, *A Time of Little Choice*, 300–302.

40 Sherburne F. Cook was the first scholar to attempt to calculate the number of fugitives from the missions (Cook, "Population Trends among the California Mission Indians" *Ibero-Americana*, XVII [1940] 399–446, esp. 425–526, rpt. in Cook, ed., *Conflict*). Cook revisited the issue of Indian fugitivism in "The Indian versus the Spanish Mission," *Ibero-Americana*, XXI (1943), 1–194, esp. 51, rpt. in Cook, ed., *Conflict*.

41 The list from 1799 is incomplete, since the padres only listed those Indians whose whereabouts were known (Baltasar Carnicer and Francisco Pujol to Diego de Borica, Apr. 3, 1799, Taylor Coll., doc. 207, Henry E. Huntington Library, San Marino, CA) [hereafter HL].

42 Marcos Antonio de Vitoria to José Antonio de la Guerra, June 3, 1818, San Fernando, De la Guerra collection [herafter DLG], folder 1016, HL; Antonio Ripoll, June 16, 1818, Santa Barbara, ibid., box 18, folder 827; Antonio Jayme to Pablo Vicente de Solá, Dec. 9, 1818, Taylor Coll., doc. 962, HL; Narciso Durán to governor, Dec. 31, 1819, Taylor Coll., doc. 964, HL; José María Zalvidea to Solá, Oct. 13, 1819, Taylor Coll., doc. 978, HL; José Viader to Solá, Nov. 1, 1819, Santa Clara, Taylor Coll., doc. 958, HL; Jayme to Solá, Dec. 9, 1818, Taylor Coll., doc. 962, HL; Cook, *Conflict*, 59–61.

43 I base this conclusion in part on the fact that after 1795 no Indians baptized at San Carlos were born while their parents were fugitives.

44 For modern introductions to the literature on Indian depopulation, see Nicolás Sánchez-Albornoz, coord., special issue of *Revista de Indias*, LXIII, no. 227 (January–April 2003); Russell Thornton, "Population History of Native North Americans," in Michael R. Haines and Richard H. Steckel, eds., *A Population History of North America* (Cambridge, 2000), 9–50; Thornton, "Health, Disease, and Demography," in Philip J. Deloria and Neal Salisbury, eds., *A Companion to American Indian History* (Malden, Mass., 2002), 68–84; see also John W. Verano and Douglas H. Ubelaker, eds., *Disease and Demography in the Americas* (Washington, D.C., 1992); Kenneth F. Kiple and Stephen V. Beck, eds., *Biological Consequences of European Expansion, 1450–1800* (Hampshire, 1997); Ann F. Ramenofsky, *Vectors of Death: The Archaeology of European Contact* (Albuquerque, N.Mex., 1987). A particularly useful examination of Indian population change in the missions of Texas is Mardith Keithly-Schuetz, "Demography of the Mission Indians," in Larsen, ed., *Native American Demography in the Spanish Borderlands*, Spanish Borderlands Sourcebooks, II, 206–231.

45 There is an extensive literature on Indian population decline in Alta California. Among the most important works are Cook, *Conflict;* Cook, *The Population of the California Indians, 1769–1970* (Berkeley, Calif., 1976); Jackson, *Indian Population Decline*. The crude death rate (CDR) is the number of deaths in a year divided by the total population at midyear and multiplied by 1,000. The crude birth rate (CBR) is the births in a year divided by the total population at midyear and multiplied by 1,000.

46 Josep Bemabeu-Mestre, "Problèmes de santé et causes de décès infantiles en Espagne (1900–1935)," *Annales de démographie historique* (1994), 61–77, esp. 70. On the Indians' nursing customs, see Rollin, "Memoire physiologique," 27.

47 Although more infants died in December, January, February, and March than other months, more were also born in those months.

48 Phillip L. Walker and John R. Johnson, "For Everything There Is a Season: Chumash Indian Births, Marriages, and Deaths at the Alta California Missions," in

D. Ann Herring and Alan C. Swedlund, eds., *Human Biologists in the Archives: Demography, Health, Nutrition, and Genetics in Historical Populations* (Cambridge, 2003), 53–77; Johnson, "The Chumash and the Missions," in CC, I, 365–75, esp. 372; Carlo A. Corsini and Pier Paolo Viazzo, "Recent Advances and Some Open Questions in the Long-term Study of Infant and Child Mortality" in Corsini and Viazzo, eds., *The Decline of infant and Child Mortality: The European Experience, 1750–1990* (The Hague, 1997), xiii; E. A. Wrigley, R. S. Davies, J. E. Oeppen, and R. S. Schofield, *English Population History from Family Reconstitution, 1580–1837*, 226, table 6.4; John Landers, *Death and the Metropolis: Studies in the Demographic History of London, 1670–1830* (Cambridge, 1993), 192; Jacques Dupâquier, "La France avant la transition démogtaphique," Guiliano Pinto and Eugenio Sonnino, "L'Italie," both in Jean-Pierre Bardet and Dupâquier, eds., *Histoire des populations de l'Europe: Des origines aux prémices de la révolution démographique*, I (Paris, 1997), 452, 501; David Sven Reher, *Town and Country in Pre-industrial Spain: Cuenca, 1550–1870* (Cambridge, 1990), 111, table 3.20; Reher, Vicente Pérez-Moreda, and Bernabeu-Mestre, "Assessing Change in Historical Contexts: Childhood Mortality Patterns in Spain during the Demographic Transition," in Corsini and Viazzo, eds., *Decline of Infant Mortality*, 39, table 2.1. See also Johnson, "Chumash Social Organization: An Ethnohistoric Perspective" (Ph.D. diss., University of California, Santa Barbara, 1988), 143–146, tables 5.2, 5.3, 5.4.

49 Wrigley, Davies, Oeppen, and Schofield, *English Population History*, 250–51, table 6.10; Reher, *Town and Country in Pre-industrial Spain*, 111, table 3.21; Reher, Pérez-Moreda, and Bernabeu-Mestre, Assessing Change in Historical Contexts," in Corsini and Viazzo, eds., *Decline of Infant Mortality*, 39, table 2.1.

50 Wrigley, Davies, Oeppen, and Schofield, *English Population History*, 250–51, table 6.10.

51 This measure has the advantage of relating births registered in a community, not to the overall population of the community, as with the crude birth rate, but rather only to those women at risk of having those births. In other words, the age-specific marital fertility rate measures the number of children produced by women at different periods in their reproductive life, commonly accepted as between the ages fifteen and forty-nine. The rate is calculated by dividing the number of births: occurring to women in a particular age cohort by the number of years women of that age cohort were exposed to the risk of bearing a child. For example, between the ages twenty and twenty-four, a married woman will have five years of exposure to the risk of having a child. If, during those five years, she has one child, her marital fertility rate will be 200 per 1,000 (1/5 × 1,000).

52 Dupâquier, "La France avant la transition démographique," in Bardet and Dupâquier, eds., *Histoire des populations de l'Europe*, 453; John E. Knodel, *Demographic Behavior in the Past: A Study of Fourteen German Village Populations in the Eighteenth and Nineteenth Centuries* (Cambridge, 1988), 257; Reher, *Town and Country in Pre-industrial Spain*, 92; Wrigley, Davies, Oeppen, and Schofield, *English Population History*, 355. It is unlikely that an underregistration of births at the mission explains the low age-specific marital fertility rates at Mission San Carlos, and the rates have been calculated using Louis Henry's method designed to compensate for underregistration of births. Indian women at San Carlos measured .004 on the Coale-Trussel Index, where a value greater than 0.20 suggests that birth control is likely and a value greater than 0.30 suggests it is certain.

53 Robert McCaa, "The Peopling of Mexico from Origins to Revolution," in Richard Steckel and Michael Haines, eds., *The Population History of North America* (Cambridge, 2000), 250.

54 Forty-six months is a long interval, suggesting that many young women lost their first child. For women who delivered in the first thirty-six months after marriage—and most likely therefore would have not lost a first pregnancy—the interval between marriage and the birth of the first child was twenty-two months.
55 Cf. Cook, *Conflict*, 415–16; and see "Book of Clothing Distribution to Indians, Mission San Buenaventura, 1806–1815," Archival Center of the Archdiocese of Los Angeles (this record appears on the last page of the book); Mariano Payeras to Tapis, Jan. 13, 1810, La Purísima, in Donald C. Cutter, ed. and trans., *Writings of Mariano Payeras* (Santa Barbara, Calif., 1995), 50. Only 37 of the 390 families remained under observation when the woman reached age fifty.
56 Of course, not all premature deaths were the result of disease. Mission burial registers record that Indians throughout Alta California died after bear attacks, insect bites, and acts of violence; some suffered fatal injuries when they were gored by cattle, crushed by wagons, or thrown from horses.
57 Rollin, "Memoire physiologique," 18, 27.
58 Cook, *Conflict*, 17–30; Milliken, *A Time of Little Choice*, 172–176, 193–200; Phillip L. Walker and John R. Johnson, "Effects of Contact on the Chumash Indians," in Verano and Ubelaker, eds., *Disease and Demography*, 127–39, esp. 133–35; Mariano Payeras to Josef Vinalls [*sic*], July 2, 1806, La Purísima, in Cutter, ed. and trans., *Writings of Mariano Payeras*, 34; Cook, "Smallpox in Spanish and Mexican ' California, 1770–1845," *Bulletin of the History of Medicine*, VII (1939), 153–91. See also Robert M. Moses, "Smallpox Immunization in Alta California: A Story Based on José Estrada's 1821 Postscript," *SCQ*, LXI (1979), 125–45.
59 Joseph A. McFalls, Jr., and Marguerite Harvey McFalls, *Disease and Fertility* (Orlando, Fla., 1984); David E. Stannard, "Disease and Infertility: A New Look at the Demographic Collapse of Native Populations in the Wake of Western Contact," in Kiple and Beck, eds., *Biological Consequences of European Expansion*, 297–322.
60 "Gonorrhea," in Kenneth F. Kiple, ed., *The Cambridge World History of Human Disease* (Cambridge, 1993), 759–60; McFalls and McFalls, *Disease and Fertility*, 310; Cook, *Conflict*, 23. The missionaries and soldiers commonly identified syphilis as *gálico*, after the *morbus gallicus* known to Europe since the late fifteenth century. See, for example, Antonio Grajera to Borica, Aug. 14, 1795, San Diego, Archives of California, C–A7, 355, BL; Arrillaga, June 19, 1797, Archives of California, C–A 55, 102, BL; Luis Argüello, Oct. 31, 1807, San Francisco, Archives of California, C–A 16, 306, BL; Ramón Abella to Solá, Jan. 29, 1817, Mission San Francisco, Taylor Coll., doc. 698, HL; Abella to Solá, July 31, 1817, Mission San Francisco, Taylor Coll., doc. 727, HL.
61 Maynard J. Geiger and Clement W. Meighan, eds. and trans., *As the Padres Saw Them: California Indian Life and Customs as Reported by the Franciscan Missionaries, 1813–1815* (Santa Barbara, CA: 1976) [hereafter *APST*], 71–80, esp. 75–76; Abella to Solá, July 31, 1817, Mission San Francisco, Taylor Coll., doc. 727, HL; Cook, *Conflict*, 26–27; Rollin, "Memoire physiologique," 23. Langsdorff quote in Langsdorff, *Remarks and Observations*, ed. Pierce, trans. Moessner, II, 125.
62 Here I follow the lead of other scholars and assume that the modern-day progression of disease is similar to that of the past. See McFalls and McFalls, *Disease and Fertility*, 260, 262, 276–77; Paolo Miotti and Gina Dallabetta, "The Other Sexually Transmitted Diseases," in Marie-Louise Newell and Jonas McIntyre, eds., *Congenital and Perinatal Infections: Prevention, Diagnosis, and Treatment* (Cambridge, 2000), 278–79. When not treated with antibiotics, gonorrhea in

men progressed to epididymitis in 58 percent of untreated cases, and 50–85 percent of those men became sterile (McFalls and McFalls, 298–299).

63 McFalls and McFalls, *Disease and Fertility*, 323, 333, 336; "Syphilis," in Kiple, *Cambridge World History of Disease*, 1029; *APST*, 105. See also Stannard, "Disease and Infertility," in Kiple and Beck, eds., *Biological Consequences of European Expansion*, 340.

64 Abella to Solá, July 31, 1817, Mission San Francisco, Taylor Coll., doc. 727, HL. Given the large number of Indians baptized at the missions and the Franciscans' awareness about when they had baptized complete villages and the last Indians from certain villages, it seems unlikely that women with children simply stayed away from the missions.

65 *APST*, 77. Fever therapy can arrest the syphilitic infection and reduce its virulence, but only once it has progressed to late syphilis (McFalls and McFalls, *Disease and Fertility*, 347). It is not clear exactly what disease the padres were referring to here when they mentioned "the itch." Perhaps they saw only the symptoms of an unknown disease. In addition to syphilis, the itch could have been scabies. Regarding the Indians' curatives, current medical science would suggest that bloodletting and -sucking did not improve the health of the sick. But Indians believed in them, and they might indeed have had some sort of salutary effect. See also Rollin, "Memoire physiologique," 18, 23–24, for the Indians' curatives and method of preparing a sweat lodge.

66 Milliken, *A Time of Little Choice*, 173; Payeras to Tapis, Jan. 13, 1810, La Purísima, in Cutter, ed. and trans., *Writings of Mariano Payeras*, 50. See also *APST*, 106. On the padre's punishment of the childless woman, see Lorenzo Asisara, in Edward D. Castillo, "The Native Response to the Colonization of Alta California," in *CC*, 1, 377–94, esp. 380.

67 *APST*, 105. Mercury was the most common treatment in the eighteenth and nineteenth centuries, but it was highly toxic. Treatment of pelvic inflammatory disease that results from gonorrhea is still quite complicated (McFalls and McFalls, *Disease and Fertility*, 282–83).

68 Payeras to [Baldomero López], Feb. 2, 1820, La Purísima, in Cutter, ed. and trans., *Writings of Mariano Payeras*, 225–28, esp. 225.

69 Ibid., 226–228. The viceroy had been alerted to the prevalence of unchecked diseases in the California missions as early as 1805; see José Vicuña Muro to José de Iturrigaray, May 10, 1805, Mexico, Archives of California, C–A 12, 62–64, BL; Iturrigaray to Arrillaga, June 6, 1805, Mexico, Archives of California, C–A 12, 64, BL.

70 Richter, *Facing East from Indian Country;* Gregory Evans Dowd, *War under Heaven: Pontiac, the Indian Nations, and the British Umpire* (Baltimore, 2002).

71 Payeras to José Gasol, Feb. 2, 1820, La Purísima, in Cutter, ed. and trans., *Writings of Mariano Payeras*, 227.

72 Testimony of runaway Indians, Aug. 12, 1797, San Francisco Presidio, AGN, CA, LXV, expediente 2, 108a–109a. I have consulted the original for my quotations and used Milliken, *A Time of Little Choice*, for the Indians' native names.

# Part III

# GENDER

Frequently sites of encounter and difference, borderlands can lay bare a society's most basic, shared assumptions through contrast with the alien. Indeed, encounter can do more than illuminate one's own values and priorities; it can redefine and deepen a shared sense of collective identity in opposition to whoever resides on the other side of a frontier. No category is more elemental to social structure and hierarchy than gender. Moreover, gendered language, images, and metaphors are frequently mobilized to serve our most basic modes of thinking about and characterizing the natural and social world. Today we may acknowledge that gender norms are specific to time and place, and that they can differ significantly between societies. But historically assumptions about what is properly masculine and feminine, applied to any variety of realms, have been so deeply ingrained in social life and language as to seem immutable, or divinely sanctioned, or "natural."

Inevitably, then, gender played a significant role in structuring borderland interactions in North America. The study of gender in such contexts encourages a focus on relationships: precisely because it invites, even demands comparison, gender analysis facilitates shared borderland stories. Pioneering work in this vein emerged in the 1980s from scholars working at the intersection of women's history and Indian history. Like scholars in other fields, borderlands historians soon began interrogating constructions of masculinity as well as femininity. Ramón Gutiérrez, Alberto Hurtado, Susan Sleeper-Smith, James Brooks, and Juliana Barr are among the borderlands scholars who have put gender analysis at the center of revelatory books. As they and others have shown, there were myriad ways in which members of one society could mobilize the perceived shortcomings of another's gender system to ridicule or dehumanize them. But perceived similarities in gender values could by the same token help bridge borderland divides and serve as a foundation for diplomacy, commerce, and even personal or collective alliance.[1]

Few essays did more to demonstrate the potential of gender analysis to illuminate borderland dynamics than Kathleen Brown's important piece, "The Anglo-Algonquian Gender Frontier." Brown takes as her subject an encounter that has since become iconic in American history, between the indigenous peoples of the Chesapeake Bay and the first English colonists at Jamestown (nearly all of whom were male). Brown reveals the startling and often contradictory ways in which the forced comparison of "culturally-specific manhoods and womanhoods" shaped perceptions of self and other in this borderland, and helped to structure the gathering regional conflict.[2]

The second chapter in this section is less an explicit exercise in gender analysis than an intimate demonstration of how attention to gendered assumptions on borderlands can illuminate interethnic relationships and imaginings. In "Virgins and Cannibals," Alan Greer takes us to seventeenth-century New France and examines European representations of two remarkable indigenous women, Marie-Thérèse Tegaiaguenta and Catherine (Kateri) Tekakwitha. Both women lived as devout members of a Catholic Mohawk community near the St. Lawrence River. Convinced that Catherine was a genuine saint, two Jesuits penned long, detailed accounts of her short life. Contrasting Catherine's holy feminine virtues with Thérèse's supposed shortcomings, these accounts open intimate windows into the gender encounter in the borderlands of New France.

## NOTES

1 Pioneering works include Sylvia Van Kirk, *"Many Tender Ties": Women in Fur-Trade Society in Western Canada, 1670-1870* (Winnipeg: Watson & Dwyer, 1980); and Jennifer S. H. Brown, *Strangers in Blood: Fur Trade Company Families in Indian Country* (Vancouver: University of British Columbia Press, 1980). For a helpful overview of the literature, see Ann M. Little, "Gender and Sexuality in the North American Borderlands, 1492–1848," *History Compass* 7:6 (Nov., 2009): 1606–1615. A very incomplete list of distinguished books in this tradition includes Ramón A. Gutiérrez, *When Jesus Came, The Corn Mothers Went Away: Marriage, Sexuality, and Power in New Mexico, 1500-1846* (Stanford: Stanford University Press, 1991); Albert L. Hurtado, *Intimate Frontiers: Sex, Gender, and Culture in Old California* (Albuquerque: University of New Mexico Press, 1999); Susan Sleeper-Smith, *Indian Women and French Men: Rethinking Cultural Encounter in the Western Great Lakes* (Amherst: University of Massachusetts Press, 2001); Brooks, *Captives & Cousins*; Sheila McManus, *The Line Which Separates: Race, Gender, and the Making of the Alberta-Montana Borderlands* (Lincoln: University of Nebraska Press, 2005); Barr, *Peace Came in the Form of a Woman*; and Bárbara Reyes, *Private Women, Public Lives: Gender and the Missions of the Californias* (Austin: University of Texas Press, 2009). Gender analyses have been prominent in work on the U.S.-Mexican border, starting with the iconic book by Gloria Anzaldúa, *Borderlands/La Frontera: The New Mestiza* (San Francisco: Spinsters/Aunt Lute, 1987). For a sampling of more recent work, see Antonia Castañeda, ed., *Gender on the Borderlands: The Frontiers Reader* (Lincoln: University of Nebraska Press, 2007).

2 Though the piece included here is a stand-alone essay, Brown's analysis is elaborated in her monograph *Good Wives, Nasty Wenches, and Anxious Patriarchs: Gender, Race, and Power in Colonial Virginia* (Chapel Hill: University of North Carolina Press, 1996).

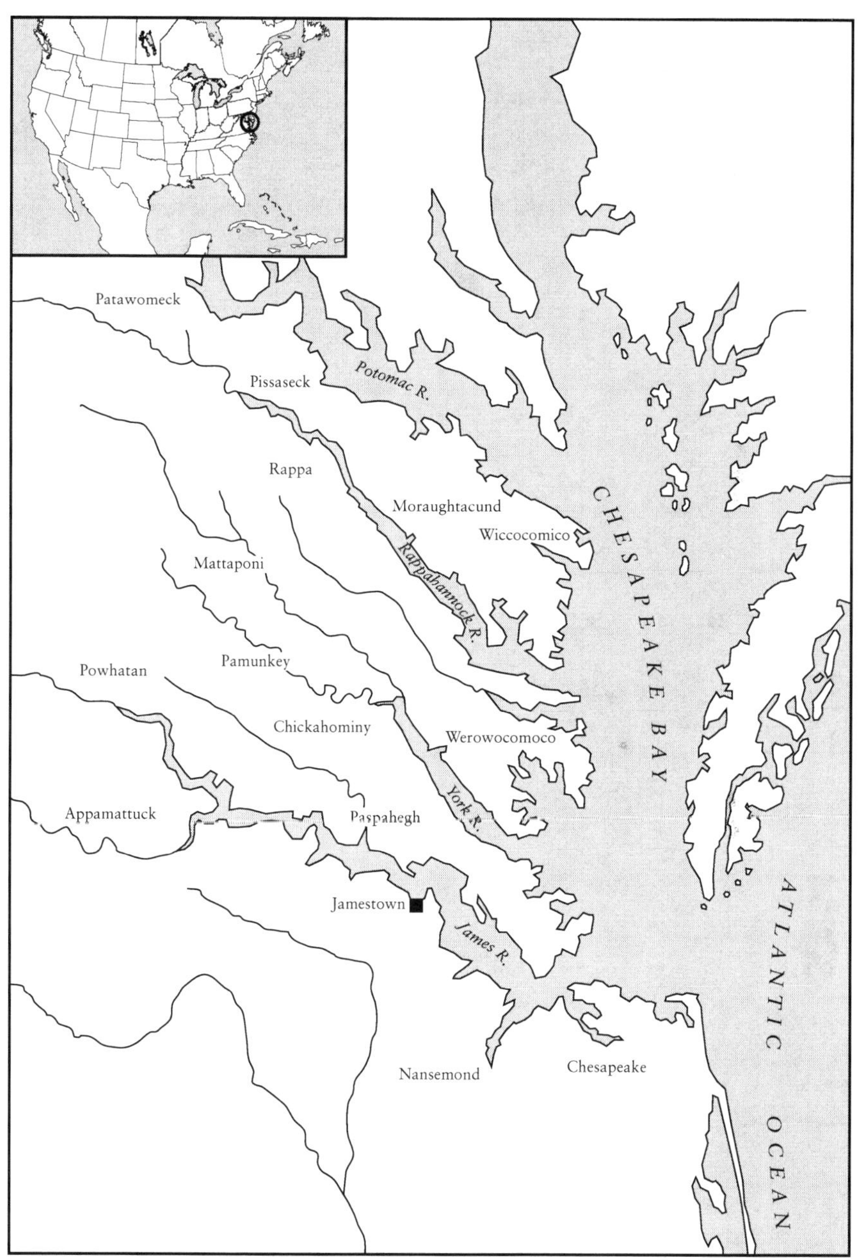


*Map 3.1* The Chesapeake

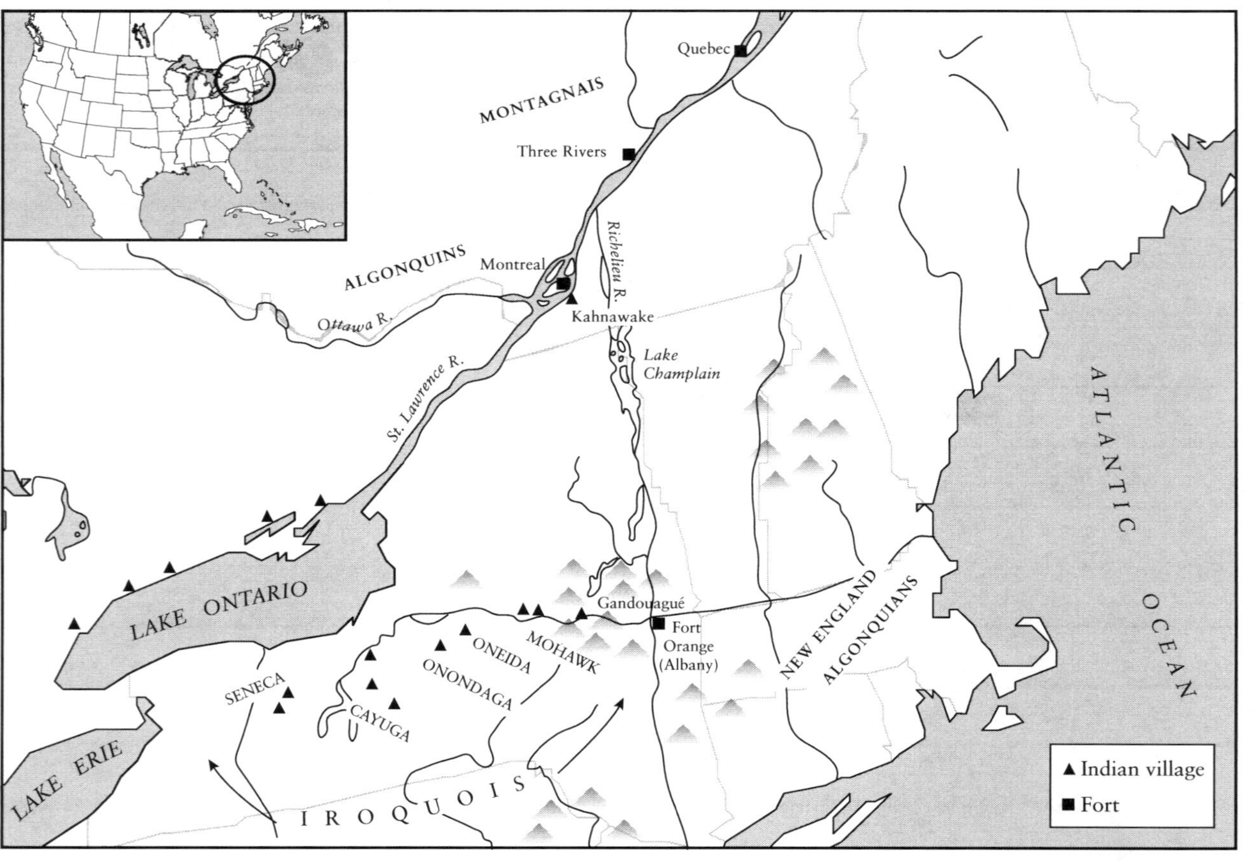


*Map 3.2* New France

# 6

# THE ANGLO-ALGONQUIAN GENDER FRONTIER

*Kathleen M. Brown*

Recent scholarship has improved our understanding of the relationship between English settlers and Indians during the early seventeenth century. We know, for instance, that English expectations about American Indians were conditioned by Spanish conquest literature, their own contact with the Gaelic Irish, elite perceptions of the lower classes, and obligations to bring Christianity to those they believed to be in darkness.[1]

Largely unacknowledged by historians, gender roles and identities also played an important role in shaping English and Indian interactions. Accompanied by few English women, English male adventurers to Roanoake and Jamestown island confronted Indian men and women in their native land. In this cultural encounter, the gender ways, or what some feminist theorists might call the "performances," of Virginia Algonquians challenged English gentlemen's assumptions about the naturalness of their own gender identities. This interaction brought exchanges, new cultural forms, created sites of commonality, painful deceptions, bitter misunderstandings, and bloody conflicts.[2]

Identities as English or Indian were only partially formed at the beginning of this meeting of cultures; it required the daily presence of an "other" to crystallize self-conscious articulations of group identity. In contrast, maleness and femaleness within each culture provided explicit and deep-rooted foundations for individual identity and the organization of social relations. In both Indian and English societies, differences between men and women were critical to social order. Ethnic identities formed along this "gender frontier," the site of creative and destructive processes resulting from the confrontations of culturally-specific manhoods and womanhoods. In the emerging Anglo-Indian struggle, gender symbols and social relations signified claims to power. Never an absolute barrier, however, the gender frontier also produced sources for new identities and social practices.[3]

In this essay, I explore in two ways the gender frontier that evolved between English settlers and the indigenous peoples of Virginia's tidewater.

First, I assess how differences in gender roles shaped the perceptions and interactions of both groups. Second, I analyze the "gendering" of the emerging Anglo-Indian power struggle. While the English depicted themselves as warriors dominating a feminized native population, Indian women and men initially refused to acknowledge claims to military supremacy, treating the foreigners as they would subject peoples, cowards, or servants. When English warrior discourse became unavoidable, however, Indian women and men attempted to exploit what they saw as the warrior's obvious dependence upon others for the agricultural and reproductive services that ensured group survival.

The indigenous peoples who engaged in this struggle were residents of Virginia's coastal plain, a region of fields, forests, and winding rivers that extended from the shores of the Chesapeake Bay to the mountains and waterfalls near present-day Richmond. Many were affiliated with Powhatan, the *werowance* who had consolidated several distinct groups under his influence at the time of contact with the English.[4] Most were Algonquian-speakers whose distant cultural roots in the Northeast distinguished them from peoples further south and west where native economies depended more on agriculture and less on hunting and fishing.[5] Although culturally diverse, tidewater inhabitants shared certain features of social organization, commonalities that may have become more pronounced with Powhatan's ambitious chiefdom-building and the arrival of the English.

Of the various relationships constituting social order in England, those between men and women were among the most contested at the time the English set sail for Virginia in 1607. Accompanied by few women before 1620, male settlers left behind a pamphlet debate about the nature of the sexes and a rising concern about the activities of disorderly women. The gender hierarchy the English viewed as "natural" and "God-given" was in fact fraying at the edges. Male pamphleteers argued vigorously for male dominance over women as crucial to maintaining orderly households and communities. The relationship between men and women provided authors with an accessible metaphor with which to communicate the power inequities of abstract political relationships such as that of the monarch to the people, or that of the gentry to the lower orders.[6] By the late sixteenth century, as English attempts to subdue Ireland became increasingly violent and as hopes for a profitable West African trade dimmed, gender figured increasingly in English colonial discourses.[7]

English gender differences manifested themselves in primary responsibilities and arenas of activity, relationships to property, ideals for conduct, and social identities. Using plow agriculture, rural Englishmen cultivated grain while women oversaw household production, including gardening, dairying, brewing, and spinning. Women also constituted a flexible reserve labor force, performing agricultural work when demand for labor was high, as at harvest time. While Englishmen's property ownership formed the basis of their political existence and identity, most women did not own property until they were no longer subject to a father or husband.[8]

By the early seventeenth century, advice-book authors enjoined English women to concern themselves with the conservation of estates rather than with production. Women were also advised to maintain a modest demeanor. Publicly punishing shrewish and sexually aggressive women, communities enforced this standard of wifely submission as ideal and of wifely domination as intolerable.[9] The sexual activity of poor and unmarried women proved particularly threatening to community order; these "nasty wenches" provided pamphleteers with a foil for the "good wives" female readers were urged to emulate.[10]

How did one know an English good wife when one saw one? Her body and head would be modestly covered. The tools of her work, such as the skimming ladle used in dairying, the distaff of the spinning wheel, and the butter churn reflected her domestic production. When affixed to a man, as in community-initiated shaming rituals, these gender symbols communicated his fall from "natural" dominance and his wife's unnatural authority over him.[11]

Advice-book authors described men's "natural" domain as one of authority derived from his primary economic role. A man's economic assertiveness, mirrored in his authority over wife, child and servant, was emblematized by the plow's penetration of the earth, the master craftsman's ability to shape his raw materials, and the rider's ability to subdue his horse. Although hunting and fishing supplemented the incomes of many Englishmen, formal group hunts—occasions in which associations with manual labor and economic gain had been carefully erased—remained the preserve of the aristocracy and upper gentry.

The divide between men's and women's activities described by sixteenth- and seventeenth-century authors did not capture the flexibility of gender relations in most English communities. Beliefs in male authority over women and in the primacy of men's economic activities sustained a perception of social order even as women marketed butter, cheese and ale, and cuckolded unlucky husbands.

Gender roles and identities were also important to the Algonquian speakers whom the English encountered along the three major tributaries of the Chesapeake Bay. Like indigenous peoples throughout the Americas, Virginia Algonquians invoked a divine division of labor to explain and justify differences between men's and women's roles on earth. A virile warrior god and a congenial female hostess provided divine examples for the work appropriate to human men and women.[12] Indian women's labor centered on cultivating and processing corn, which provided up to seventy-five percent of the calories consumed by residents of the coastal plain.[13] Women also grew squash, peas, and beans, fashioned bedding, baskets, and domestic tools, and turned animal skins into clothing and household items. They may even have built the houses of semi-permanent summer villages and itinerant winter camps. Bearing and raising children and mourning the dead rounded out the range of female duties. All were spiritually united by life-giving and its association with earth and agricultural production, sexuality and reproduction. Lineage wealth and political power passed through the female line, perhaps because of women's crucial role in producing and maintaining property. Among certain peoples, women may also have had the power to determine the fate of captives, the nugget of truth in the much-embellished tale of Pocahontas's intervention on behalf of Captain John Smith.[14]

Indian women were responsible not only for reproducing the traditional features of their culture, but for much of its adaptive capacity as well. As agriculturalists, women must have had great influence over decisions to move to new grounds, to leave old grounds fallow, and to initiate planting. As producers and consumers of vital household goods and implements, women may have been among the first to feel the impact of new technologies, commodities, and trade. And as accumulators of lineage property, Indian women may have been forced to change strategies as subsistence opportunities shifted.

Indian men assumed a range of responsibilities that complemented those of women. Men cleared new planting grounds by cutting trees and burning stumps. They fished and hunted for game, providing highly valued protein. After the last corn harvest, whole villages traveled with their hunters to provide support services throughout the winter. Men's pursuit of game shaped the rhythms of village life during these cold months, just as women's cultivation of crops determined feasts and the allocation of labor during the late spring and summer. By ritually separating themselves from women through sexual abstinence, hunters periodically became warriors, taking revenge for killings or initiating their own raids. This adult leave-taking rearticulated the *huskanaw,* the coming of age ritual in which young boys left their mothers' homes to become men.[15]

Men's hunting and fighting roles were associated with life-taking, with its ironic relationship to the life-sustaining acts of procreation, protection and provision. Earth and corn symbolized women, but the weapons of the hunt, the trophies taken from the hunted, and the predators of the animal world represented men. The ritual use of *pocones,* a red dye, also reflected this gender division. Women anointed their bodies with *pocones* before sexual encounters and ceremonies celebrating the harvest, while men wore it during hunting, warfare, or at the ritual celebrations of successes in these endeavors.[16]

The exigencies of the winter hunt, the value placed on meat, and intermittent warfare among native peoples may have been the foundation of male dominance in politics and religious matters. Women were not without their bases of power in Algonquian society, however; their important roles as agriculturalists, reproducers of Indian culture, and caretakers of lineage property kept gender relations in rough balance. Indian women's ability to choose spouses motivated men to be "paynefull" in their hunting and fishing. These same men warily avoided female spaces the English labeled "gynaeceum," in which menstruating women may have gathered. By no means equal to men, whose political and religious decisions directed village life, Indian women were perhaps more powerful in their subordination than English women.[17]

Even before the English sailed up the river they renamed the James, however, Indian women's power may have been waning, eroded by Powhatan's chiefdom-building tactics. During the last quarter of the sixteenth century, perhaps as a consequence of early Spanish forays into the region, he began to add to his inherited chiefdom, coercing and manipulating other coastal residents into economic and military alliances. Powhatan also subverted the matrilineal transmission of political power by appointing his kinsmen to be *werowances* of villages recently consolidated into his chiefdom. The central military force under his command created opportunities for male recognition in which acts of bravery, rather than matrilineal property or political inheritance, determined privileges. Traditions of gift-giving to cement alliances became exchanges of tribute for promises of protection or non-aggression. Powhatan thus appropriated corn, the product of women's labor, from the villages he dominated. He also communicated power and wealth through conspicuous displays of young wives. Through marriages to women drawn from villages throughout his chiefdom, Powhatan emblematized his dominance over the margins of his domain and created kinship ties to strengthen his influence over these villages. With the arrival of the English, the value of male warfare and the symbolism of corn as tribute only intensified, further strengthening the patriarchal tendencies of Powhatan's people.[18]

Almost every writer described the land west and south of Chesapeake Bay as an unspoiled "New World."[19] Small plots of cultivated land, burned forest undergrowth, and seasonal residence patterns often escaped the notice of English travelers habituated to landscapes shaped by plow agriculture and permanent settlement. Many writers believed the English had "chanced in a lande, even as God made it," which indigenous peoples had failed to exploit.[20]

Conquest seemed justifiable to many English because Native Americans had failed to tame the wilderness according to English standards. Writers claimed they found "only an idle, improvident, scattered people . . . carelesse of anything but from hand to mouth."[21] Most authors compounded impressions of sparse indigenous populations by listing only numbers of fighting men, whom they derided as impotent for their failure to exploit the virgin resources of the "bowells and womb of their Land."[22] The seasonal migration of native groups and the corresponding shift in diet indicated to the English a lack of mastery over the environment, reminding them of animals. John Smith commented, "It is strange to see how their bodies alter with their diet; even as the deare and wild beastes, they seem fat and leane, strong and weak."[23]

The English derision of Indian dependence on the environment and the comparison to animals, while redolent with allusions to England's own poor and to the hierarchy of God's creation, also contained implicit gender meanings. Women's bodies, for example, showed great alteration during pregnancy from fat to lean, strong to weak. English authors often compared female sexual appetites and insubordination to those of wild animals in need of taming. Implicit in all these commentaries was a critique of indigenous men for failing to fulfill the responsibility of economic provision with which the English believed all men to be charged. Lacking private property in the English sense, Indian men, like the Gaelic Irish before them, appeared to the English to be feminine and not yet civilized to manliness.[24]

For many English observers, natives' "failure" to develop an agricultural economy or dense population was rooted in their gender division of labor. Women's primary responsibility for agriculture merely confirmed the abdication by men of their proper role and explained the "inferiority" of native economies in a land of plenty. Smith commented that "the land is not populous, for the men be fewe; their far greater number is of women and children," a pattern he attributed to inadequate cultivation.[25] Of the significance of women's work and Indian agriculture, he concluded, "When all their fruits be gathered, little els they plant, and this is done by their women and children; neither doth this long suffice them, for neere 3 parts of the yeare, they only observe times and seasons, and live of what the Country naturally affordeth from hand to mouth."[26] In Smith's convoluted analysis, the "failure" of Indian agriculture, implicitly associated in other parts of his text with the "idleness" of men and the reliance upon female labor, had a gendered consequence; native populations became vulnerable and feminized, consisting of many more women and children than of "able men fitt for their warres."[27]

English commentators reacted with disapproval to seeing women perform work relegated to laboring men in England while Indian men pursued activities associated with the English aristocracy. Indian women, George Percy claimed, "doe all their drugerie. The men takes their pleasure in hunting and their warres, which they are in continually."[28] Observing that the women were heavily burdened and the men only lightly so, John Smith similarly noted "the men bestowe their times in fishing, hunting, wars and such manlike exercises, scorning to be seene in any woman like exercise," while the "women and children do the rest of the worke."[29] Smith's account revealed his discomfort with women's performance of work he considered the most valuable.

The English were hard pressed to explain other Indian behavior without contradicting their own beliefs in the natural and divinely-sanctioned characteristics of men and women. Such was the case with discussions of Indian women's pain during childbirth. In judgements reminiscent of their descriptions of Irish women, many English writers claimed that Indian women gave birth with little or no pain.[30] English readers may have found this observation difficult to reconcile with Christian views of labor pains as the source of maternal love and as punishment for the sins of Eve. Belief in indigenous women's closer proximity to nature—an interpretive stance that required an uncomfortable degree of criticism of civilization—allowed the English to finesse Indian women's seeming exemption from Eve's curse.[31] This is also why the association of Native American gender norms with animals proved so powerful for the English; it left intact the idea of English gender roles as "natural," in the sense of fulfilling God's destiny for civilized peoples, while providing a similarly "natural" explanation for English dominance over indigenous peoples.

The English were both fascinated and disturbed by other aspects of Native American society through which gender identities were communicated, including hairstyle, dress and make-up. The native male fashion of going clean-shaven, for example, clashed with English associations of beards with male maturity, perhaps diminishing Indian men's claims to manhood in the eyes of the English. Upon seeing an Indian with a full "blacke bush beard," Smith concluded that the individual must be the son of a European as "the Salvages seldome hav any at all." It probably did not enhance English respect for Indian manhood that female barbers sheared men's facial hair.[32]

Most English writers found it difficult to distinguish between the sexual behavior of Chesapeake dwellers and what they viewed as sexual potency conveyed through dress and ritual. English male explorers were particularly fascinated by indigenous women's attire, which seemed scanty and immodest compared to English women's multiple layers and wraps. John Smith described an entertainment arranged for him in which "30 young women came naked out of the woods (only covered behind and before with a few greene leaves), their bodies al painted."[33] Several other writers commented that Native Americans "goe altogether naked," or had "scarce to cover their nakednesse."[34] Smith claimed, however, that the women were "alwaies covered about their midles with a skin and very shamefast to be seene bare." Yet he noted, as did several other English travelers, the body adornments, including beads, paintings, and tattoos, that were visible on Indian women's legs, hands, breasts, and faces. Perhaps some of the "shamefastness" reported by Smith resulted from Englishmen's close scrutiny of Indian women's bodies.[35]

For most English writers, Indian manners and customs reinforced an impression of sexual passion. Hospitality that included sexual privileges, for instance sending "a woman fresh painted red with *Pocones* and oile" to be the "bedfellow" of a guest, may have confirmed in the minds of English men the reading of Indian folkways as sexually provocative. Smith's experience with the thirty women, clad in leaves, body paint, and buck's horns and emitting "hellish cries and shouts," undoubtedly strengthened the English association of Indian culture with unbridled passion:

> . . . they solemnly invited Smith to their lodging, but no sooner was hee within the house, but all these Nimphes more tormented him than ever, with crowding, and pressing, and hanging upon him, most tediously crying, *love you not mee.*[36]

These and other Indian gender ways left the English with a vivid impression of unconstrained sexuality that in their own culture could mean only promiscuity.

The stark contrast between Indian military techniques and formal European land stratagems reinforced English judgements that indigenous peoples were animalistic by nature.[37] George Percy's description of one skirmish invoked a comparison to the movement of animals: "At night, when we were going aboard, there came the Savages creeping upon all foure, from the Hills, like Beares, with their Bowes in their mouthes."[38] While writers regaled English readers with tales of Indian men in hasty retreat from English guns, thus reconfirming for the reader the female vulnerability of Indians and the superior weaponry of the English, they also recounted terrifying battle scenes such as the mock war staged for the entertainment of John Smith, which included "horrible shouts and screeches, as though so many infernall helhounds could not have made them more terrible."[39] Englishmen were perhaps most frightened, however, by reports of Caribbean Indians that echoed accounts of Irish cannibalism; George Percy claimed that Carib men scalped their victims, or worse still, that certain tribes "will eate their enemies when they kill them, or any stranger if they take them."[40] Stories like these may have led Smith to believe he was being "fattened" for a sacrifice during his captivity in December 1607.[41]

Although the dominant strand of English discourse about Indian men denounced them for being savage and failed providers, not all Englishmen shared these assessments of the meaning of cultural differences. Throughout the early years of settlement, male laborers deserted military compounds to escape puny rations, disease and harsh discipline, preferring to take their chances with local Indians whom they knew had food aplenty. Young boys like Henry Spelman, moreover, had nearly as much to fear from the English, who used him as a hostage, as he did from his Indian hosts. Spelman witnessed and participated in Indian culture from a very different perspective than most Virginia chroniclers. While George Percy and John Smith described Indian entertainments as horrible antics, Spelman coolly noted that Patawomeck dances bore a remarkable resemblance to the Darbyshire hornpipe.[42]

Even among men more elite and cosmopolitan than Spelman, a lurking and disquieting suspicion that Indian men were like the English disrupted discourses about natural savagery and inferiority. John Smith often explained Indian complexions and resistance to the elements as a result of conditioning and daily practice rather than of nature.[43] Smith also created areas of commonality with Algonquians through exchanges of gifts, shared entertainments, and feasts. Drawn into Indian cultural expressions despite himself, Smith gave gifts when he would have preferred to barter and concocted Indian explanations for English behavior.[44] Despite the flamboyant rhetoric about savage warriors lurking in the forests like animals, Smith soon had Englishmen learning to fight in the woods.[45] He clearly thought his manly English, many of whom could barely shoot a gun, had much to learn from their Indian opponents.

Most English did not dwell on these areas of similarity and exchange, however, but emphasized the "wild" and animalistic qualities of tidewater peoples. English claims to dominance and superiority rested upon constructions of Indian behavior as barbaric. Much as animals fell below humans in the hierarchy of the natural world, so the Indians of English chronicles inhabited a place that was technologically, socially, and morally below the level of the civilized English. Anglo-Indian gender differences similarly provided the English with cultural grist for the mill of conquest. Through depictions of feminized male "naturalls," Englishmen reworked Anglo-Indian relations to fit the "natural" dominance of men in gender relations. In the process, they contributed to an emerging male colonial identity that was deeply rooted in English gender discourses.

The gendering of Anglo-Indian relations in English writing was not without contest and contradiction, however, nor did it lead inevitably to easy conclusions of English dominance. Englishmen incorporated Indian ways into their diets and military tactics, and Indian women into their sexual lives. Some formed close bonds with Indian companions, while others lived to father their own "naturall" progeny. As John Rolfe's anguish over his marriage to Pocahontas attested, colonial domination was a complex process involving sexual intimacy, cultural incorporation and self-scrutiny.[46]

The Englishmen who landed on the shores of Chesapeake Bay and the James River were not the first European men that Virginia Algonquians had seen. During the 1570s, Spanish Jesuits established a short-lived mission near the James River tributary that folded with the murder of the clerics. The Spaniards who revenged the Jesuit deaths left an unfavorable impression upon local Chickahominy, Paspegh, and Kecoughtan Indians. At least one English ship also pre-empted the 1607 arrival of the Jamestown settlers; its captain was long remembered for killing a Rappahanock river *werowance*.[47]

The maleness of English explorers' parties and early settlements undoubtedly raised Indian suspicions of bellicose motives. Interrogating Smith at their first meeting about the purpose of the English voyage, Powhatan was apparently satisfied with Smith's answer that the English presence was temporary. Smith claimed his men sought passage to "the backe Sea," the ever-elusive water route to India which they believed lay beyond the falls of the Chesapeake river system. Quick to exploit native assumptions that they were warriors, Smith also cited revenge against Powhatan's own mortal enemies, the Monacans, for their murder of an Englishman as a reason for their western explorations. The explanation may have initially seemed credible to Powhatan because the English expedition consisted only of men and boys. Frequent English military drills in the woods and the construction of a fort at Jamestown, however, may have aroused his suspicions that the English strangers planned a longer and more violent stay.[48]

Equipped with impressive blasting guns, the English may have found it easy to perpetuate the warrior image from afar; up close was a different matter, however. English men were pale, hairy, and awkward compared to Indian men. They also had the dirty habit of letting facial hair grow so that it obscured the bottom part of their faces where it collected food and other debris. Their clumsy stomping through the woods announced their presence to friends, enemies, and wildlife alike and they were forced, on at least one very public occasion, to ask for Indian assistance when their boats became mired in river ooze. Perhaps worst of all from the perspective of Indian people who valued a warrior's stoicism in the face of death, the Englishmen they captured and killed died screaming and whimpering. William Strachey recorded the mocking song sung by Indian men sometime in 1611, in which they ridiculed "what lamentation our people made when they kild him, namely saying how they [the Englishmen] would cry whe, whe."[49]

Indian assumptions about masculinity may have led Powhatan to overestimate the vulnerability of Smith's men. The gentlemen and artisans who were the first to arrive in Virginia proved to be dismal farmers, remaining wholly dependent upon native corn stores during their first three years and partially dependent thereafter. They tried, futilely, to persuade Indians to grow more corn to meet their needs, but their requests were greeted with scorn by Indian men who found no glory in the "woman-like exercise" of farming. Perhaps believing that the male settlement would always require another population to supply it, Powhatan tried to use the threat of starvation to level the playing field with the English. During trade negotiations with Smith in January 1609, Powhatan held out for guns and swords, claiming disingenuously that corn was more valuable to him than copper trinkets because he could eat it.[50]

When Powhatan and other Indian peoples reminded Smith of his dependence upon Indian food supplies, Smith reacted with anger. In his first account of Virginia, he recalled with bitterness the scorn of the Kecoughtan Indians for "a famished man": they "would in derision offer him a handfull of Corne, a peece of bread."[51] Such treatment signified both indigence and female vulnerability to the English, made worse by the fact that the crops they needed were grown by women. At Kecoughtan, Smith responded by "let[ting] fly his muskets" to provoke a Kecoughtan retreat and then killing several men at close range. The survivors fell back in confusion, allowing the image of their god Okeus to fall into English hands. After this display of force, he found the Kecoughtan "content" to let the English dictate the terms of trade: Kecoughtan corn in exchange for copper, beads, hatchets, and the return of Okeus.[52] The English thus used their superior weaponry to transform themselves from scorned men into respected warriors and to recast the relationship: humble agriculturists became duty-bound to produce for those who spared their lives.[53]

Powhatan's interactions with Englishmen may also have been guided by his assessment of the gender imbalance among them. His provision of women to entertain English male guests was a political gesture whose message seems to have been misunderstood as sexual license by the English.[54] Smith, for example, believed the generosity stemmed from Powhatan's having "as many women as he will," and thereby growing occasionally "weary of his women."[55] By voluntarily sharing his wealth in women and thus communicating his benign intent, Powhatan invoked what he may have believed to be a transcendent male political bond, defined by men's common relationship to women.[56] Powhatan may also have believed that by encouraging English warriors' sexual activity, he might diminish their military potency. It was the fear of this loss of power, after all, that motivated Indian warriors' ritual abstinence before combat. Ultimately, Powhatan may have hoped that intimacy between native women and English men would lead to an integration of the foreigners and a diffusion of the threat they presented. Lacking women with whom to reciprocate and unfettered by matrilineage ties, the English, Powhatan may have reasoned, might be rapidly brought into alliance. Powhatan's gesture, however, only reinforced the English rationale for subjugating the "uncivilized" and offered English men an opportunity to express the Anglo-Indian power relationship sexually with native women.[57]

Indian women were often more successful than Powhatan in manipulating Englishmen's desires for sexual intimacy. At the James River village of Appocant in late 1607, the unfortunate George Cawson met his death when village women "enticed [him] up from the barge into their howses."[58] Oppossunoquonuske, a clever *werowansqua* of another village, similarly led fourteen Englishmen to their demise. Inviting the unwary men to come "up into her Towne, to feast and make Merry," she convinced them to "leave their Armes in their boat, because they said how their women would be afrayd ells of their pieces."[59]

Although both of these accounts are cautionary tales that represent Indians literally as feminine seducers capable of entrapping Englishmen in the web of their own sexual desires, the incidents suggest Indian women's canny assessment of the men who would be colonial conquerors. Exploiting Englishmen's hopes for colonial pleasures, Indian women dangled before them the opportunity for sexual intimacy, turning a female tradition of sexual hospitality into a weapon of war. Acknowledging the capacity of English "pieces" to terrorize Indian women, Oppossunoquonuske tacitly recognized

Englishmen's dependence on their guns to construct self-images of bold and masculine conquerors. Her genius lay in convincing them to rely on other masculine "pieces." When she succeeded in getting Englishmen to set aside one colonial masculine identity—the warrior—for another—the lover of native women—the men were easily killed.

Feigned sexual interest in Englishmen was not the only tactic available to Indian women. Some women clearly wanted nothing to do with the English strangers and avoided all contact with them. When John Smith traveled to Tappahannock in late 1607, for example, Indian women fled their homes in fear.[60] Other Indian women treated the English not as revered guests, to be gently wooed into Indian ways or seduced into fatal traps, but as lowly servants. Young Henry Spelman recorded such an incident during his stay at the house of a Patawomeck *werowance*. While the *werowance* was gone, his first wife requested that Spelman travel with her and carry her child on the long journey to her father's house. When Spelman refused, she struck him, provoking the boy to return the blows. A second wife then joined in the fray against Spelman, who continued to refuse to do their bidding. Upon the *werowance*'s return, Spelman related the afternoon's events and was horrified to see the offending wife brutally punished. In this Patawomeck household, women's and men's ideas about the proper treatment of English hostages differed dramatically.[61]

In addition to violence and manipulations of economic dependence and sexual desire, Algonquians tried to maneuver the English into positions of political subordination. Smith's account of his captivity, near-execution, and rescue by Pocahontas was undoubtedly part of an adoption ritual in which Powhatan defined his relationship to Smith as one of patriarchal dominance. Smith became Powhatan's prisoner after warriors easily slew his English companions and then "missed" with nearly all of the twenty or thirty arrows they aimed at Smith himself. Clearly, Powhatan wanted Smith brought to him alive. Smith reported that during his captivity he was offered "life, libertie, land and women," prizes Powhatan must have believed to be very attractive to Englishmen, in exchange for information about how best to capture Jamestown.[62] After ceremonies and consultations with priests, Powhatan brought Smith before an assembly where, according to Smith, Pocahontas risked her own life to prevent him from being clubbed to death by executioners. It seems that Smith understood neither the ritual adoption taking place nor the significance of Powhatan's promise to make him a *werowance* and to "for ever esteeme him as [he did] his son Nantaquoud."[63]

Powhatan subsequently repeated his offer to Smith, urging the adoptive relationship on him. Pronouncing him "a werowance of Powhatan, and that all his subjects should so esteeme us," Powhatan integrated Smith and his men into his chieftancy, declaring that "no man account us strangers nor Paspaheghans, but Powhatans, and that the Corne, weomen and Country, should be to us as to his owne people."[64]

Over the next weeks and months the two men wrangled over the construction of their short-lived alliance and the meaning of Powhatan's promises to supply the English with corn. In a long exchange of bitter words, the two men sidestepped each other's readings of their friendship as distortions and misperceptions. Smith claimed he had "neglected all, to satisfie your desire," to which Powhatan responded with a plain-spoken charge of bad faith: "some doubt I have of your comming hither, that makes me not so kindly seeke to relieve you . . . for many do informe me, your comming is not for trade, but to invade my people and possesse my Country."[65]

Smith and Powhatan continued to do a subtle two-step over the meaning of the corn. Was it tribute coerced by the militarily superior English? Or was it a sign of a father's compassion for a subordinate *werowance* and his hungry people? Powhatan made clear to Smith that he understood the extent of the English dependence upon his people for corn. "What will it availe you, to take that perforce, you may quietly have with love, or to destroy them that provide you food?" he asked Smith. "What can you get by war, when we can hide our provision and flie to the woodes, whereby you must famish by wronging us your friends." He also appreciated the degree to which the English could make him miserable if they did not get what they wanted:

> think you I am so simple not to knowe, it is better to eate good meate, lie well, and sleepe quietly with my women and children, laugh and be merrie with you, have copper, hatchets, or what I want, being your friend; then bee forced to flie from al, to lie cold in the woods, feed upon acorns, roots, and such trash, and be so hunted by you, that I can neither rest, eat, nor sleepe; but my tired men must watch, and if a twig but breake, everie one crie there comes Captaine Smith, then I must flie I knowe not whether, and thus with miserable feare end my miserable life.[66]

Ultimately, Powhatan attempted to represent his conflict with Smith as the clash of an older, wiser authority with a young upstart. "I knowe the difference of peace and warre, better then any in my Countrie," he reminded Smith, his paternal self-depiction contrasting sharply with what he labeled Smith's youthful and "rash unadvisednesse." Displeased with this rendering of their relationship with its suggestion of childish inexperience, Smith reasserted the English warrior personae with a vengeance. He informed Powhatan that "for your sake only, wee have curbed our thirsting desire of revenge," reminding him that the "advantage we have by our armes" would have allowed the English easily to overpower Powhatan's men "had wee intended you anie hurt."[67]

Although we can never know with any certainty what the all-male band of English settlers signified to indigenous peoples, their own organization of gender roles seems to have shaped their responses to the English. Using sexual hospitality to "disarm" the strangers and exploiting English needs for food, Algonquians were drawn into a female role as suppliers of English sexual and subsistence needs. Although Indian women were occasionally successful in manipulating English desires for sexual intimacy and dominance, the English cast these triumphs as the consequence of female seduction, an interpretation that only reinforced discourses about feminized Algonquians. Dependence upon indigenous peoples for corn was potentially emasculating for the English; they thus redefined corn as tribute or booty resulting from English military dominance.

The encounter of English and Indian peoples wrought changes in the gender relations of both societies. Contact bred trade, political reshuffling, sexual intimacy and warfare. On both sides, male roles intensified in ways that appear to have reinforced the patriarchal tendencies of each culture. The very process of confrontation between two groups with male-dominated political and religious systems may initially have strengthened the value of patriarchy for each.

The rapid change in Indian life and culture had a particularly devastating impact upon women. Many women, whose office it was to bury and mourn the dead, may have been relegated to perpetual grieving. Corn was also uniquely the provenance of women; economically it was the source of female authority, and religiously and symbolically they were identified with it. The wanton burning and pillaging of corn supplies, through which the English transformed their dependence into domination, may have represented to tidewater residents an egregious violation of women. Maneuvering to retain patriarchal dominance over the English and invoking cultural roles in which women exercised power, Algonquian Indians may have presented their best defense against the "feminization" of their relationship to the English. But as in Indian society itself, warriors ultimately had the upper hand over agriculturists.[68]

English dominance in the region ultimately led to the decline of the native population and its way of life. As a consequence of war, nutritional deprivation, and disease, Virginia Indians were reduced in numbers from the approximately 14,000 inhabitants of the Chesapeake Bay and tidewater in 1607 to less than 3,000 by the early eighteenth century. White settlement forced tidewater dwellers further west, rupturing the connections between ritual activity, lineage, and geographic place. Priests lost credibility as traditional medicines failed to cure new diseases while confederacies such as Powhatan's declined and disappeared. Uprooted tidewater peoples also encountered opposition from piedmont inhabitants upon whose territory they encroached. The erosion of traditionally male-dominated Indian political institutions eventually created new opportunities for individual women to assume positions of leadership over tribal remnants.[69]

The English, meanwhile, emerged from these early years of settlement with gender roles more explicitly defined in English, Christian, and "middling order" terms. This core of English identity proved remarkably resiliant, persisting through seventy years of wars with neighboring Indians and continuing to evolve as English settlers imported Africans to work the colony's tobacco fields. Initially serving to legitimate the destruction of traditional Indian ways of life, this concept of Englishness ultimately constituted one of the most powerful legacies of the Anglo-Indian gender frontier.

## NOTES

1 Spanish literature divided "barbaric" populations into two main categories: one of obedient and child-like laborers, and the other of evil, conniving and dangerous cannibals. The English similarly typed both Gaelic Irish and American Indians. See Anthony Pagden, *The Fall of Natural Man* (Cambridge: Cambridge University Press, 1986); Nicholas P. Canny, *The Elizabethan Conquest of Ireland: A Pattern Established 1565–76* (New York: Barnes and Noble, 1976), 160; Loren E. Pennington, "The Amerindian in English Promotional Literature 1575–1625" in *The Westward Enterprise: English Activities in Ireland, the Atlantic, and America, 1480–1650,* ed. K.R. Andrews, Nicholas P. Canny, and P.E.H. Hair (Detroit: Wayne State University Press, 1979), 184, 188; Anne Laurence, "The Cradle to the Grave: English Observation of Irish Social Customs in the Seventeenth Century," *The Seventeenth Century,* 3 (Spring 1988): 63–84; Nicholas P. Canny, "The Ideology of English Colonization: From Ireland to America," *William and Mary Quarterly,* 3rd ser., 30 (October 1973): 597 (hereafter cited as *WMQ*). Christianity, moreover, allowed the English to maintain the belief that their economic and imperialist motives in the Americas were part of God's work and to distinguish and devalue Indian culture; see John Smith, *The Proceedings of the English Colonies in Virginia* [London, 1612] in *Narratives of Early Virginia 1606–1625,* ed. Lyon Gardiner Tyler (New York: Barnes and Noble, 1907), 178; Karen Kupperman, ed., *Captain John Smith: A Select Edition of His Writings* (Chapel Hill, N.C.: University of North Carolina Press, 1988), 154.

2 For a useful discussion of the performative nature of identity that is especially applicable to the early modern period and the encounter of cultures in the Americas, see Judith Butler, "Gender Trouble," in *Feminism/Postmodernism,* ed. Linda J. Nicholson (New York: Routledge, 1990), 336–339.

3 For the by-now classic account of gender as a means of communicating power, see Joan Scott, "Gender: A Useful Category of Historical Analysis," *American Historical Review,* 91 (December 1986): 1053–1075. For analyses of economic, linguistic, and religious "frontiers," see James Merrell, "'The Customes of Our Country': Indians and Colonists in Early America," in *Strangers Within the Realm: Cultural Margins of the First British Empire,* ed. Bernard Bailyn and Phillip D. Morgan (Chapel Hill, N.C.: University of North Carolina Press, 1991), 117–156. In no way separate or distinct, the gender frontier infiltrated other frontiers we usually describe as economic, social, or cultural; for further elaboration see Kathleen M. Brown, "Brave New Worlds: Women's and Gender History," *WMQ,* 3rd ser., 50 (April 1993): 311–328.

4 On Powhatan's influence over neighboring Algonquian-speaking peoples, see Nancy Lurie, "Indian Cultural Adjustment to European Civilization," in *Seventeenth-Century America,* ed. James Morton Smith (Westport, Ct.: Greenwood Press, 1980), 40–42. Lurie uses the term "Confederacy" to refer to these peoples,

although she distinguishes between the "influence" Powhatan wielded and the "undisputed control" he never fully realized. Helen Rountree, *Pocahontas's People* (Norman, Ok.: University of Oklahoma Press, 1990), 3, argues that "Confederacy" is inaccurate, preferring to describe it as a "sophisticated government." See also Peter H. Wood, Gregory Waselkov, and M. Thomas Hatley, eds., *Powhatan's Mantle: Southeastern Indians in the Colonial Era* (Lincoln, Neb.: University of Nebraska Press, 1989), xv, for the use of the term "mantle." The groups under Powhatan's mantle of authority included the Pamunkey, Kecoughtan, Mattaponi, Appamattuck, Rappahannock, Piankatank, Chiskiack, Werowocomoco, Nansemond, and Chesapeake.

5 Lurie, "Indian Cultural Adjustment," 40–41; G. Melvin Herndon, "Indian Agriculture in the Southern Colonies," *The North Carolina Historical Review* 44 (July 1967): 283–297; Charles Hudson, *The Southeastern Indians* (Knoxville, Tenn.: University of Tennessee Press, 1976), 8–9, 23; Timothy Silver, *A New Face on the Countryside: Indians, Colonists, and Slaves in South Atlantic Forests, 1500–1800* (New York: Cambridge University Press, 1990), 39; J. Leitch Wright, *The Only Land They Knew: The Tragic Story of the American Indians in the Old South* (New York: Free Press, 1981), 11.

6 The secondary literature about gender and social order in England during the late sixteenth and early seventeenth centuries is vast. Among the accounts that have influenced me the most are the following: G.R. Quaife, *Wanton Wenches and Wayward Wives: Peasants and Illicit Sex in Early Seventeenth Century England* (London: Croom Helm, 1979); Anthony Fletcher and John Stevenson, eds., *Order and Disorder in Early Modern England* (New York: Cambridge University Press, 1985); Susan Cahn, *Industry of Devotion: The Transformation of Women's Work in England 1500–1660* (New York: Basil Blackwell, 1987); Susan Dwyer Amussen, *An Ordered Society: Gender and Class in Early Modern England* (New York: Columbia University Press, 1988), chapter 2, "Political Households and Domestic Politics"; Martin Ingram, *Church Courts, Sex and Marriage in England, 1570–1640* (New York: Cambridge University Press, 1987); Joan Kelly, *Women, History and Theory* (Chicago: University of Chicago Press, 1984), chapter 4, "Early Feminist Theory and the Querelle des Femmes"; Linda Woodbridge, *Women and the English Renaissance: Literature and the Nature of Womankind, 1540–1620* (Urbana, Ill.: University of Illinois Press, 1984); Constance Jordan, *Renaissance Feminism: Literary Texts and Political Models* (Ithaca, N.Y.: Cornell University Press, 1990). For a useful anthology of reprinted pamphlets and advice books, see Katherine Usher Henderson and Barbara F. McManus, eds., *Half Humankind: Contexts and Texts of the Controversy about Women in England, 1540–1650* (Chicago: University of Illinois Press, 1985).

7 For examples of gendered discourses of difference in the Irish context, see Laurence, "Cradle to the Grave"; for a classic early English account of Africans, see Richard Jobson, *The Golden Trade* [London, 1623].

8 Among the most useful accounts of English agriculture are Joan Thirsk, ed., *The Agrarian History of England and Wales,* 6 vols. (Cambridge: Cambridge University Press, 1967) vol. 4; K.D.M. Snell, *Annals of the Laboring Poor: Social Change and Agrarian England, 1660–1900* (Cambridge: Cambridge University Press, 1985); D. E. Underdown, "Taming of the Scold: The Enforcement of Patriarchal Authority in Early Modern England," in Fletcher and Stevenson, *Order and Disorder in Early Modern England,* 116–136; Ann Kussmaul, *Servants in Husbandry in Early Modern England* (Cambridge: Cambridge University Press, 1981).

9 Cahn, *Industry of Devotion,* 80–90, 158; Amussen, *Ordered Society;* William Gouge, *Domesticall Duties* (London, 1622); Richard Brathwait, *The English*

*Gentlewoman* (London, 1631); Gervase Markham, *Country Contentments or the English Housewife* (London, 1623).

10 For the terms "good wives" and "nasty wenches," see John Hammond, *Leah and Rachel, or the Two Fruitfull Sisters* (London, 1656).

11 Martin Ingram, "Ridings, Rough Music, and the 'Reform of Popular Culture,' in Early Modern England," *Past and Present,* 105 (November 1984): 79–113; Underdown, "The Taming of the Scold."

12 Ramon Gutierrez, *When Jesus Came the Corn Mothers Went Away* (Stanford, Ca.: Stanford University Press, 1991), 3–7; Hudson, *Southeastern Indians,* 148–159; Helen Rountree, *The Powhatan Indians of Virginia: Their Traditional Culture* (Norman, Ok.: University of Oklahoma Press, 1989), 135–138; William Strachey, *The Historie of Travell into Virginia Britania* [London, 1612], 89, 103.

13 Edwin Randolph Turner, "An Archaeological and Ethnohistorical Study on the Evolution of Rank Societies in the Virginia Coastal Plain" (Ph.D. diss., The Pennsylvania State University, 1976), 182–187; Rountree, *Powhatan Indians,* 45, finds Turner's estimates perhaps too high.

14 Herndon, "Indian Agriculture in the Southern Colonies," 288, 292–296, especially the reference on 292 to "She-Corn." Hudson, *Southeastern Indians,* 151–156, 259–260; Wright, *Only Land They Knew,* 8–14; Silver, *New Face on the Countryside,* 39–41, 44–52; Colonel Henry Norwood, "A Voyage to Virginia" [London, 1649] in *Tracts and Other Papers, relating principally to the Origin, Settlement and Progress of the North American Colonies,* ed. Peter Force, 4 vols. (New York, 1836; rpt, Cambridge, Mass., Peter Smith, 1947), 3: 36–37. John Smith often rendered invisible or insignificant the work of women; see Kupperman, *John Smith,* 138–139. See also Kupperman, *John Smith,* 151, 156, for Smith's description of women's role as mourners and the passage of property and political power through women.

15 Wright, *Only Land They Knew,* 8–14; Hudson, *Southeastern Indians,* 148–156, 258–260; Kupperman, *John Smith,* 105, 144, 153; Henry Spelman, "Relation of Virginia," in *Travels and Works of Captain John Smith,* ed. Edward Arber and A.G. Bradley, 2 vols. (Edinburgh: John Grant, 1910), 1: cvi.

16 Hudson, *Southeastern Indians,* 259; Kupperman, *John Smith,* 61, 163.

17 Strachey, *Historie,* 83, 74.

18 For Powhatan's clever manipulation of gender customs and symbols of power, see Strachey, *Historie,* 40, 44, 62, 65–69, and Spelman, "Relation," cxiv.

19 For a survey of changing English attitudes toward Indians in the South, see Gary B. Nash, "The Image of the Indian in the Southern Colonial Mind," *WMQ,* 3rd ser., 29 (April 1972): 197–230. See also George Percy, "Observations by Master George Percy, 1607," [London, 1607], in Tyler, *Narratives,* 17–18, and Thomas Hariot, *A Briefe and True Report of the New Found Land of Virginia* (London, 1588; rpt. New York, 1903).

20 See Smith, *Proceedings of the English Colonies,* in Tyler, *Narratives,* 178; William Cronon, *Changes in the Land: Indians, Colonists and the Ecology of New England* (New York: Hill and Wang, 1983), 47–51; Silver, *New Face on the Countryside.* See also Alfred Crosby, *Ecological Imperialism: The Biological Expansion of Europe, 900–1900* (Cambridge: Cambridge University Press, 1986), 280, for his contention that rather than being part of the landscape, Indians acted as the first wave of "shock troops" on the New World environment that cleared the way for the subsequent European migration of peoples, agricultural systems, flora and fauna.

21 Smith, *Proceedings of the English Colonies,* in Tyler, *Narratives,* 178. John Smith, "Description of Virginia," [London, 1612], in Tyler, *Narratives,* 83; Pennington,

"The Amerindians in English Promotional Literature," 189, for her summation of the argument in Robert Gray, *A Good Speed to Virginia* [London, 1609]. For Smith's recognition of native concepts of property, see Kupperman, *John Smith,* 140. Most early English commentators also noted the potential of New World abundance for exploitation by agriculturists and hunters; see for example, Percy, "Observations" in Tyler, *Narratives,* 17–18; Hariot, *A Briefe and True Report.*

22 Strachey, *Historie,* 24, 103; John Smith, "A Map of Virginia," in *The Complete Works of Captain John Smith,* ed. Philip Barbour, 3 vols. (Chapel Hill, N.C.: University of North Carolina Press, 1986), 2: 146.

23 Smith, "Description," in Tyler, *Narratives,* 102; Silver, *New Face on the Countryside,* 67.

24 V.G. Kiernan, "Private Property in History," in *Family and Inheritance: Rural Society in Western Europe, 1200–1800,* ed. Jack Goody, Joan Thirsk and E. P. Thompson (Cambridge: Cambridge University Press, 1976), 361–398; see also E. P. Thompson, *Whigs and Hunters: The Origin of the Black Act* (New York: Random House, 1975). James Axtell, *The European and the Indian: Essays in the Ethnohistory of Colonial North America* (New York: Oxford University Press, 1981), discusses the English view of "civilizing" Indians as a process of making men out of children. Although most voyagers wrote critically of Indian men, others compared them favorably to English men whose overly cultured and effeminate ways had made them weak in character and resolve; Hariot, *A Briefe and True Report.* For a critique of English effeminacy, see *Haec Vir* [London, 1620] in Henderson and MacManus, *Half Humankind;* Richard Brathwait, *The English Gentleman* (London, 1631). Strachey, *Historie,* 18, 24, 25, equated civility with manliness.

25 Kupperman, *John Smith,* 158. Smith, "Description of Virginia," in Tyler, *Narratives,* 98–99.

26 See Kupperman, *John Smith,* 138–139.

27 Kupperman, *John Smith,* 140.

28 Percy, "Observations," in Tyler, *Narratives,* 18. For an extended discussion of this theme for Virginia and elsewhere, see David D. Smits, "'The Squaw Drudge': A Prime Index of Savagism," *Ethnohistory* 29 (1982): 281–306.

29 Smith, "Description," in Tyler, *Narratives,* 101, 96–97, 103; See also John Smith, *Travels and Works,* quoted in Edmund Morgan, *American Slavery, American Freedom: The Ordeal of Colonial Virginia* (New York: W.W. Norton, 1975), 51.

30 Laurence, "The Cradle to the Grave," 66–75; Jo Murphy-Lawless, "Images of Poor Women in the Writings of Irish Men Midwives," in *Women in Early Modern Ireland,* eds. Margaret MacCurtain and Mary O'Dowd (Edinburgh: Edinburgh University Press, 1991), 201–303.

31 "Their women (they say) are easilie delivered of childe, yet doe they love children verie dearly," reported Smith; see Smith, "Description," in Tyler, *Narratives,* 99.

32 See Axtell, *The European and the Indian,* 45, 47–55, 57–60, for the deeper reverberations of different clothing and naming practices; Kupperman, *John Smith,* 100; Strachey, *Historie,* 73.

33 Smith, *Proceedings of the English Colonies,* in Tyler, *Narratives,* 153–154.

34 Hariot, *Briefe and True Report;* Percy, "Observations," in Tyler, *Narratives,* 12; Smith, "Description," in Tyler, *Narratives,* 99–100.

35 Smith, "Description," in Tyler, *Narratives,* 100; Percy, "Observations," in *ibid,* 12. For a reprint of sixteenth-century sketches of American Indians, see Theodore deBry, *Thomas Hariot's Virginia* (Ann Arbor, Mi.: University of Michigan Press, 1966).

36 Smith, *Proceedings of the English Colonies,* in Tyler, *Narratives,* 154. The horns worn by native women may have reinforced this notion of promiscuity because of English associations of horns with cuckoldry.

37 Hariot, *A Briefe and True Report.*
38 Percy, "Observations," in Tyler, *Narratives,* 10.
39 Smith, "Description," in Tyler, *Narratives,* 106. Percy, "Observations," in Tyler, *Narratives,* 6.
40 Percy, "Observations," in Tyler, *Narratives,* 6. For the history of the word cannibalism and its connection to English aspirations in the New World, see Peter Hulme, *Colonial Encounters: Europe and the Native Caribbean, 1492–1797* (London: Routledge, 1986), 45–87.
41 Smith, *True Relation,* in Barbour, *Complete Works,* 1: 59.
42 Spelman, "Relation," cxiv, cviii.
43 Smith, "Description," in Tyler, *Narratives,* 99; Strachey, *Historie,* 70.
44 Smith, *True Relation,* in Barbour, *Complete Works,* 1: 54–55. See also James Axtell, *Beyond 1492: Encounters in Colonial North America* (New York: Oxford University Press, 1992), 66.
45 Smith, *True Relation,* in Barbour, *Complete Works,* 1: 85.
46 "Letter of John Rolfe, 1614," in Tyler, *Narratives,* 241.
47 See Clifford M. Lewis and Albert J. Loomie, *The Spanish Jesuit Mission in Virginia, 1570–1572* (Chapel Hill, N.C.: University of North Carolina Press, 1953); Axtell, *Beyond 1492;* 104; Rountree, *Powhatan Indians,* 142; Rountree, *Pocahantas's People,* 15–18. For Indian investigations of Smith's possible involvement in the killing of the Tappahannock *werowance,* see Smith, *True Relation,* in Barbour, *Complete Works,* 1: 51. Powhatan spoke to Smith of other Europeans and of Roanoake; see *ibid,* 39. C.A. Weslager, *The Nanticoke Indians* (Newark, Del.: University of Delaware Press, 1986), 27, suggests that initial Nanticoke hostility to the English was a result of previous contact.
48 Smith, *True Relation,* in Barbour, *Complete Works,* 1: 39, 91.
49 Axtell, *Beyond 1492,* 101; Strachey, *Historie,* 85. See also *ibid,* 66, for an account of Warroskoyack Indians mocking the English when an Indian hostage escaped from an English ship.
50 Rountree, *Powhatan Indians,* 89; Kupperman, *John Smith,* 173.
51 Kupperman, *John Smith,* 174, for Powhatan's speech to Smith. For a Chickahominy orator's similar comments to Smith, see Kupperman, *John Smith,* 190. See also Kupperman, *John Smith,* 185, for Smith's admission of the English dependence on native corn supplies. For Smith's description of the engagement with the Kecoughtan, see Smith, *General Historie,* in Barbour, *Complete Works,* 2: 144.
52 Smith, *General Historie,* in Barbour, *Complete Works,* 2: 45.
53 Kupperman, *John Smith,* 175.
54 These sexual diplomats may well be the same women Smith claimed "were common whores by profession"; see Kupperman, *John Smith,* 156, 157.
55 Smith, "Description," in Tyler, *Narratives,* 114–115.
56 The provision of women to foreign men was a fairly common Indian diplomatic practice throughout the South as well as in Central and South America; see for example, Gutierrez, *Corn Mothers,* 16–20. This was a highly politicized form of sexual hospitality which stood in sharp contrast to the violent reaction when native women were kidnapped by foreign warriors; see Kupperman, *John Smith,* 100.
57 Axtell, *Beyond 1492,* 39, 45, 102; My interpretation is compatible with Axtell, *Beyond 1492,* 31–33, in which he claims that while Europeans stressed sharp distinctions between Europeans and non-Europeans, Indians stressed the similarities. William Strachey believed that assimilation was Powhatan's strategy for mediating English relations with other Indians outside the paramount chiefdom; see Strachey, *Historie,* 107.

58 Strachey, *Historie,* 60.
59 Strachey, *Historie,* 63; Smith, *True Relation,* in Barbour, *Complete Works,* 1: 71, for a similar tactic by Powhatan.
60 Smith, *True Relation,* in Barbour, *Complete Works,* 39.
61 Spelman, "Relation," cviii.
62 Kupperman, *John Smith,* 62, 65.
63 J.A. Leo Lemay, *Did Pocahantas Save Captain John Smith?* (Athens, Ga.: University of Georgia Press, 1992) is the most recent interpretation of this event. An ardent believer in Smith's veracity, Lemay fails to explore the degree to which Smith may have misunderstood the meaning of the near-death ritual. For primary accounts of the events, see Smith, *True Relation,* in Barbour, *Complete Works,* 1: 45; Smith, *General Historie* in Kupperman, *John Smith,* 64–65.
64 Smith, *True Relation,* in Barbour, *Complete Works,* 1: 61–67.
65 Kupperman, *John Smith,* 173.
66 Kupperman, *John Smith,* 173–175.
67 Kupperman, *John Smith,* 175.
68 Stephen R. Potter, "Early English Effects on Virginia Algonquian Exchange and Tribute," in Wood, *Powhatan's Mantle,* 151–172, especially 151, 160; Martha McCartney, "Cockacoeske, Queen of the Pamunkey: Diplomat and Suzeraine," in Wood, *Powhatan's Mantle,* 173–195; Merrell, "Customes of Our Country," 122–123; Robert Beverley, *The History and Present State of Virginia [1705],* ed. Louis V. Wright (Chapel Hill, 1947), 232–233.
69 For analyses of the devastation wrought by contact, see Hudson, *Southeastern Indians,* chapter 8; Silver, *New Face on the Countryside,* 74–83, 88, 102; Crosby, *Ecological Imperialism,* chapter 9; Merrell, "'The Customes of Our Country,'" 122–126. Powhatan himself commented upon the devastation he had witnessed in the course of three generations; see Kupperman, *John Smith,* 174. See also Wright, *The Only Land They Knew,* 24–26; Peter Wood, "The Changing Population of the Colonial South: An Overview by Race and Region, 1685–1790," in Wood, *Powhatan's Mantle,* 38, 40–42; Silver, *New Face on the Countryside,* 72, 81, 87–88, 91; Potter, "Early English Effects on Virginia Algonquian Exchange and Tribute"; Robert Steven Grumet, "Sunksquaws, Shamans, and Tradeswomen: Middle Atlantic Coastal Algonkian Women During the 17th and 18th Centuries" in *Women and Colonization: Anthropological Perspectives,* ed. Mona Etienne and Eleanor Leacock (New York: Praeger, 1980), 43–62.

# 7

# VIRGINS AND CANNIBALS

*Alan Greer*

*[Catherine Tekakwitha's brief but remarkable life inspired hagiographies written by two Jesuits, Claude Chauchetière and Pierre Cholenec. Though both authors wrote convinced of Catherine's sainthood, their narratives differed in crucial respects.]* . . . It is particularly in the area of sexuality that the two accounts diverge. Both Jesuits insist on Catherine's chastity, as well they might, for sexual purity was a prime religious virtue in the Catholic tradition and one that was considered especially crucial where saintly women were concerned. Even more than the medieval church, "the Counter-Reformation Church placed chastity above all other attributes for female religiosity."[1] Chauchetière's account certainly acknowledges Tekakwitha's "purity," but it also celebrates other virtues, her heroic "austerities," her charity and industry, as well as her strength of character in withstanding slanderous rumors of adultery; Chauchetière the mystic also emphasizes a certain ineffable holy quality in his subject. In Pierre Cholenec's biography, on the other hand, the triumph of the spirit over bodily impurity is a central theme, one that threatens to overwhelm all others.

Catherine was not simply a woman who decided to forgo sexual relations; she was someone who had never since birth been "tainted" by carnality. For Cholenec, her virginity was of paramount importance. More emphatically than Chauchetière, he argued the case for sainthood in the arena of sexuality. He even went so far as to attach the subtitle "The First Iroquois Virgin" to his 1696 manuscript "Life of Catherine Tegakouita," staking a claim to absolute priority that seems rather puzzling at first glance. Behind this seemingly absurd claim—as though no Iroquois had ever before been a virgin!—lies a complex set of religious distinctions and moral gradations in the Catholic understanding of sexual virtue. Cholenec wished to highlight this special virginal quality and even to distinguish her virginity from other, less religiously exalted, virginal states.

In many cultures around the world, sexuality is enmeshed in ideas of pollution and purity.[2] Commonly, erotic activity is considered polluting for certain individuals within a society or in specified circumstances, whereas abstinence can have a spiritually empowering effect. For example, among the Iroquois of the early colonial period, hunters and warriors habitually shunned sex to maintain their strength and enhance their luck, while certain medicinal plants were efficacious only when "put to work by chaste hands." According to Lafitau, "They attribute to virginity and chastity certain particular qualities and virtues and it is certain that, if continence appears to them an essential condition for gaining success, as their superstition suggests to them, they will guard it with scrupulous care and not dare to violate it the least bit in the world for fear that their fasts and everything that they could do besides would be rendered useless by this non-observance."[3]

In European Catholicism, there was a tendency, dating back to Saint Augustine according to one scholar, to link sexuality with original sin and therefore to consider it polluting in a general and pervasive sense.[4] While orthodox churchmen always maintained that sexual enjoyment within marriage was perfectly legitimate, there was much anxiety in the early modern period about the dangers posed by lustful impulses, even when those urges were directed toward a spouse.[5] Sex was never considered "bad" in an absolute sense (except by heretics), but it did carry a vague taint associated with human weakness and mortality. Chastity, by contrast, was a virtue, symbolized by the "pure" color white and required of all priests, nuns, and monks. The Protestant assault on clerical celibacy only served to reinforce Catholic insistence on this as a prime requisite for the dedicated religious life.

It is not surprising that celibacy emerged as a central component of the women's religious circle that Catherine belonged to at Kahnawake. Aiming as they did to appropriate French spiritual power by emulating the ways of the most religiously potent French women, they could not help noticing how much store the European nuns set by their nonmarital, asexual regimen. Even though the Iroquois tended to value abstinence in situational terms—it was a requirement of certain functions and situations rather than an attribute essential to an elevated state of existence—the spiritual seekers of Kahnawake would have been prepared to accept the basic notion of a connection between sexual abstinence and spiritual empowerment. This fundamental correspondence encouraged a cross-cultural reading of religious celibacy in spite of the untranslatability of Christian concepts such as "sin," "Virtue," and "concupiscence."

Sex for the Iroquois was not "bad," and for most purposes sexual activity did not leave any lasting contamination: it was simply incompatible with certain states and activities. Virginity was characteristic of a particular life stage, and celibacy was usually a temporary state; life-long renunciation of sex not only was a potential health hazard but also could be hard to square with an individual's responsibilities to others. The conflict between celibacy and family obligations was precisely what had long recommended that state to Old World Christians seeking religious perfection. Alongside shifting attitudes toward sexual purity and pollution ran an enduring distrust of "worldly ties" that harked back to Saint Paul's advice to the unmarried in 1 Corinthians 7: marry if you must, but stay single if you can, "that ye may attend upon the Lord without distraction." According to some interpretations, Christian celibacy was, in its origins, not so much about condemning "the flesh" as about emancipating individual believers from the constraining bonds of matrimony and kin. To return to the words of Paul's epistle, "He that is unmarried careth for the things that belong to the Lord, how he may please the Lord. But he that is married careth for the things that are of the world, how he may please his wife."[6]

This antifamily dimension of Catholic celibacy was what Iroquois people had difficulty contemplating. Self-control and the subordination of erotic urges for spiritual purposes were a part of their culture no less than that of the Europeans, but an individual existence outside the framework of clan and longhouse, and free from the marital ties that constituted these units, was harder to fathom. Men normally needed to marry in order to gain entry to a nourishing and sheltering longhouse society, and women had need of a husband for a variety of reasons; prominent among the latter was the necessity of securing the skins and meat that only a hunter could supply. Accordingly, many of the most pious Christian Iroquois seem to have found it easier to renounce sex within marriage than to forgo the social and economic dimensions of matrimony; the Jesuits mention several couples living together at the Sault "as brother and sister."[7]

Catherine was one of the few who avoided sexual and domestic entanglements with men to the end of her life. To do so, she had to resist pressures to marry, both before her conversion to Christianity and after her move to Kahnawake. Pierre Cholenec recounts the later challenges to her virginal vocation in great detail, for he considered this "one of the most beautiful passages in the story of her life,"[8] no doubt because it revolved around his favorite theme and because, in his telling, it recalled the heroic struggles of saintly European girls such as Catherine of Siena to resist parental attempts to force them into wedlock. Chauchetière makes no mention of any of this in his biography. His silence does not necessarily mean that the other Jesuit fabricated the whole story, though that is a possibility. But regardless of discrepancies over plot details, it does appear that Catherine shunned marriage and thus gained credit, from Cholenec's standpoint, for choosing the Lord in preference to any flesh-and-blood husband.

More was at stake, however, than strength of character and the renunciation of worldly ties: in proclaiming her a virgin, Cholenec surrounded his heroine with a quasi-magical quality. Anthropologists tell us that, in many cultures where purity anxieties prevail, sex is seen as a threat to the impermeability of the body; conversely, the unpenetrated body of the female virgin is especially venerated.[9] Father Lafitau reports that several native nations of the Americas accorded special status to virginal young women:

> As regards the Iroquois, whom I know a little better, they have certainly had their virgins who are so by status, whom they called *Ieouinnon*. I cannot possibly say what their religious functions properly were. All that I have been able to get out of the Iroquois is that they never left their cabins, that they were occupied in small tasks purely to keep busy. The people held them in respect and left them in peace.

European traders debauched these "vestal virgins" with brandy, continues Lafitau, and so their special status dissolved at an early stage of colonial contact.[10] Catholic Christendom was another culture in which female virgins enjoyed quasi-sacred status. From the fourth century, writes Peter Brown, "Dedicated women came to be thought of as harboring a deposit of values that were prized by their male spokesmen, as peculiarly precious to the Christian community."[11] Through the Middle Ages and the early modern period, when clergymen were expected to cultivate celibacy as one virtue among many, virginal "brides of Christ" (nuns) seemed to radiate a spiritual potency from the core of their untainted beings.

But what should we make of Father Cholenec's designation of Catherine as "the first Iroquois virgin"? Never mind Lafitau's observations about the "vestal virgins" of ancient times: there were cases in the Jesuit record from Cholenec's own time citing Iroquois, "pagans" as well as converts, who shunned sex and marriage to the end of their days.[12] In claiming this unique priority for his heroine, the Jesuit clearly has in mind factors other than simple abstinence from a physical act. The author explains in his biography:

> But what made our Catherine more blessed than all the rest and placed her in a higher rank, not only than the other Indians of the Sault, but than all the Indians who have embraced the faith throughout New France, was this great and glorious title of virgin. It was to have been the first in this new world who, by a special inspiration of the Holy Ghost, consecrated her virginity to Our Lord.[13]

Though we might think of virginity as an all-or-nothing condition, comparable in that respect to pregnancy, it turns out that for a sophisticated cleric of the seventeenth century, there were degrees and varieties of virginity.

Virginity as a Christian virtue required complete abstention from coitus, but that physical state counted for little if it was merely accidental; to merit the virgin's halo, abstention had to be intentional and religiously motivated. As a graduate in theology, the Jesuit hagiographer would surely have been aware of Thomas Aquinas's writings on the "special crown called the aureole," that "is due virginity." The philosopher insists that the aureole is not "due to the act . . . because in this case those who have the will to marry and nevertheless die before marrying would have the aureole." Instead, "virginity comes under the genus of virtue in so far as perpetual incorruption of mind and body is an object of choice . . . . Consequently the aureole is due to those virgins alone, who had the purpose of observing perpetual virginity, whether or not they have confirmed this purpose by vow—and this I say with reference to the aureole in its proper signification of a reward due to merit." "Integrity of the flesh" remains the sine qua non, but religious significance depends on the state of mind and intention for the future.[14]

To the degree that Cholenec was writing with an audience of theological experts in mind, he clearly wished to establish a claim on Catherine's behalf to that virginal crown: hence his emphasis on her struggles to avoid marriage and maintain her sexual purity. He would have been aware of the skepticism such a proposition was bound to provoke, and he presumably felt that a dramatic event was needed to distinguish Tekakwitha's story from those of other pious Indian converts. Accordingly, he consolidates and reinforces his claim by declaring that, in addition to preserving her purity, she actually took a solemn vow of perpetual virginity.

After triumphing over the pressures to marry, and after pursuing ever more painful penitential practices, Cholenec's Catherine formed a desire to "give herself entirely to the Lord by an irrevocable pledge." Such a momentous gesture was unheard of for Indians, and so, as a prudent spiritual director, he made her wait, pending additional proof of her unflagging constancy. She was overjoyed when the priest finally gave permission. Then, "on the Feast of the Annunciation, 25 March 1679, about eight in the morning," Catherine Tekakwitha took communion and promised Jesus Christ "perpetual virginity," asking him "to be her only spouse." In the same ceremony, she solemnly dedicated her virginity to Mary as well as to her son. Cholenec considered this nunlike vow "her greatest glory before God."[15]

So writes Pierre Cholenec. But what about Tekakwitha's other biographer? How does Chauchetière treat this crucial incident? Under the heading "Her Chastity" appears the following passage:

> It is the most beautiful jewel in her crown . . . . Men, God and conscience have given witness to the truth that Catherine never committed a single sin of the flesh. . . . If it had occurred to anyone to have her take a vow, the vow of chastity would not have been wanting, though she did not fail to live up to such a vow, which makes me believe that she received the merit of it. The priest was sorry after her death not to have let her make it.[16]

The wording is rather awkward, as no doubt were Claude's sentiments on the subject, but the contradiction is clear enough: Pierre Cholenec himself had declined to administer the vow of chastity while Catherine was alive, and, regretting his decision afterward, he revised the record of events.

It is apparent that the Jesuits, Claude and Pierre at least, but perhaps others as well, had argued among themselves about what to make of Tekakwitha's virginity and how to present their case to a skeptical audience of European Catholics. There are hints in Cholenec's manuscript that one missionary at the Sault (Chauchetière?) had harbored doubts shortly after the death about whether Catherine had even been a genuine virgin in the minimal, biological, sense. There had, after all, been rumors of illicit liaisons.[17] But all uncertainty had been laid to rest by the miraculous cures that God had presumably sent to signal her saintliness and thus, by implication, to verify her sexual purity. Because prayers in her name were efficacious, she must have been a virgin. This established fact, joined to all the other evidence of holiness in her life story, indicated that she possessed as much religious merit as any nun who may have dedicated her chastity to God through the holiest of vows. This is what Chauchetière means when he avers that she "received the merit" of a vow she would have taken had she been given the opportunity and whose terms she did in fact adhere to. And his colleague, following the example of innumerable hagiographers in adjusting raw historical data to the demands of religiously meaningful discourse, simply translated this virtual vow into a literal event.

The story of the fictive vow, repeated in most subsequent retellings of the Catherine Tekakwitha narrative, seems designed both to bring the larger narrative into closer conformity with standard hagiographic plots for women saints and to shore up the claim to virginal status. The emphasis on holy virginity, so much more insistent in Cholenec's shrewd writings than in Claude's more naive biography, has to be understood in light of prevailing European views of native women's sexuality. One early vulgarizer of the Tekakwitha story, a military officer who had served many years in Canada, suggested that Catherine could only have had a confused idea of what virginity was when she first came to the Sault, as "this state was too elevated to be proposed to Indians, the latter being so carnal by nature."[18] Against the backdrop of this underlying suspicion—the sense that the sexual propriety of Indians women was always in question, even when there was no particular evidence of vice—Pierre Cholenec penned his overstated defense of Catherine's virginal purity.

When Europeans and Euro-Americans of the early modern period thought about *inidas, indiennes*, or "Indian women," their views were shaped by a number of assumptions about culture, race, and sexuality. More important than any propositions consciously agreed upon were the basic mental structures—built into language and prior to reflection—by which people organized information about the world. There was a tendency, for example, to consider natives under the heading of "savages," a category that suggested an absence of effective government and personal restraint. The concept of savagery had ancient antecedents leading back to Greek views of the "barbarians,"[19] but centuries of conquest and colonization in the Americas had shaped and modified the sense of basic difference between the "civilized" and the "savage" state. Thus, Europeans of the time generally expected to find poverty, violence, and unconstrained lust among the indigenous peoples they encountered, because these were understood to be essential features that identified them as savages. (Explorers and missionaries kept coming across contrary evidence, but such puzzling anomalies were slow to affect the architecture of the imperial mind.) Certainly there was room for considerable variation in the way the savage/civilized dichotomy was deployed—in the hands of Claude Chauchetière, for one, its values were inverted to the advantage of the natives—but the sense of fundamental difference was a constant. The fact that it tended to accompany, and serve as justification for, the dehumanizing processes of colonization, conquest, and enslavement does not mean that it was simply an ideology, cynically constructed with a practical purpose in mind; rather, it represented a deeper level of mental operations.

The male/female dichotomy was another deep organizing principle that conditioned the way Europeans of the seventeenth century made sense of the world. Like the savage/civilized polarity, it was rich in overtones and adaptable, but as with the discourse on the savage, it also tended to define one element, in this case the female, as a deficient version of the other. Women had many admirable qualities, it was thought, but as a species they were less strong, less courageous, less governed by rational constraint than were men. Closer to nature and more subject to bodily appetites, they were more likely to succumb to sexual urges if they were not properly supervised.

Native women therefore seemed doubly savage in their essential nature, for they stood at the wild end of two basic polarities of European thinking. Moreover, when we remember that the moral evaluation of women in this period was primarily sexual—"vice" and "virtue" had connotations that were specific to one gender or the other—then it becomes clear that to refer to someone as an Indian in the feminine form (*indienne, iroquoise*) was to situate her in the realm of sexual disorder. Prior to anything specific that might be said was an ontological starting point suggestive of impurity. It was still possible to speak of native women as virgins or as virtuous wives—and of course the French Jesuits often did just that—but the assertion could not help conveying a sense of internal contradiction, since the manifest content of the message was at odds with the overtones of the language in which it was expressed.

The image of the native woman as it developed through centuries of European conquest and colonization in the New World tended to reflect the brutally exploitive race relations that characterized the Spanish and Portuguese empires. In the Ibero-American colonies, "white" men frequently enjoyed power over the bodies of servant women of other races. French men in seventeenth-century Canada rarely confronted indigenous women in such starkly asymmetrical power relations, but many of them did take advantage of differences in native and European customs regulating extramarital sex, reinforcing in the process the notion that Indian women were inherently promiscuous. Experience thus seemed to "prove" what racial ontology suggested: that indigenous women were more readily available to white men than were women of European origin.

Europeans also encountered sexualized images of native women in the discourses and iconography of colonialism. Once again, these tendencies were most apparent where the older empires of the Iberian powers are concerned. The stories of discovery, conquest, and colonization of the New World were rife with sexual metaphors. In what the literary scholar Anne McClintock calls "the erotics of imperial conquest," Europeans were depicted entering, possessing, and ravishing a feminized America.[20] Texts and visual images frequently used women's bodies as "the boundary markers of empire." The New World's women, like its other treasures and allurements, were there to be taken by the men from Europe; consequently, even if an individual *indienne* led a life of blameless chastity, she would still be ascribed a species identity suggestive of sexual availability.[21]

It was against this background that two New France Jesuits struggled to gain acceptance for the view that a Mohawk woman stood out as a radiant example of holiness, virtue, and—of necessity—virginal purity. Pierre Cholenec seems to have grasped the importance of this last quality better than his colleague, and so he crafted his hagiography in counterpoint: difference within difference, purity in an ambience of savage impurity. In his hagiography, Catherine's virginity, certified in and through the church, was the crucial quality that served to lift her out of the native society that had nourished and raised her. She was unique, even in the pious atmosphere of Iroquois-Catholic Kahnawake, and even among the zealous ascetics whose feats of penitence were at least as amazing as her own, even among women so devoted to religious celibacy that they cut their hair as a sign of chastity. The quality of undefiled purity distinguished her in particularly striking fashion from her bosom companion, Marie-Thérèse Tegaiaguenta, a fervent Catholic who shared many of Tekakwitha's other saintly virtues.

As a widow, Marie-Thérèse suffered from the disability of sexual experience prior to her commitment to celibacy and asceticism. Moreover, both Jesuit hagiographers imply that she had wavered between "sin" and repentance over the years following her baptism (the nature of the sin is not specified, though that term, applied to a woman, suggested sexual misconduct). Married to a non-Christian, she remained strongly affected by "the disorders of her country" even after migrating to Kentake (La Prairie), but eventually she experienced what the writers considered a true conversion about the time she encountered Tekakwitha in the spring of 1678. Their first meeting occurred not long after Catherine returned from a winter hunt, the one on which the saintly Mohawk had spent her time praying at her little oratory and imaginatively projecting her soul back to its proper home in the mission chapel. In introducing this new character to their story, the Jesuit hagiographers flash back to a hunting expedition Marie-Thérèse had participated in two years earlier, in the winter of 1675–76. This juxtaposition of two different hunt subplots, parallel stories featuring young women who were Indians but also Christians and who had to negotiate the tensions between these two aspects of their identity in the "savage" environment of the forest hunting camp, seems designed to highlight Catherine's unique excellence through contrast with another worthy, but not saintly, convert.

Chauchetière includes a brief version of Tegaiaguenta's hunt in his Life of Catherine, but Cholenec develops the subplot much more fully in his two hagiographic texts. It constitutes a long digression from the main story of Tekakwitha's life. This is how it goes:

> In the early autumn [of 1675], she had embarked with her husband and a small child, the son of her sister, to go hunting on the Ottawa River. En route, they fell in with some other Iroquois, forming a party of eleven persons, four men, four women and three children. Unfortunately for them, the snows came very late that year, so that they were unable to hunt. Consequently, after having eaten all their provisions, as well as the meat of a moose her husband killed, they faced starvation. First they ate some bits of rawhide they had brought with them to make shoes [moccasins], then they ate their own shoes [possibly their moccasins, possibly the sinews of their snowshoes], and finally they were reduced to eating grasses and the bark of trees, like animals.

Starvation in the winter forests was a danger that constantly stalked hunting-gathering peoples of the northern woodlands. With fishing streams frozen hard and roots and berries no longer available, survival hinged on the hunt for mammals, particularly large animals such as moose and caribou, whose carcasses would sustain a band for some time. Proper snow conditions were critical to hunting success, not only because animals left tracks for human predators to follow but also because animals could become bogged down in deep, crusty snow when snowshoed hunters closed in for the kill. If the weather failed to cooperate for extended periods, disaster could ensue, even for the Algonquin bands who knew the land best and whose way of life revolved around finely tuned seasonal migrations in pursuit of shifting food resources.[22] Iroquois existence was usually less tenuous, for Tekakwitha's people could depend on their corn and other field crops for easily stored provisions. However, the fur trade boom and the migration to the St. Lawrence, where agricultural conditions were marginal, had given hunting a more central place in the economy of the northern Iroquois, with the result that women and children, as well as men, were embarking on long expeditions from Kentake/Kahnawake. Marie-Thérèse's party may have been at greater risk than a more experienced Algonquin band would have been under the same conditions; certainly the Iroquois people would have been comparatively ill equipped to face the terrifying prospect of winter starvation.

In every respect, Tegaiaguenta's experience was exceptional, and as the days of relentless hunger succeeded one another, desperation set in.

> Meanwhile, the husband of the woman in question [since she was still alive at the time of writing, Cholenec leaves her unnamed] fell ill and two of the party, a Mohawk and a Seneca, went off in search of game, promising to return within ten days. The Mohawk returned on the appointed day, but he came alone, assuring the others that his comrade had died of want, but it was not without reason that they suspected him of having killed him and subsisted on his flesh while he was away. They doubted him all the more because he seemed healthy though he admitted he had taken no animals. Since it was clear that the hunting there was hopeless, they decided to leave that place, urging our Christian to abandon her husband to death, since he could no longer travel, and to save herself and her nephew. But she would never consent and, resisting bravely, she was left behind with her husband and the nephew.
>
> Two days later, the sick man died, greatly regretting he had never been baptized. She buried him and then set off after the others, carrying her nephew on her shoulders. After several days walking, she caught up with the party then making its way down the river in an effort to reach the French settlements. However, they were so weak and exhausted that, after twenty days march, they could go no further.

In the fall, they would have all traveled from Kentake by canoe, a comparatively easy mode of transport, even if they did have to toil against the current of the Ottawa River. But in this midwinter evacuation, there was no choice but to trudge over those same waters, now windswept and rock hard, the adults carrying the smaller children on their backs. Under normal circumstances, a well-fed, properly clothed native party could make excellent time traveling on foot in the winter and using snowshoes wherever the snow was deep, but this bedraggled and famished band, their feet wrapped in whatever covering they were able to improvise, must have been inching along, step by painful step.

> It was then, facing starvation, that their desperation led them to a strange resolution: they would kill one of their number to sustain the others. They cast their eyes on the widow of the Seneca and her

> two children and they asked [Marie-Thérèse] if it was permissible to kill them, and what the law of the Christians said on that point, for she was the only one of the party who had been baptized. She did not dare reply as she did not know enough about this important question and she was afraid of contributing to a homicide. More to the point, she quite naturally felt that her own life depended on the answer, for she believed that, after they had eaten the woman and her two children, as they did in fact do, she herself would then be killed.
>
> As her eyes were opened to the danger to her body, [Marie-Thérèse] also began to realize that the deplorable state of her soul was infinitely more pitiable than that of her body. She felt great horror for the disorders of her past life and the fault she had committed in going on a hunting trip without first going to confession. Asking God's pardon with all her heart, she promised that if He delivered her from this danger and returned her safely to the village, she would not only confess herself immediately, but reform her life and do penance. God wished to use this woman to make Catherine known, and so He answered her prayer and after incredible pains and exertions, five of the twelve [sic] returned to La Prairie toward the middle of the winter. Among them were this woman and her little nephew.[23]

And so Tegaiaguenta survived that ordeal of starvation and anthropophagy. Did she herself taste the flesh of the unfortunate widow or her children? Cholenec does not say one way or the other, but the anecdote about the suspiciously healthy Mohawk hunter and the obvious parallel to Marie-Thérèse's situation at the journey's end constitute a broad enough hint to the reader. In any case, as a character in the life narrative of Catherine Tekakwitha, she is, to say the least, strongly associated with cannibalism for this long digression on the ill-fated hunting expedition is almost all that we are told about her personal background. Present in all versions of the hagiography, it is one of the most vivid passages in Cholenec's 1696 manuscript and of his later published biography, even though it is quite tangential to the main plot. Evidently it was important to the Jesuit.

"Survival cannibalism" of the sort Tegaiaguenta was involved in can occur in any society, though it may be especially common among hunting peoples living in inhospitable environments. If pressed, Pierre Cholenec might well have admitted that human flesh had been eaten in his own country, and in the comparatively recent past. Indeed, he does present Tegaiaguenta's "crime" as a regrettable response to extreme circumstances rather than as normal or approved Iroquois practice.

And yet, a story recounted to European readers of Indians eating human flesh could only be read as a comment on savagery, so powerful and pervasive were the ideological effects of almost two centuries of European colonization. "Man-eater" is the epithet leveled in a multitude of societies against enemy outsiders—the term "Mohawk," for example, derives from the Algonquian word for "eater of human flesh"—and in medieval Europe, "internal outsiders" such as heretics, Jews, and witches were often accused of ritual murder and the eating of Christians. Ever since 1492, however, cannibalism and American savagery had become indissolubly linked in Europe's colonial imagination. Columbus himself introduced the word "cannibal" into Spanish, and thence into other European tongues, when he adopted the Arawaks' designation of their supposedly ferocious enemies from the Lesser Antilles: Carib/Caribal/Cannibal. What had previously been seen as a sin tended to become, with this new linguistic coinage, the defining feature of an entire sector of humanity. "Cannibals" were not simply people with a strange offensive custom; they became the quintessence of savagery, a species of humanity classified under the insignia of a monstrous crime. There were indeed countercurrents in the European cannibal discourse, critics such as Michel de Montaigne and Jean de Léry, who insisted that Brazilian cannibals possessed redeeming qualities and that European civilization was, on balance, no less cruel in its customs. But even in these relativist accounts, anthopophagy still stamped whole nations with a complete, and a fundamentally alien, identity.[24]

When Europeans of the early modern period read or heard about the Caribs of the West Indies or the Tupinambá of coastal Brazil and when they viewed woodcut images supposedly depicting their cannibal feasts, a varied blend of savage excesses enriched the scene of barbarity. The guiding assumption was that eating humans betokened a complete breakdown of civility and constraint, and so cannibalism and sexual license always seemed to go together.[25] Theodore de Bry's influential prints of sixteenth-century Brazil showed the cannibals as naked and sexualized, with women portrayed as the most forward in indulging their lusts and appetites.[26]

Pierre Cholenec made no such explicit denunciations of Marie-Thérèse, nor did he even apply the "cannibal" label to the winter incidents of 1676. But when the colonialist images and assumptions lurking in the background and conditioning the outlooks of author and reader are borne in mind, this episode in the biography of Tekakwitha seems laden with meaning. A young woman, raised as a savage, finds herself deep in the forest, a "savage" location, engaged in hunting, a "savage" pursuit. She is sexually experienced and, though baptized, still attached to the sinful customs of her people. When circumstances force her to eat human flesh (whether or not she actually indulged in cannibalism, Cholenec leaves at least a suspicion hanging in the air), that act conclusively identifies her as a tainted being, notwithstanding her later piety. All these evil associations operate as so many points of contrast that serve to highlight Catherine's fundamental purity. Entirely free of sexual contamination, the younger woman had grown up among pagan Indians without her inner nature having been affected by Iroquois "savagery." Moreover, when she went off to the forest with a winter hunting party, far from surrendering to evil, she remained immune to the savage influences of that locale and of that bloody endeavor.

Thus the story of Catherine's vow of virginity and the digression on Marie-Thérèse's cannibal adventure have a convergent tendency, both serving to dissociate the holy girl from the polluting effects of sexuality and savagery, Together they have the calculated effect of assuring the European reader that this *indienne* was not what she seemed. On the surface an Indian woman, with all that that phrase stood for at the time, she was still a saint in her essential inner being.

As the seventeenth century drew to a close, Catherine Tekakwitha's fame was spreading through the Jesuits' transatlantic network of correspondence. Versions of Chauchetière's and Cholenec's manuscript hagiographies were read in France and in the French West Indies, while Claude dispatched drawings of the Mohawk saint to acquaintances overseas. (These pictures reportedly brought relief to headache sufferers when pressed against the forehead.)[27] However, the time was not considered right to publish the astonishing news of Indian saintliness.

This was the era of the "Chinese Rites" controversy, when the Society of Jesus was under attack for compromising Catholic orthodoxy by adapting to the local culture in its missionary efforts in China. Enemies within the church had seized the opportunity to accuse the Jesuits of heterodoxy, and the once-mighty order was on the defensive, afraid to make any extravagant claims, especially in the area of overseas missions. The *Jesuit Relations* had long since been suppressed by a papacy alarmed at the dangers inherent in public discussion of Jesuit experiments in cross-cultural religion, but restrictions eased somewhat after the acute phase of the Chinese Rites controversy died down. In the early eighteenth century, French Jesuits ventured to resurrect an annual mission publication, though this time it was global in scope and not restricted, as the *Relations* had been, to New France. The *Lettres édifiantes et curieuses* took the form of reports from Jesuits (mainly French) working in Vietnam, China, California, Africa, the West Indies, and other distant lands. In the Francis Xavier tradition, they were crammed with interesting information about the flora, fauna, landscape, and human customs of exotic lands, as well as with inspiring tales of conversion; in fact, "curious" content rather outweighed "edifying" material, thus ensuring a wide readership among the secular minded. It was in the pages of the *Lettres édifiantes et curieuses* that a reworked version of Pierre Cholenec's life of Catherine Tekakwitha was published in 1717.[28]

At this point in the eighteenth century, French Jesuits were among those most closely engaged in the intellectual ferment of the time, as churchmen and early Enlightenment philosophers reassessed basic questions about human nature, the truths of religion, and the diversity of cultures.[29] Regardless of the considerations that drove Cholenec and Chauchetière to proclaim the holiness of the saintly Mohawk, the editors of the *Lettres édifiantes* likely had European philosophical issues of the day in mind when they decided to print this ninety-two-page tale of virginal perfection and wondrous cures. "Pagans" and "savages" had long played a prominent part in Western discussions of fundamental questions about what it means to be human, and in the hands of thinkers such as Rousseau and Diderot, they would continue to be called upon for that purpose down through the century.

Around 1717, Jesuit intellectuals tended to be preoccupied with the struggle against Augustinian tendencies within the church and secular deist tendencies outside it. To summarize, briefly and crudely, the way in which larger debates were played out in discussions of overseas missions, Augustinians were inclined to attribute paganism to sin and to hold out little hope for the genuine conversion of peoples outside the European cultural sphere. Whereas Augustinians would see natives as depraved and largely irredeemable, secular deists regarded them as people without religion, guided by natural reason; this view reinforced skepticism as to the universal applicability and absolute truth of Christian revelation. The Jesuits challenged both these views with a theory of universal theism that found inklings of Christian faith and instances of Christian virtue spread among the cultures of the globe; conversion therefore was only a matter of bringing to the fore a latent Christianity that was already present among pagans and savages. A comparatively favorable view of Indians, of their indigenous culture, and of their potential for Christian sanctity thus formed an integral element of Jesuit debates with opponents both within and beyond the Catholic fold.[30] The story of the Mohawk Virgin would have served the polemical purpose of demonstrating the unlimited spiritual potential even of natives raised in paganism. Since deists denied the possibility of God working outside the laws of nature, it may also have served the secondary purpose of asserting the reality of miracles.

Whatever philosophical agenda may have led to the publication of Cholenec's hagiography, it had now been published and widely disseminated. In place of the many drafts and manuscript biographies that Cholenec and Chauchetière had labored over through the previous decades—divergent, constantly under revision, limited in their circulation—there was now a printed text: permanent, authoritative, mass-produced. For almost two centuries, until Chauchetière's hagiography was retrieved from obscurity and printed in 1887, Cholenec's account defined the Tekakwitha story and served as the source for hundreds of subsequent versions of the narrative.

Seven years after the initial *Lettres édifiantes* article, the story first appeared as a freestanding book; moreover, this was a Spanish translation of Cholenec's biography, and it was published not in Europe but in the New World, *La gracia triunfante en la vida de Catharina Tegakovita, india iroquesa*, appeared in 1724 in Mexico City, capital of the viceroyalty of New Spain, a city far older, richer, and more impressive than any of the little settlements then established in French or British North America.[31] So remote from Mexico were New France and the lands of the Iroquois that hardly anyone there had heard of such places. The translator located them just east of New Mexico and the Apaches.[32] It seems that the international Jesuit network had delivered the French publication to residents of one of the order's colleges in Mexico City just at a moment when issues surrounding native women, religion, and chastity were agitating local spirits.

A convent was about to open, specially endowed for Indian nuns, and the municipal authorities were attempting to block it. *Indias* were unsuited to the religious life, according to expert witnesses testifying before the city council, because they could not be trusted to "mortify their disorderly appetites" and observe the vow of chastity. Proponents of the convent had to counter a colonialist mentality, much more pronounced in New Spain than in New France, that associated indigenous women and sexual promiscuity. Whereas natives enjoyed a high degree of cultural and economic autonomy in the Canadian setting, they were very much a subjugated people in Mexico City. Subjugated but omnipresent, they outnumbered "white" residents in the region and played a vital role in the city's labor market. As domestic servants, Indians—especially Indian women—entered the households of the urban elite, where they faced sexual and economic exploitation. With servants giving birth to mixed-race babies and with Spanish tastes being affected by Nahua aesthetics, cuisine, and child-rearing practices, anxieties about preserving boundaries between the colonizers and the colonized were bound to intensify. Hence the long tradition in New Spain of attempting to legislate racial divisions, with laws prohibiting Indians and other members of inferior races from carrying swords, taking university degrees, or entering the clergy. Honor and prestige were reserved to Spaniards of "pure blood," and that included access to religious orders.

For Indians to be accepted as nuns was particularly objectionable to colonial opinion in Mexico, for convents had a special symbolic role as reservoirs of white female sexuality and reserved procreative power. Often referred to as "Virgins" (even though some were widows and therefore honorary virgins), nuns were women with a unique claim to perfect purity on both racial and sexual grounds. In theory, every postulant in New Spain had to produce a certificate of *limpieza de sangre* guaranteeing that her blood was untainted by Jewish, Muslim, or Indian ancestry before she could take her oath of chastity.[33] The fact that Indian women did actually gain entry to nunneries as religious women of uncertain status did not alter the basic image of the convent as an island of purity radiating spiritual power over a colonial society threatened by the menace of hybridity.

In this context, *La gracia triunfante en la vida de Catharina Tegakovita, india iroquesa*, was presented as a political pamphlet in hagiographic form, and it was meant, as the preface states quite explicitly, to prove that Indian women really were capable of lifelong virginity for religious purposes. Some biographical sketches of exemplary piety on the part of Mexican native women were appended, but Cholenec's life of Tekakwitha was the central document in the volume. In a Catholic society, the sacred biography genre carried a weight and an authority that made it an ideal instrument for reconfiguring ontological assumptions about the nature of Indian women. There may have been saintly women in Spanish America whose life stories could have been recounted for this purpose, but no white clergyman had ever thought to research and record a native biography in any detail. Consequently, when the Jesuit defenders of the new convent went looking for material to fuel their polemics, they were forced to turn to the religious literature of New France, where a Catholic empire had been built upon alliance rather than conquest and where the conventions of colonial hagiography had been turned upside down.[34]

Given that it is a biography of a virgin written by a celibate Jesuit priest, sexuality forms a surprisingly prominent theme in Pierre Cholenec's account of the life of Tekakwitha. But, of course, how could the subject be avoided in a hagiographic work, when hagiography is a catalog of Christian virtues and when virtue in a woman was understood to be fundamentally sexual virtue? The special veneration long accorded to female virgins in the European Catholic tradition was another dimension of the mentality of the period that led the hagiographer to bolster his case by dwelling on Catherine's exceptional "purity." The fact that she was a "savage," a woman raised outside the constraining influence of civilization, meant that her sexual virtue was doubly uncertain and therefore doubly in need of verification and emphasis. As Indian and as woman she tended to be associated with nature a wild, unregulated, and therefore dangerous domain in the eyes of many Europeans of the seventeenth century.

Over the course of the eighteenth century, and under the influence of intellectual and artistic currents conventionally labeled "the Enlightenment" and "Romanticism," the idea of nature acquired new and generally more positive connotations. And even as settler regimes continued to subjugate or marginalize native peoples in the Americas, artists and philosophers were increasingly inclined to idealize Indians as the embodiment of simplicity, transparency, and stoic fortitude.[35] In this altered intellectual atmosphere, the story of the Mohawk saint continued to find an audience. The various poles of opposition that structured the original biography—nature/culture, savage/civilized, female/male, polluted/pure—had shifted significantly in their meaning and valence, but Tekakwitha continued to represent basic difference: she was the exotic figure onto which writer and reader projected fantasies. And in the hands of a series of novelists, these fantasies carried a barely concealed erotic charge.

François-René de Chateaubriand, a major early Romantic writer, inserted Catherine Tekakwitha into his sprawling and never completely finished novel, *Les Natchez*. Published in 1826, the work had been written in the 1790s when Chateaubriand was a Royalist exile from the French Revolution living in London. Set in the North American forests, *Les Natchez* was inspired partly by the writer's tour through the young United States, from Baltimore to Niagara Falls, and partly by his readings on France's now shattered colonial empire. His favorite source was the works of the Jesuit traveler and historian Pierre-François-Xavier de Charlevoix. In the mid-eighteenth century, Charlevoix had published massive, multivolume histories of Canada, Louisiana, other distant lands; one long chapter in the *History and General Description of New France*[36] consisted of a paraphrased version of Cholenec's 1717 sacred biography of Catherine Tekakwitha.

Chateaubriand's central theme was love and sex in the natural world of America, with the encounter of European civilization and savage North America providing the tension to his narrative. Set on the frontiers of French Louisiana and Spanish Florida, the novel contains an extended subplot about the passion of the Natchez chief Chactas for the beautiful Atala, a Catholic convert who had pledged to preserve her virginity. Another part of the narrative takes the form of a colonial love story featuring the solitary French explorer, René, who arrives in the Natchez village years later, when Chactas is an old man. The chief's lovely daughter, Céduta, is assigned to cook for the white stranger, and she instantly falls in love with him. René responds to her naive and artless devotion, but there can be no happiness for the young couple, since the native enemies of the Natchez have enlisted the aid of a French army to attack and destroy Céluta's doomed people.

On the verge of the looming holocaust, Chateaubriand shifts the scene to heaven, where saintly figures are about to implore divine intervention. A strange amalgam of Greek mythology and Catholic mysticism, all wrapped in a style derived from Milton, this celestial interlude also seems morally confused, since the object of concern slides from an imperiled "America"—apparently represented by the Natchez town about to be immolated—to "la France," the imperial power whose troops are preparing the attack. It is in the midst of this contradictory thrust that Catherine Tekakwitha makes her appearance as, at once, the personification of native North America and the guardian spirit of France. Along with Saintè Genevieve, the shepherd girl who mobilized Paris to defend itself against the barbarian Huns, Catherine appears at the head of a delegation of saints—including the Jesuit martyr Jean de Brébeuf and the medieval crusader-king, Saint Louis—to petition the Virgin Mary:

> People of France: warlike nation, nation of genius! Is it some famous conqueror whose spirit looks down from on high and protects your double empire? No, it is a shepherdess in Europe and an Indian girl in America! Geneviève, from the village of Nanterre, and you,

> Catherine of the Canadian forests, hold out your crook and your beech cross above my homeland. Preserve that naiveté and that natural charm which it surely draws from its patronesses!

The two female saints both strengthen France through their natural innocence, but thanks to her origins in the American wilds, Catherine possesses a distilled version of this quality. "Perhaps more simple even than the patron of civilized and regulated France is the patron of savage France."[37] One might well argue that the original Jesuit biographers of Tekakwitha tended to indulge in a form of spiritual appropriation, assimilating her specifically "savage" virtues to the cause of European Christendom, but Chateaubriand is much more direct, and quite explicit. Moreover, the appropriation he performs is in the interests of the French nation, not of the Catholic Church. A nationalist as well as a Romantic (and a contemporary of Herder's), the novelist had no hesitation in incorporating the qualities associated with the Mohawk maiden—naturalness, transparent sincerity, savage freedom—directly into the French national character. He was by no means the last to enlist the figure of Catherine Tekakwitha in the service of an improbable nationalist cause.

Though Tekakwitha herself is not sexualized in *Les Natchez*, she is placed in the midst of a highly eroticized story of colonial desire. In this respect, Chateaubriand's novel is at once archetypical and characteristic of its time. Almost from the beginning of American colonization, stories of love—invariably ill-fated—between a native woman and a man from Europe form a staple of the literature of travel and encounter. Typically, the Indian maiden is spontaneously and immediately attracted to the white stranger. She gives of herself with generosity and naïveté, providing food and other assistance as well as uncomplicated sex. The Pocahontas legend is only the best known of these colonial narratives. "The major feature of this myth," writes the literary critic Peter Hulme, "is the ideal of cultural harmony through romance." The relationship between colonizers and indigenous people, marked in historical reality by violence and exploitation, is transformed into a redeeming story of interracial love. Why Pocahontas, like Céluta, falls for a white stranger is never explained, but the implications are clear enough according to Hulme: "Inseparable from Pocahontas's love for Smith is her recognition of the superiority of English culture."[38]

Though built around the venerable colonial fantasy of the redeeming romance, Chateaubriand's novel is also a characteristic creation of the Romantic age. America and its indigenous inhabitants represent heightened passion and an authenticity that was felt to be lacking in Europe.[39] While one Indian maid, Ceduta, serves as the object of French lust, another Indian girl, Tekakwitha, contributes the natural force of savagery—in a spiritualized form—to the French national character. As in Cholenec's hagiographies, a figure of savage purity appears in the company of a contrasting figure of savage passion. Chateaubriand may well have injected Catholic saints into his novel, and he may well have won fame as an opponent of de-Christianization campaigns of the French Revolution, but *Les Natchez* is still the product of a secular mind. Eroticism supplies the main vehicle for the exploration of human relations, while race and nationality serve as fundamental lines of division.

Chateaubriand was not the last writer to entangle Tekakwitha in stories of sexual conquest. *Beautiful Losers,* a postmodernist novel published in 1966 by a young Leonard Cohen, before he became famous as a singer and songwriter, takes the form of an extended—and quite obscene—riff on the hagiography.[40] Comparing Tekakwitha to the recently martyred Marilyn Monroe, Cohen concocts lurid fantasies for his narrator and has him coupling in a variety of ways with the nubile virgin. Critics have commented on the carnivalesque strategy at work here, the author's use of obscenity for the traditional purpose of shocking the reader and undermining authority.[41] Equally striking, however, is Cohen's shrewdness—and he seems to have had before him nothing more than one Cholenec-inspired hagiography from the 1920s—in picking up on and caricaturing the exotic/erotic theme that runs through the writings of Cholenec, Chateaubriand, and their imitators.

## NOTES

1 R. Po-Chia Hsia, *The World of Catholic Renewal 1540–1770* (Cambridge: Cambridge University Press, 1998), 41.
2 Mary Douglas, *Purity and Danger: An Analysis of the Concepts of Pollution and Taboo* (London: Routledge and Kegan Paul, 1966), 157–58.
3 Joseph-François Lafitau, *Customs of the American Indians Compared with the Customs of Primitive Times*, ed. and trans. William N. Fenton and Elizabeth L. Moore, 2 vols. (Toronto: Champlain Society, 1974), 1:218.
4 Elaine Pagels, *Adam, Eve, and the Serpent* (New York: Random House, 1988).
5 Jean Delumeau, *Sin and Fear: The Emergence of a Western Guilt Culture, 13th–18th Centuries* (New York: St. Martin's Press, 1990), 431–45.
6 1 Corinthians 7:32, 33, 35. For discussions of early Christian celibacy, see Pagels, *Adam, Eve, and the Serpent*, 78–97; Peter Brown, *The Body and Society: Men, Women, and Sexual Renunciation in Early Christianity* (New York: Columbia University Press, 1988), passim.
7 Claude Chauchetière, *Narration de la mission du Sault depuis sa fondation jusqu'en* 1686, ed. Hélène Avisseau (1686; Bordeaux: Archives départementales de la Gironde, 1984), 51. The renunciation of sex within marriage was not unknown in Europe: see Dyan *Elliott, Spiritual Marriage: Sexual Abstinence in Medieval Wedlock* (Princeton, N.J.: Princeton University Press, 1993).
8 Pierre Cholenec, "La Vie de Catherine Tegakouita, première vierge Iroquoise," Archives de l'hôtel-dieu de Québec, 35 (*Pos*, 273).
9 Douglas, *Purity and Danger*, 158.
10 Lafitau, *Customs of the American Indians*, 1:129.
11 Brown, *The Body and Society*, 263.

12 Chauchetière, *Narration*, 41.
13 Cholenec, "Vie de Catherine Tegakouita," 49–50 (*Pos*, 286–87).
14 Thomas Aquinas, *Summa Theologica*, Supplement to the Third Part, Question 96, article 5, "Whether an aureole is due on account of virginity" (on-line edition: http://www.newadvent.org/summa/).
15 Cholenec, "Vie de Catherine Tegakouita," 50–51 (*Pos*, 288).
16 Claude Chauchetière, "La vie de la B. Catherine Tegakouita, dite à présent La Saincte Sauvagesse," [hereafter "La vie"] Archives de la société de Jésus, Canada français. St.-Jérôme, Quebec [hereafter ASJCF], 126 (*Pos*, 211).
17 Cholenec, "Vie de Catherine Tegakouita," 71–72 (*Pos*, 316).
18 Bacqueville de la Potherie, *Histoire de l'Amérique septentrionale*, 4 vols. (Paris: Brocas, 1753), 1:355.
19 Anthony Pagden, *The Fall of Natural Man: The American Indian and the Origins of Comparative Ethnology* (Cambridge: Cambridge University Press, 1982); Olive P. Dickason, *The Myth of the Savage and the Beginnings of French Colonialism in the Americas* (Edmonton: University of Alberta Press, 1984); Francis Jennings, *The Invasion of America: Indians, Colonialism, and the Cant of Conquest* (Chapel Hill: University of North Carolina Press, 1975).
20 Anne McClintock, *Imperial Leather: Race, Gender and Sexuality in the Colonial Contest* (New York: Routledge, 1995), 21–25.
21 Louis Montrose, "The Work of Gender in the Discourse of Discovery," in *New World Encounters*, ed. Stephen Greenblatt (Berkeley: University of California Press, 1993), 177–217; Peter Mason, *Infelicities: Representations of the Exotic* (Baltimore: Johns Hopkins University Press, 1998), 61–63.
22 See Paul Lejeune's account of a perilous winter hunt with the Montagnais (Innu/Naskapi) of Quebec in Relation of 1634, in Rueben Thwaites, ed., The Jesuit Relations and Allied Documents, 73 vols. (Cleveland: Burrows Brothers, 1896–1900) [hereafter JR], 7:106–15.
23 Cholenec, "Vie de Catherine Tegakouita," 31–35 (*Pos*, 267–71). This passage appears, almost word for word, in the published 1717 Life. "Lettre du P. Cholenec, missionnaire de la compagnie de Jésus, au P. Augustin le Blanc, de la même compagnie, procureur des missions du Canada," in *Lettres édifiantes et curieuses écrites des missions étrangères*, 30 vols. (Paris: N. Ledere, 1708–71), vol. 12 (1717):119–211 (*Pos*, 361–62).
24 Michel de Montaigne, "On Cannibals," in *Essays*, trans. J. M. Cohen (Harmondsworth: Penguin, 1958), 105–19; Jean de Léry, *History of a Voyage to the Land of Brazil, Otherwise Called America*, ed. and trans. Janet Whatley (Berkeley: University of California Press, 1990), 132. On cannibalism as a colonialist ideology, see William Arens, *The Man-Eating Myth: Anthropology and Anthropophagy* (New York: Oxford University Press, 1979); Pagden, *Fall of Natural Man*, 80–89; Peter Hulme, *Colonial Encounters: Europe and the Native Caribbean* (London: Methuen, 1986); Frank Lestringant, *Cannibals: The Discovery and Representation of the Cannibal from Columbus to Jules Verne*, trans. Rosemary Morris (Cambridge: Polity Press, 1997).
25 Pagden, *Fall of Natural Man*, 83.
26 Bernadette Bucher, *Icon and Conquest: A Structural Analysis of the Illustrations of de Bry's "Great Voyages"* (Chicago: University of Chicago Press, 1981), 46–64.
27 JR 64:126, Claude Chauchetière to Jean Chauchetière, 7 August 1694; Cholenec, "Vie de Catherine Tegakouita," 69, 80 (*Pos*, 313, 327).
28 "Lettre du P. Cholenec," in *Lettres édifiantes et curieuses*, 12 (1717): 119–211. See Allan Greer, "Savage/Saint: The Lives of Kateri Tekakwitha," in *Habitants*

*et marchands, vingt ans apres: Lectures de l'histoire des XVIIe et XVIIIe siècles canadiens*, ed. Sylvie Dépatie, Catherine Desbarats, and Thomas Wien (Montreal: McGill–Queen's University Press, 1998), 147–50.

29 Catherine M. Northeast, *The Parisian Jesuits and the Enlightenment 1700–1762* (Oxford: Voltaire Foundation, 1991).

30 In addition to Northeast, *Parisian Jesuits*, see Andreas Motsch, *Lafitau et l'érnergence du discours ethnographique* (Sillery, Quebec: Septentrion; Paris: Presses de l'Université de Paris-Sorbonne, 2001).

31 *La gracia triunfante en la vida de Catharina Tegakovita, india iroquesa, y en las de otras, Assi de su Nacion, como de esta Nueva-España* (Mexico City: Joseph Bernardo de Hogal, 1724).

32 Ibid., 4.

33 Ascunción Lavrin, "Women in Convents: Their Economic and Social Role in Colonial Mexico," in *Liberating Women's History: Theoretical and Critical Essays*, ed. Bernice A. Carroll (Urbana: University of Illinois Press, 1976), 257.

34 For a more detailed account of the circumstances surrounding the Mexican edition of 1724, see Allan Greer, "Iroquois Virgin: The Story of Catherine Tekakwitha in New France and New Spain," in *Colonial Saints: Discovering the Holy in the Americas*, 1500–1800, ed. Allan Greer and Jodi Bilinkoff (New York: Routledge, 2003), 233–48.

35 Anthony Pagden, *European Encounters with the New World: From Renaissance to Romanticism* (New Haven, Conn.: Yale University Press, 1993).

36 P.-F.-X. de Charlevoix, *History and General Description of New France*, 6 vols., trans. J. G. Shea (New York: Francis P. Harper, 1900), 4:283–96. (This text can also be found in Allan Greer, ed., *The Jesuit Relations: Natives and Missionaries in Seventeenth-Century North America* [Boston: Bedford Books, 2000], 172–85.)

37 François-René de Chateaubriand, *Les Natchez*, ed. Gilbert Chinard (Baltimore: Johns Hopkins Press, 1932), 167–68.

38 Hulme, *Colonial Encounters*, 137–73, 225–63; quotations at 141. In a similar vein, see Mary Louise Pratt, *Imperial Eyes: Travel Writing and Transculturation* (London: Routledge, 1992), 90–102.

39 Harry Liebersohn, *Aristocratic Encounters: European Travelers and North American Indians* (Cambridge: Cambridge University Press, 1998), 39–60.

40 Leonard Cohen, *Beautiful Losers* (New York: Viking, 1966). (A personal note: In spite of the obscenity, the only passage in *Beautiful Losers* that makes me squirm is this one: "Catherine Tekakwitha, I have come to rescue you from the Jesuits. Yes, an old scholar dares to think big.")

41 Linda Hutcheon, *The Canadian Postmodern: A Study of Contemporary English-Canadian Fiction* (Toronto: Oxford University Press, 1988), 26–30, 109.

# Part IV

# WAR

People living in borderland regions have found many ways to surmount difference and abide one another without the benefit of shared legal and political institutions. "Middle Grounds," "Colonial Pacts," and the unsung diplomatic triage of go-betweens attest to the possibility, the process, and the varieties of coexistence in borderlands. But as several of the chapters in this book have already attested, such places were nonetheless haunted by the specter of war. Borderlands often, even usually, have their origins in predatory expansion of one kind or another. As historian Charles Maier puts it in his comparative history of empire, when authority wanes "frontiers will become the site of killing, maiming, forced uprooting, and destruction of property."[1] Enduring differences in identity and interests, asymmetries of power, and the influence of other peoples on other frontiers can all trend against accommodation and toward organized conflict. Even in the midst of a broad consensus for peace, individual quarrels can quickly escalate into collective violence in the absence of shared values, politics, and institutions.

For all these reasons, violence and warfare has both generated and preoccupied American borderlands history writing since the early contact period. Canonical texts in the tradition including Bartolome de las Casas's *Brief Account of the Destruction of the Indies*, Cabeza de Vaca's *Narración* of his epic continental sojourn, and Mary Rowlandson's *Sovereignty and Goodness of God* have their beginnings in the bleak trauma of collective violence.[2] The preoccupation endured through the 19th century, inevitably, as warfare contributed to the annihilation of plural sovereignties across the continent and helped consign native peoples to assimilation or reservation life. Though some borderlands scholarship retained a focus on the subject throughout the twentieth century, increasingly framed in the context of native resistance, by at least the 1980s historians began working to decenter interethnic violence. Reacting against caricatures of native peoples that overemphasized the martial, much of the New Indian history deliberately shifted the focus to other aspects of borderland life. De-centering conflict also meant doing the same with conquest, displacement, trauma, colonialism, and (not least) colonists themselves, in order to make way for a more multi-dimensional understanding of life in indigenous borderlands. By the 1990s and early 2000s, interest in cultural fluidity, ethnogenesis, hybridity, and mutual accommodation on borderlands likewise de-emphasized collective violence in borderlands history.

Over the past decade, however, there has been a decided resurgence in the study of violence and war in borderlands. No doubt influenced to some degree by contemporary geopolitics, the renewed attention to organized violence is more simply and importantly attributable to our deepening understanding of the continent's history and of Indian agency in that history. Historians have paid more attention to territories outside of European control (the great majority of the continent's landmass for most of its post-contact history), and staggering changes have come into focus. As Ned Blackhawk has observed, the emerging narrative of this continent's borderland relationships "reads like a series of constant wars." Colonial violence, epidemic disease, new technologies, competition for markets, ecological transformation, and the displacement and migration of many tens of thousands of people fueled transformative wars throughout much of colonial and 19th century North America. More than victims, native peoples were of course agents in these tragic and monumental processes.[3]

Nowhere has warfare figured more prominently in new borderlands research than in the North American Southeast, where in the late sixteenth and early seventeenth centuries peoples throughout the region attacked and captured one another in response to a booming export market for indigenous slaves in Carolina.[4] William Ramsey's chapter examines the Yamasee War (1715–1717), a watershed confrontation that nearly ruined the colony and put an abrupt end to most commercial warring for slaves. While previous explanations for the war privileged the treachery, venality, and lawlessness of Carolina's merchants, Ramsey's piece highlights indigenous patterns of exchange and the structural character of the regional slave trade to recover the shared origins of the war.

The Southern Plains has been another site of intense scholarly interest over the past decade, and here, too, violence has emerged as an important preoccupation.[5] Aridity and a dispersed, mostly non-sedentary population made the plains effectively immune from direct European colonization. The native adoption of horses provoked profound social and political transformations that remade the political geography of the region several times over from the seventeenth through the nineteenth centuries. Amidst this intense dynamism and competition, native polities on the plains had to manage a rapidly shifting complex of relationships on multiple frontiers. "The Wider World of the Handsome Man" examines the neglected connections between peace and war on the southern plains and northern Mexico during the 1830s and 1840s. As manifestations of U.S. expansion began effecting the Southern Plains in these years, Comanches and Kiowas brokered peace with adversaries to their north and east in order to more securely and profitably raid Mexicans to their south. The intense violence of these years had dire consequences for the people of northern Mexico, and would ultimately help shape the course and outcome of the U.S.-Mexican War.

## NOTES

1 Charles S. Maier, *Among Empires: American Ascendancy and Its Predecessors* (Cambridge, MA: Harvard University Press, 2006), 110.

2 The monumental study of early preoccupation with frontier violence remains Richard Slotkin's *Regeneration Through Violence: The Mythology of the American Frontier, 1600–1860* (Middletown: Wesleyan University Press, 1973).

3 Ned Blackhawk, *Violence over the Land: Indians and Empires in the Early American West* (Cambridge: Harvard University Press, 2006), 5. The number of recent books centering borderland violence and warfare is very large. Examples include Jill Lepore, *The Name of War: King Philip's War and the Origins of American Identity* (New York: Knopf, 1998); Benjamin Heber Johnson, *Revolution in Texas: How a Forgotten Rebellion and Its Bloody Suppression Turned Mexicans into Americans* (New Haven: Yale University Press, 2003); Gary Clayton Anderson, *The Conquest of Texas: Ethnic Cleansing in the Promised Land, 1820–1875* (Norman: University of Oklahoma Press, 2005); Peter Silver, *Our Savage Neighbors: How Indian War Transformed Early America* (New York: W. W. Norton, 2007); Brian DeLay, *War of a Thousand Deserts: Indian Raids and the U.S.-Mexican War* (New Haven: Yale University Press, 2008); Karl Jacoby, *Shadows at Dawn: A Borderlands Massacre and the Violence of History* (New York: Penguin Press, 2008); Benjamin Madley, "California's Yuki Indians: Defining Genocide in Native American History," *Western Historical Quarterly* 39:3 (2008): 303–332; and the works cited below on the Southeast.

4 For recent introductions to this burgeoning literature, see Alan Gallay, ed., *Indian Slavery in Colonial America* (Lincoln: University of Nebraska Press, 2009); Sheri M. Shuck-Hall and Robbie Ethridge, eds., *Mapping the Mississippian Shatter Zone: The Colonial Indian Slave Trade and Regional Instability in the American South* (Lincoln: University of Nebraska Press, 2009); and Christina Snyder, *Slavery in Indian Country: The Changing Face of Captivity in Early America* (Cambridge: Harvard University Press, 2010). For Ramsey's broader argument, see *The Yamasee War: A Study of Culture, Economy, and Conflict in the Colonial South* (Lincoln: University of Nebraska Press, 2008).

5 In addition to two Bancroft-prize winning books [James F. Brooks, *Captives & Cousins: Slavery, Kinship, and Community in the Southwest Borderlands* (Chapel Hill: University of North Carolina Press, 2002); and Pekka Hämäläinen, *The Comanche Empire* (New Haven: Yale University Press, 2008)], recent work on the borderlands of the southern plains includes Gary Clayton Anderson, *The Indian Southwest, 1580–1830: Ethnogenesis and Reinvention* (Norman: University of Oklahoma Press, 1999); Anderson, *Conquest of Texas*; Juliana Barr, *Peace Came in the Form of a Woman: Indians and Spaniards in the Texas Borderlands* (Chapel Hill: University of North Carolina Press, 2007); DeLay, *War of a Thousand Deserts.*

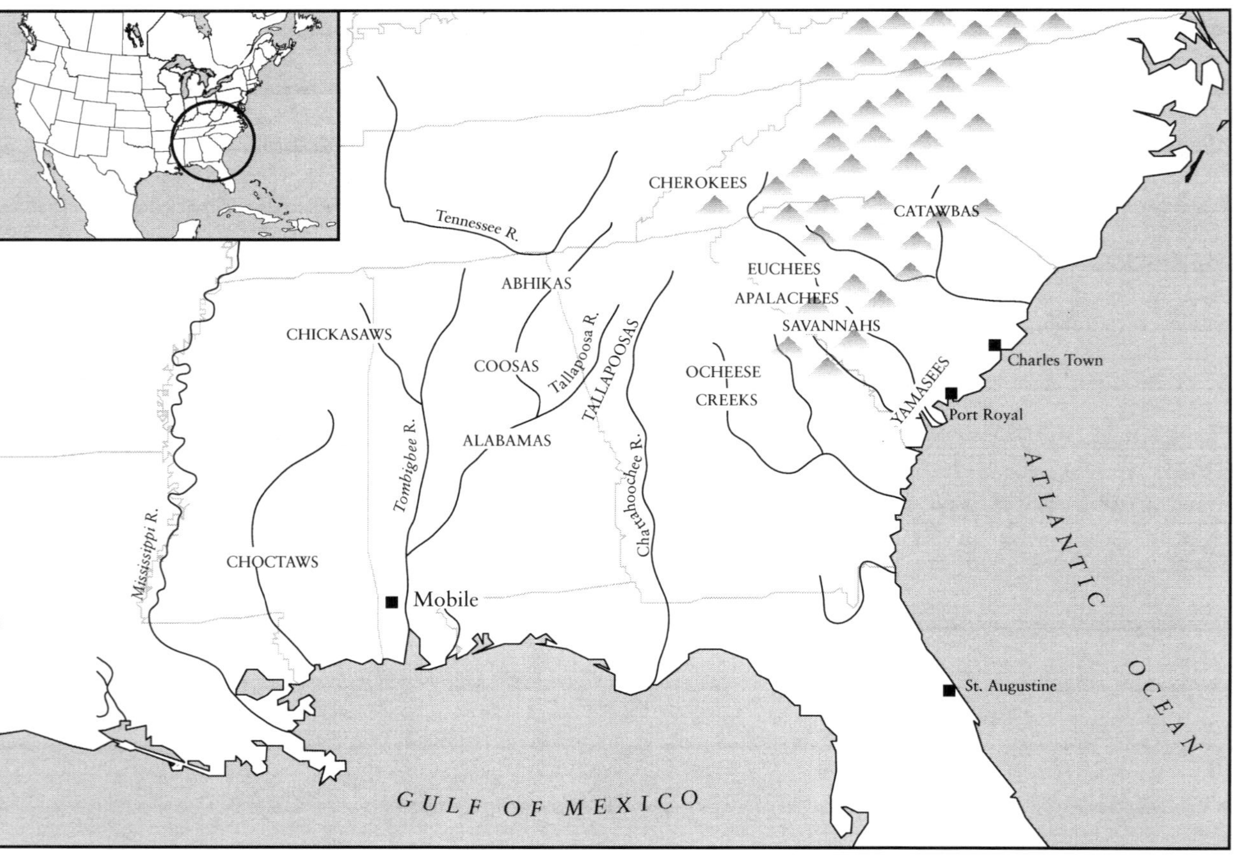


*Map 4.1* The Southeast

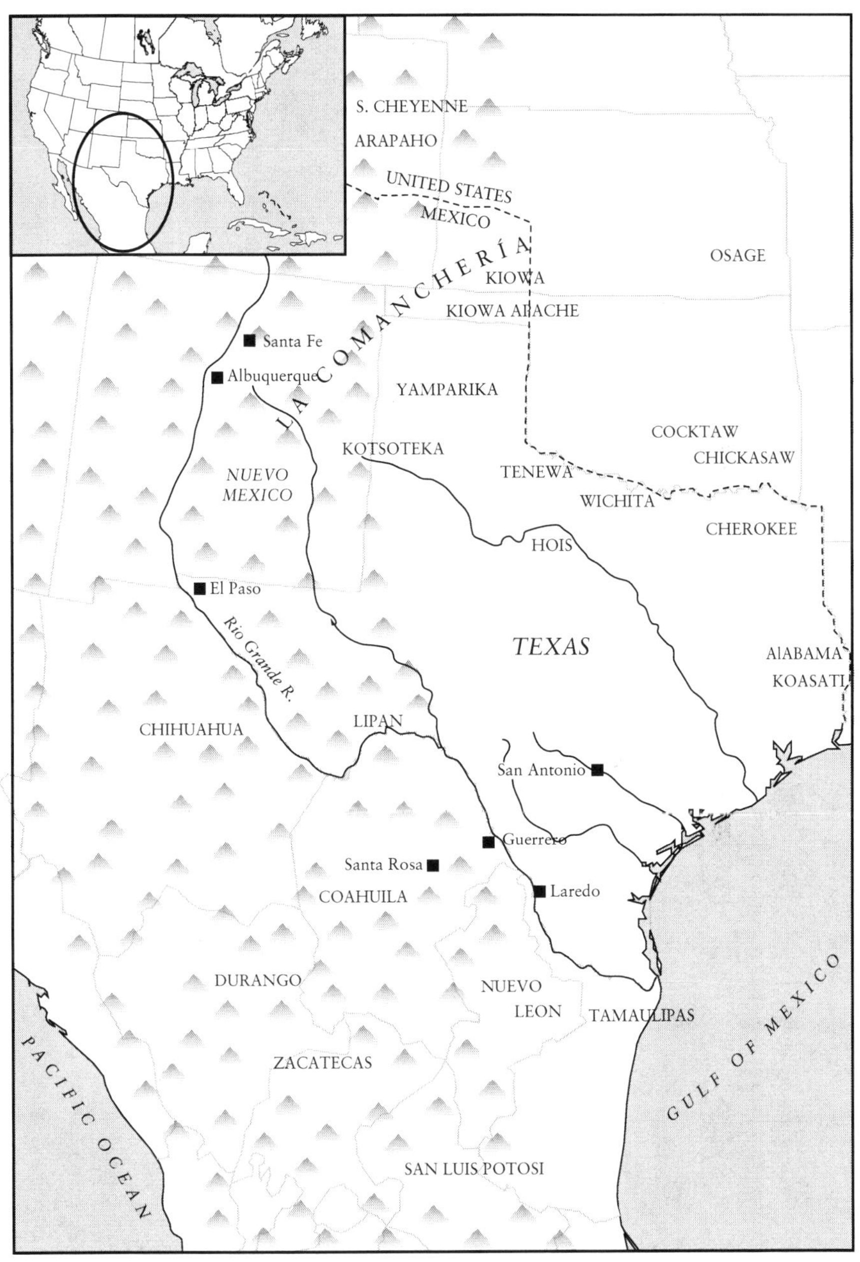


*Map 4.2* Southern Plains and Northern Mexico

# 8

# THE ORIGINS OF THE YAMASEE WAR RECONSIDERED

*William L. Ramsey*

The Reverend Francis LeJau, writing from South Carolina early in 1712, remarked on the aloof manner of the "free Indians" living near his parish in Goose Creek. "They goe their own way," he observed, "and bring their children like themselves with little conversation among us but when they want something from us." He did not identify them by nation, but, whoever they were, he felt discomfited by "something cloudy in their looks." Few other Carolinians appear to have noticed those clouds; certainly no one else wrote about them. But LeJau was correct. There were clouds, and they had been gathering in the "looks" of southeastern Indians for several years. When the storm finally broke in April 1715, it nearly washed South Carolina off the map. Warriors from virtually every nation in the South, from the Catawbas and their piedmont neighbors in the Carolinas to the Choctaws of Mississippi, joined together in one of the most potent native coalitions ever to oppose the British in colonial North America.[1]

The Yamasee War, as it has come to be known, has long been recognized as one of the most important events in southern colonial history. According to the historian Gary B. Nash, Native American combatants came "as close to wiping out the European colonists as ever [they] came during the colonial period." Southeastern Indians destroyed most of South Carolina's plantation districts and came within a few miles of Charles Town (now Charleston) during the first year of the war. By 1718, when peace returned to much of the region, over four hundred colonists and an untold number of Native American warriors had perished, making the conflict a serious candidate for America's bloodiest war in proportion to the populations involved. The war spurred extensive tribal migrations and alliance realignments that changed the diplomatic and cultural landscape of the region for the remainder of the eighteenth century, and it led directly to the collapse of South Carolina's proprietary government in 1719. British imperial responses to the war, moreover, prompted the first calls for a buffer colony to protect Carolina's southern border against Indian or even French or Spanish attacks, which culminated in the establishment of Georgia in 1733. Recent work even indicates that the war ended South Carolina's experimentation with Indian slavery and committed the colony to an exclusive reliance on African labor from 1715 onward.[2]

Despite its significance, however, the Yamasee War has attracted surprisingly little scholarly attention over the last half century, and explicating its origins in particular remains very much open to debate. Early efforts to understand the causes of the war focused mainly on the inflammatory behavior of English traders. In its most sophisticated expression, crafted in 1925 by the historian Verner Crane, this approach viewed the war as a "far reaching revolt against the Carolinian trading regime" in which Native Americans across the South rose up in anger over the "tyrannies of the Charles Town traders." John R. Swanton, writing in the same decade, also felt that the "misconduct of some traders" had been the "immediate cause" of the war but went on to add that fears of enslavement may have prompted the Yamasees to action as well. Elements of those two versions were refined, interwoven, and reiterated for a generation and, indeed, continue to influence current scholarship in subtle ways. Yet they depend on a number of premises that do not bear modern scrutiny. First, the application of moralistic judgments concerning English trade behavior makes the mistake of assuming that what is just and proper in one culture will necessarily be recognized as such in another. Second, they err in presuming that a single, uniform cause of action operated everywhere, in the same way, throughout the entire region.[3]

More recent studies have explored multicausal approaches to the war's origins that also include environmental pressures and the consequences of dependency on Anglo-Indian relations. James Merrell's work moved the discussion forward significantly by recognizing for the first time the need to consider geographical differences, and his work on the Catawbas broke new ground by assessing native perceptions and misperceptions of Europeans as filtered through the unreliable "lens" of trade. With few exceptions, however, these studies routinely fall back upon the vocabulary of abuse and misconduct pioneered by Crane and Swanton. Efforts to apply dependency theory, in particular, have demonstrated a decidedly teleological tendency. Perhaps because Anglo-Indian trade relations had such a brief history prior to the Yamasee War, dating only to the 1680s, such studies tend to accelerate the advance of trade dependence excessively. At the same time, they often oversimplify the correlation between purportedly abusive English traders and the hegemonic power supposedly conferred on Englishmen by advanced dependency. In short, they anticipate too much in too simple a manner in too little time. The present study invokes dependency theory sparingly, and only to recalibrate scholarly assumptions about its rate of progress in the colonial South, on the one hand, and to urge, on the other, a more complex treatment of its local manifestations that includes not only the behavior of English traders but economic, cultural, and social changes as well. In the process, it seeks to restore to the discussion the driving mechanism that led to Native American dependence, as the historian Richard White saw it: the market.[4]

The essay proposes an alternative explanation for the origins of the Yamasee War in which the nature of the trade itself, more than the traders, and in which efforts at trade regulation, rather than their absence, played important roles in provoking the conflict. By analyzing the extant dialogue of Anglo-Indian exchange relations, it seeks to sketch a more accurate portrait of the trade and its diplomatic implications and escape at last the gravitational pull of the vocabulary of the Crane and Swanton school. It takes as one of its working premises the symbiotic relationship between trade and diplomacy among Native American groups, recognizing that indigenous participation in commodity exchange was more than purely economic, especially during early phases of the trade. As recent scholarship has made abundantly clear, Native American approaches to exchange were embedded in complex cultural and political systems that Europeans ignored at their own peril. It is that multifaceted aspect of the trade, it is argued here, that has been missing in previous attempts to grapple with the problem. Although trade lay close to the heart of the conflagration, the Yamasee War ultimately represented a diplomatic breach between Charles Town and the native peoples of the South, fostered not only by the personal offenses of English traders but, more significantly, by long-term structural trends in the Anglo-Indian trade and finally provoked by specific diplomatic missteps with respect to trade regulation on the part of South Carolina. That the native coalition included at its height such nations as the Choctaws, Upper Creeks (Abhikas, Coosas, Tallapoosas, and Alabamas), and Catawbas, who had relatively few trade-related complaints of any sort, was almost exclusively the result of diplomatic concerns.[5]

Ultimately, in attempting to see past traditional assumptions about English trade behavior and assess the diplomatic meaning of exchange, the study seeks to do more than advance an alternate explanation for the war's origins. It begins the process of bringing the Yamasee War in a usable form into the broader ethnohistorical discussion that has already done so much to transform our understanding of the region. On a larger scale, it also seeks to establish for the first time a basis for comparative analyses between the Yamasee War and other regions, events, and epochs. Far from being *sui generis*, the origins of the war as presented here exhibit elements that are strikingly similar to the difficulties experienced in French-Algonquian trade relations in the Great Lakes region, or Pays d'en Haut, during the late seventeenth century, and they have a clear significance with respect to ongoing discussions over the influence and development of the Atlantic economy. As the war begins to figure more prominently in those broader debates, it may at last take its place beside the other great "Indian wars" of the colonial period as a historical moment of the highest importance.

As earlier accounts have emphasized, there were numerous instances of reprehensible conduct committed by English traders. But misconduct and abuse as defined in European terms does not necessarily add up to an explanation of war. Around 1711, for instance, a trader named Alexander Longe became embroiled in a bitter feud with the Euchee Indians after having "his hair torn off," possibly in a scuffle over outstanding debts. Nursing his resentment, Longe got his revenge a few years later when a Euchee warrior unwisely came to his store to purchase gunpowder. According to a Cherokee man named Partridge, the trader piled up the powder next to his unfortunate client and then "sett fier to itt and blew him up." Longe's behavior clearly qualified by European standards as "misconduct," and the Commissioners of the Indian Trade moved aggressively to prosecute him for that and other offenses. Nevertheless, Longe's actions did not preclude his enjoying the support and friendship of the Cherokee Indians, who subsequently sheltered him even as Charles Town officials sought to bring him to justice. South Carolina's regulatory diligence did more to alienate the Cherokees in this instance than had Longe's behavior. Indeed, as Carolinians languished in their fever-ridden fortifications, Longe safely spent the entirety of the Yamasee War in Cherokee country and continued trading there as an honored guest through the 1720s.[6]

Obviously, misconduct meant different things to different people. For purposes of historical analysis, the term does more to obscure than to explain the causes of the Yamasee War. Southeastern Indians had their own ideas about proper and improper conduct and, for their own reasons, submitted a large number of trade-related complaints to Charles Town officials. Those complaints need to be analyzed as far as possible on their own terms as part of a complex, ongoing dialogue between southeastern Indians and Europeans. In order to do so, however, Native and European voices must be untangled from each other and the basic outlines of the discourse restored. Many of the complaints traditionally cited as evidence of trader misconduct, for example, were not submitted by Native Americans at all. In many cases they were submitted by English traders themselves and probably represent partisan rhetoric directed at opposing trade factions. In the *Journals of the Commissioners of the Indian Trade,* by far the richest and most systematic source of such complaints, roughly 32 of the 65 cases adjudicated from 1710 to 1715 involved internecine squabbles between English traders. The 30 cases that clearly emanated from Native American sources, however, contain a wealth of information about the sometimes subtle problems plaguing Anglo-Indian relations. The priorities framed in these complaints differed in several respects from those of English traders, and the well-founded frustrations of the peoples who submitted them deserve a more thorough analysis than mass categorization as complaints about abuse. By plotting the Anglo-Indian dialogue and insisting on the importance of identity as a determinative element in the shaping of discourse, the following study seeks to build the foundation for a native interpretive perspective that revolves around specific, practical issues raised by Native Americans themselves, recognizes geographical distinctions, and acknowledges the asymmetrical distribution of power.[7]

It may be best to begin where many historical accounts of English trade behavior prior to the Yamasee War have ended: with accusations of beatings and murders. These glaring incidents figure prominently in many characterizations of the Anglo-Indian trade relationship, yet they represented a distinct minority when compared with other categories of complaint. Only five English traders were ever accused of such crimes by Native Americans in the *Journals of the Commissioners*. At Altamaha, for instance, the principal town among the lower Yamasee settlements near Port Royal, South Carolina, an Englishman named Alexander Nicholas reportedly "beat a Woman that he kept for his Wife so that she dyed and the Child within her." He later beat up "another Woman being King Altimahaw's Sister." Nicholas then proceeded to a nearby Yamasee town and beat "the Chasee [probably Chechesee] King's Wife." The headman of Altamaha finally sent word to the Commissioners of the Indian Trade in 1711 that, if Nicholas were not removed and punished, the Indians "would quit the Town." A warrant was quickly issued for his arrest. At Savano Town on the Savannah River, meanwhile, the Apalachee Indians had reason to resent the presence of Jess Crosley who, "being jealous of a Whore of his, beat and abused an Apalachia Indian Man in a barbarous Manner." At another unidentified Apalachee village, Phillip Gilliard "took a young Indian against her Will for his Wife." He reportedly got her "drunk with Rum and locked her up" and then threatened to kill the girl's mother "becaus she would not leve her Daughter behind."[8]

There is no excuse, of course, for such behavior, but there is none either for historians who have taken it at face value, for it conceals a deeper set of issues that must be considered in assessing the nature of Anglo-Indian relations. These incidents overwhelmingly involved affronts to native women. Though perhaps prevalent in the patriarchal societies of western Europe, violence against women was virtually unheard-of among many of the matrilineal societies of the indigenous South. Englishmen among the Cherokees, for instance, marveled that "the women Rules the Rostt and weres the brichess." On those occasions when domestic violence did erupt, moreover, it was invariably the women who "beat thire husbands within an Inch of thire life." Indeed, the typical Cherokee man would "not Resesst thire poure if the woman was to beate his breans out." Traders who raised their fists against native women therefore struck at more than a single victim. They attacked the social values of the community at large.[9]

Traders who married native women encountered a variety of sociocultural perils. Such unions offered immediate advantages for traders, such as kinship privileges and assistance in learning the language, but they also produced long-term problems for all concerned. The two parties brought opposing expectations and presumptions to the marriage. Native women probably anticipated that they would rule the "rostt" and wear the "brichess," while their English husbands viewed the roost and the britches as rightfully theirs. Marriages that produced offspring may have been particularly prone to trouble. The typical English trader probably expected his children to take his surname and be subject to his authority as head of the household. His native wife, on the other hand, may have anticipated that her children would belong to her lineage, as was customary, and fall primarily under the authority of herself, her mother, and her siblings. Indeed, in the typical Indian household, the dominant male figure in the lives of the children was the mother's brother, not the children's father. Such divergent agendas may have led to frequent episodes of domestic turmoil. . . .[10]

Other forms of trader abuse masked similarly complex issues. Seven of the 30 complaints levied against English traders by Native Americans in the *Journals of the Commissioners of the Indian Trade,* for instance, involved incidents of "taking away" the Indians' personal belongings. A series of resolutions passed in the Commons House of Assembly on January 26, 1702, also indicates the prevalence of this activity. Of 6 resolutions concerning traders, 5 required them to give back or make restitution for what they had taken away from someone. The expropriation of goods from Indians was practiced by many traders across much of the Southeast. Indeed, it appears to have been regarded more as an established and reputable order of business than an act of burglary. In 1713, for instance, when Cornelius Meckarty was accused by two Indian leaders of "beating two of their people that came from North Carolina and taking some cloaths from them," he produced affidavits from eyewitnesses "to prove that he had not beaten" the Indians. He apparently considered it unnecessary to defend or deny the simple act of taking away their "cloaths."[11]

The key to understanding most of these incidents is probably linked to credit. Meckarty behaved as he did, for example, not necessarily because he was perverse or abusive, though he may have been, but because the Indians in question owed him eighty-three deerskins. He probably considered himself guilty of nothing more than repossession of merchandise for nonpayment. Similarly, when William Ford went before the Commissioners of the Indian Trade on June 27, 1712, to answer charges that he had taken away a slave belonging to a Yamasee Indian named Enaclega, he defended his action on the grounds that Enaclega "owed him 39 skins and that he toock the said slave for security of his debt." Far from condemning Ford, the commissioners ordered the Indian to pay the debt in exchange for the return of the slave.[12]

In its basic form, the practice of forcible confiscation did not overtly violate indigenous norms. Among the Creek Indians, whenever a particular individual contributed less than his or her quota of labor to the tilling of the communal fields or to village improvements, the mico and his council routinely dispatched warriors to "pillage his house of such things as they [could] find." The confiscated goods were then sold and added "to the town stock." In cases involving personal debts between individuals, moreover, "if the debtor prove too negligent the creditor only goes to his house and takes the value of his debet in what he can find." These methods undoubtedly possessed a compelling logic among early historic period societies rooted in communal values, where property was generally held in common and private ownership was not yet pronounced, but English traders did not belong to that community. They did not share in the demands of communal labor, and they owned property exclusively as private individuals or, at best, as part of joint trading companies. As European markets increasingly cast their influence over the Southeast, moreover, the rate of seizures rose at an alarming rate. . . .[13]

Sometimes the intermixture of native and European worlds produced hybrid concepts that created more problems than they solved. One such case involved the practice of collecting what traders termed "relations' debts," a fusion of European credit and native devotion to communal or clan responsibility. Many traders discovered that, even if a particular Indian could not repay his debts, his family and friends, or even the leaders of the town, could often be counted on to fulfill his obligations. In one instance, a Chiaha Indian man named Tuskenehau, who had "gon to warr," returned home to find

> that the Head Men of the Cussetau Town had taken away the said Tuskenehau's wife named Tooledeha, a free woman, and her mother, a slave belonging to the said Tooskenehau, . . . upon pretence of paying some town debts due from others of the said town to Mr. John Pight when the said Tuskenehau was no wais indebted to the said John Pight or any other person trading att the said town.

The Commissioners of the Indian Trade recognized "relations' debts" as an unorthodox practice but refrained from banning it entirely. Instead, they attempted to refine it by insisting that traders first obtain the assent of all those who might be affected, after which "such relations or chief men of the town shall be liable and answerable for the payment of all such debts."[14]

Perhaps the clearest indication that issues related to credit played an important role in producing the Anglo-Indian rupture of 1715 comes from the close relationship between the outbreak of the Yamasee War in April and the seasonal nature of the credit cycle. Aside from the handful of traders who operated warehouses year-round, the majority of traders made only two trips into the interior during the course of the year: once in the fall and once in the spring. In the fall, traders laden with new merchandise arrived in villages across the Southeast and began selling their wares. Indians unable to purchase all the supplies they needed outright were extended credit. The traders then returned to Charles Town, and Indian men set out to gather as many deerskins as possible during the winter hunt, usually from about October until March. Then, as the weather improved the following spring, traders once again trekked into Indian territory, this time to purchase deerskins and collect payment of outstanding debts. In the spring of 1715, however, they found another sort of payment altogether waiting for them.[15]

There is reason to believe that several nations had run up heavy debts during the early eighteenth century. The Yamasees alone had amassed a collective trade debt of about a hundred thousand deerskins by 1711, a figure greater than South Carolina's entire yearly export total. The historian Richard Haan has suggested that the Yamasees' plight resulted from environmental and demographic factors, primarily the depletion of white-tailed deer in coastal regions and difficulties in acquiring new Indian slaves. Yet they had access to extensive hunting grounds that extended along most of the coast of modern-day Georgia and may have included portions of the abandoned Apalachee cornfields in northern Florida. It remains uncertain whether they could have denuded that region of game in only thirty years of trade, and Carolina's deerskin exports continued rising dramatically for several decades after the Yamasee War. Some ethnohistorians have even begun to question whether deer populations were in decline by the mid- to late eighteenth century, well after the trade had reached its peak. Yamasee participation in the Tuscarora War (1711–1713), moreover, swelled the number of unfortunate captives brought in for sale on the Charles Town slave market and provided Yamasee warriors with a significant new source of income. While Haan's arguments deserve consideration, credit problems among the Yamasees and several other of Carolina's oldest trading partners probably had as much to do with a rapidly deteriorating exchange rate between English pounds sterling and Carolina currency, which must have increased the price of European trade goods dramatically, and changing market demands that drastically restricted the range of permissible exchange commodities. Whatever the causes of the Yamasees' credit dilemma, such enormous sums meant that they and many other Indians were increasingly obliged "to goe to war and a'hunting to pay their debts," with very little to show for their exertions afterward.[16]

Yet indebtedness, like gender relations, cannot be applied as a formulaic constant. Not all Native Americans were debtors, and lines of credit did not extend solely from Carolina into Indian country. They sometimes ran in the other direction. The *Journals of the Commissioners of the Indian Trade* listed five separate occasions when Native creditors sought the assistance of Carolina officials in forcing English traders to pay their debts. Several of these involved Yamasee Indians, including "King Lewis" of Pocotaligo Town, where the first shots of the war ultimately broke out. At about the same time, the "Coosata King" sought action against Theophilus Hastings for the sum of a thousand deerskins. The commissioners recognized the validity of his claim and persuaded Hastings to honor his commitment. Considered alongside incidents of "taking away" and "relations' debts," the prevalence of Native creditors indicates that credit constituted a serious hot spot in the trade that produced tension on all sides.[17]

Finally, incidents related to the Indian slave trade represented one of the most common categories of misconduct attributed to English traders. Six of the 30 complaints brought by Native Americans before the Commissioners of the Indian Trade in the five years preceding the Yamasee War had to do with slavery. English traders themselves appear to have been even more concerned about it, filing 11 complaints on that issue against rival English traders. With few exceptions, the incidents stemmed from legal ambiguities involved in the process of transforming human beings from a state of freedom into forms of property. The profitability of the slave trade, for native warriors as well as for English traders, placed individual liberties at risk across the South and led many to seek their victims among vulnerable friends and allies as well as legitimate enemies. As a result, the Commissioners of the Indian Trade spent much of their time adjudicating cases in which free Indians had allegedly been sold unjustly into slavery.[18]

The commissioners appear to have approached the cases conscientiously, and they ruled in favor of the enslaved parties in a surprising number of instances, though often leaving the door open for additional evidence to reverse their decisions. On September 21, 1710, for example, they determined "that Ventusa, an Appalachia Indian, and his wife are to continew as free people," but their freedom was not unconditional. They were entitled to their liberty only until such time as "Phillip Gilliard by a hearing before the board can prove the contrary." In another case reviewed the same day, the commissioners ruled that an "Ellcombe" (elsewhere Illcombee) Indian named Wansella was "to be a free man till Mr. John Pight can prove him a slave." The Commons House of Assembly also heard such cases on occasion. On May 12, 1714, they reviewed allegations that William Bray, a trader who worked primarily among the Yamasee Indians, had sold "a free Indian woman and her two children." In contrast to the quick, if irresolute, decisions of the Commissioners of the Indian Trade, the house moved at a snail's pace, often referring cases to committees where they languished for months at a time. Such was the fate of William Bray's case. It was apparently still in committee when the Yamasee War erupted a year later.[19]

South Carolina officials never recognized the underlying patterns of the cases that came before them or else considered them unimportant. Incidents related to the slave trade, gender-specific violence, and credit inundated the Commissioners of the Indian Trade with personal anecdotes, affidavits, and details that undoubtedly obscured the larger picture. Nevertheless, those subcategories of trader misconduct suggest that Anglo-Indian relations were marred by much more than the personal failings and abuses of individual

Englishmen, reprehensible though they often were. Anglo-Indian relations were riven by distinct lines of stress that formed in particularly troublesome areas. Native complaints and irritation clustered conspicuously around those cultural, economic, and social fault zones, not around individual traders. The nature of the exchange relationship itself thus appears to have concentrated tension along these lines, and few traders could wholly avoid contributing to the problem in one way or another.

In addition to the fault zones, the complaints attributable to Native Americans prior to 1715 displayed a striking geographical pattern. Although Cherokee, Upper Creek, and Catawba voices occasionally found their way into the journals of the Commissioners of the Indian Trade or the Commons House of Assembly, the vast majority belonged to Ocheese (or Lower) Creek, Euchee, Savannah, Apalachee, and Yamasee villages. Those nations formed a coherent zone of settlement along Carolina's oldest and most lucrative trade route, extending south and southwest from Charles Town into central Georgia. The volume of complaints from that region probably reflects their deeper involvement in trade more than it does any regional differences in the behavior of English traders. At the same time, however, those nations had fewer options for European trade open to them than others. They had done much themselves, in fact, to limit their access to alternative sources of European goods between 1680 and 1704 by assisting in the destruction of the Spanish mission system in Florida. Having thus entered into what economists term a monopsony relationship with Charles Town by the first decade of the eighteenth century, one in which there is only a single buyer of goods, Yamasees, Euchees, Lower Creeks, and others may have found it necessary to engage English officials more aggressively in order to affect the terms of exchange. Even so, their prominence in the historical record should not be read simply as evidence of greater victimization. In many cases, their protests suggest they were active, intelligent participants in exchange, attempting purposefully to influence and direct the process for their own advantage.[20]

The stress fractures plaguing Anglo-Indian trade in the South were not unique and need not necessarily have resulted in warfare. They appeared at various points in other regions of North America as well. In the normal course of business in 1684, for instance, cultural, economic, and social friction led to the deaths of thirty-nine French traders in the hinterlands of New France. Cordial relations between Quebec and its native clients did not break down, however, because the two groups, meeting each other on what the historian Richard White has termed the "middle ground" between cultures, managed to resolve their differences and arrive at mutually agreeable ways of interacting with one another by observing and accommodating the cultural values of the other. Indeed, as complaints about English misconduct poured into Charles Town, Frenchmen in Louisiana and New France were engaged in some of the most adept and creative frontier diplomacy of the age. If English abusiveness no longer functions as an analytical tool, it is not immediately apparent why Carolinians and their native clients could not arrive at a similar accommodation. Why did Englishmen and Indians in the colonial South move further apart when other groups experiencing similar difficulties managed to establish a sustainable, responsive dialogue?[21]

In the aftermath of the Yamasee War, a number of Native American voices found their way into the records on this topic, and they tell a complicated story. Many accounts denied that there was a problem at all. Cherekeileigie (Cherokeeleechee) of the Lower (Ocheese) Creeks, recalling "the Yamasee Wars" in 1735, insisted that he was "not the occasion of breaking the peace at that time." He was "averse unto it because [he] lived as happily as any white man in those days in my own house . . . [and] wore as good apparel and rode as good a horse as most of them." Nevertheless, once "engaged in the wars, [he] did the English all the harm he could." Such statements make it clear that many southeastern Indians made war on South Carolina for reasons that had nothing to do with traders or the trade. Other comments, however, do cite English trade relations as a source of irritation, and, at first glance, they seem to reinforce arguments about trader misconduct. In 1747, for instance, Malatchi of the Lower Creeks recalled that "we lived as brothers for some time till the traders began to use us very ill and wanted to enslave us which occasioned a war." The Cherokees also reported in 1716 that English traders "had ben very abusefull to them of latte, and not as whitte men used to be to them formerly." According to those sources, relations between Englishmen and Indians were not always troubled. Native accusations of generalized abuse were almost always framed in comparison to earlier periods of supposed harmony. What these documents really say, therefore, is that traders and the trade, and therefore their relationship with Native America, had changed in a way that did not please Native Americans.[22]

If a mature "middle ground" had not yet emerged in the early-eighteenth-century South, Malatchi and others had nevertheless developed a clear set of ideas about the protocols of intercultural exchange that allowed them to assess the adequacy of French, English, and Spanish behavior. Although grounded in traditional notions of reciprocity, gift giving, and alliance, such ideas had undergone more than a century of contact with and adaptation to European approaches to exchange by 1715. According to the ethnohistorian Gregory H. Waselkov, a low-level but significant Spanish-Indian trade in the early to mid-seventeenth century prepared aboriginal cultures in the region for more intensive trade relations in the eighteenth century, primarily by introducing them to a broad range of material goods. The lessons learned in that trade served southeastern Indians well during the early phases of trade with South Carolina and, following the establishment of Louisiana in 1699, with the French. In the first fifteen years of the eighteenth century, however, trade relations with South Carolina began to accelerate and take on new dimensions, adding tension to the inherently delicate process of intercultural trade. Measured against previous exchange patterns, the Cherokees had no trouble recognizing that English traders were not behaving "as whitte men used to be to them formerly."[23]

The observations of Jean-Baptiste Lemoyne de Bienville, the principal architect of French Louisiana's frontier policy, may provide some insight into the nature of this new behavior. He conceded in 1715 that the English of Carolina had a natural economic advantage in that they "sold . . . merchandise very cheap and . . . took the peltries at a high price and here [in French Louisiana] it is quite the contrary." But he understood that southeastern Indians factored more into the bargain than simple economics. Unable to offer a better deal, he chose to focus French efforts instead on what he later called "*good faith* in trading" (italics mine). This meant a good deal more in practice than equitable treatment and honesty. For the first half of the eighteenth century, French Louisiana remained very much at the margins of the emerging Atlantic economy. The historian Daniel H. Usner has aptly described the colony as being involved in a "frontier exchange economy," dominated by indigenous, regional patterns of exchange rather than the demands of external markets. The informal nature of this "exchange economy" allowed Indians greater freedom to control and adapt the volume and terms of trade with Europeans to their own needs. As a result, French trade was conducted not only in "good faith" but in closer accordance with traditional forms of ceremonial gift exchange and tribute.[24]

Bienville believed that the Indians noticed and appreciated the differences between the respective English and French approaches to trade. Those differences, he felt, were most evident in relation to the trade in Indian slaves. According to Bienville, the majority of southeastern Indians had come to "despise" the English "because of the little scruple that they have against buying slaves of the nations with which they are not at war, which we [French] do not do at all." On those rare occasions when over-zealous French traders took slaves from allied nations, Bienville invariably had them returned. "Barbarians as they are," he wrote in 1711, "they do not fail to make the distinction between our sentiments and those of the English."[25]

The difference in French and English sentiments regarding Indian slaves, like their differences on other aspects of trade, was not the result of French moral superiority or English deficiency. It reflected, rather, the contrasting economic imperatives at work in Louisiana and South Carolina. Whereas Louisiana remained an insular and economically backward region, allowing Bienville to cultivate "good faith," the burgeoning South Carolina economy had come to depend on a continuous flow of unfree labor by the end of the first decade of the eighteenth century, both for use within the colony on rice plantations and for export as trade credit to other plantation colonies. Increasingly, that dependence encouraged English traders to take risks they may not have taken formerly in order to secure an adequate supply of slaves. The deerskin trade accelerated as well, transforming the trade, in the words of the historian Clowse, from "haphazard bartering . . . to a business carried on by professionals." Although English traders were able to offer goods at competitive prices, by the first decade of the eighteenth century their attention was more attuned to the demands of the Carolina and Atlantic economies than to the complaints of their native clients. In short, they had less power to shape the basic contours of trade or to fashion it to fit local conditions than did their French rivals.[26]

In some cases the influence of the market made English trade behavior seem almost suicidal. In 1706, for instance, an English trading partnership involving John Pight, James Lucas, and Anthony Probert attempted to augment its profits by having a small, English-allied, Indian nation called the Illcombees declared and taken slaves en masse. The plan encountered opposition among neighboring Indian nations, but the traders continued to pursue their aims undeterred. At length, during a "consultation" about the issue in an unidentified native "round house," their persistence almost cost them their lives. "Affraid least the Indians would rise upon them," they ordered another of their associates, Theophilus Hastings, "to loade all his guns." Even after this episode, remarkably, they remained committed to the scheme. Not until the South Carolina Commons House of Assembly stepped in and reprimanded the traders later that year did they drop their plans.[27]

Although assembled together in the same "round house," Indians and Englishmen were worlds apart on this occasion. It is not enough, moreover, to blame the failure on English misconduct, for Pight, Lucas, and Probert brought something more than their own recklessness into the round house with them: they brought the market. Even as they were loading all their guns, several members of the partnership faced legal actions in the South Carolina Court of Common Pleas for collection of debts. Both Pight and Probert were in desperate financial trouble in late 1706; Probert was sued in November by William Smith for the enormous sum of 1,500 pounds Carolina currency. He was forced to put up bail in order to continue trading. His inflexible performance in the round house had much to do with market forces beyond his control.[28]

Market influence over English traders involved much more, however, than credit stress. In the decade preceding the Yamasee War, the market effected a sweeping reconfiguration of the South Carolina Indian trade. It is a phenomenon that has entirely escaped scholarly notice thus far, perhaps because export totals for deerskins, the most obvious barometer of Anglo-Indian exchange for most of the eighteenth century, do not reflect this early transformation. Although deerskins became the primary staple of the trade and had predominated from the beginning, there was initially a trade in other types of pelts that more closely resembled the northern "fur trade." During the 1690s, black bear, panther or wildcat (listed as cat), fox, muskrat, woodchuck, otter, raccoon, and beaver pelts were traded in meaningful volumes. From 1699 to 1701, southeastern Indians received European goods in exchange for 3,373 beaver pelts, 3,675 fox furs, 1,228 otter pelts, 2,460 raccoon skins, and 529 cat skins. By the end of the first decade of the eighteenth century, however, the trade in beaver had declined drastically, while the rest had virtually disappeared as viable items of exchange. From 1713 to 1715, English traders accepted only 1,469 beaver pelts, 39 fox furs, 12 otter pelts, 7 raccoon skins, and not a single cat skin. Meanwhile, deerskin exports during the same three-year period increased by about 50,000 skins to 167,044.[29]

The market clearly lay behind this transformation. English traders purchased from their native clients only those items they could expect to sell most profitably abroad or else offered such unappealing compensation that the skill and labor involved in acquiring, for instance, panther or wildcat skins made the trade unattractive. Those economic imperatives stemmed in part from the disruption of shipping routes as a result of Queen Anne's War from 1702 to 1713 and in part from depressed European fur markets. Although additional studies on transatlantic shipping and trade need to be done, it seems likely that new British imperial legislation making South Carolina's most profitable export, rice, an enumerated commodity in 1704 had some impact as well. The legislation eliminated a number of lucrative Iberian markets for the colony's rice planters because their fall harvests could not be transshipped from English ports in time to satisfy seasonal needs. As a result, much of the colony's rice was diverted into the coastwise trade to other North American colonies. Fur shipments dependent on those pre-1704 routes may have been curtailed as a consequence. A profitable reexport system capable of serving northern as well as southern European markets did not emerge in Great Britain until the 1720s, by which time furs had disappeared from South Carolina shipping lists. Whatever the causes, Charles Town officials were painfully aware of this process. As early as 1708, the first Indian agent, Thomas Nairne, was already reminiscing about the days "when beavor was a comodity." Observing "multitudes of beavor dams" in Chickasaw country, he lamented not only the loss of revenue but also the diplomatic leverage the trade conferred against French Louisiana. "We can easiely ruin Mobile," he argued, "meerly by purchasing beavor skins." He urged the Commissioners of the Indian Trade to "study all means" by which the beaver trade might be revived, suggesting ultimately that "if it's no comodity in England" it might "be sent else where."[30]

Lost in the backwaters of the French empire, Louisiana apparently escaped such transatlantic economic pressures, but, at the other end of the Mississippi River, New France was turned inside out. Beaver was "no comodity" anywhere in the first decade of the eighteenth century. Plagued by a declining European market, interrupted shipping routes, and runaway local overproduction, profits from the Canadian beaver trade fell off spectacularly from 1696 to 1713. The collapse was so complete that the French ministry proposed at one point a total cessation of the Indian trade. It continued only because officials in New France explained to the ministry how catastrophic the diplomatic repercussions of such a move might be. Unprofitable as it had become, they argued, the beaver trade nevertheless kept valuable Indian allies in the French interest. For that reason alone, while taking a loss, Canadian merchants continued to exchange European goods for beaver pelts, consciously sublimating the demands of the market to the greater good of friendship and alliance. Much has been written on the subject of "administered" or "treaty" trade, that is, trade conducted predominantly for political purposes rather than profit. If the Canadian trade was not generally "administered," it nevertheless displayed on this occasion the wisdom to shield its native allies from the harshness of the market.[31]

Aside from the comments of Thomas Nairne, Carolina officials made no such effort to assist their native client/allies in making the transition from a mixed skin and fur trade to one based solely on deerskins during the same period. It may be argued that increased deerskin exports smoothed the transition by offsetting the decline in other commodities, but the net equivalency in economic terms concealed a drastic redeployment of labor on the part of native hunters and trappers. Such a process demanded the curtailment of diversified, probably pre-market, activities that drew on a variety of species and habitats in favor of a single, seasonal pursuit targeting a single species. The practical difficulties of that transformation, involving issues of hunting territory, technique, and technology, must have been immense.

Archaeological excavations at Upper and Lower Creek town sites in Alabama and Georgia corroborate the period of the transformation and suggest how profoundly it altered traditional lifeways. Before 1700, the Muskogee- and Hitchiti-speaking towns that later made up the Creek Confederacy routinely constructed circular winter houses, built with a sunken floor and wattle-and-daub construction techniques. The winter houses were sturdier than the rectangular summer houses and provided additional warmth and protection during cold winter months. As the commercial deerskin trade came to dominate native economic life, however, hunters were forced to extend their winter hunting expeditions for months on end. Labor formerly devoted to the construction of winter housing may have been devoted increasingly to the hunt, and the extended absence of hunters and often their families may have rendered such housing unnecessary as villages emptied during much of the winter. Not surprisingly, winter houses uniformly disappeared from villages across the region. That loss involved much more than mere architectural technique; the demise of winter housing altered the actual and social landscape of proto-Creek villages. The appearance and spatial structure of southeastern towns changed, and seasonal patterns of family life and gender relations must have shifted to fit the new order as well.[32]

In the first fifteen years of the eighteenth century, deer hunting drew Native American men farther into the Atlantic economy than ever before, and their mothers, wives, sisters, and daughters followed them. As raccoons, wildcats, foxes, muskrats, otters, and beavers disappeared from South Carolina shipping lists between 1699 and 1715, the entries for deerskins displayed, in addition to an increase in volume, a pronounced shift toward a certain method of preparation. Whereas exports had previously included large numbers of "undrest" deerskins, comprising about 30 percent of the total number of deerskins exported at the start of this pivotal period, only about 10 percent continued to be undressed by 1715. By contrast, roughly 90 percent of all deerskins exported from Charles Town from 1713 to 1715 were "half-drest," a process of partial preparation (scraped but untanned) specifically geared toward trade. Because women were generally responsible for the preparation of deerskins, this may indicate their growing involvement in at least one aspect of the trade. We may never know whether it was a voluntary strategy to maximize exchange rates or a grudging concession to market demands. Since half-dressed skins generally commanded higher prices, however, the shift benefited native consumers and may thus have represented an effort on their part to counter the largely negative developments underway at the time. Such a strategy would have been particularly useful in offsetting the deteriorating exchange rate between South Carolina currency and British pounds sterling. . . .[33]

Although an integral part of the phenomenon, Carolina traders were in part the unwitting personification of larger economic forces over which they had little control. In contrast to the scattered effects of gender-specific violence or the localized hardship of indebtedness among the Yamasees, the new economic imperatives communicated by English traders touched all native communities involved in trade relations with South Carolina. The torque thus exerted on Anglo-Indian relations further strained the inherently delicate mechanisms of intercultural exchange, already critically stressed in key areas, and placed Carolina's extensive alliance network on a tenuous footing. By 1715, South Carolina's relationship with its native clients and allies had come to depend more than ever on official acts of diplomacy from Charles Town, carried to the frontier by the Indian agent.

The office of Indian agent for South Carolina was scarcely eight years old when Thomas Nairne and John Wright, the only two men ever to hold the position, were both killed in 1715 in the Yamasee town of Pocotaligo in the opening drama of the Yamasee War. Created by the Commons House of Assembly in 1707, the agency represented the colony's most visible diplomatic connection with southeastern Native America; it was entrusted with the responsibility of adjudicating differences between Indians and traders, policing the trade, and delivering diplomatic messages to and from Indian country. Simultaneously, the assembly created a board of commissioners responsible for overseeing the Indian trade and the activities of the agent. The regulatory legislation of 1707 was part and parcel of the market phenomenon already rippling along the frontier, and, while its full economic consequences for southeastern Indians have not been recognized to date, historians have long considered 1707 a watershed year. For Converse D. Clowse, it marked the "dividing line between an Indian trade conducted informally and a regularized commerce," while Verner Crane saw it as a transformation of the Indian trade from a "profitable sideline" into a "mercantile interest second only to the exportation of rice." Scholars have traditionally agreed as well that the new regulatory legislation contributed, though indirectly, to the outbreak of the Yamasee War by failing to curtail trader misconduct and abuse. It is argued here, however, that the office of Indian agent, and particularly the two men who competed for it between 1707 and 1715, played a central, even decisive, role in provoking conflict.[34]

Although neither man by himself intended to compromise Carolina's diplomatic standing among southeastern Indians, together they produced a rare chemistry that managed to dissolve the colony's reputation utterly. Beginning as a simple competition for sole ownership of the Indian agency, which changed hands between them twice, their rivalry soon expanded into a vindictive conflict that ultimately transcended the personal enmity between Nairne and Wright and drew South Carolina traders and officials into one camp or the other. The specific circumstances of the rivalry's inception, though compelling as human drama, are perhaps irrelevant to the current discussion. Yet Wright felt himself wronged, first by his ouster as agent in 1712 and subsequently by Nairne's enthusiastic application of the regulatory laws to Wright's own trading ventures. Wright first sought legal redress through the Court of Common Pleas; from 1713 to 1715 he became a master of nuisance suits, designed to harass and annoy his enemies. They followed a common formula, citing clauses of the 1712 Act for Regulating the Indian Trade with such an emphasis on details and technicalities as to seem almost comical. He appears to have changed only a few key phrases and names from case to case in order to save time. Soon, other traders sympathetic to his cause also began filing suits, utilizing his exact format and targeting the same defendants. By the summer of 1714, Wright and his supporters were ready to move beyond nuisance suits and the Court of Common Pleas to mount a more serious challenge to the colony's regulatory administration.[35]

Wright fired the opening salvos of that broader battle on June 8, 1714, when he submitted a list of "remonstrances" to the Commons House of Assembly, accusing Nairne of "irregularities & ill practices." Only four days later, the trader John Pight revealed the full extent of the offensive when he too submitted a petition to the assembly, this time accusing the Commissioners of the Indian Trade of exercising poor judgment in a case they had decided the previous year. Although filed separately, it became clear as time went on that the two traders were coordinating their efforts, often drafting and submitting letters for their respective cases to the same people on the same or consecutive days and calling on a common pool of witnesses. Pight later testified that he had in fact spent much time at Wright's Goose Creek plantation during this period, a revelation that struck contemporaries as "very strange," since he was "notoriously known" to spend most of his time "in the Indian country."[36]

By August, Wright began to flout Nairne's authority openly on the frontier. When the agent locked up a cask of Wright's rum (an illegal commodity) in the mico's own "hous" at the Yamasee town of Pocotaligo, Wright sent two of his henchmen to take it back. They "broke open" the headman's house and carried away the rum. Nairne issued a warrant for their arrest, but the residents of Pocotaligo saw no immediate local action. The real problem of bringing Wright and his supporters to heel was another matter entirely. For the Yamasee Indians, who had seen both Nairne and Wright in the same official capacity, the incident could not possibly have made sense. It signaled the disintegration of a coherent policy and voice from Charles Town. The two agents were at war with each other. Several questions must have passed repeatedly around Yamasee council fires in late 1714 and early 1715: which man is the official agent, which man is more powerful, which man's policy is best, and *which man is to be believed*?[37]

No answers to those questions ever came from Charles Town. Beginning in November 1714, when the Commons House began considering in earnest the complaints brought to it by Wright and Pight, Thomas Nairne was forced to neglect his duties as agent and remain in town to defend himself. Likewise, the Commissioners of the Indian Trade foreswore their normal business and devoted themselves exclusively to their own defense. Virtually no routine business was conducted either by the agent or by the commissioners in the five months preceding the outbreak of the war the following April. In essence, therefore, South Carolina ended all official contact and correspondence with all corners of Native America from November 1714 onward, creating an abrupt and utter diplomatic vacuum everywhere. The colony simply disappeared on a diplomatic level, and the trade that continued pulsing outward from it carried a confusing array of messages, depending on the factional loyalties of individual traders. Alexander Longe, for instance, who had been arrested for his participation in a slave raid against the Euchees (allies of Carolina), capitalized on the confusion in Charles Town by running away to the Cherokees. Once there, he reportedly told them "that ye Einglish was goeing to macke warrs with them and that they did design to kill all their head warriers wich was ye reason he ran away." With no counterstatement forthcoming from reputable Carolina officials, the Cherokees may have found it difficult to distinguish truth from falsehood.[38]

In fact, information filtering into Cherokee territory from other Indian nations rather tended to support Longe's allegations. When the Yamasees observed English preparations to build a fort at Port Royal on the edge of their settlements, their initial concern over the cessation of diplomatic communications turned to alarm. Again, Charles Town offered no official explanation, leaving the Yamasees to search for their own answers. Some apparently became convinced that Carolina was preparing for war, and a Yamasee delegation conscientiously made a circuit of neighboring allies to warn them of the threatening English behavior.[39]

With the breakdown of diplomacy in late 1714, the trade was stripped of its political dimension just when it was needed most. The growing inflexibility of English trade behavior during the first fifteen years of the century had placed an unusually high premium on competent diplomacy from Charles Town, first to smooth over the difficulties of intercultural exchange (exacerbated by recent market developments), and second to reassure concerned clients and confirm valuable alliances. Its absence now proved fatal. As the diplomatic blackout continued into the spring of 1715, and English traders began arriving in native villages across the South to collect their debts, the situation became critical for some nations. After having "made severall Complaints without Redress," the "Creeks" (probably the Ocheeses or Lower Creeks) finally issued an ultimatum that "upon the first Afront from any of the Traders they would down with them and soe goe on with itt." The Creeks, to be clear, did not simply kill the traders outright. They issued a warning clearly intended to be heard and passed up the trading path to Charles Town. It was an effort, born of desperation, to break through the diplomatic pall that had fallen over the colony and to elicit some sort of official response. Similar warnings emanated from the Yamasee settlements around Port Royal at the same time, and they had their desired effect. Carolina officials snapped to attention, stopped their bickering, and organized their first diplomatic overture in over five months. Given the importance and delicacy of the venture, it was entrusted jointly to the colony's most experienced frontier diplomats: Thomas Nairne and John Wright.[40]

The fate of that famous effort at negotiation has become a favorite staple of Carolina lore. Meeting the Yamasees in their principal town of Pocotaligo on April 14, 1715, Nairne gave reassurances of Carolina's friendship and concern for its trading partners and promised to address their concerns. All parties shook hands amicably that evening as if the problem had been resolved. Then, in the morning, the Yamasees, adorned in red and black war paint, swarmed in upon Nairne and his colleagues, killing most of them outright. Nairne was not so fortunate. He was tortured for three days "before he was allowed to die." (Wright was killed as well, though the circumstances were not recorded.) The standard account of this incident has not changed in any of its details since the publication of *The Southern Frontier* more than seventy years ago. It is generally taken as proof that the Yamasees had already committed themselves to war and that Nairne had little chance of changing their minds. The friendly goodnight exchanges thus became a sinister facade, masking the Yamasees' deadly intentions. Yet there is a face missing from this time-honored portrait: that of John Wright. Only the previous August, the Yamasees had seen the battle between the two agents played out violently in that very town over a cask of rum. Wright's presence alongside Thomas Nairne at what may be termed ground zero of the Yamasee War inevitably raises a number of questions. Foremost among them, did he bring the same political agenda to Pocotaligo Town that had governed his actions for the last two years in the Court of Common Pleas and the Commons House of Assembly?[41]

Carolina lore also holds that, after the first pitched battle with the Yamasees, a note addressed to Gov. Charles Craven was found on one of the fallen warriors. Rumored to have included an explanation of Yamasee motives, it disappeared as quickly and completely as the musket smoke of that battle. The note, however, did and does exist. It has spent the last three centuries, astonishingly, tucked inside another letter in the British Public Record Office, where it was never cataloged on its own merit. Signed by the "Huspaw King," it was written in "gunpowder ink" and dictated to a young English boy taken captive for precisely that purpose. True to legend, it is an explanation in the Yamasee Indians' own voice of why they acted as they did. Amidst voluminous English, French, and Spanish sources, this is the only extant primary document ever produced by the Yamasees themselves during this crucial period.[42]

The first few lines of the note confirm the central role played by John Wright during those final hours of delicate negotiation. According to the Huspaw King:

> Mr. Wright said that the white men would come and fetch [illegible] the Yamasees in one night and that they would hang four of the head men and take all the rest of them for slaves, and that he would send them all off the country, for he said that the men of the Yamasees were like women, and shew'd his hands one to the other, and what he said vex'd the great warrier's, and this made them begin the war.[43]

Wright's message seems intended to stir up trouble and could hardly have been compatible with the official reassurance of peace and friendship proffered by Thomas Nairne. If he did in fact say those things, as the Yamasees asserted, he must have arranged a private meeting at some point that did not include the acting Indian agent. It would have been difficult while the main negotiations were still underway, but less so once Nairne had said his friendly good-night and gone to sleep.

Regardless of the circumstances, it now seems clear that two separate, conflicting messages were delivered to the Yamasee Indians gathered at Pocotaligo Town: Nairne's message of peace and Wright's message of war. According to Spanish accounts of Yamasee testimony shortly after the outbreak of hostilities, the assembled warriors and headmen debated the problem throughout the night, unable to arrive at a consensus. Having seen both Wright and Nairne previously in an official capacity, they knew that one of the two messages reflected the colony's true intentions. After much soul-searching and a rousing predawn oratory by a Yamasee warrior, they ultimately found it easier to believe the worst about the Carolinians. Even so, if English sources are to be believed, a number of warriors may have clung to Nairne's message of peace to the bitter end and lost their lives along with him. This was not an angry, reflexive outburst provoked by trade abuse or dependency, nor was it necessarily the first premeditated act in a grand Native American "conspiracy" to destroy South Carolina. It was, rather, an agonized, deliberate response to English diplomatic behaviors that can only be described as schizophrenic.[44]

Rather than assuming that the Yamasees orchestrated a massive conspiracy among southeastern Indian nations, we must now begin asking a whole new set of questions. How and with whom, for instance, did they form an alliance network prior to the outbreak of hostilities, and why did those allies respond as they did upon hearing the news that the Yamasees had broken off relations with South Carolina? The question is complicated by the likelihood, as Steven Oatis has pointed out, that the unified native front perceived by Carolinians masked a series of interlocking alliance networks, each acting on its own set of diplomatic considerations. The problem is too complex to receive a thorough treatment here, but the actions of the various members of the 1715 coalition suggest a few basic patterns.[45]

It is not surprising that the first native voices to break through South Carolina's diplomatic paralysis in early 1715 came from the same geographical range and set of nations that had been most vocal in protesting various trade practices over the previous fifteen years. Having become, on average, routine participants in the Carolina trade network during the mid-1680s, the Savannahs, Lower (Ocheese) Creeks (including the splinter towns of Oconee and Palachacola), Euchees, and Yamasees were more deeply engaged in trade and consequently more attuned to the tenor of the exchange relationship by 1715 than any other groups in the South. The frictions of intercultural exchange, exacerbated by disturbing market trends, demanded a continuous dialogue between those nations and Charles Town officials and made the diplomatic breakdown of late 1714 all the more conspicuous. News of open conflict between the Yamasees and the English in April 1715 undoubtedly confirmed suspicions about the meaning of Carolina's silence and drew the Lower Creeks, Savannahs, and Euchees (and the recently relocated Apalachees) into the war in short order. Along with the Yamasees, they formed the core of the native war effort. They struck the first and fiercest blows against Carolina, often in concert with each other, and ultimately refused to make peace until long after the rest of the indigenous South had resumed trade with Charles Town.[46]

Those core combatants were flanked on several sides by less enthusiastic confederates: the Upper Creeks (including Abhikas, Coosas, Tallapoosas, and Alabamas) and Choctaws to the west, and the Cherokees, Catawbas, and Carolina piedmont tribes (Waterees, Congarees, and others) to the north. Their complaints had appeared much less regularly, if at all, in the English records. Although they all participated in the spring massacres of South Carolina traders, only the Cherokees and Carolina piedmont tribes mounted additional attacks against the colony, and even they grew quiet by the end of the first summer. While the destabilizing effects of market influence and diplomatic breakdown must have shaken them, it is doubtful that the auxiliary participants would have struck at the English of their own accord. Their decision to do so ultimately depended on the interplay and compatibility of local concerns with the emergence of a powerful war movement among the core nations.

In contrast to the Lower Creeks, Savannahs, and Yamasees, the auxiliary confederates were generally influenced by two meliorating factors that set them apart in significant ways. First, they were relative newcomers to trade with Carolina. Englishmen did not move west into Upper Creek territory until the mid-1690s, and Carolinians continued to regard the Cherokees as "but little known to us" as late as 1713. The Choctaws, meanwhile, remained outside the Carolina trading sphere until 1714. Although subject to the same market-driven changes as the core nations, the auxiliary confederates felt them less intensely due to their more limited involvement in the English trade. The only exception to this rule may be the Catawbas and other piedmont nations, who had been engaged in trade with Virginia before the establishment of South Carolina in 1670. Yet here a second factor of profound significance came into play. All of the auxiliary confederates enjoyed access to alternative sources of European goods. The Upper Creeks and Choctaws reaped the benefits of direct relations with French Louisiana, while the Catawbas and their Carolina piedmont neighbors routinely welcomed Virginia traders into their villages. Although geographically remote, Cherokee consumers also managed to acquire French goods via the Tennessee and Tallapoosa river systems and Virginia goods through Catawba middlemen. Competition with Virginians on the one hand and Frenchmen on the other forced South Carolina traders to provide those groups with better terms; and, because French and Virginia traders were still willing to purchase beaver pelts and other traditional staples of the old fur trade, those nations were spared the hardships of converting abruptly to an exclusive reliance on deerskins. Consequently, participation in the war against South Carolina was a less compelling decision for Upper Creeks, Choctaws, Cherokees, and Catawbas.[47]

Discovering the means by which the auxiliaries became aligned with the core combatants in 1715 will require a separate study, analyzing each nation individually and in depth. One common element, however, deserves a brief mention here. Access to alternative sources of trade also brought rival diplomatic overtures into Upper Creek, Choctaw, Cherokee, and Catawba villages. It is clear, for instance, that Jean-Baptiste le Moyne de Bienville of French Louisiana made concerted efforts to counter English influence among the Choctaws and Upper Creeks in early 1715, distributing gifts liberally and promising attractive terms of trade. Balanced against Carolina's continuing diplomatic blackout and the power of the core nations, his message must have carried more than its usual weight that spring. For the Catawbas of the Carolina piedmont, as James Merrell has pointed out, trade rivalry between South Carolina and Virginia encouraged the belief that war with South Carolina would not affect the flow of merchandise from its colonial rival, as indeed it had not during the Tuscarora War in 1711. That war in fact had never really ended for the Catawbas and their piedmont allies, who continued fending off Tuscarora and Iroquois attacks long after Carolinians had closed the book on it. For the Catawbas, therefore, the events of 1715 may have represented less a new declaration of war than a reshuffling of alliances in mid-conflict.[48]

Each of those auxiliary participants faced a complex set of local considerations that defy generalization. Common elements shaped their decisions, to be sure, such as prospects of alternative trade, market influence, the ambiguous silence of Carolina's diplomatic voice, and finally the unambiguous clamor of warfare in April. But the nature and value of those elements differed from region to region, and among them stretched a "thousand threads" that wove them into the local reality. The enduring marvel of the Yamasee War may be that they all led to the same solution: political alignment with the core nations and token "war" with South Carolina.[49]

Only one nation in the entire region, the Chickasaws, remained loyal to the English. Significantly, they were the only nation to receive a formal declaration of friendship from the colony in the five months preceding the war. Even then, it was extended only because a Chickasaw delegation had walked five hundred miles to Charles Town for that very purpose in December 1714 and waited patiently for the Commons House of Assembly to notice them. Their example suggests how little might have been required of South Carolina to maintain peace.[50]

South Carolinas diplomatic failure from late 1714 onward became a critical problem only because the colony's trade behavior, increasingly influenced by external market demands, had become progressively less responsive to indigenous needs over the previous decade. Charles Town officials never rose to the challenge of establishing the sort of meaningful discourse with southeastern Indians that might have resolved the tensions generated by the trade. They dissolved, instead, into internecine squabbles over who should control that discourse, ultimately forcing the Yamasees and others to infer the colony's intentions. While the Yamasee response to Carolina's incoherent diplomatic communication undoubtedly colored the responses of other southeastern Indian nations, it represented only the first in a series of independent actions, each determined by its own set of local considerations.

Sprung from this politico-economic thicket, the Yamasee War produced a matrix of related consequences that influenced the terms of Anglo-Indian exchange for the next half century. As Carolina negotiated the terms of peace with southeastern Indians, an unprecedented antimarket modification of the trade emerged: the price agreement. It is generally considered a standard feature of the deerskin trade for most of the eighteenth century, but the earliest set price schedules date only to 1716. The Cherokees were the first to extort such an agreement from Charles Town in April 1716, when they received a list of permanent prices for all items "as they are allways to be sold." Prior to this, Anglo-Indian exchange rates had been determined by the market mechanism of supply and demand, requiring Indians to "bargain," "deale," and "agree for" purchase prices. The Cherokee breakthrough was followed by a fixed price agreement with the Creek Indians in 1718. Thereafter, Anglo-Indian exchange rates throughout the South were always established at a fixed level by treaty. . . .[51]

As the historian Joel W. Martin has demonstrated, moreover, the Yamasee War marked the beginning of regular, ritualized gift exchange between Charles Town and its native allies and clients. Although Carolinians had grudgingly participated in gift exchange prior to the war, their approach to the custom had been tinged with a cynical concern for profit. The prewar Carolina policy had been to reciprocate at the rate of "one half the value" of any gifts received from Native American allies. The resumption of trade relations after the war, however, was accomplished, on a nation-by-nation basis, through official ceremonies, treaties, and exchanges of gifts in which the indivisibility of trade and diplomacy became undeniably apparent. From that point onward, the colony renewed its pledge of friendship and trade annually, lavishing southeastern Indians with gifts and entertainment in order "to keep up a good understanding." Rather than rationing its goodwill as it had once done, Carolina petitioned the crown for and received a royal subsidy of three thousand pounds sterling per year for Indian presents, a practice that French Louisiana had adopted long before.[52]

Martin also argued convincingly that South Carolina's commitment to ritual gift giving collapsed shortly after the British victory in the Great War for Empire in 1763, when southeastern Indians were reduced to an exclusive reliance on British trade. If so, the Yamasee War may serve as a counterweight to that event, anchoring a distinct historical phase between 1715 and 1763 that requires treatment on its own terms. . . . New evidence concerning the "real price" or purchasing power per deerskin demonstrates a steady improvement for southeastern Indians during much of this period, suggesting again that the years between 1715 and 1763 were characterized by an exchange paradigm that differed from what had come before and what would come after. In many ways, then, the war's consequences and its origins were of one cloth and logically connected. In the midst of imperial rivalries and alien economic systems, the indigenous peoples of the North American Southeast made a series of decisions in 1715 about their place in the world and succeeded, to a surprising extent, in determining both their place in and the nature of that new world.[53]

## NOTES

1 [Francis] LeJau to the Secretary [of the Society for the Propagation of the Gospel in Foreign Parts], Feb. 20, 1712, in *The Carolina Chronicle of Dr. Francis LeJau, 1706–1717*, ed. Frank J. Klingberg (Berkeley, 1956), 109.

2 Gary B. Nash, *Red, White, and Black: The Peoples of Early North America* (Englewood Cliffs, 2000), 123. For the war's diplomatic repercussions and tribal migrations as well as the collapse of the colony's proprietary government, see Verner W. Crane, *The Southern Frontier, 1670–1732* (1925; New York, 1981), 137–68. For the decline of Indian slavery, see William L. Ramsey, "'All and Singular the Slaves': A Demographic Profile of Indian Slavery in Colonial South Carolina," in *Money, Trade, and Power: The Evolution of a Planter Society in Colonial South Carolina*, ed. Jack P. Greene, Rosemary Brana-Shute, and Randy Sparks (Columbia, S.C., 2001), 166–86.

3 Crane, *Southern Frontier*, 162–67, esp. 162. John R. Swanton, *The Early History of the Creek Indians and Their Neighbors* (1922; Gainesville, 1998), 97. For a modern example of this line of thinking, see John Philip Reid, *A Better Kind of Hatchet: Law, Trade, and Diplomacy in the Cherokee Nation during the Early Years of European Contact* (University Park, 1976), 52–55.

4 See Richard L. Haan, "The 'Trade Do's Not Flourish as Formerly': The Ecological Origins of the Yamassee War of 1715," *Ethnohistory*, 28 (Fall 1981), 341–58; and James H. Merrell, *The Indians New World: Catawbas and Their Neighbors from European Contact through the Era of Removal* (New York, 1991), 68–75, esp. 50. For efforts to explain the origins of the Yamasee War in terms of dependency theory, see James H. Merrell, "Our Bond of Peace': Patterns of Intercultural Exchange in the Carolina Piedmont, 1650–1750," in *Powhatan's Mantle: Indians in the Colonial Southeast*, ed. Peter H. Wood, Gregory A. Waselkov, and M. Thomas Hatley (Lincoln, 1989), 207; and Nash, *Red, White, and Black*, 124–26. For a concise summation of Richard White's ideas about dependency theory, see Richard White, *The Roots of Dependency: Subsistence, Environment, and Social Change among the Choc taws, Pawnees, and Navajos* (Lincoln, 1983), xiii–xix.

5 For the political significance of trade among southeastern Indians, see Joel W. Martin, "Southeastern Indians and the English Trade in Skins and Slaves," in *The Forgotten Centuries: Indians and Europeans in the American South, 1521–1704*, ed. Charles Hudson and Carmen Chaves Tesser (Athens, Ga.,1994), 308. See also Merrell, "Our Bond of Peace,'" 198–99; and James Axtell, *The Indians' New South: Culture Change in the Colonial Southeast* (Baton Rouge, 1997), 47. Some of the most rewarding efforts to gain perspective on intercultural exchange have thus far been produced by scholars of the northern fur trade; see, for instance, Arthur J. Ray and Donald B. Freeman, *"Give Us Good Measure": An Economic Analysis of Relations between the Indians and the Hudson's Bay Company before 1763* (Toronto, 1978); and Richard White, *The Middle Ground: Indians, Empires, and Republics in the Great Lakes Region, 1650–1815* (Cambridge, Eng., 1992). Perhaps the best general introduction to the substantivist position

(which takes into account native cultural approaches to economic transactions) is Marshall Sahlins, *Stone-Age Economics* (New York, 1972); see also Abraham Rotstein, "Karl Polanyi's Concept of Non-Market Trade," *Journal of Economic History,* 30 (March 1970), 117–26.

6 May 6, 1714, in *Colonial Records of South Carolina: Journals of the Commissioners of the Indian Trade: September 20, 1710–August 29, 1718,* ed. W. L. McDowell Jr. (Columbia, S.C., 1992), 56; Alexander Longe, "A Small Postscript on the Ways and Manners of the Indians Called Cherokees," ed. David Corkran, *Southern Indian Studies,* 21 (1969), 55–56, 3.

7 For one of the first efforts to untangle this trader factionalism, see Alan Gallay, *The Indian Slave Trade: The Rise of the English Empire in the American South, 1670–1717* (New Haven, 2002), 315–34. My survey of the *Journals of the Commissioners of the Indian Trade* counted only those cases from 1710 to 1715 where a clear complain ant and defendant(s) could be identified. Only two, however, involved an unidentified complainant or defendant. One additional case in 1711 involved a Yamasee request for clarification of policy with neither complainant nor defendant. I have also followed the threads of each case through the journals in order to avoid counting the same case multiple times, since the commissioners often resumed deliberations after lengthy recesses. For the first identifying references to the 32 cases involving complaints lodged by English traders against other English traders, see McDowell, ed., *Colonial Records of South Carolina: Journals of the Commissioners of the Indian Trade,* 5–6, 11–13, 17–18, 20–23, 25, 27–28, 38, 41–43, 46–47, 57–58; for the first identifying references to the 30 cases involving complaints lodged by Native Americans against English traders, see *ibid.,* 3–5, 9, 11, 18–19, 23, 26, 37–38, 42–43, 49–50, 52–53, 57, 59–60.

8 For complaints against Alexander Nicholas, see Oct. 25, 1712, in *Colonial Records of South Carolina: Journals of the Commissioners of the Indian Trade,* ed. McDowell, 37, 4. For complaints against Phillip Gilliard and Jess Crosley (identified elsewhere as Joseph Crossley), see Sept. 21, 1710, *ibid.,* 4. For other cases of beatings, see *ibid.,* 50, 52.

9 Longe, "Small Postscript on the Ways and Manners of the Indians Called Cherokees," ed. Corkran, 30. Admittedly, not all southeastern nations held women in such high esteem. The Chickasaws and Catawbas, for instance, exhibited pronounced patriarchal traits. Indeed, the Chickasaws occasionally mocked the "Ochesees" or Lower Creeks for being so obedient to their womenfolk. Significantly, however, these nations were also relatively content with English trade relations. For Chickasaw opinions of Lower Creek gender relations, see Thomas Nairne, *Nairne's Muskhogean Journals: The 1708 Expedition to the Mississippi River,* ed. Alexander Moore (Jackson, 1988), 48.

10 Theda Perdue, *Cherokee Women: Gender and Culture Change, 1700–1835* (Lincoln, 1998), 45–46; also see Robin Fox, *Kinship and Marriage: An Anthropological Perspective* (Baltimore, 1967), 97–121; and J. Leitch Wright Jr., *Creeks and Seminoles: The Destruction and Regeneration of the Muscogulge People* (Lincoln, 1989), 19.

11 For complaints about "taking away" lodged by Native Americans against English traders, see McDowell, ed., *Colonial Records of South Carolina: Journals of the Commissioners of the Indian Trade,* 11 (two accounts), 13, 38, 42, 43, 50. A. S. Salley, ed., *Journals of the Commons House of Assembly of South Carolina for 1702* (Columbia, S.C., 1932), 21. For Cornelius Meckarty's case, see Nov. 24, 1713, in *Colonial Records of South Carolina: Journals of the Commissioners of the Indian Trade,* ed. McDowell, 52.

12 For William Ford's case, see June 27, 1712, in *Colonial Records of South Carolina: Journals of the Commissioners of the Indian Trade,* ed. McDowell, 28.
13 Nairne, *Nairne's Muskhogean Journals,* ed. Moore, 34–35.
14 For early concerns about "relations' debts," see Aug. 3, 1711, in *Colonial Records of South Carolina: Journals of the Commissioners of the Indian Trade,* ed. McDowell, 15. For Tuskenehau's case, see June 12, 1712, *ibid.,* 26. For official instructions on the matter, see July 10, 1712, *ibid,* 36.
15 Louis R. Smith Jr., "British-Indian Trade in Alabama, 1670–1756," *Alabama Review,* 27 (Jan. 1974), 71; Braund, *Deerskins and Duffels,* 62.
16 For Yamasee trade debts, see Crane, *Southern Frontier,* 167. For an environmental perspective of the topic, see Haan, "'Trade Do's Not Flourish as Formerly,'" 341–58. For a discussion of late-eighteenth-century deer populations, see Gregory A. Waselkov, "The Eighteenth-Century Anglo-Indian Trade in Southeastern North America," in *New Faces of the Fur Trade: Selected Papers of the Seventh North American Fur Trade Conference, Halifax, Nova Scotia, 1995,* ed. Jo-Anne Fiske, Susan Sleeper-Smith, and William Wicken (East Lansing, 1998), 203–5. The exchange rate in terms of pounds Carolina currency per 100 pounds sterling jumped from 150 in 1712 to 200 in 1713 and then to 300 in 1714. See John J. McCusker, *Money and Exchange in Europe and America, 1600–1775: A Handbook* (Chapel Hill, 1978), 222. For a discussion of changing market demands and viable commodities, see below. July 27, 1711, in *Colonial Records of South Carolina: Journals of the Commissioners of the Indian Trade,* ed. McDowell, 11.
17 For complaints of Indian creditors, see McDowell, ed., *Colonial Records of South Carolina: Journals of the Commissioners of the Indian Trade,* 19, 42 (two accounts), 53, 57.
18 For a more detailed discussion of Indian slavery and its complications, see William L. Ramsey, "A Coat for 'Indian Cuffy': Mapping the Boundary between Freedom and Slavery in Colonial South Carolina," *South Carolina Historical Magazine,* 103 (Jan. 2002), 48–66. For complaints lodged by Native Americans about slavery, see McDowell, ed., *Colonial Records of South Carolina: Journals of the Commissioners of the Indian Trade,* 3, 4 (two accounts), 23, 26, 49. For complaints lodged by English traders against other English traders concerning the issue of Indian slavery, see *ibid.,* 6, 11, 20, 22–23 (two cases), 25, 41 (two cases), 42, 47, 57.
19 Sept. 21, 1710, in *Colonial Records of South Carolina: Journals of the Commissioners of the Indian Trade,* ed. McDowell, 3–4. May 12, 1714, Journals of the Commons House of Assembly of South Carolina, 1706–1721 (microfilm: frame 4: 255), John S. Green transcripts (South Carolina Department of Archives and History, Columbia).
20 For excellent accounts of the English-Indian attacks on the Spanish missions, see Paul E. Hoffman, *Florida's Frontiers* (Bloomington, 2002), 174–82; and Amy Turner Bushneil, *Situado and Sabana: Spain's Support System for the Presidio and Mission Provinces of Florida* (Athens, Ga., 1994), 193–95. For a speculative discussion of the diplomatic repercussions of the collapse of the Spanish mission system from a Yamasee perspective, see Bradley Scott Schrager, "Yamasee Indians and the Challenge of Spanish and English Colonialism in the North American Southeast, 1660–1715" (Ph.D. diss., Northwestern University, 2001), 167–230.
21 White, *Middle Ground,* 75, 50–93. The general utility of White's model for other regions and epochs remains a point of controversy. Scholars of the colonial South have been especially suspicious of the "middle ground," preferring to emphasize local accommodation and variation over the development of a shared trade culture. For insightful discussions of intercultural exchange, see Andrew R. L. Cayton and Fredericka J. Teure, "Introduction: On the Connection of Frontiers,"

in *Contact Points: American Frontiers from the Mohawk Valley to the Mississippi, 1750–1830,* ed. Andrew R. L. Cayton and Fredericka J. Teute (Chapel Hill, 1998), 1–15; and Leonard Thompson and Howard Lamar, "Contemporary Frontier History," in *The Frontier in History: North America and Southern Africa Compared,* ed. Leonard Thompson and Howard Lamar (New Haven, 1982), 6–10; see also Gregory H. Nobles, "Breaking into the Backcountry: New Approaches to the Early American Frontier, 1750–1800," *William and Mary Quarterly,* 46 (Oct. 1989), 641–47.

22 For Cherokeeleechee's recollections, see Patrick Mackay to James Oglethorpe, March 29, 1735, in *General Oglethorpe's Georgia: Colonial Letters, 1733–1743,* ed. Mills Lane (2 vols., Savannah, 1975), I, 152. For Malatchi's comments, see Speech by Malatchi Opiya Mico to Alexander Heron, Dec. 7, 1747 (microfilm: frame 316, reel 12), Original Manuscript Books, vol. 36, Colonial Records of the State of Georgia (Georgia Department of Archives and History, Atlanta). For the Cherokee assessment of English traders, see "Journal of the March of the Carolinians into the Cherokee Mountains," in *City of Charleston Year-book, 1894,* ed. Landgon Cheves (Charleston, 1894), 335.

23 For seventeeth-century Spanish-Indian trade, see Gregory H. Waselkov, "Seventeenth-Century Trade in the Colonial Southeast," *Southeastern Archaeology,* 8 (no. 2, 1982), 117–30. For the classic statement on the acceleration of trade in the first decade of the eighteenth century, see Converse D. Clowse, *Economic Beginnings of Colonial South Carolina, 1670–1730* (Columbia, S.C., 1971), 162–66.

24 [Jean-Baptiste Lemoyne de] Bienville to Pontchartrain, Sept. 1, 1715, in *Mississippi Provincial Archives: French Dominion,* ed. and trans. Dunbar Rowland and Albert Godfrey Sanders (3 vols., Jackson, 1927–1932), III, 187. Price differences probably had much to do with Louisiana's marginal position in the French empire. In regions where distributional problems were not as severe, Native American consumers in the early eighteenth century often preferred French goods. See W. J. Eccles, "A Belated Review of Harold Adams Innis, *The Fur Trade in Canada,*" *Canadian Historical Review,* 60 (Dec. 1979), 430–31; and Walter L. Dorn, *Competition for Empire* (New York, 1940), 254. Bienville to Maurepas, April 20, 1734, in *Mississippi Provincial Archives: French Dominion,* ed. and trans. Rowland and Sanders, III, 670–71. For Louisiana and the frontier exchange economy, see Daniel H. Usner Jr., *Indians, Settlers, and Slaves in a Frontier Exchange Economy: The Lower Mississippi Valley before 1783* (Chapel Hill, 1992), 277, 8, 26–27.

25 Bienville to Pontchartrain, Oct. 27, 1711, in *Mississippi Provincial Archives: French Dominion,* ed. and trans. Rowland and Sanders, III, 160.

26 For South Carolina's economic development, see Clowse, *Economic Beginnings of Colonial South Carolina,* 165; see also Russell R. Menard, "Financing the Lowcountry Export Boom: Capital and Growth in Early Carolina," *William and Mary Quarterly,* 51 (Oct. 1994), 659–76; Peter A. Coclanis, "The Hydra Head of Merchant Capital: Markets and Merchants in Early South Carolina," in *The Meaning of South Carolina History: Essays in Honor of George C. Rogers Jr.,* ed. David R. Chesnutt and Clyde N. Wilson (Columbia, S.C., 1991), 1–18; and R. C. Nash, "South Carolina and the Atlantic Economy in the Late Seventeenth and Eighteenth Centuries," *Economic History Review,* 45 (Nov. 1992), 677–702. The long-standing presumption that French attitudes toward Native Americans were inherently more beneficent than those of the English are explored in Cornelius Jaenen, "French Attitudes towards Native Society," in *Old Trails and New Directions: Papers of the Third North American Fur Trade Conference,* ed. Carol M. Judd and Arthur J. Ray (Toronto, 1980), 59–72.

27 A. S. Salley, ed., *Journal of the Commons House of Assembly of South Carolina, November 20, 1706–February 8, 1706/7*(Columbia, S.C., 1939), 34.

28 *William Smith v. Anthony Probert,* Nov. 12, 1706, box 2A (microfilm: frames 731–32, reel 1705–1707), Judgement Rolls, South Carolina Court of Common Pleas (South Carolina Department of Archives and History, Columbia); *Peter Mailhett v. John Pight,* Jan. 17, 1706/7, box 2A, frame 803, *ibid.* The same may be said for most of the traders cited earlier with respect to the forcible confiscation of goods and issues of credit. Most were sued for debts, including Joseph Bryan (Brynon), Phillip Gilliard, Shippy (Sheppy) Allen, Richard Gower, Samuel Hilden, and John Wright: *see John Buckley v. Joseph Brynon,* Oct. 23, 1706, box 2A, frame 758, *ibid.; Richard Beresford v. Phillip Gilliard,* 1710, box 2C, frame 143, reel 1710–1711, *ibid.; John Buckley v. Shippy Allen,* Aug. 2, 1712, box 2D, frame 2, reel 1711–1712, *ibid.; Isaac Mazyck v. Shippy Allen and Alexander Nicholas,* Aug. 2, 1712, box 2D, frame 15, *ibid.; Richard Beresford v. Richard Gower,* June 22, 1711, box 3A, frame 206, *ibid.; John Wright v. Samuel Hilden and John Cocket,* Aug. 13, 1712, box 2D, frame 81, *ibid.;* and *William Smith v. John Wright,* Nov. 4, 1706, box 2A, frame 752, reel 1705–1707, *ibid.*

29 For fur trade export totals, see America and the West Indies, Virginia: Original Correspondence, Board of Trade, 1715–1717, 5/1317, p. 178, Colonial Office (British Public Record Office, London); also available in photocopy in British Records Calendar, 1712–1716, X77.594, pp. 1–2 (North Carolina State Archives, Raleigh).

30 For new imperial regulations concerning rice and their consequences, see Clowse, *Economic Beginnings of Colonial South Carolina,* 139; see also R. C. Nash, "The Organization of Trade and Finance in the Atlantic Economy: Britain and South Carolina, 1670–1775," in *Money, Trade, and Power,* ed. Greene, Brana-Shute, and Sparks, 77; Stephen G. Hardy, "Colonial South Carolina's Rice Industry and the Atlantic Economy," *ibid.,* 115; Marc Egnal, *New World Economies: The Growth of the Thirteen Colonies and Early Canada* (New York, 1998), 100; and Peter A. Coclanis, "Bitter Harvest: The South Carolina Low Country in Historical Perspective," *Journal of Economic History,* 45 (June 1985), 254–55. Nairne, *Nairne's Muskhogean Journals,* ed. Moore, 47, 50–51.

31 For the failure of the Canadian trade, see Dale Miquelon, *New France, 1701–1744: "A Supplement to Europe"* (Toronto, 1987), 55–76; Eccles, "Belated Review of Harold Adams Innis," 422–23; and W. J. Eccles, *Frontenac: The Courtier Governor* (Toronto, 1959), 285–94. For an effort to gain perspective on the issue of "treaty trade" in light of more dominant market features, see Ray and Freeman, *"Give Us Good Measure,"* 2–9, 231–45. Early efforts to apply the theoretical framework of treaty trade to the northern fur trade may be found in E. E. Rich, *The History of Hudson's Bay Company, 1670–1870* (2 vols., London, 1958–1959); and E. E. Rich, "Trade Habits and Economic Motivation among the Indians of North America," *Canadian Journal of Economics and Political Science,* 27 (1960), 35–53.

32 Gregory A. Waselkov, John W Cottier, and Craig T. Sheldon Jr., *Archaeological Excavations at the Early Historte Creek Indian Town of Fusihatchee (Phase I: 1988–89)* (Washington, 1996); Cameron Wesson, "Households and Hegemony: An Analysis of Historic Creek Culture Change" (Ph.D. diss., University of Illinois, Urbana-Champaign, 1997); Gregory A. Waselkov and Marvin T. Smith, "Upper Creek Archaeology," in *Indians of the Greater Southeast: Historical Archaeology and Ethnohistory,* ed. Bonnie G. McEwan (Gainesville, 2000), 247; John E. Worth, "The Lower Creeks: Origins and Early History," *ibid.,* 284–85. For Creek town life and spatial organization, though at a later period, see Piker, "'Peculiarly Connected,'" 1–37, 163–274.

33 For Carolina exports to Great Britain, see America and the West Indies, Virginia: Original Correspondence, Board of Trade, 1715–1717, 5/1317, p. 178, Colonial Office (British Public Record Office); also available in photocopy in British Records Calendar, 1712–1716, X77.594, pp. 1–2. For the deteriorating exchange rate, see McCusker, *Money and Exchange in Europe and America,* 222.

34 For a political history of the Commons House of Assembly during this period, see Alexander Moore, "Carolina Whigs: Colleton County Members of the South Carolina Commons House of Assembly, 1692–1720" (M.A. thesis, University of South Carolina, 1981); see also Alexander Moore, "Royalizing South Carolina: The Revolution of 1719 and the Transformation of Early South Carolina Government" (Ph.D. diss., University of South Carolina, 1991). Clowse, *Economic Beginnings of Colonial South Carolina,* 165. According to Verner Crane, the 1707 regulatory legislation represented a victory of merchant interests over the prerogatives of the governor and his planter allies in the governor's council; see Crane, *Southern Frontier,* 120.

35 The best introduction to the early history of Nairne's problems as agent may be found in Alexander Moore, "Introduction," in *Nairne's Muskhogean Journals,* ed. Moore, 12, 16–17. For examples of Wright's nuisance suits, *see John Wright v. John Cochrane* (elsewhere Cochran), Jan. 10, 1713/14, box 5A, frame 268, reel 1714, Judgement Rolls, South Carolina Court of Common Pleas; *John Wright v. John Cochrane,* April 19, 1714, box 6A, frames 490–94, reel 1714, *ibid.; John Wright v. Alexander Parris,* Jan. 16, 1712/13, box 4A, frame 8, reel 1713, *ibid.;* and *John Wright v. John Beauchamp,* Oct. 1714, box 5A, frame 310, reel 1714, *ibid.* For an example of a copycat suit, *see Edmund Ellis v. Alexander Parris,* Sept. 21, 1714, box 6A, frame 498, reel 1715, *ibid.*

36 Journals of the Commons House of Assembly . . . 1706–1721, frames 4: 272, 285, Green transcripts. For a common example of the coordination that appears to have existed between Messrs. Wright and Pight, see *ibid.,* frame 289. For information on Pight's time at the Wright plantation, see Anne King Gregorie, ed., *Records of the Court of Chancery of South Carolina, 1671–1779* (Washington, 1950), 189.

37 Aug. 31, 1714, in *Colonial Records of South Carolina: Journals of the Commissioners of the Indian Trade,* ed. McDowell, 59.

38 Journals of the Commons House of Assembly . . . 1706–1721, frames 4: 289 ff, Green transcripts. For the complete preoccupation of Nairne and the commissioners, see McDowell, ed., *Colonial Records of South Carolina: Journals of the Commissioners of the Indian Trade,* 60–65. For Longe's behavior, see "Journal of the March of the Carolinians into the Cherokee Mountains," 334–35.

39 Larry E. Ivers, "Scouring the Inland Passage, 1685–1787," *South Carolina Historical Magazine,* 73 (April 1972), 125. For Yamasee diplomatic activities among neighboring Indian nations, see Gov. Francisco de Corcolesy Martinez ro King Philip V, July 5, 1715, Audiencia de Santo Domingo 843, Archivo General de Indias (microfilm: reel 36), 58-1-30/42, John B. Stetson Collection (P. K. Yonge Library of Florida History, University of Florida, Gainesville).

40 April 12, 1715, in *Colonial Records of South Carolina: Journals of the Commissioners of the Indian Trade,* ed. McDowell, 65.

41 For an account of the attack and Nairne's torture, see "Letter of Charles Rodd to His Employer in London," May 8, 1715, in *Calendar of State Papers, Colonial Series, America and West Indies, August, 1714–December, 1715,* ed. Cecil Headlam (London, 1928), 167–68; for the standard account of the incident, see Crane, *Southern Frontier,* 168–69. The only version of these events to depart from Crane's original portrait is the groundbreaking account in Steven James Oatis, "A Colonial Complex: South Carolina's Changing Frontiers in the Era of

the Yamasee War, 1680–1730" (Ph.D. diss., Emory University, 1999), 176. Oatis was the first scholar to question the assumption of predetermined action and to propose that the Yamasees were engaged in legitimate debate over the issue of war or peace while Nairne slept. He argued that they ultimately experienced a crisis of faith in the promises of English officials.

42 Letter of Capt. Jonathan St. Lo and Enclosure, July 12, 1715, Admiralty Office, 1:2451 (British Public Record Office); also available in photocopy in British Records Calendar, 1712–1716, 72. 1409: pp. 1–4.

43 *Ibid.*

44 Martinez to the King, July 5, 1715, Audiencia de Santo Domingo 843, Archivo General de Indias (microfilm: reel 36), 58-1-30/42, Stetson Collection. Francis LeJau reported in May 1715 that as many as 25 Yamasee peace advocates had been killed; see LeJau to the Secretary, May 14, 1715, in *Carolina Chronicle of Dr. Francis LeJau,* ed. Klingberg, 156.

45 Oatis, "Colonial Complex," 157–58.

46 For the beginnings of trade among these nations, see Chapman J. Milling, *Red Carolinians* (Chapel Hill, 1940), 84–85; Letter of Caleb Westbrooke, Feb. 21, 1684/5, in *Records in the British Public Record Office Relating to South Carolina,* ed. A. S. Salley (5 vols., Columbia, S.C., 1946), II, 8–9; James W. Covington, "Stuart's Town, the Yamasee Indians, and Spanish Florida," *Florida Anthropologist,* 21 (March 1968), 9–10; Herbert E. Bolton, "Spanish Resistance to the Carolina Traders in Western Georgia (1680–1704)," *Georgia Historical Quarterly,* 9 (June 1925), 115–30; and McDowell, ed., *Colonial Records of South Carolina: Journals of the Commissioners of the Indian Trade,* 3–65. For a narrative discussion of the Yamasee War, see Crane, *Southern Frontier,* 162–86.

47 For the origins of trade, see Crane, *Southern Frontier,* 45; Pryce Hughes to the Duchess of Ormond, 1713, in Five Pryce Hughes Autograph Letters, Proposing a Welsh Colony, 1713 (South Caroliniana Library, University of South Carolina, Columbia); and Jean-Baptiste Bernard de la Harpe, *Historical Journal of the Establishment of the French in Louisiana,* ed. and trans. Glenn R. Conrad, Virginia Koenig, and Joan Cain (Lafayette, 1971), 89. For the positive benefits of trade competition among the Catawbas, see Merrell, *Indians' New World,* 68. For a discussion of the same process in the Mississippi Valley, see Daniel H. Usner, "Economic Relations in the Southeast until 1783," in *Handbook of American Indians: History of Indian-White Relations,* ed. Wilcomb E. Washburn (17 vols., Washington, 1988), IV, 391–95. For Cherokee access to alternative trade, see Tom Hatley, *The Dividing Paths: Cherokees and South Carolinians through the Revolutionary Era* (Oxford, 1995), 22. Evidence of Virginia's continuing interest in fur trade commodities may be found in America and the West Indies, Virginia: Original Correspondence, Board of Trade, 1715–1717, 5/1317, p. 178, Colonial Office (British Public Record Office); also available in photocopy in British Records Calendar, 1712–1716, X77.594, pp. 1–2.

48 For Bienville's diplomatic overtures, see Bienville to Pontchartrain, June 15, 1715, *Mississippi Provincial Archives: French Dominion,* ed. and trans. Rowland and Sanders, III, 183; and Bienville to Pontchartrain, Sept. 1, 1715, *ibid.,* III, 186–88. For James Merrell's arguments, see Merrell, *Indians' New World,* 69–70; and Merrell, "Our Bond of Peace,"' 209. For evidence of continuing warfare between the Tuscaroras and Iroquois and the Carolina piedmont nations, see "Account of a Conference with the Iroquois," America and the West Indies, New York: Original Correspondence, Board of Trade, 1710–1715, 5/1050, p. 640, Colonial Office (British Public Record Office); also available in photocopy in British Records Calendar, 1712–1716, X77.572, pp. 1–5.

49 The textile metaphor is Herbert Butterfield's; see Herbert Butterfield, *The Whig Interpretation of History* (New York, 1965), 20.

50 For the Chickasaw delegation, see Dec. 17, 1714, in Journals of the Commons House of Assembly . . . 1706–1721, frame 4: 334, Green transcripts.

51 For the Cherokee agreement, see July 23, 1716, in *Colonial Records of South Carolina: Journals of the Commissioners of the Indian Trade,* ed. McDowell, 89. For bargaining behavior prior to set price schedules, see Aug. 3, 1711, *ibid.,* 15. For the Creek agreement, see June 3, 1718, *ibid.,* 281–82.

52 For Carolina's prewar gifting policy, see July 10, 1712, in *Colonial Records of South Carolina: Journals of the Commissioners of the Indian Trade,* ed. McDowell, 36. For Joel Martin's ideas, see Martin, *Sacred Revolt,* 62–63.

53 For the demise of gift giving after 1763, see Martin, *Sacred Revolt,* 64–65. For the rise in the "real price" of deerskins, see Edward Murphy, "The Eighteenth-Century Southeastern Indian Economy," in *The Other Side of the Frontier: Economic Explorations into Native American Economy,* ed. Linda Barrington (Boulder, 1998), 154–55.

# 9

# THE WIDER WORLD OF THE HANDSOME MAN

*Brian DeLay*

Fanny Calderón de la Barca loved a good story, and in 1841 people in Mexico City were telling stories about Comanches. Early in the year, the wife of the Spanish minister would have heard astonishing reports about an army of the Indians attacking Coahuila's state capital, Saltillo, and its surrounding towns, stealing sixteen hundred horses, taking two dozen captives, and killing one hundred and two Mexicans, including a former governor. Mexico City's press ran hundreds of stories on the north's *indios bárbaros* in 1841, and anyone claiming to have knowledge of them found an eager audience. Calderón met a colonel who thrilled her and her companions with "an account of his warfare against the Comanches, in which service he has been terribly wounded." The colonel considered them "an exceedingly handsome, fine-looking race," with remarkable resources in both trade and war. Calderón learned more from an old soldier covered in wounds from Santa Anna's ill-fated Texas campaign. The veteran evinced a "devout horror" of Comanches, and stated "his firm conviction that we should see [them] on the streets of Mexico [City] one of these days."[1]

Thanks to a surge in scholarship during the past fifteen years, we now have a sophisticated picture of the people who so transfixed the scarred soldier's "gaping audience." This recent work has enriched our understanding of Comanche ethnogenesis, economic activity, diplomacy, kinship, spirituality and ritual, gender relations and labor, honor, territorial expansion, captive-taking, hunting and pastoralism, and politics. But Comanche specialists have been curiously disinterested in what their subjects did below the Rio Grande. Though the recent work often acknowledges that Comanches and their allies increasingly seized horses and captives from Mexican settlements in the 1830s and 1840s, plains scholars have not examined these activities through the source material in present-day Mexico. Partly this reflects a more general tendency to read the modern border backward into history. It is also the case that the extraordinarily violent raiding campaigns of these decades fit poorly with the dominant themes in prereservation American

Indian historiography—resistance to colonialism and, more recently, hybridity, interdependence, and mutual accommodation.[2]

By recovering links between the southern plains and northern Mexico we can deepen our understanding of both regions. Consolidating and extending a small but important body of scholarship about Indian raiding in northern Mexico with research in Mexican archival and periodical sources, I have built a database tracking Comanche–Mexican conflict. In many ways the data from the late 1820s through the 1840s reinforce what we have come to expect from this relationship—hostilities erupting in one place while commerce and cooperation continue elsewhere. At the same time it is clear that Comanche raiding expanded and contracted in sharply defined stages. Intriguingly, these peaks and valleys coincide with well-known geopolitical events on and around the southern plains. Read alongside the often thin evidence that exists for scholars to interpret Comanche activities north of the river from the mid-1830s through the early 1840s, Mexican sources reveal striking interconnections between raiding in Mexico and events unfolding on the other frontiers of the Comanches' wider world. By making peace with dangerous Indian and Texan neighbors over the course of a decade, Comanches and their allies obtained the security necessary to launch long-distance raiding campaigns into northern Mexico. Just as important, peace agreements produced new market connections that made campaigns increasingly lucrative. This realignment of frontier relationships reached maturation in the early 1840s, by which time southern plains men were traversing several Mexican states and fueling anxious conversation in Calderón's Mexico City.[3]

Like borderlands scholarship, the broader historiographies of the U.S. and Mexico in the nineteenth century stand to gain from better understanding links between the southern plains and the Mexican north. Despite the existing work on raiding below the river, the Indians of the southern plains remain all but invisible in the national literature of nineteenth-century Mexico. Similarly, the recent advances in Comanche scholarship have had little influence on the historiography of the U.S. early republic. And yet it is clear that Comanches and their allies both reacted to and contributed to events of continental scope and significance. In the 1830s and 1840s native peoples on the southern plains faced three manifestations of U.S. expansion: Indian removal, colonization and independence in Texas, and the growing penetration of U.S. market forces into the trans-Mississippi west. These changes presented Indians in the region with dangers and opportunities. Comanches and their allies minimized the former and maximized the latter by realigning their various frontier relationships and steadily expanding their profitable raids against Mexicans. In the process they did much to shape the northern Mexico that American forces conquered in 1846. Raiding campaigns terrified most of the Mexican north, shattered vital sectors of its economy, and left its diminishing rural population divided and exhausted on the eve of the U.S. invasion.

Thus, while the story of how southern plains Indians came to invade Mexico will not fit into any of our fragmented historiographic territories, it can be a bridge between them. This article explores frontier realignment on the southern plains both as a case study in flexible and ambitious Indian policy making and as an indirect but vital conduit linking U.S. and Mexican histories in the fifteen years before the two republics went to war.

In the early 1830s, the southern plains were home to a large and dynamic coalition of Indian peoples. The most populous and diverse were the 10–12,000 Numic-speakers called Comanches, subdivided into four tribes or divisions—Kotsotekas and Yamparikas in the west, and Tenewas and Hois in the east. In rebuilding their numbers following late eighteenth- and early nineteenth-century epidemics, they had assimilated large numbers of Indian and Mexican captives, as well as Indians and non-Indians who voluntarily chose to become Comanche. Moreover, in the early nineteenth century they had made the extraordinary concession of allowing their former enemies the Kiowas and Kiowa Apaches to dwell beside them on the southern plains. Linguistically, sociopolitically, and ceremonially distinct from each other and from Comanches, the 1,500–2,000 people comprising these tribes nonetheless integrated themselves with their hosts—occasionally through marriage, often through camping and hunting together, and usually through cooperation against peoples their partners considered enemies.[5]

Like other plains Indians, Comanches and their allies depended on bison for food, trade goods, clothing, and shelter. But proximity to Mexico gave the inhabitants of the southern plains privileged access to horses, and this is what made them wealthy in comparison to their neighbors. While some Indians experimented with controlled breeding and tried to capture and break mustangs, in the early nineteenth century the ranches and haciendas of northern Mexico remained the indispensable source of horse wealth on the plains. Through trading and raiding, Comanches, Kiowas, and Kiowa Apaches had gradually come to possess more horses per capita than any other native people. Some of their richest men were said to own hundreds of animals each.[6]

By the 1820s and 1830s, however, this great wealth had provoked a security crisis across *la comanchería.* Recently arrived Cheyennes threatened southern plains Indians from the north. During the late 1820s the southern Cheyennes and their allies, principally the Arapahos, had helped push the regular Comanche range south of the Arkansas River. Inspired by Blackfeet raiders who traveled great distances to plunder Comanche and Kiowa herds, the newcomers came to covet horses as well as hunting grounds. In 1826 the famous chief Yellow Wolf led one of the first Cheyenne raids into *la comanchería,* and other parties followed upon his success. These northern threats only worsened when the St. Louis traders Charles and William Bent developed an intimate alliance with Cheyennes and Arapahos and established a trading post on the Arkansas River in the early 1830s. According to George Bent, William's son with the prominent Cheyenne Owl Woman, Comanches were "constantly being plundered" not only from the north but also from Pawnees and Osages to the east. Violence and killings often accompanied raids on Comanche herds. The botanist and traveler Jean Louis Berlandier reported that in January 1828 Osages executed thirty Comanche women and children they had taken captive in a previous raid. An extraordinary native source attests to this violence as well. From at least 1833 on, Kiowas recorded their history on calendars that memorialized two key events each year, one in summer and one in winter. The summer of 1833 is recorded as the "summer that they cut off their heads." That year Osage raiders attacked and decapitated several Kiowas—men, women, and children—dropping their heads into brass buckets for kin to discover later.[7]

It seemed that these enemies would soon be outdone by new adversaries who were literally arriving every day. Wars, coercive treaties, and finally the formal policy of Indian removal compelled mass migrations of eastern woodlands peoples onto the prairies. Shawnees, Kickapoos, and Delawares sojourned out of the north and settled on the central prairies. Cherokees, Chickasaws, Creeks, Choctaws, and eventually Seminoles also tried to rebuild their lives and their fortunes in the west. Starting in the 1820s, smaller groups of southeastern Indians had embarked on another exodus into east Texas. While there is evidence of amicable trade between the newcomers and southern plains peoples in the early 1820s, by decade's end the sources speak far more about conflict. In 1828, Berlandier noted that "almost all the peoples who came here originally from the United States of North America make war on the Comanches." In 1830, an early Anglo-Texan newspaper reported on the outbreak of "a kind of exterminating war" between Cherokees, Shawnees, Delawares, and others against the Comanches and their allies. Immigrant Indians enjoyed the critical advantage of having more and better firearms than Indians on the southern plains, including many that came from U.S. government annuities given in return for ceded lands. In 1832, for example, twenty-nine well-armed Koasati Indians (a division of the Upper Creeks) fought one hundred and fifty Comanches, apparently killing or wounding upwards of one-half. That same year Shawnees attacked the party of a prominent Hois leader outside of San Antonio, killing many, and in 1833 another Koasati party reportedly brought back seventy scalps from Comanche country.[8]

The same animals that lured enemies into their territory complicated efforts by southern plains Indians to organize an effective defense. Each day an average mustang needs ten to twelve gallons of water and enough grass to equal twenty-five pounds of hay. They also require a pound of salt per week. One study has found that a camp with a thousand horses in western Kansas would have consumed seven acres of grass each day during periods of average rainfall. In times of drought, horses could consume six times as much.

The threat of illness and disease also led to dispersion of animals and their keepers, as did the requirements of hunting and simply surviving the rigors of winter. Though a populous people, Comanches and their allies necessarily spent most of the year in small residence groups vulnerable to enemy raiders. Southern plains Indians often organized retaliatory campaigns against Cheyennes, Pawnees, Osages, and others, but, with so many adversaries, absent men exposed their families to considerable risk. The Osage attack during the "summer they cut off their heads," for example, occurred wile Kiowa men were away fighting Utes.[9]

Boxed in by enemies to the north and east, Comanches became uncomfortably dependent on a faltering relationship with Mexicans to the south and west. Following decades of intermittent warfare, Comanches had forged an alliance with Spanish authorities in the 1780s. While never perfect, the peace proved remarkably stable over the next generation until Mexico's War for Independence threw Spanish authority into disarray in the 1810s. At first certain Comanches campaigned with royalist forces, but, as confusion mounted and Indian diplomacy faltered, numbers of exiled rebels and American filibusters fled to Comanche camps and helped shift the dynamic. In 1814 and 1815, southern plains Indians launched punishing raiding campaigns against Texas, on the lower Rio Grande, and into Coahuila. Smaller parties of men continued sporadic raiding throughout the decade, often trading stolen animals to the Americans who were becoming increasingly active on the plains.[10]

After independence, many Comanche leaders had agreed to renew the peace and even sent envoys to Mexico City in 1822. But independent Mexico's Indian policies proved to be less informed, consistent, and generous than Spanish policies of the late colonial period. Young men resumed animal raids in Chihuahua, Texas, the lower Rio Grande, and even New Mexico in the mid-1820s. This led to frantic talks and, over the next few years, to a round of treaty making in Chihuahua City, San Antonio, and Santa Fe. The negotiations produced another period of uneasy calm, but by the early 1830s small groups of southern plains raiders were again plundering herds and occasionally killing or capturing Mexicans in Chihuahua. Prominent Comanches kept visiting key towns and reiterating their goodwill, but the attacks and inconsistencies left Mexican authorities angry and impatient. They continued to mouth assurances of friendship, but viewed Comanches as increasingly haughty and dangerous and privately celebrated their conflicts with Indians from the United States.[11]

The distinction would have meant little to those caught up in the fighting, but it is important to note that by gauges narrow and broad the violence of the 1810s and 1820s paled in comparison to what would follow in the next two decades. For example, Texas's Spanish governor calculated that Indian raiders had killed sixty of his people in the seven years from 1813 through 1820; Comanches killed more than one hundred people in one afternoon in the 1841 attack on greater Saltillo. A careful student of the period has found a considerable increase in the population of northern Coahuila and an "explosive" growth in animal stocks during the 1820s, despite intermittent raiding. Well into the 1830s, in other words, prominent Comanches who advocated peace worked successfully to mitigate violence against Mexicans and their property.[12]

Given the hostility they faced from other quarters, it is easy to see why. Southern plains leaders needed trade outlets where their people could exchange commodities like dressed skins, bear grease, horses, mules, and captives for agricultural goods, metal, textiles, and other manufactured products. Comanches had been the key figures in a flourishing regional trade system in the eighteenth and early nineteenth century, and growing numbers of American traders seemed to promise even more regular commercial connections. But as violence with other Indians escalated in the 1820s and early 1830s, and as men like the Bents established themselves among the Comanches' adversaries, these connections withered. Harried by enemies from multiple directions, and lacking reliable conduits into dynamic American markets, southern plains families had to rely on dull if dependable Mexican markets to the west and south for the bulk of their trade. For this reason they continued welcoming New Mexican *comancheros* into their camps, and making visits to towns and villages in New Mexico, Texas, and all along the lower Rio Grande. These were not Comanche-Mexican relationships per se, but rather local, place-specific connections between southern plains families and members of individual Mexican settlements, what James Brooks calls "borderlands communities of interest." Many of these local connections would endure no matter the broader state of affairs between Comanches and the Republic of Mexico.[13]

But by 1833 there were surely figures on the southern plains arguing that something had to change. Comanches and Kiowas saw the regional economy stagnating, their families under attack, their herds plundered, and their nominal Mexican allies increasingly distracted and disrespectful. Moreover, southern plains envoys had requested military assistance against their Indian enemies on at least two occasions, and Mexican authorities had refused both requests. The scattered raids of the early 1830s reflected a growing desire within the southern plains coalition to rearrange its unprofitable constellation of frontier relationships.[14]

The first opportunity to do so came from the East. Concerned that ongoing violence between immigrant Indians, Indians of the prairies, and the people of the southern plains might complicate the removal program, the U.S. war department dispatched a dragoon expedition to try and ease these tensions in the summer of 1834. Eight Cherokees, seven Senecas, six Delawares, and eleven Osages accompanied the expedition, as did three captives, including a Kiowa girl who had been captured during the brutal summer of 1833.

The expedition crossed into Mexican Texas and made its way to a Wichita village. There the delegates held talks with Comanche, Kiowa, and Wichita representatives, returned the captives (to the delight of their kin), and proceeded to arrange for peace between all parties. Even the long-standing enmity between the Osages and the Comanches and Kiowas began to cool when southern plains representatives embraced their old enemies in council. More formal negotiations would take place over the next few years, and the peace had its strains. Disputes would arise over hunting rights, and, rarely, over acts of violence. Nonetheless, a basically cooperative relationship existed between southern plains Indians and their eastern and northeastern neighbors from the summer of 1834 onward, and trade was its foundation.[15]

This development was the first of a series of frontier realignments that would transform the southern plains and northern Mexico alike. The peace took multiple and increasing threats and turned them into cautious commercial friendships. Peace with eastern Indians gave Comanches and their allies access to a wider variety and steadier supply of U.S. and European manufactured goods, guns and ammunition included. In turn, southern plains Indians offered processed hides and a seemingly inexhaustible supply of horses and mules, animals that eastern Indians needed more than ever as they tried to rebuild their lives and fortunes in the west. Most trade would move through Indians, but two Americans, Holland Coffee and Auguste Pierre Chouteau, established trading posts east of Comanche country in 1834 and 1835, respectively. Finally, peace had dramatic implications for movement on the southern plains. In the several years before the truce, large numbers of Comanche and Kiowa men could not go on extended campaigns without endangering their families and fortunes. After 1834, more and more men could travel with confidence.[16]

Many took their newfound freedom of movement into Chihuahua. In October 1834, more than one hundred Comanche raiders stole horses from the eastern half of the state. Another more wide-ranging campaign unfolded two months later. Comanches and Kiowas continued attacking Chihuahuan ranches and haciendas every month from January through July of 1835, killing Mexicans, capturing women and children, stealing horses and mules, and destroying all kinds of property. The most dramatic campaign of 1835 took place in May, when more than eight hundred southern plains warriors invaded the eastern districts of Chihuahua. They laid waste to the Hacienda de las Animas, driving off horses and mules, sacking and burning houses, and destroying stores of beans and corn. They finally withdrew after killing six men and capturing thirty-nine women and children.[17]

Mexicans faced a variety of obstacles in responding to large groups of Indian raiders. Arid northern Mexico's pastoral economy depended upon a dispersed population, and that made defense a losing strategy against numerous well-armed and highly mobile raiders. A string of presidios (garrisons) had contributed to security in the late colonial period, but empty treasuries and perpetual political crises consigned them to neglect after independence. Ranches and small towns sometimes bested Indian attackers, but they had no effective means to safeguard animal property and often failed even to protect their residents. Without effective defenses, northern Mexicans had to rely on diplomacy and trade to shield them against enemies and, failing that, had to send offensive campaigns into Indian territories. "Pursue them as they pursue us," an observer from Coahuila once advised. "Threaten them as they threaten us. Rob them as they rob us. Capture them as they capture us. Frighten them as they frighten us. Alarm them as they alarm us."[18]

Doubtless this is what most northerners yearned to do. And yet Mexicans trying to organize campaigns into *la comanchería* faced daunting challenges. An effective force would have to be large, and organizers would find men reluctant to participate unless their families and property could be protected in their absence. A large force of Mexicans would likely find insufficient meat on the plains, and so, if they planned on being out for any length of time, would have to march with slow-moving cattle in tow. Water and pasturage for cattle and, especially, for large numbers of horses, would be reliable only during certain times of the year. Strategists also worried about Comanche herds drinking waterholes dry before Mexicans got there, or else finding water sources poisoned, "infested with dead horses, killed intentionally by Comanches." Finally, southern plains families ranged seasonally over a huge territory and Mexicans themselves had seasonal peaks to their labor cycle, so it took tremendous resources, political capital, administrative skill, and, not least, luck, to coordinate and mobilize effective campaigns.[19]

For a variety of reasons, then, northern Mexicans found it extremely difficult to strike at plains Indians from below the Rio Grande. New Mexico would have been the ideal place from which to launch such attacks. But the isolated New Mexicans enjoyed a brisk trade with these formidable peoples and refused to wage war on them, insisting that doing so would "bring complete ruin" to their state. Thus Texas had a unique role in the security of the Mexican north, and it became the focal point for Mexico's emerging efforts at reestablishing peace with Indians on the southern plains. In 1834, Mexican authorities intensified negotiations with Cherokees and other eastern Indians in Texas who wanted formal land titles from Mexico. These Indians had not been party to the recent peace, and agreed to strike against Comanches and their allies on the plains. Tejano authorities urged their constituents to contribute funds for the anticipated campaign. At the same time, Mexican officials sought a diplomatic breakthrough with specific eastern Comanche leaders that they might then leverage into a broader peace. The commander general of northeastern Mexico ordered the resumption of gifts for prominent Comanches, and authorities in San Antonio encouraged trade. Though high-ranking officials warned against buying stolen animals, it seems that locals looked the other way when Chihuahuan horses and mules wound up in Texan markets. Commerce led to conversation, talks got underway about a new treaty, and, by August 1835, three hundred Comanches had visited San Antonio with the intention of proceeding on to Matamoros to renew a peace agreement with the Mexican Republic. Obviously, these three hundred could not speak for everyone on the southern plains. But it was a start. After the terrible campaigns of late 1834 and early 1835, it seemed that Texas could be the entryway into a renewed Comanche-Mexican peace.[20]

The Texas Rebellion demolished these hopes. When Anglo-Texan colonists and certain Tejanos rebelled against the central government in late 1835, and then defeated and captured Mexican President Antonio López de Santa Anna in April 1836, Comanches disappeared from the list of Mexico City's priorities. But Texan independence had profound and underappreciated implications for northern Mexico's relationship with southern plains Indians. Most immediately, the centerpiece of Mexico's plan for ending the current Comanche hostilities had suddenly and literally disappeared from the national map. The project of enlisting Cherokees and other eastern Indians in Texas against Comanches and their allies would now have to proceed quietly, in enemy territory, or not at all. And the peace negotiations that had been painstakingly nurtured in San Antonio had become irrelevant.[21]

The long-term consequences mattered more. For generations, San Antonio had been a key site of negotiation with plains Indians, and Tejanos like José Francisco Ruíz had been crucial intermediaries between these Indians and the Mexican government. Mexico lost these resources when it lost Texas. Most importantly, Texas had been Mexico's only realistic staging ground for offensive campaigns against Comanches and their allies. The rebellion eliminated this possibility. Indeed, it erected yet another barrier to launching an offensive from elsewhere in the north. Any military campaign into *la comanchería* would now first have to march through the independent and belligerent Republic of Texas. The only effective defense against raiders was an effective offense, and the Texas Rebellion helped insure that Mexican soldiers would never again kill Comanches in their homelands.[22]

With Mexican authority vanished from Texas and distracted throughout the northeast, southern plains raiders shifted their attention away from Chihuahua. In 1837, for the first time in more than a decade, huge campaigns began crossing the river into Coahuila, Nuevo León, and Tamaulipas. In July Mexican authorities reported one thousand Comanches attacking points on the lower Rio Grande. This campaign and others like it transformed the region. In the aftermath of the Texas Rebellion, raiders took more than a thousand horses and mules from Laredo alone, including more than four-fifths of the horses possessed by the city and its hinterland. The raiders also slaughtered animals they had no interest in driving off. The number of sheep and goats owned by families in Laredo plummeted from nearly six thousand in late 1835 to a mere fifteen hundred in 1837. Indians burned huts and fields between the Nueces River and the Rio Grande, compelling the ranching families lately established there to move back south of the great river. Meanwhile raiders went deeper into Mexican territory, seeking untapped concentrations of animal wealth and probing defenses throughout the northeast.[23]

The timing, frequency, and size of these dangerous campaigns speak to the formidable capacity of the people of the southern plains to organize themselves across families, bands, divisions, and even ethnic and linguistic lines in pursuit of shared goals. Averaging between ten and thirty people, the extended family was the most stable Comanche residence group. When attempting to raise men for a campaign, warriors could appeal to others in these family units and also to kin and affines within the larger *rancherías* or bands in which they spent much of the year. Band members were further connected through an institutionalized form of friendship, which imposed kinship obligations upon two people and also on their relatives. During summer, Comanches came together for divisional gatherings to renew social bonds, perform rituals of community integration, and hunt collectively. They generally married outside the band but inside the division, and so created kinship obligations and political support networks that bound different bands together at a variety of levels. Divisional gatherings gave leaders an opportunity to share information, mediate disputes, seek consensus on matters regarding outsiders, and, not least, organize ambitious campaigns. And though the four divisions were distinct, all Comanches moved freely throughout *la comanchería.* They traded throughout the larger region, sometimes moved across divisional lines, and commonly made pan-divisional appeals in times of war. An American observer who came to know them well considered Comanches "but one people" because of the way that men from different divisions cooperated in their Mexican campaigns. Finally, they could call on many non-Comanches when organizing raids. Most obviously they cooperated closely with Kiowas and Kiowa Apaches, but Comanches also occasionally campaigned with allies among the Wichitas and even with opportunistic Mexicans from eastern New Mexico and the lower Rio Grande.[24]

As the conflict intensified, more and more families found themselves mourning male relatives killed below the river. Kiowas memorialized several of the more prominent dead in their calendars. Emotion, honor, and tradition dictated that bereft kin seek revenge for such deaths, and protocols existed through which grieving family members could make appeals for assistance throughout the complicated social and political network on the southern plains. Ambitious young leaders seem to have championed these causes, folding revenge into the ongoing and escalating program of plundering animals and captives from the Mexican north. Many built formidable reputations doing so, capitalizing on their growing knowledge and on their reputations as effective and generous leaders to raise more and more campaigns. Among the Hois, for example, Potsanaquahip (known to Texans as Buffalo Hump) and a man we know only as Santa Anna attracted large followings and became well known for their profitable trips into Mexico. Their feats could translate into political capital; Potsanaquahip would eventually become principal chief of his division.[25]

Effective campaigners like these often relied upon captives or else Mexican collaborators, people other Mexicans referred to as *entregadores* or "deliverers," to guide them through the complex terrain below the Rio Grande. Once they knew the best routes, places of refuge, and the whereabouts of sizable herds, Comanches found large-scale operations considerably easier below the river than above it. While it was difficult to combine hunting with major long-distance military operations on the plains, the fixed targets sought by Comanche campaigners in northern Mexico were also those places with the region's highest concentration of nonequine meat. Old campsites littered with bones and, especially, the presence of thousands of slaughtered sheep, goats, pigs, and cows unused for food and rotting in heaps across the fields of northern Mexico testified to the superabundance of protein available to plains Indians on campaign below the river. Moreover, the Indians' horses enjoyed better pasturage beneath the Rio Grande during much of the year, grazed on rich grass cover while traversing low mountain ranges, and occasionally would have had access to Mexican grain stores. Abundant resources for men and mounts enabled southern plains warriors to travel in armies large enough to stay in enemy territory for weeks at a time. Northern Mexico's land, animals, and climate seemed to conspire with the raiders and magnify the sufferings of its own people.[26]

By early 1838, northern Mexicans had reason to despair. Many politicians talked about bringing the war to the enemy, but after the loss of Texas none would manage to do so. If offense was impossible, defense often seemed futile. Locals found the underfunded army more a curse than a blessing, and saw the raiders growing bolder each season. "God contain them," wrote a group of citizens calling themselves the "sufferers," "for our soldiers cannot!" The authorities seemed to agree. In April 1838, the governor of Nuevo León wrote to his superiors in Mexico City, assuring them that each raid brought his state "closer to its total destruction." Everyone expected the raids to continue getting worse.[27]

Remarkably, they did not. The raids in 1838 were if anything smaller than they had been the year before, and both the frequency and the scale of raiding contracted significantly in 1839 and during the first half of 1840. While few recognized it fully, northern Mexicans were bound together with southern plains Indians in a larger system, and changes on other frontiers of this wider world had again brought temporary respite to the towns and ranches of the Mexican north.

To the east, the Hois found themselves in sharp conflict with the newly independent Republic of Texas by the late 1830s. While President Sam Houston had championed coexistence with Indians, controversies over captives, territory, and raiding from both sides complicated Comanche–Texan relations. These tensions increased exponentially when the Indian-hater Mirabeau B. Lamar became president of Texas in late 1838 and initiated a program of active campaigning designed to drive Comanches west. In late January 1839, Lamar's Lipan Apache spies discovered "the place where the women and children of the hostile Comanches are stationed." The informants noted that the men were "absent on an excursion"; they may have been in Nuevo León participating in one of the few campaigns from that season. In mid-February, a Texan–Apache force attacked the Comanche village without warning, "throwing open the doors of the wigwams or pulling them down and slaughtering the enemy in their beds." The Texan and Indian force boasted that they killed or wounded eighty to one hundred Comanches, but made little of the fact that women, children, and aged men made up most of the dead. All told, Texans sent a dozen organized raids against eastern Comanches and their allies between 1839 and 1841, inflicting grievous damage on families and property. Mexican observers must have been reminded of how much easier it was to attack Comanches from above the Rio Grande than below it.[28]

Kiowas, Kiowa Apaches, Yamparikas, and Kotsotekas struggled with their own crises and tragedies in the late 1830s. The sources that speak to their history in this period are thinner than those concerning the Hois and Tenewas. But the Kiowa calendar indicates that raids by southern Cheyennes and Arapahos worsened in the late 1830s. The key external events from mid-decade concerned the Mexican campaigns, but the period 1837–1839 is devoted entirely to enemies from the north. Kiowas called summer of 1837 "the summer that the Cheyenne were massacred," and winter 1837–38 the "winter that they dragged the head." Summer 1838 was the "summer that the Cheyenne attacked the camp on Wolf River," an attack in which hundreds of Kiowa and Comanche men and women were said to have been killed. The winter of 1838–39 was remembered for yet another storied battle with the Arapaho. While the defenders garnered some significant victories in these years, the conflicts nonetheless kept Comanche and Kiowa families in a state of anxiety and alarm and made it exceedingly dangerous for men to leave on raiding campaigns into Mexico.[29]

There are two other factors that likely contributed to the lull in campaigns during the late 1830s. First, a good proportion of the men who had been eager raiders in the previous few years may have found that they had as many horses and mules as they could manage by late decade. A major trade outlet disappeared when Choteau's posts were closed following his death in 1838. Those families who failed to dispose of excess trade animals had to expend labor caring for them and had to make difficult choices about camping in large, relatively safe groups and moving constantly, or staying in smaller, more manageable *rancherías* and hoping for the best. This dilemma became especially keen in winter, and could mean life or death so long as the region was harried by enemies. Second, the Kiowa calendar for winter 1839–40 depicts a man covered from head to foot in spots; that is, a man suffering from smallpox. Brought to the southern plains by Osage traders, this was the same epidemic that virtually destroyed the Mandans. As is so often the case during the 1830s and early 1840s, surviving sources tell us little of this event's consequences in *la comanchería* but it is fair to assume that the tragedy sapped enthusiasm for campaigning.[30]

Reeling from loss and insecurity, southern plains Indians set out to change the regional dynamic. In the summer of 1840, Kiowas and Comanches made peace with their formidable southern Cheyenne and Arapaho enemies. The agreement was solemnized with an epic round of gifting. Cheyennes and Arapahos gave Comanches and Kiowas blankets, beads, calico, kettles, guns, and ammunition. Southern plains Indians gave their newfound allies—what else?—horses, so many horses that even "unimportant" Cheyenne and Arapaho men and women got four, five, six animals each. Perhaps there had indeed been a glut of horses on the southern plains. The agreement served multiple purposes. Most basically, it put an end to years of violence, freed families on both sides of the Arkansas from much suffering and uncertainty, and inaugurated an intense commercial relationship. Peace also meant secure hunting access to the buffalo-rich territory between the Platte and Arkansas Rivers and, as southern Cheyennes and Arapahos deepened their trading relationship with Bent's Fort, this access seems to have been uppermost in their minds. Given the paucity of source material for fleshing out the Great Peace of 1840 (we do not even know in which month it took place), scholars seeking Comanche and Kiowa motivations have often speculated that southern plains negotiators were motivated by threats from Texans and immigrant tribes. However, the Kiowas, Kiowa Apaches, and western Comanches in closest communication with Cheyennes and Arapahos had little to fear from these eastern threats, and, with one possible exception, seem not to have turned their attentions eastward in the aftermath of the Great Peace.[31]

But they did look south. Soon after the celebrations on the Arkansas, northern Mexicans experienced what was for them the most terrifying winter in living memory. Hundreds of southern plains men struck Tamaulipas and eastern Nuevo León in September, Coahuila and western Nuevo León in October, Coahuila and the northern reaches of Zacatecas and San Luis Potosí in December and January, Chihuahua and Durango in February, and Nuevo León again in February and March. It is unclear whether Hois men participated in these campaigns, given their unresolved conflicts with Texans. But an election in late 1841 brought to power a new administration in Texas that put an end to state-sponsored raids. Tentative peace negotiations began soon after and finally culminated in formal treaty in October 1844, signed by Potsanaquahip and two other Comanche leaders. Here again, the Mexican data seem to register the change. Following a lull in raiding in 1842 and 1843, campaigns became more widespread and intense than ever starting in the winter of 1844.[32]

Emerging into places that none of their kinsmen had ever laid eyes on, plains Indians became astonished at the animal wealth they discovered. Following a campaign into Zacatecas, for example, an escaped Mexican captive reported that these Indians had never before been this far south, and that one impressed warrior had exclaimed "we will go and bring more handsome lads and come back here, for there are many horses." Between 1840 and 1846, Comanches and Kiowas sent twenty-two major raiding campaigns into Mexico, averaging nearly four hundred "handsome" men each. This was double the number of large campaigns that they had organized during the previous six years.[33]

As expeditions into Mexico made greater claims on Comanche and Kiowa time and labor, their communities moved to reconcile the Mexican conflict with other dimensions of their economy. Whereas half of all large campaigns from 1834 to 1840 occurred in summer, from 1840 through 1846 three-quarters left in late autumn and winter. This insured that men would be available for bison hunts in early summer, for harvesting of the virtually hairless "summer skins," and again in late summer and early fall, when the animals came together during rut and their coats began filling out enough to use as robes. It is probably the case that southern plains men felt increasingly reluctant to miss these crucial hunting seasons because bison were becoming harder and harder to find. By 1843 or 1844, long-term overhunting for the hide trade, habitat destruction, and other factors seem to have reduced buffalo populations to the point that some Comanches and Kiowas had insufficient meat. Large-scale, long-distance raiding campaigns into Mexico therefore accounted for more and more of the region's economic activity as bison harvests declined. The war that southern plains Indians initiated against Mexico in the mid-1830s had become an integrated feature of their yearly round by the early 1840s and an essential component of their collective livelihoods by mid-decade.[34]

Neither the southern plains nor northern Mexico can be understood adequately in isolation from the other during the 1830s and 1840s. The Mexican data reveal that southern plains Indians expanded their raiding activity below the Rio Grande in four dramatic stages. These expansions followed the initial 1834 peace with Osages and immigrant Indians, the 1836 Texas Rebellion, the Great Peace of 1840, and the treaty-signing with the Republic of Texas in 1844. The loss of Texas made it virtually impossible for Mexicans to launch reprisals against Comanches, Kiowas, and Kiowa Apaches on the plains, and, by enhancing security and creating hungry new markets, each of the three peace agreements made long-distance raids into Mexico safer and more profitable. As northern Mexico sunk into insecurity and deepening poverty, most southern plains Indians experienced the exact reverse. Though it proved to be a very temporary accomplishment, by the early 1840s Comanches and their allies had nearly eliminated organized threats to their physical security. A violent, harried landscape only a decade before, the southern plains had become a plunderers' bazaar, dotted with new trading outposts at its margins and crisscrossed by Cheyennes, Arapahos, New Mexicans, Osages, Cherokees, Missourians, Creeks, Delawares, Texans, and Shawnees, all bartering for hides processed by southern plains women, and horses, mules, and captives seized by southern plains men.[35]

Did Indian leaders engineer this outcome, strategically embracing opportunities for peace with the sole aim of expanding the profitable war against Mexico? The complexities of the period cannot be reduced to so simple a formulation. Comanches, Kiowas, and Kiowa Apaches had complicated and divergent motives for making peace with Indians and Texans in this period, these motives changed over the 1830s and 1840s, and not everyone in *la comanchería* supported the agreements in any case. The alliances may also be seen as part of a broader effort by Indian peoples across the Great Plains in this period to forge strong partnerships in the face of demographic, ecological, and economic change. Still, while the sources do not give us access to high-level deliberations about regional strategy, the convergence of events above and below the river strongly suggests that Mexico played an increasingly important role in the geopolitical decisions of the period. Surely southern plains leaders anticipated the ways in which security and expanded markets would facilitate raiding campaigns into Mexico. How else can we explain the speed with which so many of them capitalized on geopolitical change by leading their men below the Rio Grande, or the tremendous resources that they devoted to this dangerous, complicated, and labor-intensive project year after year?[36]

Comanches, Kiowas, and Kiowa Apaches made their decisions at a critical moment in the history of the continent. In the summer of 1846 American troops came to conquer the impoverished, divided, and exhausted people who had paid for the economic revival of the southern plains with fifteen years of terror and tragedy. American officers denounced the Indian raiders, who continued their campaigns throughout the war, and promised that the U.S would save Mexicans from the "savage Cumanches." In truth it proved enormously beneficial to the U.S. invasion and resulting occupation that northern Mexico had already endured more than a decade of war. And, more broadly, the United States had been implicated in Comanche and Kiowa attacks upon Mexicans from the beginning. While the connections were neither as direct nor as sinister as Mexican commentators believed, the Americanization of Texas, the federal policy of Indian removal, and U.S. market penetration into the west all powerfully influenced the shifts in southern plains policy in the 1830s and 1840s.[37]

And yet there was nothing inevitable about these shifts. Given their vulnerable position at the beginning of this period, Comanches, Kiowas, and

Kiowa Apaches might have been expected to be more cautious and safeguard their imperfect alliance with Mexico. They might have viewed Texan independence, for example, as an opportunity to play one republic off against the other and coax both onto a diplomatic and commercial middle ground. Instead, they concentrated on establishing market connections with other Indians, maintained a defiant posture towards Texas into the 1840s, and, over time, forged a broad consensus supporting a lucrative and extraordinarily aggressive war against Mexico.

Only a few years after this realignment came into maturity, Comanches and Kiowas found themselves living inside the United States. Though southern plains Indians would continue to raid along the Rio Grande through the 1870s, the size and ambition of their campaigns decreased sharply in the mid-1850s. Growing settlement and traffic on the margins of *la comanchería* and increased competition for diminishing bison undermined the security that had been prerequisite for large, long-distance campaigns. Just as importantly, southern plains men met growing resistance from the new international order that their devastating Mexican raids had indirectly helped to bring about. Newly established Mexican military colonies and American forts complicated raids, while diplomatic agreements with the U.S. government undermined the audacious, unified policies that had predominated before, during, and immediately after U.S.-Mexican War. By the late 1850s Comanches and Kiowas were more commonly sending small parties into Texas and into northern-most Mexico in search of horses and slow-moving cattle. These vestiges of their bold raiding campaigns declined into the early 1870s, when the U.S. government reduced all southern plains Indians to reservations and, in so doing, confined to memories the wider world of the handsome man.[38]

## NOTES

1 Howard T. Fisher and Marion Hall, eds., *Life in Mexico: The Letters of Fanny Calderón de la Barca* (New York, 1966), 552, 509. For the hacienda, see Víctor Orozco Orozco, *Las guerras indias en la historia de Chihuahua: Primeras fases* (Mexico City, 1992), 153. For Saltillo, see "Estado que manifiesta las victimas sacrificados por los bárbaros . . . ," Saltillo, Feb. 6, 1841, C 86, E13, If, Presidencia Municipal, Archivo municipal de Saltillo, Saltillo, Coahuila. For press reports, see Antonio Escobar Ohmstede and Teresa Rojas Rabiela, eds., *La presencia del indígena en la prensa capitalina del siglo XIX* (Mexico City, 1992), cuadros 1 and 2.

2 Ralph Adam Smith and Isidro Vizcaya Canales long ago alerted scholars to the scope and violence of Comanche raiding in northern Mexico. See Ralph A. Smith, "The Comanche Invasion of Mexico in the Fall of 1845," *West Texas Historical Association Year Book* 35 (1959), 3–28; "The Comanche Bridge Between Oklahoma and Mexico, 1843–1844," *Chronicles of Oklahoma* 39 (Spring 1961), 54–69; "Indians in American–Mexican Relations before the War

of 1846," *Hispanic American Historical Review* 43 (Feb. 1963), 34–64; Isidro Vizcaya Canales, ed., *La invasión de los indios bárbaros al noreste de México en los años de 1840 y 1841* (Monterrey, 1968).

3 The data referred to in this paragraph and elsewhere in the article come from the appendix to Brian DeLay, *The War of a Thousand Deserts: Indian Raids and the U. S. Mexican War* (New Haven, CT, 2008). That appendix builds upon existing scholarship, including the previously mentioned works of Smith and Vizcaya-Canales as well as William B. Griffen, *Utmost Good Faith: Patterns of Apache–Mexican Hostilities in Northern Chihuahua Border Warfare, 1821–1848* (Albuquerque, NM, 1988); Víctor Orozco Orozco, *Las guerras indias en la historia de Chihuahua: Antología* (Ciudad Juárez, 1992); Martha Rodríguez, *Historias de resistencia y exterminio: Los indios de Coahuila durante el siglo XIX* (Mexico City, 1995); Cuauhtémoc José Velasco Avila, "La amenaza comanche en la frontera mexicana, 1800–1841" (Ph.D. diss., Universidad Nacional Autónoma de México, 1998). Though he focuses on American rather than Indian traders, David J. Weber was the first to explore in detail connections between U.S. market forces and northern Mexico's relations with independent Indians. See his seminal article, "American Westward Expansion and the Breakdown of Relations Between *Pobladores* and '*Indios Bárbaros*' on Mexico's Far Northern Frontier, 1821–1846," *New Mexico Historical Review* 56 (July 1981), 221–38.

5 For renderings of Comanche names, I follow Thomas W. Kavanagh, *Comanche Political History: An Ethnohistorical Perspective, 1706–1875* (Lincoln, NE, 1996). For the Comanche peace with Kiowas, see James Mooney, *Calendar History of the Kiowa Indians* (1889; rep. Washington, DC, 1979), 162–64. Scholars continue to debate Comanche population figures. José Francisco Ruíz, the most informed non-Indian observer of Comanches in the early nineteenth century, put their total population at ten to twelve thousand in 1828. See Jean Louis Berlandier, *The Indians of Texas in 1830,* ed. John C. Ewers, trans. Patricia R. Leclercq (Washington, DC, 1969), 121. This figure is roughly compatible with estimates of the carrying capacity of the southern plains. See William R. Brown Jr., "Comanchería Demography, 1805–1830," *Panhandle–Plains Historical Review* 59 (1986), 1–17. For Kiowas and Kiowa Apaches, see Mooney, *Calendar,* 236, 253.

6 Bernard Mishkin, *Rank and Warfare Among the Plains Indians* (1940; rep. Lincoln, NE, 1992), 19; Berlandier, *Indians of Texas,* 44: Joseph Jablow, *The Cheyenne in Plains Indian Trade Relations, 1795–1840* (1951; rep. Lincoln, NE, 1994), 15–16.

7 George E. Hyde, ed., *Life of George Bent, Written From His Letters* (Norman, OK, 1968), 37. For raiding more broadly, see ibid., 33–40. For linkages between harsh winters, small herds, and intense horse raiding on the northern plains, see Pekka Hämäläinen, "The Rise and Fall of Plains Indian Horse Cultures," *Journal of American History* 90 (Dec. 2003), 833–62. For conflicts with Osages and Pawnees, see Berlandier, *Indians of Texas*, 140; José María Sánchez, "A Trip to Texas in 1828," *Southwestern Historical Quarterly* 29 (Apr. 1926), 249–88, see p. 262. For summer 1833, see Mooney, *Calendar,* 258–59.

8 Berlandier, *Indians of Texas,* 122; *Texas Gazette* (San Felipe de Austin), June 12, 1830. For the attack near San Antonio, see Kavanagh, *Comanche Political History,* 232–33. For the Koasati, whom Berlandier refers to as Cutchaté, see Jean Louis Berlandier, *Journey to Mexico During the Years 1826 to 1834,* trans. Sheila M. Ohlendorf, Josette M. Bigelow, and Mary M. Standifer (Austin, TX, 1980), 560–61; and Ewers' identification in Berlandier, *Indians of Texas,* 124, note 167. For Comanche complaints about eastern Indian hostility, see David La Vere, *Contrary Neighbors: Southern Plains and Removed Indians in Indian Territory* (Norman, OK, 2000), 53.

9 For the challenges of keeping horse herds on the plains, see James E. Sherow, "Workings of the Geodialectic: High Plains Indians and Their Horses in the Region of the Arkansas River Valley, 1800–1870," *Environmental History Review* 16 (Summer 1992), 61–84, especially pp. 69–74; Moore, *The Cheyenne,* 49; Elliott West, *The Way West: Essays on the Central Plains* (Albuquerque, NM, 1995), 20–37. For retaliation against Cheyennes, see Hyde, ed., *Life of George Bent,* 40. For campaigns against Osages, see Berlandier, *Indians of Texas,* 67, and the testimony of Dionisio Santos, Lampazos, July 11, 1873, in Cuauhtémoc José Velasco Avila, ed., *En manos de los bárbaros* (Mexico City, 1996), 40–43. For Utes, see Mooney, *Calendar,* 258–59.

10 The conflicts of the mid-eighteenth century are discussed in detail in Elizabeth A. H. John, *Storms Brewed in Other Men's Worlds: The Confrontation of Indians, Spanish, and French in the Southwest, 1540–1795* (1975; 2nd ed., Norman, OK, 1996), 258–696. For Comanches initially helping royalists, see David J. Weber, *Bárbaros: Spaniards and Their Savages in the Age of Enlightenment* (New Haven, CT, 2005), 261. For hostilities in the 1810s, see Gary Clayton Anderson, *The Indian Southwest, 1580–1830: Ethnogenesis and Reinvention* (Norman, OK, 1999), 251–55; Kavanagh, *Comanche Political History,* 157–61.

11 For the decline in defense and diplomacy on the frontier, see David J. Weber, *The Mexican Frontier, 1821–1846: The American Southwest Under Mexico* (Albuquerque, NM, 1982), 83–121. For the variously hostile and peaceful relationships of the 1820s, see Anderson, *Indian Southwest,* 255–64; Rodríguez, *Guerra entre bárbaros y civilizados,* 148; Griffen, *Utmost Good Faith,* 139; Gaspar de Ochoa to principal commander of New Mexico, Durango, Mar. 8, 1825, frame 665, reel 4, Mexican Archives of New Mexico (microfilm) [hereafter MANM]; Antonio Elosua, copy of the armistice celebrated with the Comanche captains, San Antonio, Aug. 8, 1827, in vol. 8, p. 104, Matamoros Archives Photostats, Center for American History, University of Texas, Austin. For friction in the early 1830s, see for example José J. Calvo, circular, Chihuahua, Oct. 16, 1831, MANM 13:483. For continued diplomacy, see Comandante Principal to Comandante General, Santa Fe, Oct. 30, 1831 [letter book], MANM 13: 521; Alejandro Ramírez to Governor of Chihuahua, El Paso, July 23, 1834, in Orozco, *Guerras indias: Antología,* 237–39. For Mexican enthusiasm about the Comanches' security crisis, see Velasco Avila, "La amenaza comanche," 227.

12 For numbers killed in Texas, see Anderson, *Indian Southwest,* 255. For growth in population and herds, see Velasco Avila, "La amenaza comanche," 212–13.

13 James Brooks, "'This Evil Extends Especially to the Feminine Sex': Captivity and Identity in New Mexico, 1700–1846," *Feminist Studies* 22 (Summer 1996), 279–309, see p. 280. See also James F. Brooks, *Captives & Cousins: Slavery, Kinship, and Community in the Southwest Borderlands* (Chapel Hill, NC, 2002). For earlier trade connections, see Pekka Hämäläinen, "The Western Comanche Trade Center: Rethinking the Plains Indian Trade System," *Western Historical Quarterly* 29 (Winter 1998), 485–513. For commodities and for a glimpse of what trading visits looked like, see Berlandier, *Indians of Texas,* 47–48.

14 For the Comanche requests and Mexican refusals, see Joel R. Poinsett to Henry Clay, Mexico City, July 16, 1828, letter 145 in *Despatches from United States Ministers to Mexico, 182–1906* (Microfilm, 179 reels, National Archives Microfilm Publications, 1955); Kavanagh, *Comanche Political History,* 204–5.

15 For the dragoon expedition, see La Vere, *Contrary Neighbors,* 72–78; Brad Agnew, *Fort Gibson: Terminal on the Trail of Tears* (Norman, OK, 1980), 115–39. For later Comanche complaints over hunting and (in early 1845) over violence, see Kavanagh, *Comanche Political History,* 242–43, 274.

16 For Coffee, see Audy J. Middlebrooks and Glenna Middlebrooks, "Holland Coffee of Red River," *Southwestern Historical Quarterly* 69 (Oct. 1965), 146–62. For Chouteau and Comanches, see Kavanagh, *Comanche Political History,* 242–46. For the significance of horses among the Choctaw, see James Taylor Carson, "Horses and the Economy and Culture of the Choctaw Indians, 1690–1840," *Ethnohistory* 42 (Summer 1995), 495–513.

17 For Comanche raids into Chihuahua in 1834 and 1835, see Griffen, *Utmost Good Faith,* 143. For references to the raid on the Hacienda de las Animas, see Josiah Gregg, *Commerce of the Prairies,* ed. Max L. Moorhead (1844; rep. Norman, OK, 1954), 250.

18 Quote is from 1849, in Rodríguez, *Guerra entre bárbaros y civilizados,* 52. On dispersed landholding patterns in the lower Rio Grande, see Leroy P. Graf, "The Economic History of the Lower Rio Grande Valley, 1820–1875," (Ph.D. diss., Harvard University, 1942), 16–17; Omar Santiago Valerio-Jiménez, "Indios Bárbaros, Divorcées, and Flocks of Vampires: Identity and Nation on the Rio Grande, 1749–1894," (Ph.D. diss., UCLA, 2001), 52–60. For declining presidios, see Weber, *Mexican Frontier,* 107–21.

19 For "infested" quote, see Juan N. Armendariz, "Diario de las operaciones militares de la seccion en campaña contra los comanches sobre el Bolson de Mapimí . . . .", Cerrogordo, Nov. 1, 1844, in *El Registro Oficial del Gobierno del departamento de Durango* (Victoria de Durango), Nov. 10, 1844. On dead animals and captives thrown into water holes, see also Michael C. Meyer, *Water in the Hispanic Southwest: A Social and Legal History, 1550–1850* (Tucson, AZ, 1984), 96–97. For seasonal obstacles to campaigning, see the analysis in *El Ancla* (Matamoros), May 3, 1841.

20 Quote is from Manuel Armijo, in Weber, *Mexican Frontier,* 114–15. For a later elaboration on his concerns, see Manuel Armijo to the departmental assembly, June 27, 1845, MANM 38: 740–45. For Mexican attempts at aligning Mexicans, Anglos, and eastern Indians against Comanches, see John Holmes Jenkins, ed., *The Papers of the Texas Revolution, 1835–1836* (10 vols., Austin, TX, 1973), 1: 44, 47, 55, 67; Velasco Avila, "La amenaza comanche," 272–75, 280. For resumption of gifts, see Martín Perfecto de Cos to Domingo de Ugartechea, May 8, 1835, frame 38, roll 165 of the Bexar Archives (microfilm) [hereafter BA]. For Chihuahuan mules being sold in Texas, see José J. Calvo to Luis Zuloaga, Chihuahua, Sept. 10, 1835, in *Diario del Gobierno de la Republica Mexicana* (Mexico City), Oct. 11, 1835; Angel Navarro to the gefatura politica del departamento de Béxar, San Antonio, May 14, 1835, in BA 165: 38. For treaty talks, see Kavanagh, *Comanche Political History,* 234.

21 After 1836 Mexicans occasionally courted Cherokees for help against Texans. See for example D. W. Smith to U.S. Secretary of State, Matamoros, July 1, 1836, frames 585–96, reel 1 of *Despatches from United States Consuls in Matamoros, 1826–1906* (Microfilm, 12 reels, National Archives Microfilm Publications, 1964) [hereafter *Despatches*].

22 Velasco Avila, "La amenaza comanche," 292–93.

23 For consequences of raiding in Laredo, see Gilberto Miguel Hinojosa, *A Borderlands Town in Transition: Laredo, 1755–1870* (College Station, TX, 1983), 50–52. For raids between the Nueces and Rio Grande, see D. W. Smith to U.S. Secretary of State, Matamoros, Aug. 4, 1837, in *Despatches* 1: 700. The abandonment of this little region would eventually help Texas recruit the Polk administration to its feeble but momentous claim to a Rio Grande boundary. For the 1,000-man raid, see *Diario del Gobierno,* Aug. 10, 1837; D. W. Smith to U.S. Secretary of State, Matamoros, Aug. 4, 1837, in *Despatches,* 1: 700.

24 Quote about "one people" is from Robert S. Neighbors, in Morris W. Foster, *Being Comanche: A Social History of an American Indian Community* (Tucson, AZ, 1991), 49. For the primary and secondary sources behind this sketch see DeLay, *War of a Thousand Deserts*, 350, note 2. For hints of New Mexicans campaigning with Comanches, see for example Brooks, *Captives & Cousins,* 271, note 14.

25 For Kiowa casualties in Mexico, see Mooney, *Calendar,* 269–71, 282. For contemporary observations about vengeance on the southern plains, see Sánchez, "A Trip to Texas in 1828," 262; Berlandier, *Indians of Texas,* 67–75. For Hois setting out on revenge expeditions, see for example Thomas G. Western to A. Coleman, Washington on the Brazos, May 11, 1845, in Dorman H. Winfrey and James M. Day, eds., *The Indian Papers of Texas and the Southwest, 1825–1916* (5 vols., Austin, TX, 1966–1995), 2: 236–37; and *Telegraph and Texas Register* (Houston), Sept. 3, 1845.

26 For Mexican collaborators, see for example General-in-Chief of the Army of the North to Vicente Filísola, Matamoros, Dec. 11, 1837, in *Diario del Gobierno,* Jan. 3, 1838. For discoveries of mounds of animal remains where Comanches had made camp, see for example *Registro Oficial,* May 24, 1846. For animals slaughtered in raids, see J. M. Iglesias de Orduña to governor of Durango, Hacienda de San Salvador de Horta, Sept. 19, 1845, in *Registro Oficial,* Sept. 28, 1845. For mountain environments of Coahuila and Nuevo León, see Cornelius H. Muller, "Vegitation and Climate of Coahuila, Mexico," *Madroño* 9 (1947), 33–57.

27 For the "sufferers," see *El Mercurio* (Matamoros), Aug. 5, 1836 [supplement]. For the governor, see J. de Jesús D. y Prieto to the Secretaría de Guerra y Marina, Monterrey, April 1, 1838, C12, Correspondencia con la secretaría de Guerra y Marina, Archivo General del Estado de Nuevo León, Monterrey, Nuevo León [hereafter AGENL-MGM].

28 Quotes are from *Telegraph and Texas Register,* Jan. 30, 1839; J. H. Moore to Albert Sidney Johnston, LaGrange, Mar. 10, 1839, in Winfrey and Day, eds., *Texas Indian Papers,* 1: 57–59. For the Comanche campaign into Nuevo León in winter 1838–39, see Joaquín García to Ministro de Guerra y Marina, Dec. 9, 1838, C 12, E 44, AGENL-MGM; same to same, Mar. 23, 1839, C13, E 34, AGENL-MGM. For reports of Lipan scouts encouraging and guiding Texan raiding parties, see *Telegraph and Texas Register* for Jan. 2, 12, and 30, 1839. The history of Comanche–Texan relations in this period is best told in Gary Clayton Anderson, *The Conquest of Texas: Ethnic Cleansing in the Promised Land, 1820–1875* (Norman, OK, 2005), 108–94.

29 Kiowa dates come from Mooney, *Calendar,* 271–74. For the casualties during the attack on the camp at Wolf River (Creek), see Moore, *The Cheyenne,* 134–35.

30 For Choteau, see Janet Lecompte, "Bent, St. Vrain and Company among the Comanche and Kiowa," *Colorado Magazine* 49 (1972), 273–93, see pp. 275–79. For smallpox, see Mooney, *Calendar,* 274–75. For the 1837 epidemic on the northern plains, see R. G. Robertson, *Rotting Face: Smallpox and the American Indian* (Caldwell, ID, 2001).

31 For the gifting see George Bird Grinnell, *The Fighting Cheyennes* (Norman, OK, 1958), 63–69. For the bison "buffer zone" created by hostility between the Indians of the central and southern plains, and the significance of access to this zone for the peace, see Dan Flores, "Bison Ecology and Bison Diplomacy: The Southern Plains from 1800 to 1850," *Journal of American History* 78 (Sept. 1991), 465–85; and West, *The Way West,* 61–62. For interpretations of the peace that stress Texas and eastern Indians, see for example Flores, "Bison Ecology," 483; Elliott West, *The Contested Plains: Indians, Goldseekers, & the Rush to Colorado* (Lawrence, KS, 1998), 77; La Vere, *Contrary Neighbors,* 143; Anderson, *Conquest of Texas,* 186–87.

32 Many of these campaigns can be traced through an excellent collection of official letters reprinted in Nuevo León's newspapers: Vizcaya Canales, ed., *La invasión de los indios bárbaros*. See also Griffen, *Utmost Good Faith,* appendix; *El voto de Coahuila, Jan.* 8, 1841; *Diario del Gobierno,* Mar. 2, 1841; *El Seminario Político del Gobierno de Nuevo León* (Monterrey), Mar. 4, 1841. For the Comanche–Texan negotiations, see Minutes of the Council at the Falls of the Brazos, Oct. 7, 1844, in Winfrey and Day, eds., *Texas Indian Papers,* 2: 103–14.

33 For quote, see Antonio Sánchez Múzquiz to Sr. Secretario del despacho del Superior Gobierno de Durango, Parras, Aug. 31, 1842, in *Registro Oficial,* Sept. 8, 1842. The line of transmission (from raider—presumably in Spanish—to captive to official to official) obviously opens this quote to question. But it is worth noting that Kiowas considered good looks to be an important quality in a man, regardless of age. It was assumed that all men of highest rank should be "handsome on a horse," and in 1870 four of the twenty-five most prominent Kiowas made the list because they were handsome. See Mishkin, *Rank and Warfare,* 36, 54–55. Numbers of campaigns in this paragraph and comment on seasonality in the paragraph below are drawn from data in the appendix of DeLay, *War of a Thousand Deserts.*

34 For hunting seasons, see Frank Gilbert Roe, *The North American Buffalo: A Critical Study of the Species in its Wild State* (Toronto, ON, 1951), 116–18. See Pekka Hämäläinen, "The First Phase of Destruction: Killing the Southern Plains Buffalo, 1790–1840," *Great Plains Quarterly* 21 (Spring 2001), 101–14, for the argument that such pressures were encouraging raiding as early as the 1820s. Particularly intense campaigning seasons in 1844 and 1845 may have reflected food shortages in *la comanchería,* but it is unlikely that declining herds had much to do with raiding before then. The timing of increased raiding into Mexico coincided with diplomatic and political developments that were, through the early 1840s at least, largely independent of changes in the bison herds. Indeed, the dramatic increase in raiding in the early 1840s came at a moment when Comanche and Kiowa hunters had just obtained safe access to dense bison populations on the high plains between the Arkansas and Platte Rivers. As Flores himself remarks, the Kiowa calendar for 1841 includes the rare notation "many bison." See Flores, "Bison Ecology," 483.

35 For a glimpse of the economic revival of the early 1840s, as well as its diverse participants, see J. C. Eldredge to Sam Houston, Washington on the Brazos, Dec. 8, 1843, in Winfrey and Day, eds., *Texas Indian Papers,* 1: 251–75. For continuing *comanchero* activity in this period, see Charles L. Kenner, *The Comanchero Frontier: A History of New Mexican–Plains Indians Relations* (1969; 2nd. ed., Norman, OK, 1994), 79–80; Brooks, *Captives & Cousins,* 221–22, 269–70. For trading posts that the Bents established in western Comanche country in the early 1840s, see Lecompte, "Bent, St. Vrain and Company." For Texan trading houses established in the early 1840s, see Henry C. Armbruster, "Torrey Trading Houses," in *The Handbook of Texas Online* http://www.tsha.utexas.edu/handbook/online/articles/view/TT/dft2.html, accessed Sept. 24, 2002.

36 For peace among high plains tribes, see West, *The Contested Plains: Indians, Goldseekers, & the Rush to Colorado,* 77; Brooks, *Captives & Cousins,* 263–64.

37 For U.S. promises, see "Translation of the Spanish proclamation given to Generals Taylor and Kearny." 29th Cong., 2d sess., S. Doc. 19, 17.

38 The change in raiding is best reflected in data assembled by a Mexican claims commission in the 1870s. See *Informe de la comisión pesquisidora de la frontera del norte al ejucutivo de la union, en cumplimiento del artículo 3 de la ley de 30 de septiembre de 1872,* (Mexico City, 1874), appendix.

# Part V

# IDEAS

The great methodological challenge to writing borderlands history from multiple perspectives is imbalanced source material. In the borderlands of modern nation-states, this imbalance can follow from various obstacles to research: restricted access to archives on one side or the other of a border; major differences in the volume and type of source materials produced by the two countries; or simply the loss, destruction, or misfiling of key documents. Students of indigenous/colonial borderlands often face comparable obstacles, but find them greatly compounded by the fact that through the nineteenth century most native peoples did not write. Consequently historians are left working with a large volume of sources written by non-Indians, but precious little directly produced by the native peoples they were interacting with. The triumph of ethnohistory was in championing the requisite sensibility and refining the necessary techniques to write meaningful native history despite the source problem. But the fact remains that borderlands historians often know far, far more about some of our subjects than about others.

Nowhere is this imbalance more glaring than in the realm of ideas. The previous chapters in this volume highlighted some of the contexts within which borderlands relationships unfolded—in struggles over authority, in the face of sweeping biological changes unleashed by the Columbian Exchange, over competing definitions of masculinity and femininity, and amid the terror and transformative potential of war. All of these intense and often overlapping contexts cried out for narratives and discourses that would make sense of profound and rapid change, frame options, and sustain community in dynamic and often dangerous times. That is, these contexts demanded the mobilization of ideas as well as actions. Writing multi-vocal borderland history means attending to the narratives and discourses of multiple peoples, and this can be exceedingly difficult given the typical problem with imbalanced sources.

The chapters in this section do not solve the insolvable methodological problem, but they are exemplary of what creative historians can do to recover the interplay of ideas in borderlands relationships. Kathleen DuVal's essay examines cross-cultural debates in the borderlands of the Arkansas Valley during the early 19th century. In these years immigrant Cherokees and then British Americans moving into the region came into conflict with native peoples indigenous to the valley. Both groups of immigrants employed rhetoric about civilization and savagery while making appeals for state support, albeit in tellingly different ways. Meanwhile native Osages and Quapaws reacted by insisting upon their own conceptions of rights and sovereignty. Though attentive to the ways in which asymmetries of power condition the outcome of such borderland debates, DuVal nonetheless demonstrates the substance and urgency of the regional conversation and its significance to the U.S. policy of Indian removal.

Karl Jacoby's chapter interrogates the discourse of extermination in the U.S.-Mexican borderlands. For centuries, Spanish and then Mexican authorities had occasionally indulged in casual rhetoric about 'exterminating' the region's independent Indian peoples, most especially the diverse peoples they called Apaches. But it wasn't until the second half of the nineteenth century that non-Indians would be in a position to meaningfully pursue this dark vision. Emboldened by a rising white population, regional economic development, and an empowered post-Civil War military and state apparatus, American soldiers, ranchers, politicians, and editors held forth on the desirability and the supposed inevitability of Apache extermination. And they conspired with other peoples in the region to put rhetoric into action. Acknowledging the profound imbalance of source material, Jacoby insightfully juxtaposes this rhetoric with Apache 'narratives of horror,' indigenous histories of exterminatory violence that insisted upon the very human agency that white discourse about inevitability was meant to obscure.

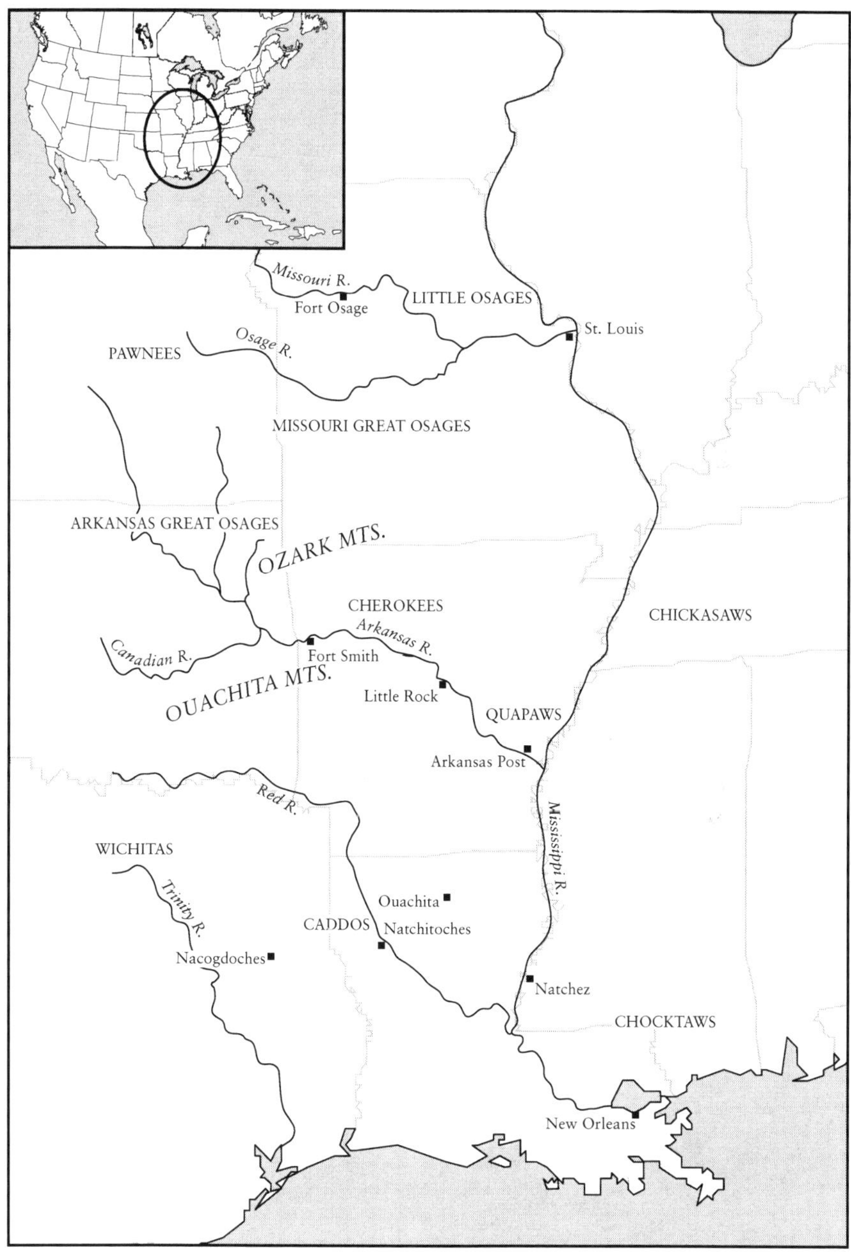


*Map 5.1* The Arkansas Valley

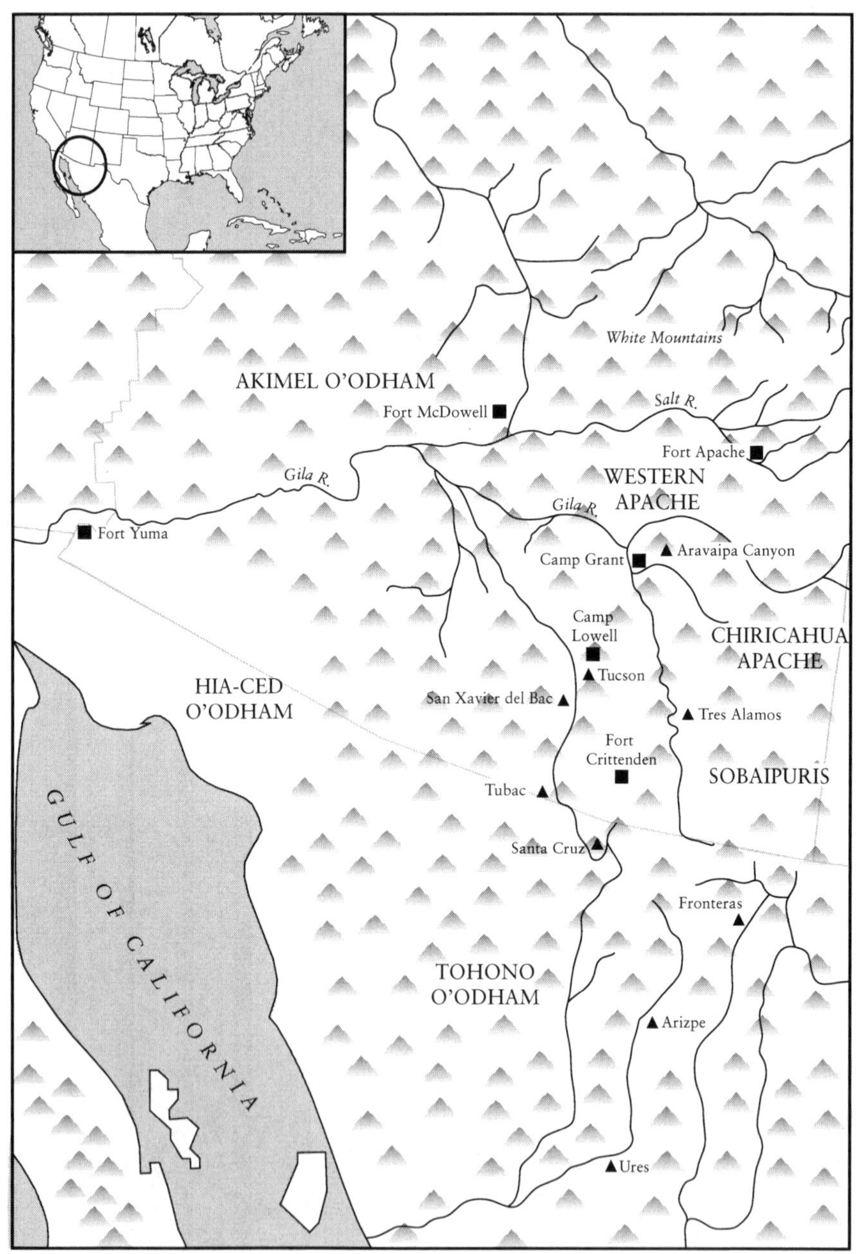


*Map 5.2* Arizona Territory

# 10

# DEBATING IDENTITY, SOVEREIGNTY, AND CIVILIZATION

*Kathleen DuVal*

In the spring of 1821, six Cherokee chiefs living west of the Mississippi wrote President James Monroe that their neighbors, the Osage Indians, were continuously robbing and killing Cherokee people and destroying their property. The chiefs requested federal assistance in their ongoing war against the Osages, reminding the president that the Cherokees had moved west of the Mississippi over the past two decades to "gratify and accommodate" their white Tennessee neighbors who had "coveted" their land. In return, the chiefs explained, Thomas Jefferson had promised any Cherokees who moved west "protection in the new and unexplored wilderness." The Cherokees charged that the United States had broken Jefferson's promise. Instead of being protected, they had been "most inhumanly murdered, butchered and plundered by a band of Savages."[1]

The place to which the Cherokees had moved, the Arkansas River Valley, was not an "unexplored wilderness." The "Savages" of whom the chiefs complained were the Osage people, who had controlled the Arkansas Valley since the early eighteenth century. The Osages, the Quapaws, and countless other Indian peoples had explored, farmed, traded, and hunted in the river valley for as long as anyone could remember. Neither was the Arkansas Valley new to Europeans. French, Spanish, and British explorers, traders, hunters, soldiers, and bureaucrats had traveled and settled in the region ever since Hernando de Soto crossed the Mississippi nearly three hundred years earlier. By labeling their new home an "unexplored wilderness" and their Indian neighbors "Savages," these Cherokees were enlisting the contemporary rhetoric and assumptions of many British-Americans in the eastern United States concerning "civilization," Indians, and the destiny of the republic.

In the early years of the nineteenth century, United States government claims to white superiority rested on culture rather than race. Most British-American officials, reformers, and missionaries simply believed that Native

Americans lived in an earlier stage of development than themselves. They proposed a "civilization" policy, advising Native Americans to secure their future in the American republic by becoming more like white farmers. To Jefferson and like-minded white easterners, the Louisiana Purchase provided the ideal space in which eastern and western Indians could train in white ways of farming, domestic production, and worship—in short, a place where "savages" could become "civilized." The fertile lands of the Arkansas Valley, halfway between the formerly French towns of New Orleans and St. Louis, would be the primary destination for southeastern Indians. However, neither eastern nor western Indians were interested in serving as passive objects of frontier development theories.[2]

Instead, various native peoples engaged in a multilateral debate over their place in the republic, a debate that revolved around issues of identity, sovereignty, cross-cultural relations, rights to resources, and, increasingly, the concepts of civilization and savagery. In the early nineteenth century, as Indian and white westward migration intensified competition for game and land, Arkansas Valley inhabitants began to look to the federal government to help resolve their disputes and couched their arguments in terms that appealed to United States policy-makers. But when local Indians and whites employed the concepts of civilization and savagery, they defined them in their own ways and used them to argue for their own rights to government protection and to land. As the Cherokee letter to Monroe demonstrates, Indians could use these concepts to argue against other Indians. Just as they had adapted the goods and economic pursuits of Europeans to their own lifeways and social structures, Indians altered the concept of "civilization" to serve their own cultural and political ends, often using it against other Indians or whites. Indians and whites alike oversimplified their own and others' cultures to argue for their own rights.

In this article I examine the arguments of four populations of the early nineteenth-century Arkansas Valley—native Osages and Quapaws and immigrant Cherokees and British-Americans. All responded to early nineteenth-century changes by drawing on their own understandings of history. The differences in their beliefs about diplomatic relations, land rights, and sovereignty reflect their diverse experiences with colonialism. East of the Mississippi, Britons and their descendants had steadily come to dominate all others. In contrast, various Indian groups had remained dominant in the West. Far from British settlements, western Indians had more autonomy as well as more influence over the less populous French and Spanish colonizers. In the colonial West, various native peoples had the power to enforce their ideas of identity and hierarchy on one another and on Europeans.[3]

In the early years of the nineteenth century, British-American power began to replace the West's multiple sovereignties, but Indians did not concede silently. Rather, they intellectualized their alternative views of the continent's future and communicated them to their rivals in a real, if losing, debate about legitimate possession and use of land, proper ways to live, and cultural differences. As was the case throughout the region's history, people's success in imposing their views depended largely on their relative strength. Ultimately, British-American settlers had the advantage both in numbers and power. . . .

Early nineteenth-century debates and conflicts in the Arkansas Valley form an essential part of the story of southeastern Indian removal. The difficulties the Cherokees faced in fighting the Osages and the lack of federal support for their efforts helped to harden many of their eastern kin's unwillingness to move west. The frustrations of applying the civilization policy to Arkansas and the pressure that irate white settlers placed on their representatives paved the way for the United States removal policy. United States-Indian relations in the 1830s were not a radical departure from previous history. Rather, the removal policy and Indian methods of resisting it grew out of conflict in the Arkansas Valley and other places where Indian and white ambitions clashed.[4]

Although white settlers' desires prevailed in the Arkansas Valley in the 1820s, Indians' alternative visions mattered, both in their own right and because they affected the ways in which British-Americans defined themselves and others. Recently, historians of African Americans have argued that race is not simply a system of beliefs imposed by whites on non-whites. . . . As recent historiography has been working, in Mia Bay's words, "to recapture the biracial history of American ideas about race," it is important to recognize that Native Americans played a similarly important role in colonial and nineteenth-century discussions of American identity. Historians have now begun to acknowledge that Native Americans, like African Americans, contested and recast Euro-Americans' accelerating racialism. Yet these studies of whites' beliefs about and policies toward Indians in the early republic have not incorporated Indians' conceptions and arguments into á cross-cultural intellectual history. . . .[5]

Like African Americans, Indians would ultimately have little power to stop the rising tide of American racism. Still, their words hold importance as alternatives to the emerging order. Even more importantly, their ability to change and to intellectualize change showed whites that it was dangerous to offer Indians equality—they might accept it.

In 1803, the Arkansas River Valley, extending east from the Rocky Mountains to the Mississippi River, became part of the United States, at least according to the two countries whose representatives signed the Louisiana Purchase. On the ground, however, most of the valley belonged to the Osage Indians. Osages had long lived to the north, near the Missouri River, and a majority still lived there in 1803. In the eighteenth century, armed with European weapons, the Osages had expanded south, with many settling near the Arkansas River. During the eighteenth century, the Osages controlled extensive lands across Louisiana by peacefully trading with selected partners and threatening, robbing, and occasionally killing uninvited white and Indian intruders. Violent protection of their lands served to keep out rivals, and the Osages' ability to bring in large numbers of furs assured a steady supply of munitions from European traders. . . .[6]

At first, the Osages expected that the Louisiana Purchase would follow the familiar pattern of European transfers. United States officials would come to the posts, speaking a different language but distributing guns, powder, ball, and blankets just as their French-and Spanish-speaking predecessors had. Indeed, when a delegation of Osage chiefs visited James Bruff, the new military commander for Upper Louisiana, they left "loaded with valuable presents & puffed up with ideas of their great superiority to other nations."[7]

Despite their pride, Osage dominance was already endangered. The threat came not from Bruff's government but from the arrival of numerous Indian outsiders who had lost vast tracts of their Ohio Valley homelands to the United States through the Treaty of Greenville. Thousands of Shawnee, Delaware, Miami, Potawatomi, Kickapoo, Sauk, Fox, Kaskaskia, and other warriors organized against the Osages in Missouri to gain access to Osage lands and to punish the Osages for their violent attacks. Under these pressures, in September of 1808, Osage Chief Pawhuska (White Hair) agreed to United States Indian Affairs Agent William Clark's proposal of a land cession.[8]

Pawhuska and other Osage chiefs did not see this land cession as the first step toward United States domination. In return for some of their eastern lands, the Osages received a pledge from the United States to provide goods, a fort and garrison for the Indians' protection, and a blacksmith to mend their weapons and tools. Moreover, much of the land that the Osages ceded actually belonged to the Quapaws, and other parts had been settled by Cherokees, Chickasaws, Choctaws, Shawnees, Delawares, and whites. Another reason that the chiefs agreed to the 1808 treaty was the hope of increasing their authority over wayward and increasingly independent Osage bands on the Arkansas River, south of the Osages' Missouri heartland. Most of the cession was in the Arkansas Valley, and the United States negotiators offered to assist in pressuring the Arkansas bands to return north.[9]

For their part, Clark and Jefferson saw the 1808 Osage treaty as an important step to Indian civilization and eventual white settlement. Eastern native peoples experiencing white encroachment and decreasing game could move onto the land that the Osages ceded. On this training ground, Christian missionaries and federal agents would teach both native Louisiana Indians and newcomers from the East how to live like whites. The Osages' agent, for example, was ordered to divert them from their hunting way of life and to "inculcate upon their minds the propriety and usefulness of a gradual introduction of the arts of civilization." By the time white farmers needed Louisiana lands, the Indians there would be autonomous farmers with lands to spare that they had formerly used for hunting.[10]

Many British-Americans identified the Osages, and the Arkansas Osages in particular, as the most uncivilized Indians in the region and the greatest challenge to the federal government's reform efforts. Traveler William Dunbar said that whites and Indians alike feared the Arkansas Osages, "a lawless gang of robbers, making war with the whole world." According to Dunbar, even other Indians called them "a barbarous uncivilized race." "The village on the Arkansaw," according to explorer Zebulon Pike, who traveled the region in 1806, "serves as a place of refuge for all the young and daring, and discontented." British-Americans interpreted Osage intimidation, not as a strategy that had allowed Osages to control the region for many decades, but as the faithlessness and ruthlessness of an uncivilized people.[11]

When United States officials instructed them to stop hunting and warring, Osages refused to accept the American model of themselves as savages in need of civilization. They rejected the notion that the United States had any right to prescribe how Osages should live. Rather than acceding to the civilization-savagery distinction, Osage leaders presumed equality between their nation and the United States, as they had with the French and Spanish in their decades in the region. Their model centered on the most basic political concepts that they shared with Europeans: national sovereignty, succession of power, and international alliance-making. According to this thinking, the Osages and the United States were separate, equal nations with more commonalities than differences.

It was in this context that Osage leaders discussed their common problems with United States leaders. On an 1804 trip to Washington, Chief Pawhuska complained to Jefferson that the Arkansas Osages were challenging his control, a problem that the United States government was also experiencing with its independent frontier settlers. Meanwhile, Arkansas Osage Chief Clermont told British-American trader Jacob Bright in 1806 that the Spanish, who claimed Louisiana from 1763 to 1800, had overstepped the bounds of legitimate international diplomacy by interfering with Osage succession. Clermont claimed that he, not Pawhuska, was the rightful chief over the entire Osage nation. He explained to Bright that, on the death of his father a decade or two earlier, the Spanish had determined that he was too young and had given the chieftainship to Pawhuska, "who had no claim to it." Because of Osage principles of succession as Clermont interpreted them, Pawhuska's treaty with William Clark was invalid—the usurper did not have the right to cede Osage lands. Clermont thus called on the United States to respect national integrity and lawful succession as mutually recognized prerogatives of independent civilizations.[12]

Rather than a paternalistic relationship wherein a culturally and politically superior government would instruct an inferior people, Pawhuska and Clermont both proposed a military alliance between equal states. Jacob Bright described how Clermont pointed to the "marks of the Tom-hock in many plaices," which he had received "in defence of white people." Calling on a history of alliances with Europeans, Clermont explained that he had cast off the epaulets that the Spanish had given him in order to adopt an American alliance. Still, he warned that the United States would need to court Osage alliance, mentioning that Cash-esegra, another Arkansas Osage chief, "liked the Spaniards." In 1806, this was a real threat. Spanish officials and soldiers occupied the Texas lands along the nation's southwestern border.[13]

To Pawhuska and Clermont, the Osage right to recognition and assistance had nothing to do with their internal behavior. Although they disagreed on who had the right to speak for their people, they agreed that the Osages were a sovereign government negotiating with another nation. Regardless of Clermont's complaints about the Spanish, this is how Europeans had previously treated the Osages. Of course European officials *tried* to influence the Osages, but the Osages generally forced Europeans to treat them as equals or even superiors. . . .

In the first decade of the nineteenth century, the Osages could still dismiss United States officials' condemnations of their culture. While the Osages had at least 1,000 fighting men, the United States army was small and stretched thin. Fewer than 2,000 troops guarded all the lands west of the Appalachians, on both sides of the Mississippi. Only sixteen men held the post on the Arkansas River, and there were fewer than 150 in all of Upper Louisiana. To make matters worse, the garrisons suffered from debilitating illnesses and a lack of supplies. Without more troops, United States officials could in no way force the Osages to accept or even consider their dichotomy of civilization and savagery.[14]

At the turn of the nineteenth century, Quapaw Indians found themselves in a much more vulnerable position than the Osages. The Osages had used European markets, their location just west of the Mississippi, and their relatively large numbers to become the region's strongest power. Living in three towns between the Osages up the Arkansas River and the European post at its mouth, the Quapaws numbered only six hundred people, one-quarter of the Arkansas Osage population. Some 15,000 to 20,000 Quapaws had lived in the Arkansas Valley in the seventeenth century, but they had suffered several devastating epidemics. To defend their homes on the lower Arkansas against encroaching Indians and whites, the Quapaws needed to establish a relationship of mutual trade and protection with the United States similar to what they had enjoyed with the French and Spanish.[15]

When United States officials arrived in the Arkansas Valley, the Quapaws called on them to assume the previous European governments' responsibilities. Quapaw chiefs carefully explained to United States official John Treat, through a French interpreter, that Europeans had lived with them "in the greatest harmony" and "frequently gave them talks and Annual Presents." The United States should be the same kind of ally. They described the Spanish as "long our Friends, who presented the Chiefs with medals and annually bestowed presents to all in our villages." They continued to make similar points throughout the years of Treat's tenure, wearing their Spanish medals and detailing the exact amounts of guns, gunpowder, ammunition, and blankets that they traditionally received.[16]

When United States officials told Quapaws that they had to "become more accustom'd to cultivating the soil" before they could receive goods and assistance, Quapaw chiefs declared that they found this order "extraordinary" because they "already do it to that extent, as enables a supply to many of the Inhabitants here both of Corn, and Horses." The Quapaws already were a settled, agricultural people who produced enough for their own subsistence and a small marketable surplus—the Jeffersonian ideal. Through their pointed arguments, the Quapaws revealed the hollowness of British-American admonitions to settle down. The Quapaws were farming more successfully than their French and Anglo neighbors at the post, to whom they sold food. Treat admitted that they "do neither hunt much or ask Credit."[17]

The Quapaws had long practiced a mixed economy. They lived in permanent towns and fed themselves largely by farming. Quapaw women grew squash, beans, and corn, cultivated fruit and nut trees, and raised domestic fowl. Unlike the Osages, the Quapaws did not range widely across the region. Quapaw men fished in the region's streams and hunted small game in the forests and meadows near their towns. Most western Indians, including the Osages, spent four to six months on hunting expeditions and took their entire villages. Quapaw hunts only lasted a matter of weeks, and Quapaw women stayed home to tend the fields.[18]

For Jefferson's imagined Indians, the United States civilization policy would work perfectly; for Indians who very reasonably asserted that they already were the kind of people that Jefferson wanted them to become, abstract theories disintegrated. Having to make a specific judgment about real Indians, American officials decided that the Quapaws fell somewhere between civilized and savage. Treat apparently did not see the irony in reporting that the Quapaws "present to us the fairest prospect of Civilization [of] any . . . Indian Tribes." Quapaw men were industrious in raising horses to sell but still acquired most of their meat from the hunt. In growing corn for the market, the Quapaws fit the agrarian ideal. However, British-American men simply could not see Quapaw women as independent yeoman farmers producing for the market. Like many whites before them, British-Americans in Arkansas believed that Indian men forced their women into the "drudgery" of farming while the men enjoyed the hunt. To white reformers, agricultural production for the market was only part of being a civilized people. Quapaw gender roles would have to change as well. Quapaws would have to cease hunting altogether and formally cede all but enough land for small family farms, on which they should build English-looking barns and fences and work their land with English-style plows.[19]

Ironically, the Quapaws' nonthreatening and largely agrarian way of life allowed the United States to ignore their arguments. United States officials' relations with the Quapaws reveal that becoming "civilized" members of the American republic meant more than not being "savage." The Quapaws could show that they had been settled and agricultural long before 1803, but without the benefit of United States protection, they would lose all of their lands to white settlers by 1824. By this time, United States officials lumped agrarian Indians in with all other Indians and drove them out of the territory. But in the early years of the Louisiana Purchase, another group arrived, who more closely fit British-American conceptions of "civilization."

In 1808, a delegation of Cherokees from the southern Appalachians informed Jefferson of "their desire to continue the hunter life." Because game was becoming scarce in their homeland, they preferred to "remove across the Mississippi river, on some vacant lands of the United States." Jefferson offered to exchange lands in Arkansas (which of course were not vacant) acre-for-acre with lands that Cherokees ceded east of the Mississippi. In the first decades of the nineteenth century, thousands of Cherokees immigrated to the Arkansas Valley, moving in between the Quapaws and Osages and probably outnumbering both.[20]

The Cherokees who went west, purportedly to continue older economic and social ways, found it more advantageous to distinguish their ways from those of western Indians. The leaders and their families were members of the Cherokee elite, including Chief Tolluntuskee and others who had been driven from power for ceding land in the East. West of the Mississippi, they had to defend themselves against the Osages, who did not acknowledge the Cherokee right to settle on their lands. Cherokees began to represent themselves as a civilized people in an uncivilized place.[21]

White visitors noticed Cherokee leaders' "highly civilized" way of life, as Thomas James put it. The gendered divisions of labor in Cherokee chiefs' families made James feel at home. When one of his hosts, the wife of John Rogers, served him a "noble meal of bacon, eggs, corn bread, milk and coffee," James praised her as a "good woman, squaw though she was." Cherokee Chief Thomas Graves impressed visitor Edwin James with his fine house, "surrounded with enclosed fields of corn, cotton, sweet potatoes, &c., with cribs, sheds, droves of swine, flocks of geese, and all the usual accompaniments of a thriving settlement." Material culture and gendered divisions of labor were central to Cherokees' display of civility. Missionary Cephas Washburn wrote that they "were building comfortable log-cabins and beginning to cultivate the soil." Washburn noted that the material property of the Arkansas Osages, on the other hand, "consisted wholly in horses, and the little stock of provisions they might have on hand, and the materials with which their lodges were covered."[22]

Cherokees could present a front of assimilation because most British-American travelers visited the homes and farms of the Cherokee elite. Based on his visit, James determined that the Arkansas Cherokees were "almost exclusively agriculturists," but in fact they were no more "exclusively agriculturists" than their neighbors. But enough elite families lived as Thomas Graves did to make the Cherokees look different. Their numerous livestock and large plantations were more visible to visitors than the practices of the Cherokee majority. Unlike most Cherokees, elite Cherokee men and women spoke English and lived in homes that looked comfortable to British-Americans. Ironically, the employment of slaves made the Cherokee elite look industrious to white observers. To avoid troubling gender implications, the Cherokee elite simply had neither Cherokee men nor Cherokee women farm, but black slaves (male and female). Thus, the Cherokees as a whole seemed less "Indian" to white visitors than even their common white neighbors.[23]

The Cherokees had little difficulty representing themselves as relatively "civilized." Cherokee economic pursuits were similar to the Quapaws, but the Quapaws' multifamily bark-covered dwellings could not compare favorably in the eyes of whites with Graves's frame house and enclosed fields and livestock. The poor white settlers who were beginning to come to Arkansas could not compete either. To many British-American travelers and officials, these settlers seemed less civilized than many of the native peoples. In opposition to Graves's neatly tended domestic animals, white settlers set pigs out to range and hunted them like game. Traveler Fortescue Cuming toured the Arkansas settlements along the Mississippi River in 1808 and reported little progress. The settlers did have domesticated livestock, he said, "but they raise neither grain nor cotton, except for their own consumption." A French hunters' and traders' village was even farther from the agrarian ideal. It seemed to him "a poor place" because such people "never look for any thing beyond the mere necessaries of life, except whisky."[24]

Traveler Henry Schoolcraft found particularly disturbing the white women living "beyond the pale of the civilized world." Their clothes and bodies "were abundantly greasy and dirty." He tried to make small talk with the women of a northern Arkansas settlement but, to his horror, found that they "could only talk of bears, hunting, and the like." He attributed the low birthrate among white families in Arkansas to these women's "disgust[ing]" appearance. In Arkansas, Schoolcraft found that "the state of society is not essentially different from that which exists among the savages," and the most obvious sign of savagery was the coarse white women. The Cherokee elite and poor white settlers defied the simple dichotomy of savage Indians and civilized whites.[25]

Cherokee chiefs claimed that, as a civilized people, the Cherokees were a natural friend of the United States. In 1813, Thomas Graves and thirty-two other leading Arkansas Cherokees wrote Missouri Territorial Governor Benjamin Howard to report incursions on their property by white bandits.

Like Quapaws, Cherokees maintained that their own agricultural pursuits qualified them for American protection. They declared, "we are indeavouring to cultivate the soil for our support." Unfortunately, they wrote, "there are a few bad men combined together for the purpose of stealing our horses." They named nineteen culprits who might, "if some measures are not taken," leave the Cherokees "destitut of property; & thereby prevented from persueing our Farms." The Cherokees encouraged United States officials to deconstruct the racial implications of the civilization policy and recognize that some Indians (such as the Cherokees) were civilized and some whites (such as the bandits) were savage.

The Cherokee chiefs also threatened to be a dangerous enemy if provoked. They informed Governor Howard that some of these "characters have solicited us to join them in killing robing & burning the Houses of the honest & industrious part of the white inhabitance." The Cherokee leaders made a distinction between the "honest & industrious" whites and the "bad" white men. By stressing their own efforts "to cultivate the soil," the Cherokees placed themselves on the side of the industrious whites. Yet mentioning that the bandits had tried to recruit them left open the possibility that the Cherokees might join the other side if the government did not protect them.[26]

Cherokee chiefs also positioned themselves as allies of the United States in the civilizing mission. In 1824, Arkansas Cherokee chiefs offered to help persuade eastern Indians that their best interest lay in migrating west, where they could escape from hostile whites and learn how to become civilized. They informed William Clark that Shawnees, Delawares, Kickapoos, Peorias, and others east of the Mississippi had asked Arkansas Cherokee Chief Tekatoka to assist with their negotiations in Washington. Tekatoka intended to comply with their request because the Cherokee nation felt "a deep solicitude in the success of said negotiation as being in its beliefs immediately connected with the preservation and future respectability of the Red people." Like white reformers, Tekatoka and other Arkansas Cherokee chiefs declared their belief that Indians' future depended on becoming civilized.[27]

Cherokee leaders adopted the civilization-savagery dichotomy but did not surrender their sovereignty. To white reformers, Indians should civilize in order to join the republic, but becoming United States citizens was not what most Cherokees had in mind, any more than did Osages or Quapaws. Rather, Cherokees portrayed their people as civilized Indians who could help advance United States objectives as long as they were treated as a civilized, separate nation.[28]

By 1813, clashes between Osage and Cherokee hunting bands had escalated into bloody war, and Cherokees were justifying the war in the terms of the civilization policy. Cherokee leaders argued that they were innocent victims of Osage aggression, while simply trying to implement United States Indian policy. In a letter to William Clark, Arkansas Cherokee chiefs alleged that for nine years "we have been trying to make friends" with the Osages, who instead insisted on fighting. The chiefs said they were simply living the way Jefferson had advised, "to raise our crops for the support of our families." They were trying to be civilized farmers, but the Osages would not let them do so in peace. Only when "provoked beyond bearing" had they taken up arms in a defensive war against the aggression of these wild Indians.[29]

Cherokee chiefs alleged that they and the United States were on the same side of a larger war for civilization. On one occasion, they persuaded Indian Agent Edward DuVal that Osages had killed a Cherokee man through "ferocious and barbarian treachery." The two nations had recently made a peace agreement, and yet several Osages "deluded" a Cherokee "by a friendly invitation" and then shot and scalped him. According to Cherokees, this incident was a "barbarian" violation of the rules of hospitality. Cherokees played by the rules, they implied, while Osages violated treaties with trickery and treachery.[30]

As Cherokees used their civilizing efforts to inspire United States assistance, they drove the Osages to submission. In 1816, the vanquished Osages agreed to a peace treaty that ceded most of their lands along the Arkansas River. For the first time, Arkansas Osages acknowledged the possible need to change. According to the local agent, Arkansas Osages asserted that because they wanted "to be treated as the Cherokee," they would try "to improve themselves in agriculture & manufacture." The Osages assumed that this cession would create a buffer zone between themselves and the Cherokees, but the Cherokees proved more diplomatically skillful. Cherokees showed the Indian commissioners who visited the disputed lands the improvements that their people had already made. The improvements impressed the commissioners, who deemed them "considerable and really valuable" and decided "it would be Just" to give the Osage lands to the Cherokees. The visual signs of Cherokee civilization outweighed the fact that they had been squatting on Osage land.[31]

Stung by Cherokee success, Arkansas Osages attempted to outmaneuver their enemies by inviting white settlers to the disputed territory. They promised United States officials they would learn to farm and produce domestic goods if the government kept the Cherokees from getting their lands. Osage representatives told Arkansas Territorial Governor James Miller in 1820 that they "never would have sold these lands to the United States to be given to other Indians, particularly the Cherokees." According to Miller, they had accepted the necessity of instruction in civilization, declaring that their "object, in selling the country, was to have the White people settle it, so as to instruct them in husbandry." Major Stephen Long reported that the Arkansas Osages "have repeatedly solicited the Americans to settle near them, alleging that they sold the land under the expectation that the Americans would become their neighbors, and teach them how to cultivate the ground, and their Women how to spin and weave, and thus enable them to live when the woods could afford them no more game for their subsistence."[32]

Arkansas Osage leaders saw the political advantages that Cherokees gained from their rhetorical position. Osages may also have genuinely feared that the declining stocks of game would make their hunting way of life untenable. They persuaded Long that they had become "sensible of the advantages the Cherokees have derived from the partial change that has been effected in their mode of life" and "zealous to imitate their example and even exceed them in their progress of becoming civilised." At least in the presence of British-American visitors, Osage leaders advocated change. Tally, one of the Arkansas Osage chiefs, gave a speech to his people in 1819 in which he urged them to "learn to do right" in their relations with other peoples. Tally explained what he meant by doing right—creating peace with neighbors by treating them with respect and generosity. Even in this vision, Osages were by no means surrendering their sovereignty, but they acknowledged their weakened position and the necessity of accommodating others.[33]

Arkansas Osages claimed that they wanted to become more like the Cherokees, but Chief Clermont also used their current way of life to justify the need for large amounts of land and game. In a speech to Major William Bradford, the commanding officer of Fort Smith, Clermont declared, "We Sold him Land but not the game on our Land." Clermont separated ownership of the land from ownership of the region's game. He used a similar argument against Cherokee hunting. The Cherokees' hogs and cattle were their property, and Clermont agreed that the Osages should not harm them. By the same rule, the region's game was Osage property. Following this reasoning, Clermont concluded that the Cherokees should not hunt the rapidly shrinking supply of game just as Osages should not steal their cattle and hogs. He compared the Cherokee ability to raise their food with the Osage need for game. "We cannot farm like the Cherokees," he said. "We have not yet learn'd how to raise Hogs Cattle and other things . . . . When we want meat . . . and clothing our dependance is in the woods—If we do not get it there we must go hungry and naked—This is not the Case with the Cherokees. If they Can't find those things in the woods their Cattle, Hogs, Corn, and Sheep will give it to them at home."[34]

Clermont claimed to accept that his people would eventually have to learn "to farm like the Cherokees." But since they had "not yet learn'd" the new ways, the chief based his people's land and hunting rights on their status as a nonagricultural people. Of course, Osage women were fine farmers, but Clermont found it as convenient to ignore this fact as did United States reformers and Cherokee chiefs. Just as the Cherokees had created an image of themselves as an exclusively agrarian society, so Clermont exaggerated his people's lack of agriculture in order to argue for land rights.

As the Osages' military options declined, rhetorical power increased in importance. Cherokees and white Americans already knew that the old modes of power were changing. In the East, as British-American representative governments gained ascendancy (backed by armies and militias), the route to influence increasingly lay in persuasion. Although from hindsight

British-American domination seems secure by the early nineteenth century, debates continued over the form that domination would take.

When Osage military strategies failed, Clermont developed a new initiative based on the needs of a people slowly becoming agrarian. But neither Clermont's, the Quapaws', nor the Cherokees' strategies would succeed as white settlers gained power in Arkansas. The United States civilization policy, Quapaw and Cherokee declarations that they had already complied, and more recent Osage arguments over the short-term application of the policy were all swept aside by the incoming flood of British-American settlers, who rejected the civilization policy entirely.

At first, white settlers in Arkansas did not employ the concepts of civilization and savagery. Early settlers had little reason or means to argue against Indians' right to their lands. The sparse white settlements consisted of isolated farms and small communities that had less access to government officials and continental trade than did Indians. But the conclusion of the War of 1812 and the introduction of the steamboat increased white immigration. The number of non-Indian settlers in Arkansas rose from fewer than four hundred in 1803 to over 14,000 by 1820, double the entire Indian population. When Arkansas became a territory in 1819, white Arkansans used their status as white yeoman farmers in a white man's republic to support their claim that their personal as well as national independence depended on exclusive ownership of the region's lands. Becoming a territory gave them a legislative assembly and delegates in Congress to argue for their rights directly. The federal government's continued efforts to move eastern Indians into Arkansas seemed to them to threaten its future prosperity and statehood. White citizens and their representatives launched a concerted effort to free Arkansas of all Indians.[35]

White Arkansans developed an argument that employed the same civilization-savagery distinction as used by the Cherokee and the United States elite. However, white settlers placed all whites on one side of the line and all Indians on the other, rejecting eastern reformers' and Cherokees' faith that Indians could cross the divide. As in earlier eastern struggles for land and legitimacy, white Arkansans decided that the distinction between savage and civilized was not developmental, but permanent. Although they did not use terms like *race* or focus their attention on skin color, they insisted that Indians were inherently and uniformly inferior to whites. Whereas federal policy-makers imagined a future equality for Indians but showed little awareness of their current realities, land-hungry white settlers knew Indians and wanted them gone.

In their petitions to Congress, white settlers drew a clear line between industrious whites and indolent Indians. One petition expressed shock that Congress was "unnecessarily lavishing large Portions of Public and Private Property on Savages while a total indifference or neglect is manifested towards their fellow citizen." The Arkansas Territorial Assembly lamented the wastefulness of letting "that Small remnant of the Quapaw tribe" retain "nearly three Millions of acres fronting on the Arkansas." In contrast to white settlers, the Quapaws left land "which would sustain fifty thousand souls . . . scarcely furrowed by a plough." Acting Arkansas Governor Robert Crittenden hoped Secretary of War John C. Calhoun would see the absurdity of letting this "poor indolent, miserable, remnant of a nation, insignificant, and inconsiderable" continue to own 250 miles of "high rich, and immensely valuable" cotton land along the navigable Arkansas River. An 1825 petition charged that if the government displaced its citizens "to give Place to Indians!!" it would not be acting as a "civilized Government." The settlers not only labeled themselves more civilized than all Indians, they accused their own government of behaving in an uncivilized manner by not protecting white settlers' property rights.[36]

Quapaw Chief Hekaton firmly rejected Anglo-Americans' growing insistence on a stark line between Indians and whites. When white Arkansans suggested that the Quapaws could give up their remaining lands and join the Caddos to the southwest in Louisiana, Hekaton said to Acting Governor Crittenden, "to leave my natal soil, and go among red men who are aliens to our race, is throwing us like outcasts upon the world." Driving home his point, the chief reminded Crittenden, "the lands you wish us to go to belong to strangers." The Caddos were different enough for Hekaton to call them "aliens" and "strangers." Nonetheless, Crittenden insisted that Indians would be better off living with Indians and, implicitly, that whites would be better off without them. He instructed the chief that, if his people remained where they were, "the whites will be continually cheating you, and will make you continually intoxicated, and will render you useless and effeminate." In contrast, "you will, by removing, get from the pestilential neighborhood of the whites, and your rifles will procure you a manly and independent livelihood." While previous officials had told the Quapaws that they could only fit in if they changed their gender roles, Quapaw men now heard that they could only be true men if they moved far away from whites.[37]

Cherokees and Quapaws insisted that Indians were different from one another and that whites and Indians could live together. They used their agricultural ways to argue that they deserved land. Osage Chief Clermont described his people's lack of agriculture to justify large land claims. When Indians spoke of civilization, they pointed to behavior, as did eastern reformers. Economics, religion, education, and ways of dealing with neighbors could all be signs of civilization. Because behavior could change, civilization and savagery could be neither permanent nor exclusive to a particular people. Disregarding Indian diversity, white Arkansans classed all Indians together as squanderers of the land. Ignoring behavior, they equated civilization and citizenship with being white.

Cherokees were appalled at this line of reasoning. When Arkansas newspapers reported a rumor that Cherokees might cede some of their Arkansas lands, a Cherokee delegation told the secretary of war that they were "astonished" at the suggestion. Describing themselves as pioneers and co-opting the white myth of the West as empty, these Cherokees claimed that they had left the land of their birth to settle a land "then uninhabited." If forced farther west, they would be "strangers in a wilderness." They would be forced to get their living from hunting because the lands to the west were "unfit for agricultural pursuits." Surely, they said, the government does not want to monopolize "all the *good* lands for our *white* brethren and give *us* the *worst*."[38]

The Cherokees had fought the Osages to stake out their place on the Arkansas River and had used their knowledge of British-American political culture to lobby Indian agents, secretaries of war, and presidents to support their claims; now they employed the methods of white settlers to argue for their place among them. In April of 1828, the territorial newspaper, the *Arkansas Gazette,* printed a letter by Nu-Tah-E-Tuil, or No-Killer. The letter referred to a memorial of the Territorial Legislature that the *Gazette* had printed, which argued against Cherokee land rights. Nu-Tah-E-Tuil called the memorial "replete with savage barbarity and injustice" and countered the accusation that Cherokees were too uncivilized to live among whites:

> What is civilization? Is it a practical knowledge of agriculture? Then I am willing to compare the farms and gardens of this nation with those of the mass of white population in the Territory. The advantage will be on our side. Does civilization consist in good and comfortable buildings? Here, if the comparison be made, we shall have the advantage over the mass of your people . . . . Does it consist in morality and religion? Our people have built, wholly at their own expense, the only Meeting house in the Territory; . . . Does it consist in school and the education of youth? I believe a larger portion of our youths can read and write than of those in your own settlements.

Nu-Tah-E-Tuil's letter identified the flaws in British-American reasoning. If the federal government wanted Indians to civilize, it should not make Cherokees leave their farms, homes, churches, and schools. If the government wanted only civilized people in its country, it should move Osages and maybe a few British-Americans west. By all of the standards that British-American leaders had cited in the past, white Arkansans should proudly claim Cherokees as neighbors, not insult them in the territory's newspaper.[39]

But white Americans' visions of their country's future did not include Indians. . . . Even whites who still believed Indians could theoretically change increasingly concurred with white settlers that Indians showed no signs of improving. In 1828, the House Committee on Indian Affairs concluded that, while Indians were capable of change, "they remain, to this hour, *a miserable and degraded race.*" Indians had two possible futures: extinction or removal "*to a more peaceable and better regulated home.*" Cherokee leaders' logic was impeccable. In their view, civilization is as civilization does. But white settlers wanted good agricultural land, and their government existed to supply it. In the 1790s, eastern states controlled Congress and the presidency. With the exception of Georgia and New York, those states had already occupied most Indian land within their borders, and their native populations had declined drastically due to disease, warfare, and emigration. Their representatives then pursued abstract Enlightenment ideas of human equality, urging Indians to assimilate.[40]

But these theorists were behind the times. Backcountry settlers had already developed a philosophy and rhetoric of virulent Indian-hating that allowed no room for Indian assimilation. As westerners obtained greater representation in Congress, federal policies began to reflect their fear and hatred toward Indians. Trans-Appalachian states insisted that Indians move across the Mississippi, and trans-Mississippi territories in turn lobbied for Indian removal even farther west. Federal officials lamented the settler passion for acquiring land, which Secretary of War James Barbour blamed for driving "in ceaseless succession, the white man on the Indian." But every time, the officials acquiesced. . . .[41]

An article in the *Cherokee Phoenix* exposed the central flaw of the civilization policy. Now that Cherokees were "prospering under the exhilarating rewards of agriculture, the rifle is again put into our hands, and the brass kettle swung to our backs, and we are led into the deep forest where game is plenty, by the hands of those who would once have had us abandon the chase. Admirably consistent." . . . Removal was structurally guaranteed to create conflict. First came intra-Indian strife between old inhabitants and immigrants, disrupting the lives of all the Indians in the now-embattled territory. Then, white squatters inevitably arrived, because they could reach any place that Indians could. British-American settlement in turn necessitated a new solution, requiring Indians to move again. Every move was justified in the name of agriculture, but every move disrupted the stability on which agriculture depends.[42]

White settlers in the 1820s employed a rigid dichotomy to argue against all Indian land claims in Arkansas. In 1825, the Territorial Assembly recommended establishing a "chain of civilised and industrious occupants" as a barrier against Indian aggression on the "frontier" by "that hord of Indians" to the west, including the Osages, Cherokees, and Quapaws. The rhetorical line between "civilised and industrious" white Arkansans and "that hord of Indians" had solidified, and there was no suggestion that Indians could become civilized. A corresponding physical line between the Arkansas territory and Indian territory would soon reflect white Arkansans' dichotomy.[43]

By 1828, the federal government extinguished all Indian claims in Arkansas. White settlers won the debate where it mattered most, on the ground. They wanted good agricultural land, and their government did not say no to them. The United States was a white man's republic where white men had the power of the vote.

In some ways, white settlers were more accurate concerning Indian realities and desires than eastern reformers. While Cherokee, Quapaw, and even Osage leaders spoke of transformation, they had no intention of assimilating to white governance and culture. Their men continued to hunt across the land, and their people lived in ways more similar to the past than some of their leaders admitted. Although they wanted peaceful relations with their white neighbors and were willing to make some concessions to achieve that goal, they were not going to surrender their identity and sovereignty. Indians had never agreed with Jefferson's vision of them as children in need of maturation. Rather, they selected the components of American ideology that served their purposes. No more eager to fit themselves into an eastern-designed mold than white settlers, Indians struggled to define the terms of change.[44]

The white settlers' error lay in describing Indians as indistinguishable and timeless—one people with no history and no future. In fact, Quapaw, Cherokee, and Osage histories were narratives of adaptability. As heavy competition in hunting and a decreasing game supply diminished the fur trade, these peoples adopted alternative economic and diplomatic strategies to retain their lands. They directly countered the long-standing assumption that Indians could only be hunters and that when game declined, they would have to keep moving west. The Quapaws stressed their economic similarity to white settlers. The Cherokee elite developed rhetoric that closely mirrored Jefferson's, using their agricultural way of life and acculturated manners to argue that Cherokees were more civilized than either white squatters or the Osages. Even the Osages suggested that they could play a part in the Jeffersonians' program of orderly frontier development. All three resisted attempts to erase tribal distinctions in favor of racial ones. Indeed, the manner in which they came to redefine the government's civilization program reinforced their biases toward other tribes and their reorientation toward the American national government.

In the long run, even the Cherokees' arguments could not protect their lands against white settlers who were also staking their claims on their status as an agricultural people. They based their definitions of civilization and savagery on white citizenship and Indian otherness, not way of life. Indeed, the very malleability of the concept of civilization made it ultimately useless in the struggle against British-American dominance because white settlers were able to mold it to their purposes.

In the 1820s, Congress acceded to white settlers' vision, preparing the way for the Indian removal policy. In the same year that the Cherokees left Arkansas, the country elected its first western President, Andrew Jackson. Jackson embodied white settlers' belief that, in his words, Indians "have neither the intelligence, the industry, the moral habits, nor the desire of improvement" to co-exist with British-Americans. Despite Indians' proven ability to adapt and their intelligence in defending their choices, Congress and presidential administrations increasingly accepted white settlers' long-standing assertion that Indians were not changing. Many officials even accepted the most profound assault on Indian sovereignty, forced removal of all eastern Indians.[45]

Indians actively participated in long-running discussions over how different peoples should live on this shared continent. As with Euro-Americans, their past experiences shaped their vision of the future, and their answers benefited their own interests more than those of others. They adapted to changing power relations and wielded older beliefs as well as newer ideas including the concepts of civilization and savagery, disagreeing with one another as often as with British-Americans. The Arkansas Valley's cross-cultural debates about the nature of societies and social development embodied a range of alternative visions for the nineteenth century that could not be reconciled with each other, forcing the United States government to abandon the belief that Indians could stop being Indians, at least in the near future. Confronted with choosing between independent Indian allies and their own citizens, policy-makers accepted white settlers' view of permanent Indian inferiority.

## NOTES

1 Arkansas Cherokees to James Monroe, Mar. 17, 1821, *The Territorial Papers of the United States,* ed. Clarence E. Carter (26 vols., Washington, DC, 1934–1962), 19: 273.

2 For the civilization policy, see Henry Dearborn to John Treat, June 23, 1807, *ibid.*, 14: 129; Cephas Washburn, *Reminiscences of the Indians,* ed. Hugh Park (Van Buren, AR, 1955), 123; Francis Paul Prucha, *The Great Father: The United States Government and the American Indians* (Lincoln, NE, 1984).

3 For the colonial West, see Colin G. Calloway, *One Vast Winter Count: The Native American West before Lewis and Clark* (Lincoln, NE, 2003); James F. Brooks, *Captives and Cousins: Slavery, Kinship, and Community in the Southwest Borderlands* (Chapel Hill, NC, 2002); Elizabeth A. H. John, *Storms Brewed in Other Men's Worlds: The Confrontation of Indians, Spanish, and French in the Southwest, 1540–1795* (1975; 2nd ed., Norman, OK, 1996); Gary Clayton Anderson, *The Indian Southwest, 1580–1830: Ethnogenesis and Reinvention* (Norman, OK, 1999).

4 For eastern Cherokee judgments of problems in the West, see, for example, *Cherokee Phoenix,* Apr. 15, 1829.

5 Mia Bay, *The White Image in the Black Mind: African-American Ideas about White People, 1830–1925* (New York, 2000), 4; Patrick Rael, *Black Identity and Black Protest in the Antebellum North* (Chapel Hill, NC, 2002). For histories of Indians' conceptions of identity and race in other places and times, see Gregory Evans Dowd, *A Spirited Resistance: The North American Indian Struggle for Unity, 1745–1815* (Baltimore, MD, 1992); Dowd, *War Under Heaven: Pontiac, the Indian Nations, and the British Empire* (Baltimore, MD, 2002); Theda Perdue, *"Mixed Blood" Indians: Racial Construction in the Early South* (Athens, GA, 2003); Daniel K. Richter, *Facing East from Indian Country: A Native History of Early America* (Cambridge, MA, 2001); Claudio Saunt, "The Paradox of Freedom: Tribal Sovereignty and Emancipation during the Reconstruction of Indian Territory," *Journal of Southern History,* 70 (Feb. 2004), 63–94; Nancy

Shoemaker, "How Indians Got to be Red," *American Historical Review,* 102 (June 1997), 625–44; John Wood Sweet, *Bodies Politic: Negotiating Race in the American North, 1730–1830* (Baltimore, MD, 2003). On Indian policy in the early republic, see Roy Harvey Pearce, *Savagism and Civilization: A Study of the Indian and the American Mind* (Baltimore, MD, 1965); Bernard W. Sheehan, *Seeds of Extinction: Jeffersonian Philanthropy and the American Indian* (Chapel Hill, NC, 1973); Robert F. Berkhofer, Jr., *The White Man's Indian: Images of the American Indian from Columbus to the Present* (New York, 1978); Reginald Horsman, *Race and Manifest Destiny: The Origins of American Racial Anglo-Saxonism* (Cambridge, MA, 1981); Anthony F. C. Wallace, *Jefferson and the Indians: The Tragic Fate of the First Americans* (Cambridge, MA, 1999).

6 Kathleen DuVal, *The Native Ground: Indians and Colonists in the Heart of the Continent* (Philadelphia, PA, 2006); Willard H. Rollings, *The Osage: An Ethnohistorical Study of Hegemony on the Prairie-Plains* (Columbia, MO, 1992).

7 James Bruff to James Wilkinson, Nov. 5, 1804, *Territorial Papers,* 13: 80.

8 Wilkinson to Dearborn, Sept. 22, 1805, *ibid.*, 228; "A Treaty Between the Tribes of Indians Called the Delawards, Miamis, Patawatimis, Kickapoos, Sacks, Foxes, Kasaskias, Scious of the River Demoin & Iowas, of the one part and the Great and Little Osages of the Other part," Oct. 23, 1805, *ibid.*, 245; Jean Ducoigne (Macouissa) to Como'l, Mar. 2, 1805, *ibid.*, 103–4.

9 William Clark to Dearborn, Sept. 23, 1808, *ibid.*, 14: 225–26; Clark to Dearborn, Dec. 2, 1808, *ibid.*, 243; Pierre Chouteau, Jr., to William Eustis, Sept. 1, 1809, *ibid.*, 316; Son of White Hair to Chouteau, Mar. 4, 1811, *ibid.*, 467; Lewis to Chouteau, Oct. 3, 1808, *ibid.*, 766; Lewis to Jefferson, Dec. 15, 1808, *ibid.*, 766; Meriwether Lewis to Thomas Jefferson, Dec. 15, 1808, *American State Papers* (38 vols., Washington, DC, 1832–1861), Indian Affairs, 1: 766; "Treaty with the Osage," Nov. 10, 1808, *Indian Treaties, 1778–1883,* ed. Charles J. Kappler (New York, 1972), 96; Gilbert C. Din and Abraham P. Nasatir, *The Imperial Osages: Spanish-Indian Diplomacy in the Mississippi Valley* (Norman, OK, 1983), 359.

10 Dearborn to Pierre Chouteau, July 17, 1804, *Territorial Papers,* 13: 31–32; Jefferson to Benjamin Hawkins, Feb. 18, 1803, in *The Writings of Thomas Jefferson,* ed. Albert Ellery Bergh (20 vols., Washington, DC, 1907), 10: 362–63.

11 William Dunbar, "The Exploration of the *Red,* the *Black,* and the *Washita* Rivers," *Documents Relating to the Purchase and Exploration of Louisiana* (Boston, MA, 1904), 68, 167; Pike to Wilkinson, Aug. 30, 1806, *Zebulon Pike's Arkansaw Journal: In Search of the Southern Louisiana Purchase Boundary Line (Interpreted by his Newly Recovered Maps),* ed. Stephen Harding Hart and Archer Butler Hulbert (Colorado Springs, CO, 1932), 61.

12 Jacob Bright to Dearborn, Dec. 20, 1806, "Jacob Bright's Journal of a Trip to the Osage Indians," ed. Harold W. Ryan, *Journal of Southern History,* 15 (Nov. 1949), 512; Jefferson to Chiefs and Warriors of the Osage Nation, July 18, 1804 (reel 2), Letters Sent by the Office of the Secretary of War Relating to Indian Affairs, 1800–1824 (M15, RG 75, National Archives, Washington, DC); John Joseph Mathews, *The Osages, Children of the Middle Waters* (Norman, OK, 1961), 299; Treat to Dearborn, Nov. 18, 1806, Letter Book of the Arkansas Trading House (National Archives, Washington, DC).

13 Bright to Dearborn, Dec. 20, 1806, "Jacob Bright's Journal," 512, 517. It is more likely that Clermont received his scars defending his lands from intruders than defending whites.

14 Extracts from the Travels of Perrin du Lac, 1802, *Before Lewis and Clark: Documents Illustrating the History of the Missouri, 1785–1804,* ed. and trans. Abraham Phineas Nasatir (St. Louis, MO, 1952), 706; Chouteau to Dearborn,

Nov. 19, 1804, *ibid.*, 759–60; George Peter to Wilkinson, Sept. 8, 1805, *Territorial Papers,* 13: 231; Dearborn to Daniel Bissell, Nov. 7, 1803, *ibid.*, 10; Elijius Fronmentin and Richard Waters to Bruff, Sept. 19, 1804, *ibid.*, 61; Bruff to Wilkinson, Nov. 5, 1804, *ibid.*, 79–80; Wilkinson to Dearborn, Aug. 10, 1805, *ibid.*, 180, 182; Treat to William Davy, Apr. 15, 1806, Letter Book; Wallace, *Jefferson and the Indians,* 216; Francis Paul Prucha, *A Guide to the Military Posts of the United States, 1789–1895* (Madison, WI, 1964), 143; Roger E. Coleman, *The Arkansas Post Story: Arkansas Post National Memorial* (Santa Fe, NM, 1987), 147; *Annals of St. Louis in Its Territorial Days from 1804 to 1821,* ed. Frederic L. Billon (New York, 1971), 23–24, 92; James Neal Primm, *Lion of the Valley: St. Louis, Missouri* (1981; 2nd ed., Boulder, CO, 1990), 105–6, 137.

15 W. David Baird, *The Quapaw Indians: A History of the Downstream People* (Norman, OK, 1980), 10, 37; William Dunbar, *Life, Letters and Papers of William Dunbar of Elgin, Morayshire, Scotland, and Natchez, Mississippi, Pioneer Scientist of the Southern United States,* ed. Mrs. Dunbar Rowland (Jackson, MS, 1930), 210–11; Treat to Dearborn, Dec. 31, 1806, Letter Book.

16 Treat to Dearborn, Mar. 27, 1806, *ibid.*; Treat to Dearborn, May 20, 1806, *ibid.*; Treat to Dearborn, Nov. 18, 1806, *ibid.*; Treat to Dearborn, Jan. 7, 1808, *Territorial Papers,* 14: 164–65.

17 Treat to Dearborn, Mar. 27, 1806, Letter Book; Treat to Davy, Sept. 1, 1806, *ibid.*

18 Baird, *Quapaw Indians,* 9–10; Treat to Dearborn, Nov. 15, 1805, Letter Book.

19 Treat to Dearborn, Mar. 27, 1806, *ibid.* For more on English demands on Indians, see James Axtell, *The Invasion Within: The Contest of Cultures in Colonial North America* (NewYork, 1985), 136–78.

20 "Treaty with the Cherokee," July 8, 1817, *Indian Treaties,* 140–44; Jefferson to Cherokees of the Upper Towns, Jan. 9, 1809 (reel 2), Letters Sent by the Office of the Secretary of War Relating to Indian Affairs; Jefferson to Cherokees, Jan. 9, 1809, *ibid.*

21 "Treaty with the Cherokee," July 8, 1817, *Indian Treaties,* 140–44; William G. McLoughlin, *Cherokee Renascence in the New Republic* (Princeton, NJ, 1986), 109, 145–60, 164.

22 Thomas James, *Three Years among the Indians and Mexicans* (St. Louis, MO, 1916), 104, 237, 239; Edwin James, "Account of an Expedition from Pittsburgh to the Rocky Mountains Performed in the Years 1819, 1820," in *Early Western Travels,* ed. Reuben Gold Thwaites (32 vols., Cleveland, OH, 1904–1907), 17: 17–18; Washburn, *Reminiscences of the Indians,* 115.

23 James, "Account of an Expedition," 17: 17–18; Perdue, *"Mixed Blood" Indians,* 64–65. For the Cherokee elite, see Nathaniel Sheidley, "Origins of the First New South: Manhood, Capital, and the Making of a Native American Elite in the Post-Revolutionary Southeast," unpublished article.

24 Fortescue Cuming, "Sketches of a Tour to the Western Country," *Early Western Travels,* 4: 298–99; Treat to Dearborn, Nov. 15, 1805, Letter Book; John Billingsley, "Letters from an Early Arkansas Settler," ed. Ted R. Worley, *Arkansas Historical Quarterly,* 11 (Winter 1952), 327; Walter N. Vernon, "Beginnings of Methodism in Arkansas," *Arkansas Historical Quarterly,* 31 (Winter 1972), 359, 367; *Arkansas Gazette,* Feb. 4, 1860; James, "Account of an Expedition," 17: 31–33; Baird, *Quapaw Indians,* 11.

25 Henry Schoolcraft, *Rude Pursuits and Rugged Peaks: Schoolcraft's Ozark Journal, 1818–1819,* ed. Milton D. Rafferty (Fayetteville, AR, 1996), 52–53, 55, 74, 63.

26 Cherokees to Benjamin Howard, Apr. 27, 1813, *The Life and Papers of Frederick Bates,* ed. Thomas Maitland Marshall (2 vols., St. Louis, MO, 1926), 2: 239–41.

27 Cherokee Chiefs to Clark, Oct. 17, 1824, U.S. Office of Indian Affairs, St. Louis Superintendency, Field Records, 1813–1853 (Kansas State Historical Society, Topeka).
28 On Indians' joining the republic, see Jedidiah Morse, *Report to the Secretary of War of the United States, on Indian Affairs, Comprising a Narrative of a Tour Performed in the Summer of 1820* (New Haven, CT, 1822), 36; Pearce, *Savagism and Civilization*; Berkhofer, *White Man's Indian*; Horsman, *Race and Manifest Destiny*.
29 Arkansas Cherokee Chiefs to Clark, July 11, 1817, *Territorial Papers,* 15: 304; Arkansas Cherokee Chiefs to Monroe, Mar. 17, 1821 (reel 3), Letters Received by the Office of the Secretary of War Relating to Indian Affairs, 1800–1824 (M271, RG 75, National Archives).
30 Edward DuVal to James Barbour, May 31, 1826, *Territorial Papers,* 20: 260.
31 Lovely to Clark, May 27, 1815, *ibid.*, 15: 57; Lovely to Monroe, May 27, 1815, *ibid.*, 49; Clark, Ninian Edwards, and Auguste Chouteau to William Crawford, June 30, 1816, *ibid.*, 151–52.
32 James Miller to John C. Calhoun, Mar. 24, 1820, *Territorial Papers,* 19: 153–55; Stephen Long to Thomas Smith, Jan. 30, 1818, *ibid.*, 7. For references to declining game, see Arkansas Cherokees to Monroe, Mar. 17, 1821, *ibid.*, 273; Clermont, speech to William Bradford, Sept. 15, 1821, *ibid.*, 321; Clark to Osage Nation, n.d., U.S. Office of Indian Affairs, St. Louis Superintendency, Field Records (Kansas State Historical Society, Topeka).
33 Long to Smith, Jan. 30, 1818, *Territorial Papers,* 19: 7; Thomas Nuttall, *A Journal of Travels into the Arkansas Territory during the Year 1819,* ed. Savoie Lottinville (Norman, OK, 1980), 212–13.
34 Clermont, speech to Bradford, Sept. 15, 1821, *Territorial Papers,* 19: 320–21.
35 Daniel H. Usner, Jr., *Indians, Settlers, and Slaves in a Frontier Exchange Economy: The Lower Mississippi Valley before 1783* (Chapel Hill, NC, 1992), 114; Treat to Dearborn, Nov. 15, 1805, Letter Book; James Logan Morgan, *1820 Census of the Territory of Arkansas (Reconstructed)* (Newport, AR, 1984), 92.
36 Petition to Congress by Inhabitants of Arkansas County, Nov. 2, 1818, *Territorial Papers,* 19: 11–12; Petition to Congress by the Arkansas Territorial Assembly, Dec. 8, 1823, *American State Papers,* Public Lands, 4: 1; Robert Crittenden to Calhoun, Sept. 28, 1823, *Territorial Papers,* 19: 559; "Petition to the President by Citizens of Miller County," n.d., 1825, *ibid.* 20: 138–39.
37 *Arkansas Gazette,* Nov. 30, 1824.
38 Cherokee Delegation to Barbour, Mar. 12, 1825, *Territorial Papers,* 20: 4–5.
39 *Arkansas Gazette,* Apr. 23, 1828.
40 *Report of the House Committee on Indian Affairs, Regarding Indians Removing Westward,* Jan. 7, 1828, House Document No. 56, 20th Congress, 1st Session (Washington, DC, 1828), *The United States and the Indians,* vol. 5, Ayer Collection (Newberry Library, Chicago, IL); Reginald Horsman, "The Indian Policy of an 'Empire for Liberty,'" *Native Americans and the Early Republic,* ed. Frederick E. Hoxie, Ronald Hoffman, and Peter J. Albert (Charlottesville, VA, 1999), 54–55.
41 Barbour to John Cocke, Feb. 3, 1826, U.S. Congress Register of Debates, 19th Congress, 1st Session, vol. 2, part 2, appendix, 40.
42 *Cherokee Phoenix,* Sept. 17, 1828.
43 "Memorial to the President by the Territorial Assembly," n.d. [1825?], *Territorial Papers,* 20: 128.
44 William L. Anderson, *Cherokee Removal: Before and After* (Athens, GA, 1991), viii–ix.
45 Andrew Jackson, Fifth Annual Message to Congress, Dec. 3, 1833, *A Compilation of the Messages and Papers of the Presidents* (20 vols., New York, 1897), 3: 1252; Prucha, *Great Father,* 70–72.

# 11

# "THE BROAD PLATFORM OF EXTERMINATION"

*Karl Jacoby*

In 1864, an Anglo-American rancher in Arizona named King Woolsey dispatched a letter to the territory's military commander. Woolsey had recently led a number of civilian expeditions against the local Apache peoples, and he felt obliged to defend his extra-legal violence to territorial authorities. "As there has been a great deal said about my killing women and children," he wrote, "I will state to you that we killed in this Scout 22 Bucks 5 women & 3 Children. We would have killed more women but [did not] owing to having attacked in the day time when the women were at work gathering Mescal [cactus]. It sir is next to impossible to prevent killing squaws in jumping a ranchería even were we disposed to save them. For my part I am frank to say that I fight on the broad platform of extermination."[1]

By literally and figuratively underscoring the word "extermination" in his correspondence, Woolsey invoked the nineteenth century United States' most common term for discussing the fate of North America's indigenous peoples. Records from the period are saturated with references to Native American extermination—as possibility, promise, threat, even humour. Nine years after Woolsey composed his letter to Arizona's military authorities, the artist Charles Stanley Reinhart created a cartoon for *Harper's Weekly* that depicted a sullen Indian slumped by an open window while a juvenile Uncle Sam complained to his mother, personified by that other symbol of American nationhood, Columbia. In response to his mother's queries, "Little Sammy" stated "Boo hoo! I got all his playthings, an' I kicked him into the corner, an' I was a-goin' to chuck him out er the winder, when he up an' slapped me. An', ma, wouldn't you please Exterminate him?"

Investigating how the concept of extermination shaped nineteenth century interactions with Native Americans ought to compel the attention of far more than just students of the "dark and bloody ground" of the American West. Although often treated by U.S. and non-U.S. historians alike as the foundation of a perceived American exceptionalism, the efforts of the United States to assert control over the western reaches of North America correspond with one of the globe's pre-eminent ages of imperial expansion—the long nineteenth century, during which Germany, France, Great Britain, and other European powers scrambled to claim vast portions of Africa, Asia, and the Pacific. As Ben Kiernan and others have noted, the agrarian and Utopian ideologies of "civilization" and "progress" that animated these imperial projects often contained a dark inner core—a "logic of elimination" in the words of Patrick Wolfe—in which the dominance of newly arriving settlers was predicated upon the disappearance of indigenous societies. By the nineteenth century, this logic acquired much of its power from contemporary thought about the natural world, especially the notion of the extermination of species. As none other than Charles Darwin put it in *Descent of Man,* "At some future time period . . . the civilized races of men will almost certainly exterminate, and replace, the savage races throughout the world."[2]

What this blending of the human and the natural obscured (often conveniently so) was how precisely the predicted disappearance of Native Americans was to take place. Was it a purely natural process, akin to extinction? Or was it an explicit policy, brought about by direct human action? The American commentator George Ellis highlighted the stakes underlying these "interesting and exciting questions" in 1882:

> Not unfrequently, in place of the milder word *extinction* the sterner word *extermination* is boldly used to define the alternative fate of the Indians. The difference between the words hardly needs to be morally defined here. One may speak of the extinction of the Indians as a result which might follow from natural agencies, irresistible and not requiring any external force to insure it. Extermination implies the use of violent measures to effect it.[3]

This essay revisits the issues Ellis and many others raised in the nineteenth century through a close investigation of the territory that produced Woolsey and his actions in support of "the broad platform of extermination." In so doing, it situates itself at the uneasy intersection of genocide studies and Native American history. The reason for this unease can be traced to the fact that, unlike scholars of genocide, who focus on the perpetrators of mass violence, practitioners of the so-called "new Indian history" have sought to recover the historical agency of Native Americans and recast Indians as active co-creators of a "New World for all" in North America. This difference reflects not simply differing academic agendas but also the fact that for many present-day Native American communities, the narrative of Indian decline and disappearance central to genocide studies can itself be an object of suspicion. Dwelling on past annihilations is sometimes seen in Native communities as reinforcing mainstream notions of Indians as "vanished" and therefore undercutting present Native efforts to reclaim treaty rights, establish federal tribal recognition, and otherwise assert sovereignty. Indeed, it is revealing to note that as much as the recent flowering of academic histories from Native American scholars foregrounds the brutalities visited upon their communities, this literature seldom employs genocide as a way to describe the violence of the past, favouring instead less charged terms such as colonialism.[4]

In keeping with the belief that interpretative issues of the sort that the tension between genocide studies and Native American history raises are most fully revealed in a specific setting, the pages below attempt to unravel how extermination operated among both settlers *and* Native Americans in a small but revealing corner of nineteenth century North America. The targets of the extermination campaigns of Woolsey and his compatriots were the diverse array of Athapaskan peoples known to outsiders as Apaches and to themselves, depending on dialect, as *Nnēē* or *Ndee* ("the People"). The Apache had been exposed to European colonialism since the arrival of the Spanish in the borderlands in the sixteenth century.[5] Over the intervening centuries, by alternately raiding and trading with European colonists, Apache bands incorporated an array of "Old World" goods, such as livestock and cotton cloth, into their daily lives. Although Apache communities suffered dramatic violence during these years as well, it was not until after the United States acquired much of northern Mexico in the 1840s and 1850s that the Apache faced the greatest threat to their existence. Spanish and Mexican officials had spoken upon occasion of their hopes for the "total extermination" of the Apache, or of discovering "the most serious and efficient means to exterminate these nomadic tribes." But only with the arrival of large numbers of Anglo-American settlers and the U.S. Army in the borderlands in the mid-nineteenth century would these visions of extermination become, as we shall see, a tangible possibility.[6]

The term at the centre of so much nineteenth century thought about indigenous peoples can be traced to the Latin word *exterminatus,* meaning beyond (*ex*) a boundary (*terminatus*). By the early 1800s, however, extermination had acquired in contemporary Anglo-American usage a far harsher edge. As Richard Trench observed in his 1873 work, *A Select Glossary of English Words Used Formerly in Senses Different from their Present,* "our fathers, more true to the etymology" understood exterminate to mean "to drive men out of and beyond their own borders." But, reported Trench, extermination "now signifies to destroy, to abolish." Likewise, noted Trench's contemporary Charles John Smith, "[e]tymologically, the word [exterminate] might mean expulsion, but, as a fact, is never so used." Rather, extermination had become to mean "[t]o utterly destroy, and so take away from the place of occupation." As such, extermination was, according the Smith, synonymous with "eradication" and the opposite of "colonization."[7]

This juxtaposition of extermination and colonization emerged in sharp relief as Euro-American settlers began to establish ranches and mines in what became in 1863 Arizona Territory. Although a number of the region's indigenous peoples, most notably the Tohono O'odham (Papago), Akimel O'odham (Pima), and Xalychidom Piipaash (Maricopa), developed productive trade relations with the newcomers, settlers nonetheless found their vision for the region challenged by raids from other Native communities. In the face of these conflicts, the complex mosaic of indigenous peoples in Arizona Territory, with their marked linguistic, political, and cultural differences, became reduced for most incoming settlers down to the two categories—peaceful or hostile—with the term Apache applied to any group believed to be among the latter. "Excepting the Pirnas and Maricopas," recalled one army officer, "the Indians were all called Apaches."[8]

To many settlers, the solution to this "Apache" threat was correspondingly simple. "Extermination is our only hope, and the sooner the better," declared a writer for the *Arizona Miner* in 1864. "There is only one way to wage war against the Apaches," agreed the Arizona mine owner Sylvester Mowry. "A steady, persistent campaign must be made, following them to their haunts—hunting them to the 'fastnesses of the mountains.' They must be surrounded, starved into coming in, surprised or inveigled—by white flags, or any other method, human or divine—and then put to death."[9] As one newspaper headline summed up the prevailing mood in the territory, "Arizona Settlers Preparing for the Extermination of the Apache."[10]

With the Civil War soon reducing the U.S. military presence in the region to a minimum, much of this attempted extermination was undertaken by civilian patrols, occasionally guided by skilled Tohono O'odham, Akimel O'odham, or Xalychidom Piipaash trackers. The Connecticut-born judge, Joseph Pratt Allyn, for example, noted upon his arrival in the territory in 1863 that "a war of extermination has in fact already begun. [Apache] Indians are shot wherever seen." The judge witnessed several organizational meetings for civilian campaigns, at which settlers not only volunteered their own services as "Indian hunters" but also contributed towards a bounty "for Indian scalps." Such undertakings, according to Allyn, were remarkably popular. "[P]ersons were constantly coming in who wished to join the party, one and all believing and talking of nothing but killing Indians," he noted. "It is difficult to convey . . . an adequate idea of the intensity of this feeling."[11]

Although distinct from the U.S. Army's campaigns against the Apaches, these scouting expeditions nonetheless enjoyed a degree of official support. At one meeting Allyn attended, for instance, the federally appointed governor of Arizona, John Goodwin (a graduate, ironically enough, of Dartmouth College, a school founded to educate Indian youth) encouraged the assembled "Indian hunters" through a speech that, in Allyn's words, "took all by storm" through its call for "the extermination of the [Apache] Indians."[12] A few years later, King Woolsey, the advocate of "the broad platform of extermination" would receive a "resolution of thanks" from the Arizona Territorial Legislature for leading "civilian volunteers" against the Apache.[13]

The majority of such volunteers adopted a policy of killing whatever "Apaches" they encountered on their patrols. "[I]t was the rigid rule all over the country," noted one settler, "to shoot these savages upon sight." In the minds of many Arizonians, the elusiveness of their Apache foes justified their indiscriminate violence. As one put it, "We have a horror of them [the Apache] that you feel for a ghost. We never see them, but when on the road are always looking over our shoulders in anticipation. When they strike, all we see is the flash of the rifle resting with secure aim over a pile of stones." Since Americans seldom possessed the skills to deter such raiders, they responded by attacking whatever Apaches they did encounter, on the assumption that, even in the absence of direct evidence, these "savages" were doubtless involved in past or future assaults on Americans.[14]

This logic transformed extermination into a central feature of what the historian Philip J. Deloria has termed the notion of "defensive conquest": the belief that Euro-Americans were forced into aggression as a result of Indian violence.[15] Fundamental to this concept was the settlers' projection of their desire for extermination onto the Apache. The true authors of extermination, asserted most Euro-Americans in Arizona, were not themselves but the region's Native Americans. "The Indians really have possession of this Territory," claimed one settler. "It is feared that the Hualapais, the Yavapais, and the different tribes of Apaches, with some straggling Navajoes, have combined for the purpose of exterminating the whites." The rains of several ancient irrigated settlements in the new territory—in truth the abandoned villages of the ancestors of the Tohono O'odham and Akimel O'odham—proved to Americans that the Apaches "have been waging for ages . . . unceasing war against the cultivator of the soil." Having supposedly annihilated the farmers who had created these earlier settlements—for Native Americans were, in the Euro-American mind, "perpetually engaged in the work of exterminating each other"—the Apaches were now attempting to do the same to the territory's "Anglo-Saxon" newcomers.[16]

If the stated goal of the mid-nineteenth century civilian campaigns was to preempt the Apaches' attempted extermination of the territory's Euro-Americans, the unstated goal was to call the Apaches' very humanity into question, often through acts designed to emphasize the Indians' animal-like qualities. While on a scout designed to "chastise [the Apache] into peace," for example, the newly arrived settler Daniel Ellis Conner witnessed one of his fellow participants cut the heads off five Apaches slain in the encounter and, much as he would with any other wild animal, use the dead men's brains to tan a deer hide ("[t]he best buckskin I ever seed," the man contended, "was tanned with Injun brains").[17]

Such settlers deployed violence towards the Apache not simply as a tool but as a form of grotesque spectacle, intended to demonstrate the Apache's subhuman status. Conner recalled one Arizona farmer who, when he discovered

Apaches sneaking into his corn patch, ambushed the offending Indians, killing two. The man then placed the Apaches' corpses on a platform overlooking his field as if they were human scarecrows—akin, in Conner's words, "to the action taken by old ladies sometimes, to keep the hawks away from the chickens."[18] King Woolsey engaged in a similar parading of dead Apaches. In 1861, Woolsey killed an Apache leader with a shotgun blast. "[D]etermined to make a conspicuous mark of the dead chief," he dragged the man's body to a nearby mesquite tree and hung the corpse by the neck, where it dangled for several years for all to see.[19]

As such gory displays of Apache remains indicates, among many settlers, the Apache had come to be perceived as little more than, in the words of one, "the most savage wild beast"—and not just any animal, but one of the "meaner brutes," to be killed wherever possible. Indeed, it was *canis lupus,* the wolf, that provided Euro-Americans with their pre-eminent point of comparison for Arizona's Apaches. Some writers noted that Apaches and wolves haunted the same "hungry waste" and attributed Apache tribal names to the Indians' seeming closeness to wolves. As an 1868 article in *The Overland Monthly* put it, "The Coyoteros are so named from a fancied or real similitude to the coyote, a small prairie wolf."[20] Such comparisons underscored the unredeemably predatory nature of Apaches and wolves alike. "The wolf still is, he always will be, a savage; so has been, so always will be, the Apache," asserted J. S. Campion in 1878.[21] Labelling the Apache "the wolf of the human race" served in turn to minimize the humanity of those victimized by the settlers' anti-Apache violence.[22] Sylvester Mowry, for example, called for the "massacre of these 'human wolves,'" while John Cremony of the U.S. Boundary Survey spoke of the Apache as "a biped brute who is as easily killed as a wolf."[23]

For such writers, the metaphor of *canis lupus* to describe the Apache also achieved another objective. Not only did the wolf summon up images of skulking deceitfulness and inhuman savagery; wolves had long been the subjects of state-supported exterminationist campaigns designed to eliminate a predator who, much like the Apache, was perceived to threaten settler livestock. The payment of bounties for wolf scalps was a venerable Euro-American tradition, dating to a 1630 measure in Massachusetts, and was continued by many states throughout the nineteenth century. The wolf was also the long-standing target of communal hunts, intended to exterminate all the wolves in a given vicinity. In 1818, for instance, 600 settlers in Hinkley, Ohio, launched a "war of extermination upon the bears and wolves" in which 17 wolves were killed and scalped for the local predator bounty.[24]

If the original impulse for exterminating the wolf arose from the fact that these predators were "so destructive to valuable property," by the nineteenth century wolves had been transformed from mere nuisances into the very antithesis of the ordered agrarian landscape that settlers were attempting to create across North America. Writers thus spoke of efforts to obliterate the wolf as part of an epic, Manichean struggle. Wolves had become "evildoers . . . [who] deserve[d] to be destroyed," animals whose "crimes" justified the "natural right of man to exterminate" them. As the nineteenth century wolf hunter Ben Corbin put it: "The wolf is the enemy of civilization, and I want to exterminate him."[25]

It was in this atmosphere of mass, state-supported enthusiasm for wolf extermination that many of the measures that had first been developed to eliminate wolves—community hunts, scalps, and bounties—were applied to Apaches in Arizona. "A thousand dollars reward for every Apache brought in, dead or alive,' was the cry of the Arizona Legislature," reflected the editors of *Everywhere* magazine at the turn of the century. "It was the same sort of bounty that used to be offered for wolf-scalps."[26] Not surprisingly, the extension of extermination tactics from wildlife to human beings encouraged acts of extreme brutality towards the Apache. The settler Alonzo Davis recalled that in the 1860s some of his neighbours laced several sacks of sugar with strychnine and then left the bags where they were sure to be found by local Apaches. "One package was put into a greasy sugar sack and accidentally (?) left by the big rock where we cooked our supper. The other was put upon an Indian trail running out to Rock Springs." Davis confessed that this incident "may seem harsh to people who know nothing of conditions on the old frontier, but it was the only way we could get hold of those natives who never would stand and fight." Davis might have added that the technique he and others (including, inevitably, King Woolsey) employed against the Apache—leaving poisoned food for an elusive foe—had long been familiar to those seeking to exterminate wolves.[27]

Euro-American efforts to lower their Apache foes to the status of animals nonetheless foundered upon an unresolved paradox. As much as the bestialization of the Apache helped justify settler efforts to exterminate them, what made the Apache such a threat in the first place was their all-too-human understanding of Anglo intentions—the very feature that allowed them to raid Euro-American settlements with such seeming ease. Moreover, reducing their opponents to mere animals risked diminishing settlers' ongoing struggle over the borderlands into little more than an unequal contest between humans and lesser animals. If only to elevate themselves, Euro-Americans needed to endow the Apache with a degree of humanity. The travel writer Samuel Cozzens encapsulated the instability of Anglo-Americans' bestialization of the Apache in his 1876 work *The Marvellous Country.* Cozzens simultaneously claimed that Apaches "resemble[d] the prairie wolf,—sneaking, cowardly, and revengeful" *and* depicted the Chiricahua Apache leader Mangas Coloradas (*Gandazistichíídń* "The One with Reddish Sleeve Covers") as a "noble . . . specimen of the Indian race . . . straight as an arrow, his physique splendid."[28]

The fragility of settler attempts to bestialize the Apache as wolf-like others was perhaps most apparent when Euro-Americans confronted those who seemed most unlike vicious predators: Apache non-combatants such as the very aged or the very young. Conner, for example, considered "the worst case of brutality" that he witnessed in 1864 to be the shooting and scalping of "an old gray-headed squaw" by a fellow member of an expedition against the Apache. Indeed, revulsion at the man's behaviour was widespread enough that his fellow settlers subjected him to a "drumhead court martial," although it is unclear from Conner's account whether it was the killing of the elderly woman or her subsequent mutilation that occasioned most objections.[29]

The exercise of violence against Indian children was even more fraught. At several points, Conner depicted expeditions in which the participants treated infants almost as if they were innocent of the quarrels of the adult world. When one settler raid stumbled across three abandoned babies in a camp from which the adult Apaches had all fled, Conner and his compatriots left the infants behind in the hope that their relatives, presumably hiding nearby, would soon reclaim them. Similar practices were followed by at least some U.S. Army units in the region: as one soldier reported after an attack, "most of the papooses we left to be picked up by their friends."[30]

Still, violence against children was not unknown—in fact, it was unavoidable, given the American penchant for attacking camps of sleeping Native Americans. As the military commander of Arizona, General George Crook, acknowledged, "[i]n surprise attacks on [Apache] camps women and children were killed in spite of every precaution; this cannot be prevented by any foresight or order of the commander any more than shells fired into a beleaguered city can be prevented from killing innocent civilians." Conner discovered the truth of Crook's statement first hand when during an attack on an Apache camp, his companions fired upon what they thought was an escaping Indian male. Closer examination revealed that their target had been a woman with an infant on her back and that the attackers' shot had not only killed the woman but also broken the baby's leg. "[T]he men," Conner reported, decided that the appropriate action was to "kill it [the injured child] to put it out of its misery." While considered distasteful, this death excited little controversy among the participants, presumably since the initial wounding of the child was not considered intentional. Nor did anyone comment on the fact that a leg wound was not necessarily a fatal injury.[31]

In contrast, the conscious targeting of children generated far more unease, as revealed in a series of incidents involving Conner and a settler known as "Sugar-foot Jack." In the course of yet another campaign against the Apache, a band of American civilians, having found an Indian camp, proceeded to burn the shelters and supplies to prevent any surviving Apaches from reclaiming them. In his search of the encampment, Sugarfoot Jack happened upon an Apache infant, whom he tossed into one of the fires and watched burn alive. Observing Sugarfoot's behaviour, several other Americans attempted to rescue the baby or at least to reclaim "the little, black, crisped body" from the flames. But "the skin peeling off every time it was touched made the 'boys' sick," and they left the dead child in the still-smoldering ashes. Meanwhile, Sugarfoot Jack located yet another Apache infant. Soon he could be seen to "dance it upon his knee and tickle it under the chin and handle the babe in the manner of a playful mother." When he tired of this game, Sugarfoot drew his pistol, a heavy dragoon revolver. Placing his weapon against the child's head, he pulled the trigger, "bespatter[ing] his clothes and face with infant brains."[32]

Sugarfoot's callous treatment of these Apache infants, in Conner's words, "threw the apple of discord into our ranks." Noting the repugnance that his behaviour had occasioned among his compatriots, Sugarfoot prudently retreated into the brush, leaving the rest of the party to debate the appropriate forais of warfare against the Apaches. Some Americans "thought that it was no harm to kill an Indian of any age, size, or sex," nor did they much care how such killing was done. Others declared that "they could not nor would not support such brutality" and refused to participate in any campaign that countenanced a policy of intentionally targeting Indian women and children. The two sides proved so incapable of reconciling their differences that eventually the party split. Of the original group of one hundred or so, 17 (of which Conner was one) quit the campaign. An ex-soldier with similar qualms about the campaigners' goal of exterminating all the Indians they encountered joined the dissidents a few days later. The man apparently felt strongly enough about absenting himself from the expedition that he was willing to travel alone for several days across a terrain filled with Apaches seeking revenge for the Anglo raiders in their midst.[33]

Despite the obvious challenges in generalizing from this single experience, the break up of this campaign may give us a rough sense of the proportion of "ordinary men" in mid-nineteenth century Arizona who opposed the most extreme forms of violence against Native Americans. If Conner's counts are correct, a little less than 20 percent of those on the campaign opposed a policy of total extermination. Given that those Euro-Americans concerned about killing Apache women and children likely would not have joined such an expedition in the first place, it may be that the proportion of settlers opposed to extermination might be even higher, although still a probable minority of the Anglo-American population in Arizona. (Note, too, that Conner and his fellow dissidents expressed far fewer qualms about killing adult males.)[34]

The limits to settler bestialization of the Apache acquire yet another layer of complexity if we note that the same public that regularly clamoured for the extermination of wolf-like Apache also demonstrated considerable anxiety about other forms of violence towards animals. The leading newspapers in Arizona, the *Weekly Arizonan* and the *Arizona Citizen,* both featured prominent editorials in the early 1870s condemning cruelty to livestock and calling for the territorial legislature to pass an animal welfare law. In addition, the *Citizen* urged reforming the severe, animal-like punishments, such as branding, meted out to disobedient soldiers in the territory, which it considered "opposed to the dictates of humanity." It was not the case, in other words, that Anglo-American settlers stood apart from the moral reform movements sweeping Europe and the Americas in the latter half of the nineteenth century. Yet at the same time that settlers were expanding their ethical compass in certain directions, developing increased empathy for domestic animals and fellow members of their own society, they were also struggling to devise new ways of expressing difference. This dynamic crystallized in the peculiar form of bestialization attached to the Apache—the comparison of the Apache not to animals in general but to a specific, feared predator already subject to extermination campaigns.[35]

Much like their civilian counterparts, the U.S. Army also grappled with the question of what forms of violence were appropriate to use on the Apache. Moreover, for all its aspirations of a professional detachment in the use of force, the army found itself as prone as settlers to portraying the Apache as animal-like others. Expeditions became in many military dispatches "hunts"; the Apache inevitably "wolves." The 1867 report of the U.S. Secretary of War, for example, referred to fighting Apaches as "more like hunting wild animals than any kind of regular warfare" and noted that the Apaches "like wolves . . . are ever wandering." As the U.S. Army officer Davis Britton, posted to Arizona a decade later put it, "[W]e hunted [Apaches] and killed them as we hunted and killed wolves."[36]

The dilemma of how far the military should go in exterminating these Apache "wolves" manifested itself most clearly during the short-lived Confederate occupancy of Arizona Territory. Marching west from Texas, Lieutenant Colonel John Baylor and his men occupied Arizona in the summer of 1861 and soon set about organizing a campaign to "clean out the Apache Indians." In March of 1862, Baylor ordered his subordinates to entice the Apaches into treaty negotiations, kill the adults, and enslave the children. "[U]se all means to persuade the Apaches or any tribe to come in for the purpose of making peace, and when you get them together kill all the grown Indians and take the children prisoners and sell them to defray the expense of killing the Indians. Buy whisky and such other goods as may be necessary."[37]

Baylor's willingness to undertake extermination in such a duplicitous manner disgusted Jefferson Davis, the president of the Confederacy. Davis denounced Baylor's plan when a copy of it reached his desk as "an infamous crime" and demanded an investigation into the Colonel's behaviour. Although Baylor offered as an excuse the rumour (quickly disproved) that the Congress of the Confederate States had passed a law "declaring extermination to all hostile Indians," the centrepiece of his defense was that for an opponent such as the Apache—prone to "barbarities almost beyond conception"—the only remedy was the "extermination of the grown Indians and making slaves of the children."

Such a solution seemed eminently moral to Baylor. Southern slave-owners had long condoned the peculiar institution as a method for domesticating the savage peoples of Africa. Given that numerous scientists at the time maintained that "[a]s relates to the mental cultivation and improvement, the Indian and African races resemble the inferior animals," Baylor was puzzled why the "extension of that system [slavery] to the youth of the Indian race [was] a measure deserving of rebuke." Yet as willing as he was to lead the Confederacy into a prolonged, bloody war to ensure African Americans' enslavement, Jefferson Davis balked at exterminating Apache adults. Despite his pressing demands for manpower, Davis ordered the Confederate Secretary of War, G. W. Randolph, to remove Baylor from command and revoke his authority to raise troops.[38]

The Union army, which reoccupied Arizona in 1862, adopted a policy towards the Apache that, on its face, seemed less harsh than Baylor's; it certainly excited less internal debate among Union officials. In practice, however, it, too, laid the groundwork for the potential extermination of the Apaches. Upon his arrival in the territory, James H. Carleton, the commander of the U.S. forces, declared that the Apaches "should not be fired upon or molested until they committed toward us some act of hostility. They were to be the aggressors so far as this column was concerned." Though this arrangement held for several months, its proffered leniency, in the minds of Carleton and his aides, justified the severest of measures should the Union's good will be abused. As First Lieutenant Ben C. Cutler of the California Column advised a subordinate in early 1862, "[i]f the Tontos [Apaches] are hostile he is to shoot or hang every one he sees." When in Carleton's view an Apache band violated the truce with Union forces a few months later, the colonel called for devastating reprisals on the Indians "for their treachery and their crimes": "There is to be no council held with the Indians nor any talks. The men are to be slain whenever and wherever they can be found."[39]

Unlike Baylor, Carleton did not envision engaging in deceptive parlays or enslaving Apache children after exterminating their parents. But to many observers, the ultimate difference was slight: the disappearance of the Apache from the Territory seemed as likely under Union as Confederate rule. Carleton's cavalrymen soon adopted a marching song that went as follows:

*We'll whip the Apache*
*We'll exterminate the race*
*Of thieves and assassins*
*Who the human form disgrace*

James McNulty, a surgeon with the California Column, concluded: "[the Apaches'] race is nearly run. Extinction is only a question of time."[40]

In a telling juxtaposition, it so happened that Carleton's campaigns against the Apache in Arizona coincided with the U.S.'s effort to codify it rules of war. The ongoing Civil War, arguably the first example of industrialized, total war in human existence, had fostered the need among Union leaders for clear guidelines for their campaigns in the Confederate heartland, where they confronted for the first time large civilian populations and widespread guerilla resistance. For advice, Union officials turned to a former Prussian solider turned law professor named Francis Lieber. The resulting "Lieber Code," approved by President Lincoln on April 24, 1863, as General Order No. 100, established policies for dealing with prisoners and for distinguishing between civilians and combatants. Significantly, however, Lieber's rules only applied to certain kinds of opponents. His code drew a sharp distinction between "barbaric" and "civilized" military practices, with the implication that the Apaches' behaviour released the U.S. from following the same moral standards that applied to the Southern secessionists. Thus, although the U.S. was engaged in two conflicts at the same time in the 1860s—one against the Confederacy, another against Indian peoples in the West—it saw fit to practice a quite different form of "total war" in these two campaigns. The U.S. sought to defeat Confederates, but it never contemplated exterminating them as it did with the Apache.[41]

As Euro-Americans grappled with the problem indigenous groups such as the Apache posed for their agrarian vision of the American West, the Apaches in turn wrestled with the far more pressing problem of their attempted extermination. Accessing Apaches' perspectives on the vast wave of violence breaking over them in the latter half of the nineteenth century presents numerous challenges. In particular, sources documenting the Apache point of view tend to be sparse—in part because the hundreds of Apaches killed during this time left no record of their experiences, in part because the accounts of most Apache survivors remained in the far more perishable realm of oral testimony, and in part because the Apache often favoured non-verbal forms of communication, such as cutting one's hair to signal grief at a family member's death. Nonetheless, from the few available fragments one can piece together at least a partial view onto Apache experiences of this painful period in their history. These materials underscore the Apaches' efforts not only to rescue their lives and humanity in the face of their bestilization by outsiders but to depict extermination not as a natural, inevitable process, but one connected to definite human actions.[42]

Even prior to the American annexation of their homeland, the Apache possessed a tradition of what one folklorist has termed "narratives of horror," detailing their experiences with Spanish and Mexican colonists. The defining feature of such narratives was the mass murder of an Apache community in a supposedly peaceful Mexican village. Seeking trade, an Apache party would visit a Mexican town, where they would be received cordially, often with gifts of alcohol. Once lulled into a false sense of security—a condition exacerbated by the disorienting effects of the liquor—the Apache found themselves under attack from, as one put it, "our treacherous friends[,] the Mexicans."[43]

Different towns provided the setting for these tales, depending on each band's experiences. But such narratives of horrors circulated widely, shared not only between groups of Apache but with outsiders as well. Upon encountering a group of American fur trappers in the 1820s, for example, one "indignant" Apache community described how "a large party of their people had come in to make peace with the Spaniards, of which they pretended to be very desirous; that with such pretexts, they had decoyed the party within their walls, and then commenced butchering them." Almost three decades later, one of the leaders of the Chiricahua Apache, *Gandazistichíid* ("The One with Reddish Sleeve Covers" or Mangas Coloradas), offered a similar account of his encounters with Mexican trickery:

> Some time ago my people were invited to a feast; aguardiente, or whiskey, was there; my people drank and became intoxicated, and were lying asleep, when a party of Mexicans came in and beat out their brains with clubs. At another time a trader was sent among us from Chihuahua. While innocently engaged in trading . . . a cannon concealed behind the goods was fired upon my people, and quite a number were killed. Since that, Chihuahua has offered a reward for our scalps, $150 each . . . How can we make peace with such people?

The prevalence of such episodes led the Chiricahua Apache Jason Benitez, "an eyewitness to the Casas Grandes massacre" in which Mexicans attacked his kins-people after giving them liberal quantities of liquor the night before, to reflect that the history of this era was little more than "a series of treacherous attacks made upon us by whites or Mexicans."[44]

Such stories of treachery imparted lessons both obvious and subtle to their Apache listeners. Most immediately, the tales reinforced Apache beliefs as to the perils of trusting those outside one's clan or local group. The apparent generosity of others, these stories suggested, often masked an ulterior motive. Many accounts also contained a pointed critique of the deleterious effect that alcohol had upon the Apache, clouding their judgment and rendering them liable to deception.

Similar anxieties manifested themselves in the tense parlays with Americans in the 1860s. In 1864, for example, a group of Apaches met to negotiate with a number of U.S. Army officers. During the encounter, the Apache pointed to the experience of the neighbouring Navajo Indians to voice their suspicion that the Americans were interested not in peace but rather in extermination. "They said that the Zuñis [a nearby group of agricultural Indians] had told them that after the Navajoes surrendered we had killed all the men, and left none alive but the women and children, of whom we made slaves."[45] During a similar parlay two years later, an Apache elder proclaimed, "he was opposed to making peace. The whites were only doing it to kill them." Although the army tried to persuade the Apache otherwise by offering them a cow, the Indians remained "apprehensive of treachery." That night, apparently convinced by the elder's warnings, the Apache slipped away, leaving behind many of their goods in their haste to escape what they believed to be their imminent extermination.[46]

Although Apaches often responded to Euro-American settlers through violence of their own, Apache hostilities nonetheless unfolded in a culturally specific pattern. Central to the Apache conceptualization of violence was the existence of a sharp divide between raiding (perhaps best translated from the Apache language as "to search out enemy property") and warfare ("to take death from an enemy"). Only the latter activity sought to exact casualties, usually in revenge for Apache losses; the former normally limited itself to seizing useful goods such as livestock.[47] Even in the late 1860s, after years of bitter conflict with settlers bent on exterminating them, many Apache bands maintained this division. While the distinction between raiding and warfare was frequently lost on Euro-Americans, observers could not help but notice the curious behaviour of the supposedly wolf-like Apache. In the spring of 1866, for example, after seizing a group of freight wagons outside Tucson, the Apaches amused themselves by aiming arrows at the Anglo teamsters' chests, releasing their bow strings with their right hands, and catching their arrows with their left. Having demonstrated their ability to kill the teamsters but their refusal to do so, the Apache then allowed the men to depart unharmed. Similar incidents occurred with enough regularity that the Arizona press, for all its advocacy of exterminating the Apache, admitted in 1869 that "instances are known where the Apache, after having captured teams, 'had yet the power but not the will to hurt,' and permitted those of the party who survived the combat just decided in his favor to depart unmolested."[48]

Nor was Apache violence during the nineteenth century limited solely to conflicts between themselves and settlers. Conflicts also took place between the Apache and other indigenous groups—including not only traditional Native opponents such as the Tohono O'odham and Akimel O'odham but also rival Apache bands. Even though settlers tended to think of their foes as parts of a single, unified "Apache nation," the borderland's Apache communities were in fact divided into scores of politically separate and, at times, mutually suspicious bands. Hostilities between these groups were not unknown, and it was ultimately by exploiting this divide and enlisting the members of one Apache band to fight another that the U.S. managed to achieve military dominance over the Apache in the closing decades of the nineteenth century. Apaches found the Apache-on-Apache violence that the U.S. Army unleashed among them particularly unnerving, not only because it was harder to evade fellow Apaches than soldiers or settlers, but because the military demanded extreme forms of behaviour such as the decapitation of "renegade" Apaches.

As the Chiricahua Apache leader Geronimo (*Guyaałé* "The Yawner") complained during a parlay with the army, "Sometimes a man does something and men are sent out to bring in his head. I don't want such things to happen to us. I don't want that we should be killing each other."[49]

To many nineteenth century Euro-Americans, the conflict with the Apache was not an isolated struggle over scarce resources or for social dominance in a remote corner of the U.S.-Mexico borderlands. Rather, it was but one facet of a planetary process, in which American Indians, along with the native peoples and animals of Australia, Tasmania, the Pacific Islands, and elsewhere, were fated to disappear in the face of "civilization." The nineteenth century heyday of European imperialism, of which the American West was an integral part, thus can also be considered, in the language of the day, the era of global extermination. Indeed, perhaps no better summation of this period—its blending of animal and human images, its embrace of terms such as extermination tied to contemporary thinking about the natural world—can be found in the phrase that Joseph Conrad so famously articulated at century's end in *Heart of Darkness:* "Exterminate all the brutes!"[50]

While there is much to be gained in reckoning with how to apply present-day definitions, such as Raphael Lemkin's twentieth century neologism, genocide, to the brutalities of the nineteenth century, there are also virtues to be found in following Conrad's footsteps and assessing the past on its own terms. To apply the concept of extermination to nineteenth century incidents of mass violence in no ways diminishes the horror of these events. Nor does it lessen their moral repugnance, for even within the moral universe of the nineteenth century, there were those who saw fit to decry extermination. "To exterminate the aborigines of the forest and the mountains," contended E.A. Graves, Indian Agent in New Mexico in the 1850s, for example, "is a policy that no enlightened citizen or statesman will propose or advocate."[51]

What rooting an analysis of historic atrocities in a term like extermination does allow, however, is a deeper understanding of how violence functioned in the past: the cultural practices in which it was embedded, the internal tensions it contained, the responses of indigenous peoples to it. One might even venture a periodization of violence, with the nineteenth century constituting the age of extermination, and the era of genocide representing only the period after the term's coining in 1943. Such a formulation does not imply that genocide did not take place before the mid-nineteenth century or that extermination ended in the 1940s; only that the dominant reference point underwent a profound shift at this moment in time.

For its part, the "new Indian history" reminds us that taking the past on its own terms requires paying much more attention to those whom colonists sought to displace. As the nineteenth century borderlands reveal, even in an era dominated by a discourse about the extermination of Indian peoples, Native Americans adopted a diverse array of responses to outside pressures. If all Native groups in the borderlands experienced the oppressions of colonialism, some, such as the Tohono O'odham and Akimel O'odham, unlike their "Apache" neighbours, never became the targets of Euro-American campaigns of extermination. Moreover, in a few cases, Indian communities assisted settlers' exterminatory campaigns against other indigenous groups. Such experiences—and the thorny questions of culpability that they raise—also need to be considered part of the Native experience of colonial violence.

Above all, closer attention to indigenous experiences can help us unravel the conceptual confusion at the heart of the Euro-American concept of extermination. Anglos often employed extermination in a way that blurred human and natural agency, with the implication that extermination resulted less from conscious human acts than from inevitable natural laws. The remarks of Charles Caldwell in the early nineteenth century—"Civilization is destined to exterminate them [American Indians], in common with the wild animals, among which they have lived"—offer a telling example of the age of extermination's disconcerting vagueness. Was "civilization" here a decision-making entity or just a bundle of social traits? Would the predicted extermination be brought about through the direct application of violence or through more indirect means? Was the extermination of Native Americans to be accomplished in an identical manner to that of "wild animals"?[52] In contrast, Apache "narratives of horrors" about their betrayal and massacre at the hands of outsiders cut through such obfuscations, highlighting the very human decisions underlying the terrifying violence that Apache communities suffered during the age of extermination. At the very moment when settlers were attempting to bestialize the Apaches as wolf-like others, the Apaches, it turns out, were endeavoring to accomplish the opposite: to denaturalize the violence of colonialism and show its all-too-human face.

## NOTES

1 King Woolsey to Gen. Carleton, March 29, 1864. Plaintiff's Exhibit No. 95, Box 401. Western Apache, Docket 22, Records of the Indian Claims Commission, RG 279, National Archives—Washington, DC. Emphasis appears in the original.

2 Charles Darwin, *The Origin of Species by Means of Natural Selection and The Descent of Man and Selection in Relation to Sex* (Chicago: Encyclopedia Britannica, 1952 [1871]), p 336; Ben Kiernan, *Blood and Soil: A World History of Genocide and Extermination from Sparta to Darfur* (New Haven: Yale University Press, 2007), pp 29–33; Patrick Wolfe, "Settler colonialism and the elimination of the Native," *Journal of Genocide Research,* Vol 8, No 4, 2006, p 388. For more on the relationship between Darwin and genocide, see Tony Barta, "Mr. Darwin's shooters: on natural selection and the naturalizing of genocide," *Patterns of Prejudice,* Vol 39, No 2, 2005, pp 116–137.

3 George E. Ellis, *The Red Man and the White Man in North America* (Boston: Little, Brown, 1882), pp 4, 588.

4 For a useful overview of some of the tensions between genocide studies and Native American history, see Michael A. McDonnell and A. Dirk Moses, "Raphael Lemkin as historian of genocide in the Americas," *Journal of Genocide Research,* Vol 7, No 4, 2005, pp 501–529. For examples of recent Native-authored histories, see Jennifer Nez Denetdale, *Reclaiming Diné History: The Legacies of Navajo Chief Manuelito and Juanita* (Tucson: University of Arizona Press, 2007); Ned Blackhawk, *Violence over the Land: Indians and Empires in the Early American West* (Cambridge: Harvard University Press, 2006); Waziyatawin Angela Wilson, *Remember This! Dakota Decolonization and the Eli Taylor Narratives,* with translations from the Dakota Text by Wahpetunwin Carolynn Schommer (Lincoln: University of Nebraska Press, 2005); Steven J. Cram, *The Road on Which We Came: A History of the Western Shoshone* (Salt Lake City: University of Utah Press, 1994). Of these works, only Wilson's makes passing reference to the U.N. Convention on the Prevention and Punishment of the Crime of Genocide. Wilson, *Remember This,* p 54.

5 For such a mythologized American Indian group, the Apaches have been remarkably understudied by ethno-historians. The best short introductions are perhaps Keith Basso, "Western Apache," in: Alfonso Ortiz (Ed.), *Handbook of North American Indians,* Vol 10, *Southwest* (Washington, DC: Smithsonian Institution Press, 1983), pp 462–488; and Dale Curtis Miles and Paul R. Machula, *History of the San Carlos Apache.* Rev. ed. (San Carlos, AZ: San Carlos Apache Historic and Cultural Preservation Office, 1998). For more on Apache terms for themselves, see Willem J. de Reuse, *A Practical Grammar of the San Carlos Apache Language,* with the assistance of Phillip Goode (Munich: Lincom, 2006), 478; and Dorothy Bray (Ed.), *Western Apache-English Dictionary: A Community-Generated Bilingual Dictionary,* in collaboration with the White Mountain Apache Tribe (Tempe, AZ: Bilingual Press/Editori al Bilingüe, 1998), p 287.

6 Bernardo de Gálvez, *Instructions for Governing the Interior Provinces of New Spain, 1786,* ed. and trans. by Donald E. Worcester. (Berkeley: Quivara Society, 1951), pp 38, 41, 43; José María Tornei, *Memoria del secretario de estado y del despacho de guerra y marina, leida á las cámaras del congreso nacional de la República Mexicana, en enero de 1844* (México: Imprenta de I. Cumplido, [1844]), p 53. David J. Weber argues that Spanish references to extermination in the eighteenth century implied a tactic of total war rather than a little desire to kill every member of a given Indian community. See Weber, *Bárbaros: Spaniards and Their Savages in the Age of Enlightenment* (New Haven: Yale University Press, 2005), pp 150–151. The contrary position can be found in Ricardo León García and Carlos González Herrera, *Civilizar o exterminar: Tarahumaras y Apaches en Chihuahua, siglo xix* (México: Centro de Investigaciones y Estudios Superiores en Antropología Social, 2000).

7 Richard Trench, *A Select Glossary of English Words Used Formerly in Sense Different from their Present* (London: MacMillan, 1873), p 91; James Donald (Ed.), *Chamber's Etymological Dictionary of the English Language* (London and Edinburgh: W&R Chambers, 1878), p 170; Charles John Smith, *Synonyms and Antonyms* (London: Bell and Daldy, 1867), p 168. See also Kiernan, *Blood and Soil,* pp 15–16.

8 Camillo C.C. Carr, "The days of the empire—Arizona, 1866–1869," *Journal of the United States Cavalry Association,* Vol 2, No 4, 1889, pp 3–22, in: Peter Cozzens (Ed.), *Eyewitnesses to the Indian Wars, 1865–1890* (Mechanicsburg, PA: Stackpole Books, 2001), p. 19.

9 *Weekly Arizona Miner,* October 26, 1864; Sylvester Mowry, *Arizona and Sonora: The Geography, History, and Resources of the Silver Region of North America* (New York: Harper and Brothers, 3rd ed., 1864), p 68.

10 *Washington Post,* September 17, 1881.

11 John Nicolson, (Ed.), *The Arizona of Joseph Pratt Allyn: Letters from a Pioneer Judge* (Tucson: University of Arizona Press, 1974), p 68.

12 Ibid., pp 70, 76; *Arizona Miner,* November 30, 1866 and January 26, 1867.

13 *Acts, Resolutions and Memorials Adopted by the First Legislative Assembly of the Territory of Arizona* (Prescott: Arizona Miner, 1865), pp 69–70, 78–79.

14 Daniel Ellis Conner, *Joseph Reddeford Walker and the Arizona Adventure,* Donald J. Berthrong and Odessa Davenport (Eds.) (Norman: University of Oklahoma Press, 1956), p 188; Wesley Merritt, "Incidents of Indian campaigning in Arizona," *Harper's New Monthly Magazine* 80:459 (April 1890), pp 725–731, in Cozzens (Ed.), *Eyewitnesses to the Indian Wars,* p 156.

15 For more on "defensive conquest," see Richard White, "Frederick Jackson Turner and Buffalo Bill" in; James R. Grossman (Ed.), *The Frontier in American Culture* (Berkeley: University of California Press, 1994), pp 6–10; and Philip J. Deloria, *Indians in Unexpected Places* (Lawrence: University Press of Kansas, 2004), pp 15–21.

16 *The War of the Rebellion: A Compilation of the Official Records of the Union and Confederate Armies.* Series 1, Volume L (Washington, DC: GPO, 1897), p 1247; William A. Bell, "On the basin of Colorado and the great basin of North America," *Journal of the Royal Geographical Society of London,* Vol 39 (1869), p 104; John Cremony, "The Apache race," *The Overland Monthly* 1, September 1868, p 203. For a similar trope east of the Mississippi, see Patrick Brantlinger, *Dark Vanishings: Discourse on the Extinction of Primitive Races, 1800–1930* (Ithaca: Cornell University Press, 2003), pp 50–52.

17 Conner, *Joseph Reddeford Walker and the Arizona Adventure,* pp 227–228, 302–303.

18 Ibid, pp 304–305.

19 J. Ross Browne, *Adventures in the Apache Country: A Tour Through Arizona and Sonora* (New York: Harper and Brothers, 1869), p 100.

20 Susan E. Wallace, *The Land of the Pueblos* (Troy, NY: Nims & Knight, 1889), p 143; John Cremony, "The Apache Race," *Overland Monthly* 1, September 1868, p 203.

21 Campion quoted in Ellis, *The Red Man and the White Man in North America,* 101.

22 Nantan Lupan [pseudo.], "An Apache Dance," *Outing,* June 1893, p 190.

23 *Army and Navy Journal,* April 27, 1872, in Cozzens (Ed.), *Eyewitnesses to the Indian Wars,* 113; Mowry, *Arizona and Sonora,* 68; John Cremony, *Life Among the Apaches* (San Francisco: A. Roman, 1868), p 188. See also Sherry L. Smith, *The View from Officers' Row: Army Perceptions of Western Indians* (Tucson: University of Arizona Press, 1990), pp 157–158.

24 Rick McIntyre (Ed.), *War Against the Wolf: America's Campaign to Exterminate the Wolf* (Stillwater, MN: Voyageur Press, 1995), pp 30, 41–46; James A. Tober, *Who Owns the Wildlife? The Political Economy of Conservation in Nineteenth-Century America* (Westport, CT: Greenwood Press, 1981), pp 23–24; William Cronon, *Changes in the Land: Indians, Colonists, and the Ecology of New England* (New York: Hill and Wang, 1983), pp 132–134; Virginia DeJohn Anderson, *Creatures of Empire: How Domestic Animals Transformed Early America* (New York: Oxford University Press, 2004), pp 147; Thomas R. Dunlap, *Saving America's Wildlife* (Princeton: Princeton University Press, 1988), p 5.

25 W. Weissenbom, "On the influence of man in modifying the zoological features of the glove," *The Magazine of Natural History 2,* March 1838, p 124; William T. Hornaday, *Wild Life Conservation in Theory and Practice* (New Haven: Yale University Press, 1914), pp 140–141; Corbin quoted in Bruce Hampton, "Shark of the plains: early western encounters with wolves," *Montana: The Magazine of Western History* 46, Spring 1996, p 2.

26 "The passing of the Indian?" *Everywhere* 24, March 1909, p 47. The editors overstated the bounty for Apache scalps by close to a factor of ten. See also Stanton Davis Kirkham, *The Ministry of Beauty* (San Francisco: Paul Elder, 1907), p 121.

27 Alonzo E. Davis, *Pioneer Days in Arizona by One Who Was There,* pp 106–107, Huntington: MS Film 135. The settler King Woolsey also used strychnine against Indians on at least one occasion. See John G. Bourke, *On the Border with Crook* (Lincoln: University of Nebraska Press, 1971 [1891]), p 118. For more on the extermination campaign against wolves in the nineteenth century, see Peter Coates, "'Unusually Cunning, Vicious, and Treacherous': The Extermination of the Wolf in United States History," in: Mark Levene and Penny Roberts (Eds.), *The Massacre in History* (New York: Bergahn Books, 1999), pp 163–184; Jon T. Coleman, *Vicious: Wolves and Men in America* (New Haven: Yale University Press, 2004); and Stanley P. Young, "Nux Vomica and the Wolf," (unpublished paper in possession of author). I am indebted to Jon T. Coleman for sharing this last document with me.

28 Samuel Cozzens, *The Marvellous Country: Or, Three Years in Arizona and New Mexico* (Boston: Lee and Shepard, 1876), pp 83, 118–119. The possible translation of Mangas Coloradas's name was provided to me by the Apache linguist Willem de Reuse (personal communication, July 19, 2007). A similar paradox surrounding slavery's dehumanization is explored in David Brion Davis, *Challenging the Boundaries of Slavery* (Cambridge: Harvard University Press, 2003), pp 6–7.

29 Conner, *Joseph Reddeford Walker and the Arizona Adventure,* p 232.

30 Walter Scribner Schuyler to George Washington Schuyler, September 29, 1872, WS 79, Huntington Library; Conner, *Joseph Reddeford Walker and the Arizona Adventure,* p 232.

31 Crook quoted in Karl H. Schlesier, *Josanie's War* (Norman: University of Oklahoma Press, 1998), p 81; Conner, *Joseph Reddeford Walker and the Arizona Adventure,* p 232.

32 Conner, *Joseph Reddeford Walker and the Arizona Adventure,* pp 266–267.

33 Ibid, pp 266–268.

34 The issue of what brings "ordinary" men to commit acts of extraordinary violence is at the heart of Christopher Browning, *Ordinary Men: Reserve Police Battalion 101 and the Final Solution in Poland* (New York: HarperCollins, 1992).

35 *Weekly Arizona Miner,* April 30, 1870 and July 27, 1872; *Weekly Arizonan,* January 1, 1870, January 8, 1870, and February 26, 1870; *Arizona Citizen,* February 4, 1871, March 2, 1872, and October 12, 1872. Branding with a "D" or "T" was a military punishment for desertion or theft. For later articles decrying animal brutality, see *Arizona Daily Citizen,* August 5, 1893, and August 7, 1893. For an insightful discussion of the downsides of the rise of the idea of animal and human rights, see Lynn Hunt, *Inventing Human Rights: A History* (New York: W.W. Norton, 2007), pp 209–214.

36 *Report of the Secretary of War, 1867* (Washington, DC: GPO, 1867), pp 91, 129; Davis Britton, *The Truth About Geronimo* (New Haven: Yale University Press, 1929), p 50.

37 *The War of the Rebellion: A Compilation of the Official Records of the Union and Confederate Armies,* Series 1, Volume IV (Washington, DC: GPO, 1902),

pp 20–21; *The War of the Rebellion,* L, pp 399, 942. For more on the Confederate occupation of Arizona, see L. Boyd Finch, *Confederate Pathway to the Pacific: Major Sherod Hunter and the Arizona Territory, C.S.A.* (Tucson: The Arizona Historical Society, 1996).

38 *The War of the Rebellion: A Compilation of the Official Records of the Union and Confederate Armies,* Series 1, Volume XV (Washington, DC: GPO, 1886), pp 857, 914, 917, 919; Finch, Confederate Pathway to the Pacific, p 176. For the comparison of African Americans and Native Americans to "inferior animals," see Charles Caldwell, "On the unity of the human race," *The North American Medical and Surgical Journal* 12, October 1831, p 388.

39 *The War of the Rebellion,* L, p 929, 1147; *The War of the Rebellion,* XV, pp 579–580.

40 Andrew E. Masich, *The Civil War in Arizona: The Story of the California Volunteers, 1861–1865* (Norman: University of Oklahoma Press, 2006), pp 63–64; *The War of the Rebellion,* L, p 367.

41 For the original text of Lieber's code, see *The War of the Rebellion: A Compilation of the Official Records of the Union and Confederate Armies.* Series 3, Volume III. (Washington, DC: GPO, 1899), pp 148–164; and *The War of the Rebellion: A Compilation of the Official Records of the Union and Confederate Armies,* Series 3, Volume II (Washington, DC: GPO, 1899), pp 301–309. For more on the contrast between the U.S. Army's treatment of Confederates and American Indians, see Peter Maguire, *Law and War: An American Story* (New York: Columbia University Press, 2001), pp 36–40; Mark Grimsley, *The Hard Hand of War: Union Military Policy Toward Southern Civilians, 1861–1865* (New York: Cambridge University Press, 1995), p 18; and Mark Grimsley, "'Rebels' and 'Redskins': U.S. military conduct toward white southerners and Native Americans in comparative perspective,": in Mark Grimsley and Clifford J. Rogers (Eds.), *Civilians in the Path of War* (Lincoln: University of Nebraska Press, 2002), pp 137–161.

42 On the uses of silence in Western Apache culture, see Keith Basso, "To Give Up on Words," in: Keith Basso and Morris Opler (Eds.), *Apachean Culture, History and Ethnology,* Anthropological Papers of the University of Arizona No. 21 (Tuscon: University of Arizona Press, 1971); and Granville Goodwin, *The Social Organization of the Western Apache* (Chicago: University of Chicago Press, 1942), pp 518–521.

43 Jason Betzinez with Wilbur Sturtevant Nye, *I Fought with Geronimo* (Harrisburg, PA: Stackpole, 1959), p. 82; Joseph C. Jastrzembski, "Treacherous towns in Mexico: Chiricahua Apache personal narratives of horrors," *Western Folklore* 54 (July 1995), pp 169–196. See also the tale related by Geronimo in J. Lee Humfreville, *Twenty Years Among Our Hostile Indians* (New York: Hunter, 1899), pp 196–197.

44 Timothy Flint (Ed.), *The Personal Narrative of James O. Pattie of Kentucky* (Chicago: Lakeside Press, 1930 [1831]), p 114; Mangas Coloradas quoted in Thomas Edwin Farish, *History of Arizona* (Phoeniz, AZ: N.p., 1915), II, p 151–152; Betzinez, *I Fought with Geronimo,* pp 1, 80.

45 Report of Julius Shaw, July 14, 1864, in *War of the Rebellion, L,* pp 370–376.

46 Report from Fort McDowell, June 21,1866, p 3, Clarence Bennett Papers, MS 69, Arizona Historical Society.

47 Keith H. Basso (Ed.) *Western Apache Raiding and Warfare: From the Notes of Grenville Goodwin.* (Tucson: University of Arizona Press, 1971), pp 16–17.

48 *Weekly Arizonan,* May 15, 1869, p 3; June 4, 1870, p 3; *Arizona Weekly Citizen,* August 24, 1872, p 2. See also Vance Wampler, *Arizona: Years of Courage, 1832–1910* (Phoenix: Quail Run Publications, 1984), pp 127–128.

49 Geronimo quoted in *Letter from the Secretary of War, Transmitting Correspondence Regarding the Apache Indians* (51st Congress, 1st sess., Sen. Executive Doc, No. 88), 12. Translation of Geronimo's name provided by Apache linguist Willem de Reuse (personal communication, July 19, 2007). The larger issues connected to indigenous views of genocide are taken up in Jeff Ostler, "The question of genocide in U.S. history" (paper in possession of author).

50 Joseph Conrad, *Heart of Darkness,* Robert Kimbrough (Ed.) (New York: W.W. Norton, rev. ed., 1971), p 51. See also Sven Lindquist, *"Exterminate all the Brutes": One Man's Odyssey into the Heart of Darkness and the Origins of European Genocide,* trans, by Joan Tate (New York: New Press, 1996). The global discourse on the extinction of indigenous peoples is explored in Brantlinger, *Dark Vanishings,* pp 1–16.

51 *Annual Report of the Commissioner of Indian Affairs, 1854* (Washington, DC: Beverley Tucker, 1854), p 389.

52 Caldwell, "On the unity of the human race," p 388.

# Part VI

# CROSSINGS

By the close of the nineteenth century, the governments of the United States, Mexico, and Canada had extinguished plural sovereignty throughout nearly all of North America. Indigenous peoples obviously still lived in the continent in large numbers (though the early 20th century would see their demographic nadir), and in certain cases maintained considerable autonomy over their internal affairs. And tribes would continue the struggle over sovereignty throughout the 20th and 21st centuries, on a variety of fronts. But by 1900, nearly everywhere in the continent states had final authority over vital questions concerning native land, resources, politics, economy, law, education, even family and culture. Where once the continent had been fractured into hundreds of borderlands—a vast, shifting jigsaw of sovereign polities with distinct if contested claims to territory—now North America's sovereign geography had been brutally simplified into two immense borders dividing Canada and Mexico from the United States.

State boundaries were nothing new, of course; and, as the chapters by DuVal and Jacoby made clear, expanding states exerted real power in borderland regions long before 1900. But for most of the nineteenth century border policy as such meant little to people's daily lives. To pick just one example, Mexico criminalized American immigration into the state of Coahuila y Texas in 1830, and indifferent American 'illegals' (with their African-American slaves) simply flocked across the Mexican border in greater numbers than ever before, rebelling against Mexican rule five years later.[1]

Borders took on considerably more substance by the late nineteenth century. Starting around the second half of the nineteenth century, empires and nation-states around the world tried to master space by harnessing new technologies: steamships, railroads, telegraphs, and new firearms technologies, most obviously, but also breakthroughs in industry, medicine, international finance, and agriculture. A new emphasis on territoriality held out the promise of greater control of resources and of people. Pursuing that promise meant projecting power at territorial borders.[2] In North America, nation-states partnered with each other to constrain Indians' cross-border mobility.

Though these partnerships were often halting and contentious, Mexico and the United States cooperated against Comanches, Kiowas, Apaches, and Yaquis, and Canada and the United States did the same against Iroquois, Sioux, Blackfeet, Métis, and other peoples around the northern border.[3] The subjugation of Indian polities accelerated regional connection to global capitalism. It made large (white) mining, ranching, and agricultural operations possible, led to dramatic increases in the non-native population, and encouraged greater and greater capital investment in both borderlands—all processes critical to and accelerated by the arrival of railroads. These transformations invited the growth of state power at different sites along the international borderlands. Though haltingly, incompletely, and often haphazardly, states began crafting and enforcing laws to manage movement across national boundaries.[4]

In the process states and the people they sought to govern had to grapple with many of the same basic issues so vexing to earlier borderland relationships. Most fundamentally, no matter how regulated, delimited, or militarized, modern borderlands are still sites of plural sovereignty. Everyone in the U.S.-Mexican and U.S.-Canadian borderlands seeking to make, enforce, or navigate policy is working near the hard spatial limit of state authority. To cross over the line is to enter a different and independent system of law and authority, a reality that affords both dangers and opportunities for individuals and for state sovereignty. The Columbian Exchange continues apace, and on both borders state regulation began partly in efforts to manage the crossing of animals, plants, and pathogens over national boundaries.[5] Critiques of supposedly deviant gender norms have been deployed on both borderlands to create and sustain hierarchies of power. Unsurprisingly, men and women of color have usually been the targets of this enduring borderland refrain.[6] Interstate war has long seemed unlikely on North America's international borders (with prominent exceptions, as when forces under Pancho Villa invaded the American Southwest and the U.S. Army invaded northern Mexico a century ago during the Mexican revolution). But the lure of economic opportunity and the fragmentation of authority invite competition that has often resulted in collective violence, from cross-border raiding campaigns to filibusters to the present-day warfare between cartels over prized drug-routes. And the borderlands continue to be particularly intense sites for discursive struggles over national identity, citizenship, race, justice, modernity, and rights.[7]

The essays in this last section of the volume reflect both the novelties and the continuities characterizing the continent's modern borderlands. All three chapters interrogate evolving state power in border regions, and uncover the perils and the possibilities people face when crossing national boundaries. Lissa Wadewitz's chapter examines the Pacific salmon fishery in the waters between western Washington and southwestern British Columbia. During the late nineteenth and early twentieth centuries, fishermen from both countries found their livelihoods threatened by conservation laws their governments enacted to govern salmon stocks. Environmental legislation frequently hurt working or poor people, but regulations proved especially difficult to enforce in borderlands precisely because that was where state power ended. Men from both countries evaded the laws simply by fishing over the line. In the process they improved their own fortunes, but also did lasting damage to the fishery.[8]

Erika Lee's chapter "Enforcing the Borders" considers Chinese exclusion from and immigration to the United States from the vantage point of both international borderlands. In defiance of the Chinese Exclusion Act (1882), thousands of Chinese immigrants entered the U.S. from Canada and Mexico. Lee demonstrates how their efforts to enter the country, and the varied state responses, differed north and south. Throughout she weaves a shared borderland story tacking back and forth between very different actors and perspectives. The exclusion acts and Chinese responses to them created the country's initial preoccupation with illegal immigration, and did much to shape racialized discourse surrounding borderland immigration generally.[9]

Finally, Geraldo Cadava interrogates the uneven development of the post-WWII U.S.-Mexican borderlands, through shared stories around both a north/south *and* an east/west axis. Postwar policies in both countries gradually fortified the border, but also encouraged population growth, development, and cross-border markets for goods and labor in places like ambos Nogales, a growing metropolitan region bisected by the international boundary. But just sixty miles west, in the similarly bisected lands of the Tohono O'odham nation, underdevelopment and state neglect remained the postwar norm. Comparing the shifting fortunes of people living in and crossing over these horizontal and vertical dividing lines, Cadava reveals the complex interplay of modernity and abandonment on the modern borderlands.

## NOTES

1 For Texas, see the classic work by David J. Weber, *The Mexican Frontier, 1821–1846: The American Southwest Under Mexico*. (Albuquerque: University of New Mexico Press, 1982), 158–78.

2 For technology, see Daniel R. Headrick, *Power Over Peoples: Technology, Environments, and Western Imperialism, 1400 to the Present* (Princeton, N.J: Princeton University Press, 2010). For territoriality, see Charles S. Maier, "Consigning the Twentieth Century to History: Alternative Narratives for the Modern Era," *American Historical Review* 105:3 (2000): 807–31.

3 On this point see for example Shelly Bowen Hatfield, *Chasing Shadows: Indians Along the United-States-Mexico Border, 1876–1911* (Albuquerque: University of New Mexico Press, 1998); David McCrady, *Living with Strangers: The Nineteenth-Century Sioux and the Canadian-American Borderlands* (Lincoln: University of Nebraska Press, 2006). For earlier Iroquois experiences with borders, see Alan

Taylor, *The Divided Ground: Indians, Settlers and the Northern Borderland of the American Revolution* (New York: Knopf, 2006).

4 See especially Samuel Truett, *Fugitive Landscapes: The Forgotten History of the U.S.-Mexico Borderlands* (New Haven: Yale University Press, 2006); and Rachel St. John, *Line in the Sand: A History of the Western U.S.-Mexico Border* (Princeton University Press, 2011).

5 See for example Jennifer Seltz, "Epidemics, Indians, and Border-Making in the Nineteenth-Century Pacific Northwest," and Rachel St. John, "Divided Ranges: Trans-Border Ranches and the Creation of National Space along the Western Mexico-U.S. Border," both in Johnson and Graybill, eds., *Bridging National Borders in North America*, 91–115, 116–140.

6 For instance, see Sheila McManus, *The Line Which Separates: Race, Gender, and the Making of the Alberta-Montana Borderlands* (Lincoln: University of Nebraska Press, 2005); Alexandra Minna Stern, "Nationalism on the Line: Masculinity, Race, and the Creation of the U.S. Border Patrol, 1910–1940," in Truett and Young, eds., *Continental Crossroads*, 299–324.

7 See for example Eric V. Meeks, *Border Citizens: The Making of Indians, Mexicans, and Anglos in Arizona*, (Austin: University of Texas Press, 2007) Katherine Benton-Cohen, *Borderline Americans: Racial Division and Labor War in the Arizona Borderlands* (Cambridge, Mass: Harvard University Press, 2009); Monica Perales, *Smeltertown: Making and Remembering a Southwest Border Community* (Chapel Hill: University of North Carolina Press, 2010).

8 See Wadewitz's new monograph, *The Nature of Borders: Salmon, Boundaries, and Bandits on the Salish Sea* (Seattle: University of Washington Press, 2012).

9 For an elaboration of her argument in this essay, see Erika Lee, *At America's Gates: Chinese Immigration During the Exclusion Era, 1882–1943* (Chapel Hill: University of North Carolina Press, 2003).

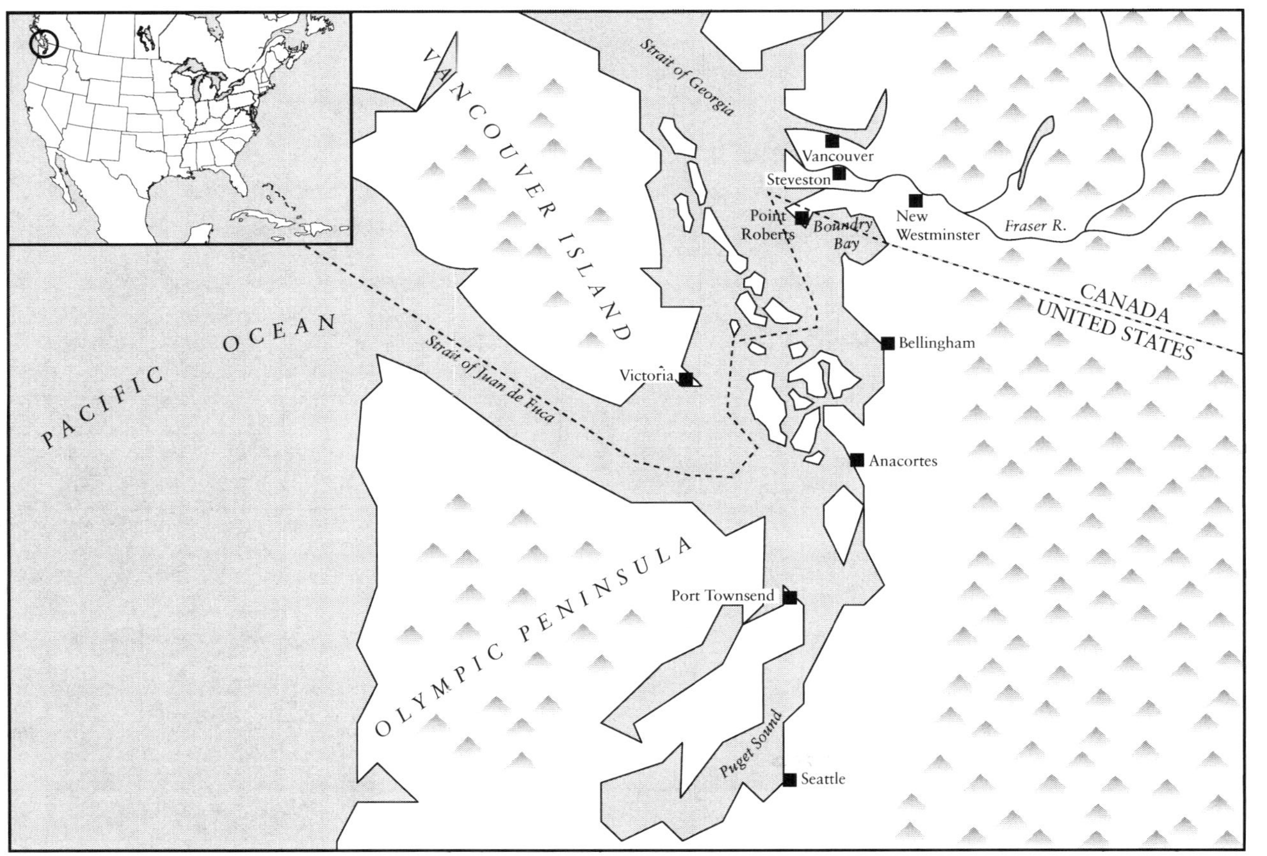


*Map 6.1* The Pacific Northwest

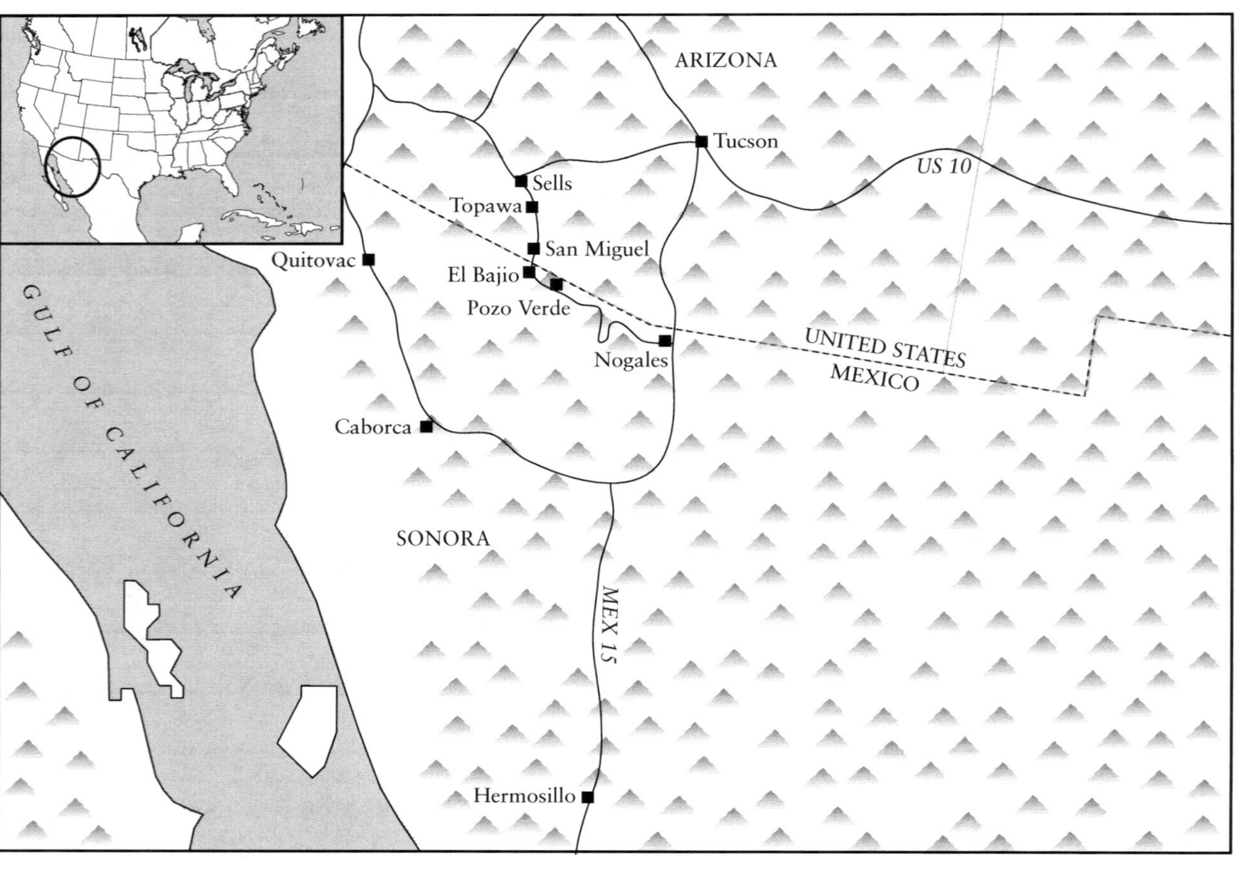


*Map 6.2* Western U.S.-Mexican Borderlands

# 12

# FISHING THE LINE

*Lissa Wadewitz*

In the waning summer months of 1895, George Webber, a U.S. customs inspector in Puget Sound, expressed his exasperation in trying to police the water border between Washington and British Columbia. In particular, he was frustrated with Canadian fishing boats illegally crossing the border to help themselves to what Webber deemed an American possession—salmon taken in the numerous fish traps at that peninsula. "If you try to get to them," Webber complained of the Canadian vessels, "they will steam away for a hundred yards across the line and then lay and laugh at you." The only way to catch them, he advised, was "to wait your chance, and the first time you can get aboard them in American waters to make the seizure."[1]

Webber's laments echoed repeatedly from his perch in the salmon infested waters of Puget Sound as he struggled to uphold U.S. customs laws and protect U.S. fisheries from the depredations of what he perceived as fish-hungry northern neighbors. Indeed, Webber's experiences with the Canadian fishing vessels at the turn of the century highlight several crucial issues regarding the connections between political borders and environmental policies and practices that beg further study.

Borders are not merely abstract political and economic entities; they divide, restrict, and mitigate the lives of the people living along their edges. Although American historians acknowledge this phenomenon with respect to the southern border of the United States, we have not looked at our northern border with the same level of diligence and inspiration. Historians interested in the intersections of social and environmental history should be particularly concerned with how working-class or poor peoples (designations often directly tied to issues of ethnicity) interacted with their natural surroundings and how conservation legislation came to affect them and the quality of their lives. As some scholars have shown, the creation of national parks and forests and other conservation legislation in the United States interfered with poor peoples' subsistence lifeways in some areas by pushing them out of designated spaces and restricting their methods of resource procurement. Peoples living in border regions underwent similar processes, but they were able to take advantage of political realities to achieve their subsistence needs by crossing the borders between the United States, Canada, and the international seas of the Pacific; these resources included both subsistence goods and wages.[2]

The designation of the U.S.–Canadian political border and the ready access to international waters in the western Puget Sound region contributed to economic and social changes in the late nineteenth and early twentieth centuries that, in turn, exacerbated rates of environmental exploitation. The evolution of the Pacific salmon fishing industry in western Washington and in southwestern British Columbia from approximately 1880 through the 1930s provides an excellent lens through which to examine these claims. Although the creation of the international boundary had some positive economic impacts on the lives of the region's inhabitants, with the onset of conservation laws governing the fisheries, the existence of the border ensured higher catches of salmon than might otherwise have been possible. In short, the border contributed to the decline of the Pacific salmon runs while simultaneously offering the region's fishermen greater financial opportunities.

The life cycle of the Pacific salmon precipitated many of the border tensions that have touched the western U.S.–Canadian boundary. The main species of Pacific salmon begin their lives in rivers or lakes, migrate to the oceans where they spend their formative years, and then return to ascend their natal rivers and spawn in the same place as their ancestors. The Fraser River run of salmon has been of particular interest to policymakers since the late nineteenth century because their return path passes through the Strait of Juan de Fuca—the same body of water that divides British Columbia from Washington. As a result, residents of both countries have access to the salmon before they return to the Fraser River system in British Columbia proper. This fact of mutual access has given rise to years of controversy and negotiation between the United States and Canada, and has had a significant impact on the fishing activities in the region as well as the health of the runs.[3]

Concern about the future health of the salmon runs prompted some early efforts at conservation on both sides of the border, but these early restrictions were not very extensive, nor were they effectively enforced. Stricter laws on the Canadian side of the border, together with the placement of efficient American fish traps at Point Roberts, enabled fishermen on the American side of the border to catch a much larger proportion of Fraser River salmon. Recognizing this, both governments made efforts to negotiate a fair compromise with respect to the Fraser River fish as early as the 1890s, but a successful treaty was not achieved until 1937.[4]

Although the policymaking record indicates that Americans catching a larger proportion of the Fraser River salmon was a sensitive point in negotiations, a review of the U.S. Customs records for the 1880s through the early 1900s suggests that fishermen from both sides of the border caught and sometimes stole the salmon passing through American waters and illegally transported them across the border for purchase by Canadian canneries—often under cover of darkness and fog. In other words, fishermen were able to avoid the more stringent Canadian fishing regulations, cross the fluid water border, and retreat with their scaled booty to the Fraser River canneries.

Once the salmon started running, Point Roberts, an otherwise sleepy, largely uninhabited peninsula that juts just south of the Washington–British Columbia border into official Washington waters, transformed into a buzzing, multicultural waterscape as fishers and cannery workers from "up and down Sound" converged at her coordinates in honor of the salmon. The white, Indian, mixed-blood, and Japanese fishermen from both sides of the border came in boats numbering in the hundreds as they mingled together awaiting the cargo for which they had come. If it was a good year, the sockeye run would fill out by about the middle of July or early August, and the most intense fishing of the season would be under way. The mood was festive and somewhat frenzied as the fish were caught and delivered to the various canneries around the Sound.[5]

The U.S. Customs records overflow with tales regarding Canadian fishermen crossing the border to fish in American waters or load up with the salmon caught at the efficient Point Robert traps. Apparently this was a common occurrence by the late 1890s, by which time the Pacific salmon fisheries had become quite profitable on both sides of the border, and the Puget Sound fisheries were gaining ground versus their Fraser River counterparts. Some of the steamers coming over from the British Columbia side to purchase fish conducted the entire transaction within legal parameters, whereas others risked capture in order to avoid the hassle and time associated with reporting. The frequency of the border crossings for salmon was determined by the path of the runs, which often stayed on the American side of the line until they turned north to the mouth of the Fraser River. While smaller vessels simply crossed over to fish in American waters, larger steamers stole to the boundary line in the middle of the straits and were met by canoes or sloops loaded with fish from the traps. The scows and sloops would then transfer the fish—often numbering in the thousands—to the Canadian vessels for delivery to the Fraser River canneries.

The customs officers policing the western U.S.–Canadian border around the turn of the century had many forces working against them in their quest to control smuggling, illegal crossings, and border fishing. They were notoriously understaffed, frequently overworked, and often not well trained or supervised. These problems grew in scope as immigration and customs laws became increasingly more stringent and complex. Even when their powers were clearly defined, the nature of the border environment—particularly the fluid water border of the greater Puget Sound region—made it extremely difficult to control border crossings and natural resource usage. In addition, the fledgling nature of the force on the Pacific at that time and lack of respect for its authority sometimes prevented the customs officers from effectively performing their duties. In such cases, the customs agent had little recourse, and in at least one such instance, the "seized" vessel simply steamed away. Others continued in their pursuit of fish in spite of the presence of customs officers, and at least one group of angry Indians went so far as to confront one official at gunpoint to demand the return of their seized boat. As a result of these conditions, the U.S. Customs patrols were not very effective at policing the American border. Seizures of fish and vessels are sprinkled throughout the letters from this period, but if hundreds of Fraser River fishing boats illegally crossed the border on a daily basis during the height of the salmon runs as the records indicate, the chance of getting caught with illegal fish was low, and the rewards were worth the risk.

Border fishing linked each class of people living and fishing up and down the Sound to their natural surroundings and its resources in varying and complex ways. Many of the American fish trap and cannery owners in the Point Roberts region were troubled by the success of the British Columbia canneries in buying up Point Roberts salmon, as they frequently saw these sales as cutting into their profits. Indeed, American cannery owners were extremely frustrated at their inability to control the actions of the fishermen, many of whom were American and Canadian Indians. Yet the frustrations and concerns of the cannery men and fish trap owners must be viewed with a cautious and sophisticated eye, for the shifting nature of national capital and ownership in the traps at Point Roberts and in the various canneries around the Sound not only color their concerns as ones of complex financial interest but also suggest that the group's ranks were split in intricate ways. How these capital and national interests clashed or aligned with environmental ones is an important question that needs to be investigated further.

Border fishing was a different issue for the fishermen themselves, but it still offered both threat and opportunity. In fact, the evidence indicates that both independent fishermen and fishermen who had promised a portion of their catch to a cannery could manipulate the border fish markets to get a better price for their fish from year to year. As Customs Officer Ira B. Myers reported in August 1883, as Indian and white fishermen selling fish to Canadian canneries in that year received as much as 50 percent more for their catch, the Canadian canneries were naturally dominating the market. And the best prices were not always on the Canadian side—the practice worked both ways and shifted with the changing economic tides.[6]

In addition to fishermen using the border to get better prices for their fish, the boundary line also offered other fish workers the ability to get higher wages for their work. White American citizens and Indians often crossed the border with the fish runs to work in British Columbia fisheries, but being white or Indian made border crossing a relatively easy venture at first. On the other hand, though usually risking deportation due to the increasingly strict immigration laws in both British Columbia and the United States,

Japanese fishermen and Chinese cannery workers also used the limited flexibility that the border offered. Often these workers would cross the boundary by both land and sea in search of employment in the fisheries or at other ventures once the fishing season came to a close. For example, in his report to the Collector of Customs, Deputy Collector Walker stated he believed that upwards of three thousand Japanese fish workers would try to cross the border by stealth as soon as the Canadian fisheries closed their doors. He claimed he caught more than thirty Japanese laborers trying to cross the line in just a few days' time; twenty-six of those failed to convince him that they should not be deported. Chinese cannery workers were also in high demand on both sides of the border, but faced significant competition from Native workers in British Columbia and tougher regulations regarding their movement into the United States after the Exclusion Act of 1882. Still there are hints that their border crossings often followed patterns similar to those of the Japanese.[7]

While Indian fishermen and workers were crucial to the success of the early fisheries and the border trade, the designation of the international border held special meanings and consequences for Native American and First Nation fishing communities in Washington and British Columbia. The line dividing the United States from Canada also divided bands of Coast Salish peoples bound together via highly significant kinship ties. In addition to the emerging reservation systems and the effects of the growing salmon canning industry, the boundary obstructed Salish patterns of land and sea use, interfered with their spiritual activities, and fractured their traditional system of salmon fishing site assignment. U.S. Customs officials and Indian agents recognized that the border arbitrarily divided Native communities, but as with the newly imposed reserve system, did not know how to reshape Indian behavior to the new boundaries. As one western Indian agent wrote of the issue, the Natives "are intermarried and visit back and forth continually, and . . . the boundary line of nations has heretofore had but little influence with them or their intercourse with each other; so that to prevent entirely their going on to that side is next to impossible." Initially, customs officials allowed Indians some leeway in their border crossing activities, although their reasons are unclear. Perhaps this leniency was due to cultural sensitivity, but more likely it was due to the fact that as the Northwest Indians were still feared and considered dangerous, officials simply wanted to avoid trouble. By the early 1900s, this laissez-faire approach to Indian crossings began to fade, and increasing numbers of seizures of Indian vessels for illegal border crossings appear in the American record.[8]

The border and increasingly strict customs officials altered the character and accessibility of Indian fisheries on both sides of the boundary. Many Native groups had long traditions of fishing at Point Roberts and other points in Puget Sound. On top of the exclusionary tactics employed by fish trappers at Point Roberts, and the discriminatory laws against Indian fishers in American waters, more rigorous border crossing rules for Indians could only serve to further exacerbate their access to traditional fishing sites. For example, when the Lummi Indians brought suit against the Alaska Packers Association (APA) in the 1890s for denying access to their customary fishing sites at Point Roberts—fishing rights that were guaranteed in the Lummi treaty with the U.S. government—the APA strategically used the border in crafting its defense. The witnesses for the defense repeatedly claimed that contrary to Lummi claims, the tribe did not have a long tradition of fishing at Point Roberts. Indeed, they insisted that the only Indians who had the right to such claims were the Saanich and Cowichan of southwestern British Columbia. Acknowledging an Indian presence on the peninsula projected the illusion of truthfulness, but arguing that such claims were limited to Canadian Indians skillfully utilized the international divide between the fishery and the Canadian Indians. Winning the suit essentially protected the company from further Indian incursions emanating from either side of the boundary line.[9]

Records of the fish sellers and poachers themselves, especially if they were engaged in illegal activities, are difficult to find. Bert Jones, otherwise known as both "Spider" Jones and "Fish Pirate" Jones, stole fish from the fixed traps that peppered Puget Sound in the late nineteenth and early twentieth centuries. According to Jones, he and numerous other fish rustlers would sneak to the traps—often in bad weather and without lights—and take fish from the traps while the night watchmen were asleep. Other times he would pay the watchmen to look the other way while he took the fish. "The watchmen figured the fish were made for everybody and they wanted their share. Everybody wanted to make money," Jones asserted. Ironically, as the efficiency of the corporate fish traps enabled Jones to take thousands of fish at a time, he had no trouble selling to a ready audience of buyers.

Although Jones apparently made the fish-rustling business pay and enjoyed the adventure involved, other factors influenced his decision to become a fish poacher. "Oh, gosh, I used to be a crook," Jones admitted. "But I wasn't any more crooked than they were. They fished their traps during the closed season and were just as bad as me." Jones' reaction to the illegal fishing engaged in by the trap owners raises important questions about local people's reactions to the rise of wage labor, the class distinctions that attended different types of gear and work positions in the fishing industry, and local people's own sense of acceptable levels of resource use. Jones apparently justified his illegal activities by the fact that the trap owners themselves refused to abide by the laws put in place to allow the escapement of salmon necessary for their future health. In fact, he was stealing from thieves himself—thieves who had no respect for the very natural resources they depended on for their wealth. As long as they obeyed the law, Jones claimed, so would he. "But if they start to steal the fish out of season," he declared, "I'll have a little hand in it myself."[10]

Life along the U.S.–Canadian water border in the late nineteenth and early twentieth centuries was lively, fascinating, and growing increasingly complicated with each passing year. Fishing the line held different meanings for the various groups of people living and working in the Puget Sound region, and these constantly shifted according to changes in the economy, regulations, and border policing efforts. While the border meant both opportunity and hardship for those people engaged in the region's fisheries, it meant devastation for the Fraser River salmon. Unbalanced regulations and irregular enforcement on both sides of the border during the crucial decades of unbelievable growth in these respective national salmon industries allowed fishers to use the border to their advantage to take larger numbers of fish. National loyalty and patriotic verve further exacerbated the economic competition among fishers and canneries in the region during these early years and fueled the forces behind overfishing, as Garret Hardin's tragedy of the commons seemed to play out to near perfection.[11] On the other hand, the border also provided opportunities to some of the region's fishers. The people who lived along the boundary and who fished the line may have been able to use the border to enhance their incomes and subsistence levels. But as the decline in the numbers of salmon attests, the sacrifice was great and the rewards were uneven.

## NOTES

This essay is an expanded version of a paper presented at the conference the American Historical Association—Pacific Coast Branch, Vancouver, British Columbia, August 2001.

1 George Webber, Inspector, Point Roberts, to Collector of Customs J. C. Saunders, Port Townsend WA, August 27, 1895, U.S. Customs Service, Puget Sound Collection District, RG 36, box 103, file 3.
2 See Louis S. Warren, *The Hunter's Game: Poachers and Conservationists in Twentieth-Century America* (New Haven: Yale University Press, 1997) and Karl Jacoby, *Crimes against Nature: Squatters, Poachers, Thieves, and the Hidden History of American Conservation* (Berkeley: University of California Press, 2001).
3 On the salmon life cycle, see Joseph E. Taylor III, *Making Salmon; An Environmental History of the Northwest Fisheries Crisis* (Seattle: University of Washington Press, 1999), 5–6. For more information on the problems posed by the route of the salmon through the Strait of Juan de Fuca, see James A. Crutchfield and Giulio Pontecorvo, *The Pacific Salmon Fisheries: A Study of Irrational Conservation* (Baltimore: Johns Hopkins University Press, 1969), 122–27.
4 Sara Singleton, *Constructing Cooperation: The Evolution of Institutions of Comanagement* (Ann Arbor: University of Michigan Press, 1998), 61–62.
5 Charles McLennan, Deputy Collector Inspector, Blaine, to Collector Andrew Wasson, Port Townsend WA, May 5, 1892, RG 36, box 62, file 2.
6 Ira B. Myers, Inspector, (no located listed) to A. W. Bash, Collector of Customs, District of Puget Sound, August 9, 1883, RG 36, box 169, file 4; A. M. White,

Port Angeles WA, to H. F. Beecher, Collector of Customs, Port Townsend WA, December 4, 1885, RG 36, box 73, file 3; H. K. Bickford, Deputy Collector, Port Angeles WA, April 25, 1893.

7 Samuel Walker, Immigrant Inspector, New Whatcom, to Collector F. D. Huestis, Port Townsend WA, September 2 and 7, 1900, RG 36, box 107, file 1.

8 Bruce Miller, "The 'Really Real' Border and the Divided Salish Community," BC *Studies* 112 (Winter 1996–97): 65.

9 *The U.S. v. The Alaska Tacking Association, 1895–1897,* RG 21, U.S. Circuit Court Western District of WA, Northern Division—Seattle Civil and Criminal Case files 1890–1911, box 82, case 482.

10 "Bert Jones: Fish Pirate," in Ron Strickland, *River of Pigs and Cayuses: Oral Histories from the Pacific Northwest* (San Francisco: Lexikos, 1984), 8–11, 13.

11 Garret Hardin, "The Tragedy of the Commons," *Science* 162 (December 1968): 1243–48. According to Hardin, human beings were compelled to exhaust those resources owned "in common," as there was no incentive to inspire contrary action.

# 13

# ENFORCING THE BORDERS

*Erika Lee*

In September 1924 a Chinese male immigrant named Lim Wah entered the United States illegally from Mexico. His goals were to find work and to join his father, a farm laborer in northern California. Legally excluded from the United States, Lim paid an American $200 to bring him from Mexicali, Mexico, to Calexico, California. They waited until night and then crossed the border, ending up in San Francisco three days later. The Chinese exclusion laws (in effect from 1882 to 1943) greatly hindered Chinese immigration to the United States, but as Lim Wah's case demonstrates, they did not serve as the total barriers that exclusionists had hoped for. Deteriorating political and economic conditions in south China, the availability of jobs in the United States, the U.S. Bureau of Immigrations harsh enforcement procedures at regular ports of entry such as San Francisco, and the Chinese belief that the exclusion laws were unjust—all had the unintended consequence of turning illegal immigration via the borders into a profitable and thriving business.[1]

It is estimated that at least 17,300 Chinese immigrants entered the United States through the "back doors" of Canada and Mexico from 1882 to 1920.[2] The number of Chinese entries pales in comparison with that of contemporary border migrants from Mexico, and recent scholarship has all but ignored this early history of Chinese exclusion in the northern and southern borderlands. Nevertheless, I argue that Chinese immigration to and exclusion from the United States had transnational consequences that transformed the northern and southern borders into sites of contest over illegal immigration, race, citizenship, immigration policy, and international relations. Considering Chinese immigration and exclusion from the vantage point of the borders illustrates both the racialization of U.S. immigration policy and the importance of the Chinese diaspora in the Americas. It also demonstrates how a seemingly national issue can sometimes be understood only in a wider, transnational context. Race, borders, and immigration policy in the United States, Canada, and Mexico became intertwined at the turn of the twentieth century over the issue of Chinese immigration and exclusion.

Prior to the 1870s, American immigration laws were aimed at recruiting, rather than restricting, foreign immigration. The Chinese Exclusion Act (1882) marks the first time in American history that the United States barred an immigrant group based on race and class. It excluded Chinese laborers and allowed only a few select classes of Chinese merchants, students, teachers, travelers, and diplomats to apply for admission to the country. The act also represents the first time that illegal immigration was defined as a criminal offense in U.S. law. The new policy also provided for the deportation of Chinese in the country illegally. When Chinese responded to exclusion by taking advantage of legal loopholes and cracks in the government's enforcement practices, they became the country's first illegal immigrants, both in technical, legal terms and in the context of popular and political representations. Subsequent American immigration laws barred certain excludable aliens, such as contract laborers, convicts, idiots, and persons likely to become public charges or afflicted with a contagious disease. But until both illegal immigration and border enforcement changed in response to the 1924 immigration act, Chinese immigrants remained the main practitioners of illegal immigration and the main immigrant targets of government scrutiny.[3]

Chinese border crossers highlighted the weaknesses in American immigration law and tested the sovereignty of the United States in relation to immigration for the first time. They forced U.S. immigration officials to deal with two interrelated problems: stopping illegal immigration at the nation's borders and expelling illegal immigrants already residing in the country. The U.S. reaction signaled a new imperialist assertion of national sovereignty in the form of border control and the imposition of American nativism, immigration laws, and enforcement practices on both Canada and Mexico. The ways in which this played out in the north and south, however, differed. In the north, U.S. efforts centered on "border diplomacy" based on a historically amicable diplomatic relationship and a shared antipathy for Chinese immigration. In contrast, control over the southern border relied less on cooperation with Mexico and more on border policing, a system of surveillance, patrols, apprehension, and deportation. Both methods eventually proved successful in closing the northern and southern borders to Chinese immigration. In doing so, they laid the foundations for racialized understandings of the "illegal immigrant problem" and of American border enforcement and nation building at the beginning of the twentieth century.

The most numerous and earliest border crossings occurred along the Canadian border. Some of the first illegal border crossers were most likely Chinese residents of the United States who had immigrated to Canada to work for the Canadian Pacific Railway Company (CPR) in the 1870s and then found themselves excluded from the United States after the 1882 Chinese Exclusion Act. Others went straight to Canada from China with the intention of eventually entering the United States. The largely unguarded boundary between the United States and Canada made such border entries feasible and relatively easy to execute.[4] Moreover, although Chinese immigrants in Canada were targets of racial hostility, Canada's Chinese immigration laws contrasted sharply with those of the United States. Instead of imitating the U.S. practice of direct exclusion of Chinese laborers, Canada's efforts to restrict Chinese immigration were indirect. In 1885 Canada's Chinese Immigration Act imposed a fifty-dollar head tax to be collected by each ship captain at the point of departure. Thus, though the United States explicitly singled out all Chinese laborers (and, for all intents and purposes, most Chinese immigrants), Canada's early measures allowed entry to every Chinese provided that he paid the landing fee.[5]

Although the intent was to restrict Chinese immigration, Canada's head tax system was not a sufficient deterrent. Canada was such a convenient back door into the United States that the tax reduced the appeal of immigration *to* Canada but did not reduce the appeal of secondary immigration to the United States *through* Canada. Other aspects of Canadian immigration laws seemed to facilitate Chinese illegal immigration across the border. Chinese immigrants destined for the United States were permitted to remain in the dominion for ninety days without paying the head tax and could presumably cross the border at will during that time. Those who had paid the head tax could also easily leave Canada.[6] The relatively lenient Canadian laws combined with the increasingly stringent U.S. Chinese exclusion laws led directly to a rise in illegal border entries. After the United States passed the Scott Act (1888), which nullified the U.S. return permits of an estimated 20,000 Chinese laborers, 773 Chinese immigrated to Canada. In 1892, 3,264 more Chinese immigrated to Canada following the U.S. passage of the Geary Act, which extended the exclusion of any additional Chinese laborers from the United States for another ten years and required those already in the country to register with the federal government. Witnesses at U.S. congressional hearings in 1890 and 1891 estimated that 300 to 2,000 Chinese entered illegally each year.[7] Even after Canada raised its head tax to $100 in 1900, American officials complained that the Canadian laws "practically nullified . . . the effective work done by the border officers."[8]

Chinese border crossers took advantage of established smuggling networks involving opium and other contraband substances along the U.S.-Canadian border. The Vancouver–Puget Sound area was known as a "smugglers' paradise" in the opium trade, and Chinese and their American or Canadian guides used the same smuggling boats and routes to make the journey to the United States. The cost of crossing the border along this route ranged from $23 to $60 in the 1890s. One decade later, border crossing through Washington State could cost up to $300.[9] Other popular entry points were along the northeastern border. The completion of the Canadian Pacific Railway, which stretched several thousand miles from Vancouver, British Columbia, to Montreal, Quebec, allowed immigrants to enter at a western seaport in

Canada and then travel across the country to the east, where entry into the United States was even less guarded. Aided by Chinese already in the United States and white Americans looking for a ready profit, the business of transporting Chinese through Buffalo, New York, for example, became well organized and very profitable. In 1909 one newspaper reporter found that two to four Chinese were brought into Buffalo weekly, at a price of $200 to $600. Chinese were also commonly brought from the Canadian border to Boston and New York City in groups ranging from two to seventy-five in number. Corrupt immigration officials and judges along the border facilitated the illegal entry of Chinese by either masterminding the routes or admitting Chinese immigrants into the country in exchange for money.[10]

Thus, until 1923, when Canada passed a more complete exclusion bill, it remained a convenient route into the United States for anyone willing and able to pay the head taxes. This migration across the border prompted one Oregon magazine editor to complain that "Canada gets the money and we get the Chinamen," and reporters wrote about the growing "Chinese leak" coming in from Canada. As U.S. immigration officials began to understand the magnitude of the problem facing them along the U.S.-Canadian border, they also looked warily to the south and correctly predicted that the Mexican boundary would "undoubtedly be the next point of attack."[11]

As in Canada, in Mexico immigration policies regarding Chinese contrasted sharply with American laws, creating another back door into the United States. When the United States passed its exclusion law, both Chinese and Mexican authorities were encouraging Chinese migration to Mexico. The Chinese government believed that Mexico and other Latin American countries were convenient alternatives to the United States, where racial hostility and discriminatory laws placed Chinese at risk. Likewise, Mexican officials believed that foreign immigration was an essential ingredient in the development and modernization of the country's infrastructure during the Porfiriato, the rule of President Porfirio Díaz from 1876 to 1911. Attempts to attract Europeans—considered the most desirable immigrant group—failed. Instead, Chinese came in significant numbers and increasingly moved into local trade and commerce, meeting new demands for goods and services in the newly expanding society. After China and Mexico signed the Treaty of Amity and Commerce in 1899, Chinese immigration to Mexico increased. Like their fellow migrants in the north, the Chinese in Mexico also faced racial hostility, and an organized anti-Chinese movement developed in the early 1900s, reaching a climax during the 1930s. However, it did not result in the legal restriction of Chinese immigration. One reason was that though Mexican officials found Chinese immigrants "undesirable," they also admitted that Chinese labor was beneficial and necessary. Anti-Chinese sentiment in Mexico also did not hinder secondary migration to the United States. The open border continued to facilitate both Mexican and Chinese immigration to the United States.[12]

By 1906 U.S. government attempts to curb Chinese illegal entries along the northern border had proved effective enough that the business of illegal immigration shifted south. Soon thereafter, the Mexican border was considered the greatest trouble spot in relation to Chinese illegal immigration. One immigrant inspector went so far as to say that legitimate immigration via Mexico was "a joke, a hollow mockery." It was estimated that 80 percent of the Chinese arriving at Mexican seaports eventually reached the border. From 1907 to 1909, 2,492 Chinese were arrested by U.S. officials for illegal entry along the Mexican border. Mexican statistics on Chinese immigration also suggest that from 1,000 to 2,000 Chinese migrated illegally to the United States per year during the Porfiriato.[13]

Chinese immigrants choosing the circuitous route through Mexico usually disembarked in Ensenada, Manzanillo, Mazatlán, or Guaymas and then took either another steamer going north or the railroad, making sure to disembark well before the trains had reached the United States, where immigration officials were tracking passengers. Entry west of El Paso, Texas, was especially popular for those wishing to go to the West. In fact, the town was known as a "hot-bed for the smuggling of Chinese." Those headed to the eastern states might take a sea route to Florida, Louisiana, Mississippi, and other Gulf Coast states. Some Chinese simply walked across the line by themselves or hitchhiked a ride northward. Law Ngim, for example, found his way north, crossed the border, rested on the side of the road, and then waved down a car to take him to San Francisco in the 1920s. Others hired guides and engaged in highly organized plans. In 1903 one "band of fifteen to twenty Chinamen" was found camped out in a "safe house" about seventy-five miles southeast of San Diego. While the Chinese hid inside the building, their Mexican guides went into town to buy provisions and make further preparations. The average cost for a guide ranged from $25 to $75 in the 1890s, depending on where the crossing took place. By the 1930s, it had increased to $200.[14]

As in Canada, Chinese border migration in the south was built on an established foundation of U.S.-Mexican trade and smuggling networks that thrived in southwestern border towns. There Chinese border crossings were an "open secret," and American immigration officials along the southern boundary complained that Chinese illegal immigration was "carried on with the cognizance if not with the concealed cooperation of the local [Mexican] authorities." Chinese illegal immigration depended on those established networks, and Chinese on both sides of the border could be counted on to provide assistance. Newly arrived Chinese immigrants in Mexico were provided with American money, Chinese-English dictionaries, Chinese American newspapers, and American railroad maps. Immigrant guidebooks to Mexico also circulated, and fraudulent immigration documents manufactured in Mexico arrived at the El Paso post office "almost daily." One Bureau of Immigration report complained that both laborers and merchants in the Chinese community of El Paso "banded together as one man for the purpose of concealing . . . those Chinese coolies who have crossed the line." Rumors of hidden, underground chambers or rooms built between the ceilings and roofs of Chinatown businesses spread among El Paso residents and immigration officials alike.[15]

The "banding together" of the Chinese of El Paso with the Chinese coming in from Ciudad Juárez, Mexico, reflects not only the transnational connections between and among Chinese immigrant communities in the United States and Mexico but also the fluidity of the border region for Chinese illegal immigrants. Indeed, much like contemporary migratory activity in the U.S.-Mexican borderlands, Chinese immigration and exclusion along both the northern and southern borders resembled "a world in motion" made up of shifting and multiple identities and relationships constructed for the purpose of illegal migration.[16]

One of the best examples of that multiplicity involves racial crossings, attempts by Chinese to pass as members of another race in order to cross the border undetected. Even though Chinese migration to both Canada and Mexico dated from as far back as the middle of the nineteenth century, Chinese were not viewed as "natural" inhabitants of the northern and southern borderlands like Mexicans or Native Americans. Indeed, the mere presence of Chinese along the border could raise suspicion among government officials. Some Chinese immigrants and their guides thus learned, beginning in the early 1900s, to try to pass as Mexican or Native American as they crossed the border. Although such elaborate strategies were by no means the only way to cross the border undetected, they were indeed effective. In 1904 the *Buffalo Times* reported that it was not uncommon for white "smugglers" to disguise the Chinese as Native Americans crossing from Canada to the United States in pursuit of trade. They would be dressed in "Indian garb," given baskets of sassafras, and rowed across the border in boats.[17]

Racial crossings were common along the southern border as well. In 1907 special government inspectors reported on a highly organized, Chinese- and Mexican-run illegal immigration business headed by the Chinese Mexican José Chang in Guaymas. Chinese immigrants landed in Mexico on the pretense that they had been hired to work in the cotton fields there. Chang then brought them to his headquarters in Guaymas, where letters from the immigrants' United States relatives were distributed and further preparations for the border journey were made. One of the most important steps in Chang's operation involved disguising the newly arrived Chinese as Mexican residents. The Chinese cut their queues and exchanged their "blue jeans and felt slippers" for "the most picturesque Mexican dress." They received fraudulent Mexican citizenship papers, and they also learned to say a few words of Spanish, especially "Yo soy mexicano" (I am Mexican). As in the case of the Native American disguise, the Mexican one was supposed to protect Chinese should they be "held up by some American citizen" while attempting to cross the border. The Mexican disguise was apparently quite successful. In 1907 the immigrant inspector Marcus Braun traveled undercover to Mexico to investigate Chinese, Japanese, and European immigration through Mexico to the United States. In Mexico City he uncovered the use of fraudulent Mexican citizenship certificates and photographs by Chinese to facilitate their entry into the United States. On examination of the photographs, Braun expressed amazement that it was "exceedingly difficult to distinguish these Chinamen from Mexicans." To make his point even clearer, he included in his report two "exhibits" of the fraudulent citizenship papers as well as photographs of Chinese on a steamship, emphasizing that the Chinese in question could easily pass as Mexican without detection.[18]

Racial crossings were not confined to the northern and southern borders. One government report on the illicit entry of Asian and European immigrants via Cuba described a particularly successful strategy of "painting the Chinese black" to disguise them as part of the steamships crew. They apparently "walked off the steamer in New Orleans without trouble." In Mobile, Alabama, an immigrant inspector reported a project to bring in newly arrived Chinese from Mexico and then "disguise the Chinamen as negroes." Mobile was apparently a popular destination point because it was home to one man—referred to by fellow Chinese as "Crooked Face"—whose specialty was disguising Chinese immigrants as African Americans.[19]

Chinese immigrants in effect traded their own racial uniforms, which elicited suspicion in the borderlands, for others that would allow them to blend into particular regional and racial landscapes. In the north, the dominant racial "others" were American and Canadian Indians. In the Southwest, they were Mexicans and American Indians, and in the South, they were African Americans. Chinese illegal immigrants learned to use the ways race marked each particular regional landscape to their own advantage in order to enter the country undetected.

If Chinese racial crossings reflected the multiple, hybrid nature of the borderlands, then the multiracial character of the Chinese illegal immigration business defined the border as a contact zone where people—mostly men—of different races, classes, and nationalities met and sometimes formed fragile alliances. The most numerous smugglers were white American or European immigrant men working with Chinese accomplices and organizers. Many were often already involved in illegal activities. Others apparently participated in the business on the side. Either their regular occupations or their geographical locations facilitated covert activities. In Seattle the locomotive engineer Billie Low and the fireman Bat Nelson took advantage of Low's railroad connections to bring both Chinese immigrants and opium into the United States from Vancouver. In Bay St. Louis, Mississippi, a government informant reported, "a certain ring of Greeks" who owned a store and factory were "running Chinese" through Mexico. The store and factory provided substantial housing for the newly arrived immigrants as well as cover for the illegitimate activities. Even those working in the highest levels of law enforcement were involved in the business of Chinese illegal immigration. In 1908 several witnesses and government informants came forward with evidence that the former chief of police Edward M. Fink was "the leader of one of the gangs of smugglers" in El Paso.[20]

American Indians were also known to guide Chinese into the country, especially across the northern border. In the south, however, the Papago Indians "seemed to have a natural antipathy for Chinese," according to the immigrant inspector Clifford Perkins, and thus were routinely hired as government informants to help apprehend Chinese illegals. Mexicans were often the primary guides across the southern border, and they made a handsome profit from selling provisions to Chinese and guiding them. In 1912 Luis Fernandez, Jordan Felize, and Wong Gong Huey of Mexicali joined Ethel Hall, Muy Fat, Lin Fat, and Chin Man of San Francisco in a transnational "notorious smuggling ring" that came under government scrutiny. Multiracial alliances forged in the underground business of illegal immigration, however, could be fragile. For example, Mexicans were not always working on the same side as the Chinese. Some Mexicans might be paid informants, employees of the U.S. Bureau of Immigration, or even witnesses in courts, while others refused to assist Chinese lest their actions call unwanted attention to themselves. Fragile or formal, the multiracial relationships and alliances made Chinese illegal immigration possible and profitable.[21]

Though the business of illegal immigration relied on an ability to function beyond and below the sight of government authorities, illegal Chinese immigration became the very public symbol of the continuing "Chinese problem" that had inspired the passage of the Chinese Exclusion Act in the first place. As a result, Chinese border crossers became the public image of a new type of immigrant—the "illegal." The American public learned about Chinese border crossings through sensationalist regional and national newspaper reports, magazine articles, and government investigations. The reportage borrowed extensively from existing racial stereotypes of Chinese, often merging the illegal aspect of their migration with coexisting charges that Chinese were either cunning criminals or "coolies" whose immigration constituted a harmful invasion of inferior and unassimilable aliens. As Robert G. Lee has illustrated, beginning in the 1850s, the racialized character of "John Chinaman" in American plays, songs, minstrel shows, and fiction created and reinforced the popular representation of Chinese immigrants as both "pollutants" who endangered American society with their alien presence and unfree, servile coolies who threatened the white working class. By the 1880s "John Chinaman" also came to be the primary image through which Chinese illegal immigration was explained in both popular magazines and political discourse.[22]

The San Francisco–based weekly illustrated journal the *Wasp* was one of the first publications to articulate and illustrate fears of Chinese illegal immigration from Canada and Mexico with a two-page, color illustration entitled "And Still They Come!" Printed in 1880, while anti-Chinese politicians were still laying the groundwork for the eventual passage of the 1882 Chinese Exclusion Act, the cartoon played on fears of future Chinese illegal immigration from the north and south. Having just failed to enact the 1879 Fifteen Passenger Bill that would have limited to fifteen the number of Chinese passengers on any ship coming to the United States, the supporters of Chinese exclusion worked tirelessly to keep the specter of an alien Chinese invasion alive and well. "And Still They Come!" articulated the Chinese exclusion message perfectly. It portrays two endless streams of slant-eyed "Johns" or Chinese coolies disembarking from overcrowded steamships and flowing into the United States. Their racial difference is clearly marked and communicated through exaggerated racial features inscribed onto the bodies of the Chinese figures and through alien Chinese dress and hair. The dark slits that are supposed to be eyes are mere physical manifestations of the surreptitious, sneaky nature of the Chinese. Their loose-fitting garments, broad coolie hats, Chinese baskets, and shoes emphasize the alien customs that will pollute America. Finally, the long, rattail-like braided plaits of hair worn by the Chinese men represent a cultural anomaly that is both sexually and racially ambiguous and threatening. Entering surreptitiously through two back doors labeled "British Columbia" and "Mexico," the Chinese gleefully flout U.S. attempts to bar them. They easily evade an eaglelike Uncle Sam who is trying in vain to shut America's main gates to a third wave of Chinese coolies entering by sea. With his back turned toward the Chinese entering from the north and south, Uncle Sam is oblivious to the larger threats posed by the open borders and fails to notice the Chinese thumbing their noses at him, U.S. law, and the sovereignty of the American nation. As a symbol of the imminent invasion of Chinese, the two steamships docked in British Columbia and Mexico sag with the weight of countless Chinese hanging from the spars and streaming down the gangplank into the United States. On the distant horizon, dozens of Chinese vessels and even air balloons filled with Chinese leave China and make their way to the shores of the United States. Each ship and balloon is marked by the number fifteen, alluding to the unsuccessful Fifteen Passenger Bill and demonstrating how the cunning Chinese would undoubtedly evade and take advantage of Americas ineffectual immigration and border policies through an outright invasion.[23]

Beginning in the 1890s, after Chinese border entries had indeed become a reality, the specter of the Chinese illegal immigrant received more national press coverage. Speakers before the U.S. Congress likened the influx of Chinese from Canada to the "swarming of the Huns" in early European history.[24] In 1891 *Harper's New Monthly Magazine* published an exposé written by the journalist Julian Ralph. Titling the piece "The Chinese Leak," Ralph explained in detail the strategies used by Chinese to enter the United States from Canada and Mexico. Lax Canadian laws, "wily" Chinese, and profit-hungry Canadian and American smugglers and "pilots" all figured prominently in Ralph's investigation. Four illustrations accompany the article. One, simply titled "John," portrays a young, disheveled Chinese male walking, presumably across the border. His queue trails in the wind behind him. His dress and shoes are distinctly Chinese, and the slant of his eyes is overemphasized. Here, the image of "John Chinaman" connects the standard racialized caricature of Chinese immigrants as alien coolies to the new phenomenon of illegal immigration. Ralph's text running alongside the image elaborates on the connection. Readers are told that John and other Chinamen who crossed the border were especially "impenetrable," "shrewd," and "intelligent trickster" members of their race. The inhuman conditions to which Chinese subjected themselves in order to enter the United States were also taken by Ralph to be signs of Chinese racial inferiority. In 1891 Ralph witnessed the interdiction of the *North Star,* a "tiny" smuggling boat in "desperately bad condition" that frequently carried as many as thirty Chinese males in her hold from Victoria, British Columbia, to the United States. Noting the small stature of the Chinese and their "raisin-like adaptability . . . to compressed conditions," Ralph observed that it would have been difficult, if not unthinkable, to transport "men of any other nationality" in the same fashion. A more graphic image entitled "Dying of Thirst in the Desert" accompanies Ralphs exploration of Chinese border crossings in the south and portrays an abandoned, parched, and dying Chinese male in the desolate southwestern desert. His canteen empty and his hat and walking stick abandoned on the desert floor beside him, this John crawls on his bony, clawlike hands and knees toward the U.S. border. In stark contrast to the comfortable, middle-class lives of *Harper's* readers, the shocking illustration sensationalized the phenomenon of Chinese illegal immigration. Although it could be perceived as a somewhat sympathetic image that pointed to the desperate measures Chinese were willing to take to enter the United States, "Dying of Thirst in the Desert" nonetheless reinforced racialized notions of Chinese criminality, alienness, racial inferiority, and difference and the threat of invasion with the very same depiction of desperation and tragedy.[25]

Not surprisingly, the construction of the Chinese illegal immigrant was especially strong in the American West and in the northern and southern border regions where most of the illicit migration took place. Both American and Canadian newspapers located in the border regions regularly and actively covered the smuggling of Chinese from the north into the south. All the major newspapers in Buffalo, New York, for example, covered Chinese illegal immigration in minute detail. One *Buffalo Evening News* article prominently displayed a stereotypical image of a disheveled, menacing, and subhuman Chinese male under the headline "Wily Tricks Played by John Chinaman and His Smugglers." Contending that the evasion of exclusion laws was common among the "wily" and "heathen" Chinese, the newspaper warned that the "smuggling business" would continue to "flourish and defy authorities." Explicitly connecting the new threat of illegal Chinese immigration with the standard anti-Chinese rhetoric from the 1870s, the headline was accompanied by a few lines from Bret Harte's popular anti-Chinese poem first published in 1871:

> Which is Why I Repeat (and I'm Free / to Maintain) That for Ways That / Are Dark and for Tricks / That Are Vain, the / Heathen Chinee is / Peculiar.

In another article, a Chinese immigrant who was caught trying to enter the country illegally was described as a "Chink" who used his "long, talon-like nails" in a struggle with law enforcement officials.[26]

Also significant is the persistent use of the terms "smugglers," "smuggled," and "imported" by both journalists and government officials to describe Chinese crossing the border. Such terminology invoked earlier charges that Chinese immigrants were merely "imported coolies" and furthered the racialization of Chinese as inferior immigrants under the control of powerful, clandestine organizations and individuals. The connections made between smuggled goods such as liquor and drugs and Chinese border crossers also painted Chinese immigrants as contraband commodities that did not belong in the United States and that disrupted communities. Sensationalist newspaper accounts fed the public's appetite, but while they focused attention on the Chinese and used existing racial stereotypes to explain why Chinese crossed the border, they ignored the role of U.S. immigration laws in creating and fostering Chinese illegal immigration in the first place.

Chinese immigrants may have been the first immigrants to enter the United States illegally, but by the early 1900s they were joined by a much larger number of immigrants of other origins who also chose the border as an alternative to the rigorous immigration inspection at American seaports. Syrians, Greeks, Hungarians, Russian Jews, Italians, and some "maidens" from France, Belgium, and Spain were the main groups entering through Canada and Mexico. All were suspected of having been denied entry at the Atlantic ports of entry, but the back door of Canada offered them a second chance. In the late nineteenth and early twentieth centuries Canadian immigrant inspection processes were considerably less rigorous than U.S. procedures and consisted mainly of a limited health screening. Both European and Asian immigrants quickly learned to buy steamship tickets for Canada and then attempt a border crossing into the United States. Exact statistics of those who entered the country illegally are not available. One sensationalist congressional report claimed that as many as 50,000 European immigrants entered via this route in 1890 alone, but more accurate Bureau of Immigration estimates place the figure at "several thousand" each year in the early 1900s.[27] American officials were consistently frustrated by what they deemed overly lax immigration laws in Canada. As the immigrant inspector Robert Watchorn explained in a 1902 report, "much that appears menacing to us is regarded with comparative indifference by the Canadian government." As a result, Watchorn claimed, "those which Canada receives but fails to hold . . . come unhindered into the United States." By 1909 general immigration via the Canadian and Mexican borders was so great that the U.S. Bureau of Immigration identified them as gateways second in importance only to New York.[28]

Even though both Europeans and Asians were illegally crossing the borders into the United States, the discourses concerning the immigrant groups differed sharply, reflecting an existing American racial hierarchy that viewed European immigration—even illegal immigration—as more desirable than Asian immigration. That the category of the illegal immigrant was, from its inception, a highly racialized one is clear from the differences between U.S. officials' discussion of the challenges posed by European immigrants who crossed the border and their discussion of those posed by Chinese immigrants. U.S. immigration officials were certainly concerned about the large numbers of European immigrants evading inspection at the regular ports of entry by crossing the borders. The U.S. government suspected that those immigrants were particularly likely to become diseased or public charges, and the back door European immigration from Canada caused some alarm. Nevertheless, unlawful entries by Europeans were not defined as a threat to the American nation as Chinese illegal immigration was. In 1890 Secretary of the Treasury William Windom, whose agency administered U.S. immigration laws until 1903, articulated that distinction most clearly. Illegal European immigration from Canada was noted as a potential problem, but the attitudes toward European immigration in general remained welcoming and supportive and reflected the view that Europeans—even illegal immigrants—were still future American citizens. "Our country owes too much in greatness and prosperity to its naturalized citizens to wish to impede the natural movement of such valuable members of society to our shores," Windom noted. The next year Windom merely noted an increase in the number of European aliens crossing the northern border illegally and made a general suggestion for increased border inspection. In later years, European immigrants crossing the border illegally were commonly portrayed in government reports as "forlorn," "unfortunate victims of unscrupulous agents in Europe" who were misled and overcharged in the border migration scheme. In other words, the European immigrants arriving via the borders were coming in violation of the law, but they were an exception to the generally acceptable population of European immigrants as a whole. They were not a reflection on *all* European immigrants.[29]

On the other hand, government officials characterized the threat of Chinese migration along the border in highly racialized terms that evoked an immigrant invasion, suggested threats to national sovereignty, and cast suspicion and blame on the entire race. The same year Windom praised the country's "naturalized citizens" of European immigrant heritage, he warned in alarmist terms of the "organized attempts . . . by Chinese laborers to *force* their way into the United States by way of Mexico, British Columbia, and Canada." The next year he warned that the department was "unable . . . to withstand the *great influx* of Chinese laborers along our Canadian border. . . . They are at liberty to *invade* our territory." Similarly, the commissioner-general of immigration blamed the border enforcement problem on the "difficulties inherent in the character of the Mongolian *race*" and the entries of Chinese through Mexico were characterized as an "evil, constant and systematic evasion of our laws."[30]

The racialization of Chinese immigrants as "illegal" also contrasted sharply with the government's treatment of Mexican immigrants crossing the U.S.-Mexican border. Compared to the estimated 17,000 Chinese who entered the country illegally from 1882 to 1920, approximately 1.4 million Mexicans migrated largely unrestricted into the United States from 1900 to 1930. Though some nativists argued that the large influx of "Mexican peons" entering the country in the 1920s was just as dangerous as the "Chinese invasion" of earlier years, before 1924 anti-Mexican nativism worked differently, in practice, than the anti-immigrant sentiment targeting Asians. Instead of excludable aliens, Mexicans were more often characterized as long-term residents of the Southwest or as "birds of passage" who returned to Mexico after the agricultural season ended.[31] Mexican immigration was not wholly unregulated, but it did exist in a state of "benign neglect," and "little attention" was paid to Mexicans who crossed the border into the United States. Indeed, though the immigration service began to record entries and to inspect aliens at the southern border in 1903, the procedures did not apply to Mexicans at all.[32]

The reasons behind the differential treatment are directly related to the expansion of the southwestern economy from the 1890s through the 1920s and the related need for a steady pool of labor. The curtailment of Asian and southern and eastern European immigrant labor beginning in 1882 and continuing through 1924 made Mexico a logical source for new labor. There were immigration restrictions directed against Mexicans, including the Immigration Act of 1917, which imposed a literacy test and an eight-dollar head tax on Mexican immigrants, but until the late 1920s, companies and agriculturalists were highly successful in evading those requirements. U.S. officials at the border also consistently allowed Mexican migrants to avoid the head tax and literacy test. In 1905 Hart Hyatt North, the commissioner of immigration in San Francisco, reported matter-of-factly that Mexicans and Indians were "crossing at will" at Mexicali and other points along the line without either immigration or medical inspection. But the Chinese, he warned, warranted the government's full and "most vigilant attention." In the eyes of the government and the public, Chinese were the "illegals," and they became the targets of concerted government efforts to control illegal immigration. American newspapers in the Southwest during the early 1900s reported on "Chinese wetbacks" instead of Mexican ones. In effect the border was controlled both to facilitate Mexican immigration and to restrict Chinese immigration.[33]

Identifying Chinese and not European or Mexican immigration as the dangerous illegal immigration had direct consequences for immigration officials' dealings with all Chinese immigration. The first was the government's blanket association of Chinese immigration with illegality. The mere presence of Chinese along the border was enough to raise suspicions among government officials. Chinese residents of El Paso, for example, complained to the government that they were routinely suspected of being illegal immigrants and were treated with "undue harshness and strictness." The categorization of Chinese in the northern and southern border regions as illegal immigrants also led to the dehumanization of all Chinese immigrants. Government officials described them as "contraband," as if they were the same as a banned drug or product being smuggled into the country. Investigators' reports routinely referred to the subjects of their inquiry as "this chink" or "these two chinks." The reward system offered by the government to those who gave information leading to the arrest of Chinese found in the country unlawfully also reinforced the dehumanizing categorization of Chinese as smuggled goods, rather than as individuals. In 1908 the government paid G. W. Edgar, a Seattle farmer, an established fee of "five dollars per Chinese head" or two hundred and fifty dollars for "fifty or more Chinamen" in exchange for information that would lead to the arrest of Chinese immigrants found in the country illegally.[34] Last, the categorization of Chinese as illegals gave the arguments of anti-Chinese exclusionists even more power and legitimacy and furthered the racialization of Chinese as undesirable, threatening, and now illegal immigrants. It also permeated the ideology and practice of policing, eventually closing the border to Chinese immigration. That the conflation of "Chinese" with "illegal" was embedded in border policy was made explicitly clear when the immigration service established a special department whose primary responsibility was to deal with illegal aliens. Its name was the Chinese Division.[35]

Such sensationalist and institutionalized categorizations of Chinese as illegal immigrants highlighted grave weaknesses in American immigration law. Primarily concentrating on immigrant entry through the seaports, United States restrictive immigration legislation largely ignored the country's lack of control over its own land borders. As one Border Patrol inspector commented in 1924, the nation's immigration laws provided "locked doors," but there was no "connecting wall between them" due to the open borders. The United States responded by devising a border enforcement policy to assert its sovereignty and control over the northern and southern borders and to protect the American nation within. The assertion, I argue, was part of the larger practice of extending American laws, ideologies, and systems of control to other countries, a practice that characterized American imperialism in the late nineteenth and early twentieth centuries. Indeed, the process of Chinese exclusion, traditionally defined within the confines of domestic or U.S.-Chinese relations, spilled over many national boundaries. Border anxiety and U.S. immigration policy were directly linked to, and products of, U.S. expansionism.[36]

If we understand imperialism, as Matthew Frye Jacobson has recently suggested, to encompass both a "projection of vested interest in foreign climes . . . and overt practices of political domination," it becomes clear that restricting Chinese immigration via U.S. border enforcement was inextricably tied to the expansion of U.S. imperialism from its inception. At its very foundation, Chinese exclusion had always been justified and articulated through the language of American national sovereignty and self-preservation, American nation building and empire building. U.S. immigration law explicitly equated threats posed by Chinese immigration with threats to national sovereignty. Two Supreme Court cases, *Chae Chan-ping v. United States* (1889) and *Fong Yue Ting v. United States* (1893), asserted that the state held the same rights and duties to curb the foreign menace of immigration as it did to protect its citizens in time of war. Such Supreme Court decisions and domestic, federal immigration laws as the Chinese Exclusion Act of 1882 thus protected the American nation within and served as expressions of American sovereignty. As the American empire advanced across the Pacific Ocean, colonizing Hawaii and the Philippines in 1898, both American anti-Chinese nativism and assertions of American sovereignty followed the flag. After the annexation of Hawaii in 1898, Congress prohibited all immigration of Chinese to the islands despite strenuous Hawaiian protests. In 1902 the final Chinese Exclusion Act included a section prohibiting Chinese immigration to the Philippines as well. In both cases the United States took the unusual step of prohibiting the free movement of certain peoples *within* the empire, as Chinese immigrants already in Hawaii and the Philippines were prohibited from entering the mainland United States. Like the export of capital, politics, religion, and culture, immigration laws and immigration control thus came to be understood and experienced as a central aspect of American imperialism. The "white man's burden" involved not only uplift and civilization of savage peoples abroad but also protection of Americans from the foreign menaces plaguing the mainland United States as well.[37]

As the cases of Canada and Mexico illustrate, the projection of American interests—in the form of anti-Chinese nativism and legislation—extended beyond the United States and its territories. Through an increasingly rigid set of Chinese exclusion laws, the United States had protected itself from the menace of Chinese immigration, yet it still remained vulnerable because of the lax supervision of immigration in Canada and Mexico. Increasingly, the United States began to assert its right to extend its immigration agenda to neighboring sovereign countries. One immigration official justified tough measures at the border by citing the "law of self-preservation." If Chinese illegal immigration through Canada was indeed "a threat against our very civilization," as the U.S. commissioner-general of immigration said in 1907, then extending the American legal reach into a foreign country to control the threat was a logical outcome.[38] Though it could control its newly annexed territories, the United States could not force its immigration agenda onto Canada and Mexico. Instead, U.S. officials employed a variety of other measures to extend U.S. immigration control into the interiors of its northern and southern neighbors and to induce both countries to cooperate with the United States by adopting compatible immigration laws. The United States achieved that through two new arms of imperialism in modern America: border diplomacy and border policing.

Northern borderland scholars write that historically the international boundary at the forty-ninth parallel was largely ignored as both people and goods (legal and illegal) crossed the border uninterrupted and without interference. After border disputes between the United States and Canada were resolved in the eighteenth century, the lack of significant geographical, racial, linguistic (except in the case of Quebec), or religious barriers between the American and Canadian populations helped construct and reinforce the notion of the Canadian-American border as "the world's longest undefended border." The success of Chinese border crossings through Canada does partially support the perception that the boundary line was nothing more than an arbitrary mark in the landscape.[39] Nevertheless, recent scholarship has suggested that the Canadian border was not a racially neutral site and that it underwent a major transformation in immigration control by the 1890s.[40] Indeed, Chinese immigration and exclusion were the primary lenses through which the border was demarcated and racialized. Because Canada's immigration policies clashed with American goals of Chinese exclusion and facilitated illegal entry, the United States increasingly viewed the northern border as a site to be controlled and enforced. Initially frustrated and derisive of Canada's immigration policies, U.S. immigration officials eventually turned to border diplomacy. The mutual antipathy of Canada and the United States toward Chinese immigration and the historically amicable relations between the two countries fostered cooperation and finally control of the northern border.

Early border enforcement was an inherently difficult task. The number of inspectors was too small to monitor the large expanse of land. As a result, one of the government's first imperatives was to increase the number of inspectors along the border. In 1902 the total force numbered only 66 inspectors, mostly along the northern border. The next year, the number had increased to 116, again mostly along the U.S.-Canadian border. By 1909, 300 officers and other employees of the immigration service were committed to work along both borders. Another source of difficulty was that too many people and institutions benefited from the illegal immigration. They included the Canadian government itself, which collected the revenue from the head tax imposed on Chinese but did not have to suffer the repercussions of increased Chinese immigration to its shores. From 1887 to 1891, revenues from the Chinese head tax equaled $95,500 or about $3,000 a month. Canadian officials were blunt in their opinions. They publicly recognized that the Chinese came to Canada "mainly to smuggle themselves across the border." As one prominent observer explained to an American journalist in 1891, "They come here to enter *your* country. You can't stop it, and we don't care."[41]

The U.S. government turned to three main strategies: pressuring Canada to assist the United States in enforcing the Chinese exclusion laws, moving the enforcement of immigration law beyond the border to the Canadian ports of entry where Chinese first entered, and encouraging Canada to adopt Chinese immigration laws that were more compatible with American goals. All measures reflected the new U.S. imperialist assertion of national sovereignty over its borders and marked the extension of American immigration control beyond its own territory. The goal, as Commissioner-General of Immigration Terence Powderly put it in 1901, was to reinforce the border to the point where it was so "airtight" that no one would be able to "crawl through."[42]

U.S. officials first suggested that all ports of entry along the Canadian border be closed to Chinese immigration, but they reluctantly conceded that such a drastic measure would interfere with free trade between the two countries. Instead, beginning in 1894, the U.S. Bureau of Immigration began to extend U.S. immigration law and control into Canadian seaports through the Canadian Agreement. The agreement, made between all Canadian transportation, steamship, and rail companies and the U.S. commissioner-general of immigration, allowed U.S. immigration inspectors to enforce U.S. immigration laws on arriving steamships and on Canadian soil at specifically designated border points. They were instructed to conduct examinations of all United States-bound Asian and European immigrants arriving in Canada in exactly the "same manner" and with the "same objectives" as in the examinations of all arrivals at American seaports. Those who passed inspection were issued a certificate of admission to present to border officers when entering the United States. Those who failed to do so were returned to Canadian railway companies, who were required to return the individual to Canada.[43]

The general 1894 agreement initiated transnational immigration control for both Asian and European immigrants along the border, but the problem of Chinese illegal immigration continued to vex U.S. immigration officials.

Even with the Canadian Agreement, they remained unable to establish the same level of control over Chinese immigration through Canada that they had institutionalized for Chinese sailing directly to the United States. Chinese passengers on Canadian steamship lines, for example, were not required to undergo the rigorous predeparture physical examinations that those bound for the United States were subjected to. Nor were they automatically placed in detention and prevented from receiving mail and visitors while awaiting inspection as their counterparts in the United States were. U.S. officials believed that such gaps in enforcement made it easier for newly arriving Chinese to be coached for their U.S. immigration inspections. With study and practice, they could more easily survive the exhaustive interrogations designed to ferret out fraudulent claims of the right to be admitted into the United States.[44] Thus, because Canadian regulation of Chinese immigration remained different from U.S. procedures and prevented U.S. officials from fully controlling the Chinese immigration "problem," the U.S. government began to consider more specific and drastic remedies.

In 1903 Powderly successfully negotiated a new agreement with officials of the Canadian Pacific Railway Company, which operated both the transcontinental Canadian railway and the main line of passenger and cargo ships between China and Canada. Unlike the earlier 1894 agreement, the new initiative placed more border controls on Chinese immigrants exclusively. The agreement first required the CPR to examine all Chinese persons traveling on its steamships to determine "as reasonably as it can" that United States-bound passengers claiming to be admissible were in fact entitled to enter under U.S. law. CPR officials in effect agreed to interpret and enforce U.S. immigration law. Second, the company agreed to deliver *all* Chinese passengers seeking admission into the United States under guard *directly* to U.S. inspectors stationed at four designated ports along the Canadian border (Richford, Vermont; Malone, New York; Portal, North Dakota; and Sumas, Washington). By having the CPR hand over the Chinese immigrants directly to the U.S. government and by processing the Chinese at the designated immigration stations, the U.S. Bureau of Immigration was able to control the movements of Chinese immigrants more closely and to mirror the rigid procedures and detention conditions governing Chinese immigrants at American seaports.[45]

Believing that compliance with such an agreement would be detrimental to its profitable trans-Pacific steamship business, the Canadian Pacific Railway Company was at first reluctant to agree to the U.S. government's demands. Threats that the entire border would be closed unless the CPR agreed to the proposed terms, however, eventually led the company to sign the agreement. The Canadian government itself was not a formal party to the agreement but certainly consented to its terms and means of enforcement. Relations had been strained between the two countries over the issue of border enforcement. The agreement, American officials noted, was mutually satisfactory.

The United States gained protection "from the evils of unrestricted immigration," and Canada realized "the extensive benefits" resulting from the loss of friction with its southern neighbor. The 1903 agreement was quite successful. Just one year after the agreement had been signed, the immigration service could report that "no Chinese person from China can enter the United States through Canada without submitting to an examination by Bureau officers. At present there are but a few Chinese coming to this country by way of Canada." With those results achieved, the U.S. Bureau of Immigration officials applauded their counterparts for their cooperation and "cordial spirit of friendship for us and for our exclusion policy." By 1908, inland border inspection points had been established across the boundary to regulate all cross-border migration.[46]

Another explicit goal of American border policy in the north was to "induce" Canada to adopt immigration laws similar to those of the United States. Agreements with Canadian transportation companies were effective but could only extend U.S. control to immigrants who were destined for the United States. Chinese increasingly claimed Canada as their final destination and then crossed the border surreptitiously. As a result, American officials grumbled that the relaxed attitudes toward immigration in Canada were detrimental to the United States. Full control of the borders required *transnational* efforts. American laws might become increasingly restrictive, but as the secretary of the treasury pointed out in 1891, "Any legislation looking to exclude will fail of its full purpose so long as the Canadian government admits Chinese laborers to Canada."[47] To remedy the gaps in immigration control, the U.S. Bureau of Immigration engaged in numerous negotiations with its counterpart in Canada. In 1903 both homegrown anti-Chinese sentiment and "patient and persistent" pressure from U.S. Bureau of Immigration and Department of Justice officers motivated Canada to increase its head tax on Chinese immigrants from $100 to $500. The increased head tax proved a strong deterrent to potential Chinese border crossers. In 1912 Canada also agreed to end the practice of admitting Chinese immigrants into the country if they had already been denied entry into the United States. Finally, in 1923, Canada drastically transformed its regulation of Chinese immigration to mirror U.S. law more closely. The 1923 Exclusion Act completely abolished the head tax system and instead prohibited *all* people of Chinese origin or descent from entering Canada. Consular officials, children born in Canada, merchants, and students were exempted.[48]

Unlike earlier acts, the 1923 Canadian bill was finally the effective barrier to Chinese exclusion that American immigration officials had supported. During the next twenty-four years, only fifteen Chinese persons were admitted into Canada. The bill was repealed in 1947. The reach of American regulation of Chinese immigration into Canada was thus made complete with the 1923 bill.[49] That Canada's 1923 exclusion law closely resembled the U.S. regulation of Chinese immigration was no coincidence. Pressure from both anti-Chinese activists within the dominion and from their neighbors to the south resulted in the convergence of American and Canadian policies. Border diplomacy based on a shared antipathy toward Chinese immigration in defense of the Anglo-American nation proved effective and finally closed the border to Chinese immigration.

Increased Chinese illegal entries via Mexico were a direct outgrowth of successful border enforcement in the north. Much to the U.S. governments chagrin, in 1906 it found that Chinese immigrants, "having been practically defeated at every turn along the Canadian frontier," were increasingly turning their attention to the opportunities of entry via the southern border of the United States. Unlike the northern border, the southern border had always been marked by conquest and contestation between the United States and Mexico. No "'undefended' border" like the one to the north, the U.S.-Mexican border has been described by the border studies scholar Gloria Anzaldúa as an "*herida abierta*" (an open wound). Boundary disputes lasted well into the early twentieth century, and the border was routinely the site of activities that tested the relationship between Mexico and the United States: Indian raids, banditry, smuggling, and revolutionary activities. Chinese immigration and exclusion introduced further conflict as the border region became the site of U.S. immigration control and enforcement.[50]

As Chinese immigration and exclusion along the northern border did, Chinese illegal immigration through Mexico set in motion an American assertion of national sovereignty through the imposition of American nativism, immigration laws, and enforcement practices along the border and in Mexico. However, due to the different immigration goals in the United States and Mexico and the tense relations between them, the form and content of border enforcement in the south contrasted with the practices along the northern border. Unlike Canada, Mexico did not have extensive or consistently enforced immigration laws aimed at Chinese or other immigrants. Mexico also did not require any examination of aliens entering the country, and in general its immigration policies were designed to recruit, not restrict, labor. Although Chinese were targets of periodic racial hostility, they played a vital role in the economy from which both Mexican and American businesses operating in Mexico benefited. The United States could not simply "piggyback" or extend its own immigration policies onto an already existing framework in Mexico as it had in Canada.[51]

Moreover, though Canadian officials eventually complied with U.S. immigration law and prerogatives, Mexican officials were more reluctant to do so. In 1907 the U.S. government undertook initial talks with President Porfirio Díaz in the hope he would allow more American control over Chinese immigration entering through Mexico. The American immigrant inspector Marcus Braun reported to Díaz that it was the intention of the United States to institute an agreement similar to the Canadian Agreement made with Canadian transportation companies. As in Canada, the United States wanted direct control over Chinese arrivals in Mexico. President Díaz expressed concern that American control over Chinese immigration would result in a loss of valuable labor needed in Mexico.[52]

Lower-level Mexican officials also resisted U.S. efforts to track Chinese immigrants entering from Mexico. In 1907 U.S. officers in El Paso tried to send inspectors over to Ciudad Juárez every day to meet the incoming trains. They were instructed to "take a good look at every Chinaman who arrived," so that they might be able to identify him in case he should later be caught in the United States. As one official reported in 1907, however, the surveillance of Chinese in Mexico had to be abandoned because the authorities in Ciudad Juárez "threatened our officers with arrest if they should take pictures or descriptions of any Chinamen to come through." Mexican transportation officials also showed little inclination to assist American immigration officials in the quest to bar illegal Chinese entries. One meeting with an agent for the Mexico-Canadian Steamship Company demonstrated this clearly. When asked to cooperate, the agent reportedly remarked that his next ship would carry about 300 Chinese as far north as Guaymas. "For all I know they may smuggle into the United States and if they do I do not give a d—n, for I am doing a legitimate business." After 1910 U.S. immigration officials seem to have been more successful, although they were not granted official jurisdiction in Mexico as they were in Canada.[53]

Like other cross-border interactions at the turn of the century, Mexican cooperation with American immigration officials was thus ambivalent and inconsistent at best. American goals of Chinese exclusion were seen as a threat to Mexico's own labor needs, and it was simply unclear to both the Mexican government and the transportation companies what benefit was to be gained by allowing American immigration officials to exercise so much power within their country. Moreover, Mexican reluctance may have been tied to larger concerns about the increased American presence in the country overall. The end of the nineteenth and the beginning of the twentieth centuries constituted a period of increasing American economic penetration into Mexico, especially in the northern state of Sonora. Mexican state-building activities also played up anti-American themes. Although the transnational economy benefited both regions, border relations—of which Chinese immigration and exclusion soon became a part—embodied this ambivalence.[54]

Southern border enforcement thus presented very different challenges to the U.S. immigration service than its northern counterpart did and led to an alternate approach. Instead of using border diplomacy and cooperation, the U.S. Bureau of Immigration closed the southern border to Chinese immigration through policing and deterrence. Immigration officials at the border were charged with the mission of preventing illegal entries in the first place and of apprehending those caught in the act of crossing the border.[55] To accomplish this, they imposed a three-pronged system of transnational surveillance within Mexico and the United States, patrols at the border, and raids, arrests, and deportations of Chinese already in the United States.

Surveillance of Chinese immigrants in Mexico involved a large informal and formal network of immigration officers, train conductors, consular officials, and Mexican, Indian, and American informants. American diplomatic officers routinely warned U.S. immigration officials on the other side of the border of new Chinese arrivals in Mexico. A typical telegram came from Clarence A. Miller, stationed at Matamoros, warning of an upcoming "flood on the Mexican side" in November 1909 and urging immigration officers to "keep up their vigilance to a high point."[56] Government surveillance of Chinese immigrants in Mexico also involved elaborate undercover investigations by special immigration service agents. The immigrant inspector Marcus Braun, who surveyed the Mexican border situation, first suggested a "Secret Service Squad" charged with watching the Chinese in Mexico in 1907. By 1910 the immigrant inspector Frank R. Stone, praised as "one of the best criminal investigators" in the immigration service, went undercover as a smuggler to investigate the Chinese operations in El Paso. Stone unearthed a wealth of evidence, including fraudulent U.S. certificates of residence (that is, green cards) that Chinese in the United States were required to hold under the 1892 Geary Act. He also found counterfeit seals of two immigration officials and judges of the U.S. District Court for the Northern District of California. Stone's investigation resulted in twelve indictments for conspiracy: four against the Chinese principals and masterminds of the operation, three against Mexican "river-men" who were known for their ability to ford the Rio Grande, one against a Mexican driver, and four against Chinese immigrants holding fraudulent U.S. documents. Stone was also able to photograph the four Chinese leaders (in one photo, Stone himself posed with the suspects), the exact locations where immigrants usually crossed the border, the fraudulent immigration documents, and the adobe huts that served as safe houses. Beginning in the early 1900s, Mexican informants and government witnesses also regularly tracked the movements of Chinese immigrants within Mexico by taking photographs of potential border crossers. The photographs were then sent to the immigration offices at Tucson, Arizona, to be used to identify newly arrived Chinese as ones who had recently passed through Mexico.[57]

The burden of enforcement work along the Mexican border lay in the detection and arrest of "contraband Chinese" and the prosecution of those who assisted in their unlawful entry. The earliest attempts to control the southern border were centered on an increased number of officers along the border "maintaining a much closer patrol, night and day" and a "very vigorous policy with regard to the arrest of Chinese found in this country in violation of the law." The goal of patrolling the border was inherently difficult because of the magnitude of land to be covered as well as the paucity of officers to patrol it. As Braun complained to the commissioner-general of immigration in 1907, all the rivers, carriage roads, pathways, highways, and mountain trails needed to be patrolled. "There is a broad expanse of land with an imaginary line, all passable, all being used, all leading into the United States. The vigilance of your officers stationed along the border is always keen; but what can a handful of people do?"[58]

In response, the immigration service increased the number of immigrant inspectors every year. The first patrol officer in the south was Jeff Milton, who in 1887 resigned from the Texas Rangers and became a mounted inspector with the U.S. Customs Service in El Paso. In the early 1900s, Milton was hired by the immigration service as a U.S. immigration border guard in the El Paso district. His primary duty was to "prevent the smuggling of Chinese from Mexico into the United States." With a territory covering the vast stretches of border from El Paso to the Colorado River, he was known as the "one-man Border Patrol." By 1904 there were an estimated eighty mounted inspectors patrolling the border for illegal Chinese entrants. The so-called "line riders" of the Customs Service continued to "pick up any suspects they ran into," and Milton expanded the scope of his job to "pick up Hindus and Japanese" as well. In 1908 the special Chinese Division was established in the U.S. Bureau of Immigration, which took over the responsibility for dealing with illegal aliens, including the work of the patrol officers. From 1907 to 1909, 2,492 Chinese were arrested by U.S. officials for illegal entry along the Mexican border.[59]

Despite the strengthened border patrol, the inspectors could not catch every Chinese attempting to enter the country illegally. Indeed, it was this inability that led to the formulation and practice of the third feature of the government's border policy: extending border enforcement into the interior cities and regions of the United States and instituting a "vigorous policy" of raids, arrests, and deportations of suspected illegal immigrants. "Let it be known," Commissioner-General Frank Sargent declared in 1906, "that even thickly settled city districts will not afford, as in the past, a safe harbor for those who clandestinely enter." By 1909 a system of interior enforcement was in place, and many of the activities of the service were directed toward "ridding the country of undesirable aliens." The immigration service assigned special agents, commonly known as "Chinese catchers," to find and arrest Chinese unlawfully in the country. Those with high records of arrests and deportations were "celebrated" in the local press and transferred throughout the country to spread their expertise. The Chinese inspector Charles Mehan, for example, began his career in San Francisco, which was widely known as the most difficult port of entry for Chinese. Recognized within the service and by supporters of Chinese exclusion for his rigid interrogations and energetic enforcement of the Chinese exclusion laws, Mehan was called "one of the most celebrated Chinese catchers" in the newspapers and was transferred to El Paso to deal with the problem of Chinese border crossings from Mexico. In 1899 he was transferred to Canada.[60]

Border surveillance, policing, and deportation proved successful in stemming illegal Chinese border entries from Mexico. The numbers of Chinese arrested and deported for unlawful residence in the United States increased. In 1899 the ratio of Chinese admitted to Chinese deported was 100:4. By 1904 the ratio was 100:6l.[61] Border enforcement also became more centralized. In 1907 the border states were consolidated and reorganized into the Mexican Border District, containing Arizona, New Mexico, and most of Texas. Demonstrating the importance of Chinese immigration in shaping general border enforcement, the first commissioner hired to manage the new Mexican Border District (which supervised all foreign immigration across the border) was Frank W. Berkshire, who had overseen the Chinese service along the New York–Canadian border and in New York City.[62]

At the same time, conditions in Mexico, including revolution and increasing anti-Chinese sentiment, placed additional barriers to Chinese immigration. By 1911 the border division reported that it was "no longer acting upon the defensive." Immigration officials also observed that by World War I, a decline in Chinese attempts at entry along the southern border led the immigration service to transfer its Chinese inspectors away from the region.[63] In 1917 Congress provided that aliens who entered the country by land from places other than those designed as ports of entry or who entered without inspection (as many Chinese crossing the borders had done) could be taken into custody and deported without any legal procedure. By 1926 the commissioner-general of immigration declared that "the smuggling of Chinese over the land boundaries, which was a vexatious problem in the past, has been greatly reduced."[64]

Different Chinese immigration goals and policies in the United States, Canada, and Mexico as well as different relationships between the United States and its neighbors led to the evolution of distinct border policies. While the northern border was eventually closed through U.S.-Canadian border diplomacy and a mutual antipathy toward Chinese immigration, southern border enforcement policies were the product of conflicting Chinese immigration policies in the United States and Mexico as well as inconsistent cooperation between the two countries. Border diplomacy thus gave way to border policing designed to deter and apprehend illegal Chinese immigrants already at the border and within the United States. By the 1920s, both the northern and southern borders were effectively closed to Chinese immigration. While Chinese border entries did not completely end, they ceased to warrant the level of attention and response within the immigration service that they had at the turn of the century.

From 1882 to 1924, however, Chinese immigration and exclusion along the U.S.-Canadian and U.S.-Mexican borders had transformed immigration policy, the border region, and American border enforcement. Chinese immigrants—racialized as perpetual foreigners—became the first group in the country marked as "illegal immigrants." The U.S. Bureau of Immigration's first division to deal primarily with illegal immigration was, after all, called the Chinese Division, making "Chinese" synonymous with "illegal" in the same way "Mexican" is racialized now. Indeed, Chinese immigration and exclusion along the northern and southern borders appears to have been an important trial run for the U.S. Bureau of Immigrations much larger efforts to control Mexican immigration in later years. In both cases, the racialization of political discourse and policy on immigration has been central to the ideological, legal, and political definitions of national membership and national identity.

In the wake of increased illegal immigration from Mexico since the 1970s, attitudes and responses to illegal immigration by both the American public and the U.S. government echo earlier responses and sentiments from the Chinese exclusion era. Metaphors of war, for example, are commonly used in contemporary border enforcement discourse as they were at the end of the nineteenth century. Words, phrases, and even political initiatives such as "invasion," "conquest," and "save our state" have been consistently deployed by xenophobes and others, revealing a highly racialized perspective on the new immigration, especially illegal immigration. Much as "John Chinaman and his smugglers" were the dominant public image of the illegal immigrant during the Chinese exclusion era, undocumented immigrants from Mexico became the nearly exclusive focus of government and public concern at the end of the twentieth century.[65]

Significant differences exist as well. The Chinese exclusion laws may have laid the foundations of U.S. border control and enforcement beginning in the late nineteenth century, but those early state efforts pale in comparison with recent campaigns to control immigration. In particular, the government's first attempts to enforce the northern and southern borders during the Chinese exclusion era have increased exponentially, turning the U.S.-Mexican border into a militarized zone designed to deter illegal immigration at any cost. Instead of "Chinese catchers" and "line riders," the government relies on surveillance in the form of night scopes, motion sensors, and communications equipment as well as jeeps and a fourteen-mile triple fence on the U.S.-Mexican border south of San Diego. With newly hired border inspectors mandated by Congress, the Border Patrol became one of the government's largest police agencies in the late 1990s. The United States currently spends $2 billion a year to build walls and manage a twenty-four-hour patrol of the border. During the Chinese exclusion era, the number of "mounted inspectors" patrolling the line was around 80. In 2001, the Border Patrol had 9,400 agents.[66]

In the wake of the terrorist attacks on the United States on September 11, 2001, issues of transnational immigration policies and border control have been pushed to the very forefront of U.S. and international policy. Several of the suspected hijackers who took control of the commercial flights that crashed into the World Trade Center in New York City and the Pentagon in Washington, D.C., spent time in Canada and allegedly entered the United States from the north. In the months following the attacks, policy makers have renewed their focus on increased border security, especially along the northern border. Like critics of Canada's allegedly lax Chinese immigration policies during the 1890s, contemporary American politicians blame Canada for allowing foreigners to enter with false or no passports, apply for asylum, travel freely, and raise funds for political activities while their asylum applications are pending. Canada's open doors, it is argued, increase the risk to American national security.[67] Likewise, the racialized categorization of Arabs and Muslims as "terrorists" follows on the heels of racialized characterizations of Chinese and later Mexicans as "illegal immigrants." Recent suggestions for increased border security also echo earlier efforts first articulated during the Chinese exclusion era. In the early twentieth century, U.S. government officials sought to induce Canada to adopt Chinese immigration policies that more closely mirrored U.S. laws. In late September of 2001, Paul Cellucci, the U.S. ambassador to Canada, publicly called for Canada to "harmonize its [refugee] policies with those of the United States." President George W. Bush sketched out a vision of a "North American security perimeter" in which transnational immigration controls would be central.[68] As of this writing, there is little agreement on what such a "harmonization" would mean. Nor is it clear how U.S. and North American border policies might change. What is certain is that in the United States' "new war" against terrorism, transnational border enforcement and immigration policies will undoubtedly remain central issues facing the United States, Canada, and Mexico in the twenty-first century, just as they were over one hundred years ago.

## NOTES

1 The Chinese Exclusion Act of 1882 prohibited the immigration of Chinese laborers for a period of ten years and barred all Chinese immigrants from naturalized citizenship. Act of May 6, 1882, 22 Stat. 58; Testimony of Lim Wah, Dec. 2, 1932, file 12020/22130, Case Files of Investigations Resulting in Warrant Proceedings (12020), 1912–1950, San Francisco, Records of the Immigration and Naturalization Service, RG 85 (National Archives, Pacific Branch, San Bruno, Calif.).

2 Since illegal immigration is difficult to quantify and detect, this estimate is speculative. It is drawn from: U.S. Department of Commerce and Labor, *Annual Report of the Commissioner-General of Immigration to the Secretary of Commerce and Labor: For the Fiscal Year Ended June 30, 1903* (Washington, 1903), 102; George E. Paulsen, "The Yellow Peril at Nogales: The Ordeal of Collector William M. Hoey," *Arizona and the West,* 13 (Summer 1971), 113–28; C. Luther Fry, "Illegal Entry of Orientals into the United States between 1910 and 1920," *Journal of the American Statistical Association,* 23 (June 1928), 173–77.

3 On pre-1875 immigration law, see Gerald L. Neuman, "The Lost Century of American Immigration Law, 1776–1875," *Columbia Law Review,* 93 (Dec. 1993), 1834–38. For the provisions of the Chinese Exclusion Act, see Act of May 6, 1882, sec. 7, 11, 12, 22 Stat. 58. For post-1882 general immigration laws, see Act of Aug. 3, 1882, 22 Stat. 214; Immigration Act of 1891, 26 Stat. 1084; Act of Feb. 5, 1917, 39 Stat. 874; Act of May 26, 1924, 43 Stat. 153. On the 1924 change in immigration law, see Mae M. Ngai, "The Architecture of Race in American Immigration Law: A Reexamination of the Immigration Act of 1924," *Journal of American History,* 86 (June 1999), 67–92.

4 Resident Chinese laborers who had been in the United States at the time of the act were allowed to reenter. David Chuenyan Lai, *Chinatowns: Towns within Cities in Canada* (Vancouver, 1988), 52. The earliest reports of illegal border crossings by Chinese appear in northwestern newspapers in June and July 1883. See "Chinese in B.C.," *Port Townsend Puget Sound Argus,* June 15, 1883; "More about the Chinese," *ibid.*, July 9, 1883.

5 Act of July 20, 1885, ch. 71, 1885 S.C. 207–12 (Can.); Patricia E. Roy, *A White Man's Province: British Columbia Politicians and Chinese and Japanese Immigrants, 1858–1914* (Vancouver, 1989), 59–63.

6 Department of Commerce and Labor, *Annual Report of the Commissioner-General of Immigration . . . 1903,* 97.

7 Statistics are compiled from Canadian Royal Commission on Chinese and Japanese Immigration, *Report of the Royal Commission on Chinese and Japanese Immigration* (1902; New York, 1978), 271, as cited in Qingsong Zhang, "Dragon in the Land of the Eagle: The Exclusion of Chinese from U.S. Citizenship" (Ph.D. diss., University of Virginia, 1993), 238; and U.S. Congress, House, Select Committee on Immigration and Naturalization, *Investigation of Chinese Immigration,* 51 Cong., 2 sess., 1890, H. Rept. 4048, serial 2890, p. 1.

8 Act of July 18, 1900, ch. 32, 1900 S.C. 215–21 (Can.); U.S. Department of Commerce and Labor, *Annual Report of the Commissioner-General of Immigration to the Secretary of Commerce and Labor: For the Fiscal Year Ended June 30, 1910* (Washington, 1910), 143; U.S. Department of Commerce and Labor, *Annual Report of the Com missioner-General of Immigration to the Secretary of Commerce and Labor: For the Fiscal Year Ended June 30, 1911* (Washington, 1911), 159.

9 Lai, *Chinatowns,* 23; Julian Ralph, "The Chinese Leak," *Harper's New Monthly Magazine,* 82 (March 1891), 520–23; Roland L. De Lorme, "The United States Bureau of Customs and Smuggling on Puget Sound, 1851–1913," *Prologue,* 5 (Summer 1973), 77–88; Hyung-chan Kim and Richard W. Markov, "The Chinese Exclusion Laws and Smuggling Chinese into Whatcom County, Washington, 1890–1900," *Annals of the Chinese Historical Society of the Pacific Northwest* (1983), 16–30; Department of Commerce and Labor, *Annual Report of the Commissioner-General of Immigration . . . 1903,* 98–99.

10 U.S. Congress, Senate, *Reports on Charge of Fraudulent Importation of Chinese,* 49 Cong., 1 sess., 1886, S. Doc. 103, p. 8; James Bronson Reynolds, "Enforcement of the Chinese Exclusion Law," *Annals of the American Academy of Political and Social Science,* 34 (no. 2, 1909), 368; U.S. Department of Commerce and Labor, *Annual Report of the Commissioner-General of Immigration to the Secretary of Commerce and Labor: For the Fiscal Year Ended June 30, 1904* (Washington, 1904), 137–41; Stanford Lyman, *Chinese Americans* (New York, 1974), 106. On corrupt federal judges, see U.S. Department of Commerce and Labor, *McGettrick Certificates: List of Chinese Cases Tried before Former U.S. Commissioner Felix W. McGettrick, for the District of Vermont, from December 11, 1894, to June 24, 1897* (Washington, 1906).

11 Ralph, "Chinese Leak," 515; Department of Commerce and Labor, *Annual Report of the Commissioner-General of Immigration . . . 1903,* 101.

12 Ching-Hwang Yen, *Coolies and Mandarins: China's Protection of Overseas Chinese during the Late Ch'ing Period (1851–1911)* (Singapore, 1985), 292; Raymond B. Craib III, *Chinese Immigrants in Porfirian Mexico: A Preliminary Study of Settlement, Economic Activity, and Anti-Chinese Sentiment* (Albuquerque, 1996), 8, 22, 24; Evelyn Hu-DeHart, "Racism and Anti-Chinese Persecution in Sonora, Mexico, 1876–1932," *Amerasia Journal,* 9 (no. 2, 1982), 2–4, 13.

13 On the new threat to the Mexican border and U.S. government estimates, see U.S. Department of Commerce and Labor, *Annual Report of the Commissioner-General of Immigration to the Secretary of Commerce and Labor: For the Fiscal Year Ended June 30, 1906* (Washington, 1906), 98; "Report by Marcus Braun, U.S. Immigrant Inspector, New York, to Hon. Frank P. Sargent, Commissioner General of Immigration, Dept. of Commerce and Labor, Washington, DC, dated Feb, 12, 1907," file 52320/1, Subject Correspondence, Records of the Immigration and Naturalization Service, rg 85 (National Archives, Washington, D.C.). U.S. government estimates are included in J. W. Berkshire to Commissioner-General of Immigration, April 16, 1910, file 52142/6, *ibid.;* Zhang, "Dragon in the Land of the Eagle," 372. For Mexican statistics, see Evelyn Hu-DeHart, "Immigrants to a Developing Society: The Chinese in Northern Mexico, 1875–1932," *Journal of Arizona History,* 21 (Autumn 1980), 275–312, esp. 282–83.

14 Berkshire to Commissioner-General of Immigration, Oct. 17, 1907, file 52212/2, part 1, Subject Correspondence, Immigration and Naturalization Service Records (Washington, D.C.); Testimony of Law Ngim, May 17, 1931, file 12020/19153, Case Files of Investigations, Immigration and Naturalization Service Records (San Bruno, Calif.). On the organized smuggling attempts, see Charles W. Snyder to Commissioner-General of Immigration, Nov. 11, 1903, folder 22, box 2, Hart Hyatt North Papers (Bancroft Library, University of California, Berkeley). On the cost of border crossing, see "Report by . . . Braun . . . Feb. 12, 1907"; U.S. Department of Commerce and Labor, *Annual Report of the Commissioner-General of Immigration to the Secretary of Commerce and Labor; For the Fiscal Year Ended June 30, 1902* (Washington, 1902), 75; U.S. Department of Commerce and Labor, *Annual Report of the Commissioner-General of Immigration to the Secretary of Commerce and Labor: For the Fiscal Year Ended June 30, 1907* (Washington, 1907), 110; Ralph, "Chinese Leak," 524; Paulsen, "Yellow Peril at Nogales," 113–28; and Testimony of Lim Wah, Dec. 2, 1932, file 12020/22130, Case Files of Investigations, Immigration and Natutalization Service Records (San Bruno, Calif.).

15 Ralph, "Chinese Leak," 524; Department of Commerce and Labor, *Annual Report of the Commissioner-General of Immigration . . . 1907,* 111; Craib, "Chinese Immigrants in Porfirian Mexico," 8. On cross-border networks, see Department of Commerce and Labor, *Annual Report of the Commissioner-General of Immigration . . . 1907,* 110; "Digest of, and Comment Upon, Report of Immigrant Inspector Marcus Braun, dated September 20, 1907," file 51630/44D, Subject Correspondence, Immigration and Naturalization Service Records (Washington, D.C.); and Burton Parker to Secretary of the Treasury, June 5, 1909, file 52516/7, *ibid.* On Chinese in El Paso, see U.S. Department of Commerce and Labor, *Annual Report of the Commissioner-General of Immigration to the Secretary of Commerce and Labor: For the Fiscal Year Ended June 30, 1905* (Washington, 1905), 95–96.

16 Gloria Anzaldúa, *Borderlands/La Frontera: The New Mestiza* (San Francisco, 1987), preface.

17 *Buffalo Times,* Jan. 18, 1902, p. 5. See also *New York Times,* Nov. 29, 1896, p. 1; *ibid,* June 10, 1891, p. 1.
18 "Report by . . . Braun . . . Feb. 12, 1907," 30–33; Department of Commerce and Labor, *Annual Report of the Commissioner-General of Immigration . . . 1907,* 110–11.
19 "Report of Inspector Feri F. Weiss to Commissioner-General of Immigration In re: Cuban Smugglers," April 4, 1925, file 55166/31, Subject Correspondence, Immigration and Naturalization Service Records (Washington, D.C.); Feri F. Weiss to Commissioner-General of Immigration, Feb. 25, 1925, *ibid.* My thanks to Libby Garland for these sources. P. H. Shelton to Commissioner-General of Immigration, Aug. 15, 1911, file 53161/2-A, *ibid.*
20 On the Seattle activities, see Thomas M. Fisher to Commissioner-General of Immigration, May 7, 1917, file 53788/3, *ibid.* On Chinese illegal immigration through Mississippi, see M. R. Snyder to S. E. Redfern, Feb. 2, 1911, file 53161/2, *ibid.* On the corrupt El Paso police chief, see Richard H. Taylor to Commissioner-General of Immigration, Oct. 24, 1908, file 52212/2, *ibid.*
21 On American Indians, see Clifford Allan Perkins, *Border Patrol: With the U.S. Immigration Service on the Mexican Boundary, 1910–54* (Washington, 1978), 23. On Mexicans, see Department of Commerce and Labor, *Annual Report of the Commissioner-General of Immigration . . . 1910,* 146; and Berkshire to Commissioner-General of Immigration, Sept. 19, 1912, file 53507/32, Subject Correspondence, Immigration and Naturalization Service Records (Washington, D.C.). On Mexican informants, see *Preventing Immigration of Chinese Labor from Canada and Mexico,* 1891, H. Rept. 2915, cited in Leon C. Metz, *Border: The U.S.-Mexico Line* (El Paso, 1989), 365; and Perkins, *Border Patrol,* 23.
22 On the construction of "John Chinaman," see Robert G. Lee, *Orientals: Asian Americans in Popular Culture* (Philadelphia, 1999), 9, 22, 32. Illegality became a racially inscribed category for Mexicans in the 1924 Immigration Act, according to Ngai, "The Architecture of Race in American Immigration Law," 67–92.
23 Both the Senate and the House passed the Fifteen Passenger Bill, demonstrating national and bipartisan sup port for Chinese exclusion. A presidential veto blocked its enactment. See Andrew Gyory, *Closing the Gate: Race, Politics, and the Chinese Exclusion Act* (Chapel Hill, 1998), 3–6. "And Still They Come!," *Wasp,* Dec. 4, 1880, p. 280.
24 Ralph, "Chinese Leak," 516. See also U.S. Treasury Department, *Annual Report of the Commissioner-General of Immigration to the Secretary of the Treasury: For the Fiscal Year Ended June 30, 1897* (Washington, 1897), 758; U.S. Department of the Treasury, *Alleged Illegal Entry into the United States of Chinese Persons: Letter from the Secretary of the Treasury . . .,* 55 Cong., 1 sess., 1897, Sen. Doc. 167, p. 153; Zhang, "Dragon in the Land of the Eagle," 349–50; Department of Commerce and Labor, *Annual Report of the Commissioner-General of Immigration . . . 1904,* 149, 626.
25 Ralph, "Chinese Leak," 516–19, 522, 444.
26 *Buffalo Evening News,* Feb. 1, 1904, p. 9; *Buffalo Morning Express,* Jan. 29, 1901, p. 6; "Big Chinese Haul," *ibid.,* Feb. 19, 1902. On Bret Harte, see Lee, *Orientals,* 39, 68–69, 91; and Ronald Takaki, *Iron Cages: Race and Culture in Nineteenth Century America* (New York, 1979), 223.
27 European immigrants are described in "Report by . . . Braun . . . Feb. 12, 1907." For statistics, see U.S. Congress, Senate, *Report of the Select Committee on Immigration and Naturalization,* 51 Cong., 2 sess., 1891, S. Rept. 3472, vii, cited in Ramirez, *Crossing the 49th Parallel,* 42; Treasury Department, *Annual Report of the Commissioner-General of Immigration . . . 1902,* 39.

28 Treasury Department, *Annual Report of the Commissioner-General of Immigration . . . 1902,* 40–41; U.S. Department of Commerce and Labor, *Annual Report of the Commissioner-General of Immigration to the Secretary of Commerce and Labor for the Fiscal Year Ended June 30, 1909* (Washington, 1909), 13.

29 U.S. Treasury Department, *Annual Report of the Secretary of the Treasury on the State of the Finances for the Year 1890* (Washington, 1891), lxxv; U.S. Treasury Department, *Annual Report of the Secretary of the Treasury on the State of the Finances for the Year 1891* (Washington, 1891), lxii; Department of Commerce and Labor, *Annual Report of the Commissioner-General of Immigration . . . 1902,* 40, 42.

30 Treasury Department, *Annual Report of the Secretary of the Treasury . . . 1890,* lxxvi. Emphasis added. Treasury Department, *Annual Report of the Secretary of the Treasury . . . 1891,* lxiv–lxv. Emphasis added. Department of Commerce and Labor, *Annual Report of the Commissioner-General of Immigration . . . 1902,* 71. Emphasis added. "Report by . . . Braun . . . Feb. 12, 1907."

31 This would change dramatically after 1924. As Mae Ngai has shown, Mexicans increasingly became characterized as dangerous foreigners and "illegal immigrants." Sanchez, *Becoming Mexican American,* 18–19. For the post-1924 period, see Ngai, "Architecture of Race," 91. On nativism directed against Mexican immigrants, see Frederick Russell Burnham, "The Howl for Cheap Mexican Labor," in *The Alien in Our Midst; or, Selling Our Birthright for a Mess of Pottage,* ed. Madison Grant and Charles Stewart Davison (New York, 1930), 45, 48. On Mexicans as "birds of passage," see Lawrence Cardoso, *Mexican Emigration to the United States, 1891–1931* (Tucson, 1980), 22; Sanchez, *Becoming Mexican American,* 20; and Abraham Hoffman, *Unwanted Mexican Americans in the Great Depression: Repatriation Pressures, 1929–1939* (Tucson, 1974), 30–32.

32 U.S. Immigration and Naturalization Service, "Early Immigrant Inspection along the U.S./Mexican Border" <http://www.ins.gov/graphics/aboutins/history/articles/mbtext2.htm> (Feb. 15, 2002).

33 Sanchez, *Becoming Mexican American,* 19–20; Hoffman, *Unwanted Mexican Americans in the Great Depression,* 30–32; Mark Reisler, *By the Sweat of Their Brow: Mexican Immigrant Labor in the United States, 1900–1940* (Westport, 1976) 8–13, 24–42; Hart Hyatt North to Frank Sargent, March 9, 1905, file 13618, Segregated Chinese Records, Chinese General Correspondence, Immigration and Naturalization Service Records (Washington, D.C.); Metz, *Border,* 365.

34 For Chinese complaints from El Paso, see Ng Poon Chew to Daniel Keefe, July 30, 1910, folder 1, box 3, Ng Poon Chew Collection (Asian American Studies Library, University of California, Berkeley). For a description of Chinese as "contraband," see F. H. Larned, "Memorandum for the Commissioner-General," Oct. 27, 1913, file 53371/2A, Subject Correspondence, Immigration and Naturalization Service Records (Washington, D.C.). On investigations of "chinks," see [signature illegible] to Brother Larned, April 19, 1901, file 52730/53, *ibid.* The agreement between the government and G. W. Edgar is outlined in Larned to Inspector in Charge, Seattle, Washington, Oct. 26, 1908, file 52214/1, part IV, *ibid.*

35 Perkins, *Border Patrol* 9.

36 Mary Kidder Rak, *Border Patrol* (Boston, 1938), 1. On U.S. imperialism, see Amy Kaplan, "'Left Alone with America': The Absence of Empire in the Study of American Culture," in *Cultures of United States Imperialism,* ed. Amy Kaplan and Donald Pease (Durham, 1993), 16–17.

37 Matthew Frye Jacobson, *Barbarian Virtues: The United States Encounters Foreign Peoples at Home and Abroad, 1876–1917* (New York, 2000), 4, 6, 26–38, 93; *Chae Chan-ping v. United States,* 130 U.S. 606 (1889); *Fong Yue Ting v.*

*United States,* 149 U.S. 698 (1893). On the extension of Chinese exclusion to Hawaii and the Philippines, see Act of July 7, 1898, 30 Stat. 750; Act of April 30, 1900, 31 Stat. 141; and Wu Ting Fang to John Hay, Dec. 12, 1898, Notes from the Chinese Legation in the U.S. to Department of State, 1868–1906, Records of the U.S. Department of State, RG 59 (National Archives, Washington, D.C.). The best account of Chinese immigration to Hawaii is Clarence E. Glick, *Sojourners and Settlers: Chinese Migrants in Hawaii* (Honolulu, 1980). See also Edward C. Lydon, *The Anti-Chinese Movement in the Hawaiian Kingdom, 1852–1886* (San Francisco, 1975).

38 "Report by . . . Braun . . . Feb. 12, 1907"; Frank P. Sargent, "Memorandum," c. 1905, file 52704/2, Subject Correspondence, Immigration and Naturalization Service Records (Washington, D.C.).

39 For descriptions of the U.S.-Canadian border as open and undefended, see John W. Bennett and Seena B. Kohl, *Settling the Canadian-American West, 1890–1915: Pioneer Adaptation and Community Building* (Lincoln, 1995), 13; Roger Gibbins, "Meaning and Significance of the Canadian-American Border," in *Border and Border Regions in Europe and North America,* ed. Paul Ganster et al. (San Diego, 1997), 315–32; Ralph, "Chinese Leak," 521; and De Lorme, "United States Bureau of Customs and Smuggling on Puget Sound," 77–88.

40 Sheila McManus, "Their Own Country: Race, Gender, Landscape, and Colonization around the 49th Parallel, 1862–1900," *Agricultural History,* 73 (Spring 1999), 168–82; Ramirez, *Crossing the 49th Parallel,* 39.

41 For statistics on inspectors in 1902, see Department of Commerce and Labor, *Annual Report of the Commissioner-General of Immigration . . . 1903,* 46. For statistics for 1909, see Marcus Braun, "How Can We Enforce Our Exclusion Laws?," *Annals of the American Academy of Political and Social Science,* 34 (no. 2, 1909), 140–42. Ralph, "Chinese Leak," 516.

42 Vincent J. Falzone, *Terence V Powderly, Middle Class Reformer* (Washington, 1978), 182.

43 The agreement underwent several revisions to permit additional transportation companies to become signatories and to perfect implementation of its terms. At the same time, the U.S. government began to place inspectors along the border. Inspectors were stationed at Quebec, Montreal, Halifax, Vancouver, and Victoria beginning in 1895. On threats to close the border entirely, see Department of Commerce and Labor, *Annual Report of the Com missioner-General of Immigration . . . 1904,* 137. On the original Canadian Agreement, see Marian L. Smith, "The Immigration and Naturalization Service (INS) at the U.S.-Canadian Border, 1893-1993: An Overview of Issues and Topics," *Michigan Historical Review,* 26 (Fall 2000), 127–47; "Canadian Agreement," Sept. 7, 1893, file 51564/4A-B, Subject Correspondence, Immigration and Nationalization Service Records (Washington, D.C.); and U.S. Bureau of Immigration, *Annual Report of the Commissioner-General of Immigration to the Secretary of the Treasury for the Fiscal Year Ended June 30, 1896* (Washington, 1896), 13. For amended versions, see Treasury Department, *Annual Report of the Commissioner-General of Immigration . . . 1902,* 46–48; and "Digest of . . . Report of . . . Braun . . . September 20, 1907."

44 "Digest of . . . Report of . . . Braun . . . September 20, 1907," 30–34.

45 Department of Commerce and Labor, *Annual Report of the Commissioner-General of Immigration . . . 1904,* 138; "Digest of . . . Report of . . . Braun . . . September 20, 1907," 29–30; U.S. Treasury Department, *Annual Report of the Commissioner-General of Immigration For the Fiscal Year Ended June 30, 1901* (Washington, 1901), 52; U.S. Bureau of Immigration, *Compilation from the Records of the Bureau of Immigration of Facts Concerning the Enforcement of*

*the Chinese-Exclusion Laws: Letter from the Secretary of Commerce and Labor, Submitting, in Response to the Inquiry of the House, a Report as to the Enforcement of the Chinese-Exclusion Laws* (Washington, 1906), 94.

46 On threats to close the border, see "Digest of . . . Report of . . . Braun . . . September 20, 1907," 32. Immigration officials cited the benefits of the Canadian Agreement in "Memorandum in re Proposed Mexican Agreement" included in Berkshire to Commissioner-General of Immigration, Jan. 15, 1908, file 51463/B, Subject Correspondence, Immigration and Naturalization Service Records (Washington, D.C.); Department of Commerce and Labor, *Annual Report of the Commissioner-General of Immigration . . . 1904,* 138; Department of Commerce and Labor, *Annual Report of the Commissioner-General of Immigration . . . 1906,* 94; and Department of Commerce and Labor, *Annual Report of the Commissioner-General of Immigration . . . 1911,* 159–60. On inland border inspection points, see Smith, "Immigration and Naturalization Service (INS) at the U.S.-Canadian Border," 127–35.

47 The term "induce" was first used in "Report by . . . Braun . . . Feb. 12, 1907." On changes in immigrants' strategies at the border, see Zhang, "Dragon in the Land of the Eagle," 323; Smith, "Immigration and Naturalization Service (INS) at the U.S.-Canadian Border," 127–30. On the need for fuller cooperation from Canada, see Treasury Department, *Annual Report of the Secretary of the Treasury . . . 1891,* lxv.

48 Act Respecting and Restricting Chinese Immigration, ch. 8, 1903 S.C. 105–11 (Can.); Department of Commerce and Labor, *Annual Report of the Commissioner-General of Immigration . . . 1904,* 138. On Canadian–U.S. negotiations, see, for example, John H. Clark to U.S. Commissioner-General of Immigration, July 16, 1912, file 51931/21, Subject Correspondence, Immigration and Naturalization Service Records (Washington, D.C.). Act of June 30, 1923, ch. 38, 1923 S.C. 301–15 (Can.); H. F. Angus, "Canadian Immigration: The Law and Its Administration," in *The Legal Status of Aliens in Pacific Countries,* ed. Norman MacKenzie (New York, 1937), 63–64.

49 Peter Ward, *White Canada Forever: Popular Attitudes and Public Policy toward Orientals in British Columbia* (Montreal, 1978), 133; Robert E. Wynne, "Reaction to the Chinese in the Pacific Northwest and British Columbia, 1850–1910" (Ph.D. diss., University of Washington, 1964), 483.

50 Bureau of Immigration, *Compilation from the Records of the Bureau of Immigration of Facts Concerning the Enforcement of the Chinese-Exclusion Laws,* 12–33; Lauren McKinsey and Victor Konrad, *Borderlands Reflections—the United States and Canada* (Toronto, 1989), iii; Anzaldúa, *Borderlands,* 3; Linda B. Hall and Don M. Coerver, *Revolution on the Border: The United States and Mexico, 1910–1920* (Albuquerque, 1988), 7.

51 "Report by . . . Braun . . . Feb. 12, 1907"; Marcus Braun to Commissioner-General of Immigration, June 10, 1907, file 52320/1-A, Subject Correspondence, Immigration and Naturalization Service Records (Washington, D.C.); Evelyn Hu-DeHart, "Coolies, Shopkeepers, Pioneers: The Chinese of Mexico and Peru, 1849–1930," *Amerasia Journal,* 15 (no. 1, 1989), 92–98; Hu-DeHart, "Racism and Anti-Chinese Persecution in Sonora, Mexico," 16.

52 Braun to Commissioner-General of Immigration, June 10, 1907, file 52320/1-A, Subject Correspondence, Immigration and Naturalization Service Records (Washington, D.C.).

53 Department of Commerce and Labor, *Annual Report of the Commissioner-General of Immigration . . . 1907,* 112; R. L. Pruett to Braun, May 11, 1902, file 52320/1-A, Exhibit "B," Subject Correspondence, Immigration and Naturalization

Service Records (Washington, D.C.). For the post-1910 period, see Delgado, "In the Age of Exclusion," 241–42, 250–52.

54 "Memorandum in re Proposed Mexican Agreement"; Miguel Tinker Salas, *In the Shadow of the Eagles; Sonora and the Transformation of the Border during the Porfiriato* (Berkeley, 1997), 16, 161; Hall and Coerver, *Revolution on the Border,* 11, 15; Delgado, "In the Age of Exclusion," 241–42, 250–52.

55 Department of Commerce and Labor, *Annual Report of the Commissioner-General of Immigration . . . 1909,* 142.

56 Department of Commerce and Labor, *Annual Report of the Commissioner-General of Immigration . . . 1907,* 130; Keefe to Supervising Inspector, El Paso, Texas, Nov. 26, 1909, file 52265/6, Subject Correspondence, Immigration and Naturalization Service Records (Washington, D.C.); Berkshire to Commissioner-General of Immigration, Feb. 15, 1910, file 52142/6, *ibid;* Clarence A. Miller to Assistant Secretary of State, Oct. 11, 1909, file 52265/6, *ibid.*

57 "Report by . . . Braun . . . Feb. 12, 1907"; Frank R. Stone to Berkshire, April 23, 1910, file 52801/4A, Subject Correspondence, Immigration and Naturalization Service Records (Washington, D.C.); Berkshire to Commissioner-General of Immigration, May 7, 1910, *ibid.;* Perkins, *Border Patrol,* 11, 23.

58 Department of Commerce and Labor, *Annual Report of the Commissioner-General of Immigration . . . 1906,* 95; Braun to Commissioner-General of Immigration, June 10, 1907, file 52320/1-A, Subject Correspondence, Immigration and Naturalization Service Records (Washington, D.C.).

59 John M. Myers, *The Border Wardens* (Englewood Cliffs, 1971), 16–17, 23; Rak, *Border Patrol,* 6; Perkins, *Border Patrol,* xii, 9; "The U.S. Border Patrol: The First Fifty Years," *I & N Reporter* (Summer 1974), 3; Immigration and Naturalization Service, "Early Immigration Inspection along the U.S./Mexican Border"; Zhang, "Dragon in the Land of the Eagle," 372.

60 Department of Commerce and Labor, *Annual Report of the Commissioner-General of Immigration . . . 1906,* 95; Department of Commerce and Labor, *Annual Report of the Commissioner-General of Immigration . . . 1909,* 132; "New Chinese Inspector," *El Paso Herald,* June 27, 1899, in box 8, Chinese General Correspondence, Immigration and Naturalization Service Records (Washington, D.C.).

61 Here deportation figures apply to those found to be in the country unlawfully. They do not include immigrants denied entry upon arrival. Department of Commerce and Labor, *Annual Report of the Commissioner-General of Immigration . . . 1904,* 148.

62 Immigration and Naturalization Service, "Early Immigration Inspection along the U.S./Mexican Border."

63 The commissioner-general of immigration reported that southern border strategies to curb Chinese illegal immigration were yielding results as early as 1905. Department of Commerce and Labor, *Annual Report of the Commissioner-General of Immigration . . . 1905,* 94. On the border conditions in 1911 and during World War I, see Department of Commerce and Labor, *Annual Report of the Commissioner-General of Immigration . . . 1911,* 146; and Perkins, *Border Patrol,* 49. On conditions in Mexico that diminished Chinese illegal immigration, see Salas, *In the Shadow of the Eagles,* 171.

64 Act of Feb. 5, 1917, sec. 19, 39 Stat. 889; Zhang, "Dragon in the Land of the Eagle," 375–76; R. D. McKenzie, *Oriental Exclusion; The Effect of American Immigration Laws, Regulations, and Judicial Decisions upon the Chinese and Japanese on the American Pacific Coast* (Chicago, 1927), 158.

65 Juan Perea, *Immigrants Out! The New Nativism and the Anti-Immigrant Impulse in the United States* (New York, 1997), 73; Kevin R. Johnson, "Race, the Immigration

Laws, and Domestic Race Relations: A 'Magic Mirror' into the Heart of Darkness," *Indiana Law Journal,* 73 (Fall 1998), 1137; Claudia Sadowski-Smith, "Reading across Diaspora: Chinese and Mexican Undocumented Immigration at Land Borders," in *Globalization on the Line: Culture, Capital, and Citizenship at U.S. Borders,* ed. Claudia Sadowski-Smith (New York, forthcoming).

66 *Washington Post,* Oct. 1, 1996, p. Al; *ibid.*, April 5, 1996, p. A17; "Immigration Overhaul," *Migration News,* 3 (Oct. 1996) <http://migration.ucdavis.edu/mn/archive_mn/oct_1996-01mn.html> (Feb. 15, 2002); *New York Times,* May 27, 2001, p. Al4.

67 *Chicago Tribune,* Sept. 26, 2001, p. 9; *New York Times,* Oct. 1, 2001, p. B3; Dennis Bueckert, "Canadian Sovereignty Called into Question in Fight against Terrorism," Oct. 3, 2001, Canadian Press Newswire, available at Lexis-Nexis Academic Universe; *National Post* (Toronto), Oct. 4, 2001, pp. Al, A15; *New York Times,* Oct. 4, 2001, p. B1; *Seattle Times,* Oct. 10, 2001, p. Al.

68 *National Post* (Toronto), Oct. 1, 2001, p. A10.

# 14

# BORDERLANDS OF MODERNITY AND ABANDONMENT

*Geraldo L. Cadava*

Only sixty miles west of tall steel border walls in Ambos Nogales on the U.S.-Mexico border, people pass casually through staggered fences on the Tohono O'odham reservation. These border spaces are adjacent points along the same international boundary, but the contrast between them could not be more apparent. Nogales, Arizona, and Nogales, Sonora, together are known as Ambos Nogales and assert a single community identity despite different histories (the Spanish word *ambos* means "both"). Ambos Nogales has continuous border fencing, storefronts, and homes that crowd as close to the international line as laws permit, and hundreds of U.S. and Mexican government agents police everything that moves across the border. Heading west from the city, steel walls turn into chain link and barbed wire fences, and vehicle barriers spaced far enough apart for cattle and people to cross through. These fences soon reach the lands of the Tohono O'odham, a binational indigenous group divided by the border. Their borderlands remain rural, sparsely populated, and comparatively less policed. They lack the fortress-like walls that symbolize the border's militarization; brick and mortar businesses that represent cross-border commerce; and customs and immigration compounds that embody U.S. and Mexican states on the frontiers of both nations.[1]

This article explains how two borderlands so close together developed so differently. It begins in the mid-nineteenth century, with the demarcation of the border after the U.S.-Mexico War, but moves quickly to the mid-twentieth century. After World War II, the U.S.-Mexico border region boomed. Hundreds of thousands of people with varied citizenships, races, and identities streamed into borderlands cities. U.S. and Mexican officials enforced the border, but they also encouraged cross-border social, cultural, and economic exchanges that promoted harmonious international relations and shared visions of progress and modernity. These developments, however, did not affect Ambos Nogales and the Tohono O'odham nation in the same way.[2]

The construction of international gateways in Ambos Nogales during the 1960s symbolized the border region's modernity, contrasting with the comparative abandonment of O'odham lands and people. By the late 1960s, U.S. and Mexican states saw border cities as symbols of the frontier's capitalist development, while often viewing sparse O'odham lands as synonymous with O'odham antimodernity. Those differences became imprinted upon the land, confirming the literary scholar Mary Pat Brady's argument that the border is "a state-sponsored aesthetic project" intertwined in the "swirl" of history and narrative. Post–World War II ideas about modernity and abandonment—the state-sponsored aesthetics examined here—put in sharp relief U.S. and Mexican histories of capitalist development, border regulation, and citizenship based on national belonging; support of state projects and ideologies; and access to services. Finally, during the late twentieth century, even though the appearances of these borderlands remained different, perceptions of them converged as many increasingly saw the entire border as a zone of criminality.[3]

The contrast between these two border spaces during the postwar era demonstrates a paradox made visible by the historian Samuel Truett: state visions of a uniform border were at odds with the reality of a border that national governments invested in, developed, and tightly policed in certain areas, while leaving others comparatively unattended. It is a paradox that represents contradictions within U.S. and Mexican approaches to the border: both nations encouraged and engaged in cross-border quests for modernity but then abandoned areas and peoples that did not conform. These approaches segmented metropolitan Ambos Nogales and the Tohono O'odham nation into quadrants—Nogales, Arizona; Nogales, Sonora; O'odham land in Arizona; and O'odham land in Sonora—enabling comparisons between Mexicans and indigenous peoples, Anglos and Mexicans, and indigenous peoples in Arizona and Sonora.[4]

Focusing on the recent histories of borderlands within Ambos Nogales and the Tohono O'odham nation offers new perspectives on North American borderlands more broadly. As a field, borderlands history has focused on Spanish, Mexican, and early American borderlands into the nineteenth century, when imperial relationships were still being determined, nations were still being formed, and racial categorization was more fluid. The few works that move into the twentieth century argue that U.S. borders hardened by the 1930s as a result of new immigration restrictions, establishment of the border patrol, and depression-era xenophobia. These works then leap forward to connect those developments with present phenomena. But contemporary meanings of the border owe as much to the period after World War II as to earlier moments, remaining fluid into the present. Even with nation-states consolidating by the early twentieth century and borderlands becoming borders, as the historians Jeremy Adelman and Stephen Aron have argued, national governments still struggled to maintain authority in the border region—through not only armed enforcement but also the deployment of ideas about modernity and abandonment.[5]

Comparing these borderlands also illuminates transnational histories of Mexicans, indigenous peoples, and North Americans. Scholars have written histories of binational indigenous groups straddling the U.S.-Mexican and U.S.-Canadian borders. They also have written about indigenous groups and Mexicans together, offering either transnational histories of the pre–World War II period or nation-based histories of the postwar era. A comparison of postwar U.S., Mexican, and indigenous borderlands grounded in transnational archival research enables insights that histories of one group on both sides of the border or two groups on one side cannot, challenging traditional assumptions about relations among nations, groups, and individuals.[6]

A comparison of Ambos Nogales and O'odham borderlands enables other new perspectives as well. These border spaces provide opportunities for conceiving of distinctions between particular border segments, but migration, economic, and kinship practices undermine the rigidity of perceived differences. Many observers, even historians, have presumed an ontological divide between a modern United States and a primitive Mexico. Ambos Nogales and O'odham borderlands challenge that understanding by tilting the border's east-west axis ninety degrees to reveal mid-twentieth-century understandings in both Mexico and the United States of a modern Ambos Nogales and primitive Tohono O'odham nation. But these borderlands were more complicated still. Officials and reporters noted the modern habits of O'odham in Arizona and Sonora; conversely, border vice in Ambos Nogales manifested the disorder and backwardness more commonly associated with the Tohono O'odham nation. As such, the border became a point not only of division or unity but also of multiple refractions of meaning.[7]

Soon after the 1848 Treaty of Guadalupe Hidalgo, which formally ended the U.S.-Mexico War, the 1854 Gadsden Purchase cut through the Mexican state of Sonora and annexed an additional 30,000 square miles of land to the United States. U.S. and Mexican surveyors marked the new international line between Sonora and Arizona, which formed part of New Mexico Territory until 1863. For many, the border became an opportunity for profit. Wagon-based freight companies, transnational mining interests, and cross-border cattle ranches became industries of moving goods between the United States and Mexico. So did cross-border raids. Article 11 of the Treaty of Guadalupe Hidalgo singled out Native Americans and obligated the United States to prevent their raids into Mexico, even though U.S. filibusters and "white Cowboys" raided as well. The raids prompted early calls for border enforcement, but the physical character of the border remained unchanged into the late nineteenth century, when locomotives led to the growth of Ambos Nogales. Until then, sporadically placed cairns were the only objects that let anyone know where one country ended and the other began.[8]

The railroad's arrival in this borderland region signified industrialization and an emerging capitalist economy. The U.S. Southern Pacific Railroad and the Southern Pacific Railroad of Mexico met in Nogales, linking the border with the Mexican interior. When railroads arrived, the U.S. and Mexican governments erected customshouses to regulate international exchange, which in turn led to the creation of ancillary occupations including customs brokers, border agents, and importers and exporters. Border towns became border cities, and national governments resurveyed the boundary line, seeking to clearly demarcate the border as new businesses crowded against it. In 1897 President William McKinley created "a public reservation of a strip of land sixty feet wide" on the U.S. side of the border where businesses could not operate. As they sought to make the boundary a more concrete reality, government officials replaced cairns with guardhouses and obelisks.[9]

Just as market capitalism reshaped the border within Ambos Nogales, it also affected the Tohono O'odham land base. From the seventeenth century onward, Spanish, Mexican, and U.S. political regimes enacted laws that prioritized private land ownership. Bourbon reforms during the late Spanish colonial period and Mexican legislation during the early to mid-nineteenth century expedited the division of communal lands into private plots. Following the U.S.-Mexico War, the United States did the same. After first establishing O'odham reservations at San Xavier and Gila Bend in 1874 and 1882, the U.S. government passed the 1887 Dawes Act—or General Allotment Act—which divided communal lands and redistributed them to individuals and families. Some O'odham became ranchers and small farmers, while others sought off-reservation work alongside Mexicans, in mines, on farms, and on railroads. Market-oriented capitalism and popular movements against it helped spark the Mexican Revolution, which, along with World War I, transformed Nogales and O'odham borders again.[10]

The border militarized as U.S. soldiers guarded the international line in the wake of Pancho Villa's 1916 raid on Columbus, New Mexico, and as revolutionary violence threatened to, and sometimes did, cross the border. At the same time, O'odham ranchers in Arizona complained that Mexican soldiers stole their cattle and horses, driving them deep into Sonora where they were difficult to recover. In response to O'odham demands for protection the United States established the Sells Reservation in 1916 and built the first border fence on O'odham lands. Security concerns also drove border policies during World War II, but so did the rise of cross-border commerce. Fearing enemy invasions, U.S. and Mexican governments required border residents to register with local authorities and closed segments of the border. Residents of Ambos Nogales carried special border-crossing cards, and U.S. officials padlocked reservation gates. But the simultaneous growth of cross-border exchange also triggered an economic and demographic boom. The 1934 Indian Reorganization Act had prompted the Tohono O'odham to adopt a constitution, establish tribal government, and increase participation in regional capitalist economies. Meanwhile, Mexican government officials appealed to the United States for financial assistance with infrastructural developments that were part of the binational defense effort and would benefit cross-border commerce into the postwar era.[11]

After World War II, customs and immigration gateways in Ambos Nogales symbolized the modern transformation of border cities. Not long after the war ended, local officials, businessmen, and economic boosters pressured their national governments to build new ports of entry and facilitate international exchange, the economic livelihood of border communities. The imminent completion of a highway from the border to Mexico City had many in Ambos Nogales worried that the cities would not be able to accommodate the anticipated traffic increase. A 1953 report by the Nogales, Arizona, Chamber of Commerce characterized cross-border traffic as "very bad," and predicted that following completion of the road to Mexico City the situation "will become impossible." The report offered impressive statistical data to support gateway construction, which promised to facilitate the rapid passage of vehicles in and out of the region. Between 1951 and 1952 local border traffic—individuals who crossed by foot or automobile and remained in the border region instead of traveling to the interiors of Mexico or the United States—increased by 3 million people, from 9 million to 12 million. Between 1949 and 1952 the value of exports that passed through Ambos Nogales to Mexico increased from $18 million to $41 million, and the value of imports into the United States increased from $25 million to $42 million. In 1952 Mexico invited even more retail trade by making Nogales, Sonora, a free-trade zone. On a Sunday in 1953, "a day of no particular significance," the author of the chamber of commerce report observed bumper-to-bumper traffic stretching from the border deep into Mexico. Business was booming and something had to be done, not only to solve the problem of congestion but also because doing nothing would be an opportunity lost.[12]

Supporters of new gateways prepared information pamphlets, deluged politicians with requests for support, and invited government representatives to the border to decide where a new gate might be placed. All agreed that new international gateways were necessary but had yet to determine their form. During the early 1950s, ports of entry in Nogales, Arizona, stood at Grand and Morley Avenues, two of the city's busier commercial strips. One leading proposal, supported by business owners tired of trucks idling in front of their stores, was to establish a third gateway west of the downtown business districts especially for trucks (Ambos Nogales got a third gate, but not for decades). For the moment, the U.S. government planned to improve the Grand Avenue gate and widen the one at Morley Avenue. Planning took place in consultation with Mexican businessmen, engineers, and government representatives. But according to U.S. officials, because Mexico was unable at the time to say what the "final outcome of their deliberations" would be, the United States moved forward on its own.[13]

As government officials and border residents made these plans, the *Saturday Evening Post* published a profile of Ambos Nogales in May 1952 that economic boosters could not have written better themselves. Brushing aside past conflicts to suggest how much the cities had progressed, the author wrote, "A two-nation border town where Mexicans and gringos used to kill each other on sight, Nogales is now the place where Anglos and Latins mix like peaches and cream." Just months after the article appeared, Congress passed the restrictive McCarran-Walter Act over President Harry S. Truman's veto. The act extended a national origins quota for immigration and, at the height of Cold War–inspired fear, allowed the deportation of immigrants and naturalized citizens suspected as subversives. But in the gateway proposals, nobody openly suspected that an increased flow of people across the border would mean trouble. Government officials in Ambos Nogales still reported subversive activities—marijuana busts, prostitution, and wartime black markets in oil and rubber—but in the two decades after World War II, these concerns paled next to promotions of cross-border economic development. Residents of Ambos Nogales fought for their gateways and won, and then they waited. Politicians and businessmen hoped to have the gateways finished by January 1954, at the peale of trucking, tourist, and vegetable-importing seasons, but government bureaucracies did not fund the projects until 1963.[14]

As if to make up for lost time, the border gateways were executed on a much larger scale than either the United States or Mexico had imagined. Instead of undertaking simple expansions, the U.S. and Mexican governments built new border complexes. The design and appearance of the projects on each side of the border differed greatly. The Mexican edifice had two large arches that resembled the wings of a bird. Seen from above, the arches looked like an airplane headed north, toward the United States. Just south of the monument stood a circle of flags representing nations throughout the Americas. Nogales, Sonora, also got a new customs facility, a new telephone building, an overhauled telephone grid, an "ultra-modern" railroad station, and a new pediatrics and maternity hospital. The U.S. building, meanwhile, was rectangular, nondescript, and functional—a two-story, steel-frame building with exterior walls made of blue mosaic tiles. The ground level was for automobile and pedestrian inspection facilities, while the second floor housed offices of the Immigration and Naturalization Service, Public Health Service, and U.S. Customs. Mexico spent $12 million on its border projects; the United States spent $1.9 million. Architects chosen to design these projects further suggest the different approaches taken by Mexico and the United States. Mexico chose Mario Pani, one of the country's most prominent modernist architects. Pani's many buildings could be seen throughout Mexico City, including several at the National Autonomous University of

Mexico. One newspaper described him as "Mexico's top young architect." Meanwhile, the U.S. government chose the Tucson architect Emerson Scholer, whose later obituaries praised his designs for local hospitals, schools, and libraries, but not the work he did on the border. The *Nogales Herald* put it simply: the project in Sonora was "more elaborate" than the one in Arizona.[15]

Mexican construction crews sliced away portions of the hillsides that hemmed in downtown Nogales, Sonora, suggesting through this literal transformation of the landscape the importance that Mexico attributed to the border projects. During the early 1960s, the Mexican government attempted to make the northern border region attractive for investment, tourism, and settlement by combating images of its remoteness and backwardness. During the mid-twentieth century, Mexican leaders recognized the area as one of the country's main engines of economic and demographic growth. In 1960, U.S. tourists spent $520 million there compared with $150 million in Mexico's interior. Also, salaries in northern Mexico were higher than in other parts of the country, in part because goods in the North cost more due to the influx of U.S. dollars. The average annual income in northern Mexico was $652 per person, 135 percent higher than the $280 one could expect to make elsewhere. As a result, northern Mexico's population exploded in the decades after World War II, becoming the country's fastest growing region. It grew by more than 83 percent during the 1950s, compared with 34 percent in the rest of Mexico. Between 1940 and 1960, the population of Nogales, Sonora, in particular, nearly tripled, growing from 14,000 to 38,000. Pani's designs for the new gateway reflected these developments, evoking the Brazilian architect Oscar Niemeyer's 1950s designs for Brasilia, the capital of Brazil, the layout of which also resembled an airplane. Aviation-themed designs demonstrated not only the influence of modernist architecture throughout Latin America but also the popularity of technological innovations enabling the cross-border movement of people and goods among the Americas.[16]

Sonoran border projects signified not only industrial development but existential maturation as well. Established in 1961 by President Adolfo López Mateos, the National Border Program (Programa Nacional Fronterizo, or PRONAF) became the grandest of Mexico's efforts to link the border region's postwar economic and technological development with Mexican modernity itself. López Mateos called PRONAF a "top priority" of his domestic policy, and PRONAF director Antonio Bermúdez—the former director of the nationally owned oil company Pemex and former mayor of Ciudad Juárez—said, through "urbanization, new highways and beautiful public buildings . . . Mexico is making a complete change in the image of its northern cities." The projects in Nogales would make the city a "showplace," he continued, echoing claims that PRONAF would convert the border region into a "show window 1600 miles long." Putting words into practice, the

Mexican government budgeted $300 million for PRONAF projects along the northern border.[17]

Mexico's extravagant opening ceremony heightened the sense that modernity had arrived in Sonoras largest border city. On November 12, 1964, the day the gateway opened, López Mateos visited Nogales with his cabinet. He boarded a train at the new depot and took a three-mile ride to the border, where he unveiled a plaque and spoke before a crowd of thousands. After Nogales he visited a dam near Hermosillo and toured farms surrounding Navojoa. With his whirlwind tour of Sonoran progress complete, he returned to Mexico City by nightfall. Upon learning that López Mateos had traveled to Sonora, Arizona newspapers reported, local officials and business leaders vowed that "efforts will be made to bring a prominent American here for the occasion." Planners invited President Lyndon B. Johnson, Senator Barry Goldwater, Senator Carl Hayden, and others. None of those invited attended except Arizona's governor-elect Sam Goddard. The incongruity of attendance by Mexico's highest official and a state official from Arizona suggested a discrepancy in how U.S. and Mexican officials viewed the projects. But mismatched efforts were typical in many U.S.-Mexican diplomatic ceremonies; Mexican officials frequently projected displays of pomp, modernity, state influence, and wealth for their northern neighbors.[18]

Despite the unfavorable comparisons it received, the new U.S. border building also signified modernity in the Arizona border region. Construction of the Arizona gateway coincided with the 175th anniversary of the U.S. Customs Service, first established in 1789 by Congress and signed into law by George Washington. On January 1, 1964, President Johnson declared that 1964 would be "United States Customs Year." To link that national commemoration with the new customs building in Arizona, state officials declared that November 1964 would be "U.S. Customs Month in Arizona." The anniversary inspired lectures by officials and businessmen, who described customs collections as necessary to provide revenue, regulate commerce, prevent fraud, thwart smugglers, and protect U.S. agriculture, industry, and labor. They told the story of Arizona's first collector of customs, George Christ, who rode the "iron horse" into the territory during the 1880s. Explaining how things had changed since then, one speaker noted that when Christ came to Arizona—George Christ, that is—there was "no fence between the two countries." Speakers in 1964 considered his arrival pivotal because it gave "the small community of crude adobe structures a position of importance as a port of entry."[19]

As during the 1950s, not a single U.S. or Mexican report on the projects mentioned immigration restriction as a factor motivating their construction. In 1964—the same year that the U.S. and Mexican governments ended the Mexican guest worker arrangement known as the bracero program and the U.S. Congress was debating a new immigration and nationality act—Ambos Nogales politicians and residents were more concerned with securing their ability to engage cross-border commerce than with securing the border itself. Because Mexico and the United States demonstrated similar interests, the border projects also suggested that Ambos Nogales embodied national and internationally shared ideologies of modernization and economic development.

The new gateways enabled even greater increases in cross-border exchange into the 1970s. Customs collections grew exponentially each year after the new gates opened. In 1964–1965, agents in Nogales, Arizona, collected $9 million, which "shattered all records" for the Arizona district and were even greater than those collected in San Diego and El Paso. Leaders of the West Mexico Vegetable Distributors Association, headquartered in the city, became powerful lobbyists and demanded yet another port of entry. The result was the construction in 1974 of a truck inspection station west of downtown, which many in the city had lobbied for in the early 1950s. To recognize the significance of trade in Ambos Nogales, Presidents Luis Echeverría Alvarez and Gerald R. Ford met there later that year. After their meeting, commerce between Arizona and Sonora continued unabated, even though debates about border criminality soon eclipsed public celebrations of international commerce like those of the mid-1960s.[20]

The idea during the 1960s that the border at Nogales could be a "show window" to promote Mexico contrasted sharply with the image projected by Tohono O'odham borderlands. Mexico and the United States shone a spotlight on progress in certain border spaces, while ignoring others. Whereas metropolitan Ambos Nogales became a symbol of the modern U.S.-Mexico border, the Tohono O'odham nation remained a borderlands marked by abandonment, despite rhetoric in both countries of indigenous uplift and investment in indigenous communities. Nogales and O'odham borderlands evolved side by side, but with different results.

Even if the border on O'odham lands had no customs house or steel barriers and few government agents to patrol the international line, it served some of the same functions as the border in Ambos Nogales. Like gateways in Ambos Nogales, the San Miguel gate presented informal opportunities for profit. One newspaper claimed that every weekend scores of O'odham would "swarm" San Miguel, where Mexican O'odham sold chimichangas and tortillas; fruits and vegetables; and crafts at a deep discount compared with stores in the United States. Also like in Ambos Nogales, legal trade operated alongside a black market in illicit goods, especially liquor, which was prohibited on Arizona's O'odham reservation. The San Miguel gate also created a quandary for authorities seeking to enforce cultural and political boundaries. U.S. officials noted how, as a matter of "habit" or "tradition," the border at San Miguel was "always open" to O'odham who crossed "without hindrance." During the 1950s, though, U.S. authorities attempted to corral O'odham cross-border movements to official ports of entry. When O'odham complained, Indian Affairs commissioner Glenn Emmons acknowledged that the new policy contrasted with the "promiscuous crossing" of earlier years. Believing they were O'odham instead of Mexican or U.S. citizens, the "idea of citizenship" as belonging to one nation or the other for the first time "became of any importance" to them, Emmons claimed. Finally, in contrast with the Ambos Nogales border, the San Miguel gate divided indigenous lands in the United States and Mexico.[21]

After the Gadsden Purchase, each country established different practices for acknowledging aboriginal title, which shaped O'odham relationships to land in Arizona and Sonora from the nineteenth century onward. Simply put, the United States created reservations while Mexico created *ejidos,* or communal lands granted by presidential decree. Beginning in 1874, with the creation of the San Xavier Reservation southwest of Tucson, the U.S. government established reserves ostensibly to protect O'odham from the onslaught of nonindigenous migrations following the territory's incorporation into the union. The United States then established the Gila Bend Reservation in 1882 and the Sells Reservation in 1917. Nonindigenous peoples protested at every step the creation of reservations, decrying the resulting "lack of access" to O'odham lands and claiming that O'odham were racially unfit to cultivate them. Still, over time the United States acknowledged titles based on habitation "since time immemorial," or habitation in the "Indian fashion," the technical term by which U.S. government officials recognized migratory land use.[22]

Mexico's *ejidos* remained vulnerable to encroachment despite being granted by the president himself. O'odham in Sonora also claimed longtime habitation of their land, arguing that Moctezuma had given it to them. But because they were unable to prove their title, the Mexican government granted them *ejidos* as *dotaciónes,* or endowments, instead of *restituciones,* recoveries of land that the government acknowledged had once belonged to indigenous peoples. Beginning during the Mexican Revolution and reaching a high point during the presidency of Lázaro Cárdenas (1934–1940), Mexico carved up national lands in Sonora that held various legal statuses, including *ejidos.* The Mexican government did not "officially" distinguish between indigenous people such as the O'odham and mixed-race mestizo peasants, who could also receive *ejido* lands. *Ejidos,* therefore, rarely represented the reclamation of traditional O'odham homelands or claims to sovereignty. In the central valleys of Sonora, Yaqui Indians and nonindigenous small farmers received a majority *of ejido* lands. While the O'odham in the northern part of the state received some small *ejido* allotments near the border, cattle ranches—largely exempted from Cárdenas-era agrarian reforms—surrounded and often impinged upon their holdings.[23]

Even though Mexican government officials did not explicitly articulate land policies in the language of *mestizaje* and *indigenismo*—two postrevolutionary ideologies related, respectively, to the veneration of the country's mixed-race population and to the incorporation of indigenous peoples into mainstream society—the creation of *ejidos* did have the effect of those ideologies. Their creation led to the absorption of many Sonoran O'odham into Mexican towns, or the "Mexicanizing" of the "Indian himself," as President Cárdenas put it. The Mexican state, particularly *indigenistas,* the intellectual and political elite who advocated indigenous progress first through assimilation then through pluralism, upheld these ideologies as social and cultural ideals. *Mestizaje* and *indigenismo* supposedly represented a renewed commitment to indigenous progress, and contemporaries interpreted them as progressive because they countered ideas about Anglo supremacy then prevalent in Europe, the United States, and elsewhere. But the supporters of those ideals ignored the racial hierarchies that continued to exist in Mexico, as well as the impact that incorporation had on traditional O'odham landholdings.[24]

Because the United States granted reservations, O'odham land in Arizona appeared to benefit from government protections that Sonoras O'odham land did not. But despite the insulation that reservations nominally guaranteed, reservations did not prevent encroachment. Throughout the twentieth century, O'odham in Arizona struggled against forces that threatened to strip away their land or use it in a way they had not approved. When the U.S. government allotted individual parcels of land or created reservations, it left Native Americans the right to lease or sell the land as they chose. This provision aligned with government interests in capitalist development and encouraged many Native Americans to lease to outside mining, ranching, and oil interests. On the Sells Reservation, O'odham who lived closest to Tucson and Nogales were most likely to negotiate with outsiders. These O'odham, according to the historian Eric Meeks, were "generally more receptive to the prospect of private property" and chose to "abandon the older practice of village government by consensus." The decision to grant outsiders access to their lands created rifts between O'odham communities on the Sells Reservation. Therefore, notwithstanding the establishment of reservations in the United States, efforts to dispossess O'odham of their territories and resources was an experience common to O'odham on both sides of the border.[25]

Still, even more than reservations, *ejidos* were islands surrounded by a rising tide of nonindigenous peoples who persistently threatened O'odham land. Despite postrevolutionary agrarian reforms intended to protect communal land, Sonoran O'odham protested encroachments into the late twentieth century. A particularly provocative case unfolded in 1957, when the director of Mexico's National Indigenous Institute (Instituto Nacional Indigenista, or INI), Alfonso Caso, sent his associate, the anthropologist Alfonso Fabila, to investigate complaints by O'odham living on Sonoras Pozo Verde and El Bajío *ejidos.* Fabila traveled from Mexico City to one O'odham settlement after another, where he collected ethnographic data that led him to conclude that mestizo encroachment had created an "alarming situation," which, if allowed to continue, would constitute a "grave injustice."[26]

According to the O'odham, the aggressors were members of the Zepeda-Wood family, who owned a cumulative 70,000 hectares of land in northern Sonora along the international border. Jesús Zepeda was the patriarch of the family. His son was Rudolf Zepeda, a vice president of the Valley National Bank of Phoenix. His daughter was Fresia Zepeda, who had married a U.S. citizen named Robert Wood. They owned the land together, revealing the dense family and commercial connections that shaped cross-border relations between Anglos and Mexicans. But O'odham complaints likewise revealed how the border region's indigenous communities could be victims of those collaborations. Particularly troubling, the O'odham and Fabila both agreed, was the fact that foreigners owned Mexican land along the border. The O'odham claimed that Hermosillo's Colonization Commission, the local branch of the national agency responsible for disbursing land, had sold the Zepeda-Wood property despite knowing that foreigners could not own land within sixty miles of the border.[27]

While foreign ownership of Mexican land made O'odham complaints against the Zepeda-Woods somewhat distinctive, Fabila learned of similar encroachments during his travels. Representatives for the 250 O'odham in Caborca, 50 in Quitovac, and 40 in Sonoita recounted how the Colonization Commission in Hermosillo divided up O'odham land to sell it to mestizos and other nonindigenous peoples. Invaders enclosed the property they purchased with wire fences, marked with their own brands cattle that belonged to O'odham ranchers, diverted O'odham water sources, and inhibited O'odham animals from grazing. Finally, when the O'odham complained, nobody listened. In Caborca, O'odham governor José Antonio Acosta told Fabila that, on the very day of their interview, the Colonization Commission had announced the boundaries of O'odham properties it planned to acquire. In Quitovac, another O'odham told him that when Manuel Ávila Camacho campaigned in 1940 to become the president of Mexico, he promised to mark clearly the boundaries of O'odham lands. But after becoming president, he "did nothing."[28]

Having suffered injustices for decades, many O'odham claimed that the Mexican government had abandoned them. Since 1928, when a presidential decree established the Pozo Verde *ejido,* Mexico had been sending representatives of various government agencies—agricultural specialists, irrigation engineers, livestock veterinarians, indigenous-affairs experts, and foreign relations advisers—to do "everything necessary" to develop O'odham land and defend it against "all forms of plunder." But because the federal government also turned a blind eye to divisions and sales of O'odham land by state agencies such as the Colonization Commission, its mandate lacked credibility. While government interventions on their behalf brought short-term comfort to some O'odham, evidence over the course of the twentieth century reveals a Mexican government that neglected its O'odham citizens. Many O'odham, at least, believed this to be true. As one O'odham representative put it, the actions of the Colonization Commission demonstrated that the Mexican government only considered "mestizos as Mexicans" and granted "better concessions to American colonists," who benefitted from their "contacts with the governors of the state" and their "greater cultural and economic resources." The American colonist Rudolf Zepeda substantiated O'odham suspicions. During Fabila's conversations with him, Zepeda, in the same breath that he claimed a right to national lands, offered a list of the prominent men he counted as friends, including President Adolfo Ruiz Cortines and Secretary of Foreign Affairs Luis Padilla Nervo.[29]

The Mexican government and nonindigenous mestizos, however, did not believe that they had abandoned the O'odham, but rather that the O'odham had abandoned them by refusing to fall in line with postrevolutionary visions of a modern Mexican state. For members of the Zepeda-Wood family, that rationale had a culturally and racially biased bent. According to Robert Wood's son, Sonoran O'odham were obstacles to overcome, a bunch of "lazy, drunken . . . thieves." His uncle Rudolf Zepeda also considered O'odham a "problem," arguing for their removal inland to a proposed "Mexican O'odham Reservation." Coming as Zepeda did from Arizona, the placement of indigenous peoples on reservations must have seemed a natural solution. Even though Mexican Americans also were victims of racial discrimination, they nevertheless distinguished themselves from indigenous peoples. Zepeda established a contrast between himself and Sonoran O'odham by noting that his bank offered loans to mestizo cattle ranchers, indicating that his business supported the goals of the Mexican government, while O'odham endeavors did not. Even Fabila, whose writings revealed him to be an advocate for the O'odham, sometimes reinforced that logic by comparing the productivity of mestizo and O'odham farms. Not only did mestizo farms produce greater quantities of fruits and vegetables, he explained, but a greater diversity as well. Mexican farmers produced oranges, grapes, peaches, apricots, and watermelons—much of which made its way to the United States through Ambos Nogales—while O'odham farmers grew only melons. Fabila also succumbed to stereotypes about the O'odham as "wandering people," which contributed to false perceptions of them as unorganized members of free-floating groups rather than coherent communities.[30]

Descriptions of O'odham lack of productivity and dispersal mirrored Fabila's musings on the desolation and remoteness of their lands, homes, and selves. Even though metropolitan Ambos Nogales and O'odham lands both experienced deadly heat, Fabila argued that O'odham lands were dangerous to outsiders. Many "who are not from this region," he wrote, "already have died" in this "unfamiliar" and "hostile" environment. Moreover, O'odham homes were "rudimentary," made of ocotillo branches, adobe, and earthen floors. Fabila noted with surprise every time he encountered "modern" accoutrements such as sewing machines, American-made beds, and pewter and aluminum pots. Similarly, despite their "bad" hygiene and "open air" defecation, he noted their "modern" haircuts, leather jackets, and shoes. U.S. reporters made similar statements about Arizona O'odham. A 1962 *Los Angeles Times* article quipped, "The 20th Century has arrived, although 60 years late." Pick-up trucks replaced the "horse and wagon," and Native Americans used knives, forks, "cups, plates, telephones and furniture." In a sense, these statements highlighted the supposed success of U.S. and Mexican assimilation projects. But they also perpetuated notions that indigenous peoples on both sides of the border lived outside modernity. That tension led Fabila to waver awkwardly between proclaiming that O'odham in Sonora were economically stable and that their situation was desperate. His participation in the circulation of these ideas demonstrated how prevalent conceptions of modernity grounded in maximized productivity, mastery of nature, and ordered settlement—as in Ambos Nogales—had become. To become productive citizens, many believed, the O'odham needed to strive toward those goals. Their failure to do so implied their betrayal of the states that claimed to protect them.[31]

For nonindigenous mestizos, nothing symbolized Sonoran O'odham's abandonment of Mexico more than their increasing emigration to the Sells Reservation in Arizona. Since the border's creation, O'odham had traveled back and forth across it, but over time their movements became increasingly unidirectional, from Sonora to Arizona. Until the early twentieth century, binational residence was common, as many O'odham worked seasonally in both states. Migration patterns changed, not only because Sonoran O'odham sought access to services provided on the Sells Reservation but also because of the border region's changing economic environment. The growth of mining, ranching, and agricultural industries in the United States drew O'odham from both sides of the border into regional economies of labor and consumption. Sonoran and Arizona O'odham increasingly found work in Arizona cities as wage laborers at ranches, farms, and mines; and as domestics, railroad workers, truck drivers, and construction workers. They made trips back to their home villages only for social, family, and religious gatherings. Fabila described similar developments in Sonora, noting his encounters with "urbanized O'odham" working for mestizos. As a result of O'odham migrations, by 1960 Arizona's O'odham population grew to more than 10,000, Sonora's O'odham population dwindled to less than 1,000, and Tucson became home to the largest O'odham population anywhere.[32]

To the Mexican government, O'odham emigration was a stinging reminder of Mexico's inability to provide for its citizens and of the increasing power of the United States relative to its own. Rudolf Zepeda portrayed O'odham emigrants as a more immediate threat, claiming that, in conspiracy "with the leaders of Sells," they planned to "move the border between Mexico and the United States further into Mexico." Zepeda's claim was fanciful, but it evinced fears of the looming influence of Arizona's Sells Reservation. Mexico's INI director Alfonso Caso only learned of O'odham complaints, in fact, because U.S. Bureau of Indian Affairs (BIA) agents brought them to his attention. Sonoran O'odham reached out first to Sells Indian Agency superintendam

Alden Jones because the BIA had helped them in the past. Jones forwarded their complaints to the former BIA commissioner John Collier, who forwarded the news to Mexico's famed anthropologist and government official, Manuel Gamio. Gamio then informed Caso, who instructed Fabila to investigate. The wide circle that O'odham complaints traveled before reaching Mexican officials—from Sonora to Arizona to New York to Mexico City and, finally, back to Sonora—offered clear evidence of the mutual betrayal and distrust felt by Sonoran O'odham and the Mexican government.[33]

The increasing dependence of Sonoran O'odham on services provided by the Sells Reservation further heightened that sense of division. Foremost among these services were schooling for O'odham children, medical attention, and even places to pick up mail. Because there was no school for O'odham children in Sonora, a bus from Arizona picked them up at the San Miguel gate and took them to reservation schools where they learned English. The Mexican government tried at least twice to establish schools that served their O'odham communities—in 1945 and 1950—but these efforts failed because teachers fled their posts. Because there were no hospitals for O'odham in Sonora, many sought treatment in Sells. Sonoran O'odham, moreover, depended on priests from Arizona who visited them to baptize children, perform marriage ceremonies, and say mass. Finally, because there was no post office nearby, Sonoran O'odham often had mail sent to them in Topawa, San Miguel, Sasabe, and elsewhere in Arizona.[34]

BIA agents recognized that U.S. influence potentially compounded O'odham alienation from the Mexican government, but they argued that responsibility to correct that problem rested with the Mexican government and mestizos who invaded their land. The "Papagos of Sonora are Mexican citizens and can be good citizens," Jones wrote, but that will not happen if the "only government they know is the [U.S.] Papago Indian Agency, the only education they receive is the one given them by American schools, the only non-indigenous language they speak is English, and the only contact they have with other Mexican citizens is with Mexicans who oppress them." The BIA therefore continued to provide services.[35]

American teachers schooling Sonoran O'odham in English, American priests serving O'odham religious needs, and American doctors vaccinating indigenous children aggravated Mexican officials who felt impotent when confronted with the reality of a stronger nation providing for its citizens. Whenever Mexican officials had the opportunity, they argued for diminishing the influence of the Arizona O'odham and the BIA. Their insecurities about the O'odham inversely influenced their drive to display Mexico's modernity, strength, and power at the gateway in Ambos Nogales. But their vague statements about limiting U.S. influence failed to address the fact that the ground beneath their feet had already shifted, and the gulf had widened not only between Sonoran O'odham and the Mexican government but also between Sonoran O'odham and O'odham in Arizona.

The border itself became a point of demarcation for the rifts that had grown between the O'odham in Arizona and Sonora. Each group came to inhabit different "ethnic spaces," as the historian Cynthia Radding has described the union of land and community. Because of their multiple migrations—not only south and north but also west and east between reservations and cities in Arizona, as between *ejidos* and cities in Mexico—many O'odham lost their traditional language and cultural practices. In general, when Sonoran O'odham learned a nonindigenous language they learned Spanish, while Arizona O'odham learned English. Sonoran O'odham "lost" the arts of basketry, pottery, and weaving, but Arizona O'odham maintained them, in part to satisfy the demands of American tourists who created a market for O'odham crafts. Naming broader socioeconomic disparities, while at the same time articulating the Sells Agency's motivation for working to eliminate them, Jones explained, "it's difficult for us to remain content and satisfied on our side of the border, seeing that the O'odham in Arizona are improving in health, they have better education, and advance in everything having to do with their prosperity, while their brothers on the other side of the border lose what little they have." To be sure, Jones could make claims about the advancement of Arizona O'odham only in relation to O'odham in Sonora. At midcentury, fewer than 40 percent of Arizona O'odham spoke English, less than 20 percent could read or write, only two of every three O'odham children in Arizona enrolled in school, and only one in three attended regularly. Arizona's Supreme Court only granted O'odham the right to vote in 1948, making them some of Arizona's most marginalized citizens into the mid-twentieth century. The O'odham in Arizona and Sonora were indeed brothers (and sisters), as Jones had noted, but by the mid-twentieth century the international boundary had precipitated changes that made them unrecognizable to each other. Describing the consequences of these transformations, one scholar wrote: "slowly, the two sides drifted apart."[36]

For two decades after World War II, the experience of modernization and abandonment shaped borderlands in Ambos Nogales and the Tohono O'odham nation. In Ambos Nogales, the United States and Mexico built new international gateways that physically imprinted modernity on the land. Meanwhile, O'odham borderlands often signified modernity's flip side, allowing U.S. and Mexican states to justify their abandonment. Perceptions of difference between these borderlands eroded as many observers began proclaiming that criminality increasingly characterized the border as a whole.

Increased Mexican migrations changed perceptions of Ambos Nogales. Post–World War II promotions of international commerce culminated with the 1965 establishment by the Mexican government of the Border Industrialization Program (BIP), which facilitated the construction of one thousand *maquiladoras* between Tijuana and Matamoros. These factories, owned by global corporations, exploited Mexican labor to manufacture goods sold around the world. The BIP constituted Mexico's effort to provide work for nationals returning from the bracero program, which had ended in 1964. But it also encouraged the migration of hundreds of thousands of workers from Mexico's interior to the border region. By the 1980s, *maquiladoras* accounted for half of the income generated in Nogales, Sonora. The area's population had tripled between 1940 and 1960. It tripled again between 1960 and 1980, and yet again between 1980 and 2000, reaching 400,000 inhabitants. Once in the border region many migrants moved north to the United States, with or without papers.[37]

In combination with economic downturns in Mexico and the United States in the 1970s and 1980s, the rising numbers of Mexican immigrants in the United States sparked intense racism against Mexicans in general, regardless of their citizenship or immigration status. In the same year that Mexico established the BIP, the U.S. Congress passed the Immigration and Nationality Act of 1965, which removed limits on family reunification visas and led to increased immigration from Latin America and Asia. As more immigrants arrived, vigilante groups patrolled the border, and several newspapers rearticulated stereotypes of Mexicans as thieves, drug smugglers, and competition for jobs. Facing extreme pressure, the U.S. Congress, after fifteen years of debate, passed the Immigration Reform and Control Act of 1986, which included employer sanctions, increased border enforcement, and amnesty provisions.[38]

Cross-border tourism industries, export-import businesses, and *maquiladoras,* all of which signified the modernity of Ambos Nogales during the mid-twentieth century, continued to generate great profits. But public conversations about the border focused increasingly on border enforcement rather than cross-border economic exchange. The arched gateway on the Sonoran side of the border still stood, but its magnificence had faded. It became obscured by new and higher border walls constructed during the 1970s and 1990s, and by groups of migrants gathered in plazas awaiting their opportunity to enter the United States, either by climbing over the border wall or tunneling under it. U.S. tourists still visited Nogales to buy alcohol, cheap medicine, and sex, and cars still drove through the wings designed by Pani. But passersby, viewing the gateway through the lens of globalization, associated it with the arches of McDonald's instead of the wings of a plane.[39]

Meanwhile, conditions on O'odham lands remained poor. Despite an increase in job creation, federally sponsored programs such as ones for economic development, relocation, self-determination, land grants, and monetary compensation for land largely failed to improve the O'odham's economic situation. Some became relatively prosperous ranchers and land leasers; others became integrated into regional power structures as cultural brokers and leaders of O'odham government. But the vast majority lived in poverty. Many lived without electricity or running water, suffered continued encroachments upon their lands, and eventually left Mexico. The abandonment of O'odham lands left a vacuum that opened the way for migrants and smugglers. During the 1970s, the Tohono O'odham Tribal Council granted the U.S. Border Patrol greater access to O'odham lands to police the movement of people and drugs. The O'odham themselves participated in smuggling operations. While the historian Robert Perez has argued that O'odham smuggling activities constituted acts of "resistance" against their "trajectory from abundance to scarcity," the tribal council, seeing smuggling as a negative development, called for tighter enforcement. Finally, increased smuggling led customs officers—twelve O'odham men on horseback looking for illegal activities—to patrol reservation lands for the first time.[40]

The O'odham expressed cross-border solidarity in response to the increased pressures from immigration, smuggling, and state failures to solve these problems no matter how many government agents patrolled their lands. During the late 1970s, the Tohono O'odham Tribal Council called on the U.S. and Mexican governments to recognize land on both sides of the border as O'odham "patrimony"; guarantee their right to cross the border freely; protect their lands and resources; and open up tribal enrollment to Sonoran O'odham, entitling them to share land-claims awards. One particularly provocative resolution suggested that Sonora cede Mexico's O'odham lands to the United States, to be held in trust for all O'odham, or, alternatively, establish a government-recognized reservation within Sonora. These efforts culminated twenty years later, in 2000, with the unsuccessful demand that the United States grant citizenship to all O'odham in Arizona and Sonora.[41]

Despite expressions of solidarity, many Sonoran O'odham rejected help from their so-called brothers living north of the border. During the 1990s, O'odham from Quitovac, Sonora, expressed "energetic protest" against the meddling of Arizona O'odham, arguing that Arizona O'odham thought only of their own economic interests as determined by the United States, The Sells Agency, they concluded, negatively affected the "progress of our communities" and "pitted us against the programs and authorities of our own Mexican government." Solicitation of Mexican support, however, did not suggest renewed faith in the Mexican state. As a group from Caborca explained, during the twentieth century the Mexican government repeatedly denied "rights and privileges" promised by the Mexican Revolution. During the late twentieth century, the O'odham articulated more clearly than ever the failure of Mexico's efforts to protect them. In both Mexico and the United States, citizenship guaranteed access to services, and the lack of citizenship did not always prevent access. Nevertheless, citizenship failed to protect indigenous peoples against encroachment and other injustices. The O'odham therefore increasingly echoed emerging indigenous demands throughout the Americas for justice and autonomy.[42]

During the early twenty-first century, U.S. anti-immigrant activists and security hawks called Arizona's borderlands the most dangerous of the southern border's two-thousand-mile expanse. Arizona became the leading point of undocumented entry, and the second-leading point of drug seizure behind Texas, a state with a border more than three times as long as Arizona's. In a sense, this narrative of modernity and abandonment offers a history of the present that demonstrates how the United States and Mexico wrought this situation. But a comparison of Nogales and O'odham borderlands also offers historical lessons for how to think about the U.S.-Mexico border, and all North American borderlands, more broadly.

Post–World War II projects of modernity in Ambos Nogales demonstrated U.S. and Mexican hopes for what the border region might become. But their vision largely excluded O'odham who lived only sixty miles away. During the late twentieth century, the ephemeral quality of the Nogales border projects and the continued poverty of O'odham on both sides of the border demonstrate U.S. and Mexican disinvestment in the border region as a whole, except for national security operations that have received lavish funding. But even though concepts of modernity and abandonment were associated most clearly during the mid-twentieth century with Ambos Nogales and the Tohono O'odham nation, respectively, those concepts were not confined to one or the other of these spaces. Instead, the border refracted these and other ideologies every which way, undermining conceptions of an ontological divide between the United States and Mexico and demonstrating the deep sense of affinity and alienation experienced by borderlands residents. Understanding these dynamics in no way guarantees we will solve problems that have mired North America's borderlands in so much injustice, violence, and inequality; but ignoring them, choosing to see borders as a single uniting or dividing line rather than multiple lines at once, guarantees that we will not.

## NOTES

1 Tohono O'odham enemies called them Papagos, or "bean eaters." In 1986 Papagos changed their name to Tohono O'odham, or "people of the desert." I use O'odham or Tohono O'odham instead of Papago, except in quotations. On the Papago name change, see Philip Burnham, "O'odham Linguist Comes to Washington," *Indian Country Today*, Jan. 4, 2006, p. C1; and Eric V. Meeks, *Border Citizens: The Making of Indians, Mexicans, and Anglos in Arizona* (Austin, 2007), 16, 228.

2 Geraldo L. Cadava, *The Heat of Exchange: Cultures of Commerce and Migration in Arizona and Sonora's Post–World War II Borderlands* (Cambridge, Mass., forthcoming). On border enforcement since the 1920s, see Kelly Lytle-Hernández, *Migra! A History of the U.S. Border Patrol* (Berkeley, 2010).

3 Mary Pat Brady, *Extinct Lands, Temporal Geographies: Chicana Literature and the Urgency of Space* (Durham, N.C., 2002), 52.

4 Samuel Truett, *Fugitive Landscapes: The Forgotten History of the U.S.-Mexico Borderlands* (New Haven, 2006), 9.

5 On North American borderlands through the late nineteenth and early twentieth centuries, see Truett, *Fugitive Landscapes;* Ned Blackhawk, *Violence over the Land: Indians and Empires in the Early American West* (Cambridge, Mass., 2006); Brian DeLay, *War of a Thousand Deserts: Indian Raids and the*

*U.S.-Mexican War* (New Haven, 2008); Pekka Hämäläinen, *The Comanche Empire* (New Haven, 2008); Katherine Benton-Cohen, *Borderline Americans: Racial Division and Labor War in the Arizona Borderlands* (Cambridge, Mass., 2009); and Rachel St. John, *Line in the Sand: A History of the Western U.S.-Mexico Border* (Princeton, 2011). On how nation-states consolidated and borders hardened by the early twentieth century, see Jeremy Adelman and Stephen Aron, "From Borderlands to Borders: Empires, Nation-States, and the Peoples in Between in North American History," *American Historical Review,* 104 (June 1999), 814–41.

6 For a call to do transnational and broadly comparative borderlands research, see Ramón Gutiérrez and Elliott Young, "Transnationalizing Borderlands History," *Western Historical Quarterly,* 41 (Spring 2010), 48. On binational indigenous groups, see Jeffrey Schulze, "Trans-Nations: Indians, Imagined Communities, and Border Realities in the Twentieth Century" (Ph.D. diss., Southern Methodist University, 2008); Kenneth Dean Madsen, "A Nation across Nations: The Tohono O'odham and the U.S.-Mexico Border" (Ph.D. diss., Arizona State University, 2005); and Benjamin H. Johnson and Andrew R. Graybill, eds., *Bridging National Borders in North America: Transnational and Comparative Histories* (Durham, N.C., 2010). For transnational scholarship on Mexican, North American, and indigenous histories before World War II, see Karl Jacoby, *Shadows at Dawn: A Borderlands Massacre and the Violence of History* (New York, 2008). For a work on Mexicans, Tohono O'odham, and North Americans in Arizona that relies exclusively on U.S. archives and secondary sources for its discussion of O'odham in Sonora, see Meeks, *Border Citizens.*

7 On perceived ontological divides between the United States and Mexico, see Mauricio Tenorio-Trillo, "On *La Frontera* and Cultures of Consumption: An Essay of Images," in *Land of Necessity: Consumer Culture in the United States–Mexico Borderlands,* ed. Alexis McCrossen (Durham, N.C., 2009), 336.

8 Jacoby, *Shadows at Dawn*, 95, 97–100; DeLay, *War of a Thousand Deserts*, 294–303; Benton-Cohen, *Borderline Americans*, 61; St. John, *Line in the Sand*, 39–62.

9 On the meeting in Ambos Nogales of U.S. and Mexican rail networks, see Daniel Lewis, *Iron Horse Imperialism: The Southern Pacific of Mexico, 1880–1951* (Tucson, 2007); and Alma Ready, ed., *Nogales Arizona, 1880–1980, Centennial Anniversary* (Nogales, 1980), 6. William McKinley quoted in J. B. Bristol, "History of Nogales: Facts concerning Nogales and Santa Cruz County, Arizona," March 1928, p. 6, MS 401, Fred Rochlin Papers (University of Arizona Library Special Collections, Tucson).

10 Cynthia Radding, *Wandering Peoples: Colonialism, Ethnic Spaces, and Ecological Frontiers in Northwestern Mexico, 1700–1850* (Durham, N.C., 1997), 180; Schulze, "Trans-Nations," 76; Meeks, *Border Citizens,* 26, 29–30, 50, 58.

11 On Pancho Villa's raid, see Friedrich Katz, *The Life and Times of Pancho Villa* (Stanford, 1998), 560–77. Schulze, "Trans-Nations," 79–81, 189; Madsen, "Nation across Nations," 68; Constanza Montana, "Papago Indians' Gate Admits Illegal Aliens, Narcotics, and Liquor," *Wall Street Journal,* June 9, 1986, p. 1; Meeks, *Border Citizens,* 128–38; Cadava, *Heat of Exchange,* chap. 1.

12 Nogales, Arizona, Chamber of Commerce, "Outline of Crossing Problems at Port of Nogales," Jan. 30, 1953 (microfilm CD 1, PDF no. 9, MSS 1), Personal and Political Papers of Senator Barry M. Goldwater (Arizona Historical Foundation, Hayden Library, Arizona State University, Tempe); Alma Ready, *City of Nogales, Nogales Arizona, since 1880* (Nogales, 1978).

13 Louis Escalada to Barry Goldwater, Feb. 10, 1953 (microfilm CD 1, PDF no. 9, MSS 1), Personal and Political Papers of Goldwater; Sam Marcus to Goldwater,

telegram, March 2, 1953, *ibid.;* Goldwater to Don Smith, March 4, 1953, *ibid.;* Ernest Martan to Goldwater, telegram, March 6, 1953, *ibid.;* W E. Reynolds to Goldwater, March 13, 1953, *ibid.;* Smith to Goldwater, March 23, 1953, *ibid;* Margaret M. Moore to Goldwater, May 18, 1953, *ibid.*

14 Neil Clark, "Nogales," *Saturday Evening Post,* May 24, 1952, pp. 26–27; Hanson Sisk to Goldwater, July 24, 1953 (microfilm CD 1, PDF no. 9, MSS 1), Personal and Political Papers of Goldwater; C. R. Long, "The Customs Service," speech to the Rotary Club of Nogales, Arizona, March 21, 1958, MS 1136, folder 69, box 8, Papers of the United States Customs Service, District of Nogales, 1892–1977 (Arizona Historical Society, Tucson). On subversion and vice during the 1940s and 1950s, see Mexican government spy reports, boxes 92, 192, Secretaria de Gobernación, Departamento de Investigaciones Politicas y Sociales (Mexican National Archives, Mexico City).

15 "Nogales, Son. Improvement Program Well Under Way," *Nogales International,* July 19, 1963, p. 1; Hanson Sisk, "Border Traffic," *Nogales Herald,* Feb. 7, 1964, p. 1; Polly Benn, "Construction of Gateway at Nogales on Schedule," *Nogales International,* May 8, 1964, p. 1; "Rites Set for Architect Scholer," *Arizona Daily Star,* Nov. 3, 1979; "Emerson Scholer Services Sunday," *Tucson Citizen,* Nov. 5, 1979. On Mario Pani, see the special issue on Mexican architecture of the French architectural magazine *L'Architecture d'Aujour d'Hui* (no. 109, Sept. 1963), 14–15, 18–21; Louise Noelle, *Arquitectos contemporáneos de México* (Contemporary architects of Mexico) (Mexico City, 1989), 119–23; Manuel Larrosa, *Mario Pani, arquitecto de su época* (Mario Pani, architect of his time) (Mexico City, 1985), 99–106.

16 Sergio Calderón Valdes, ed., *Historia general de Sonora* (General history of Sonora) (5 vols., Hermosillo, 1985), V; Stephen Niblo, *Mexico in the 1940s: Modernity, Politics, and Corruption* (Wilmington, 1999); Ruben Salazar, "Fence, River Divide U.S., Mexico Cultures," *Los Angeles Times,* Jan. 7, 1962, p. J1; and "Ambos Nogales Economy Mingles," *Nogales Herald,* Feb. 19, 1964, p. 4.

17 "Nogales, Son. Improvement Program Well Under Way," 1; "Official in Charge of Mexico's National Frontier Program on Inspection Trip to City," *Nogales International,* Dec. 25, 1963, p. 1; "Tourism's Economic Value Impresses Mexico Leaders Says Former Nogales Man," *ibid.,* Dec. 24, 1965, p. 1. On Mexico's National Border Program, see Evan R. Ward, "Finding Mexico's Great Show Window: A Tale of Two Borderlands, 1960–1976," in *Land of Necessity,* ed. McCrossen, 196–214.

18 "New Border Gateway at Nogales Completed," *Nogales International,* Nov. 13, 1964, p. 1; "President of Mexico Visitor in Nogales," *ibid.*; "Sen. Hayden Not Coming," *ibid.*

19 "November U.S. Customs Month in Arizona," *ibid.,* Nov. 6, 1964, p. 1; "History of Customs Service Given by Speaker at Rotary Meeting," *ibid.,* April 17, 1964, p. 1; Polly Benn, "Customs Service in Limelight Friday at Project Dedication," *ibid.,* Nov. 20, 1964, p. 4; Long, "Customs Service," 6.

20 "Customs Collections Up $456,134.95 over 1963–64 Figures for Period," *Nogales International,* Feb. 12, 1965, p. 1; "Customs Collections at Arizona Ports, 1964–65 Fiscal Year, Greatest in History of District," *ibid.,* July 2, 1965, p. 1.

21 Montana, "Papago Indians' Gate Admits Illegal Aliens, Narcotics and Liquor," 1; Charles Hillinger, "Border No Barrier to Indian Tribe," *Los Angeles Times,* June 7, 1977, pp. Al, Bl; Alden W. Jones to John Collier, Dec. 21, in "Apuntes sobre los Papagos de Sonora" (Notes on the Papagos of Sonora), by Alfonso Fabila, typescript, pp. 40–41 (Information and Documentation Unit for the Indigenous Peoples of Northwestern Mexico, College of Sonora, Hermosillo); Alfonso Fabila to Alfonso Caso, March 6, 1957, *ibid.,* 41–44; Fabila, "Apuntes sobre los Papagos

de Sonora," 18, 26, 31; Glenn Emmons to Goldwater, Jan. 26, 1955 (microfilm CD 1, PDF no. 9, MSS 1), Personal and Political Papers of Goldwater.

22 Christian W. McMillen, *Making Indian Law: The Hualapai Land Case and the Birth of Ethnohistory* (New Haven, 2007), 86–103; *Papago Tribe of Arizona v. United States,* 19 Ind. Cl. Comm. 394, 426 (1968). The Indian Reorganization Act of 1934 reversed the 1887 General Allotment Act's provision of distributing individual parcels of land and reestablished reservation lands held in common. The establishment of O'odham reservations during the allotment era was therefore anomalous. See Meeks, *Border Citizens,* 57–58; and Madsen, "Nation across Nations," 68.

23 "O'odham Timeline," in *Diagnóstico de las localidades O'otham* (Diagnosis of O'odham towns), by Instituto Nacional Indigenista, Unidad Caborca (Caborca, 1991), 1–14; Radding, *Wandering Peoples,* 171–207; Adrian A. Bantjes, *As if Jesus Walked on Earth: Cardenismo, Sonora, and the Mexican Revolution* (Wilmington, 1998), 123–50.

24 On *indigenismo,* see Alexander S. Dawson, *Indian and Nation in Revolutionary Mexico* (Tucson, 2004); and Emilio Kourí, "Manuel Gamio y el Indigenismo de la Revolución Mexicana" (Manuel Gamio and the Indianism of the Mexican Revolution), in *Historia de los intelectuales en América Latina: Los avatares de la "ciudad letrada" en el siglo XX* (History of intellectuals in Latin America: Transformation of the "lettered city" in the twentieth century), ed. Carlos Altamirano (Buenos Aires, 2010), 419–32.

25 Meeks, *Border Citizens,* 33, 55–56; Bernard L. Fontana, *Of Earth and Little Rain: The Papago Indians* (Flagstaff, 1981), 87.

26 Fabila to Caso, March 6, 1957, in "Apuntes sobre los Papagos de Sonora," by Fabila, 41–44.

27 "O'odham Timeline"; Fabila, "Apuntes sobre los Papagos de Sonora," 9; Fabila to Caso, March 6, 1957, *ibid.,* 41–44; Marina Byerby Check Cinco and Gilberto Carrillo Pérez to Guillermo Espinosa Velasco, Oct. 30, 1991, in *Diagnóstico de las localidades O'otham,* by Instituto Nacional Indigenista, n.p.

28 Fabila, "Apuntes sobre los Papagos de Sonora," 8–11; Fabila to Caso, March 6, 1957, *ibid.,* 41–44.

29 "O'odham Timeline"; Fabila, "Apuntes sobre los Papagos de Sonora," 8–10; Jones to Collier, Dec. 21, 1956, *ibid.,* 40–41; Fabila to Caso, March 6, 1957, *ibid.,* 41–44.

30 Fabila to Caso, March 6, 1957, in "Apuntes sobre los Papagos de Sonora," by Fabila, 41–44; Fabila, "Apuntes sobre los Papagos de Sonora," 6–7, 12, 16.

31. *Ibid.,* 6–7, 16–17, 25, 29; Charles Hillinger, "Wind of Change Sweeps Indian Reservations," *Los Angeles Times,* Nov. 12, 1962, p. 31; Fabila to Caso, March 6, 1957, in "Apuntes sobre los Papagos de Sonora," by Fabila, 41–44.

32 Schulze, "Trans-Nations," 9, 191, 195; Jones to Collier, Dec. 21, 1956, in "Apuntes sobre los Papagos de Sonora," by Fabila, 40–41; Fabila to Caso, March 6, 1957, *ibid.,* 41–44; Meeks, *Border Citizens,* 45, 60–61, 69, 220. O'odham census estimates vary widely. I chose the conservative estimate of 1,000 Sonoran O'odham at mid-century, even though some sources estimate fewer than 500. For examples, see Fontana, *Of Earth and Little Rain,* 75; and María Macrina Restor Rodríguez, "Papago," spreadsheet with demographic and historical data compiled from several published sources, n.d. (in Geraldo L. Cadava's possession).

33 Fabila to Caso, March 6, 1957, in "Apuntes sobre los Papagos de Sonora," by Fabila, 40–41; Jones to Collier, Dec. 21, 1956, *ibid.,* 40–41.

34 *Ibid.,* 25, 34–35; Jones to Collier, Dec. 21, 1956, *ibid.,* 40–41.

35 Jones to Collier, Dec. 21, 1956, *ibid.,* 40–41.

36 Radding, *Wandering Peoples,* 175; Fabila, "Apuntes sobre los Papagos de Sonora," 33; Madsen, "Nation across Nations," 76–78; Jones to Collier, Dec. 21, 1956, in "Apuntes sobre los Papagos de Sonora," by Fabila, 40–41; Ben Markland, "Lore Abounds in Villages of Papagos Tribe," *Chicago Daily Tribune,* April 2, 1950, p. E9; Alden Stevens, "Voice of the Native; Arizona's and New Mexico's Redskins Could Swing the Election in Those Two States," *New York Times,* Nov. 2, 1952, p. SM65; Schulze, "Trans-Nations," 195–96.

37 Charles Hillinger, "An International Tale of Two Cities," *Los Angeles Times,* Feb. 9, 1986, p. H22; Alicia Schmidt Camacho, *Migrant Imaginarles: Latino Cultural Politics in the U.S.-Mexico Borderlands* (New York, 2008), 248–53.

38 On the rising number of Mexican immigrants and racism, see Cadava, *Heat of Exchange,* chap. 5. On the Immigration and Nationality Act of 1965, see Mae M. Ngai, *Impossible Subjects: Illegal Aliens and the Making of Modern America* (Princeton, 2005), 254–64. For examples of newspapers rearticulating negative stereotypes of Mexicans, see Jeff Smith, "Burglary! Border Vigilantes Feared," *Tucson Daily Citizen,* Feb. 4, 1977; and Carol Trickett, "Friendly Border Town's Problems," *Yuma Daily Sun,* Sept. 29, 1976. See also Christine Marin, "They Sought Work and Found Hell: The Hanigan Case of Arizona," *Perspectives in Mexican American Studies,* 6 (1997), 98. On the Immigration Reform and Control Act of 1986, see Christine Marie Sierra, "In Search of National Power: Chicanos Working the System on Immigration Reform, 1976–1986," in *Chicano Politics and Society in the Late Twentieth Century,* ed. David Montejano (Austin, 1998), 131–53.

39 Gilberto Rosas, "The Fragile Ends of War: Forging the United States-Mexico Border and Borderlands Consciousness," *Social Text,* 25 (Summer 2007), 81–102.

40 *Larry* Rohter, "A Tribe's Bitter Drug Lesson: Nothing Is Sacred," *New York Times,* March 5, 1990, p. A4; Hillinger, "Border No Barrier to Indian Tribe," Al, Bl; Resolution 42–77, May 31, 1977, folder 2 of 5, box 236, Tohono O'odham Tribal Council Resolutions, Records of the Papago Agency, Bureau of Indian Affairs, RG 75 (National Archives, Riverside, Calif.); Robert Perez, "Confined to the Margins: Smuggling among Native People of the Borderlands," in *Land of Necessity,* ed. McCrossen, 249; Resolution 24–75, May 7, 1975, folder 2 of 6, box 234, Tohono O'odham Tribal Council Resolutions, Records of the Papago Agency, Bureau of Indian Affairs.

41 Resolution 42–79, May 14, 1979, folder 2 of 4, box 237, Tohono O'odham Tribal Council Resolutions, Records of the Papago Agency, Bureau of Indian Affairs; Resolution 43–79, May 14, 1979, *ibid,;* Resolution 44–79, May 14, 1979, *ibid.;* Resolution 45–79, May 16, 1979, *ibid.* See also Guadalupe Castillo and Margo Cowan, eds., *It Is Not Our Fault: The Case for Amending Present Nationality Law to Make All Members of the Tohono O'odham Nation United States Citizens, Now and Forever* (Sells, 2001), 10, 13, *44;* Meeks, *Border Citizens,* 227–28; and "Informe final de la segunda cumbre de los Pueblos Indígenas de las Américas sobre la frontera, Distrito de San Xavier, Nación Tohono O'odham, de 7 a 10 de Noviembre del 2007" (Final report of the second summit of the indigenous peoples of the Americas regarding the border, San Xavier District, Tohono O'odham nation, November 7–10, 2007), *International Indian Treaty Council,* http://www.treatycouncil.org/PDF/E_C19_2008_4_CRPl_ES.pdf.

42 Quitovac O'odham to Arturo Warman G., Feb. 11, 1991, in *Diagnóstico de las localidades O'otham,* by Instituto Nacional Indigenista, n.p.; Caborca O'odham to C. Ramon Rivera Montaño, Oct. 24, [ca. 1990–1991], *ibid.;* Quitovac O'odham to Ignacio Almada Bay, May 6, 1990, *ibid.;* Cinco and Pérez to Velasco, Oct. 30, 1991, *ibid.*

# PERMISSION ACKNOWLEDGEMENTS

*The editor and publishers wish to thank the following for permission to reproduce copyright material:*

Richard White, "Marriage and Homicide on the Middle Ground," from his *The Middle Ground: Indians, Empires, and Republics in the Great Lakes Region, 1650–1815* (Cambridge: Cambridge University Press, 1991), 50–93.

Cynthia Radding, "The Colonial Pact," from Donna J. Guy and Thomas E. Sheridan, eds., *Contested Ground: Comparative Frontiers on the Northern and Southern edges of the Spanish Empire* (Tucson: University of Arizona Press, 1998), 52–66.

James H. Merrell, "Conversations in the Woods," from his *Into the American Woods: Negotiators on the Pennsylvania Frontier* (New York: W.W. Norton, 1999), 179–224.

Virginia DeJohn Anderson, "King Philip's Herds: Colonists, Indians, and the Problem of Livestock in Early New England," William & Mary Quarterly, 3rd Series, 51:4 (Oct., 1994): 601–624.

Steven W. Hackel, "Dual Revolutions in the California Missions," from his *Children of Coyote, Missionaries of Saint Francis: Indian-Spanish Relations in Colonial California, 1769–1850* (Chapel Hill: University of North Carolina Press, 2005), 65–123.

Kathleen M. Brown, "The Anglo-Algonquian Gender Frontier," from Nancy Shoemaker, ed., *Negotiators of Change: Historical Perspectives on Native American Women* (New York: Routledge, 1995), 26–49.

Alan Greer, "Virgins and Cannibals," from his *Mohawk Saint: Catherine Tekakwitha and the Jesuits* (Oxford: Oxford University Press, 2005), 171–92.

William L. Ramsey, "'Something Cloudy in Their Looks': The Origins of the Yamasee War Reconsidered." *Journal of American History* 90:1 (June, 2003): 44–75.

Brian DeLay, "The Wider World of the Handsome Man: Southern Plains Indians Invade Mexico, 1830–1846," *Journal of the Early Republic* 27:1 (Spring, 2007): 83–113.

Kathleen DuVal, "Debating Identity, Sovereignty, and Civilization: The Arkansas Valley after the Louisiana Purchase," *Journal of the Early Republic* 26:1 (Spring, 2006): 25–58.

Karl Jacoby, "'The Broad Platform of Extermination': Nature and Violence in the Nineteenth Century North American Borderlands," *Journal of Genocide Research* 10:2 (2008): 1–19.

Lissa Wadewitz, "Fishing the Line: Political Boundaries and Border Fluidity in the Pacific Northwest Borderlands, 1880–1930s," from Sterling Evans, ed., *The Borderlands of the American and Canadian Wests: Essays on Regional History of the Forty-Ninth Parallel* (Lincoln: University of Nebraska Press, 2006): 299–308.

Erika Lee, "Enforcing the Borders: Chinese Exclusion along the U.S. Borders with Canada and Mexico, 1882–1924," *The Journal of American History* 89:1 (June, 2002): 54–86.

Geraldo L. Cadava, "Borderlands of Modernity and Abandonment: The Lines within Ambos Nogales and the Tohono O'odham Nation," *Journal of American History* 98:2 (September, 2011): 362–383.

# INDEX